Research Methods

FROM THEORY TO PRACTICE

Ben Gorvine
Northwestern University

Karl Rosengren
University of Wisconsin—Madison

Lisa Stein
Northwestern University

Kevin Biolsi
KB Statistical Services

New York   Oxford
OXFORD UNIVERSITY PRESS

Oxford University Press is a department of the University of Oxford.
It furthers the University's objective of excellence in research,
scholarship, and education by publishing worldwide. Oxford is a
registered trademark of Oxford University Press in the UK and
certain other countries.

Published in the United States of America by Oxford University Press
198 Madison Avenue, New York, NY 10016, United States of America.

© 2018 by Oxford University Press

Library of Congress Cataloging-in-Publication Data

CIP data is on file at the Library of Congress
ISBN number: 978-0-19-020182-1

9 8 7 6 5 4 3 2 1

Printed by LSC Communications, United States of America.

Brief Contents

Contents

CHAPTER 7   Survey and Interview Approaches   145

Preface

Research Methods: From Theory to Practice is designed primarily for students who want to or will be expected to conduct research or for those who want to understand research as it occurs from the "inside." As its name suggests, this text guides students through the entire research process—from learning about the wide range of current methods, to the first step of developing a research question, and through the final stage of writing up and publishing results.

Our first goal for this book is to provide new researchers with the knowledge and skills they need to begin ethical, creative research. Although this book focuses primarily on psychological research, its content is relevant for anyone interested in doing research in the social and behavioral sciences. Our second and closely related goal for this book is to help students become not only producers of research, but also educated consumers of the research they encounter daily in online news sources, blogs, social media, and printed newspapers and magazines. These reports often provide brief snippets from actual research, but with an unstated marketing bias. We believe that every educated adult in our society should know when to trust these accounts and how to evaluate them.

Given the large number of research methods books on the market, someone could reasonably ask why another book on this topic is necessary. Because two of us have taught research methods and helped redesign the research methods classes at Northwestern University and the University of Wisconsin, we feel there is a need for a novel approach to this course. In our experience, we have found that the majority of current research methods texts are not written with the notion that students will conduct their own research projects, nor do they provide beginning students with much guidance about becoming involved in research.

By contrast, *Research Methods: From Theory to Practice* delves into the practical challenges that face new researchers. For example, although most current textbooks include information on ethics, we devote an entire chapter to describing how to negotiate an institutional review board, much of it drawn from our personal experience working on and with such boards. Our final chapter gives detailed information on presenting research at conferences and how to find the right publication outlet for research, a topic we think will be particularly valuable as more and more undergraduates work toward these goals.

We also include two chapters on statistics. This may seem odd given that most colleges and universities require a separate statistics course prior to a research methods course. However, we have seen that many students taking research methods need at least a refresher, if not a more comprehensive review, of statistical material. Additionally, a number of colleges and universities are moving toward an integrated sequence of statistics and research methods courses, an approach we feel is quite productive. These statistics chapters provide up-to-date information about current controversies regarding the continued use of null hypothesis testing with a view to what the future might hold for data analysis, while also providing students with a requisite understanding of the traditional model. We also present material on research over time (or developmental approaches), neuroscience, qualitative research, case study approaches, single-subject experimental designs, and meta-analysis. Although we acknowledge that few undergraduates will use these methods in their undergraduate careers, we feel that this information will make them better critical consumers of research wherever they encounter it.

FEATURES

Research Methods: From Theory to Practice contains a number of distinct features. Each chapter begins with an **Inside Research** section drawn from interviews of leading psychological researchers whose work exemplifies the content of that chapter. Their shared experiences about their research studies, struggles, and career choices help demystify and personalize the research process and capture some of its inherent excitement for students. We have also interspersed researcher quotes that provide insights into particular issues throughout the textbook. An **Abstract** presents an overview of what will be covered in the chapter. A **Flow Chart** depicts the organization of the research process and important choice points. The flow chart in Chapter 1 provides an overview of the entire research process, emphasizing iterative aspects of research. Flow charts in subsequent chapters zoom in on sections of the initial flowchart relevant to the material covered in the chapter. Each chapter includes at least one **Media Matters** section that analyzes and evaluates how a particular research study or general topic relevant to the chapter is portrayed in the mass media. **Practical Tips** boxes highlight central concepts introduced in each chapter and a **Chapter Summary** recaps the key issues. Two pedagogical elements conclude each chapter. The first is **Up for Discussion**, which offers a series of thought questions meant to push the reader beyond the text to consider wider applications of the material. The second is a list of **Key Terms** defined in the **Marginal Glossary** within each chapter. Although many terms are specific to research methods and analysis, others come from diverse areas of psychology to broaden students' understanding of the field. Our **Accompanying Instructor's Manual** not only presents standard material such as chapter outlines, slides, and exam questions, but also includes details and examples regarding how to conduct data analysis in SPSS and R. These analyses are based on the examples provided in the chapters.

ORGANIZATION

Whereas many instructors like to assign chapters in a textbook in the order in which they appear, our own experience has taught us that this can be difficult in a research methods class, especially one that requires students to conduct mini-research projects. In a sense, to be a skilled researcher and critical consumer of research, you need to know all of the material covered in this book to start with. This is clearly not practical or possible. For this reason, we have designed chapters to stand alone as references for a particular method or issue, so that they might be used in an order that best fits an instructor. We have also placed a chapter on ethics early in the book and presented material on ethics throughout the text to reflect our belief that ethical concerns should be considered throughout the research process. In our own research methods courses, we include in almost every class a brief discussion of ethical issues relevant to a particular method or gleaned from a recent press account.

ACKNOWLEDGMENTS

A book like this takes some time and a lot of help! We are particularly thankful for Jane Potter at Oxford University Press for convincing us that we should write this book. We are grateful to Lisa Sussman at Oxford University Press for her careful editing of the text and for guiding us through the entire process. We also thank the many reviewers and students who read drafts of chapters, as well as the many students who have taken our research methods classes. Your thoughts and comments have undoubtedly made this a better book! We thank the following reviewers:

Michael D. Anes, Wittenberg University

Suzette Astley, Cornell College

Jodie Baird, Swarthmore College

Levi R. Baker-Russell, University of Tennessee

Cole Barton, Davidson College

Timothy Bickmore, Northeastern University

Caitlin Brez, Indiana State University

Kimberly A. Carter, California State University, Sacramento

Janessa Carvalho, Bridgewater State University

Herbert L. Colston, University of Wisconsin–Parkside

Elizabeth Cooper, University of Tennessee, Knoxville

Katherine Corker, Kenyon College

Randolph R. Cornelius, Vassar College

Amanda ElBassiouny, Spring Hill College

Catherine Forestell, The College of William & Mary

Judith G. Foy, Loyola Marymount University

Ronald S. Friedman, University at Albany, State University of New York

Kathleen Geher, State University of New York, New Paltz

Frank M. Groom, Ball State University

David Haaga, American University

William Indick, Dowling College

Mark A. Jackson, Transylvania University

Kulwinder Kaur-Walker, Elizabeth City State University

Victoria Kazmerski, Pennsylvania State University, Erie

Marina Klimenko, University of Florida

Nate Kornell, Williams College

Rebecca LaFountain, Pennsylvania State University, Harrisburg

Huijun Li, Florida A&M University

Stella G. Lopez, University of Texas at San Antonio

William McKibbin, University of Michigan, Flint

Lindsay Mehrkam, University of Florida

Kathryn Oleson, Reed College

Bonnie Perdue, Agnes Scott College

Bill Peterson, Smith College

Thomas Redick, Purdue University

Monica Riordan, Chatham University

Melissa Scircle, Millikin University

Elizabeth Sheehan, Georgia State University

Angela Sikorski, Texas A&M University Texarkana

Meghan Sinton, College of William and Mary

Mark Stellmack, University of Minnesota

Janet Trammell, Pepperdine University

Andrew Triplett, Loyola University Chicago

Laura Butkovsky Turner, Roger Williams University

Barbara J. Vail, Rocky Mountain College

Luis A. Vega, California State University, Bakersfield

John L. Wallace, Ball State University

Mark Whiting, Radford University

Ryan M. Yoder, Indiana University–Purdue University, Fort Wayne

Finally, we thank all of our families. Ben thanks Amy for her endless patience with the length and scope of this project and her invaluable help in designing several of the figures in the chapter on experimental methods. He also thanks his daughters, Emma and Sophie, for their love and for providing the motivation to push through this project. Karl thanks Sarah for listening to many crazy research ideas and helping to turn them into more practical ones, as well as providing support on a daily basis. Karl also thanks his daughters, Emily and Julia, for their love and support. Lisa thanks Daniel for his constant encouragement, invaluable IT support, and take-out dinners and Madeline, Emma, and Owen for making everything worthwhile. Kevin thanks Carol, Lauren, and Megan for their love, encouragement, and support.

Introduction to Research Methods

INSIDE RESEARCH: MARTHA ARTERBERRY

Professor and Department Chair,
Department of Psychology, Colby
College

As an undergraduate at Pomona College I discovered I liked to do research, especially the idea of asking questions and finding the answers. I was taking a statistics course, and I really enjoyed using data to test hypotheses. (My students think I'm crazy when I tell them this.)

At the same time, I was fascinated by the study of art history. In my art history classes, I thought a lot about how an artist represents the world in a painting or an idea in a three-dimensional sculpture. Also, I used to spend summers making pots. I loved ceramics, especially making bowls and goblets, and thinking about the motor actions that allowed me to create these three-dimensional shapes, sometimes upside-down on a potter's wheel, and thinking about how others eventually will perceive them.

It all came together for me when I took a seminar on perception, as a visiting student at Swarthmore College, from Philip Kellman. He had a "baby lab," and I remember being intrigued. I had no idea there was even an area of research called infant perception. I asked, "What *is* a baby lab and can I work there?" He let me volunteer and that was the first time I did hands-on psychological research. I loved it, and I still love it.

My research in the baby lab made me realize that perceptual psychologists, like artists, also think a lot about how to represent the world. Human perceivers may not be creating something on a canvas, but they're trying to make sense of the information. It was through art that I got interested in perception, and the question of how it all starts got me to babies. The intersection of all these different areas is a great example of the power of a liberal arts education.

An overarching theme in my research asks the question: What information enables us to perceive the world and how does the ability to use this information develop? My initial work focused on infants' perception of depth and three-dimensional object shape. More recently, I am interested in what information infants use to group objects together, a process called categorization. Working with young participants who don't talk adds another layer of complexity to my research. Infant perception researchers use creative methods that allow us to infer what a baby might perceive or know. It is like cracking a code! It is another challenge to the research process, but one that makes it even more fun to do.

Martha Arterberry has combined her interests in areas as diverse as statistics, art history, and infant development to study how human beings come to perceive the world. She uses a variety of research methods, such as observing children's behavior, electroencephalograms, and an eye tracker to quantify eye movements. Her work is at the forefront of an explosion in research on the development of perception.

Research Focus: Perception and cognition in infants, children, and adults

THE RESEARCH PROCESS

This flowchart provides an overview of the research process, emphasizing the iterative aspects of research. Flowcharts in subsequent chapters zoom in on sections of this flowchart relevant to the covered material.

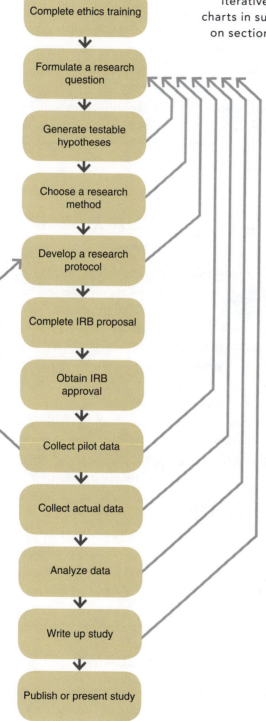

Chapter Abstract

In this chapter, we discuss the importance of research methods and their relevance not only to the scientific process but also to daily life. We explore various approaches to evaluating the constant, ubiquitous stream of reports of research findings in the media and advertising, as well as results published in scholarly journals. We present examples of fraudulent and unethical researchers to help instill a healthy skepticism of all research findings. Finally, we introduce the fundamental distinction between science and pseudoscience and present a flowchart depicting the research process that will guide the organization of subsequent chapters.

WHY YOU SHOULD CARE ABOUT RESEARCH METHODS

There are two main reasons why you should know something about research methods. First, such knowledge helps you better understand research findings reported in the media—whether digital, broadcast, or print—and advertisements. How can you tell whether the claims made are justifiable and believable? In the past few years alone, companies and researchers have claimed that listening to Mozart boosts IQ, wearing magnetic bracelets reduces pain and motion sickness and promotes better balance, drinking coffee and red wine promotes health, drinking pomegranate juice reduces cholesterol and boosts heart health, and drinking diet soda may increase women's risk for depression. Are any of these claims true? How would you find out?

Second, understanding research methods can aid in many of your everyday decisions. In terms of both physical and psychological well-being, a deeper knowledge of methods can help you make good health-care decisions. In terms of being a consumer, this knowledge can help you evaluate advertising claims made about a new car, television, or computer so that you can make the best possible choice.

Another good reason to know about research is so that you can conduct your own research. Doing research can be a fun, creative, and rewarding experience, but becoming a skilled researcher requires a certain amount of knowledge. Our hope is that by reading this book, you will acquire the knowledge to be a better consumer of research and to conduct your own research project.

METHODS FOR EVALUATING CLAIMS

One way to evaluate research claims made by researchers, reporters, or health care–related websites is to simply accept them at face value because they are based on the opinions of experts. After all, if some expert did not support the claim, it would not appear in the news or on the Web, right?

Do you blindly trust experts cited in a newspaper or online? How do you know who you can trust? Many reports do not even mention a specific expert, so how can you determine whether the report and reporting provide an accurate description of trustworthy results?

A second approach for evaluating claims is to read and evaluate the actual research. But often you will find competing accounts that are difficult to interpret without extensive knowledge of a particular field of study. How, then, do you evaluate the claims found in different sources and come to your own conclusion? This evaluation process becomes easier as you gain experience and learn to judge the quality of the research and conclusions.

A third method for evaluating claims is to search for similar results, or converging evidence, about claims made in news releases (in print or online) and original research. **Converging evidence** refers to results from multiple research investigations that provide similar findings. But when you begin to search for converging results, you may be confronted with a diverse set of facts and opinions that can be difficult to sort out.

Finally, you could conduct your own research project to test the claims, but many individuals do not have the knowledge or resources to conduct such tests. We will delve into this approach over the course of this book; much of the book is targeted to help you design and conduct your own research project.

Converging evidence Results from multiple research investigations that provide similar findings.

The Extraordinary Coffee Bean

As an introduction to evaluating particular claims that appear in the media, we present two reports about coffee and consider how you might evaluate their veracity. We examine issues of expertise, reading, and evaluating past research; the importance of finding convergent evidence; and particular aspects to look for in a report of a research finding.

For many years, reports about the health benefits of caffeine have circulated in the media. A *New York Times* article highlighted in Figure 1.1 suggests that caffeine consumers have a lower death rate than individuals who abstain from caffeine. Should we trust Jane Brody and her reporting? How can we know whether the research she reported really supports the claim that is being made?

There are multiple ways to evaluate the report. First, you could try to find out who conducted the original research. Was it a trained, objective researcher or someone hired by Starbucks or some other coffee supplier? The blurb in Figure 1.1 does not contain this information, but if you look at the original press report (Brody, 2012), you will find that Dr. Neal Freedman and his colleagues conducted the study. Dr. Freedman is listed as an epidemiologist at the National Cancer Institute, and the research was published in *The New England Journal of Medicine*. He seems like a trained researcher, so perhaps we should accept the findings. But skepticism is a good trait when reading newspapers or websites, and we will explore in the next section why trusting the experts may or may not be a good thing.

Having Your Coffee and Enjoying It Too
By JANE E.BRODY [NY TIMES, June 25, 2012]

A disclaimer: I do not own stock in Starbucks nor, to my knowledge, in any other company that sells coffee or its accoutrement. I last wrote about America's most popular beverage four years ago, and the latest and largest study to date supports that earlier assessment of coffee's health effects. Although the new research, which involved more than 400,000 people in a 14-year observational study, still cannot prove cause and effect, the findings are consistent with other recent large studies. The findings were widely reported, but here's the bottom line: When smoking and many other factors known to influence health and longevity were taken into account, coffee drinkers in the study were found to be living somewhat longer than abstainers, Further, the more coffee consumed each day—up to a point, at least— the greater the benefit to longevity. The observed benefit of coffee drinking was not enormous— a death rate among coffee drinkers that was 10 percent to 15 percent lower than among abstainers. But the findings are certainly reassuring, and given how many Americans drink coffee, the numbers of lives affected may be quite large.

FIGURE 1.1. The benefits of coffee.

Second, you could dig for converging evidence from other websites or news outlets. Do multiple sites provide converging evidence? Unfortunately, not all of them will cover the same aspects of a story. The press release *Green Coffee Diet—Free Offer: The Magic Weight Loss Cure for Every Body Type* (shown in Figure 1.2) discusses how Dr. Oz (from the popular *Dr. Oz* television show) suggests that taking green coffee bean supplements can lead to "magic weight loss" (Weight Loss Pills Network, 2016). Is Dr. Oz an expert on caffeine or weight loss? Is he even a real doctor? How should we evaluate these two reports, and should we drink coffee or take green coffee bean supplements, or both?

Third, you could use knowledge of research methods to help you evaluate the claims. We will go into this approach in more detail shortly. Here, we describe potential approaches you can use as you encounter research claims reported in the media.

Trust the Experts

Trusting the experts is a common strategy. After all, the *New York Times* and other newspapers would not report inaccurate or wrong information, would they? One piece of information to help you determine accuracy is whether the news report is based on an original research study, an interview with the lead researcher, or some **secondary source**. Even if the report lists the journal that published the research, you still cannot be sure it is based on the original data. Many scientific journals (or periodicals with scientific-sounding names) publish secondary reports of research, meaning they are not the original source. The problem with using secondary sources is exemplified by the old game of "telephone," where one

Secondary source
An article or reference in which the author describes research that has previously been published.

Chlorogenic acid levels

Low   High

Roasted   Green
coffee bean   coffee bean

Magic Weight Loss Cure for Every Body Type: The green coffee bean is the latest buzz in the "battle of the bulge." Since recently being studied on the popular Doctor Oz television show, millions of people are praising this so called "miracle weight loss pill." Surprisingly, many people who struggle daily with their weight have yet to hear about this powerful supplement

What has the scientific community so excited about green coffee bean extract is that people don't have to do anything different when taking this food supplement. They don't need to exercise, and they don't need to diet; they just appear to lose pounds fast.

Green Coffee Extract Helps Burn More Fat: Let's cut to the chase: The most recent study on the green coffee bean published in the Diabetes, Metabolic Syndrome and Obesity journal followed a group of 16 adults who supplemented with green coffee bean for only 12 weeks. Over the course of the study, the subjects lost an average of 17 pounds each—this was 10.5% of their overall body weight and 16% of their overall body fat! There were no side effects reported. This is very exciting information and one reason why I think that green coffee bean could be an effective weapon against the obesity epidemic in our country.

FIGURE 1.2. Press release for green coffee diet.

person whispers a phrase in the ear of the next person and so on down the line, so that by the time the message gets to the end of the line, it sounds nothing like the original. The same holds true for research findings—the farther you get from the source, the less accurate the information becomes.

If the press release quotes the lead researcher, you can generally assume that the report is based on the original research and not some secondary source. But how can you tell whether the lead researcher is trustworthy? Generally, if researchers are faculty members or scientists at known universities or research institutes (such as the National Cancer Institute or the National Institutes of Health), you can assume they are highly qualified experts in their particular field. But even experts have biases and vested interests, and some skepticism is always warranted (see "Media Matters: The Persistent Autism–Vaccine Myth"). For example, it is always useful to know who paid for the research. Did Dr. Freedman and his colleagues receive payment by coffee producers or suppliers to conduct their research?

Even researchers from respected universities sometimes cross the line. In 2010, the Stanford University School of Medicine confronted scandals involving conflict-of-interest issues with a number of prominent researchers. In one instance, a psychiatrist allowed a pharmaceutical company to ghostwrite a book on pharmacology. Another case involved 12 Stanford physicians who accepted relatively large sums of money (some more than $100,000) for speaking engagements involving talks about the drugs made at that pharmaceutical company (Reid, 2010). It is important, especially if a particular drug or product is being advocated, to determine who is sponsoring the research and whether the researcher

The Persistent Autism–Vaccine Myth

When Andrew Wakefield claimed in 1998 that he had found a link between the onset of autism and the measles, mumps, and rubella (MMR) vaccine, he set off a public opinion firestorm that burns in the media to this day. Although Wakefield's findings did not hold up under scrutiny, some parents shunned not only MMR but also *all* vaccines for their children and encouraged others to follow their example.

Wakefield's mythical autism–vaccine connection stands as a powerful cautionary tale of what can happen when fraudulent research meets mass media amplification and parents desperate to find an explanation for their children's suffering. According to one medical anthropologist, the controversy surrounding childhood vaccines has been a factor in "the long-term erosion of public trust in science" (Gross, 2009).

In the past 15 years, the antivaccination movement, joined by the celebrity Jenny McCarthy, who blamed MMR for her son's symptoms of autism (Lowry, 2014), has rallied around Wakefield. It has contributed to an increase in measles and mumps in Europe and the United States, and significant outbreaks of whooping cough in California in 2010 and 2015 because some parents have refused to vaccinate their children (Gross, 2015; Hiltzik, 2014a). Moreover, scientists and public officials refuting the autism–vaccine link have routinely received malicious e-mails, phone calls, and even death threats (Gross, 2009).

Newspaper headlines and broadcast news trumpeted Wakefield's research linking autism and the MMR vaccine, citing its appearance in *The Lancet*, a prestigious peer-reviewed medical journal founded in London in 1823. Wakefield, a gastroenterologist, led the study (Hiltzik, 2014b). It comprised 12 developmentally challenged children, 9 of whom were showing some signs of autism (Deer, 2011). Wakefield reported that the parents had noted the onset of some of the children's behavioral symptoms immediately after receiving the MMR vaccine, and he presented these observations as fact (Deer, 2011). As Brian Deer detailed in an investigative report in the *British Medical Journal*, the paper is rife with discrepancies, including falsified data and misreported or changed time frames, symptoms, and diagnoses (Deer, 2011).

Wakefield argued that the children suffered from "regressive autism" caused by colitis. Specifically, he proposed that the measles virus caused a leaky gut, sending toxic substances into the bloodstream and eventually the brain in a syndrome he calls "autistic enterocolitis" (Gross, 2009). The combination of the three vaccines into one was the culprit, he said, and separating them into three separate vaccines would be safer (Gross, 2009).

What Wakefield did not reveal in the article or in his subsequent press conference was his work on a rival measles vaccine (Gross, 2009). He had received funding in 1997 from a Norfolk solicitor (lawyer) with whom he was working on a lawsuit against the manufacturers of MMR (Deer, 2011).

The Lancet published a retraction of Wakefield's paper in 2010, and many reputable news outlets eventually reported on allegations against his research and his denial of any wrongdoing. Britain's General Medical Council banned Wakefield from practicing medicine (Hannaford, 2013), citing unprofessional conduct. Over the next few years, a range of media outlets denounced Wakefield's research and conduct (e.g., "The Aftermath," 2013).

But the damage had been done. Parental online groups continue to support Wakefield's claims, and

Wakefield promoted his theories in the book *Callous Disregard* (2010), in public speaking events, and online (Hannaford, 2013).

Signs are beginning to emerge, however, of a growing media backlash to the antivaccination movement. Interestingly, posts on social media regularly encourage parents to vaccinate their children, pointing to reports on the surge in cases of measles and whooping cough (e.g., Ingraham, 2015). Perhaps media will, in the end, put out the fire it helped to create.

has a bias, vested interest, or conflict of interest that should make you skeptical about the validity of the findings.

You can usually determine the source of a researcher's funding by checking the original publication and the researcher's website. Although investigators are typically required to disclose this information, some unethical researchers fail to provide it or, in some cases, as did members of the Stanford faculty, say they did not know it was required.

Unfortunately, sometimes even well-known researchers from respected universities engage in fraud. In 2011, Diederik Stapel, a prominent and widely published social psychologist, admitted that he had faked data about research findings on stereotyping, discrimination, advertising, and situations where individuals appeared to prefer negative feedback to praise (Aldhous, 2011). His research was reported in a number of top scientific journals, including *Science*, one of the most prestigious publications on science news and research. A number of junior researchers alleging scientific misconduct uncovered Stapel's fraud. Close investigation of the data in many of these studies suggested a number of anomalies, including surprisingly large experimental effects and data that lacked any outliers.

Another case of scientific misconduct rocked the campus of Harvard University in 2010, when the psychologist Marc Hauser was accused of fabricating and falsifying data in experiments funded by the U.S. government (Carpenter, 2012). Members of Hauser's own research team called into question the truthfulness of his research findings on biological origins of cognition and morality. Like Stapel's work, Hauser's work was published in *Science*, as well as other leading scientific journals (*Cognition, Proceedings of the Royal Society*). Eventually, Hauser was found to have engaged in a number of instances of scientific misconduct, and he resigned from Harvard.

Both of these examples highlight the idea that knowledge of research methods helps you evaluate the validity of research claims. If the data look too good—or the claims too shocking or grandiose ("Lose weight like magic")—to be true, they probably are. These examples also underscore the idea that you should approach press releases and even research published in high-quality scientific journals with a skeptical eye. Do not always assume the expert is right.

Martha Arterberry:
"Results often have several interpretations, so it is important to look at the data and generate and evaluate the conclusions for yourself. Don't rely on others to do this, not even the experts!"

Read and Evaluate Past Research

Another way to evaluate claims in the mainstream media is to search out and read the published research on the topic. With a strong background in research methods, you are in a better position to recognize particular flaws in the design, method, analysis, or inferences drawn from the data that might make it difficult to trust the claims made by an author, manufacturer, or researcher. As with looking for converging reports across different popular press outlets, such as the *New York Times* and the *Chicago Tribune*, it is always useful to examine a number of research articles to evaluate a particular claim. Chapter 4 includes more detail about how to find and evaluate relevant research articles. Researchers do not always agree—and if they do not, you will need to track down more articles to evaluate the validity of an overall claim. In some cases, if an equal number of studies support or refute the claim, you may be left with no clear conclusion.

Search for Convergence

As mentioned previously, another good way to evaluate a claim made in the mainstream media or scholarly journals is to look for converging evidence. Ideally, you want to find multiple websites or research articles that provide the same or similar information and conclusions. This does not always lead to a simple answer. For example, when one of the authors was helping his daughter with a report on the jazz trumpeter Louis Armstrong, he could not find any definitive information about Armstrong's birthdate. Some sites listed it as July 4, 1900, whereas others reported it as August 4, 1901. The latter was eventually confirmed as the actual birthdate when a baptismal certificate was found (http://www.satchmo.com/louisarmstrong/). However, it took some time for various publications and websites to come to a consensus. As late as 2010, Columbia University's radio station celebrated Armstrong's birthday with a broadcast of his music from July 3 to July 5, suggesting some still believe his birthday is July 4 (Walkington, 2010).

Replication The process through which either the original researcher or the researchers from an independent laboratory repeat the investigation and obtain the same or highly similar results.

With specific research findings, a person knowledgeable about research and methodology will look to see whether the results have been replicated. **Replication** occurs when researchers achieve the same or highly similar results after repeating a study or experiment. Although you should still be skeptical if the original researcher is the only one to replicate the results, if the results hold up over time and are reported by independent laboratories and researchers, you can be fairly confident of their validity.

How to Evaluate the Quality of Reported Research

Conclusion validity Making the determination as to whether a researcher's claims are valid or justified.

As shown in our coffee bean example, media routinely report on new research findings, and determining whether a researcher's claims are valid or justified, a concept referred to as **conclusion validity**, can be tricky. We will discuss this concept in more detail in Chapter 5.

Several pieces of information will help you evaluate the quality of the research that backs up an article's claims. First, does the article list the names of the researchers? If it does, you can use this information to determine whether the lead researcher has basic qualifications and experience.

Second, does the article, website, or press release identify where the research was conducted? Although research is conducted at different types of institutions (academic and nonacademic), knowing the particular institution can help you determine whether the researchers have the necessary resources and support structure to conduct high-quality research. You should avoid assuming that all findings coming from a well-known research institution are of the highest quality, however. The pressure to produce and publish results at some of the most competitive research institutions may lead researchers to cut corners. As we emphasized earlier, it is *always* useful to evaluate research reports with a critical view. However, one of the problems with advanced training in many disciplines is that individuals become hypersensitive to flaws in research, setting standards that are unattainable by even the most thoughtful, careful researchers. If possible, determine what can be learned or taken away from any research article, even after you have taken design flaws into account. Conducting your own research will eventually help you understand the practical considerations of all research and the fact that all researchers must make compromises.

Third, has the research been published (and, if so, in what type of journal) or is it based on preliminary findings? Often, researchers will present preliminary findings at national and international conferences where other researchers can comment on and evaluate them through a peer-review process. It is common to see press releases based on findings reported at conferences. But in other cases, researchers may go straight to the media with what they think is a novel or "hot" finding, bypassing the review process that occurs when a finding is presented in a scientific forum or journal. You should always be skeptical about research that reports preliminary findings that have not been either presented at a scientific conference or published in a respected journal.

Preliminary Findings.   In fact, there are many instances where a study's preliminary results are not supported when the entire data set is collected. In a number of famous cases, researchers went straight to reporters, who championed what they thought was a breakthrough finding, only to find out that the researchers' claims based on preliminary data could not be verified. One such example is "cold fusion" (Taubes, 1993), the idea that a nuclear reaction can occur at room temperature, which opened up the possibility of cheap, almost limitless energy. Ultimately, repeated failures to replicate the results led the scientific community to dismiss the claim, after large sums of research funds were expended.

In a more recent case, researchers at the European Organization for Nuclear Research (CERN) reported that they had recorded particles traveling faster than the speed of light, a phenomenon judged impossible by Einstein's theory of special relativity. In this case, the researchers themselves doubted the result and asked the scientific community to confirm it or find the problem with their experiment, which they labeled the OPERA project (Sample, 2011). Antonio Ereditato, one of the lead researchers, stated, "We are very much astonished by this result, but a result is never a discovery until other people confirm it. When you get such a result you want to make sure you made no mistakes." When a second team of researchers attempted to replicate the study, they failed to find evidence of particles traveling faster than light. That result, combined with the finding that an important fiber-optic cable used in the original experiment was loose, potentially resulting in faulty data, ultimately led scientists to reject the original claim. As this example suggests, a crucial aspect of good science is ensuring that results can be replicated, especially if they seem too good to be true or go against the bulk of established theory and research. It is important to realize that breakthroughs do occur in science, however, and novel findings are often slow to be accepted. Thus, although skepticism can serve to police a scientific discipline, if taken to an extreme it can also impede the advance of science.

Peer-reviewed journals Scholarly journals whose editors send any submitted article out to be evaluated by knowledgeable researchers or scholars in the same field.

Published Research.   Different types of publications serve as outlets for disseminating research. Researchers generally try to publish in high-quality scientific and scholarly journals, which are collections of scholarly papers published by academic or research organizations. Most journals have standards for acceptance that guarantee a certain level of quality for the research found between their covers. By and large the highest-quality research will be published in journals that have a peer-review process.

We will discuss the peer-review process in depth in Chapter 16, but in brief, **peer-reviewed journals** send any submitted article out to knowledgeable researchers or scholars in the same field. The reviewers (usually a minimum of two) evaluate the manuscript in terms of the adequacy of overall writing, research methods, statistical analyses, and inferences drawn from the study.

Martha Arterberry:

"Nonsignificant findings are difficult to interpret and often difficult to publish; however, they are useful (when real and not due to study limitations) because we learn about the full range of a behavior or process. For example, we learn more about an outcome when we can identify what does and does not predict it."

Recognizing higher-quality journals becomes easier as you gain expertise in your chosen field. High-quality journals usually reject many more research studies than they publish, with some journals having rejection rates as high as 95%. But the rejection rate is only one of a number of factors that experts in a field use to evaluate journals. Other factors include the expertise of the journal editor and editorial board (these individuals choose reviewers and make decisions about what to publish in the journal), the scope of the journal (does it target a narrow scientific or more general audience?), and a history of publishing high-quality research. A research study published in a less prestigious journal may signal that the researcher made a number of compromises, which made determining the validity of the conclusions difficult. For example, to keep the costs of conducting a research project within budget, a researcher may choose to have a relatively small number of participants or use a less desirable method or technology for collecting the data. These choices may in turn lead the reviewers to question the strength of the conclusions that can be drawn from the research.

How Cognitive Biases and Heuristics Affect Your Judgment

Regardless of whether you are evaluating a newspaper report, website blurb, or journal article, it is important to realize that a number of factors influence the judgments and decisions that people make (Kahneman, 2011). These factors also influence you as you evaluate the validity of various claims and as you construct, design, and conduct your own research. These factors may also affect participants in your research studies as they respond to questions and situations that you have created. Daniel Kahneman and other researchers (Gilovich, Griffin, & Kahneman, 2002; Kahneman, Slovic, & Tversky, 1982) have outlined several of these factors, labeled cognitive biases and heuristics.

Cognitive biases are ways of thinking that push you to respond in a particular way in certain situations. **Heuristics** are simple procedures that often help us find adequate but less-than-perfect solutions to difficult problems. Sometimes these ways of thinking and simple procedures lead to highly effective problem solving, but at other times they yield surprisingly bad decisions. Many are related and operate in similar ways to influence how we process information and make decisions. It is worth noting that all of these cognitive biases and heuristics operate outside of our conscious control. Unfortunately, ample evidence suggests that an awareness and understanding of a particular bias or heuristic does not protect you from it (Kahneman, 2011). However, we argue that being conscious of these biases and heuristics can help you recognize when they might be active and counteract them with deliberate, conscious processes.

A variety of biases and heuristics can influence individuals evaluating and conducting research. One overarching framework for explaining these biases and heuristics is the **cognitive miser model**. This model refers to decision making where we attend to only a small amount of information, using as much prior information and experience as possible (Fiske & Taylor, 2013). Although the cognitive miser model can occasionally lead to appropriate decisions, you can easily imagine how not evaluating all of the information on a certain topic could lead to crucial errors. You can overcome this bias in your own research by reading the background literature as thoroughly as possible. The more you know about past research in an area, the less likely you will be to draw on a small amount of information in making important decisions.

The **availability heuristic** (Kahneman, 2011) describes how an individual overestimates the likelihood of an event that comes easily to mind, making it more difficult for a researcher to consider important any information that is not as prominent. For example, selective reporting by the media of dramatic yet relatively rare events, such as child abduction, may lead us to believe such events occur much more frequently than they actually do. A similar bias involves **discounting base-rate information** in favor of anecdotal evidence (Kahneman, 2001). This bias occurs when you make a decision, such as buying a new car, based on a friend's experience (good or bad) rather than on detailed source knowledge, as might be found in *Consumer Reports'* yearly evaluation of cars.

Cognitive bias Approach to thinking about a situation that may lead you to respond in a particular manner that may be flawed.

Heuristic Simple procedure that assists people in finding adequate but often imperfect solutions to difficult problems.

Cognitive miser model A cognitive bias that leads individuals to attend to only a small amount of information to preserve mental energy.

Availability heuristic A cognitive process that leads individuals to overestimate the likelihood of events that come easily to mind.

Discounting base-rate information A cognitive bias that leads individuals to favor anecdotal evidence over more detailed information that is available.

Anchoring A heuristic that leads individuals to use a particular value as a base for estimating an unknown quantity and adjust their estimate based on that quantity, even if the value given is entirely arbitrary.

One of the most powerful and well-documented heuristics is **anchoring**, the tendency to use a particular value as the basis for estimating an unknown quantity, even if the starting value given is entirely arbitrary. In the original demonstration of this concept, Tversky and Kahneman (1974) asked students whether the percentage of African nations in the United Nations was larger or smaller than one of two given anchors: 10% or 65%. Students who saw the anchor of 10% gave an average estimate of 25%, whereas those who saw the anchor of 65% gave an average estimate of 45%.

Anchoring has been shown to have powerful effects in real-world contexts. For example, a study of real estate agents who were asked to assess the value of an actual house on the market showed that providing two different values for the asking price of the same house—even when accompanied with a range of other information—had a major impact on the realtors' estimates; those given the larger anchor had much higher estimates of the home's value, whereas those given the smaller anchor had much lower estimates. This occurred despite the realtors' belief that the asking price had not affected their self-reported estimates (Northcraft & Neale, 1987). From a research perspective, being aware of the anchoring heuristic can help you design and construct better survey or interview questions. Similarly, knowing about this heuristic can help you evaluate whether the results in someone else's research may have been influenced by this approach.

Framing effect
A cognitive bias caused by seemingly inconsequential differences in wording in a question or problem that lead respondents to vary their choices.

Framing is a similar bias that can influence respondents who are answering questions on a survey or interview. This bias is caused by the manner in which a question is "framed," or worded. **Framing effects** occur when what might be thought of as inconsequential changes in the wording in a question influence the decision a respondent makes (Kahneman, 2011). For example, a patient may be more likely to agree to a particular medical procedure when it is framed as having an 85% chance of success than when it is presented as having a 15% chance of failure. There has been considerable focus on the impact of framing a choice in terms of a positive (a gain frame) or negative (a loss frame) perspective in the fields of social psychology (e.g., Higgins, 2000), medicine (e.g., Armstrong, Schwartz, Fitzgerald, Putt, & Ubel, 2002), and economics (e.g., Kahneman & Tversky, 1979).

Stroop effect
A specific cognitive bias influenced by knowledge, where reaction time slows when you print a color word in an ink color that differs from the actual word.

Both anchoring and framing effects refer to how particular knowledge can influence the way that we think and make decisions. An especially striking example of how knowledge can influence behavior is the well-documented **Stroop effect** (Stroop, 1935), which provides a classic example of a cognitive bias influenced by knowledge. The effect refers to the slowed reaction time that occurs when you print a color word in an ink color that differs from the actual word (e.g., the word "RED" is printed in blue ink). When people are asked to identify the physical color of the ink, their reactions are slowed by the interference of the word, which provides conflicting information; in effect, the perception of the word and the automatic extraction of the word's meaning interfere with the process of naming the color. The impact of knowledge here should be clear: if you did not know the meaning of the word red or if it were printed in a language that you did not know, there would be no effect.

Other biases that can influence your ability to both evaluate and conduct research include the overconfidence bias and the belief perseverance bias, which may lead you to over value yourself (self-serving bias) or your laboratory group (in-group bias). The **overconfidence bias** refers to a finding that individuals are often highly confident in a decision even when it has little or no relation to how correct that decision might be. The **belief perseverance bias** occurs when individuals cling to a theory even when they are presented with contradictory evidence. Researchers have found that theorists and investigators are often considerably resistant to knowledge change (Chinn & Brewer, 2000; Kuhn, 1962). The **self-serving bias** occurs when you perceive yourself (or your own research) more favorably than is warranted. In a sense, you can consider that you always have a vested interest in yourself and your research. Relatedly, the **in-group bias** refers to individuals favoring their own social group over people outside their group. In terms of research, these biases can create a tendency to view your own or your laboratory's research more positively than that produced from other individuals or laboratories.

Two other noteworthy cognitive biases are the tendency to infer causality from randomly correlated events and to perceive order in random events. We refer to these two effects more generally as the **causality bias** (Rosengren & French, 2013), or the tendency to assume that two events are causally related because of proximity of time and place, when in fact no such causal relation is present. A number of fascinating websites document many meaningless correlations, including http://tylervigen.com/. This site reports that the divorce rate in Maine is highly correlated with the U.S. per-capita consumption of margarine and that the U.S. per-capita consumption of cheese is highly correlated with the number of people who have died becoming tangled in their bedsheets. Although the connections suggested by these correlations are likely coincidental, the website serves as a warning to researchers and consumers of research that just because a finding is statistically significant, it is not necessarily meaningful. Likewise, we should be very careful about inferring causality from correlations.

Two other effects that are not strictly viewed as cognitive biases or heuristics can also influence the choices made by researchers: mood effects and decision fatigue. **Mood effects** refer to judgments and memory that can be influenced by positive or negative moods. **Decision fatigue** occurs when an individual's ability to make a rational decision is negatively impacted after making many decisions. Although the social psychology literature has extensively examined both of these effects (e.g., Baumeister, 2003; Forgas & Bower, 1987) and decision fatigue has been investigated with respect to its impact on judicial decisions (e.g., Danziger, Levav, & Avnaim-Pesso, 2011), these effects can influence the research process as well. Both of these effects can influence not only the judgment of researchers as they engage in the many decisions involved in the research process, but also subjects

Overconfidence bias A cognitive bias where an individual is highly sure of his or her response or decision, although that choice has little relation to the correctness of the choice or decision.

Belief perseverance bias A cognitive bias that leads individuals to maintain a belief or theory even when confronted with considerable counterevidence.

Self-serving bias A cognitive bias that leads to the tendency to perceive or favor your own views and beliefs over those of others.

In-group bias A cognitive bias to view members of your own social group more positively than members outside of your social group.

Causality bias The tendency to assume that two events are causally related because of proximity of time and place, when in fact no such causal relation exists.

Mood effect Influence on decision making that occurs because of either a positive or a negative mood state.

Decision fatigue
A phenomenon that occurs when the quality of decision making declines as an individual is required to make a large number of decisions in a short period of time.

participating in research. For this reason, it is important to consider whether the research environment may impact the participants' overall mood and whether the number of choices you ask your subjects to make may lead to decision fatigue.

This discussion of cognitive biases and heuristics should not lead you to conclude that your own judgments are always flawed or incorrect. Rather, we hope that this serves as a cautionary tale, an antidote to the cliché that you should always "follow your gut." Even highly experienced researchers can fall prey to biases and heuristics. We argue that a background knowledge of cognitive biases and heuristics can make individuals better consumers of knowledge and better researchers, regardless of their field of study. Ultimately, in the same way that we encourage you to be skeptical of reports that you encounter in the popular media, you should be equally skeptical of your own quick judgments and evaluations.

Conducting Your Own Research to Evaluate Claims

We believe that conducting your own research is the best way to gain a more sophisticated understanding of research and the potential problems associated with a particular research study. When you attempt to do research on your own, you become acutely aware of practical issues that may lead to a flawed research process.

Researchers must compromise on issues involving participant selection or experimental design because of a number of different constraints, which can include a lack of resources, difficulty in obtaining the desired population, or concerns with the safety and confidentiality of participants. For these and other reasons, no research study is perfect. Therefore, a knowledgeable researcher or consumer of research must learn to evaluate whether the limitations in the study make it difficult to draw reasonable conclusions from the data. In some cases, flaws in the research may render conclusions provided by the researchers unsubstantiated. But in most cases, issues with the way a research study is designed and carried out may mean only that the results should not be generalized much beyond the context of the original study. Much of the rest of this book is devoted to teaching you how to design and conduct your own research project. Yet, even if you do not go on to conduct research yourself, the material in this book should help you become an educated consumer of research.

DISTINCTION BETWEEN SCIENCE AND PSEUDOSCIENCE

Pseudoscience
Explanation that is presented with the veneer of science, but does not fundamentally conform to valid scientific methods.

Many scientists like to think that the boundary between science and **pseudoscience**—explanations that are presented as scientific but do not comply with a valid scientific method—is clear-cut and that these two approaches to inquiry are easy to identify. In practice, the distinction is often less clear. Arthur C. Clarke (1962) recognized the porous boundary between the two when he said, "Any technology distinguishable from magic is insufficiently advanced" (p. 36). Indeed, if you consider the technology that you use on a daily basis—from your smartphone and tablet computer to the Internet—these tools would have been viewed as impossible or the result of magic 100 years ago. The realm of science shifts with increases in knowledge and technology. However, some aspects of the scientific approach, including the overall goals of science and the scientific method, distinguish it from more pseudoscientific claims.

The Goals of Science

The goals of science can be placed into three broad categories: to describe, to explain, and to predict. Consider how these goals apply to the Stroop effect mentioned previously:

- *Description.* What happens when we present respondents with color words that conflict with their meaning (e.g., "BLUE" presented in red ink)? We see that it takes longer for people to name the ink color of a color word if the word does not match the color.
- *Explanation.* Why does a conflict between a color word and its ink color lead to longer color-naming times? When we read a familiar word, we cannot help but extract meaning from the word, and when meaning conflicts with perception, it can interfere with the color-naming task.
- *Prediction.* What do we predict would happen if we were to use words that are not color terms, but might suggest color (e.g., "grass," "banana")? Perhaps even color-suggestive words can lead to interference, but maybe not to the same degree as actual color terms.

These three goals—to describe, explain, and predict—interact in complex ways. For example, we use descriptions and explanations to help us make predictions, and we use explanations and predictions to help us design studies that allow for novel descriptions. In many ways, these goals set science apart from pseudoscience, but more important, the characteristics of the scientific method differentiate these two approaches.

The Scientific Method

Good science differs from pseudoscience in its use of a strict set of principles referred to as the **scientific method**. This approach requires that research be objective, consistent (or reliable), conducted in a public manner, based on established procedures and past knowledge, and driven by a quest for knowledge and truth.

Objective. The first key aspect of the scientific method is its emphasis on objectivity. From a research perspective, **objectivity** refers to the idea that researchers strive for the truth rather than attempt to find results that support their own beliefs or theory. The ideal of objectivity requires that research be conducted in a way that produces unbiased results. Objectivity is most easily understood when contrasted with **subjectivity**, which stems from

Scientific method An approach that seeks to generate explanations for observable phenomena with an emphasis on objectivity and verifiable evidence.

Objectivity Approaching knowledge as a quest for the truth, rather than as an attempt to find results that support one's own beliefs or theory.

Subjectivity Approaching knowledge from the standpoint of an individual's own beliefs, experiences, and interpretations.

an individual's own beliefs, experiences, and interpretations. In science, researchers try hard to be objective and not allow their own beliefs, emotions, or biases to interfere with the pursuit of greater knowledge. Although complete objectivity is impossible (unless perhaps you are a Vulcan from the *Star Trek* series), the research enterprise should be driven as much as possible by data rather than your own biases.

Reliability The idea that an investigation or measurement tool should yield consistent findings if researchers use the same procedures and methods repeatedly.

Consistent.   A second key aspect of the scientific method involves **reliability**, which refers to the idea that an investigation should yield consistent findings if researchers use the same procedures and methods again and again. Ideally, it is important to determine whether research can be replicated within a research group, as well as across independent research teams. If a result is obtained only by a single researcher or single research team working in one laboratory—and cannot be confirmed by other, independent laboratories—then there is reason for skepticism. Researchers should welcome attempts to replicate their work, as was the case in the CERN example mentioned earlier. Often the difference between pseudoscience and science comes down to the fact that science, if performed correctly, yields results that can be replicated widely, whereas pseudoscience is more likely to yield results that are not replicable.

Public.   The third important characteristic about science is that it exists in the public realm. Results from experiments and investigations are discussed within laboratory groups, presented at national and international conferences, and published in journals. Many of these journals (including many online ones) employ rigorous procedures to evaluate the importance of the research, the quality of the research methods, and the validity of any claims made by researchers.

Even after an article has been published, other researchers will often attempt to replicate the study or question the methods used or the validity of interpretations drawn from the data. In many ways, the scientific approach involves a relatively constant stream of evaluation and criticism. Pseudoscientific claims will often not be open for public discussion, and the methods used (and even the actual data) may not be provided for scrutiny and evaluation in a public way.

Based on Established Principles and Past Knowledge.   A fourth aspect that separates science from pseudoscience is the central role of explanation in science. That is, the explanation given for a phenomenon must be based on established principles and past knowledge. This is one reason why the scientific community did not accept the result of the OPERA team working at CERN—the data did not fit with the established laws and theories of physics. In contrast, pseudoscientific claims often provide explanations that are not testable or are based on an individual's claims that cannot be supported by actual data and rigorous testing. Often individuals promoting pseudoscience ask the consumer to "believe" them and their story. For example, the press release for the "magic weight loss cure" of the green coffee diet asks consumers to blindly trust Dr. Oz's personal opinion about green coffee beans and buy the green coffee extract.

Driven by a Quest for Knowledge and Truth. A final way in which science and pseudoscience differ is that individuals involved in science are generally searching for knowledge and truth (Thagard, 2012) rather than support for a particular idea or belief. Yet, pseudoscience often comes disguised as science. For example, makers of "power band" bracelets touted their product in videos that asked consumers to test the products themselves. The bracelets, which include a hologram (see Figure 1.3) that is purported to interact with individuals' natural energy fields to

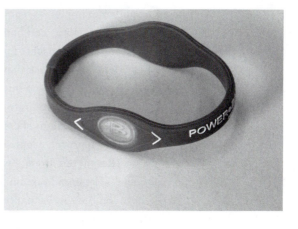

FIGURE 1.3. Power bands were endorsed by well-known athletes, but they were ultimately shown to be no more effective than wearing a regular elastic band.

promote athletic ability, were not based on any known science and were ultimately shown to be no more effective than wearing a simple elastic band (Brice, Jarosz, Ames, Baglin, & Da Costa, 2011). Interestingly, many professional athletes and celebrities, even ones who were not paid to endorse the product, have worn these bracelets. Some likely adopted the technology out of fear that their competitors might be gaining an edge, but others may have accepted the so-called "science" behind the advertising. Well-known athletes such as Shaquille O'Neal and David Beckham were reported to advocate wearing the bracelets. Such testimonial evidence (particularly from celebrities) should send up a red flag.

In lieu of valid empirical evidence, a company may resort to high-profile anecdotes in hopes of persuading consumers of their pseudoscientific claims. As the cognitive psychologist Keith Stanovich (2012) argues, testimonials are incredibly persuasive but also harmful to society, leading to investments of time and resources in disreputable products and ideas. Stanovich notes that claims from such vivid testimonial evidence can overwhelm people's weighting of solid, scientifically grounded data. This is another example of the bias of accepting anecdotal information over base-rate data, discussed earlier.

As is often the case when science and pseudoscience face off, however, science ultimately wins. After a number of empirical studies of the efficacy of power bands provided results that suggested they had no discernable impact on improving the balance and stability of the individuals wearing the bands, the manufacturer admitted that there was no "credible scientific evidence" to support its claims and eventually filed for bankruptcy ("Power Band Bracelets a 'Scam,'" 2011). Dr. Andrew Deardon of the British Medical Association Wales suggested that the power bands were basically pseudoscience ("Power Balance Band Is Placebo," 2010).

Another example of pseudoscience masquerading as science can be found in the attempts to promote "creation science" or the theory of "intelligent design." These closely aligned approaches focus on finding scientific support for the biblical narrative of creation and evidence that the only reasonable explanation for the world is that it was the product of some intelligent being. Both of these approaches grew out of attempts by religious groups to ban the teaching of evolution or to provide equal or more time to biblical versions of creationism. After repeated failures in courts, proponents of the biblical approach adopted more scientific labels (creation science) to bolster their claims (Rosengren, Brem, Evans, & Sinatra, 2012). Proponents of this view have even founded a Creation Museum. However, their repeated use of the statement "Prepare to believe" on their website ultimately undermines their claim (http://creationmuseum .org/). No true scientist would ask you to "believe" without providing some credible evidence. Rather, it is the scientist's task to convince you through evidence and rational explanation.

In summary, science seeks to accurately describe phenomena in the world, to provide a rational explanation for these phenomena, and to use the information gained through research to make predictions about future events or situations. Psychology does not have a strong history of accurate prediction. As the field progresses, however, improved methods of describing psychological phenomena and more accurate explanations of those phenomena should ultimately yield better predictions of what an individual or group might do in the future. Good science is grounded in skepticism, acknowledges the limitations of methods and interpretations, and asks both the general public and the scientific community to examine the data, evaluate the research, replicate the findings, and ultimately judge the validity of the claims.

DISTINCTION BETWEEN APPLIED AND BASIC RESEARCH

Applied research
Research that generally seeks to address a practical issue or problem.

Scholars and researchers often make the distinction between applied and basic research. **Applied research** generally seeks to address a practical issue or problem. This type of research is thought to have more immediate value because it focuses on real-world problems and attempts to find specific solutions to those problems. Research designed to make solar energy panels more efficient and economical is one example of applied research. Within psychology, investigations into the efficacy of a particular kind of behavioral intervention for children with attention deficit hyperactivity disorder would be an example of applied research.

Basic research
Research that strives to advance knowledge within a particular area of science.

Basic research strives to advance knowledge within a particular area of science. Basic research may focus on testing a particular theory or the exploration of a particular phenomenon. Physicists at CERN, for example, conduct basic research to find evidence that supports the fundamental laws of physics. The 2012 discovery of the Higgs boson—the so-called "God particle"—provides a nice example of basic research that was designed to find evidence for a particle that was assumed to exist more than 50 years ago. This discovery serves to confirm some basic physical laws but, at least for the moment, has had no real practical or applied significance.

The line between applied and basic research is not always clear and straightforward. Applied research often fails to find solutions to vexing problems, and basic research often yields findings that solve long-standing practical problems. Both kinds of research can provide real value to society. For example, the basic psychological research on judgment and decision making has led researchers to rethink applied problems in education ("Why don't students understand evolution?"), medicine ("Why don't people do what their doctors tell them to do?"), and economics ("Why do people buy lottery tickets?"). Stanovich (2012) argues that it is a mistake to view the distinction between applied and basic research solely in terms of whether the research has practical applications. He suggests that the distinction is mainly one of time. "Applied findings are of use immediately," he wrote. "However, there is nothing so practical as a general and accurate theory" (Stanovich, 2012).

THE RESEARCH PROCESS AND ORGANIZATION OF THIS BOOK

Figure 1.4 provides an overview of the research process and also, for the most part, the organization of this book. Note that the flowchart presents arrows going down the center to illustrate the most efficient pathway from the start of a research project to final write-up. Virtually no research project follows this pathway. Rather, most projects involve a highly iterative process captured by the arrows that circle back up the chart. These arrows are meant to convey the idea that as researchers progress through the research process, questions and issues pop up that cause them to reconsider previous plans. These questions and issues can lead to a reformulation of the original research question or a change in the overall research method or specific protocol.

We emphasize that the research process is open and nonlinear, with many different choices that can alter the focus or direction of the project. Each of these steps also requires a set of choices and tasks that we will describe in the chapters to come. In our view, the first step of the research process involves ethics training. As a researcher working within a college or university system, you are required to complete ethics training. Chapter 2 sets the stage by reporting on the often disturbing history of research, including that which has been conducted in the field of psychology. Chapter 3 addresses ethical issues and aspects of ethics training, including how to complete an institutional review board application and tips on receiving speedy approval. Chapter 4 leads you through the process of choosing an area of research and formulating a research question. Chapter 5 explains how to generate a testable hypothesis, identify variables of interest, and begin to design an experiment.

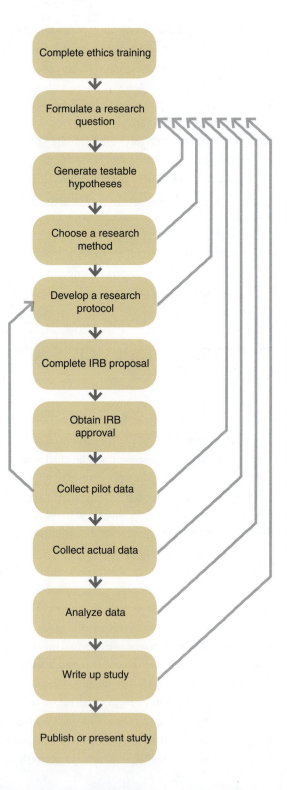

FIGURE 1.4.   Flowchart of the research process.

Chapter 6 discusses developing your research protocol, in particular how to obtain a sample, choose measures, conduct a power analysis, and formulate an analysis plan.

Chapter 7 addresses the design and construction of interviews and surveys, which are becoming increasingly popular with the advent of online technology. Chapter 8 focuses on experimental designs, which are widely considered the gold standard for scientific inquiry. Chapter 9 covers variations on standard experimental designs, including quasi-experimental single-case and factorial approaches. Chapter 10 presents the major types of nonexperimental designs—meaning designs that do not apply an experimental control, such as observation, case studies, archival research, and meta-analysis. Chapter 11 introduces basic methods and techniques in neuroscience, an area of research with increasing prominence in psychology and related fields. Chapter 12 explores research over age and time, which examines developmental changes that take place over study participants' life spans. Chapters 13 and 14 lead you through the process of analyzing and interpreting your raw data and drawing appropriate conclusions through the use of statistics. Chapter 15 describes how to accurately report your results in a clear, readable article and to identify your target audience. The book concludes with Chapter 16, which offers tips on presenting your research to the wider scientific community at conferences and in the pages of scholarly journals.

PRACTICAL TIPS

Practical Tips for Research Methods

1. Be an educated and critical consumer of research reports wherever you encounter them.

2. Learn how to evaluate sources of information.

3. Do not trust a single source—look for converging information from a variety of sources.

4. Realize that cognitive biases and heuristics influence researchers, participants, and you.

CHAPTER SUMMARY

Through our analysis of sample media reports, it should be apparent that knowledge of research methods is invaluable to vetting the barrage of research findings that confront people daily. Strategies such as identifying the researchers, their funding, and motives, as well as reading and evaluating past research, should help you determine what findings to take seriously and what to disregard. Remember, every reported research finding requires a critical eye. Knowledge of research methods will also provide a template for conducting your own research, a subject we delve into in later chapters.

Up for Discussion

1. Researchers from Cornell University and the University Jena in Germany conducted a study that appeared in the journal *Environment and Behavior* in December 2015. Results showed that diners ordered significantly more items, including alcoholic beverages, when served by wait staff with a high body mass index compared with wait staff with a low body mass index. Several news outlets, including the *Wall Street Journal* and *USA Today*, ran stories on the study. Do you think the findings are noteworthy and/or valid? Why or why not? What bias might the researchers suffer from?

2. Although researchers have shown that there is no evidence to support Andrew Wakefield's claim that the measles, mumps, and rubella vaccine leads to autism, the belief that it does remains strong. What biases and heuristics might influence the continued belief that vaccines cause autism? How might you as a researcher or scientific writer counteract those beliefs?

3. As we discussed in this chapter, it is important to obtain converging evidence to support research claims. Why might people so often avoid doing just that? Why do we prefer the one-off study to looking critically at scientific claims?

Key Terms

Anchoring, p. 14

Applied research, p. 20

Availability heuristic, p. 13

Basic research, p. 20

Belief perseverance bias, p. 15

Causality bias, p. 15

Cognitive bias, p. 13

Cognitive miser model, p. 13

Conclusion validity, p. 10

Converging evidence, p. 5

Decision fatigue, pp. 15, 16

Discounting base-rate information, p. 13

Framing effect, p. 14

Heuristic, p. 13

In-group bias, p. 15

Mood effect, p. 15

Objectivity, p. 17

Overconfidence bias, p. 15

Peer-reviewed journals, p. 12

Pseudoscience, p. 16

Reliability, p. 18

Replication, p. 10

Scientific method, p. 17

Secondary source, p. 6

Self-serving bias, p. 15

Stroop effect, p. 14

Subjectivity, p. 17

2

The Ethical Imperative

INSIDE RESEARCH: JENNIFER E. LANSFORD

Research Professor,
Sanford School of Public
Policy, Duke University

In high school I thought I wanted to be a clinical psychologist because I volunteered in a peer-counseling program that I really liked. But my first psych class in college was developmental psychology, and my professor offered me a position as a research assistant in his lab. I became interested in researching parent–child relationships, particularly the issues of parents' warmth (displays of affection) versus control (rules and discipline) and how those affect the development of their children. At first I studied how parents influenced their children's peer relationships by looking at and coding videotapes of their interactions with their kids. I would tally up the number of times each parent showed a certain behavior—like when they made a strong demand or did something affectionate—and then the number of times the children showed the same behaviors, and then looked for correlations between what the parents were doing and the children were doing.

I eventually developed a special focus on parenting and the development of aggression in children in different cultural contexts. Now I'm conducting a collaborative study of parenting in nine countries, including the United States. It's fascinating, and I feel fortunate to have found a career I love so much.

Even so, we have some challenges, like any research. One has to do with ethical issues. Any time we conduct research we have consent forms that parents sign before participating, and the children sign statements of assent, too. The form says we have an ethical obligation to report signs of suspected child abuse and neglect. And in all of the IRB (Institutional Review Board) materials we submit to get our studies approved, we say we will report any cases of suspected child abuse. It's a big issue. There have been a few times in the course of our work where we've been concerned for one reason or another about a child's safety. Those become really tricky issues. If we have concerns, we've reported them to child protective services for them to follow up on. But you struggle internally with that—am I doing the best thing for a child in that situation?

Jennifer Lansford encounters different kinds of ethical issues in her research on aggression and other behavior problems in youth. In her international studies on the effects of parents' disciplinary techniques on children's development, she must contend with various standards of research ethics in nine countries, as well as individual cases of suspected child abuse. Her work has been published in many leading psychology journals.

Research Focus: Parenting and child development in different cultural contexts

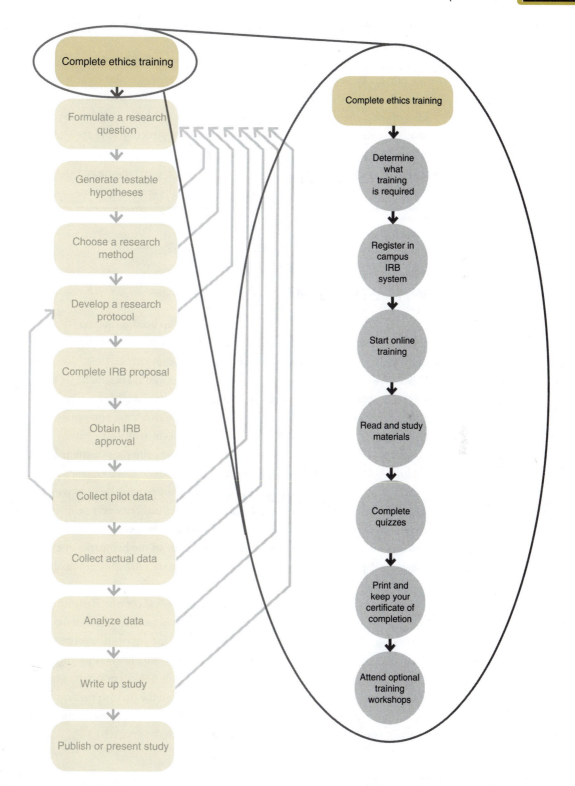

Chapter Abstract

In this chapter, we introduce the basic ethical framework that guides research in psychology, provide some historical context for the evolution of ethical standards in social science research, explain the function and role of the institutional review board (IRB), and explore a few of the contemporary high-profile cases that have kept issues of research ethics in the news. This chapter provides the foundation for our instruction in the research process. We believe that ethical principles are central to the conduct of good scientific research in psychology and that researchers must have a thorough understanding and knowledge of ethical principles *before* beginning any other aspects of the research process.

WHY ETHICS MATTER

Our placement of ethics in research at the front of this book is intentional. As Hesse-Biber and Leavy (2006) cogently argue, the trustworthiness of the research process and the findings themselves depend on the moral integrity of the researcher.

Many researchers will say that they know what is and is not ethical, as if ethical issues were clear-cut and obvious. But many are neither. For example, is it ethical for doctors to recruit their own patients to participate in research that drug companies are paying the doctors to conduct? Many physicians see no problem with this, arguing that it is both common practice and the only way to recruit the right sample of participants. In fact, recruitment of patients has become a relatively common practice among clinical psychologists. Yet, many other behavioral scientists see this as potentially coercive or a conflict of interest, because researchers are often in positions of authority over people they are trying to recruit. In these situations, chances that participants could give completely voluntary, **informed consent** are slim. Informed consent, one of the hallmarks of ethical research, means that participants agree to take part in a study *after* they are made aware of the potential risks.

Informed consent
Agreement of a participant to take part in a study, having been made aware of the potential risks.

Consider, for example, a patient with a rare form of cancer who is admitted to a hospital, where she is approached by a doctor who presents herself as the foremost expert on that cancer. The doctor says she would like to enroll the patient in an experimental drug treatment. The pharmaceutical company that makes the drug likely is paying the doctor as a consultant. The patient is potentially dying and really not in a position to say "no." Ideally, some firewall would exist between the researcher and the patient; perhaps another doctor not involved directly in the patient's care or not being reimbursed by the pharmaceutical company would talk to the patient about enrolling in the drug trial.

One useful way to think about **ethics** and research is that ethical conduct in research reflects the social responsibility that the researcher has to society at large. Ideas about social responsibility do change as a society's ethics evolve, however; for instance, child labor in the United States was once common, but now laws ban this practice. When researchers follow best practices from an ethical standpoint, they help maintain the relationship of trust between the researcher and society.

Practically speaking, ethics in psychology refers to a set of standard practices that promote the safety and dignity of humans and address issues of fairness. Many psychologists treat these standards as well established, when in truth they are not. As we discuss later in this chapter, the storied history of ethical violations by researchers—not only in psychology, but also in other academic fields—makes the maintenance of this trust all the more essential (see "Media Matters: David Reimer"). The ethical mandate for researchers goes above and beyond regulatory requirements dictated by federal and state law, which are best considered the minimum standards to which a researcher must adhere.

The onus for maintaining the bond of trust falls squarely on the shoulders of the researcher. But to fulfill this obligation, researchers must understand ethical standards and principles. Without this background, researchers cannot make ethically sound judgments in designing, implementing, analyzing, and disseminating their findings.

Ethics are not stable, universal principles; rather, they evolve over time and depend on the particular context in which the research is being conducted. Although some philosophers (e.g., Kant, Sartre) have argued that our actions should be guided by moral imperatives based on universal laws such as the Golden Rule (treat others as you would like to be treated), many others argue that ethics are socially mediated, not a universal code of conduct. Although the ethical principles outlined in this chapter are designed to provide a base for making ethical decisions, how these principles are interpreted and enforced varies from university to university, from community to community, from state to state, and from country to country. This variation makes cross-cultural research like Jennifer Lansford's particularly challenging because what is or is not viewed as ethical may vary extensively across cultures.

Ethical guidelines can even vary within regions of the same country. Consider how differently U.S. states view corporal punishment in school (currently no states have passed laws prohibiting corporal punishment in homes). According to the Center for Effective Discipline, 31 states have outlawed corporal punishment—often called "paddling"—but other states, such as Florida, Texas, and Indiana, still allow it. As a second example, the legality of video recording police officers or other individuals in public places without their permission varies from state to state. But in this case, we cross the line between what is ethical and what is legal. These two constructs, although related, are often independent. Certain behavior may be legal but unethical, whereas other behavior might be considered ethical, but

Ethics Conduct in research that reflects the social responsibility that the researcher has toward society at large.

Jennifer Lansford:
"We had originally wanted to include India in the study on parenting styles across different cultural contexts, but we could not get approval from an Indian university to adopt U.S. ethical guidelines. The researchers pointed out that the United States hadn't ratified the United Nations' 1989 Convention on the Rights of the Child. They said, 'Why would we conform to U.S. ethical standards when you haven't even ratified this convention?' It was an interesting perspective because the United States tends to put itself on a pedestal in saying we're going to make sure these countries are doing things the right way."

David Reimer

Of all the ethical violations in research throughout history, one of the cruelest is the case of David Reimer, an unwitting subject of one researcher's experiment gone very wrong. Reimer's treatment by an ambitious "expert" stands as a cautionary tale of what can happen when researchers care more about their theories than their participants.

Bruce Reimer and his twin brother, Brian, were born in 1965 to a young couple in Winnipeg and were, by all accounts, normal baby boys. At the age of eight months, they underwent circumcision at a nearby hospital. The doctor used an electrocautery needle instead of a scalpel and inadvertently burned off Bruce's penis (Colapinto, 2000); reconstructive surgery was not advanced enough at that time to restore it (Walker, 2004).

Janet and Ron Weimer visited several doctors, none of whom offered solutions. Distraught and unsure of where to turn, the Reimers saw by chance a television show featuring a researcher named Dr. John Money, a sexologist at Johns Hopkins University (BBC Horizon, 2005). Money was a pioneer in the new field of sex change surgery, and he appeared alongside a transgender woman.

"[Money] was very charismatic, seemed highly intelligent, and seemed very confident of what he was saying," Janet recalled. "The transsexual certainly made an impact because she was a very feminine-seeming woman. And I thought, 'Here's our answer, here's our salvation, here's our hope'" (BBC Horizon, 2005).

Janet wrote to Money explaining her son's condition, and he invited them to bring Bruce to his gender identity clinic in Baltimore. What Money didn't tell the Reimers was that he had long searched for such a case to prove his theory about "nurture over nature" in sexual identity (Colapinto, 2000). Money believed that gender was basically neutral for the first two years of life and that environment could make a baby adopt either a male or a female sexual identity. The Reimers gave him the perfect experiment for his hypothesis, complete with the built-in matched control of Brian. Money proposed raising Bruce as a girl and giving him estrogen supplements. Money told the couple that they must never reveal the truth to their children or the experiment would fail. They agreed and renamed Bruce Brenda (Colapinto, 2004).

Money's hypothesis soon turned out to be flawed, although Janet followed his instructions to socialize Bruce as a girl. At age 2, Brenda tore off her dresses, and as she grew, she developed a clear preference for Brian's toys. When she went to school she had trouble making friends, got into physical fights, and was ridiculed by peers for her boyish manners and gait. By the time she was 10, Brenda expressed sexual attraction for girls (Walker, 2004).

"It was so obvious to everyone, not just to me, that she was just masculine," Janet said (BBC Horizon, 2005).

Money, meanwhile, met with the Reimer twins every year and recorded his observations that the gender reassignment was succeeding, despite all evidence to the contrary. His textbook *Man & Woman, Boy & Girl* (1972), written with the psychiatrist Anke A. Ehrhardt, included a chapter on the success of Bruce/Brenda, and the case became famous (Money & Ehrhardt, 1972).

When the Reimer twins were in their early teens, a local psychiatrist convinced the parents to reveal the truth. Brenda changed his name to David and began to dress like a boy. He received testosterone injections and had several surgeries to return to his male state. "Suddenly it all made sense why I felt the way I did. I wasn't some sort of weirdo. I wasn't crazy," he said

(Colapinto, 2004). The media began reporting on Reimer when another researcher inspired him to go public with his tragic experiences.

Unfortunately, David's newfound sense of self was short-lived. Although he eventually married a woman, David struggled with depression and was devastated by Brian's death at the age of 37. He wound up separated from his wife, unemployed, and financially destitute. David committed suicide in 2004.

John Colapinto, who wrote about David in *As Nature Made Him: The Boy Who Was Raised as a Girl* (2001), observed that media accounts of David's suicide emphasized his recent troubles. "Surprisingly little emphasis was given to the extraordinary circumstances of his upbringing" (Colapinto, 2004).

Money continued to publish accounts of his success with Bruce/Brenda through the 1970s, until a psychologist named Milton Diamond wrote a myth-shattering paper published in *Archives of Pediatrics and Adolescent Medicine* (Diamond & Sigmundson, 1997). Money died in 2006 of complications from Parkinson's disease (Carey, 2006).

potentially be illegal. Just as the ethical landscape may vary over time and place, the legal landscape also may vary considerably.

Part of being a good researcher is consciously thinking about the ethical aspects of your own research and design. Most researchers will say that in general you should not lie to subjects in your research or to your colleagues or to the public in writing up your research or that you should not make up data or steal others' ideas. But most, if not all, research includes ethical gray areas that a researcher should consider. For example, sometimes participants decide they do not want to complete a study. Is it ethical to reward those who complete the study? If so, when does the size of the reward become coercive? Is it ethical to punish participants who leave a study early by deducting funds from the payment, taking away course credits, or requiring them to do some other, more onerous activity? Many issues related to subject recruitment, informed consent, and other research procedures and policy are somewhat controversial and not clear-cut.

COMPLETING ETHICS TRAINING

The flow chart at the beginning of the chapter outlines the initial steps that you must take to become a researcher. All academic institutions in the United States and many other countries require that researchers who engage in research with humans or nonhuman animals undergo some sort of ethical training. The first step in the process is to determine what kind of training your institution requires. Most U.S. academic institutions require online ethics training.

To gain access to these online programs, you must typically register (provide your name and campus affiliation) with your local IRB, the organization that oversees research on most campuses. Registration enables the IRB to keep track of who has completed the training necessary to be allowed to conduct research.

We talk more about online training programs and what they include in Chapter 3. Briefly, online training involves reading about the history of ethics as it pertains to research and thinking about particular ethical problems. The training is often broken up into specific chapters, some of which are required for all researchers and others that are required for researchers conducting certain kinds of research (e.g., research with children). Each chapter generally ends with a short quiz that must be passed to complete the training.

After completion of the required training, most online programs allow you to print a certificate of completion. If you plan to work in a research laboratory, the faculty member or lead investigator may ask that you bring in a copy of the certificate. Although completion of the formal training is all that is required, thinking about ethics should be an ongoing process. For this reason, we recommend that you attend optional training workshops periodically. These workshops are often offered by local IRBs a couple of times a year and can be found at certain national conferences where research is being presented.

We now turn to the history of ethics, which helps put current practices within the context of society's evolving views of research practices. The history is not pretty, which is one reason why we present the guidelines and restrictions early on. We urge you to think about ethics as you read about others' research and as you begin your own.

HISTORY OF ETHICS

Rules designed to ensure ethical practices in research are a surprisingly recent phenomenon. In fact, the U.S. government had virtually no guidelines for medical research or experimentation before the start of World War II in 1939 and did not begin to define *legitimate* research or regulate experiments until the mid-1960s. Prior to that point, doctors and researchers relied on informal professional codes of conduct and personal ideas about right and wrong.

The Nuremberg Code of 1947

Nuremberg Code of 1947 A group of 10 standards that guide ethical research involving human beings.

Contemporary ethical research guidelines have their roots in the **Nuremberg Code of 1947**, which comprised 10 standards that guided ethical research involving human beings. The first standard asserted that subjects must not only consent to participate in the experiment, but also have the legal capacity to give consent. For instance, prisoners, minors, and people with mental disabilities could not participate in experiments. The code grew out of the war crimes trial of Nazi doctors who had performed experiments such as forcing concentration camp prisoners to stand in tanks of ice water for several hours to research the prevention and treatment of hypothermia and infecting healthy subjects with malaria to test the effectiveness of various drugs.

Although the Nuremberg Code influenced many international ethics statements, the U.S. medical establishment did not adopt it until 1953, nor did it have much effect on the everyday methods of American researchers once the code was adopted (Stark, 2012). Many American medical professionals did not consider the Nuremberg Code guidelines relevant; they perceived the experiments as motivated by Nazi immorality, not in any way the result of researchers working without regulations (Rothman, 1991).

The Declaration of Helsinki

Despite the groundwork laid by the Nuremberg Code, a gaping hole remained in the governance of human experimentation. Many researchers resisted ethics codes because they were hesitant to relinquish authority and personal discretion in the doctor–patient relationship (Stark, 2012). In 1953, members of the World Medical Association's medical ethics committee suggested producing an ethics statement on human experimentation, but nothing was formalized until 1964, when the association approved the **Declaration of Helsinki**. The declaration broadened Nuremberg Code guidelines, stating, "It is the mission of the doctor to safeguard the health of the people." The document also made an important distinction between therapeutic and nontherapeutic clinical studies—in other words, research conducted to help sick patients versus experiments performed for purely scientific goals—and created rules governing both types of endeavors (Katz, 1972).

The National Institutes of Health

The years after World War II saw a huge increase in medical experimentation on human subjects, particularly in studies funded and conducted by the **National Institutes of Health (NIH)**, the U.S. government's main agency responsible for biomedical and health-related research. For almost 20 years, researchers conducted an array of experiments on humans, unfettered by regulations and many of them troubling.

In 1953, the NIH opened on its grounds the Clinical Center, a research hospital that played a pivotal role in the development of contemporary ethics in research. For the first time, the U.S. government began conducting medical research on healthy participants (who were called "Normals," as opposed to sick patients) who lived at the center for extended periods of time and participated in a variety of experiments.

To define parameters around this new area of research and to deflect criticism and particularly lawsuits, NIH administrators created the **Clinical Research Committee**, a group of scientists given the power to approve or modify experiments. The committee became the prototype for today's IRBs, which are described in depth later in the chapter.

The first studies approved by the committee involved injecting radioisotopes, which World War II government researchers were eager to explore, into healthy patients in the

Declaration of Helsinki Formalized in 1964, this international proclamation broadened the Nuremberg Code guidelines from 1947, stating, "It is the mission of the doctor to safeguard the health of the people."

National Institutes of Health (NIH) The U.S. government agency primarily responsible for biomedical and health-related research.

Clinical Research Committee A group of scientists given the power to approve or modify experiments, originally created by administrators at the National Institutes of Health. It is the prototype for today's institutional review boards.

hope that such treatment would eventually cure a range of diseases. Other early studies included the testing of heart drugs and, in the 1950s and 1960s, the psychedelic drug LSD (Stark, 2012).

In addition to the research carried out within its Clinical Center, NIH funded studies at other institutions as part of its Extramural Program. One such study in 1964 at New York's Jewish Hospital for Chronic Disease spurred the type of lawsuit that NIH leaders had long feared. Clinical researchers had injected 22 patients with cancer cells without first obtaining their consent. When a patient sued the hospital, the hospital in turn argued that the parent organization of NIH (the Public Health Service) was also liable. Although the NIH eventually escaped the suit unscathed, its lawyers insisted on building a firewall between NIH funding and research conducted outside its walls. They required that all NIH-funded studies be reviewed and approved by an ethics committee at the institution hosting the research (Stark, 2012).

NIH's resolve to address ethical violations by researchers was strengthened in 1966, when the *New England Journal of Medicine* published an article by Dr. Henry Beecher of Harvard Medical School, a seasoned investigator (Beecher, 1966). In the article, Beecher listed studies conducted at the nation's most prestigious university medical school clinics and laboratories that endangered the health of subjects without their knowledge (Rothman, 1991). Among Beecher's examples was a study in which researchers infected 15 mentally disabled children and young adults with hepatitis. His cases also included studies in which researchers withheld known effective treatment. In one instance, researchers wanting to investigate the relapse rate of typhoid fever withheld treatment of a drug called chloramphenicol—which had been shown to dramatically reduce mortality—from 157 charity patients, 36 of whom died (Katz, 1972).

Tuskegee Syphilis Study

Although Beecher's exposé brought ethical violations to light, abuses continued. It was not until 1972, for instance, that the mainstream media broke news of the infamous Tuskegee Syphilis Study. In 1932, the U.S. Public Health Service, in conjunction with the Tuskegee Institute in Alabama, began a study of syphilis with nearly 400 impoverished black men (Jones, 1981). The study's goal was to learn from autopsies the effects of syphilis on the body. The men were never told they had syphilis and received no treatment. They were simply told they were being treated for "bad blood"—a local term for several illnesses, such as anemia, syphilis, and fatigue. For enrolling in the study, they received free medical exams, free meals, and free burial insurance. When the study began, there was no cure for syphilis. But as the years went by, researchers withheld treatment with penicillin, which by 1947 had become the standard cure for the disease (Jones, 1981). As a result, dozens of men died and many women and children were infected. In addition, the study dealt a profound blow to the trust that many African Americans have for the country's public health-care efforts, which resonates to this day.

HISTORY OF ETHICAL ISSUES IN PSYCHOLOGY

Medical researchers are not the only ones with a history of failing to protect human subjects—psychologists have also conducted their fair share of ethically questionable studies. Consider the cases of Stanley Milgram, who performed a series of experiments on obedience from 1963 to 1965, and Philip Zimbardo, who carried out a prison simulation study at Stanford University in 1971.

Milgram wanted to explore the justifications given by accused Nazi war criminals at the Nuremberg Trials for acts of genocide committed during World War II (Figure 2.1). In particular, Milgram wanted to know how easy it would be to convince ordinary people to commit atrocities. (The short answer: pretty easy.) Milgram's original study deceived participants about the purpose of the research. Researchers told participants they were taking part in an experiment on memory and learning, but they were really examining how far participants would go in obeying researcher's demands. When they first arrived at Milgram's laboratory, participants met with a researcher in a lab coat and were introduced to another participant, a middle-age man named Mr. Wallace. (In fact, Mr. Wallace was an accomplice in the study, called a **confederate**.) The researcher had Mr. Wallace and the participant draw slips of paper to determine who would be the "teacher" and who would be the "learner"; in truth, all participants were teachers and Mr. Wallace was always the learner. Then the researcher attached electrodes to Mr. Wallace that were connected to an imposing-looking "shock" machine, and he told participants to administer shocks of varying levels to Mr. Wallace, depending on how he performed on a test of word pairs.

As Mr. Wallace got answer after answer wrong, the researcher urged participants to deliver higher and higher voltages. At a certain level, Mr. Wallace would scream in pain

Confederate An accomplice in a study who is unknown to the participant(s).

FIGURE 2.1. Main defendants at the Nuremberg Trials. Front from left: Rudolf Hess, Joachim von Ribbentrop, Hermann Göring, and Wilhelm Keitel.

(although he was pretending—he was not receiving any shocks) and volunteers would become upset. As the experiment continued, Mr. Wallace twitched and writhed, at one point begging the researcher to stop the study (Milgram, 1963). Yet, in response to commands to continue, about 65 percent of the participants delivered shocks all the way to what they believed was the maximum amount: 450 volts. The research protocol generated considerable short-term stress and potential long-term harm for those who complied and administered the highest shock level. Many psychologists found Milgram's studies unethical, in particular his callous observations of the obvious suffering of the participants while they decided whether to continue shocking the subject (Baumrind, 1964). Others, however, insisted that Milgram had provided invaluable information about obedience to authority.

Even more controversial was Zimbardo's Stanford Prison Experiment (Haney, Banks, & Zimbardo, 1973a, 1973b), which involved a group of 24 young male college students who had agreed to take part in a study on the psychological effects of prison life. The experiment began with a surprise mass arrest of participants in Palo Alto, California, on a Sunday morning in front of friends and neighbors, who were not informed about the nature of the study. Researchers randomly divided participants into guards and prisoners, the latter of whom were led to cells in the "Stanford County Jail," which was really a basement laboratory (Haney, Banks, & Zimbardo, 1973a). Guards donned uniforms and sunglasses and carried clubs. After searching, stripping, and delousing prisoners, the guards forced them to wear smocks, rubber sandals, nylon stocking caps (to simulate shaved heads), and heavy ankle chains—all designed to make prisoners feel powerless, emasculated, uncomfortable, and oppressed. To drive this point home, guards referred to them only by the number on their smocks.

Zimbardo soon observed a dramatic shift in behavior among members of both groups. Although they had not received any specific training, the guards made up their own set of rules, such as demanding prisoners to do push-ups—sometimes while a guard or prisoner was stepping on their backs—for perceived insubordination. The guards grew increasingly abusive. The prisoners responded in turn by rebelling, ranging from verbal taunts, to placing mattresses against doors, to tearing off their smocks and nylon caps. The guards then separated the prisoners, giving some preferential treatment over others and then taking it away without warning. Eventually, the guards denied prisoners access to toilets at night, so the prisoners had to use buckets in their cells that the guards would not let them empty often. One by one, prisoners began to show signs of extreme emotional distress, such as sobbing, screaming, and refusing to eat. Within a matter of days, Zimbardo reported, the prisoners were "disintegrated, both as a group and as individuals. . . . The guards had won total control of the prison, and they commanded the blind obedience of each prisoner" (Zimbardo, 1999). Zimbardo ended the study, which he had planned to run for two weeks, after six days.

Neither Milgram's nor Zimbardo's experiment would muster government approval today, thanks to sweeping changes to ethical standards instituted in the past 25 years.

Interestingly, however, modifications of both of these studies have been replicated in recent years in somewhat different ways.

In 2001, the British Broadcasting Corporation (BBC) conducted and filmed a replication of the Zimbardo study, recreating many key elements of the original study. However, it added safeguards that were not part of the original research protocol and also sought approval of university ethics committees (a particularly interesting step for a television production, which presumably did not require such an approval!). While seeking to recreate the stress of the original Zimbardo protocol, the BBC team also included three safeguards: (1) two independent clinical psychologists who were consultants for the study and who were on site or on call 24 hours a day; they could intervene and remove anyone from the study if a problem arose; (2) paramedics and security guards who monitored the study and were also empowered to intervene as needed; and (3) a five-person independent ethics panel that could modify or terminate the study at any point if members had serious concerns. Additional resources can provide further details about this interesting replication if you would like to read more (British Broadcasting Corporation, 2001; Haslam & Reicher, 2007).

In a similar vein, Burger (2009), a professor at Santa Clara University, conducted a replication of the famous Milgram study and found comparable results. As with the BBC replication, Burger added several safeguards to his design so that it would pass ethical muster. First, in his design, the hypothetical shock levels only went up to 150 volts (rather than 450 volts in Milgram's study). This much lower cutoff was based on analysis of Milgram's data, which indicated that knowing what a participant would do up to 150 volts would provide good predictive information about what he or she would likely do next. Actually putting participants through the potential stress of a manipulation up to 450 volts was unnecessary. Second, Burger screened out potential participants who might have an adverse reaction to the study. Third, participants were given repeated written reminders that they were free to withdraw from the study at any time and that they would still be paid. Fourth, experimenters gave participants a sample shock so that they could see the generator was real, but the sample shock had 15 volts (as opposed to 45 volts in Milgram's design). Fifth, participants were informed immediately after the study that no real shock had been administered; in the original Milgram study, it is unclear how much time elapsed between the end of the study and when participants were told of the deception. Finally, parallel to a BBC safeguard, a clinical psychologist monitored the study and was empowered to end the study early if undue stress was observed. Both the BBC and the Burger replications are evidence that ethical, creative scientists can often devise ways to conduct research that might otherwise be considered unethical in ways that are, in fact, ethical by modern standards. Achieving this can take a great deal of effort, but is worthwhile.

In addition to being replicated by researchers, both the Milgram and the Zimbardo studies remain a fascinating subject for movie directors, who have portrayed them in several feature-length films. Most recently, *Experimenter* (2015) and *The Stanford Prison*

Experiment (2015) explored the profound and often uncomfortable truths about human nature revealed in these studies.

Lest you think that contemporary psychologists no longer involve themselves in ethically questionable enterprises, we offer three relatively recent examples. In 2007, a stunning reality television show, *Kid Nation*, was aired. The premise of the show was that 40 children, ages 8 to 15, were placed in a privately owned town in New Mexico and left to design their own society and governance, without the aid of adults (Viruet, 2014). The *Lord of the Flies* sort of premise may have made for good television, but it also showed a remarkable lack of ethical sense. Most disturbing from the standpoint of the field of psychology, the show's producer, Tom Forman, indicated that a child psychologist was present off camera while the show was being filmed, presumably to monitor the situation (*Kid Nation*, n.d.).

Readers familiar with the controversial "Robbers Cave" experiment (Sherif, Harvey, White, Hood, & Sherif, 1961) will likely note a number of similarities between that study and *Kid Nation*. In an attempt to develop a social psychological model of intergroup conflict, Sherif conducted a study in which two groups of 11- and 12-year-old boys were observed over three weeks as they formed separate groups and then competed for different rewards at a 200-acre summer camp in the Robbers Cave State Park in Oklahoma. Even at the time of the study (well before modern ethics boards), ethical concerns were raised about the potential violation of the participants' rights. Because a number of fights broke out among the participants and the potential for violence arose, the researchers terminated the study early.

A second example comes straight from one of the most politically divisive issues of the early 21st century: the use of torture in prisoner interrogations. After the September 11, 2001, terrorist attacks on the United States, a number of psychologists served as consultants for interrogators at the Abu Ghraib, Bagram, and Guantanamo military prisons that were used to hold suspected terrorists. The American Psychological Association (APA) even drafted new formal policies supporting psychologists' involvement in these activities (Pope, 2011). As you might imagine, debates about the ethics of psychologists being complicit in what many have described as a policy of state-sanctioned torture has led to explosive controversy (see "Media Matters: The Highest Order of Hypocrisy").

Our final example comes from a recent controversy about a Facebook study that involved intentionally skewing the content of participants' news feeds to be more positive or negative than normal to manipulate their moods. Although academic psychologists served as consultants for the study, details of the research emerged indicating that a Cornell University ethics board did not preapprove the study (as would be the normal procedure), but was consulted after the fact (Sullivan, 2014). Much of the public uproar stemmed from the revelation that participants in the study were offered no option for informed consent. We offer these examples to make the point that, although the cases of Milgram and Zimbardo have become historical footnotes, the struggle and debate in the field around what constitutes ethical conduct are ongoing.

MEDIA MATTERS

The Highest Order of Hypocrisy

Any ethical violation in psychological research reflects poorly not only on the individual researchers conducting the study, but also on the profession as a whole. Therefore, revelations about the APA's involvement with Central Intelligence Agency (CIA) torture of political detainees after the terrorist attacks of September 11, 2001, came as a severe blow to the field of psychology.

The APA, the largest association of professional psychologists in the United States and the world, plays a leading role in setting standards for research, practice, and education. One of its stated goals is "to advance the creation, communication, and application of psychological knowledge to benefit society and improve people's lives" (Soldz, Raymond, & Reisner, 2015).

Yet, for years the APA secretly collaborated with the government to justify the torture of prisoners detained at Guantanamo Bay and other military facilities (Risen, 2015). APA officials protected psychologists who took part in the CIA's so-called "enhanced interrogation" program (American Psychological Association, 2015). The program included waterboarding (simulated drowning), prolonged noise stress, sexual humiliation, degradation of religious beliefs, isolation, and sensory and sleep deprivation (Mayer, 2005). Notably, both the American Medical Association and the American Psychiatric Association publicly prohibited their members in 2006 from participating in military and civil interrogations (Mathis-Lilley, 2015).

When confronted, the APA initially denied its involvement. "[There] has never been any coordination between APA and the Bush administration on how APA responded to the controversies about the role of psychologists in the interrogations program," said the APA spokeswoman, Rhea Farberman (Risen, 2015).

A U.S. Air Force program called Survival, Evasion, Resistance, and Escape (SERE) inspired many of the CIA's interrogation techniques. Several psychologists familiar with SERE advised interrogators at Guantanamo and elsewhere after September 11 (Mayer, 2015). "If you know how to help people who are stressed, then you also know how to stress people, in order to get them to talk," said Jonathan Moreno, a bioethicist at the University of Virginia (Mayer, 2015).

James Mitchell was a former APA member trained in SERE (Mathis-Lilley, 2015). According to one CIA counterterrorism expert, at one point Mitchell advocated treating an al-Qaeda suspect like a dog (Mayer, 2015). The CIA rejected Mitchell's recommendation (Mayer, 2015).

In April 2015, a group of health professionals and human rights activists issued an independent review that detailed the APA's complicity beginning at least as early as 2003 (Soldz et al., 2015). The report showed proof that, at that time, the APA had several contacts with Mitchell and his business partner, Bruce Jessen, communications that the APA had consistently denied (Soldz et al., 2015). The involvement intensified in 2004, when the Bush administration was under intense scrutiny for leaked photos of its abuse of prisoners at Abu Ghraib (Soldz et al., 2015). Prompted by the Bush administration, APA officials invited select psychologists and behavioral scientists in the government to a private meeting to discuss the role of psychologists in the interrogation program (Risen, 2015). In 2005, the APA issued new guidelines approving the involvement of its members in the interrogation program (Risen, 2015).

According to the 2015 independent review, "The APA's complicity in the CIA torture program, by allowing psychologists to administer and calibrate permitted harm, undermines the fundamental ethical standards of the profession. If not carefully understood and rejected by the profession, this may portend a fundamental shift in the profession's relationship with the people it serves" (Soldz et al., 2015).

The APA responded to the independent report and media analysis with a ban in August 2015 on any involvement by psychologists in national security investigations by the U.S. government, including noncoercive interrogations (American Psychological Association, 2015). "These actions by APA's council are a concrete step toward rectifying our past organizational shortcomings," said Nadine J. Kaslow, an APA past president and a member of a special committee that received the independent review. "We are now moving forward in a spirit of reconciliation and reform" (American Psychological Association, 2015).

Yet, some believe the APA has a long way to go in making amends. Anne Speckhard, a professor of psychiatry at Georgetown University and contributor to the *Washington Post*, worked in Iraq with the Department of Defense to rehabilitate detainees who adhered to militant jihadi ideology (Speckhard, 2015). "For me the APA ban is simply sidestepping responsibility for what the organization failed to do, and still has not done, in regard to the psychologists who took part in harsh interrogations or witnessed and abetted 'soft' torture or so-called enhanced interrogation techniques," she wrote. "Those psychologists should have been, and should still be, called up on ethics charges and have their APA memberships revoked. . . . It is also pure foolishness to tell all of us who risked our lives doing the right thing that we can no longer guide the military, the intelligence community and others who will certainly continue to use harsh techniques if not guided otherwise" (Speckhard, 2015).

The Belmont Report

Spurred in part by revelations of the Tuskegee Syphilis Study and ample historical evidence of maltreatment of human subjects, a group of ethicists, physicians, scientists, and others met at the Belmont Conference Center in Maryland. These people, who were part of the National Commission for the Protection of Human Subjects of Biomedical and Behavioral Research, met for four days in 1976 to derive basic ethical principles that would guide researchers as they performed studies with human subjects. That meeting and members' collaboration afterward yielded the **Belmont Report**, which was published in 1979. Whereas previous ethics codes listed specific rules, the Belmont Report provided three general principles to guide the application of regulations:

Belmont Report
Developed in 1976, it is a series of basic ethical principles to guide researchers as they perform studies with human subjects.

- *Respect for persons*, which dictates that researchers protect the autonomy of participants, obtain their informed consent, and treat them with courtesy;
- *Beneficence*, which reinforces researchers' obligation to do no harm and at the same time maximize the study's potential benefits; and
- *Justice*, which calls for the fair administration of carefully considered procedures and nonexploitive selection of participants, so that people of all races, ethnicities, and incomes can benefit from research.

APA Guidelines

As will become evident in the discussion of the APA's ethical guidelines (http://www.apa.org/ethics/code/index.aspx), psychology as a field also demands a higher set of standards than just the minimum requirements outlined in the Belmont Report. This demand for ethical rigor is particularly critical for a field that has often suffered from a perceived (although undeserved) lack of credibility in the public domain (Stanovich, 2012). The APA based its current guidelines on five principles that build on the tenets of the Belmont Report:

- (A) *Beneficence and nonmaleficence,* which calls for protection of a patient's welfare.
- (B) *Fidelity and responsibility,* which requires psychologists to be trustworthy and accountable.
- (C) *Integrity,* which concerns honesty and accuracy in clinical practice.
- (D) *Justice,* which seeks to provide equal access to psychology for all.
- (E) *Respect* for people's rights and dignity, which obliges psychologists to treat patients as worthy individuals and to protect their privacy, confidentiality, and self-determination.

THE INSTITUTIONAL REVIEW BOARD

Today, nearly 4,000 committees—known as **institutional review boards (IRBs)**—are active in almost every U.S. hospital, university, and organization that supports research. These IRBs are responsible for protecting the health and well-being of research participants, and they are liable for the research they approve (Stark, 2012). IRBs ensure that researchers treat participants with respect, consider potential risks and benefits, and secure the confidentiality of participants and their data.

The IRB reviews proposals submitted by researchers prior to the start of a research project, evaluating the proposals in light of the ethical principles outlined by the APA. The IRB also approves the start of a study and ensures that the research complies with both institutional and federal guidelines and rules related to the conduct of research. Much of the process can be daunting to first-time submitters and even seasoned researchers, but there are ways to more smoothly navigate the steps. In Chapter 3, we will provide some tips from our own experience with submitting proposals and serving on a social behavioral IRB committee.

Institutional review board (IRB) A committee that is active in almost every U.S. hospital, university, and organization that supports research. These boards are responsible for protecting the health and well-being of research participants, and they are liable for the research they approve.

Organization of the IRB

There are two aspects of the IRB organization. The first is the committee itself, and the second is the staff that supports the committee and completes the preliminary review of applications.

The Committee.   By federal regulation, the IRB committee must comprise at least five members, including one individual whose research focus is in the sciences, one individual whose research focus is nonscientific, and at least one individual who has no affiliation with the institution conducting research. The "science person" is usually an active researcher in the behavioral or biomedical sciences, whereas the "nonscientist" researcher is often from the humanities. The "nonaffiliated" individual is generally someone from the local community, often connected to local churches, medical facilities, or community organizations.

Committees often have additional members with some expertise in issues pertaining to children or prison populations. Larger research institutions will often have multiple committees, one or two of which might focus on social-behavioral research (including psychology) and others that specialize in reviewing biomedical research (which may include some psychological research). It is imperative that the appropriate committee reviews the research because standards can vary widely between social-behavioral and biomedical IRB panels, even at the same institution.

Staff Members.   IRBs also have a number of staff members who typically do an initial review of the proposal to ensure that it has been fully completed, that all the proper forms (e.g., consent forms, copies of surveys or questionnaires) have been included, and that the information within the proposal is consistent. These individuals, sometimes called "compliance officers," generally find the details the researcher has neglected and will send questions and required changes to the researcher prior to sending the proposal on to the committee for further review. Of all IRB committee members, staff members are the people you should get to know. Having a good working relationship with them can help ease the approval process.

Collaborative Research

Collaborative research Research conducted by scholars at different institutions (generally all of the affiliated institutions will need to approve the research from an ethics perspective).

Collaborative research is research conducted by researchers at different institutions. Generally, all affiliated institutions will need to grant approval. Engaging in collaborative research often leads to situations in which local differences in IRB culture and procedures can become glaringly and frustratingly obvious. If researchers on a collaborative project will only be involved in the planning and working with deidentified data (data in which the identifying information about participants has been removed) and will not be interacting with human subjects, their institutional IRB may not require them to obtain approval. However, other institutions with which the project is associated may require that approval. As with most IRB issues, it is always better to ask a member of the IRB for clarification than to assume it is all right to proceed with your research.

Cross-cultural research Research that occurs in countries with different ethical rules and regulations, often with few or no standing institutional review board committees.

The rules and regulations involving IRBs have been developed for research conducted in the United States. **Cross-cultural research** may occur in countries with different ethical rules and regulations, with few or no standing IRB committees. In such cases, researchers conducting research funded by U.S. agencies must establish a local IRB to oversee the research and obtain approval of the IRB from the U.S. government, which requires meeting certain guidelines. Laying the groundwork for international IRBs can be time-consuming and tedious, as Jennifer Lansford learned when she had to coordinate the formation of IRBs in eight countries as part of the international study on children's development and parenting.

Mission Creep

In recent years, an interesting set of issues has emerged around the role of IRBs regarding the notion of "**mission creep**," the expansion of IRB oversight to include areas unrelated to the protection of human subjects, such as evaluating questions researchers want to ask in qualitative research. A growing number of researchers complain that ethics boards have become increasingly rigid and constrain their very ability to conduct research.

Although he wrote specifically about the Canadian ethics review process, Haggerty's (2004) characterization of mission creep could also be applied to the institutional review process in the United States. Essentially, Haggerty observes that regulatory systems (i.e., IRBs and their responsibility as specified by the Department of Health and Human Services) are expanding to include more activities, and the regulation of research activities themselves has also intensified. Haggerty suggests that more and more ethics boards are examining activities peripheral to the main research focus and defining harm and risk quite broadly, to the point where some ethics boards regard any change in a research participant's condition or disruption of his or her routine as a potential harm. For example, IRBs now routinely ask to see the questions on a survey, and even a minor wording change in a question on a survey could be subject to IRB review.

Haggerty similarly points out that definitions of risk used by many boards have expanded such that they require researchers to proactively manage any problematic outcome that *might* occur, however unlikely. Finally, he highlights that well-intentioned informed consent policies have made certain types of research entirely unworkable (e.g., participant observation), while creating substantial (and sometimes insurmountable) barriers to research that employ deception as part of its protocol. This raises the possibility that, with more rigid and expansive IRB oversight, entire areas of scientific inquiry on high-profile, controversial issues may fall outside of the realm of permissible study.

In a widely read editorial in *Science*, a group of researchers similarly underscored the problems of mission creep, contending that the IRB system has become bogged down in excessive paperwork and spends too much time on activities that pose little or no risk to participants. They argue that these trends carry the risk of alienating researchers to the extent that they will intentionally flout IRB guidelines, which they perceive as irrelevant, arbitrary, and unenforceable (Gunsalus et al., 2006).

Jennifer Lansford:
"I've spent countless hours working on getting IRB approval on all kinds of issues, and it really felt like a thorn in my side for a while. When conducting research in another country, it is best to be sensitive to local traditions and practices, while maintaining the high ethical standards advocated by the American Psychological Association."

Mission creep The problem of the expansion of institutional review board oversight to include areas unrelated to the protection of human subjects.

A survey of neuroscience faculty, trainees, and staff similarly highlighted this disaffection with the IRB system, with many indicating that the review board often impeded ethical research insofar as time spent by researchers responding to tangential IRB requests could actually take time away from real measures to ensure participant safety (Illes, Tairyan, Federico, Tabet, & Glover, 2010). Indeed, an increasing number of reports indicate that the current structure and scope of IRB review imposes many costs to researchers, including expenditures of time or money and constraints placed on the research itself (Silberman & Kahn, 2011).

IRB Reform

In response to these concerns about mission creep, there have been a number of calls for reform to IRB systems. For example, Gunsalus and colleagues (2006) point out that researchers must take the basic responsibility for ethical conduct and that IRBs should be used as a resource, rather than the ultimate source of ethical judgments. They also suggest the creation of a national clearinghouse to support both IRBs and researchers. Such a clearinghouse would provide examples of both good and poor practices from a range of disciplinary perspectives and would provide a better perspective on what is meant by risk and harm in different human research settings.

Beskow, Grady, Iltis, Sadler, and Wilfond (2009) propose implementing a research ethics consultation service that would complement or supplement the current IRB structure. In their view, such a service should be available to all those involved in the research enterprise—for example, both investigators and IRB staff—to deal with particularly complex or thorny issues. Others have suggested that the remedy to current IRB problems lies in better communication between ethics boards and researchers, as well as more clarity within boards about their ethical mandate (Illes et al., 2010).

In addition, substantial changes to the U.S. Department of Health and Human Services regulations have been recently proposed, including exempting all survey and interview studies with adults from IRB review, having a single IRB responsible for oversight of multisite studies (rather than the current arrangement, where a multisite study requires the approval of each local IRB), and instituting greater standardization and streamlining of study consent forms. Although these well-intentioned changes come with their own set of possible hazards (e.g., breaches of confidentiality, failure of a single IRB to appreciate the conditions affecting informed consent at [foreign] locations; Lo & Barnes, 2011), they provide evidence of the ongoing robust discussions around reform.

Jennifer Lansford: *"The age of consent differs across countries. For example, in the United States, 18 is considered the legal age at which someone can provide their own informed consent, but this age is 15 in Sweden."*

DEFINING RESEARCH

To fully contextualize the role of the IRB, you must understand what exactly constitutes research. Although this might appear simple at first, the U.S. Department of Health and Human Services's legal definition of research is vague enough to leave substantial room for debate: "A systematic investigation, including research development, testing and evaluation, designed to develop or contribute to generalizable knowledge" (U.S. Department of Health and Human Services, 2009). **Generalizable knowledge** is a broad term that refers to a variety of information: conclusions drawn from data gathered in a study, principles of historical or social development, underlying principles or laws of nature that have predictive value and can be applied to other circumstances for the purpose of controlling outcomes, explanations about past study results, and predictions of future results.

Because this definition leaves much room for interpretation, institutions (and their IRBs) tend to differ in the particular distinctions they draw. For example, Northwestern University's IRB excludes the following from the category of human subjects research (Northwestern University Institutional Review Board, 2012):

- Case reports based on work with a patient (i.e., a case study) with no prior intent of public dissemination;
- Data collected as part of course-related activities where an instructor is evaluating the use of a technique within the classroom;
- Research involving death records, autopsy records, or cadaver specimens (with the exception of some protected health information);
- Journalism activities where there is no hypothesis being tested;
- Oral history without intent to draw conclusions or generalized findings;
- Activities related to quality improvement or assurance in a hospital or classroom setting;
- Research using data from a publicly available, deidentified data set; or
- Some types of biological research utilizing deidentified human biological specimens.

Although the reasons for excluding these categories and others from the definition of research vary, as a general principle, activities that are not intended to produce generalizable knowledge *and* test particular hypotheses via a systematic investigation tend not to be counted as research. For example, a systematic investigation that does not seek to produce generalizable knowledge, such as quality improvement within an organization, is not considered research. Journalistic activities conducted by individuals outside of behavioral science departments are also not considered human subjects research by the IRB.

By contrast, systematic attempts to evaluate a particular hypothesis or hypotheses and to apply findings to a broader context are considered research. As a practical guideline, investigations intended to be published in an academic journal or presented at an academic meeting likely qualify as research. Table 2.1 provides a comparison of activities that are considered research versus those that are considered nonresearch. It is always best to check

Generalizable knowledge Refers to a variety of information: conclusions drawn from data gathered in a study; principles of historical or social development; underlying principles or laws of nature that have predictive value and can be applied to other circumstances for the purpose of controlling outcomes; explanations about past study results; and predictions of future results. Such knowledge defines the boundaries of research that is regulated by institutional review boards.

Table 2.1.   Distinguishing research from nonresearch for purposes of the Institutional Review Board

Activities Considered Research	Activities Not Considered Research
Any methodology used with intent to systematically draw conclusions outside of the immediate environment being studied	Case studies/case reports
	Evaluation of classroom techniques
Experimental studies that manipulate environmental conditions	Most research involving deceased subjects
	Journalism activities
Survey/observational studies	Oral histories
	Quality improvement/quality assurance
Studies with identifiable (nonanonymous) participants	Secondary data analysis using public, deidentified data sets
	Some biological research using deidentified human biological specimens

with your local IRB about whether they consider your project "research" and whether it falls under the purview of the IRB.

ETHICAL CONSIDERATIONS FOR RESEARCH WITH NONHUMAN ANIMALS

Some researchers have argued that more people should consider switching to research with animals because the IRB process for conducting research with humans has grown unwieldy (Rice, 2011). There are considerable ethical issues related to using nonhuman animals in research. These issues include whether animals should be used in research at all; what kinds of research should or should not be allowed with animals; what particular species of animals are appropriate for use in research; and what levels of care and treatment should be required. Similar to changes that have occurred in our ethical perspectives on the treatment of human subjects, views about research on animals both inside and outside the research laboratory have changed greatly over time (Figure 2.2). Generally, nonhuman animals used in research are treated better today than they were 50 years ago. Additionally, acceptable research methods today are somewhat more restricted than in the past, especially in the case of the use of nonhuman primates in research.

Why Use Animals in Research?

The best place to start a discussion of nonhuman animal research is to ask, "Why should research with animals be conducted at all?" The first reason is that animal research can provide a useful model for exploring the impact of some event on health and behavior that can be applied to humans. For example, we have gained substantial knowledge from animal research about how particular diseases progress and how these diseases might be effectively treated. We have also learned from animal models about the impact of impoverished environments (e.g., nutritional or maternal deprivation), detrimental environments (e.g., exposure to drugs, pollution, or toxins), and enriched environments (e.g., stimulating environments that encourage physical activity). Although it is possible to investigate some of these issues with humans, studies with animals can be more highly controlled, enabling greater causal inferences. In many cases, animal research can answer important research questions about improving humans' health and well-being that cannot be effectively studied using other methods.

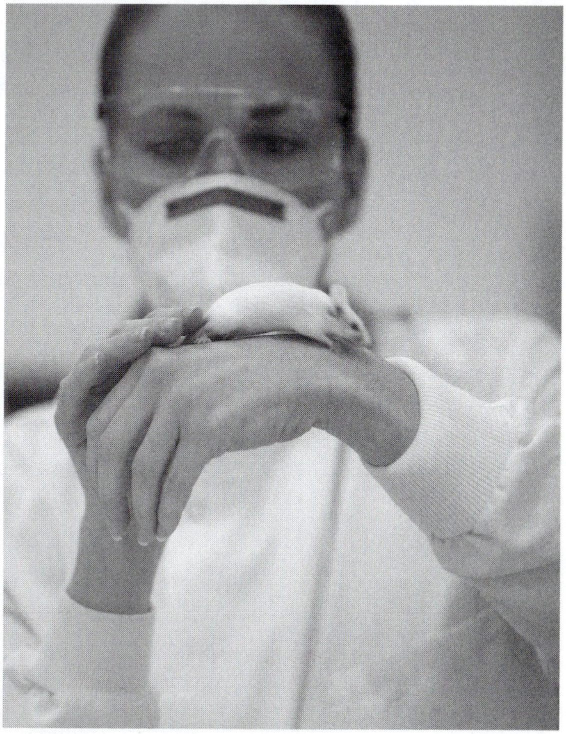

Another reason for using animals in research is that it allows the exploration of research questions that cover long periods of the life span and even across generations.

FIGURE 2.2.   Views about what is acceptable research on animals both inside and outside the research laboratory have changed over time.

By studying animals, such as mice, that reach maturity quickly and have relatively short life spans, we can examine important questions related to the interaction of genes and environments and how this interaction plays out over time. These animal models also enable the exploration of whether particular influences might impact the next generation. For example, researchers (Gapp et al., 2014) have found that male mice that have experienced severe stress have sperm with altered RNA. When the sperm of these mice are used to fertilize an egg, the resulting offspring show behavioral and metabolic differences related to the altered RNA. This dramatic finding would be impossible and unethical to conduct in humans.

What Animals Are Used in Research?

The vast majority (~95%) of psychological research using animals is conducted with rodents (e.g., mice, rats; http://speakingofresearch.com/facts/). Researchers studying various aspects of perception use different animal models to examine subjects, such as the development of vision (e.g., fish, cats) and hearing (e.g., chinchillas). Nonhuman primates have been used to study a wide range of topics, including the causes and treatments of particular diseases, visual processing, and the impact of different types of deprivation and enrichment. Over time, the use of nonhuman primates in research has declined, in part because of the cost of research, changing views of how these animals should be treated, and increased pressure from animal rights groups. However, as laboratory research with nonhuman primates has declined, researchers have been using field observations of primates in natural habitats. Thus, animal research should not be equated with invasive laboratory procedures.

How Are Animals Protected?

Institutional Animal Care and Use Committee (IACUC) Review committee responsible for protecting the health and well-being of nonhuman animals involved in research. These committees are the equivalent of institutional review boards, but for researchers who involve animals in their investigations.

Similar to human research, conducting research with animals requires oversight from a research review board called the **Institutional Animal Care and Use Committee (IACUC)**. IACUCs follow ethical guidelines and federal laws similar to those of IRBs, but ones that are specifically written with respect to issues related to animal care and research. These rules and guidelines must comply with the Public Health Service Policy on Humane Care and Use of Laboratory Animals (Public Health Service, 2002). Federal law requires at least five members of the IACUC: a doctor of veterinary medicine responsible for activities involving animals at the institution; a practicing scientist conducting research involving animals; someone who is not a scientist (e.g., an ethicist or lawyer); and someone who has no other affiliation with the institution other than the IACUC. The APA also has guidelines for researchers working with nonhuman animals (American Psychological Association, 2012).

The protection of animals involved in research goes well beyond the research situation because the researchers (and institution) are responsible for providing a home for the animals when they are not directly involved in a research project. Some faculty even argue that the general standard of care required is such that most animals are housed under conditions that are much nicer than their faculty offices. Researchers studying nonhuman primates have argued that the quality of care the animals receive is the equivalent of providing them with a middle-class home with complete medical care (Bennett, 2015, personal communication).

As with all research, the choice of methods and whether to involve nonhuman animals should be determined by the research question and ethical considerations. It is also important to realize that animal research has led to breakthroughs in our knowledge about diseases, interventions, and interactions between genetics and the environment.

Practical Tips for Conducting Ethical Research

1. Always consider your obligations to society at large as the backdrop for any research that you conduct.

2. Keep the general principles for research from the Belmont Report and the APA ethics code in mind as you design your research.

3. Be aware of the rules and regulations that apply to your particular research.

4. Consult with your IRB to clear up any ambiguities about whether your activities constitute research and what category of research they might fall into.

CHAPTER SUMMARY

The first issue you must grapple with as a researcher is recognizing the importance and complexity of ethical guidelines. Research ethics are hardly precise; they are constantly evolving and depend on the particular context in which the research is conducted. As you have learned, the history of research is marred by arrogance, thoughtlessness, and disregard for the welfare of participants by researchers all over the world. Psychological research has also violated ethical standards and caused long-term negative effects for participants. Benchmarks such as the Nuremberg Code, the Declaration of Helsinki, the Belmont Report, and the APA Ethical Guidelines were designed to set limits on the power of researchers over their subjects and institute safeguards for people not able to speak for themselves. Yet, despite these proclamations and the formation of IRBs, ethical abuses continue to this day. We hope that as you move forward in the research process, you will keep in mind that your first goal should be to conduct an ethical study.

Up for Discussion

1. The ethical problems that placebo groups can present are often underappreciated. What is the specific ethical challenge that a placebo (a treatment that has no therapeutic effect) control group may present in a research design? Under what circumstances should researchers worry, and when should they be less concerned? Given the power of a placebo group in a research design, are there ever circumstances where the ethical concerns could rule out the use of the placebo altogether?

2. Anyone who conducts psychological research is required to do online training. Some see it as valuable, whereas others see it as a waste of time. What are the benefits and problems of this model? To what extent do you feel ethical issues are clear? Do you think discussion and debate about them are important? Is online training likely to be effective in improving the ethical behavior of researchers? Why or why not?

3. Would the ethical violations experienced by David Reimer and his family happen today? Do you think that the more open online atmosphere regarding ethical training and issues prevents or at least makes it harder for such egregious violations to occur?

Key Terms

Belmont Report, p. 40

Clinical Research Committee, p. 33

Collaborative research, p. 42

Confederate, p. 35

Cross-cultural research, p. 42

Declaration of Helsinki, p. 33

Ethics, p. 29

Generalizable knowledge, p. 45

Informed consent, p. 28

Institutional Animal Care and Use Committee (IACUC), p. 48

Institutional review board (IRB), p. 41

Mission creep, p. 43

National Institutes of Health (NIH), p. 33

Nuremberg Code of 1947, p. 32

3

Negotiating the Institutional Review Board Process

INSIDE RESEARCH: KATHLEEN MURPHY

Social and Behavioral Sciences
IRB Manager, Northwestern
University

I first became involved in ethics as a social worker. I have my masters and PhD in social work, and I started out dealing with professional ethics at the National Association for Social Workers. As the chair of the ethics board, I ran into lots of standards of practice—professional standards, state laws, national expectations, regulations around mental health and confidentiality—this morass of information that told people what to do. I was more concerned about teaching people ethical decision making.

When I first got involved with IRB it was really before "IRB" became a significant consideration for social, behavioral, and educational research. At that time it was much better known for what was happening with biomedical research and the exploitation of subjects. But once I began to dig into ethics in research, I discovered that psychologists, sociologists, social workers, and a myriad of others in the social sciences were involved in all kinds of research that was equally harmful. Once I decided to really study ethical decision making—in terms of "What's the right thing to do or the wrong thing to do in any situation?"—the IRB became a natural environment for me to make a contribution. It's a place where I feel invigorated, excited, and intellectually stimulated by the challenges of balancing the protection of participants in research with the needs of research. Research is extremely important, and it has to be done in a way that is respectful of participants. Participants represent the central contribution to the research of social scientists. They're instrumental to the conduct of research. But there has to be this balance.

While important, I have never thought that federal regulations should be the primary motivation for protecting participants. I really think that the ethical principles of the Belmont Report should be central to the discourse. I love the principles of Belmont. It's the most clear, precise government document I have ever read or probably will ever read. The three ethical principles discussed in the Belmont Report are three of the five most commonly discussed in moral philosophy: autonomy, justice, and beneficence. They are the guiding principles for how I think about what we do on the IRB. Whenever I am talking to a class I tell people, "Google Belmont. Download it. Read it. If you want to understand the mission and purpose of the IRB, Belmont is the best."

Kathleen Murphy joined Northwestern University's institutional review board after having successful careers as a social worker in private practice and later as a data librarian at Northwestern. In addition to her clinical practice, she has specialized in professional ethics and taught research methods to social workers and librarians. Her unique perspective and professional experience have enabled her to help steer the Social and Behavioral IRB at Northwestern toward a broader consideration of moral and ethical standards in its consideration of proposals.

Research Focus: Developing and directing Northwestern's Human Subject Protection Program

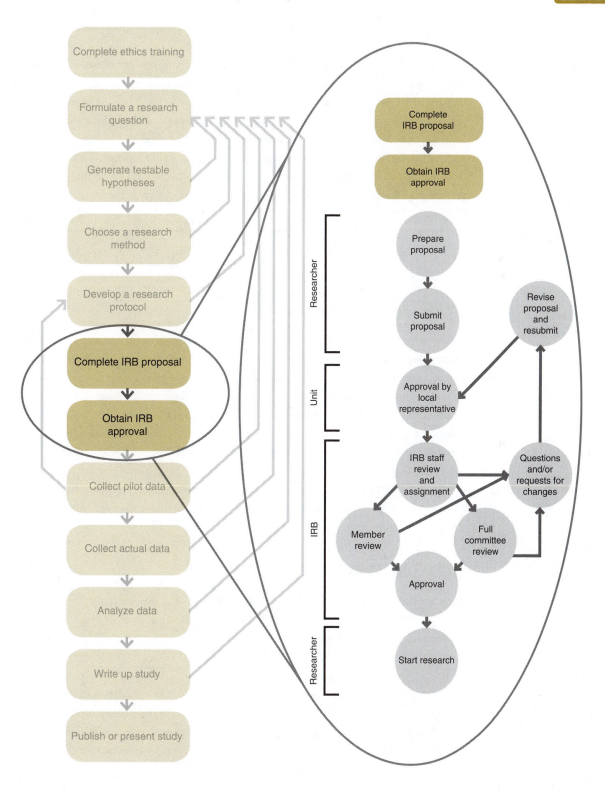

Chapter Abstract

In Chapter 2, we covered some of the long history of transgressions committed against human subjects in research and the establishment of institutional review boards (IRBs) in the United States. Now, we explore the best ways to approach an IRB with the goal of gaining approval for your study. Many researchers, even seasoned ones, find the IRB process both daunting and frustrating. Researchers who do not have much experience with this process can feel that they have entered a fun house full of smoke and mirrors. Our goal in this chapter is to blow away the smoke and realign the mirrors to aid you in this process. A prototypical flowchart of the IRB application process is shown at the beginning of the chapter.

TYPE OF IRB REVIEW

Exempt research
Research that does not require institutional review board review.

After you have determined that your particular activities qualify as research and, therefore, require scrutiny by an IRB, you must determine what kind of review is needed. IRBs sort reviews into three groups (exempt, expedited, and greater than minimal risk) based on definitions by the U.S. Department of Health and Human Services. **Exempt research** includes work evaluating educational practices in established educational settings. It also includes the use of survey, interview, or observational procedures where subjects are not identified or public behavior is being observed. IRBs will expedite research that presents minimal risk to participants or involves a minor revision to an already approved protocol (Fisher & Vacanti-Shova, 2012). Any research that involves **greater than minimal risk** of harm or discomfort exceeding that encountered in everyday daily life requires vetting and discussion by the full IRB committee.

Greater than minimal risk research
Research that may pose substantial risk to participants and requires a full institutional review board review.

STEPS IN THE IRB PROCESS

There are three main steps in the IRB process: ethics training, preparation of the proposal, and submission of the proposal to the IRB. Each step presents its own challenges, but there are several things you can do to make the process run more smoothly.

Step 1: Complete Ethics Training

Collaborative Institutional Training Initiative (CITI) An educational program that provides training in human subjects research at more than 1,100 participating institutions.

Federal regulations require researchers to obtain training in the protection of human subjects, but they do not outline how this training must be accomplished. Most research institutions offer individual or group training, done increasingly online. Currently, the **Collaborative Institutional Training Initiative (CITI)** provides training to researchers at more than 1,100 participating institutions. According to CITI's website, more than 35,000 individuals complete some kind of CITI training each month.

CITI's training modules, which have either a social-behavioral or biomedical focus, are designed for anyone who performs research with human participants. They provide a brief history of research and the key ethical principles that should guide the research process. CITI offers additional modules designed for researchers working with specific populations (e.g., children, prisoners, and other vulnerable populations). Each module ends with a short quiz; most institutions require that researchers score at least 80% on each quiz to complete the training, although individuals can repeat the training and quizzes as often as necessary.

Each institution may require a subset of modules for any individual participating in the research process, so what is required differs by institution. However, the training is usually transferable, so a researcher who moves to a new institution is not usually required to repeat all the training (provided the new institution is affiliated with CITI). Most institutions now require recertification (also done online) either every one or every three years.

Federal agencies that fund research, such as the National Institutes of Health and the National Science Foundation, also require training in research ethics. The National Institutes of Health offers an online module that researchers must complete, and the National Science Foundation requires that individuals receiving its grants take a course on responsible research conduct. However, each institution is allowed to design its own course or method for meeting the ethics requirement, provided that the course meets some general guidelines.

Step 2: Prepare Proposal

Most colleges and universities that have active research programs will have some sort of online system for submitting your IRB application, a significant improvement over paper applications. Unfortunately, these systems may be somewhat difficult to navigate because they often:

- Are designed for medical rather than social-behavioral research;
- Are provided by a vendor who has written an all-purpose software program that may not have been sufficiently customized for the researcher;
- Contain ambiguous questions that even seasoned researchers are not sure how to answer; or
- Provide few guidelines about how to address particular issues.

These difficulties highlight the importance of getting to know IRB staff members and working with them rather than against them, because they can guide you to helpful resources. However, particular IRBs vary in the extent to which they encourage or allow researchers to contact them directly. Additionally, some IRBs now provide templates for consent as well as documents that outline the necessary parts of the IRB application. Use them and the process will go much more smoothly.

Although there may be some variation across institutions, IRBs will request a set of information from researchers seeking approval to conduct research with human participants. This information will likely include a brief abstract of your research, a more detailed protocol, identification of participants and how they will be recruited, details about informed consent, and research materials.

Abstract A brief summary that outlines the specific aims of your research and why the research is important.

Abstract.   Generally, the application will require a brief **abstract** that outlines the *specific aims* of your research and *why the research is important*. You should write the abstract and all sections for a general, educated audience. Remember that some IRB committee members come from nonscientific disciplines and the general community. If they cannot understand your plan and why it is important, then the IRB process will go through more iterations than necessary.

Some IRB members consider involving participants in unimportant research unethical and have clear biases against certain types of research. This relates to a tension between two different forms of research: **quantitative research,** which involves using numerical data and statistical techniques to examine the questions of interest, and **qualitative research**, which focuses on gathering in-depth information on topics through the use of open-ended and exploratory methodology. For instance, some quantitative researchers may consider qualitative research that is not explicitly hypothesis driven unethical. For this reason, it is essential that researchers clearly explain the importance of their proposed research, since even exploratory/qualitative research is arguably grounded in a goal of examining specific research questions.

Quantitative research The use of numerical data and statistical techniques to examine questions of interest.

Qualitative research The use of open-ended and exploratory methodology, which focuses on gathering in-depth information on topics of interest.

Protocol document A document that summarizes an intended research project, including the specific aims, background and importance, participants, methods, and predicted results.

Protocol.   Most IRBs will also require a **protocol document** that summarizes the entire project, including the specific aims, background and importance, participants, methods, and predicted results. Some IRBs will also ask for accompanying articles or references that provide additional background.

We believe that researchers tend to provide too much detail in these protocols and in their applications in general; it is best to provide only a basic outline of the research project that focuses on issues related to the protection of human subjects. Providing excessive details opens you to the problem of mission creep, which we explored in Chapter 2 (see Gunsalus et al., 2006), because the IRB may see them as an invitation to comment on issues not directly relevant to the ethics of your research. Generally, all of the information in the protocol will have to be included in other sections of the application. Although this is redundant, failing to put this information in the protocol document will cost you time in the review process.

Another issue to consider is whether to provide general or specific information about the research *methods*. Some IRBs will want to see all the stimuli you will use with your subjects and every question you plan to ask, whereas others may not. Learn about your IRB's requirements before submitting the complete application; it will prevent headaches later.

For example, if your research involves showing adults images of objects on a computer screen, giving a general description of the stimuli may help you avoid having to send a revised IRB application every time you decide to alter the stimuli later. However, if the photographs are graphic or potentially disturbing, the IRB may request to see all of the images you plan to use.

Identification of Participants.   You will need to include information on the number of participants, how you will recruit them, and any inclusion and exclusion criteria you will use. Most important, your subject selection should be equitable, meaning you should look for socioeconomically and racially diverse participants and not rely on a single population (i.e., upper-middle-class people, men); everyone should have an equal share of participating in research. A growing number of IRBs are asking researchers to justify a homogenous participant group. In addition, your recruitment should be noncoercive; participation should be clearly voluntary, and the recruiting process should respect the autonomy of participants.

Often IRBs will request copies of flyers, e-mails, and phone scripts that will be used to recruit participants. Your local IRB can provide guidelines for what to include in these materials. If not, however, it is easier to ask an IRB representative than to go through multiple iterations. Also, it is usually better to overestimate the number of participants you will include in your research because IRBs do not like it when you exceed the number for which you have been approved. Because of the logistics of collecting data, researchers sometimes collect more data than they expect. This is considered a violation of research protocol. No real guideline on this exists, but we suggest inflating your subject number by at least 50% (and more if you are conducting online research because the numbers can grow quickly if you do not set limits in the survey software). Inflating your subject numbers prevents you from having to complete paperwork explaining why you ran more participants than was approved. Although adding participants to your psychology experiment may not seem like a big deal, in medical research, especially in those studies designed to test the efficacy of some kind of treatment, running additional participants may increase the overall risk.

Informed Consent.   A crucial part of the application will require you to provide information about how you will obtain **informed consent**. Many IRBs provide templates of consent that include both required and optional aspects. Consent forms should be written in clear language that is appropriate for the age or reading level of your participants. The information should also be consistent with your protocol and other sections of the IRB application—inconsistency among documents can slow the approval process.

Informed consent
Agreement of a participant to take part in a study, having been made aware of the potential risks.

The consent document is required to include the following information, which will also be addressed in other parts of the application:

- Invitation to subjects to participate in research.
- Evidence that participation is voluntary.
- Assurance that participants' responses will be kept confidential after they are collected.
- Assurance that participants' personal information will be kept private.
- Description of what participants will be asked to do.
- Risks and benefits for participants.
- Costs to participants or payments expected.
- Alternatives to participation.
- A place for participants' and researchers' signatures.

The truth is, *all research has risks* (see "Media Matters: When Informed Consent Can Mean Life or Death"). Do not under- or overstate the risks in the consent form or application. For example, if your research requires hours of mind-numbingly boring responses on a keyboard, merely note, "This research involves no more than minimal risk; there is no more risk than encountered in everyday life." Do not say, "This research involves no more than minimal risk; however, you may get bored, fall asleep, and hit your head on the keyboard."

Even if research does not pose risk to an individual, risk can occur at the community or group level. This has occurred with certain populations in the past, including the Havasupai Indians (Harmon, 2010; Sterling, 2011), a small tribe living in the Grand Canyon that suffers from an unusually high incidence of Type 2 diabetes. Starting in 1990, the Havasupai gave DNA samples to an Arizona State University geneticist in hopes that research could tell them more about their risk factors or provide treatment options. The research did not yield a link between a genetic variant and diabetes within their samples. However, the researchers continued to use the DNA samples to investigate other diseases, such as schizophrenia, metabolic disorders, and alcoholism, thereby violating the participants' right to privacy. The participants were not told about this change in protocol. When the Havasupai discovered the additional studies, they sued the university, which ultimately paid $700,000 to 41 of the tribe's members, returned the blood samples, and provided other forms of assistance to the community.

Other populations, such as prisoners or detainees (Pont, 2008) and individuals with illnesses or conditions such as HIV (Faden & Kass, 1998), also require special consideration as research subjects, for example, with issues of voluntary consent and confidentiality. Pregnant women, fetuses, and neonates (and children in general) are also considered vulnerable populations requiring special considerations.

Deidentified data
Data for which any information that may be used to identify participants (e.g., name, address, phone number) has been removed.

Researchers normally handle the issue of confidentiality by removing identifying information from the participants' data (resulting in **"deidentified" data**), storing data on a

When Informed Consent Can Mean Life or Death

In March 2013, the Office for Human Research Protections (OHRP) declared that in a 2004–2009 study of the effects of higher and lower oxygen levels on extremely premature infants, researchers at 23 academic institutions—including Stanford, Duke, and Yale—failed to tell parents about the increased risk of blindness and death (Tavernise, 2013). News of OHRP's allegations made headlines in a range of publications and broadcasts, highlighting the seriousness of the situation and high-stakes implications to a highly vulnerable participant group.

In a letter to the University of Alabama at Birmingham (the lead site in the study), OHRP concluded that babies who received high oxygen levels were more likely to become blind, and those who received low levels were more likely to die. The agency charged that researchers "had sufficient available information to know, before conducting the study, that participation might lead to differences in whether an infant survived, or developed blindness, in comparison to what might have happened to a child had that child not been enrolled in the study" (Office for Human Research Protections, 2013).

The study, which appeared in 2010 in *The New England Journal of Medicine*, involved infants who were born at 24 to 27 weeks of gestation, a high-risk category that is susceptible to blindness and death (Carlo et al., 2010). According to consent forms signed by parents, researchers randomly assigned babies to either a high-oxygen group or a low-oxygen group by a "flip of the coin," not by infants' individual needs. The only risk mentioned in the consent form was for a skin abrasion by an oxygen-monitoring device. Of the 654 babies in the low-oxygen group, 130 died; 91 of the 509 babies in the high-oxygen group developed serious eye ailments.

However, Michael Carome, a physician and deputy director of Public Citizen, a consumer advocacy organization, observed that the infants who did not participate in the study were actually in worse health two years later and therefore at greater risk for death (Tavernise, 2013). Carome called OHRP's investigation and charges "not a valid way of doing science."

In June 2013, OHRP announced that it was stopping action against the University of Alabama (Hoffman, 2013). Although it repeated its charge that researchers had not fully informed parents of the study's risks, OHRP admitted that federal guidelines regarding researchers' obligations needed to be clarified (Hoffman, 2013). OHRP hosted a public meeting to debate the subject in August 2013. Carome told the panel, which comprised representatives from OHRP, the U.S. Department of Health and Human Services, the National Institutes of Health, and the U.S. Food and Drug Administration, "Every infant in the study received experimental interventions that were not standard of care" (Office for Human Research Protections, 2013, p. 8).

Recommendations for participant safeguards that emerged from the debate included greater coordination between OHRP, the Office of Civil Rights, and the U.S. Food and Drug Administration to provide more guidance about activities allowed under existing regulations and new regulations to build an ethical framework that includes the responsibility of health-care providers and systems to learn and improve care (Office for Human Research Protections, 2013, pp. 136–137). Although OHRP's original criticism of the infant study was reported extensively in mainstream outlets, coverage of the OHRP debate was limited to journals such as *Science* and *Nature*. This follows a pattern of reporting on research: the media tend to jump on a controversial or exciting topic (such as the autism–vaccine myth discussed in Chapter 1) and then leave it as another appears. What is missing is follow-up on the long-term fallout and results.

password-secured computer or in a locked file cabinet, and allowing access only to research team members. It is also best to store any information that connects participants to their data in a separate location, such as a password-protected file or a separate locked file.

Step 3: Submit Proposal for Review

After completing the application, the researcher submits the proposal. At this stage the department head or a representative in the researcher's unit generally gives it cursory approval. The proposal then goes to an IRB staff member, who reads it and flags problems. Common problems include the following:

- Insufficient detail or information;
- Conflicting information in different parts of the application;
- Missing elements in the consent document; or
- Failure to use approved templates or language that were provided by the IRB.

The most widespread error applicants make is writing IRB proposals as if they were intended for high-level researchers. Less common problems include failure to recognize a conflict of interest or underestimating the risk to participants.

Expedited research
Research that may be reviewed by the institutional review board through accelerated procedures.

Depending on the nature of your research and your local IRB's efficiency, proposals can be approved in a week or 10 days for exempt or **expedited research** proposals. Projects involving more complicated designs, greater than minimal risk, or a risk of breach of confidentiality will be referred to the full board to review. Most full boards meet only once or twice a month, so if your research is time-sensitive you should plan accordingly. If the proposal is clearly written, with keen attention to detail, it will likely be approved in one meeting, perhaps with some minor requests for modifications. Proposals that are poorly written, pose clear risks for participation or loss of confidentiality, or involve a conflict of interest may take more than one IRB meeting to resolve. The flowchart at the beginning of the chapter contains a number of feedback loops that can lengthen the time to approval.

WAYS TO SPEED THE APPROVAL PROCESS

There are a few things you can do to speed up the IRB approval process. First, get to know your IRB members and ask them questions directly as you prepare your application; do not necessarily rely on other researchers for this information (although rules about who can contact the IRB directly vary by institution, so check first). Often a quick phone call or e-mail can resolve an issue that would have involved considerable back-and-forth. More difficult issues may require a face-to-face meeting with a staff or committee member.

Second, treat IRB members as you would like to be treated—if you are respectful of them, they will treat you with respect. Most IRBs are understaffed and overworked, so be patient and appreciative of their time commitment. Kathleen Murphy, for example, reviews between 10 and 15 proposals every day. If you have a time-sensitive project, alert your IRB so they can potentially prepare to expedite the process. They are more likely to consider your request if you have already established a positive relationship with them.

Third, investigate how your local IRB defines exempt or expedited research and what constitutes more than minimal risk. If your research is determined to include more than minimal risk, you may receive approvals for aspects that pose no more than minimal risk and then be required to submit a revision to gain approval for the riskier aspects of the research. Studies posing more than minimal risk require an outline of steps that you will take to minimize risks and a clear explanation of how the benefits of the research outweigh the risks. Often, participants themselves receive no direct benefits from participating in research. This is fine, as long as the knowledge gained from the research is considered beneficial to society at large. In this case, merely state, "Although there are no direct benefits to individual participants, knowledge gained from this research will greatly enhance our knowledge of [ ]."

A final suggestion, especially if you are new to research (or new to an institution), is to consider asking a colleague for a recent IRB protocol that has been approved. This can help you navigate some of the issues related to getting approval at your host institution. Even if you follow your colleague's proposal carefully, however, expect to make a number of changes prior to gaining approval because different reviewers may have slightly different suggestions on what your research requires.

KEEPING PROPER RECORDS

Once the IRB approves your research, it is vital that you keep proper records of participants and maintain the research data in a secure place. Most IRB committees review research projects annually to ensure that participants have been treated ethically, to check that proper records have been kept, and to evaluate potential changes to risks.

Research records must include accurate, up-to-date counts of the number of participants who have been included in the study and a signed consent form for every participant, unless the researcher has applied for a waiver of consent. You must also keep track of the number of individuals who dropped out of the study and their reasons for dropping out. All of this information, like your research data, should be stored in a secure place. The committee will review the patterns of dropout to determine whether they signal causes for concern.

Kathleen Murphy:

"Applicants need to address the concerns and the issues of the IRB, which is the protection of participants in research. While a researcher's theoretical model or philosophy of education may be important to their faculty advisor, it's not to us. We need to know at a granular level the details of how the researcher is going to get access to and interact with their participants. We need to know what they are going to say, how they will protect subjects' privacy and confidentiality, how they're going to balance risks with benefits, and how whatever it is that they're doing has some purpose, so they're not wasting people's time."

Although there are often no set guidelines for how long you should keep consent forms (the American Psychological Association states that you should keep "study materials" for at least five years postpublication), storing them in a secure location until all the data on a research project have been collected is a good, ethical practice. Often the rules and guidelines for storage of information related to research have been established at the university level. These override lower-level guidelines, so if you have any questions about storage of research materials, check with university or college policy.

The data for each participant should also be stored in a secure location, typically a password-protected computer in a research laboratory with limited access or in a locked file cabinet in either the principal investigator's (usually a faculty member) office or a secure part of the laboratory. Storage of large quantities of data can be problematic and costly, so as you design your research, consider the form your data will be in and how you plan to store and maintain it.

ETHICAL CHALLENGES IN RESEARCH

A number of interesting examples illustrate the complexities of ethics in research. These examples deal with participant coercion, special populations, participant risks, conflict of interest, deception, illegal activities, Internet research, and research with nonhuman animals. Many of these examples raise more questions than answers about what exactly constitutes ethical conduct.

Participant Coercion

Coercion The act of taking away someone's voluntary choice to participate through either negative or positive means.

In recruiting participants, researchers must pay special attention to the potential for **coercion**—the act of taking away someone's voluntary choice to participate, through either negative or positive means. Coercion presents an interesting challenge because it can slip by undetected. General agreement exists that participation in research should always be voluntary, but what about the seemingly harmless case in which a researcher who is teaching a class wants to recruit from students within the course? (This a common occurrence in a university setting.) The coercive element is that students may feel compelled to participate in the research as a requirement to do well in the class or to please their professor—even if they are given assurances to the contrary.

Consequently, researchers typically build a "firewall" between themselves and potential participants so that they do not know which students choose or refuse to participate (i.e., the students' identities are kept anonymous). Often teachers will ask a colleague who is not teaching the course to request the students' participation and collect the actual data, which are then deidentified.

Again, a good working relationship with the IRB can be invaluable to researchers who must request exceptions. "We don't allow teachers to recruit their own students for research," Murphy says. "However, sometimes teachers can have a really good reason for doing research in the classroom. If that's the situation, make your case for how you can do that in a way that the teacher is not recruiting his or her own students."

The compensation of participants presents another potentially coercive situation. The ethical standard is that compensation should correspond to what is being asked of participants. If the compensation is "too good to refuse," then prospective participants might feel they cannot possibly turn down the study. For example, a $50 payment for a 10-minute survey would likely fall into this category.

One final case of coercion involves the recruitment of patients/participants by the same individuals who are conducting the research. In the field of psychology, this most often comes up in psychotherapy outcome research. As with recruiting students in a class, the underlying concern is that patients might feel obligated to participate as a condition of the treatment or to please their therapist. Again, the best safeguard is to create a firewall so that someone other than the treating psychologist requests participation and protects the identity of participants, as well as those who choose not to participate. In some cases, this can be a greater challenge than in a classroom study because of the particular requirements surrounding confidentiality for patients.

Special Populations

Working with special populations can also create unique ethical challenges for researchers. We will briefly consider three categories—prisoners/detainees, children, and nonhuman animals—to provide insight into the ethical issues related to conducting research with these groups.

Prisoners. Research with prisoners poses obvious ethical challenges; given the prisoner's state of incarceration, it is even more critical to ensure that any decisions to participate in research are truly voluntary. U.S. Department of Health and Human Services regulations provide some useful guidance, requiring that an IRB include a prisoner or reasonably qualified prisoner representative, as well as close scrutiny of the compensation to ensure that it does not exceed the general living conditions of prisoners, to an extent that would compromise their free choice. The regulations also emphasize that the risks incurred by prisoners must not exceed research risks posed to other populations (U.S. Department of Health and Human Services, 2009).

Children. Research with children presents both legal and developmental issues that interface with ethical concerns. From a legal standpoint, a minor cannot provide the consent to participate in research. As a result, the consent process in research with children takes on an additional layer: a parent or legal guardian must provide the legal consent for participation, and the minor child must provide assent to participate (i.e., they must still agree to take part in the study). If a child is too young or for any reason has trouble understanding and responding to verbal or written information (e.g., the child is an infant or has some disability), only parental consent is required.

From a developmental standpoint, child assent must be acquired with language and techniques that are understandable and appropriate for the child's age. With preschool-age children, assent is typically acquired verbally, but with older children and adolescents, assent often resembles the formal, written consent process. In research with children, both the legal consent *and* the child's assent must be obtained to move forward. In narrow circumstances, a waiver of parental consent may be allowed—but only when circumstances make it evident that obtaining such consent is impossible (e.g., in the case of child neglect or abuse) and researchers have made assurances of protections for the child participants.

Nonhuman Animals.   Research involving nonhuman animals also requires a review process to obtain approval to conduct research (Akins & Panicker, 2012), specifically to ensure that animals receive humane treatment. In 1966, Congress passed the **Laboratory Animal Welfare Act** that stipulates guiding principles for the treatment of animals in research and led to the establishment of the Institutional Animal Care and Use Committee. This committee works in a similar way as the IRB, but includes a veterinarian who oversees all research (see Chapter 2).

Laboratory Animal Welfare Act
Legislation that stipulates guiding principles for the treatment of animals in research.

Participant Risk

Another ethical challenge that researchers confront deals with circumstances where research *might* involve more than just minimal risk—but it is unclear whether it does. Three interesting examples include the use of the well-known Beck Depression Inventory as a research tool, the recent replications of the famous obedience work of Stanley Milgram (1963), and the Stanford Prison Study (Haney, Banks, & Zimbardo, 1973).

Assessing Depression.   The Beck Depression Inventory (Beck, Steer, & Brown, 1996) is a widely validated brief survey measure often used as a screen for depression in research. The BDI-II includes one item that asks participants about suicidality, leading many IRBs to worry that the question itself might prompt suicidal behavior. In some cases, IRBs have required that the suicide question be dropped from the inventory, presenting a threat to the validity of the measure as it was intended to be used (we discuss the issue of validity in detail in Chapter 5). There is vigorous debate about the obligations of researchers once they have asked such a question—that is, if identifiable participants endorse the suicidality item, does the researcher have a duty to protect the participants and/or find them treatment?

Ethics boards have not offered a consistent answer to these questions. However, a large randomized control study ($N = 2,342$ students in six high schools in New York) explicitly examined the issue of whether asking about suicidal ideation (having thoughts about suicide) and behavior increases this ideation and risk. The study examined high school students both with and without prior depressive symptoms or other risk factors (e.g., substance abuse or prior suicide attempts) and found that students exposed to questions about suicide in a survey were no more likely to report suicidal ideation than students who were not presented with the survey (Gould et al., 2005). The best approach when facing a potential research risk is to have an effective plan in place to deal with the risk and to confer with your local IRB about best practices.

Replication of Milgram's Obedience Study and the Stanford Prison Experiment.
Jerry Burger's (2009) replication of the Milgram obedience study (see Chapter 2) provides another interesting example for examining ethical issues related to participant risk. Milgram's (1963) study and Zimbardo's studies (Haney et al., 1973) are still widely cited as examples of research that crossed an ethical line, albeit one that had not yet been formally drawn at the time of their work. Many researchers have thought that because of the potential for harm, neither of these studies could ever be replicated given current federal regulations and ethical standards. However, both of these studies have been replicated.

Based on an analysis of Milgram's data, Burger argued that one needed to follow the procedure only to the point of the "shock" of 150 volts (where the confederate first complained) to make solid predictions about obedience in the rest of the protocol. Thus, Burger was able to replicate essential components of Milgram's highly controversial study, and he did so without creating the distress in participants that formed the core of the ethical debate about the original work.

As discussed in Chapter 2, the Stanford Prison Experiment has also been replicated, but not without controversy (Reicher & Haslam, 2006; Zimbardo, 2006). In this case, two British social psychologists (S. Alexander Haslam and Stephen D. Reicher) replicated the original study with 15 male participants who were assigned to be either guards or prisoners. In this replication, there was considerably more discussion of ethical issues and oversight of the research team. An added ethical twist involved the British Broadcast Corporation (BBC) filming the experiment and broadcasting it. Interestingly, the BBC study was also halted after six days when the "prisoners" were found to experience severe levels of stress (Wells, 2002). In their approach, Haslam and Reicher (2012) focused more on ways in which the prisoners attempted to resist the "tyranny of abuse" that was the focus of the earlier work by Zimbardo.

With all the critiques of IRB oversight within the research community, it is important to note that IRBs play a crucial role in research. In the replication of controversial research, the IRB regulations stimulated researchers to be creative and to push themselves to find a way to answer complex and important research questions without jeopardizing participants' rights. IRB regulations improved the overall research that was conducted.

Conflict of Interest

Conflict of interest
A situation in which financial or other considerations may compromise or appear to compromise a researcher's judgment in conducting or reporting research.

Yet another set of interesting ethical issues arises around questions of **conflict of interest** for researchers. Although the research process is held out as impartial, researchers who are funded by agencies with a particular stake in the results provoke, at minimum, the appearance of a conflict of interest that can call into question the capacity of the researcher to do the work with required objectivity.

Questions around conflict of interest often arise when corporate funding undergirds particular research, for example, when a drug company commissions a study on the effectiveness of a particular medication. Researchers are encouraged in such circumstances to be aware of and mitigate any conflicts of interest to the extent possible. Ultimately, however, the only "remedy" for such a conflict is full disclosure so that the community of scholars can account for the conflict in vetting the research findings.

An interesting recent example comes from the research of Kiki Chang, a professor of psychiatry and behavioral sciences at Stanford University Medical Center. Chang's work centers on understanding and treating childhood bipolar disorder, particularly with psychotropic medications (e.g., Chang et al., 2009). Chang has often been criticized because much of his research funding comes from the same pharmaceutical companies whose products he is researching. Chang, for his part, points out that there is a difference between the appearance of conflict and an actual conflict of interest and notes that much of the research on medications would not exist without private funding sources (Gaviria et al., 2008).

Deception

The use of deception in research continues to be one of the most controversial and lively areas of discussion for IRBs and ethicists. High-profile research such as Milgram's study (and the resulting firestorm) set the bar high for justifying the use of deception in contemporary research.

Active deception
The giving of false information to study participants.

Passive deception
The withholding of some study details from participants.

Deception is generally categorized as being either moderate or mild, with the requirement that more moderate forms of deception include a thorough debriefing at the conclusion of the study. Deception usually takes one of two forms: **active deception**, in which participants are given false information, and **passive deception**, in which some details of a study are withheld. The Milgram study, for example, used active deception by leading participants to falsely believe they were administering shocks. This study also used passive deception by not revealing to participants that the main topic of interest was obedience to authority figures. Whether active or passive, deception is only considered justifiable by the significance of the research—the question being answered must be important enough to allow for the temporary breach of ethics.

Beyond the cost–benefit analysis of the research's importance, deception is viewed as justifiable only if a researcher can demonstrate that no other methods are available to study the given topic. For example, Claude Steele and Joshua Aronson (1995) performed a groundbreaking demonstration of the concept of **stereotype threat**—the activation of a negative belief about a particular group that influences members of that group to under-perform in certain situations. For example, African Americans have been found to under-perform on the verbal portion of the Graduate Record Examination (GRE) if the instructions describe it as an intelligence test, and females have been found to underper-form on math tests if they are told the questions are very difficult. In these studies, partic-ipants cannot know that they are being **primed**—given cues that push their thinking in a certain direction—about stereotypes regarding their race or gender before completing high-stakes academic tasks. The priming is only effective if it is done covertly; that is, de-ception is necessary. It is hard to envision any other way to study this phenomenon be-cause if participants knew about the priming, the study would undoubtedly lose its effectiveness.

One final, important distinction about deception: while **debriefing**—giving partici-pants study information that was initially withheld and the reasons for doing so—at the conclusion of a study is required when there has been deception, dehoaxing may also be required for more substantial forms of deception. **Dehoaxing** involves ensuring that partic-ipants who have been deceived are fully aware of the deception to prevent future harm. In the Milgram study, dehoaxing consisted of ensuring that participants understood that they were not administering real electric shocks to the confederate "learner."

Illegal Activities

Because researchers in psychology often study areas of human behavior where they are likely to encounter illegal activities, the question of what to do if you discover such behav-iors in the course of research is a thorny one. In many cases, the very ability to study a par-ticular topic (e.g., illicit drug use, underage drinking) depends on the assurance of participants' confidentiality or anonymity.

Researchers are generally not considered by law **mandated reporters**, that is, individuals who have a legal obligation to report incidents such as elder or child abuse to the authori-ties. Still, some IRBs require the notification of appropriate authorities when researchers encounter cases of suspected abuse. As a result, decisions about what to do fall into an area of ethics that requires balance, judgment, and common sense. On the one hand, researchers must honor the right to privacy and the various assurances they have made to participants.

Stereotype threat The activation of a negative belief about a particular group that influences members of that group to underperform in certain situations.

Priming The presentation of cues to push thinking in a certain direction.

Debrief To give participants study information that was initially withheld and the reasons that information was withheld.

Dehoax To make participants fully aware of any deception to prevent potential harm.

Mandated reporters Individuals who, by virtue of their role, possess a legal obligation to report incidents such as elder or child abuse to the authorities.

On the other hand, as responsible citizens and members of society, researchers also may face a moral imperative to act, particularly if someone is directly in harm's way.

Internet Research

Our final topic in research ethics is the expanding frontier of research involving the Internet—an excellent illustration that ethics, rather than being a static set of rules, is an evolving set of practices that shift with context and culture. Because of the rapid growth of work involving the Internet, formal ethical codes and standards have not been able to keep up with all the emerging, complex issues. But many IRBs now include guidelines for Internet research.

One of the biggest challenges is the blurring of the line between public and private information online. Although research traditionally has involved assurances of privacy for participants, both the expectation of privacy and the practicality of maintaining it are much more questionable when it comes to online research.

Although the guidelines are still evolving, researchers must employ safeguards for research participants wherever possible. Online survey tools offer a basic illustration of this. Most tools provide mechanisms for the secure transmission of data and may also allow researchers to tailor settings to ensure anonymity. Be sure to use such online mechanisms to replicate the required participant protections. However, be aware that confidentially can be breached (albeit with some effort) if too much potentially identifying information is provided online.

PRACTICAL TIPS

Practical Tips for Negotiating the IRB Process

1. Understand what is involved with ethics training and proposal preparation with your IRB.

2. Get to know your IRB staff members.

3. Follow the steps that might speed up the approval process, such as maintaining communication with your IRB, treating IRB members with respect, and obtaining a recently approved IRB application from a colleague.

4. Maintain accurate and up-to-date records of your research.

5. Be aware of ethical challenges to your research, such as the potential for coercion, populations requiring special consideration, studies posing more than minimal risk to participants, and studies involving deception.

6. Avoid conflicts of interest.

7. Be aware of the issues involved in Internet research, especially confidentiality and the blurring of public and private information.

CHAPTER SUMMARY

If your research requires IRB approval, you will need to complete ethics training; prepare a proposal generally composed of an abstract, a protocol summarizing the project, and information on the participants and on informed consent; and submit the proposal for review. Getting to know the members of your IRB can speed up the approval process, as can treating IRB members with respect and considering and understanding potential risks ahead of time.

As should be clear from the discussions in this chapter, ethics are both context and time sensitive, evolving in response to changes in social norms and values. As a researcher, you should always think about the ethics of your own research, be vigilant of protecting the rights and welfare of your participants, and strive to conduct your research with the highest level of ethical standards. If you have any questions, talk to other researchers and your new friends at your local IRB.

Up for Discussion

1. In 1994, Alan Sokal, a mathematical physicist at New York University, submitted a sham article to the cultural studies journal *Social Text*, in which he reviewed current topics in physics and mathematics. Trying to be funny, Sokal drew moral conclusions that he felt would appeal to fashionable academic commentators who question scientists' claims of objectivity. Editors of the *Social Text* did not recognize that Sokal's article was a hoax, and they published it in the journal's spring/summer 1996 issue. Sokal subsequently revealed the hoax in another journal, *Lingua Franca*. Was Sokal's behavior ethical? Why or why not?

2. A psychologist working in Business School X submitted fake resumes to companies to see whether individuals with different personal characteristics were likely to be called for an interview. It turns out that personal characteristics mattered. Was the psychologist's approach to testing his hypothesis ethical? Why or why not?

3. Dr. Y is a researcher who is an expert in lung cancer. She has been approached by a drug company to run a clinical trial involving a new treatment for lung cancer. Dr. Y also runs a medical practice where she routinely sees patients with lung cancer. Is it ethical for Dr. Y to recruit patients from her own practice?

   Psychology Professor Z needs more data to submit his research to an important conference. He is teaching a class with 72 students—just the number he needs to finish his study. Can he ethically recruit students from his class?

   If you answered the questions differently for Dr. Y versus Professor Z, why did you answer differently? If your answer was the same for Dr. Y versus Professor Z, why was it the same?

Key Terms

Abstract, p. 56

Active deception, p. 66

Coercion, p. 62

Collaborative Institutional
Training Initiative (CITI), p. 54

Conflict of interest, p. 66

Debrief, p. 67

Dehoax, p. 67

Deidentified data, p. 58

Exempt research, p. 54

Expedited research, p. 60

Greater than minimal risk
research, p. 54

Informed consent, p. 57

Laboratory Animal Welfare Act,
p. 64

Mandated reporters, p. 67

Passive deception, p. 66

Priming, p. 67

Protocol document, p. 56

Qualitative research, p. 56

Quantitative research, p. 56

Stereotype threat, p. 67

4

Starting Your Research

INSIDE RESEARCH: DANIEL SIMONS

Professor, Department of
Psychology, University of
Illinois at Urbana–Champaign

I went to Carleton College, a liberal arts school, and I was trying to decide whether to major in English or French or physics. I really had no idea. My first year I took an introductory psychology class and liked it, and took another class and liked it, and I ended up taking a couple more. I liked thinking critically about behavior . . . the objectivity of the scientific method appealed to me.

I took a lot of psychology classes, and cognitive psychology probably was my least favorite, even though it is the area I eventually chose for my honors thesis and graduate work. I liked the methodology. I liked what the tools of cognitive psychology allowed me to study, but I didn't particularly like the topics cognitive psychologists studied. At the time, I found a lot of the studies trivial or uninteresting. I still do.

I prefer doing research that generalizes to something in the world that we care about. A lot of cognitive psychology focuses on tasks and questions that are interesting in theory but that might not have any relevance to the real world. It might, but a lot of research makes little attempt to make that connection between the tasks you do in the lab and what people do in the real world. That's a central guiding principle for my research. I don't want to research just because it's of interest to cognitive psychologists. I want to do things that will be of interest to cognitive psychologists, but that also will have some relevance to people who aren't in cognitive psychology.

I tend to focus more on behavioral research—what people see, what they do, what they think—and I'm less interested where in the brain that happens. But I use a wide range of techniques—everything from survey research to judgments about simple displays on computers.

Daniel Simons and his collaborator, Christopher Chabris, won the Ig Nobel Prize in 2005 for showing that even individuals in gorilla suits can be rendered invisible when people focus attention on something else. The Ig Nobel Prize, which is awarded by the magazine *Annals of Improbable Research*, celebrates research achievements that first make people laugh and then make them think.

Research Focus: Mechanisms of attention, perception, memory, and thinking

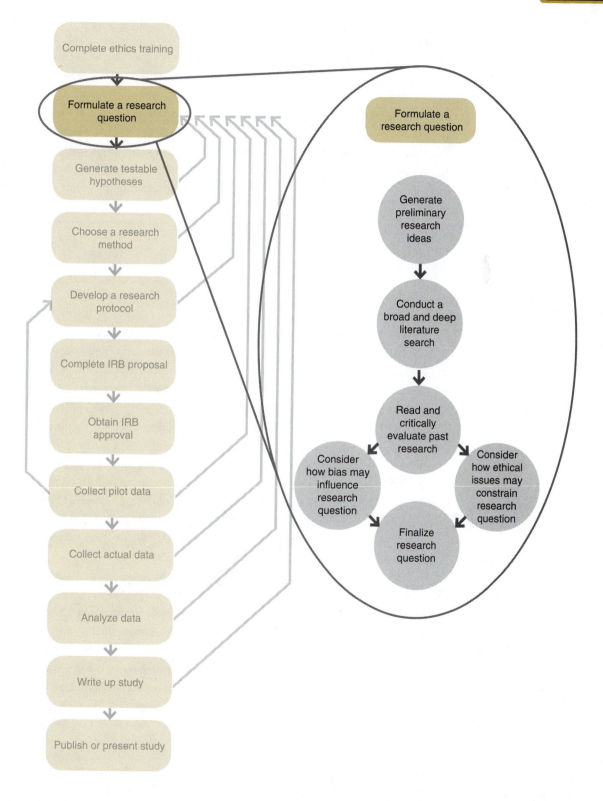

Chapter Abstract

In this chapter, we will guide you through the process of choosing an area of research and narrowing your ideas to a specific question. We start with helping you locate sources of ideas and inspiration for research ideas—including books, journal articles, classes, and ongoing research projects—and then give you tips on how best to glean information from them, in particular how to most effectively read journal articles. We delve into the foundation of theory, touching on its broad categories in psychology, and then discuss the importance of theory in defining your research question, hypotheses, methodology, and analysis strategy. We conclude with how to avoid common problems in starting your research.

Daniel Simons:

"When I get stuck I switch to one of the other ten projects that are going on. I tend to keep a lot of projects because I tend to get bored easily."

Martha Arterberry (Chapter 1):

"Students should read the literature to see what other people have found and find a place where they can join in that conversation, to extend an understanding of the phenomenon or the question."

CHOOSE A RESEARCH TOPIC

The most daunting task of the research process is choosing a topic to study. Psychology is a vast field full of unanswered questions to address. This can make the choice of a specific topic overwhelming—even for seasoned researchers. Experienced researchers often work on multiple projects, all in various stages of completion, ranging from the idea and design stages to data collection, analysis, and the final write-up. Often, different lines of research will serve to cross-fertilize one another, providing novel directions for further research.

But novice researchers do not have that luxury. Trying to pick your first research topic can be paralyzing. The good news is you do not have to come up with an amazing, grand new idea, just some area of human behavior that you would like to explore. The best way to approach it is through questions: What is interesting to you as a human being? What is one thing that you have always wondered about? What makes people behave the way they do? What follows are a few ideas and resources to get you started.

Hit the Books

Our first suggestion is to read and read broadly, because no research idea is truly novel—it either builds on past research or attempts to repudiate past research. But what should you read? Introductory textbooks for general topics that you find interesting provide a good place to look for ideas that can help you narrow your research focus. When you find a topic that interests you, track down some of the classic studies mentioned in the text. These articles should help frame the research in a broader theoretical context. Then, find some more recent scholarly articles on the topic.

Search for Research Articles

In the era of the Google search, many students are content to find research articles through the "brute force" methodology of a keyword search—either directly into a search engine such as Google Scholar or using the keyword search feature in a database such as **PsycINFO**. Although this method may be effective, it is often inefficient, either requiring that you (a) know all (or at least many of) the relevant keywords or (b) are willing to sift through dozens, or even hundreds, of potential references to cull the most relevant.

PsycINFO A database specific to psychology journals and related references.

Although it is not practical for us to list all of the possible ways to find research articles, here are several alternative strategies to simply searching by keywords:

1. Search the *Annual Review of Psychology* and *Current Directions in Psychology*. The *Annual Review of Psychology* is an edited volume that provides comprehensive reviews of trends and significant developments in the field. The *Annual Review* can be a good place to get a general sense of a broad area of research. It can also be an excellent (and comprehensive) source of references for a particular topic; the reference sections of review articles are especially valuable resources. *Current Directions in Psychology* is another journal resource that provides briefer updates on trends and developments in the field.

2. Use the advanced search features on PsycINFO. When simple keyword searching yields too many results, the advanced search features can be extremely useful. For example, you can designate that you are only interested in articles from a particular range of years (useful if you are only looking for the most current work on a topic) or specify that you only want peer-reviewed material. You can also specify the type(s) of article that you are seeking (for example, only empirical studies or only meta-analyses—statistical reports on the findings found across several studies) or narrow your search to only look at research with particular age groups.

3. Use the subject listings to target your search. For any given article that you find on PsycINFO, a list of subjects will be provided. The subjects serve as clues for how the particular piece of work is classified and organized along with similar works. For example, an article on peer rejection for children with attention deficit hyperactivity disorder might include subject headings like "Attention Deficit Disorder with Hyperactivity," "Friendship," "Peer Relations," and "Psychosocial Development." Once you identify the main subject headings for an article of interest, conducting a more targeted PsycINFO search with those subject headings can be helpful for finding similar articles.

4. Look at the cited references for relevant articles that you locate. One handy feature of PsycINFO is that, for any article you locate, you can follow a link to see the references that are cited in that particular piece of work. If an article is relevant to your particular

research focus, then it is likely that at least some of the articles that they cite will also be relevant. In effect, you can benefit from the diligence of previous researchers in identifying the important literature on a topic.

5. Follow a particular cited reference or author forward in time. PsycINFO and Google Scholar also make it easy to take a particular reference—or a specific author—and follow the work forward in time. In other words, when you find an article that is important to the research you are doing, you can look to see who has subsequently cited that article. (This is the flipside of the strategy mentioned in number 4.) In this way, you will be able to see related work that has occurred since the dissemination of a particular article.

6. Consult with a reference librarian. Librarians are trained to find information quickly and efficiently. A brief meeting or consultation with a reference librarian may help you better define your key search terms and find the material you need. Librarians will also point you to resources and services that you may not be aware exist. For example, most libraries offer an interlibrary loan service that, with some lead time, can track down articles and books at other institutions.

The Art of Reading Research Articles

Once you have located empirical research articles published in high-quality journals, one of your biggest challenges will be the task of reading the articles. Like many difficult tasks, proficiency in reading this work comes from repeated exposure and practice. That said, there are some strategies and questions to ask that can help as you begin to read research literature.

We recommend that you become a nonlinear reader. Unlike other works that you may read, it often does not make sense to read a research article from front to back in the way that you would read a novel. Instead, it is more than acceptable (and often advisable) to skip around and cull the article for key pieces of information. In your first run through, start with a quick reading, where you search for key phrases and information (e.g., "The goal of this research is . . . ," "Our hypotheses were . . . ," "Major implications include . . ."). If the article is relevant to your topic and interests, then you can go back and do a thorough reading for details.

To know what to look for, you must first understand the basic anatomy of a research article. Although there is some minor variability in formatting across different journals, most research articles are split into four broad sections: introduction, method, results, and discussion. In addition to these sections, most articles begin with an **abstract**—a brief summary of the article's purpose, methods, major findings, and implications—and end with a reference section that contains a list of other works that were used in designing the particular research. To facilitate your reading of research articles, we have provided a handout at

Abstract A brief summary of a research article's purpose, methods, and major findings. Abstracts are typically about 150 to 300 words in length.

the end of this book (Appendix) that you can use to take notes on the key information as you read.

Abstract.   A good place to start reading any article is the abstract, but resist the temptation to stop there. The abstract will give you a brief overview of the topic, findings, and implications of the article. It can be an invaluable tool for screening an article (and making an initial determination as to whether it is worth reading further or whether the article relates to your interests and questions). But be warned, it does not provide enough information to allow for a thorough understanding of the work. You also may need to go beyond the abstract to fully determine the relevance of an article to your interests.

Introduction/Literature Review.   Typically, the introduction of the paper starts by broadly articulating the problem or issue being studied, summarizing the previous work that has been done on the topic—known as a **literature review**—and explaining how the current work fits in and answers specific questions to advance our knowledge in the given area of research. The end of the introduction includes the particular hypotheses or predictions of the researchers. After reading this section, you should be able to answer the following questions: (1) What are the problem areas—both broad and specific—that have led the researchers to study this problem and generate hypotheses? Why does the topic matter? (2) What are the central research questions? (3) What is the research hypothesis?

> **Literature review**
> A summary of previous research that has been done on the topic, typically located in the introduction of the paper.

Method.   The method section lays out the specifics of how the research is conducted. It is incumbent on the researchers to describe their methods in enough detail that other researchers can attempt to replicate the findings (as part of the larger scientific research cycle). Traditionally, this section is further subdivided into participants, materials, and procedures sections. The participants section describes who was studied; the materials section describes what measures/instruments/techniques were used; and the procedures section details how it was done. After reading the method section, you should be able to answer the following questions: (1) Who is being studied (sample size and demographics)? (2) What are the key variables that were measured in the research? If the study is experimental, you should also be able to identify the independent and dependent variables. (See Chapter 5 for a more detailed discussion of these concepts.) (3) How have the researchers operationalized those variables (i.e., defined them in measurable terms)? (4) What methods are used to collect the data, and what sorts of controls are in place to deal with potential error and false variables? How do the methods allow for distinguishing among various possibilities?

Results.   Because of the technical nature of the results section, this is probably the section most often skipped by novice (or weary!) readers. But in many ways, it is the heart of the research article. You should plan on reading this section, even if you do not understand all of the statistical analyses being used. The results section gives you the raw, complete findings without the researchers' interpretation or spin. As such, it is an important place to begin your own evaluation of what the research has found, before you read the researchers' take on the meaning of their work. After reading the results section, you should be able to answer the following questions: (1) Broadly speaking, what are the methods of data analysis—qualitative, quantitative, or both? (2) Based on the analyses, what did the researchers find with respect to each of their hypotheses? Were their hypotheses supported?

Discussion.   The discussion section of the article is where the authors offer their interpretation of the findings and how they believe the results should be understood and applied. A well-written discussion section not only articulates the meaning of the findings, but also explains how the findings fit into the larger context of other work in the area. In addition, the discussion section will typically spell out the limitations of the research and make particular recommendations for future work in the area. After reading the discussion section, you should be able to answer the following questions: (1) What are the major conclusions of the authors? What are the implications for this area of research? (2) Are the conclusions reasonable and well grounded in the actual findings? (3) What are the caveats and major limitations of the research?

References.   It is easy to want to disregard the list of references at the end of an article, but this can be an invaluable source of related works. If you determine that a particular article is relevant to your interests/topic, then the reference section should be used as a springboard for finding additional materials. For an excellent and detailed resource to assist you in deeper reading of research literature, we suggest *Reading and Understanding Research* by Locke, Silverman, and Spiruduso (2010).

Take a Variety of Psychology Classes

Although it may seem like obvious advice, psychology classes offer another great source of ideas for research topics. Our advice is to look for instructors who are genuinely interested in the topic area and known as great instructors. We advise students early in their academic career to experiment with different classes. Unfortunately, many students focus only on topics that pertain to the clinical side of psychology, but interesting work is occurring in many different areas.

One example is the cognitive research conducted by Daniel Simons. In the 1990s, Simons began studying **change blindness**, a phenomenon in which people fail to notice significant changes in a visual scene or within their own environment. His book *The Invisible Gorilla: And Other Ways Our Intuitions Deceive Us*, co-written with Christopher Chabris, details his experiment in which participants watched a video of two teams of

Change blindness
A phenomenon in which people fail to notice significant changes in a visual scene or within their own environment. Research has shown that people often do not realize when large details of a visual scene have been changed.

students—one wearing white shirts and the other black—moving around and passing basketballs (Chabris & Simons, 2010; Simons & Chabris, 1999). Participants were asked to count the number of passes made by players wearing white while ignoring any passes made by players wearing black. Halfway through the video, a female student wearing a gorilla suit walks into the middle of the group of players, stops, faces the camera, thumps her chest, and walks away. When the video ended, participants were asked whether they noticed anything unusual. About half of them said they did not (Chabris & Simons, 2010).

Researchers have since replicated that experiment many times under many different conditions, and the results are always the same—*half the people fail to see the gorilla.* Simons attributes the error in perception—or **inattentional blindness**—to participants' lack of attention to an unexpected object (see "Media Matters: Much Attention Paid to Inattentional Blindness"). What prompted the book, however, was not the participants' failure to perceive the gorilla, but their consistent surprise on learning they had not seen it. Simons uses this example to write about the illusion of attention, the fact that most of us experience far less of our visual world than we think we do. Simons's research has been widely read, inspired further research on inattentional blindness, and had an enormous impact on the way people think of their ability to observe the world around them.

As you read and take classes, think about how what you have been learning relates to your everyday experiences in working and interacting with people. Does it fit? Are there observations that do not seem to coincide with what you have been reading and learning? Observations by one of this book's authors of his children interacting with photographs and small toys went against a particular theoretical perspective. It led him to collaborate with other researchers to investigate these behaviors in more controlled settings (see DeLoache, Pierroutsakos, Uttal, Rosengren, & Gottlieb, 1998; DeLoache, Uttal, & Rosengren, 2004).

Get Involved in an Ongoing Research Project

Probably the most effective way for coming up with a new research idea is to get involved in an ongoing research project, which you can do in a number of ways. If you are at a college or university where the faculty regularly conducts research, one of the best places to start is to look at faculty web pages. If the description of their research looks interesting, read some of their papers. Then try to set up an appointment to meet with them about their research. Faculty members generally have a quota of how many students they will take on and perhaps other criteria, such as having completed a research methods course. If your first choice does not have any positions available, try a different faculty member. A number of institutions also set up unpaid research internships during the summer. Some schools have formal programs, such as the **Summer Research Opportunity Program**, that are designed to provide individuals from diverse backgrounds with research experience under the guidance of

Inattentional blindness An error of perception where people do not pay attention to an unexpected object (e.g., a gorilla walking across a basketball court).

Summer Research Opportunity Program A summer research program designed to provide individuals from diverse backgrounds with research experience in a laboratory. Many schools have these programs.

Much Attention Paid to Inattentional Blindness

You do not have to look far for examples of major media outlets' misrepresentation of research, and we have included several of them in this book. But not every news report on scientific research is wrong, of course. There are meticulous journalists who do their homework, check and recheck their facts with researchers, portray the research in context, and even cover subsequent studies that try to replicate the original findings.

A prime example is the media coverage of the research on inattentional blindness by Christopher Chabris and Daniel Simons. When the scholarly journal *Perception* published the results of their invisible gorilla experiment in 1999, mainstream media outlets were understandably interested (Simons & Chabris, 1999). After all, the findings were funny, fascinating, counterintuitive, and fairly easy to grasp. A wide range of newspapers, news magazines such as *Newsweek* and *The New Yorker*, television shows such as *Dateline NBC*, and radio stations such as National Public Radio covered the story. Chabris and Simons's 2010 book, *The Invisible Gorilla: And Other Ways Our Intuitions Deceive Us*, garnered even more widespread and in-depth attention (*The Guardian*, *The Washington Post*, and *The New York Times*, among many others).

Part of the credit must go to Simons, who worked hard with reporters to ensure they understood the research. "In general, my experiences with most media coverage of my work has been excellent," Simons said. "They don't always get every detail, but most journalists I've worked with are conscientious and interested in getting the science right. They also know how to convey science to a broader audience. The few bad experiences I've had have all been with television productions. Although some television programs do an excellent job of conveying the science, others are more interested in entertainment and are less careful about getting the findings right. I've had more bad experiences when my work was covered without my involvement than when I have worked directly with a journalist."

The thorough coverage of Chabris and Simons's research has encouraged media attention to follow-up studies on inattentional blindness. A 2009 study by researchers at Western Washington University (Parker-Pope, 2009) examined the level of distraction experienced by cell-phone users, to the point where the majority of them did not notice a clown on a unicycle going by them.

Another result of solid media coverage of the original study is the spread of the concept of inattentional blindness throughout other disciplines and into a broader cultural consciousness. Roberta Smith, an art critic for the *New York Times*, expresses surprise at the psychological phenomenon in her review of a group art show in New York in 2013: "One phrase that [the artist] seems to have pulled from thin air is labeled 'Inattentional Blindness,' a painting that features the writer Linda Stone lamenting that 'We've evolved from multitasking to continuous partial attention'" (Smith, 2013).

Errol Morris, an acclaimed filmmaker known for movies such as *The Thin Blue Line* and *The Fog of War: Eleven Lessons from the Life of Robert S. McNamara*, interviewed Simons and his former collaborator Dan Levin in his exploration of film audiences' perception of continuity errors, that is, discontinuities in scenes, such as a glass of water appearing in one shot and disappearing in the next. In introducing Simons's research, Morris called inattentional blindness "an issue that also has enormous relevance for how we look at film and how we look at the world" (Morris, 2008).

Simons and Chabris have gone on to write articles for several general publications, weighing in on a variety of topics related to perception and memory. In 2015, they commented in *Slate* magazine on the scandal that erupted when the NBC news anchor Brian Williams admitted that he was not shot down in a helicopter in 2003 during the U.S. invasion of Iraq, an experience he had recounted for years. Chabris and Simons offered some potential explanations for Williams's retraction, including "ordinary, unintentional memory distortion" (Chabris & Simons, 2015). They offered readers 10 tips for not creating false memories of their own, cautioning, "Memory science shows that it's nearly impossible to distinguish an honest mistake from a deliberate deception" (Chabris & Simons, 2015).

---

a faculty member. The Summer Research Opportunity Program provides students with a stipend and regular workshops in addition to hands-on experience working on a particular faculty member's research.

Working in a research laboratory can be extremely helpful for gaining experience in the research process and seeing the process unfold from idea generation to design, implementation, and then analysis and reporting of results. As a part of a research team, you may have the chance to observe the interplay of theory and data, the challenges of getting a study to run smoothly, the excitement of processing the first couple of participants in a new study, the thrill of running the initial statistical data analyses to examine the results, and the potential challenges faced when the data contradict or fail to support the original hypotheses. These are the kinds of things that make conducting research much more fun than merely being a consumer of research. Asking important research questions, designing an appropriate method to address those questions, and ultimately obtaining an answer to the questions you have proposed can be truly exhilarating.

Even better than getting involved in just one laboratory is working in at least two different laboratories, if your schedule allows. This provides you with multiple potential recommenders should you decide to pursue application to graduate school and also exposes you to multiple subareas within psychology. Since you never know what you might find interesting, breadth of exposure is better the earlier you are in your psychology education.

Not all research is fun and games, however, and not all laboratory research experiences are the same. Make sure that your experience involves more than simply data coding or data entry. Although these relatively low-level tasks are necessary parts of the research process, they can be time-consuming and monotonous. Ideally, you should try to work in a laboratory that provides you with a wide range of research experience and has some sort of regular laboratory meeting, where the mechanics of research are discussed along with more theoretical issues. Many laboratory meetings also include reading and discussing current research in the field related to ongoing projects.

Martha Arterberry (Chapter 1):

"My favorite moment in research arrives when I can take a look at the data that have been collected. I say, 'It's a data day!' It's exciting to see if your study worked. You've been waiting a while. Is it a bummer if it doesn't work out as you expected? Sure, but you still learn something."

Research can be frustrating. Many times the data analyses do not yield clear or even interpretable results, which can lead to hours of searching for methodological or theoretical reasons to explain the results. But overall, faculty members who do research enjoy what they are doing and are deeply committed to investigating a certain set of research questions. If you are part of a well-functioning research program, you should find the research process challenging but intellectually rewarding. Gaining experience in a research laboratory has also become expected for students interested in pursuing advanced degrees in psychology and related fields.

LET THEORY GUIDE YOUR RESEARCH

Once you have identified an area of research that interests you, you must determine in what ways theory will guide your research inquiry. The debate around the role of theory in psychological research is long-standing, and there is no singular, authoritative answer to the question. Some researchers say that theory drives their research methods, whereas others say their methods are not informed by an underlying theory.

Although there is no consensus that a theoretical framework is an essential prerequisite to conducting your research, having theory available can facilitate the research process. In this section, we discuss the ways in which theory can help define your initial research questions, hypotheses, methodology, and analysis strategy. Although theory offers clear benefits in all of these areas, adhering to a particular theoretical framework can come with pitfalls, which we also consider.

Theory Operates on Different Levels

Formal scientific theory A belief grounded in a body of empirical research, as opposed to a common-sense or naive theory.

For the most part, the researcher who conducts formal research is concerned with **formal scientific theories**, rather than what are known as **common-sense** or **naive theories**—implicit, everyday beliefs. Common-sense theories can be correct and harmless, but they can also bias research questions, choice of method, and interpretation of results, especially for the novice researcher. For example, many individuals hold common-sense theories about whether genetics or the environment determines intelligence and whether this trait is stable or changeable. If a researcher starts with the assumption that intelligence is stable and inherited, she will design and conduct her research in a very different manner than if she holds the opposing assumptions that intelligence involves environmental influences.

Common-sense theory (see also **naive theory**) An implicit, everyday belief that influences how individuals reason about events.

Naive theory (see also **common-sense theory**) An implicit, everyday belief that influences how individuals reason about events.

One researcher, Carol Dweck, has examined the effects of common-sense theories of intelligence (Dweck, 2002a, 2002b). These are everyday beliefs about what make people smart and whether someone's intellectual skills are fixed or can be changed. Dweck has shown that students who hold an "entity" theory of intelligence, which assumes that intelligence is a stable, unchangeable internal characteristic, are unlikely to take on more challenging tasks and are potentially at risk for academic underachievement. Students who hold an "incremental theory" of intelligence assume that intelligence is malleable and can be increased through hard work and effort. Dweck and her colleagues have also shown that these different common-sense views of intelligence can influence the type of praise and feedback that parents and teachers provide children, often leading to results that are the opposite of what was intended (Dweck, 1999; Dweck & Reppucci, 1973; Mueller & Dweck, 1998).

Investigators (Leslie, Cimpian, Meyer, & Freeland, 2015) have also argued that the gender imbalance in some scientific disciplines may be attributed to a somewhat similar view of the role of intelligence. Specifically, Leslie and colleagues (2015) found a greater gender imbalance in fields where individuals feel that innate talent (i.e., "raw brilliance") is the key requirement for success rather than fields where individuals believe that success is not determined by "brilliance." They argue that this result is based on the stereotype that fewer women have raw intellectual brilliance than men. Disciplines such as math, physics, and philosophy are fields that are believed to require raw intellectual talent, and these fields in the United States have a smaller percentage of women who have PhD's (~30% or lower). In contrast, fields such as education and psychology are not thought to require raw intelligence, and these fields have a much higher percentage of female PhD's (~70%). The main point is that these common-sense theories or beliefs influence students, parents, teachers, and even experts in different fields.

For the purposes of our discussion, the concept of theory can also refer to either framework theories or specific theories. **Framework theories** provide a broad perspective and set of assumptions about an area of inquiry, whereas **specific theories** focus on narrower questions and offer more precise predictions.

Developmental psychopathology, a subfield of psychology that examines when children (and older individuals) deviate from the normal pathway of development, might be considered a framework theory for the study of abnormal psychology. Abnormal psychology examines how, when, and why individuals depart from typical psychological states and behaviors. Developmental psychopathology asserts a number of overarching principles, including the idea that researchers must consider the dynamic interplay between normal and atypical (different) development in the understanding of psychopathology (Sroufe, 1990). This idea serves as a framework for understanding how different pathologies emerge and change over the course of development. However, this idea does not provide specific insights into a particular disorder or behavior. In contrast, the work on "expressed emotion" (high levels of hostility, yelling, fighting, and criticism) in the study of schizophrenia might be considered a specific theory insofar as it offers a set of narrow predictions about the relationship between certain characteristics of a family environment and psychiatric symptoms (Butzlaff & Hooley, 1998). Arguably, both framework and specific theories play a major role in shaping research questions, hypotheses, methodologies, and analysis strategies.

Framework theory
A formal explanation that provides a broad perspective and set of assumptions about an area of inquiry.

Specific theory
A more focused explanation and set of assumptions that deal with a particular area of inquiry.

Developmental psychopathology
A subfield of psychology that looks at when children (and older individuals) deviate from the normal pathway of development.

The Role of Theory in Forming Research Questions

Theory can be invaluable as you form your initial research questions. Although we have already discussed the range of origins from which your initial research questions may emerge, using previous research and reading the work of theorists who have come before is a powerful approach for setting your initial research agenda. Because your research questions and interests will often be broad and ambitious, a theory can help you focus and narrow the scope of that inquiry. The downside of this narrowing, however, is the risk that a given theory may limit your inquiry too much by restricting the types of questions that you might ask. This interplay between the focus that a theory can provide and the restrictions that it may impose highlights both the risks and the benefits of using theory in the early stages of the research process.

In some cases, having the theory—or at least competing theoretical ideas—is essential for guiding research from the onset. A good example of this comes from the seminal work of Michelene Chi (1978). Chi was interested in determining whether maturity or knowledge (expertise) was the central driving force for cognitive development in the area of memory recall; essentially, she wanted to test the effects of what is popularly known as "nature versus nurture" on memory by looking at whether older adults had better recall (which would confirm the nurture theory) because they were trained experts, as opposed to children. Chi's study involved the theory of **domain-specific** expertise—the view that people can develop different areas of expertise, such as in language or mathematical skills, to different degrees. She speculated that this kind of area-specific expertise might override the traditional "deficits" of younger children in the area of memory. To determine which was more important, she pitted child chess experts against college-age novices in a task to recall pieces on a chessboard and found that the child experts performed at a higher level. In contrast, on a traditional number recall task, the college students performed at a superior level to the child experts. The research questions around the role of knowledge, expertise, and maturation would never have been asked without the theory to drive the initial inquiry.

The frameworks that theories provide can also define a research agenda at the most basic level. A vivid example of this can be seen in the contrast between the approaches of traditional **clinical psychology**, which integrates science, theory, and practice to treat patients' psychologically based distress, and **positive psychology**, the scientific study of strengths and virtues that enable individuals and communities to thrive. Each approach offers a fundamentally different set of values about the nature of human strength and deficit. Whereas clinical psychology has traditionally studied mental health and illness from the perspective of pathology (the causes and effects of disease), proponents of positive psychology have argued that the focus of inquiry should be on human strength, intelligence, and talent (Seligman & Csikszentmihalyi, 2000). As a consequence, the very questions that a traditional clinical psychology researcher might ask (for example, about the causes of depression) differ from the questions a researcher coming from positive psychology would posit

Domain specific
The idea that knowledge and/or expertise in different areas is not based on an underlying general capability, but rather determined by particular capabilities or experiences within an area.

Clinical psychology
The area of psychology that integrates science, theory, and practice to treat patients' psychologically based distress.

Positive psychology
An area of psychology that focuses on studying the strengths and virtues that enable individuals and communities to thrive.

(for example, about the ways in which resilience and optimism can buffer an individual from depression).

Whatever the possible constraints using theory present, it is also important to consider whether any question can ever truly be approached atheoretically (without using theory). Although some might worry that using a theory to form initial research questions unnecessarily focuses your framing of the issues, others might question the very existence of an atheoretical research question. Even if you are not using a formalized theory, you are always operating from underlying theoretical assumptions. In many cases, those assumptions are from your own naive psychology or common-sense ideas. To the extent that we are always working from preexisting ideas, an honest self-assessment of your own assumptions and biases is an important part of the research process.

Theory May Shape Hypotheses

In addition to its role in the formation of research questions, theory also has a function in shaping hypotheses. The assumptions embedded within a particular theory can help to define the particular predictions that you, the researcher, might make about a given topic.

An illustration from a well-known area of psychological inquiry is instructive here. Festinger's (1957) elegant articulation of **cognitive dissonance**—the notion that we are uncomfortable holding conflicting cognitions (thoughts) simultaneously and that we are motivated to reduce this discomfort (or "dissonance") by changing our existing cognitions to bring about a more consistent belief system—has spawned numerous studies examining the role of such dissonance in changing attitudes and beliefs. The theory of dissonance has led to hypotheses that would otherwise be seen as counterintuitive—for example, the prediction that individuals who were paid less to complete a monotonous task would report that the task was more important than those who had been paid more. The researchers found that participants who were not paid well and spent a lot of time on a very boring project justified their effort by suggesting the project was important (Festinger & Carlsmith, 1959).

Cognitive dissonance
The idea that we are uncomfortable holding conflicting thoughts simultaneously and that we are motivated to reduce this discomfort (or "dissonance") by changing our existing thoughts to bring about a more consistent belief system.

Theory and Methodology Reinforce One Another

The interplay between theory and **methodology**—the body of practice, procedures, and rules that regulate a discipline—is also an interesting area to consider. On the one hand, theory can both define and lead to the selection of a particular methodology. On the other hand, advances in methodology can drive changes in theory (and practice).

First, consider the ways in which theory defines and leads to the selection of a particular methodology. Two popular methodological approaches serve as good examples. The first comes from the study of infant cognitive development, the "preferential looking" paradigm. In studies that use looking time methodology, babies are presented with an object, photo, or short event (called a "novel visual event") until they tire of looking at it—this is known as **habituation**. They are then presented with a variation of the event that differs from the

Methodology
The body of practice, procedures, and rules that regulate a discipline.

Habituation
Diminished response to a stimulus that comes about through repeated exposure to that stimulus.

first event in some particular manner, and the amount of time they spend looking at the variation is measured. The assumption is that if infants look for a longer time at the variation of the event, then they are discerning something important about the event. This methodology has been used to argue that babies possess an understanding of basic physics by presenting them with "impossible" physical events (Spelke, 1985). In these studies, infants are first habituated to normal physical events, such as a ball dropping. Then researchers compare their looking time with that of another dropping event. In the control condition, the ball drop follows normal physical laws (e.g., principles of gravity and solidity) and in the experimental condition, infants witness an impossible event (e.g., the ball falls and then appears below a solid surface).

In another set of studies, Wynn habituated infants to one or two objects moving behind screens. In the control condition, infants saw the similar type of movement that indicated either one of two objects and they did not increase their looking time. In the experimental condition, researchers presented infants with a surprising event—one object was either added or removed to the display in a way that violated expectations. Infants in the experimental condition looked longer, suggesting they recognized the change in number. Wynn and others have suggested that this indicates that infants have basic mathematical concepts (Wynn, 1992).

Although it may sound simplistic, the theory that leads researchers to select the preferential looking methodology is the underlying notion that babies are smart and that they come into the world equipped with numerous understandings about how their environment works. Without that basic assumption, a researcher would not be inclined to use the preferential looking methodology in the first place.

A second example of how theory can define and lead to the selection of a particular methodology comes from the intersection of developmental psychology and behavioral genetics. In an effort to parse out the relative contributions of genetic and environmental factors in development, for a number of years, researchers have used a "twin study" methodology in which they measure twins raised in the same family environments on a variety of characteristics. Both monozygotic (identical) and dizygotic (fraternal) twins are studied because monozygotic twins share 100% of their genetic material, whereas dizygotic twins share, on average, only 50%.

The paradigm involves comparing the two different types of twins on traits, with the notion that any similarity between the monozygotic twins above and beyond the dizygotic twins should be a result of genetic factors (Neale & Cardon, 1992). Just as the preferential looking methodology discussed previously is based on a theory that infants are innately intelligent, twin study methods are also based on a fundamental theoretical assumption— that a range of behaviors and traits is largely genetically determined. As with the looking time methodology, without that assumption, a researcher would be unlikely to be interested in selecting a twin study methodology.

In addition to the important ways in which your theory leads to the selection of particular methodologies, the availability or discovery of new methodologies can also motivate shifts in theory. The preferential looking methodology was revolutionary for the field of developmental psychology because it allowed researchers to examine questions about infant cognition previously thought to be unanswerable because of infants' lack of language. Other relatively recent methodological innovations that have shifted the very nature of psychological research and theory include the implicit association task, which has advanced the study of prejudice and the notion of the unconscious (a topic we will delve into more deeply in Chapter 5); advancing technologies that allow the study of the brain via imaging (e.g., functional magnetic resonance imaging) and measurement of electrical activity (e.g., event-related potentials, covered in Chapter 11); and gene sequencing.

Interplay between Theory and Analysis Strategy

Although theory can influence research questions, hypotheses, and methodologies in fundamental ways, its impact is perhaps most profound in the ways that it shapes how researchers analyze their data. The theoretical orientation of many researchers governs the approach they take to data analysis. In this case, your preexisting theory dictates the predictions that you have for your study, and these in turn influence the ways in which you go about analyzing your data. At a more practical level, considering your analysis strategy as you develop your research question can prevent confusion and frustration when you run your analyses.

Not all researchers will say that their analysis is driven by their theoretical orientation or even their research question. For example, researchers working with infants tend to use a limited number of methods, and these methods (e.g., habituation) are accompanied by a particular data analysis approach (e.g., the looking times in the experimental and control conditions are examined using a *t* test).

Yet other researchers engage in a process known as **data mining** that many consider atheoretical (but that can and perhaps should be driven by assumptions and theories). In this approach, researchers use high-powered statistical approaches to examine large data sets for previously undetected patterns. Data mining is common in a number of fields, such as econometrics (Hoover & Perez, 1999), medicine (Bellazzi & Zupan, 2008), and epidemiology (Obenshain, 2004). Although some researchers may view atheoretical approaches to data exploration as "fishing expeditions," as researchers gain greater access to large and complicated data sets, these types of explorations are likely warranted.

A similar argument about the role of theory and analyses can be seen in the use of one- versus two-tailed hypothesis testing. As you may recall from your statistics class, these "tails" refer to the upper and lower ends of the normal distribution (see Figure 4.1). These tails represent large deviations from the mean score on some variable of interest. Consider the case of intelligence. Most researchers think that intelligence is a normally distributed trait. Imagine you have developed a new drug that you think might influence intelligence. If you have knowledge that enables you to predict that the drug would boost intelligence, then it is

t test A statistical approach that compares the difference between the means and variance between two groups.

Data mining The use of advanced statistical techniques to search large data sets for meaningful patterns.

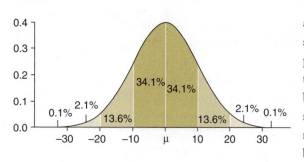

FIGURE 4.1.   Normal distribution.

appropriate to employ a one-tailed approach to test your specific, directional hypothesis. However, as a rule, most psychologists use two-tailed tests that do not presume that the intervention (or drug in this case) will influence the behavior in a particular direction (i.e., the drug might make you smarter or dumber). This two-tailed approach may appear somewhat atheoretical because it ignores background information, but it is likely adopted as a more conservative approach (i.e., one that places a higher bar for being able to report a statistically significant result).

Proponents of the two-tailed hypothesis testing approach would argue that free exploration of data—unfettered by specific theoretical assumptions—can allow for important discoveries that might otherwise be missed. Indeed, the history of science is full of anecdotes of unsought and unanticipated discoveries. Perhaps the most famous of these in psychology is Pavlov's accidental discovery of classical conditioning principles while studying the process of salivation in dogs. Although Pavlov's discovery was not a function of statistical exploration per se, if we insisted that researchers stick only to their original agendas and theories, they could never make such serendipitous discoveries. Large, publicly available data sets such as the U.S. Census or National Longitudinal Study of Adolescent Health (from the University of Michigan's Institute for Social Research) provide particularly fertile sources for data exploration that may yield interesting findings in the absence of a particular driving theory.

Needless to say, debate around data exploration continues. Meehl (1990) offers a biting critique of the hazards of such exploration, which he refers to as "testing of correlational predictions from weak substantive theories in soft psychology" (p. 195). He argues that in social and natural science there is a "crud factor" such that "everything correlates to some extent with everything else" (p. 204). To illustrate the crud factor, he highlights a number of presumably meaningless findings that emerge from a data set drawn from questionnaires administered to 57,000 high school seniors in 1966. These findings included a number of statistically sound but seemingly uninterpretable differences between children from four different Lutheran Synods (Missouri, American Lutheran Church, Lutheran Church in America, and Wisconsin). Some of the differences that emerged from the data include the fact that children from the Wisconsin Synod were less likely to have siblings than children from the Missouri Synod; Missouri Synod children were more likely to play a musical instrument or sing than American Lutheran Church children; and Lutheran Church in America children were more likely to belong to organized nonschool groups than Wisconsin Synod Lutherans. Through a range of similar examples, Meehl builds the case against the use of weak (or nonexistent theory) in informing statistical analyses.

There are ways in which the data themselves can be defined by theory. Data do not exist outside of the theory that defines them—even if that theory is unacknowledged or implicit. As Holton (1973) eloquently argues in his work, *Thematic Origins of Scientific Thought*, theoretical thought itself is based on empirical data and data analysis and, as such, it is difficult to make a separation between data and theory. As much as theory shapes the ways in which you collect and interpret your data, data and theory are ultimately inseparable. And, at a basic level, data do not exist outside of the theory that defines them. For example, the habituation data that are often collected in research with infants cannot be separated from the theory that suggests that learning can be measured by looking at attentional focus.

Theory Can Lead to the Problem of Confirmation Bias

A strong theoretical orientation, however, can pose problems. One potential problem is **confirmation bias**, which is the tendency to give the most weight to information that supports your theory, potentially discounting or ignoring data that go against your strongly held theoretical bias. An example of this problem is captured in Tim O'Brien's cartoon depicting a researcher who has just blown up his laboratory equipment (see Figure 4.2). Even though his experiment clearly failed, he justifies the outcome, saying, "I totally meant to do that." In this case, the existing theory could be that the researcher is a highly skilled, competent

Confirmation bias
The tendency to give the most weight to information that supports your theory, potentially discounting or ignoring data that go against your strongly held theoretical bias.

"*I totally meant to do that.*"

FIGURE 4.2.   Tim O'Brien cartoon showing confirmation bias in interpretation of data.

Let's walk him and pitch to the bishop."

FIGURE 4.3.   *New Yorker* cartoon showing how "theory" can alter the interpretation of "data."

chemist, and the only way the data (the explosion) can support that theory is if this outcome is interpreted as intentional. Confirmation bias illustrates the importance of thinking about your own theoretical biases (both common sense and scientific) and how these biases might influence (in positive and negative ways) the design of your research studies, how you interpret your results, and especially how you handle data that go against your theory.

Figure 4.3 provides an example of how a theory can lead to different interpretations of data. Each of the three finalist captions from the *New Yorker* leads to a completely different interpretation of the cartoon, with one focusing the reader on the age of the batter, one equating baseball and chess (provided by a prominent social psychologist), and one providing a relatively bad pun.

AVOID COMMON PROBLEMS IN STARTING YOUR RESEARCH

Probably the biggest challenge we see students face is coming up with the initial idea for research. Although we provided some methods and ideas for generating research ideas at the beginning of this chapter, we also advise you to research a topic that you find fun and interesting. This will make the task of searching for relevant literature, reviewing research that has been done before, and defining your own research question much easier and more rewarding.

Often novice researchers believe that they must do something completely new and different. This is an impossible task and most (honest) seasoned researchers will tell you that their own research builds and extends previous research, rather than being completely new and original. So think of your own research in this same way: think about extending existing research in a novel direction, rather than trying to come up with a research idea that will save the world or win you a Nobel Prize. But at the same time, you want to extend previous work in important ways. So, we would generally advise you to avoid a minimalist approach—often referred to as "incremental" research—that merely extends the age range of participant populations used in past research or examines a novel participant population, unless these extensions can be justified on theoretical or methodological grounds as important contributions.

One other common problem we find is that novice researchers often attempt to measure too many things, which leads to complex designs and often uninterpretable results. It is generally best, especially in an initial foray into a research area, to examine a small number of variables. Answering one research question always leads to others, and for most researchers this becomes a lifelong process. We hope it will become that for you as well.

PRACTICAL TIPS

Practical Tips for Starting Your Research

1. When deciding on your first research topic, make sure it is a doable project—do not try to win the Nobel (or Ig Nobel) Prize by being overly ambitious or grandiose.

2. Be prepared to make mistakes and learn from them—your second research project will be better than your first.

3. Do a thorough reading of the literature—you should become an expert on the topic.

4. Look for key sections of a research article rather than reading the entire article from start to finish.

5. Get involved in a faculty member's research—join a laboratory.

6. Look for opportunities in laboratories that provide you with a full range of research experiences.

7. Spend some time thinking about your own theoretical biases and how they might influence you as a researcher.

CHAPTER SUMMARY

Starting any new project can be difficult, and this is especially true in research. However, the array of suggestions listed in this chapter should help you find a topic that engages and sustains your interest throughout the process. Once you discover that topic, using targeted research tools to investigate scholarly journal articles and books will save you time and yield much better, faster results than a general online search. Just as important in coming up with a research question is recognizing the central role that theory plays in all research and understanding how it can help you in the next step: choosing a design.

Up for Discussion

1. Some researchers say that they conduct research with no underlying theoretical assumptions. Do you think that it is possible to conduct research atheoretically? Why or why not?

2. Do you think data mining is a legitimate way to identify new scientific findings, or do you think your questions always need to be driven by *a priori* hypotheses?

3. We have argued throughout this chapter that assumptions influence how people conduct research. What underlying assumptions—including both common-sense and formal theories—might influence the way you think about a problem? Do you have perspectives on human behavior that would lead you to design methods in a particular way?

Key Terms

Abstract, p. 76

Change blindness, p. 78

Clinical psychology, p. 84

Cognitive dissonance, p. 85

Common sense
  theory, p. 82

Confirmation bias, p. 89

Data mining, p. 87

Developmental
  psychopathology, p. 83

Domain specific, p. 84

Formal scientific theory, p. 82

Framework theory, p. 83

Habituation, p. 85

Inattentional blindness, p. 79

Literature review, p. 77

Methodology, p. 85

Naive theory, p. 82

Positive psychology, p. 84

PsycINFO, p. 75

Specific theory, p. 83

Summer Research Opportunity
  Program, p. 79

t test, p. 87

Focusing Your Question and Choosing a Design

INSIDE RESEARCH: DIANE C. GOODING

Professor of Psychology and Psychiatry, University of Wisconsin–Madison

I study schizophrenia, which is one of the most severe of all the psychiatric disorders. Although we know that it has genetic origins, we still don't know what causes it, and we don't know how to prevent it. We've made progress in identifying individuals at higher risk for developing schizophrenia, for example, people who are genetically related to someone with schizophrenia. We know that there are certain age periods where we're more likely to see the onset of schizophrenia. But we don't know who among those at-risk people will get it and who won't. My research is driven by two questions: How can we better identify people at heightened risk and intervene early enough to make a difference in their prognosis, and how can we develop better treatments to maximize the functioning and well-being of people with schizophrenia?

I use a variety of methods to research these questions, including cross-sectional studies, behavioral tasks, and questionnaires. My first research focused on smooth pursuit eye movements, an individual's ability to visually follow a slowly moving target. Impairment in these eye movements is now recognized as one of the specific genetic markers of liability to schizophrenia.

One of the most powerful methods I use is the longitudinal method, where you collect two or more observations of the same participants over a period of time. In my line of research, it's important to include a psychiatric comparison group. It's not enough to compare one group of psychiatric patients to a group of healthy controls and say, "Hey there's a difference." Well, that's not really that surprising, is it? I mean one is a group of psychiatric patients who are probably medicated and have a lot of problems, so you would expect there to be a difference. And, when you find that difference, it's difficult to say whether the results reflect psychiatric disorders in general, or if they tell you something unique about that specific disorder. It's much more powerful to include a second patient group that's matched as closely as possible to the first patient group.

For example, in some of my studies I've had two patient groups, with one made up of schizophrenia patients and the other bipolar patients. They were both outpatient groups, they both had psychotic symptoms, but the difference was one group, the bipolar group, had mood symptoms and one group had schizophrenia symptoms. Both groups displayed abnormal performance on some eye movement tasks, but I found that the group with schizophrenia symptoms was more deviant than the other. In another study, I found that bipolar patients looked just like healthy controls in terms of a working memory task, but the schizophrenia patients did not. That was very important in showing that working memory task impairments are really a characteristic trait deficit of schizophrenia.

Cognitive neuroscience and psychophysiology have really advanced our understanding of schizophrenia and the related disorders. I think now we really appreciate how schizophrenia is primarily a cognitive disorder, rather than being just an emotional disorder as was previously thought.

I love research because I love mysteries; conducting research on schizophrenia is very much like working on one aspect of a very complex puzzle along with other people. I'm trained as a clinical psychologist, but the reason I went into research was because I felt that I could help more people this way, and I still believe that. I'm very active in the National Alliance on Mental Illness (NAMI) and a couple of grassroots organizations with mental health consumers, so I see the suffering. I'm in the trenches with people who have serious and persistent mental illnesses. I believe that all research in psychology—from clinically-focused research to intervention-focused research—has the ultimate goal of improving mental health and ameliorating suffering, especially if you keep it grounded in real problems.

Diane C. Gooding has devoted her career to studying the biological bases of psychotic disorders, in particular schizophrenia, and to improving the detection and treatment of these disorders. Her research articles, which have appeared in numerous prestigious journals and reference books, are frequently cited. She has won several teaching awards and has worked with state and local groups that support patients with psychotic disorders and their families.

Research Focus: *Schizophrenia and schizophrenia-spectrum disorders*

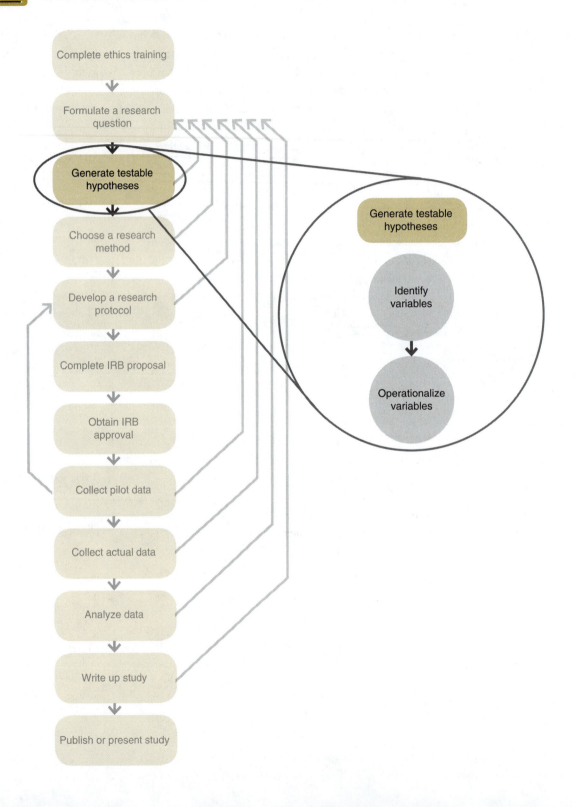

Chapter Abstract

Once you have chosen an area of study and narrowed the scope of your research to a specific question or set of questions, the time has come to more clearly define your goals. The next step is to create hypotheses, identify variables of interest, evaluate particular methods, and begin to design the experiment. We start this chapter with the problem of defining the goal of your research, and then we discuss general issues related to choosing a research methodology.

DEFINE YOUR GOAL

The first step in your research endeavor is defining your goal, which will require you to specify your research question or questions. As we suggested in Chapter 4, how you go about this will be informed, at least in part, by your review of previous research literature and theories, your experience working in research labs with others, and your own ideas and ingenuity. The quality of your research question determines the rest of your research—for better or for worse—so doing a thorough, thoughtful job at the outset is essential.

Defining a research question in the abstract is difficult, so we will use an example to anchor our discussion throughout the chapter. Our example comes from a controversial product that has been popular among parents of young children in recent years: the *Baby Einstein* videos.

Suppose you are interested in testing the claim that such products boost the intelligence of young children. How would you begin to tackle this question? In the following sections, we will discuss the steps involved in designing your study: how to frame a research question and form testable hypotheses, **operationalize** and define your variables, choose your methodology, and weigh the benefits and limitations of both quantitative and qualitative approaches. Along the way, we will also consider the issues of validity and reliability that are central to the choices you make as a researcher. **Validity** refers to the extent to which your methodology accurately enables you to capture the "reality" of the behavior or concept that you are investigating—in other words, are you actually studying what you claim to be studying? **Reliability** refers to the consistency of your chosen methodological approach, that is, is your approach dependable? Can you obtain the same or similar results if you repeat your study or specific measurements?

Define the Research Question

Articulating the initial question ("Do *Baby Einstein* videos boost young children's intelligence?") is just the beginning. The real challenge is to put the question in terms that are

---

Diane Gooding:

"Regardless of the size or scope of your research project, it's really important that you take the time to think carefully about your research question and make sure that you operationalize your variables in a valid and reliable manner. This is important whether you rely solely on interview measures and questionnaires, use observations and behavioral tasks, or incorporate neuroimaging in your research."

Operationalizing
The process by which a researcher strives to define variables by putting them in measurable terms.

Validity Overall, this concept refers to the idea that your measurements and methodology allow you to capture what you think you are trying to measure or study. There are a number of different types of validity.

Reliability This concept refers to the extent to which you can repeat your measurements and/or methods and obtain the same or highly similar results.

Falsifiable
The concept that researchers can test whether the hypothesis or claim can be proven wrong.

Atheoretical research
The idea that a given approach is not driven by an underlying theory or set of assumptions.

Diane C. Gooding:

"The interplay between theory and methods is very important in my work. One theory developed by Paul Meehl centers around a construct called schizotypy, associated with heightened risk for the development of schizophrenia. Meehl argues that there will be a range of outcomes, from people who are really psychotic to those who might not show any psychological disorder. Due to this theory, studying people who are assumed to possess schizotypy on the basis of their lab or questionnaire responses may be as informative as studying clinical patients."

testable, **falsifiable** (able to be proved wrong), and definable in scope. However, before doing any of this, it is important to recognize your own theoretical assumptions as a researcher, as we argued in Chapter 4.

Recognize Background Assumptions.   The best way to recognize your own assumptions is to openly and honestly outline the theory that undergirds your research and to use that theory to shape your research questions and hypotheses. Bear in mind that the theory that shapes your background assumptions can be personal ("naive") or formal (academic) or both.

Background assumptions often go unrecognized, and many experienced researchers will assert that they conduct their work **atheoretically** (without using theory). These claims notwithstanding, we believe that research is rarely, if ever, approached completely atheoretically.

All researchers are driven by a set of background assumptions based in common-sense theories that apply to their work. In fact, most of us hold fundamental ideas about how the world works, and these ideas inevitably inform how we address a research question. Consider the powerfully stated philosophical notion that underlies the work of the early 20th century behaviorist John Watson: "Give me a dozen healthy infants, well-formed, and my own special world to bring them up in, and I'll guarantee to take any one at random and train him to become any type of specialist I might select—doctor, lawyer, artist, merchant-chief, and yes, beggar-man and thief" (Watson, 1913). With reference to our *Baby Einstein* question, you might imagine that if you held Watson's view of the power of environment, you would be inclined to hypothesize enormous potential effects for the videos on the intelligence of young children.

In addition to acknowledging your background assumptions, you can also examine the motivations that bring you to conduct research in the first place. In terms of our *Baby Einstein* example, you would need to ask yourself about your personal investment in the question. For example, are you being paid by the company to demonstrate the effectiveness of its product? Are you a disgruntled consumer who purchased the videos and now believes them to be ineffective? Are you a parent who wants to make his or her baby smarter? Whatever your agenda, being honest with yourself and acknowledging possible bias is the best way to make sure that bias does not unduly shape your research. The assumptions of *Baby Einstein*'s creators would undoubtedly align well with John Watson's view, that is, that infants have unlimited learning potential in all areas. If you held the same assumptions and were powerfully motivated by a desire to sell a product, you would need to implement particular safeguards in the research process to protect against your own expectations, which would bias the findings.

Form Testable Hypotheses.   An important step in formulating your research project is crafting a **testable hypothesis** that will guide your investigation. Some might think of a hypothesis as informal, as a guess. In science, however, a hypothesis must be specific and testable. In our *Baby Einstein* example, we might believe that the videos work—but such a hypothesis is too vague to test (see "Media Matters: Baby Geniuses"). A testable hypothesis must be specific in its prediction. We could hypothesize that a group of children exposed to several hours of the videos per week (for some specified amount of time) will show higher levels of intelligence on a standardized measure than children who spend several hours watching non–*Baby Einstein* videos. This hypothesis is testable because it makes a particular prediction that can be supported or refuted through the collection of relevant data or information.

Ensure Your Hypothesis Is Falsifiable.   There must be a way to know whether your hypothesis is false, that is, if the videos do not boost intelligence. In the case of a study where you are measuring gain versus no gain, it is not difficult to see how a hypothesis could be falsifiable; the best way to falsify the idea that the videos boost intelligence would be to show no significant measurable gains in intelligence scores for children who are exposed to the videos.

However, some theories in the history of psychology have defied falsifiability. Among them are Sigmund Freud's personality elements in his structural theory of personality (id, ego, superego). Freud's concepts of the id, ego, and superego are unconscious processes that have no real way of being objectively measured today (and perhaps even in the future). What sort of test could researchers conduct to definitively counter Freud's idea of the id as the driving force for our basest instincts?

Another prominent example of a theory that has defied falsifiability is Noam Chomsky's **language acquisition device**. Chomsky's hypothesis that children have a specialized aspect of their brain, a language acquisition device, that has evolved to encode key principles of language and grammatical structure is for the most part untestable. It is difficult to imagine an experiment that could show that humans have, in fact, no innate capacity for acquisition of language.

Finally, Jean Piaget, a noted developmental psychologist, hypothesized key constructs of **assimilation**, the taking in of new information to cognitive structures in the brain, and **accommodation**, the changing of these internal structures—or **schemas**—to take in that information, which are for the most part untestable.

Each of these examples involves unconscious, unobservable, and unmeasurable processes that are difficult if not impossible to study empirically. Researchers would struggle and likely fail to construct a hypothesis for an experiment that would falsify their existence. Yet, the lack of falsifiability of these concepts does not mean that they are untrue. Rather, their lack of falsifiability places them outside the realm of scientific inquiry.

It is possible that with methodological innovations, concepts once considered unfalsifiable may, in fact, become falsifiable. Freud's notion of the unconscious serves as a

Testable hypothesis A claim that makes a specific prediction that can be supported or refuted through the collection of relevant data or information.

Language acquisition device Noam Chomsky's hypothetical construct within the human mind that explains the innate capacity for acquiring language.

Assimilation A concept of Piaget's (a cognitive developmental psychologist) that refers to a process where internal mental structures take in new information and fit it in with existing structures (schemas).

Accommodation A concept of Piaget's (a cognitive developmental psychologist) that refers to a process where internal mental structures change as a function of maturation and taking in new information (assimilation).

Schema A concept of Piaget's (a cognitive developmental psychologist) that refers to internal mental structures.

Baby Geniuses

Unlock the "little genius" within your infant! Increase the cognitive development of your toddler, who will be counting numbers and decoding language before you know it! Your baby can learn to read! Such were the initial claims of companies selling video products (and later, a variety of tools) that pioneered the so-called "baby genius industry" in the late 1990s and early 2000s.

Most media outlets ignored these extraordinary statements at first, even if the videos proved immediately popular with parents. Scant early reports on the baby genius phenomenon focused on the trend of younger and younger children being immersed in electronic media. One newspaper article cited a 2003 study of young children's media habits by the Henry J. Kaiser Foundation, which showed that 32 percent of children aged 6 months to 2 years were watching *Baby Einstein* videos. According to one mother, "You want to make sure you're doing everything you can for your child, and you know everyone else uses '*Baby Einstein*,' so you feel guilty if you don't" (Lewin, 2003).

By 2006, however, baby genius products had come under intense media scrutiny. The Campaign for a Commercial-Free Childhood (CCFC) filed a complaint with the Federal Trade Commission against the Walt Disney Company, which by then owned *Baby Einstein*, and the Brainy Baby Company for false and deceptive advertising. Although the Federal Trade Commission decided not to take action, Disney removed some product testimonials from its website and said that it would better substantiate its educational claims in the future (CCFC, 2007).

Then, in 2007, the *Journal of Pediatrics* published a study by researchers at the University of Washington (Zimmerman, Christakis, & Meltzoff, 2007), which issued a press release for the study suggesting that

regular viewing of the videos might even cause harm to children. The correlational study was based on telephone interviews of approximately 1,000 parents of children ages 2 to 24 months. The authors concluded that for every hour per day spent watching baby DVDs and videos, infants ages 8 to 16 months understood an average of six to eight fewer words than babies who did not watch them (Pankratz, 2007).

Media and parenting blogs jumped on results of the University of Washington study, and the researchers appeared on the *Today* show. The chief executive officer of Disney, Robert Iger, subsequently demanded that the university retract the press release, a request the university rejected. Yet, a couple of years later Disney offered a full refund to consumers who bought *Baby Einstein* videos from 2004 to 2009, eventually paying out $100 million; the company also stopped claiming that the products were educational (Martin, 2011).

Meanwhile, the founders of *Baby Einstein*, Julie Aigner-Clark and Bill Clark, filed an open-records complaint against the University of Washington for access to the researchers' raw data, saying they wanted to try to replicate the study. The University of Washington refused several times, first on the basis of ensuring privacy rights for human research subjects and then claiming that one of the researchers had ordered the data destroyed in 2008. The university eventually found backup documents and handed over the data and a settlement of $175,000 to Clark (Martin, 2011).

More recently, CCFC targeted Fisher-Price's Laugh & Learn mobile apps for toddlers in a 2013 complaint with the Federal Trade Commission, again charging that marketing materials made educational claims not backed by scientific evidence. This time around, however, media reaction was more subdued. *Slate* magazine even took issue with CCFC's tactics, arguing that such apps were merely a different kind of toy for children to play with (Rosin, 2013). Although the first babies to watch *Baby Einstein* videos had reached middle school without reaching the intellectual heights of Einstein, they had not suffered long-term damage either.

---

fascinating example. Although at one time many psychologists would have asserted that we could not verify the unconscious, today many argue that the **Implicit Association Test** (Greenwald, McGhee, & Schwartz, 1998) actually measures implicit cognition, that is, thoughts and attitudes about which a person is not consciously aware. A relatively new technique used by social psychologists, the Implicit Association Test measures reaction time to investigate the strength of association between people's mental representations.

In one example of the Implicit Association Test designed to examine different evaluations of gender described by Nosek, Greenwald, and Banaji (2007), subjects were presented with images (e.g., male or female faces), words (e.g., pleasant or unpleasant words), or combinations of images and words (e.g., male faces and pleasant words, female faces and unpleasant words). The subjects were required to respond quickly with different key presses in response to a particular set of items (e.g., left key for male faces and pleasant words, right key for female faces and unpleasant words). By examining differential reaction times, investigators were able to make inferences about unconscious processes of the subjects related to their evaluation of males and females. The notion is that faster responses on the test indicate more strongly held associations; as such, the technique has been used as a way to examine prejudicial attitudes without having to worry about people concealing their true attitudes because of social desirability.

Debates abound regarding the validity of the interpretation that faster reaction time indeed quantifies strength of attitudes. From a methodological standpoint, however, the bottom line is that this technique provides an opportunity for supporting or falsifying at least some aspects of Freud's notion of cognitive processes outside of conscious awareness.

Some ideas, such as the belief in extrasensory perception, often wrongly assumed to be outside of the realm of scientific inquiry, can also be falsifiable (Shermer, 1997) and hence the focus of scientific inquiry. In 2011, Daryl Bem published a controversial set of findings that he argued provided evidence for so-called precognitive abilities (Bem, 2011), the capacity to predict an event at greater-than-chance levels before it occurs. Although the

Implicit Association Test A test of implicit cognition that measures participants' reaction time to investigate the strength of association between people's mental representations.

specific questions of the validity of the findings and Bem's interpretations are beyond the scope of this chapter (suffice it to say that his methodology and analyses provoked a firestorm of criticism), the point is that the idea of precognitive abilities is, in fact, empirically testable and, therefore, falsifiable.

A final note about falsifiability: the key characteristic of a falsifiable theory is a theory-specific prediction that can be confirmed or refuted **empirically**, meaning that the prediction is based on observations or experiences that can be verified. As Wellman and Gelman (1992) note, scientific theories can be divided into two categories: framework (or foundational) and specific. On the one hand, although a **framework theory**, such as behaviorism, can guide the formation of a **specific theory**, it does not in and of itself provide hypotheses that can be falsified. On the other hand, specific theories are "detailed scientific formulations about a delimited set of phenomena" (Wellman & Gelman, 1992, p. 341). As such, they provide a good source of precise predictions that can be falsified. When you construct a testable hypothesis, you are always, at some level, testing a specific theory. In our *Baby Einstein* example, your *framework* theory relates to ideas about the malleability of human intelligence (see the discussion in Chapter 4 of Carol Dweck's research on this topic). That is, do you view intelligence as a raw, innate ability that is relatively immune to experience, or do you view it as something that can be improved through hard work and experience? Your *specific* theory proposes that the particular materials in the videos, when provided to children in particular dosages at particular points in time, will lead to particular, measurable increases in intelligence.

Identify Variables

Before you actually test your specific hypotheses, you must complete the crucial task of **operationalizing** your variables. In the case of *Baby Einstein*, the glaring challenge involves the definition of intelligence. If we want to test whether watching particular videos makes children smarter, then we first must agree on what we mean by "smarter." In psychology, the question of how to best define intelligence has a narrative almost as long as the history of the field itself. Yet, debates surrounding intelligence within psychology are actually debates about operationism, not the essential nature of intelligence. **Operationism** (Stanovich, 2013) posits that scientific concepts must be observable and measurable. In contrast, **essentialism** asserts that a scientific theory must provide information about the fundamental (or essential) properties of a phenomenon. As Stanovich (2013) notes, science cannot answer the essentialist questions; it can only address things in terms of operationism. He relegates the essentialist questions to the domains of philosophy and religion.

When it comes to intelligence, the questions we ask are questions of operationism. For example, should we conceptualize and measure intelligence as a single, unified factor (Spearman, 1904); as two broad areas of interrelated abilities (Horn & Cattell, 1967); or as a series of independent domains (Gardner, 1983)? Although you could argue that each of these

Empirical Based on observations or experience that can be verified.

Framework theory World views or global explanations based on a broad set of assumptions of how the world (or an important aspect of it), in general, works. These assumptions are not likely to be falsifiable.

Specific theory A detailed set of explanations about a particular, well-defined set of phenomena.

Operationism The idea that scientific concepts must be observable and measurable. It is related to operationalizing one's variable.

Essentialism Scientific claim that there exist certain fundamental (or essential) properties.

conceptualizations has an underlying essentialist assumption, it is impossible for psychology to solve the essentialist question about what intelligence truly *is* at a fundamental level. Instead, psychology helps us to tackle the operationist question of how to best measure intelligence, in this case by providing different possibilities for the factors that make up intelligence.

For our *Baby Einstein* study, we would have to pick our operationalization of intelligence as a precondition for designing our study. Do we want to hypothesize that the videos increase Spearman's notion of general measures of intelligence? Or perhaps that they enhance fluid intelligence (i.e., speed of processing) in Horn and Cattell's terms? Or maybe the videos are most effective for the domain of musical intelligence, as defined by Gardner. Once we select our preferred definition of intelligence, we would be ready to select a measurement tool to use with our participants—in this case, some sort of intelligence test. We would also need to operationalize the exposure to the video content. Although this is an easier task than defining intelligence, it would be equally important to clearly define what it means to receive a "dosage" of the videos (i.e., how much time watching the video, on how many different occasions).

CHOOSE A RESEARCH METHODOLOGY

Researchers choose a particular research method for many different reasons. Some researchers always use the same methodology in all or almost all of their research, whereas other researchers use a wide variety of methods. There is no single best method that should be used in all circumstances. The key point to keep in mind is that your research question should always drive the choice of method and *should interest you*.

Choosing a research method requires you to consider several issues. The first issue concerns the point at which you are entering the research process. Are you investigating a relatively understudied set of behaviors, or are you attempting to forge a new direction in a well-established field? Often researchers working in understudied or less well-established areas use methods that are exploratory and that enable the researcher to isolate a small number of variables from the myriad variables that could be investigated for more in-depth study. For example, researchers just starting in a new domain of inquiry might use an observational design or open-ended interviews to help narrow and define the research question. In his classic research on the stickleback fish, Tinbergen (1951) began with natural observations that helped him develop more specific hypotheses, which he could then test in highly controlled experiments.

Second, researchers in more established fields might use a relatively small number of experimental methods and designs that are accepted by the majority of researchers in a particular field. For example, much of the research on how infants reason about the world uses a standard methodology known as habituation (see Martha Arterberry's research: Bornstein, Mash, Arterberry, & Manian, 2012). In this particular method, infants are

Amy Bohnert (Chapter 6):

"What are the questions I'm trying to answer? I balance that with feasibility. Part of feasibility involves money. If you have money you can design a slightly different study, where you determine what the questions are first, then think about feasibility and practical issues second."

Correlational design A research method that is designed to uncover underlying causes related to certain phenomena, but that attempts to understand how different variables are related to one another.

Causal design A research method designed to understand what causes or explains a certain phenomenon.

Quantitative research Research that results in data that can be numerically measured.

repeatedly presented with a set of stimuli that share important features (e.g., a set of male faces). After repeated exposures, the infants become bored and look less at the stimuli (i.e., they become "habituated"). Once the infants' looking time decreases below a predetermined criterion, researchers change the stimuli for one group (known as the experimental group) of infants, for example, by replacing male faces with female faces. If infants recognize the change in stimuli, their looking time generally increases (i.e., they become "dishabituated"). A second group of infants (the control group) will receive additional examples of the original stimuli set (e.g., more male faces), and generally they will continue to be "bored" by the repeated exposures. We will discuss this type of experimental design in more detail in Chapter 8. The main idea is that researchers may use particular methods because they are the established ones in a particular discipline, with the notion that they have been vetted by the scientific community (meaning they are assumed to be both valid and reliable methods, concepts we will examine shortly).

Other issues that influence your choice of method include the cost of doing the research, whether you have the proper tools or technology available, and, of course, whether the research you are interested in can be done in a manner that is ethical and safe to study.

Obviously, you cannot use your preferred research method if you do not have the financial resources or technology available. But you can often devise low-cost methods using simpler technologies to creatively address the same or a related research question. One thing to remember, however, is that no method is perfect and that no single research study can provide the final, definitive evidence that answers your research question. It is also the case that using multiple methods can help establish the validity of a particular finding.

Yet another issue depends on whether you are attempting to understand (1) a *relation* between two or more variables or (2) what *causes* a particular behavior. Often, researchers will first use a method known as a **correlational design**, which helps uncover a relation between a set of variables. Once a relation has been established, researchers may use a **causal design** to explore a potential connection between the variables of interest. Ethics may also constrain design choices, because a causal design may not be possible for some research questions. For example, researchers studying the effects of domestic violence on child development can only examine their questions through a correlational design, since any sort of causal manipulation would be clearly unethical.

Quantitative Research Approaches

When selecting a design, researchers can choose from qualitative or quantitative research. **Quantitative research** is any systematic study that yields numerically measured data that lie on some sort of continuous scale. In quantitative research designs, measurement is typically determined *a priori*, that is, before the study is conducted. In quantitative research, statistical analyses are used to answer the questions at hand. Although use of statistics defines quantitative research, quantitative research can be either experimental or nonexperimental. The choice of a particular method often depends on available resources and the nature of the question being asked, because some questions are more amenable to one method or another. Discussion of the advantages and limitations of experimental and nonexperimental approaches follows.

Experimental Methods. Experimental methods are often held up as the gold standard for scientific research because they possess a set of powerful advantages. Such methods refer to a group of approaches where the environment of the research setting is tightly controlled and often (although not always) conducted within a formal laboratory setting. Within that controlled environment, the conditions are carefully crafted so that any differences found between groups can be attributed to the intentional variations in the procedures to which the participants are exposed. In addition to this level of control, the experimental method includes the important technique of **random assignment**, that is, participants are assigned by chance to either an **experimental group** (the participants who receive the experimental treatment) or a **control group** (the participants who do not receive the experimental treatment).

This procedure enables the researcher to assume that any variation among the participants will be randomly distributed across the two groups. The random variation across groups on the variables of interest should lead the groups to be highly similar at the start of the experiment. And, by accommodating preexisting differences between participants, a researcher can be more confident that whatever differences do emerge are a result of the actual experimental manipulation.

Consider an experiment designed to investigate the impact of a new drug on children's attention. The experimental group would receive the new drug and the control group would not receive the drug. As participants are recruited to the study, they would be randomly assigned to either the experimental group (and receive the drug) or the control group (and not receive the drug). Using random assignment, the existing variation among children in attention should be equally distributed in both the experimental and the control group. Thus, the researcher would expect to find highly similar attention levels in both groups at the start of the study. If the researcher finds that, after taking the new drug for some time, children in the experimental group have higher attention levels than those of the control group, she can infer that the drug has an impact on attention levels. We provide a much more detailed explanation of experimental designs in Chapter 8.

What might an experimental design to examine the effectiveness of *Baby Einstein* look like? Although we will discuss an actual study shortly, we will first discuss the broad parameters of an experimental approach to the topic. Imagine a study where a group of young children and their parents are recruited and randomly divided into two groups: (1) an experimental group where the children come to a laboratory setting and watch the videos

Random assignment The assignment of subjects to different conditions in an experiment by methods that rely on chance and probability so that potential biases related to assignment to conditions are removed.

Experimental group In an experimental design, the set of participants that receives a special treatment with the goal of determining whether the treatment impacts the outcome.

Control group In an experimental design, the set of participants who do not receive the experimental treatment. This group is compared with the experimental group.

with their parents for a designated amount of time every week for several months and (2) a control group where the children come to the laboratory setting with their parents for an equivalent amount of time and are simply instructed to interact and play during the sessions. Because the company claims that the videos increase vocabulary, at the end of the visits, both groups of children are tested on their understanding of a list of vocabulary words. Although other procedures could be implemented to tighten this design—and the actual research does, in fact, have additional controls in place—the basic features of the experimental method can be seen here: conditions that differ only in terms of the variable of interest (watching the videos) and random assignment of participants to one of those conditions.

The example just related contains two major constructs, or variables, that are relevant to our study. The first is the **independent variable**, a factor that is manipulated or systematically varied in an experiment. It is the factor that you are hoping will have an effect on the **dependent variable**, which is the response of interest that the experimenter thinks is influenced by the independent variable. In our *Baby Einstein* study, the independent variable is the exposure to the videos (or lack of exposure for the control group), and our dependent variable is vocabulary learning.

Two additional types of variables relevant to experimental methods are moderating and mediating variables (Baron & Kenny, 1986). **Moderating variables** *influence* the direction or strength of the relationship between independent and dependent variables. For example, suppose you are studying the relationship between a particular counseling intervention and a patient's well-being and find that the intervention leads to increased well-being (see Frazier, Tix, & Barron, 2004). You also find that the intervention increases well-being for women to a greater extent than for men. In this case, sex serves as a moderating variable: the strength of the relationship between well-being and the intervention depends on the participant's sex. However, we would not necessarily conclude that sex explains or causes the relationship.

In contrast to moderating variables, **mediating variables** play a causal role, or explain the relationship between two other variables. For example, differing levels of social support might drive (mediate) the relationship between well-being and counseling (i.e., females tend to garner more social support from their social network and respond better to the intervention). In this example, social support serves as a mediator.

A major advantage of an experimental setup, assuming it has been done with proper care, is that you *can*, in fact, draw conclusions about causality. In other words, if you find that the children in the video group have greater vocabulary retention, you can assert that the videos caused this greater learning.

A major, frequently cited disadvantage of experimental methodology is its artificiality. This concern relates to the concept of validity, that is, the extent to which the study captures the reality of the topic. When a topic is studied in a controlled laboratory setting, critics assert that lack of resemblance to the "real world" may call the applicability

Independent variable
A factor that is systematically varied in an experiment.

Dependent variable
The response that is measured by the experimenter that is thought to be related to levels of the independent variable.

Moderating variable
A variable that influences the direction or strength of the relationship between independent and dependent variables, for example, socioeconomic status.

Mediating variable
A variable that explains the relation between two other variables.

of the results into question. Although this is not a trivial concern and one that researchers must take seriously, some have argued that such a critique may be overstated because it ignores the very purpose of experimental methods: "the artificiality of scientific experimentation is not a weakness but actually the very thing that gives the scientific method its unique power to yield explanations about the nature of the world" (Stanovich, 2013, p. 105).

Nonexperimental Methods.

Nonexperimental methods comprise a group of approaches that do not attempt to manipulate or control the environment, but rather involve the researcher using a systematic technique to examine what is already occurring. In a nonexperimental study, the researcher designs ways to measure phenomena as they naturally occur.

Nonexperimental methods have some primary advantages. The first is one of validity (discussed in greater detail later in this chapter). Essentially, when you observe and measure a phenomenon as it naturally occurs, you can be assured that your data are a reasonably unadulterated reflection of reality. Second, it is often impossible—logistically, ethically, or both—to experimentally manipulate some phenomena. For example, if you want to study the health effects of chronic smoking, you are unlikely to be able to systematically assign people to a heavy smoking group so that you can compare them with more moderate smokers or nonsmokers. Researchers also cannot randomly assign a participant to variables such as age or gender. In such cases, your best bet is to use nonexperimental methods to discern relationships and trends.

Nonexperimental methods also have some disadvantages. One major limitation involves the determination of causality. When using nonexperimental methodology, researchers cannot conclusively assume causal relationships between variables, even if they are fairly certain about the nature of such relationships. The reason for this goes back to one of the advantages of experimental methodology. In an experimental design, you benefit from the ability to randomly assign participants to carefully controlled conditions so that you can attribute any difference between participants to the experimental manipulation. Without this careful control and random assignment (which allows you to assume that your groups are equivalent), any relationships between variables that you discover are purely correlational; we can say that particular phenomena are associated, but we cannot state the direction of that association or whether the association is caused by some third, unmeasured variable.

Let's return to the *Baby Einstein* example as an illustration. Imagine that we conducted a nonexperimental study to examine the relationship between exposure to the videos and babies' word learning. In our study, we took two already existing groups of babies—one whose parents played the videos for their children for the past few months and a second who have never seen the videos. We find that the group of babies who have been exposed to the videos have learned a significantly greater number of words than the babies who have not

Nonexperimental methods A group of research approaches that do not attempt to manipulate or control the environment, but rather involve the researcher using a systematic technique to examine what is already occurring.

been exposed. Can we conclude that the videos are responsible for this difference, that is, that they caused the babies to learn more words?

As tempting as that conclusion might be, the answer is no. Without experimental control and random assignment, we cannot be sure that the differences between the groups are not a result of some third variable, some other factor related to both of the relevant variables at hand (video watching and word learning). For example, there may be preexisting differences between the groups of parents and babies who are likely to use the videos versus those who do not use them. Parents of babies who view the videos may be more verbal with their children in the first place or may have access to other resources that the parents of the non–video users do not have.

The other major limitation to nonexperimental research is that the data derived from such studies do not allow you to draw conclusions about directionality of effects. Although the *Baby Einstein* example may be less relevant here, consider another example from the intelligence literature: the positive association between intelligence and socioeconomic status. Although it is well established that higher levels of intelligence are associated with higher levels of income, what is the direction of this effect? Is it that being more intelligent in the first place helps you to get a job and accrue resources that put you in a higher socioeconomic stratum? Or does socioeconomic advantage supply you with resources (books, access to high-quality education) that foster higher levels of intelligence? One possibility is bidirectionality—that is, the causal arrow may go in both directions. But without the benefit of an experimental design (which would be hard to envision with this topic), we are left to speculate about the nature of this association.

Qualitative Research Approaches

Qualitative research
Investigations where researchers infer meaning or patterns from the data that are reduced to a numerical assessment.

Whereas quantitative research focuses on obtaining information that can be "quantified" or counted, **qualitative research** emphasizes meaning (Willig, 2012). That is, qualitative researchers are generally interested in participants' subjective experience; they try to understand the way participants experience some event and what the experience means to them. Often these researchers will examine behavior in context, focusing on language and actions to understand how participants make sense of a particular event.

Willig (2012) suggests that different types of qualitative research vary in terms of the emphasis placed on the role of theory in guiding the research. For some qualitative researchers, the goal may be providing a detailed description of some type of experience without much interpretation. For others, the goal may be to provide an interpretation or explanation of an experience.

In other words, different qualitative researchers come at the research from different assumptions and framework theories. For some researchers, a key assumption underlying the work is that qualitative analysis provides knowledge that informs us about the real world (i.e., realism). Another researcher may assume that all knowledge and experience is subjective (i.e., relativism). A third qualitative researcher may have an implicit political agenda and believe that research should advance that agenda.

Like quantitative approaches, no single qualitative approach is accepted by all researchers. Rather, researchers approach their work from this perspective in different ways. Drisko (1997) captures the diversity and sometimes conflicting nature of qualitative approaches: "In this family [of approaches] there are some close relations, some distant relations, some extended kin, some odd cousins, and a few nasty divorces." Some qualitative approaches are similar and even complementary, whereas others stem from different core assumptions that researchers may view as incompatible. Indeed, whereas some qualitative and quantitative researchers see the other broad approach (qualitative or quantitative) as valuable for adding complementary information, others see the alternative approach as completely incompatible with their research goals.

The Role of Theory.   We discussed the role of theory and theoretical biases in guiding research questions and methodology in Chapter 4. This issue is more complex with respect to qualitative approaches because some qualitative researchers argue strongly that data—rather than some overarching theoretical perspective—should drive the research process. This idea is based on an approach known as **grounded theory** (Glaser & Strauss, 1967; Heath & Cowley, 2004). Researchers using this atheoretical approach spend a significant amount of time looking for themes that emerge from the data. Therefore, the grounded theory approach is often referred to as a **bottom-up approach** because the data (the bottom) help create the theory that organizes the ideas. In contrast, a **top-down approach** generally uses a particular theory to interpret the data that have been collected.

Imagine, for example, that you want to examine the impact of tai chi, a Chinese martial art involving slow, patterned movements and meditation, on practitioners' quality of life. You could conduct a semistructured interview with some tai chi practitioners that examined their experiences practicing tai chi. A researcher using a bottom-up approach would read the interviews looking for particular themes that emerged from the data (see Yang et al., 2011). One theme that emerged from the study by Yang et al. was that many older adults who regularly practiced tai chi felt that it provided a strong sense of spiritual well-being. In contrast, a researcher using a top-down approach might search the interview data for some predetermined themes. For example, a number of researchers have found that tai chi enhances older adults' **self-efficacy** (defined as "situation-specific self-confidence"; Bandura, 1977), which seems to positively relate to physical function (i.e., balance and walking ability) in older adults (Li et al., 2001).

Bottom-up approaches generally involve **induction,** a process where novel ideas and concepts emerge from exploration of data. In contrast, top-down approaches belong to the

Grounded theory
An explanatory framework that assumes researchers should allow themes to emerge from the data and adopt a more atheoretical approach.

Bottom-up approach
The idea that the data should drive the formation of theory.

Top-down approach
The view that theory constrains the manner in which data or information are interpreted.

Self-efficacy Situation-specific self-confidence.

Induction A process where novel ideas and concepts emerge from exploration of data.

Hypotheticodeductive method A view of scientific methodology that uses quantitative data to teach a particular hypothesis or theory.

hypotheticodeductive view of the scientific method, in which more quantitative approaches use data to test a particular theory. Pure hypotheticodeductive approaches are rarer in psychology and the social sciences than many researchers and theorists think (Thagard, 2012). This method works best in areas of inquiry where researchers can make precise predictions based on well-established theories. If these researchers applied a top-down approach to the same data, they might develop a coding scheme before looking at the transcripts of the interview. This coding scheme might focus on the evidence of particular concepts, such as self-efficacy and physical performance. For instance, researchers might look for words and statements related to those two concepts, such as, "After tai chi practice I feel more confident in my balance" (self-efficacy) and "tai chi has really helped my balance" (physical performance).

Description versus Interpretation.   Qualitative approaches also differ in whether their goal is to merely describe the data or to uncover the meaning of an experience from the data (Willig, 2012). Researchers taking the former perspective attempt to capture the quality and richness of participants' experience "in their own words." In contrast, researchers taking a more interpretative view try to go beyond the words and descriptions to find hidden or nonobvious meanings derived from the experience. Within psychology, descriptive accounts generally dominate. However, in the case of the tai chi study mentioned earlier, the researchers went beyond description to explore what tai chi practice meant to the older adults (Yang et al., 2011).

Realism versus Relativism.   Whereas most quantitative approaches strive to arrive at a better understanding of events and/or objects in the real world, only some qualitative approaches take this perspective. Indeed, many qualitative researchers view a truly objective understanding or description of the world as a myth. Rather, researchers with a

Relativist perspective The focus by qualitative researchers on how participants construct meaning from a particular event or experience.

relativist perspective focus on how participants construct meaning from a particular event or experience. These researchers do not claim that their research truthfully captures some aspect of the real world; they focus on *how* individuals who participate in particular experiences construct meaning.

This realist versus relativist account has sparked considerable debate between quantitative and qualitative researchers. In the fields of anthropology and sociology, these debates have caused theoretical battlegrounds that often lead to schisms within departments and even within the larger disciplines. A version of this debate played out very publicly when Alan Sokal, a physicist, submitted an article to a special issue of the decidedly relativist *Social Text*, a journal of postmodern cultural studies, which focused on the so-called "Science Wars." The Science Wars (Ashman & Barringer, 2001; Parsons, 2003) involved some relatively heated dispute between scientists who took a realist view and postmodernist scholars who took a relativist perspective.

Sokal's paper was inspired by *Higher Superstition: The Academic Left and Its Quarrels with Science*, a book by Gross and Levitt (1994) that took a realist view. Sokal (1996) adopted a relativist perspective in describing quantum gravity, arguing that physical reality was nothing more than a social and linguistic construct. The publication of the paper and revelation that it was in fact a hoax was used as evidence against the relativist approach. This event stimulated heated discussions on many campuses. Part of the debate concerned the ethics of submitting material that you know is wrong to a scholarly journal. Although the vitriol associated with this event has dissipated, realists and relativists have reached no real reconciliation. Within psychology, a more realist perspective dominates.

The Role of Politics.   Although many researchers strive to remain apolitical in their research or see no role for politics within the pursuit of greater scientific knowledge, some qualitative researchers argue that all research is inherently political. What they mean is that research and research findings can be used to enhance a particular group (e.g., reported ethnic differences in IQ can enhance the educational status of some individuals belonging to a certain ethnic group) or used to impair a particular group (e.g., reports that males and females differ on some measure, such as mathematical aptitude). Researchers taking a political approach argue that all research has an underlying agenda, determined in part by the institutional and cultural values that permeate any type of scientific inquiry. To these researchers, specific research can never be disassociated from the cultural and institutional frameworks that govern the research process. Researchers who take a political approach focus on providing a voice for underrepresented groups and practicing research in an egalitarian manner; they often give participants the chance to collaborate in the research process (Willig, 2012). These researchers are concerned with differential power relations between researchers and participants, and they strive to lessen that difference. Feminist psychology is one example of a branch of psychological inquiry often viewed as holding a political as well as scientific agenda (Burman, 1997; Crawford & Unger, 2000).

Jonathon Haidt, a prominent social psychologist, has argued that the field of social psychology has been quite partisan, with little tolerance of nonliberal researchers or conservative viewpoints (http://people.stern.nyu.edu/jhaidt//postpartisan.html/). In his view, the field has a decidedly liberal bias. He and other colleagues (Duarte et al., 2015) recommend that steps be taken to increase the political diversity in social psychology.

ADVANTAGES OF MULTIPLE APPROACHES AND METHODS

Because quantitative and qualitative approaches, and experimental and nonexperimental methods, all have their own strengths and weaknesses, the ultimate research strategy is often to employ multiple approaches and methods to study any given topic. In studying our *Baby Einstein* videos, why not conduct qualitative research, as well as a more quantitative approach? Why not use nonexperimental and experimental methodologies that look at children and parents both in their natural environment and in the laboratory setting? Using multiple methods does require more time and resources, but it allows you to satisfy concerns about the validity of any single approach. Some researchers have even suggested using methodological approaches in a particular sequence, that is, to initially study a topic with more qualitative and nonexperimental approaches to get "the lay of the land" and then, once you have a good sense of the issue, follow up with more structured and rigorous experimental methodology. Again, it is important to remember that no single method or approach is perfect, and ultimately your research question should drive the choice of method.

As discussed in Chapter 1, a key aspect of the scientific method involves the notion that results can be replicated. We discussed the importance of this idea with respect to replicating results using the same methods over time and with different experimenters, especially ones from independent laboratories. In fact, Daniel Kahneman has argued that psychologists should routinely work with other researchers in their field who work in other, independent laboratories to replicate each other's research (Yong, 2012). But another important way to provide support for a research finding is to obtain converging evidence for that finding using a variety of different methodological approaches. Replication of results involves the related concepts of reliability and validity.

Test–retest reliability When measures given more than once obtain the same or highly similar results.

Equivalent forms reliability When two different versions of a scale or assessment are used and result in similar levels of performance.

RELIABILITY AND VALIDITY

The concepts of reliability and validity are two of the most important concepts in research methods. Reliability is generally defined as a measure of the consistency of results obtained using the same or similar measures. In contrast, validity is a measure of whether a variable or assessment actually captures what it is supposed to capture. Figure 5.1 shows how the general concepts of reliability and validity relate to one another. As shown in Figure 5.1, these concepts are related but not equivalent.

Researchers use a variety of approaches to assess the reliability of a particular measure, including **test–retest reliability** (when measures given more than once obtain the same or highly similar results) and **equivalent forms** (when two different versions of a scale or assessment are used and result in similar levels of performance). Researchers are often concerned with another type of

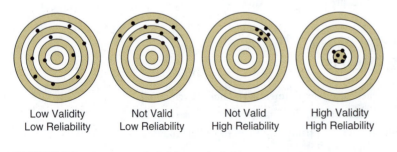

Low Validity   Not Valid   Not Valid   High Validity
Low Reliability   Low Reliability   High Reliability   High Reliability

FIGURE 5.1.   Concepts of reliability and validity.

reliability, labeled **internal consistency**. This form of reliability concerns the degree to which items within an assessment are measures of the same thing. Table 5.1 lists common forms of reliability, definitions, and examples.

Like reliability, there are a number of different types of validity, including construct validity, internal validity, external validity, and conclusion validity. **Construct validity** assesses the extent to which a particular variable or measure actually captures what it is meant

Internal consistency
The degree to which items within an assessment are measures of the same thing.

Construct validity
A measure of the extent to which a particular variable or measure actually captures what it is meant to capture.

Table 5.1.   Types of reliability

Term	Definition	Example
Reliability	A general measure of the consistency of your assessment, usually measured by specific forms of reliability.	If measures of infant intelligence are reliable, then one should be able to obtain the same intelligence score over different assessments. Reliability is often assessed by examining the correlation between different assessments. If the correlation approaches $r = 1.0$, the two assessments are highly reliable.
Test–retest	A measure of the consistency of results obtained using the same assessment tool on multiple occasions.	If you measure an infant's IQ today, how likely are you to obtain the same score tomorrow or at some later date using the same test? Typically measured by calculating the correlation between the two different scores measured at two different times. Researchers must be careful to consider effects that arise from repeated testing. Taking the same test twice can lead individuals to change their responses—because they have learned something or because their views have changed.
Equivalent forms	A measure of the consistency of results obtained on different, but equivalent forms of the same assessment tool.	You design two forms of your infant IQ measure that involve different, but equivalent items. If you have high reliability, the results you obtain using the different forms should yield the same values (as measured by a correlation between the scores obtained on the two forms).
Internal consistency	A measure of how much the scores on items within an assessment yield the same values—to what extent are items within the assessment correlated with each other?	You design your infant IQ measure with multiple items that assess "numerosity" (having a general sense of number, even at a young age). If you have high internal consistency, then one item that reflects a greater sense of numerosity will yield similar values as a second item that also reflects a greater sense of numerosity.

(continued)

Table 5.1. Types of reliability *(continued)*

Term	Definition	Example
Split half	Within a test, this is a measure of internal consistency where the scores on half the items on an assessment are correlated with the scores on the other half of the assessment.	In an IQ test made up of 100 items, to what extent do the scores obtained on a random selection of 50 items correlate with those obtained on the remaining 50 items?
Cronbach's alpha (α)	Within a test, this is a measure of internal consistency that measures the average correlation between all items in the assessment. This measure is equivalent to obtaining the average of all possible split-half reliabilities.	An IQ test with a high α-value is one where the items with the assessment tool are all highly correlated with one another.
Interrater reliability	A measure of agreement in the scores provided by two or more different raters.	Two different experimenters make independent assessments of an infant's IQ; to what extent are the scores from one experimenter consistent with those obtained by the other experimenter? Generally assessed using a statistic known as kappa (κ).

Internal validity An assessment of whether a particular variable is the actual cause of a particular outcome.

External validity A measure of the degree to which the conclusions drawn from a particular set of results can be generalized to other samples or situations.

Conclusion validity An assessment of the degree to which the inferences drawn from the study are reasonable.

to capture. **Internal validity** assesses whether a particular variable is the actual cause of a particular outcome. **External validity** refers to the degree to which the conclusions drawn from a particular set of results can be generalized to other samples or situations. Finally, **conclusion validity** refers to the degree to which the inferences drawn from the study are reasonable. Examples and definitions of the different types of validity are provided in Table 5.2.

RAISING CHILDREN'S INTELLIGENCE: WHAT WORKS?

Now that we have spent the better part of this chapter using the *Baby Einstein* videos as an example, you might be curious as to what the research has actually found in terms of the extent to which these videos boost young children's intelligence. Although a variety of researchers have examined this issue, a recent study by DeLoache et al. (2010) is representative of the findings.

Table 5.2. Different types of validities

Term	Definition	Example
Construct validity	The degree to which a variable actually captures the construct or behavior it is meant to measure.	Does "IQ" as measured by an assessment designed to measure intelligence in infants actually measure infants' intelligence?
Face validity	The degree to which a measure "appears" to assess the behavior of interest.	Do other people agree that the intelligence assessment you designed actually measures intelligence?
Content validity	The degree to which a measure assesses the key dimensions of a construct or behavior.	Does the IQ assessment you designed measure all aspects of intelligence or does it only measure verbal, or spatial, or quantitative intelligence?
Predictive validity	The degree to which an assessment correlates with a future measure of a construct or behavior.	Is "IQ" measured in infancy highly correlated with measures of intelligence assessed in later childhood and even adulthood?
Concurrent validity	The degree to which an assessment is correlated with an outcome measure at present.	Is "IQ" as measured by the Stanford–Binet Intelligence Scale highly correlated with performance on a problem-solving task given in the same testing session?
Convergent validity	The degree to which two assessments designed to measure the same construct or behavior actually do measure the same thing.	Is intelligence as measured by the Stanford–Binet Intelligence Scale highly correlated with intelligence as measured by the Wechsler Adult Intelligence Scale?
Discriminant validity	The degree to which two assessments designed to measure different constructs or behaviors are in fact measuring different things.	Does a high school achievement test measure something different than the Stanford–Binet Intelligence Scale or is performance on both assessments highly correlated?
Internal validity	The degree to which a particular variable is actually the cause of a particular outcome.	Does watching *Baby Einstein* videos boost intelligence? Or do the parents who play these videos for their children do other things that are actually the cause of any increases in intellectual performance?
External validity	The degree to which the conclusions drawn from the results of an investigation can be generalized to other samples or situations.	Do the results obtained in a study of the efficacy of *Baby Einstein* videos to boost intelligence in middle-class infants generalize to children from different classes and cultures?
Ecological validity	The degree to which the results obtained in a laboratory study generalize to real-world situations.	Do the results obtained in your laboratory measuring the relation between intelligence and mathematical problem-solving performance capture the relation between these two variables?
Conclusion validity	The degree to which the conclusions or inferences drawn from the results are reasonable.	Are the results of a study suggesting that watching 30 minutes of *Baby Einstein* videos improves infants' intelligence believable?

Diane Gooding:

"One of my research questions focused on a type of eye movement known as an 'antisaccade,' where the person moves their eyes immediately to the opposite side of a horizontally displaced target. I was interested in whether antisaccade task deficits might be a marker of schizophrenia. In order to answer my research question of whether antisaccade task performance showed test–retest reliability, I had to use a longitudinal design and test my patient groups and healthy controls at two different time points. The research question really helped to determine what type of method I would use."

In their study, a group of 12- to 18-month-old children were placed in one of three experimental conditions: (1) a video with interaction condition, where the parent and child watched the video together at least 5 times per week for a 4-week period (for a total of at least 10 or more hours in 20 or more separate episodes of viewing); (2) a video with no interaction condition identical to the first condition, except parents did not watch the video with the child; or (3) a parent teaching condition where children were not exposed to the videos, but parents were instructed to try to teach the 25 words featured on the video however they wanted. There was also a fourth control condition with no intervention, which provided a baseline for natural vocabulary growth.

The operationalization of intelligence was simple (and not as lofty as the grand debates alluded to earlier in this chapter): the number of new words learned by the children after a four-week period. The findings, although perhaps disappointing to promoters of the *Baby Einstein* series, were clear: the children who viewed the video in the four-week conditions did not learn any more words than did the control group. In fact, the most word learning occurred in the no-video parent teaching condition (supporting what many parents intuitively know—that in-person interaction with one's children is irreplaceable).

The merits of the *Baby Einstein* product aside, this study illustrates some of the central principles discussed in this chapter: the importance of operationalizing your variables clearly, the challenges of selecting a research approach and set of methods, and the consequences of those choices for the validity and reliability of your study. In this case, DeLoache and colleagues opted for an experimental design with a relatively straightforward operationalization of intelligence that allowed for a direct test of one of the claims of the *Baby Einstein* product. Of course, their particular set of choices would not be the only way to study the issue, and it is always worth considering the benefits of other methods (nonexperimental methods and qualitative approaches) that might yield other insights about the effectiveness of such products.

Lest we leave you feeling too discouraged about the prospects for raising children's intelligence with early interventions, it turns out that a number of common-sense practices can be quite effective. Based on a series of meta-analyses, Protzko, Aronson, and Blair (2013) conclude there is support for four major categories of intervention to raise young children's intelligence: dietary supplements for pregnant mothers and neonates (specifically long-chain polyunsaturated fatty acids); enrollment of children in particular early educational interventions; interactive reading with children; and enrollment of children in preschool. As an educated consumer of product claims, we hope you were already skeptical of the notion that simply setting children down in front of a video could enhance their intelligence. It is worth noting (and it is surely not accidental) that the majority of the interventions that *do* work require active parental engagement with children.

Practical Tips for Focusing Your Question and Choosing a Design

1. Define a reasonable goal for your research, one that is doable given your time and resources.

2. Spend time considering your own background assumptions and theoretical perspective and how they might influence your research.

3. Spend time thinking about how to operationalize your key concepts and how they can fit into a testable hypothesis.

4. Do not let the methods drive your research. Make sure your research question drives your choice of methods.

5. Do not be afraid to experiment with different methods.

6. Consider whether more than one method might be useful for providing converging evidence for your results.

CHAPTER SUMMARY

Our hypothetical *Baby Einstein* study in this chapter illustrates the issues involved in defining your goal once you have decided on an area of research that interests you. Knowing the assumptions and background theory that undergird your research will help you shape your research questions and hypotheses. Keep in mind that a solid research question should be testable, falsifiable, and definable. Recognizing your own background assumptions—and they are present at some level—will also aid you in determining which approach to take and which methodology to use, whether quantitative, qualitative, experimental, nonexperimental, or a combination of all of them.

Up for Discussion

1. Making sure your hypotheses are testable and falsifiable is a hallmark of the scientific method, and some would suggest that it is also the clear, bright line between questions that can be subjected to scientific inquiry and those that cannot. What sorts of questions would you place outside of the realm of falsifiability? Besides the examples given in the chapter, are there any concepts or hypotheses within the field of psychology that you can think of that have "failed" the falsifiability test? Can you think of examples of concepts that we would have once classified as unfalsifiable that no longer are?

2. Quantitative and qualitative research approaches are often presented as contrasting methodological approaches, with quantitative methodologies dominating the field of psychology in recent years. Why do you think quantitative methods have enjoyed such popularity among researchers? If you were asked to make the case for qualitative approaches, what might you say? What benefits of qualitative research might be underappreciated?

3. Paying attention to both reliability and validity is essential for researchers seeking to do the best possible work. Some have observed an interplay between the two, such that choices made to increase validity of measurements may decrease reliability, and choices made to increase the reliability of measurements may have an adverse effect on validity. Imagine that you are a researcher seeking to establish the effectiveness of a psychotherapy to help people better manage anxiety. In designing your study, what specific types of reliability and validity would you be most concerned about? What sorts of trade-offs might you be willing to make to maximize particular types of reliability or validity?

Key Terms

Accommodation, p. 99

Assimilation, p. 99

Atheoretical research, p. 98

Bottom-up approach, p. 109

Causal design, p. 104

Conclusion validity, p. 114

Construct validity, p. 113

Control group, p. 105

Correlational design, p. 104

Dependent variable, p. 106

Empirical, p. 102

Equivalent forms reliability, p. 112

Essentialism, p. 102

Experimental group, p. 105

External validity, p. 114

Falsifiable, p. 98

Framework theory, p. 102

Grounded theory, p. 109

Hypotheticodeductive method, p. 110

Implicit Association Test, p. 101

Independent variable, p. 106

Induction, p. 109

Internal consistency, p. 113

Internal validity, p. 114

Language acquisition device, p. 99

Mediating variable, p. 106

Moderating variable, p. 106

Nonexperimental methods, p. 107

Operationalizing, p. 97

Operationism, p. 102

Qualitative research, p. 108

Quantitative research, p. 104

Random assignment, p. 105

Relativist perspective, p. 110

Reliability, p. 97

Schema, p. 99

Self-efficacy, p. 109

Specific theory, p. 102

Testable hypothesis, pp. 98, 99

Test–retest reliability, p. 112

Top-down approach, p. 109

Validity, p. 97

Developing Your Research Protocol

INSIDE RESEARCH: AMY BOHNERT

Associate Professor,
Clinical and Developmental
Psychology, Loyola University
Chicago

I took my first psych course at the University of Michigan, and I loved it. It was a gigantic class. I hadn't thought a lot about why people do what they do and the psychological component involved in it. My professor was very psychoanalytic, and I enjoyed learning about Freud's defensive mechanisms and the things people do in response to anxiety. My mom was a counselor, so you could say I came by some of it naturally.

I started volunteering at a children's hospital in Ann Arbor and was fascinated by kids. I was transcribing the research of a sociologist, and he told me that the field of clinical psychology was really demanding and that I'd have to work hard. That made it more enticing to me. I thought, "Good, sign me up!" That was the summer after my sophomore year, and my interest grew from there.

I did my first research as an undergrad. I was interested in helping kids cope with cancer, and I found a professor who studied friendships between children with illness. We developed this idea of what friendships looked like broadly—their social networks and how they made friends. It developed into an interesting project investigating peer relations in children with traumatic brain injury (TBI; Bohnert, Parker, & Warschausky, 1997). We found that children with TBIs were less competent socially than a control group, and that children with more severe injuries had greater difficulty managing conflict with peers, coordinating play, and developing intimacy in close relationships. We also found that girls were more likely than boys to have lasting friendships that predated the injury. This project that I started as an undergraduate was my first psychology publication.

In my post-doc at Vanderbilt University, I worked with my mentor on a paper about organized activity involvement for at-risk kids. We found that even if kids were at-risk in the 8th grade, if they were involved in a high school activity, they were at a lower risk by their senior year. That study had a lot of interesting clinical implications. It got people thinking about the role of activities as a protective factor in clinical levels of problems.

My advisor at Vanderbilt, Judy Garber, suggested that I study organized activities as a factor that could help kids develop normally, in a healthy way. She was interested in kids with depression and with risk factors for depression, like a maternal history of depression. She had data on organized activities, and we published three papers with those data. That experience was the springboard for my career.

Over the last several years, I've coordinated evaluation efforts for a Chicago non-profit organization called Girls in the Game, which provides programs on sports and fitness, nutrition and health education, and leadership development for girls ages 6–18. It's been really fun establishing a partnership with them. Our work shows that their program works in different areas, so that Girls in the Game can be more successful in garnering grants to provide more programs. There's a direct link between our work and the impact that the organization has on its participants.

Amy Bohnert studies how organized activities can help children overcome difficulties, prevent behavioral problems, and encourage better emotional and social adjustment. She has designed and conducted dozens of studies involving a wide range of participants who come from diverse socioeconomic backgrounds.

Research Focus: How various contexts, especially organized extracurricular activities, may serve a protective role in development

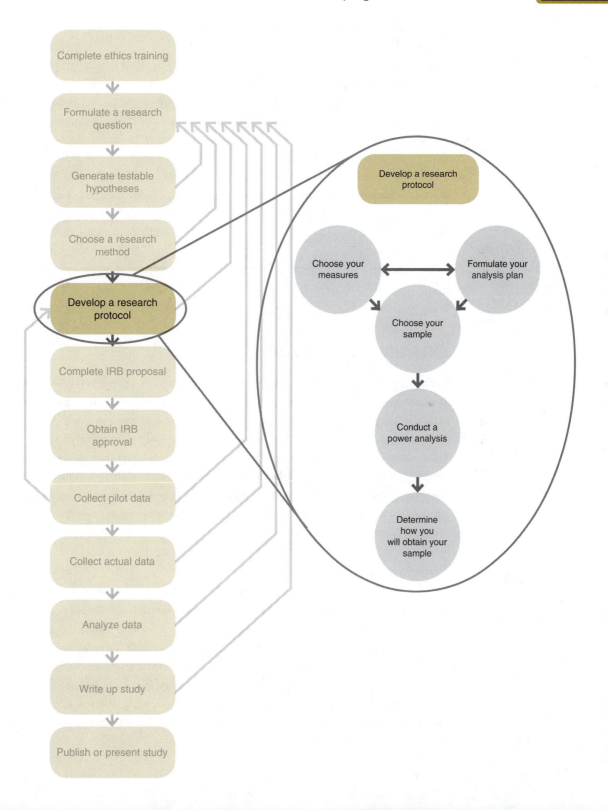

Chapter Abstract

Once you begin to develop your protocol, you have finally reached the nuts-and-bolts stage of designing a research study. In Chapter 5, we discussed the initial steps of how to define and shape your research questions and hypotheses. We also reflected on some of the big-picture decisions you will need to make as you grapple with the numerous trade-offs involved in selecting your broad methodological approach. In future chapters, we will explore the various specific methodologies and designs at your disposal. Before you consider these specific methods, however, you must address four key aspects of research design: obtaining your sample, choosing your measures, conducting a power analysis, and formulating your analysis plan. Although we present these four aspects in a particular order, they are all interrelated. It is helpful to think about them in a simultaneous rather than sequential fashion.

Amy Bohnert:

"Recruiting participants can be frustrating, especially when you're getting samples that aren't as large as you'd like. Small data sets are limited by what you can do in terms of statistics and analyses, and you have less ability to find statistically significant effects because you have limited power. I recommend taking out advertisements, making announcements at schools, or sending letters or emails to attract a sample that is large enough for your study."

Population The entire group of individuals relevant to your research.

OBTAIN YOUR SAMPLE

Before you launch almost any study in psychology, you must determine how you will obtain participants. Although this may seem easy, the availability of certain individuals—for instance, left-handed cello players with at least five years of experience playing in an orchestra—may constrain your research. Whether you are located in a large, diverse urban setting or in a more homogeneous rural college or university setting may affect your ability to conduct research. For example, if you wish to study children or adults with certain medical disorders (e.g., autism, schizophrenia), you are more likely to find them in urban areas near hospitals or medical schools. Leave yourself adequate time to recruit your sample, especially since the process can be time-intensive.

Populations versus Samples

You must first consider the population that will be the focus of your study. The **population** refers to the entire group of individuals relevant to your research. Note that a population in this sense is a moving target that always depends on your research question. For example, if you want to study attitudes that students hold about financial aid at a particular university, then the population of interest would be all of the students at that given university—not all of the students at many universities or across the country. If you are studying the level of boredom (or excitement) of research methods students reading this textbook for a particular class, then all the students in that class form the population of interest—not all the students in the university.

In considering potential participants, you must decide which criteria you will use to include or exclude individuals from the population of interest. This is an essential step in developing your research protocol and enables you to refine the specific definition of your population. For example, if you are studying depressed adults, the inclusion criteria might be that participants are men between the ages of 35 and 44 with diagnosed major depressive disorder. By extension, you are excluding younger and older men and all women.

In almost all research studies, studying the entire population of interest is not a possibility. If your population is a single class (as in our example of readers of the unnamed exciting textbook), then perhaps your study can involve that entire population. But, more commonly, psychological research populations are too large or spread across too many geographical regions, making them impractical to study in their entirety. Imagine trying to study all depressed adults in the United States, all married couples in the Midwest, or all middle school students in New York City. In such cases, we focus our research on a **sample**—a subset of individuals drawn from the population.

Sample A subset of individuals drawn from the population of interest.

Representative Samples

In putting together a research sample, most researchers try to gather a **representative sample,** one that shares the essential characteristics of the population from which it was drawn. For instance, the first author often demonstrates sampling in his undergraduate statistics course with candy. He gives students a pack of M&Ms and asks them to compare the distribution of the different colors (red, green, orange, yellow, blue, brown) in their individual bags with the distribution of colors across all manufactured M&Ms as reported by Mars, Inc. The idea is that each snack pack is a sample of the larger population of manufactured M&Ms and—unless there is reason to believe that the packaging process is systematically biased toward certain colors—each individual bag serves as a representative sample of that larger population.

Representative sample A sample that shares the essential characteristics of the population from which it was drawn.

Do I Need a Representative Sample?   Why should we worry about getting a representative sample? The answer brings us back to the discussion of external validity from Chapter 5, and it wholly depends on your research topic. If your goal is to make an externally valid conclusion that applies to the outside world, then having a representative sample matters. For example, if you want to show the efficacy of a particular form of psychotherapy for people with anxiety disorders, then you will need a representative sample of individuals with anxiety disorders. If you fail to have a representative sample, your conclusions could not be extended generally to people suffering from anxiety disorders.

Not all research, however, requires representative samples. Imagine you are studying a perceptual phenomenon such as the well-known Stroop effect. As discussed in Chapter 1, the Stroop effect is a delay in reaction time that occurs when the name of a color is printed in a color different from the word itself (e.g., the word "RED" is printed in blue ink). When people are asked to report the color of the mismatched print, their reaction time is slower than if the word and color match (i.e., the word "RED" is printed in red ink). This perceptual interference phenomenon would arguably not differ across various segments of the population, since many researchers of perceptual phenomena assert that they are relatively universal. A researcher examining the Stroop effect might not be concerned about gathering a representative sample. However, even in this example the research results might vary as a function of literacy or education levels. Members of a college or university community tend to think that they and their peers represent the general population. However, only about 30% of 18- to 24-year-olds are enrolled in degree-granting institutions (National Center for Education Statistics, 2011), and literacy rates vary greatly by region and ethnic group (National Center for Education Statistics, 2006). Be careful about assuming you are studying a universal process that holds for all samples or populations.

That said, it is always worth considering whether a phenomenon is universal enough to let you dismiss sampling concerns. Some critics charge that psychologists tend to assume more universality than they should. For instance, psychologists may assume that the well-known Müller–Lyer illusion, which involves perception of the length of various lines (see Figure 6.1), produces similar effects across all groups. Cross-cultural studies have found, however, that perception of the illusion varies across different cultural groups (Alam & Srivastava, 1977; Davis & Carlson, 1970). In one set of studies, Segall, Campbell, and Herskovits (1966) presented individuals from 15 different communities with the Müller–Lyer illusion and four other geometric illusions. The researchers found that both European and American samples were more susceptible to the illusion, judging various lines to differ in length when in fact the lines were equivalent, than were non-Western samples. The researchers suggested that these results reflect differences in everyday experiences in different cultures. People who spend more time in a "carpentered world," which has lots of straight lines and edges and more two-dimensional representations, such as line drawings, are more susceptible to these illusions than people who do not live in such an environment.

Similarly, Masuda and Nisbett (2001) found that U.S. and Japanese participants differed in their

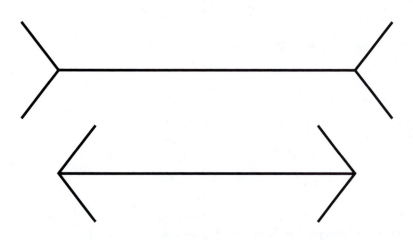

FIGURE 6.1.   Müller–Lyer illusion. The two lines are actually the same length.

perceptions of underwater scenes consisting of fish and other objects. Japanese participants showed more skill in remembering both contextual information and information about relationships than their American counterparts, arguably because of the greater attention to context in Japanese culture. In contrast, U.S. participants tended to remember more about individual fish than their Japanese counterparts. Even the experience of perceptual phenomena does not appear to be universal.

The College Sophomore "Problem"?   Related to the representative sample debate, psychological researchers are often criticized for their overreliance on undergraduates from introductory psychology participant pools (often termed the "college sophomore problem," with apologies to any sophomores reading this text). Although these students provide a convenient sample, using them to examine a research question for which they do not represent the general population can harm the validity of your findings. This might not be a major concern if you were studying perceptual phenomena such as the Stroop effect, but you would be more concerned if you were studying people's attitudes toward current events.

Henrich, Heine, and Norenzayan (2010) have argued that "WEIRD" samples (Western, educated, industrialized, rich, and democratic) may be among the least representative groups to the extent that we look for samples that resemble humans on a global level (see "Media Matters: WEIRD Science"). In their analysis, WEIRD samples are often outliers in a broad range of domains, from spatial reasoning to self-concept. As a result, Henrich et al. contend that some of psychology's claims about human nature based on this unusual subpopulation are problematic at the least.

However, opinions about the significance of this problem range widely. A recent analysis by Cooper, McCord, and Socha (2011) argued that college sophomores are virtually identical to comparison groups of other adults in terms of personality (using the classic "Big Five" dimensions: openness, conscientiousness, extraversion, agreeableness, and neuroticism) and politics. If so, the college sophomore problem may not be as big a deal as previously thought.

Regardless of where researchers land on these issues, most agree that you must be vigilant in considering whom you will study and what conclusions you can legitimately draw based on your samples. You should always consider how your sample might influence your ability to generalize to other samples and the population of interest.

Labeling Populations

Labeling your populations of interest, regardless of their origins and characteristics, requires some thought and care. The truth is, members of any group may not agree on a proper label. Some individuals, for instance, like to be referred to as "Hispanic" or "Indian" or "black," whereas others prefer "Latino" or "Native American" or "African American." We

WEIRD Science

How similar are human beings in the way they think and process the world? Although we look different, form different communities, and observe different rituals, underneath it all we must share the same cognitive mechanisms. In other words, a brain is a brain, no matter whether it lives in Borneo or Manhattan. Right?

For decades, almost all psychology researchers would have answered a resounding "yes!" to that question. They assumed that findings from studies conducted with test participants in the industrialized West were generalizable to all human beings.

But, as Henrich et al. (2010) suggested, perhaps claims about participants from WEIRD countries cannot, in fact, be generalized to the global population. Their study, which appeared in the journal *Behavioral and Brain Sciences*, concluded that participants from WEIRD countries tend to be more individualistic, analytic, concerned with fairness, existentially anxious, and less conforming than those from non-WEIRD societies.

At first, media response to their findings consisted mainly of commentary on psychology and academic websites, such as PLoS blogs, many of which passionately endorsed the study. "If you have one blockhead colleague who simply does not get that surveying his or her students in 'Introduction to Psychology' fails to provide instant access to 'human nature,' this is the article to pass along," proclaimed one blogger on *Neuroanthropology.net* (Downey, 2010).

Aside from a *New York Times* article that also supported the study's findings (Giridharadas, 2010), commentary stayed in the blogosphere until almost three years after the study was published. Then, *Pacific Standard*, a magazine covering environmental, sociopolitical, and public policy issues, published an in-depth article that traced the research of Joe Henrich, one of the lead authors, from his early days as a graduate student through the researchers' reaction to the WEIRD study (Watters, 2013).

Slate magazine ran an article written by a behavioral neuroscientist who applied the WEIRD theory to a study on the loss of virginity and subsequent sexual satisfaction in adulthood (Brookshire, 2013). The participants were—you guessed it—college undergraduates. Brookshire discussed brain development in adolescence and the dangers of extrapolating outcomes from these young participants to the general population. She argued that although some studies conducted with WEIRD populations may be generalized (at least to the rest of the WEIRD population), those concerning topics such as sexuality and social punishment should not be.

Why has the potentially revolutionary WEIRD theory received such little (and delayed) attention from the mainstream media? Does it involve the complexity of the topic, which requires an in-depth understanding of multicultural environments as well as neuroscience? At this point the WEIRD theory remains a minority psychological opinion that requires further confirmation. However, the study's implications would be enormous for researchers, who would have to spend a great deal more time and money expanding their participants beyond the convenient pool of college undergraduates. Stay tuned.

recommend asking a few members of the sample group, someone close to them, or an organization advocating for their needs how they want to be identified. You may also consider asking a member of the sample group to be part of the research team. If this is not practical or possible, find out as much as you can about the target population, including its history of labels. However, be aware that journal editors may request particular labels when you submit work for publication (see Chapter 15).

Once you decide on a label, be consistent in referring to your different sample groups. For example, if you use "white," it is best to use "black" as an identifier. If you use "African American," it is best to use "European American."

Many researchers are interested in studying groups that differ in some way from the typical, healthy undergraduate. As with any population, it is important to define your population of interest when you design your study and select participants, but these special populations require even deeper consideration than others.

Generally, when researchers refer to "nonstandard" or "atypical" populations, they mean participants who vary in important ways from the general population. Although we use these labels to explain particular research issues, you should always be extremely careful and respectful about how you refer to research participants in any study. Aside from offending members of the group you hope to study, using labels viewed as insulting by your participants may influence their honesty and willingness to provide accurate information or participate at all. Using particular labels may convey unintended messages to both the readers of your work and the group you are studying. In the case of people with particular medical conditions, you should consult with experts or advocates of the group for the preferred terminology (these experts may also be essential for recruiting these populations).

Usually researchers are interested in the dimension on which the nonstandard group varies. For example, the case studies of Phineas Gage (a man who suffered a brain injury when an iron rod shot through his head), Nadia (a young girl with autism and extraordinary drawing ability), and H.M. (a patient who underwent neurosurgery to alleviate seizures and was subsequently unable to remember recent events; see Chapter 10) involve the study of atypical individuals. Researchers chose to study them because they assumed the brains of these three remarkable individuals differed in important ways from the brains of individuals who did not have iron rods driven through their heads, autism, or neurosurgery to alleviate recurring seizures.

The "appropriate" label can change over time or vary between subgroups or even individuals. For example, the label for individuals born with a genetic disorder involving an extra 21st chromosome has changed considerably since an English doctor, John Langdon Down, first categorized the common characteristics of this anomaly (Down, 1866). In his original paper, Down referred to "the large number of idiots and imbeciles which come under my observation." Although it is hard to imagine that anyone ever thought referring to people as "idiots" and "imbeciles" was appropriate, past psychological and medical research is filled with such belittling terms. Over the years, labels have "progressed" to

"Mongoloid" and "mentally retarded" (Global Down Syndrome Foundation, 2011). It is important to recognize that atypical samples tend to be quite heterogeneous. Many people assume that individuals with a diagnosis of Down syndrome or autism spectrum disorder are similar, but there is considerable variability in how these atypicalities manifest.

Even within the special education field, researchers have struggled for appropriate labels. Researchers and practitioners have used "intellectually and developmentally disabled," "cognitively disabled," "intellectually challenged," and "differently abled" to describe particular nonstandard groups. Today, the preferred label for individuals with this genetic disorder is people with Down syndrome (Global Down Syndrome Foundation, 2011). "People-first language," a term that first appeared in 1988, seeks to avoid dehumanization of people by emphasizing the dignity of the individual over the disability. Over the past few decades, various organizations and advocacy groups have published guidelines on what is known as disability etiquette (Folkins, 1992).

Random Samples

Random sampling
A method in which every member of a given population has an equal chance of being selected into a sample.

Researchers often argue for the need to do **random sampling**—a method in which every member of a given population has an equal chance of being selected into the sample. This approach offers the most straightforward method for obtaining a representative sample. To return to our M&M example, imagine you have a giant barrel of 10,000 candies, but rather than counting all the M&Ms of different colors, you want to estimate the distribution by taking a subset of those M&Ms. To select a random sample (suppose you want 100 in your sample), you would need a methodology in which every M&M in the barrel has an equal chance of being selected for your sample, perhaps by shaking up the barrel and then dipping in a scoop to select 100 candies.

Generally speaking, for random sampling to work, you must replace samples that you draw from a population so they do not affect the overall probability that others will be selected. The easiest way to understand this is with a standard deck of cards. Suppose that you want to take a random sample of cards from the deck. You shuffle the deck after selecting each card. If you do not replace the card you selected each time before selecting the next one, then the probability of selecting any subsequent card increases each time. Your chance of selecting any given card the first time is 1/52 and it becomes 1/51 the second time, 1/50 the third time, and so forth.

You would not select the same person from the population more than once, because this would violate statistical assumptions about the independence of observations and potentially skew your results. His or her replacement into the population (i.e., putting the person back into the metaphorical deck so that he or she can be selected again) retains the equal probability of selecting any given member. When dealing with large populations, researchers often do not worry about replacement, because the probability changes minimally between the selection of each individual into the sample.

Problems with Random Sampling.   Although random sampling is viewed as the gold standard for selecting participants, there are often practical barriers to assembling a truly random sample. Successful random sampling assumes that you have complete access to the entire population of interest. If you sample students at a university, the population is known and listed in a centralized place, and you could conceivably use the registrar's records to randomly select your sample.

However, many populations are not so thoroughly indexed and organized. For example, what if you wanted a random sample of the residents of the city of Chicago? There is no single comprehensive record of the city's entire population, so you would have to use incomplete methods. Traditionally, researchers would use the phone book for randomly selecting participants. Although this method is somewhat dated, we can still use it to illustrate the point.

A phone book included an extensive listing of many of the city's residents, but also systematically excluded some groups of individuals. Historically, phone books were thought to undersample those from lower-income brackets who might not be able to afford a home phone (Taylor, 2003). Although that bias may still be a factor today, phone books are also limited in utility because they include only landlines and, therefore, exclude the ever-growing group of people who use only cell phones. They also exclude individuals who choose not to be listed in the phone book. Depending on your research questions, individuals with unlisted numbers may respond differently than those who list their numbers (Moberg, 1982; Roslow & Roslow, 1972). Basically, using a phone book to gather a random sample will leave you with a biased sample because the listings themselves are a biased population. This example highlights the dilemma of random sampling in the real world.

Alternatives to Random Sampling.   Whereas true random sampling can be either impractical or impossible, alternative methodologies offer some of the benefits of random sampling. Following are a few of many such methodologies.

Stratified random sampling, one of the most common alternatives, divides a population into homogeneous groups along some key dimension (for example, race/ethnicity) and then randomly samples from within each of the subgroups. This approach may ensure greater representativeness because relatively smaller groups are represented among your strata in proportion to the original population. This methodology is often used to ensure that minority groups are adequately represented in a sample. Say that only 5% of your population of M&Ms is red. In true random sampling, it is possible that in a sample of 100 M&Ms you might end up with only 1 or 2 red candies, or even zero. A stratified random sampling approach would guarantee that 5% of your sample will consist of red M&Ms—in other words, that you will continue sampling M&Ms until you reach that 5% threshold.

A related alternative is the **oversampling** approach, in which you intentionally overrecruit underrepresented groups into your sample to ensure that you will have enough representation of those groups to make valid research conclusions. To return to our obsession

Stratified random sampling A technique whereby a population is divided into homogeneous groups along some key dimension (for example, race/ethnicity), and then random samples are drawn from within each of the subgroups.

Oversampling The intentional overrecruitment of underrepresented groups into a sample to ensure that there will be enough representation of those groups to make valid research conclusions.

Nate Silver and the 2012 Election

The importance of sampling was perhaps best highlighted in the 2012 presidential campaign, with its extensive press coverage of an array of polls leading up to Election Day. The proliferation of political polls in recent years has confused many voters, who cannot be sure of the polls' accuracy and do not know who to believe. Although a number of political polls turned out to be wildly inaccurate in the 2012 election, the statistician Nate Silver predicted the presidential winner of all 50 states correctly in his FiveThirtyEight .com blog. He had also correctly predicted the winner of 49 of 50 states in the 2008 presidential election.

Why has Silver succeeded in his predictions where other pollsters have failed? Much of his success seems to come down to building models using probability and statistics that employ as much aggregate data as possible and avoiding theoretical models or single sets of observations to draw conclusions. He continuously updates his predictions on his blog, showing the probability of various outcomes based on constant aggregating of polling data from many sources.

At a basic level, we might argue that Silver's sample—because it combines many samples and polls—ends up being the most representative of the actual population of voters on Election Day. His work also highlights the importance of using multiple methods and samples to provide converging evidence. He outlined his procedures and various assumptions in his 2012 book, *The Signal and the Noise*.

with M&Ms, if your sample is only 100 M&Ms and 5 red M&Ms will not be enough to draw valid conclusions, then you might oversample the red M&Ms (deciding, for example, to ensure that 20% of your sample is red). For a real-life example of the importance of sampling, see "Media Matters: Nate Silver and the 2012 Election."

Nonprobability Samples

Nonprobability sample A sample in which members of the population are not all given an equal chance of being selected.

What about situations when gathering a representative sample does not matter? In such cases, random sampling (or its variations) may not be required, and a **nonprobability sample**—one in which members of the population are not all given an equal chance of being selected—may be an appropriate option.

Convenience sampling A method of sampling that makes use of the most readily available group of participants.

One of the most common ways to acquire a nonprobability sample is through **convenience sampling**. Many undergraduate students (particularly in research methods courses) use this method because, as the name suggests, it draws on the most readily available group of participants. In a convenience sample, you typically recruit people who are easily accessible. For example, you could obtain a convenience sample of undergraduates by asking friends on your dorm hallway to participate in your survey on attitudes toward gun control.

Snowball sampling A method of sampling in which participants are asked to help recruit additional participants.

A related type of nonprobability sampling is **snowball sampling**, in which participants are asked to help recruit additional participants. Although snowball sampling is a nonsystematic approach (like convenience sampling), it does have the potential advantage of helping a researcher access a difficult or hidden population. If you were conducting a study of undocumented immigrants, for example, a snowball sample might be the best way to gather a sample of reasonable size.

With any sort of nonprobability sample, you should always be aware of the hazards of **self-selection**, that is, that participants select themselves into a particular sample (or opt out of participation). Ultimately, you cannot avoid the phenomenon of self-selection in sampling. The best a researcher can do is try to account for it by understanding and, in some cases, measuring the factors that might lead participants to opt in or out.

Self-selection
An instance where participants electively place themselves into a particular sample (or they opt out of participation).

Online Samples

One of the most prominent and popular ways to collect samples today is online. Numerous online resources offer a ready source of participants, such as the Mechanical Turk (MTurk) platform. Although social science researchers have used MTurk for only a few years, it has become more and more popular because of its low-cost, large participant pool and convenient system for recruitment and compensation.

Other online systems for generating surveys, such as SurveyMonkey and Qualtrics, have also grown in popularity and in some cases offer services for gathering samples. Both SurveyMonkey and Qualtrics also provide extensive tools for constructing, structuring, and presenting your survey. You can choose from a variety of question or item types, including rating scales, multiple-choice questions, and open-ended questions and determine whether items are presented in fixed or randomized orders. You can also allow the survey to branch off into customized sets of questions for respondents who answer a question in a particular way. For example, if you are studying dating behavior, you might ask different follow-up questions for respondents who indicate their last dating experience was positive compared with those who rated it as negative.

One concern that is often raised about online samples is the extent to which they may (or may not) be representative of their intended populations. Emerging evidence suggests that many of these samples—especially MTurk—do a reasonably good job of representing the demographic diversity of the larger population. In fact, Buhrmester, Kwang, and Gosling (2011) argue that the diversity of the MTurk sample surpasses other standard Internet samples and many U.S. college samples. They argue that although MTurk may not be effective for sampling specific targeted populations, it does a pretty good job of population random sampling.

Similarly, Scherpenzeel and Bethlehem (2011) contend that as larger portions of the population go online, the concern that online participants cannot represent the larger population has diminished. They do point out, however, that certain segments of the population will be easier to sample online than others (e.g., young, working, single people are more readily accessed online than elderly or non-Western populations).

On the whole, the evidence indicates that online samples are here to stay and that they do an acceptable job, at least in some domains, of providing diverse, representative samples.

Depending on your research question, however, you may want to collect multiple samples from different populations with the hope of providing converging evidence for your findings. It might be useful to see whether the results you obtain using MTurk are similar to or different from those obtained from a group of psychology undergraduates.

Paying Participants

We discussed participant payments briefly in Chapter 2—in particular, whether payment alters participants' perspective on the risk associated with research and unduly influences them to participate (Grady, 2005). Some research suggests that when it is appropriately scaled, payment does cause participants to downplay risks (Bentley & Thacker, 2004). Here, however, we focus briefly on whether payments help recruit and potentially increase the diversity of your sample.

More and more researchers pay people to complete surveys, participate in interviews, or take part in experiments. Researchers believe that this approach improves participant recruitment, helps recruit a more diverse sample, leads participants to take their participation more seriously, and assists with participant retention in studies with multiple sessions. However, data on this issue are not entirely clear. One reason is that potential benefits of incentives can interact in complex ways with particular research questions.

Although paying participants may help with recruitment and retention, it may also have detrimental effects on effort and behavior, particularly when payment is based on participants' performance (Bonner & Sprinkle, 2002; Camerer & Hogarth, 1999; Kamenica, 2012). Behavioral economists have begun to consider how incentives make up only part of the choices that guide behavior. They also argue that how choices are framed and the number of options provided influence the impact of any incentive. Kamenica (2012) suggests that paying participants to do inherently interesting tasks or perform prosocial acts, or paying participants too much or too little, may be counterproductive.

So how should you decide whether to pay your participants? And, if you decide to pay participants, what is the right amount? Luckily, many other researchers have already addressed this issue. Look for related research in your area that has already been published; check the methods section for whether the researchers paid their participants and, if so, how much. You can also call your local institutional review board representatives and ask them for advice because they have likely encountered similar research.

CHOOSE YOUR MEASURES

Once you have determined how you will obtain your sample, the second step in establishing your research protocol is figuring out which measures you will use. Although your selection of measures will vary greatly depending on your research topic and the age and characteristics of your sample, there are some overarching considerations for how you go about this task. We discuss two of those broad topics here: determining your scale of measurement and considering the reliability and validity of your chosen instruments.

Remember, when you choose measures for your research, you do not need to reinvent the wheel. There may already be established measurement tools available for many topics you come up with, and many of these tools have a significant base of research to support their validity and reliability. For example, the Beck Depression Inventory is a widely used self-report measure to assess depression (Beck, Ward, Mendelson, Mock, & Erbaugh, 1961). You should always search the prior work on your topic before you begin to hammer out the specifics of your research protocol.

As you choose your research measures, you will also need to consider the issue of **measurement error**. Any given instrument will exhibit some difference between the actual or true value of what you are measuring and the result obtained using the measurement instrument. This difference, or error, is something that researchers must accept, because no single measurement instrument can ever be perfect. Some measurement tools are better than others, but awareness of the ever-present problem of measurement error is essential for thoughtful research design.

Measurement error
The difference between the actual or true value of what you are measuring and the result obtained using the measurement instrument.

For instance, research has found that older adults tend to slow down their walking speed when they talk more often than younger adults do when talking and walking. This dual-task effect, a situation where one task (e.g., talking) interferes with another (e.g., walking), has been found in older adults to be related to street-crossing behavior (Neider et al., 2011) and an increased risk of falling (Beauchet et al., 2008; Bootsma et al., 2003). Measuring walking speed is relevant to this discussion.

A traditional, low-cost way to measure walking speed is to have two individuals record walking speed over a set distance with stopwatches. If you try to do this with a partner, you will quickly see that this approach can be prone to errors. If the distance is relatively short, say 10 meters, and the observers are not synchronized at the start and finish, then the measurement error could exceed what you might expect from the manipulation, in this case the addition of the second task. You can fix some of these problems by automating the timing with an electronic system that is triggered in the same way for each participant. But even these systems are not perfect. In fact, no measurement system is truly perfect.

As a researcher, you must consider the amount of error that is built into your measurement tool. Even measures such as reaction time that are captured by key presses on a computer are influenced by aspects of technology, such as the responsiveness of the key press, the refresh rate of information on the computer screen, and the speed of the computer processor. Although improvements in technology and computer processing speeds reduce many of these issues, they will never go away completely.

Scales of Measurement

Although an introductory statistics textbook would cover the issue of scale of measurement extensively, here we define the four scales of measurement and only briefly discuss the benefits and detriments of each one. We cover the scales in ascending order of complexity—nominal, ordinal, interval, and ratio. The more complex scales contain more information, and interval and ratio scales are often preferred for research instruments because they contain the most quantitative information. See Table 6.1 for a summary of characteristics of each of these scales.

Nominal scale
The most basic measurement, when scale points are defined by categories.

Nominal Scale.   The most basic measurement is a **nominal scale**, which is defined by categorical measurements. When a measurement is categorical, the values assigned to the different categories have no numerical meaning, that is, the numbers mark information about the category, but nothing else. Nominal data answer questions about "how many"

Table 6.1.   The four basic scale types

Scale type	Characteristics	Examples
Nominal (categorical)	Responses are unordered categories. Although responses might be assigned numbers for coding purposes (e.g., Democrat = 1, Republican − 2, etc.), the numerical assignments are arbitrary.	Political party affiliation (Democrat, Republican, Libertarian, Green) Sex (male, female) Religious affiliation (Christian, Jewish, Buddhist, Hindu, Muslim, etc.)
Ordinal (rank order)	Responses are ordered ("greater than" or "less than" relationships make sense).	Rankings of students according to aggressiveness Preference rankings (e.g., "I like X most, Y second most, . . .") Likert items (e.g., a 5-point response scale from "strongly disagree" to "strongly agree"; are often treated as interval*)
Interval	Responses are numerical and the differences between points on the scale are numerically meaningful.	Temperature in degrees centigrade or Fahrenheit IQ test scores Many scales in behavioral research Likert items (e.g., a 5-point response scale from "strongly disagree" to "strongly agree"; are often treated as interval*)
Ratio	Responses are interval AND there is a meaningful 0 value. Ratios (e.g., response X is twice that of response Y) have meaning for these types of scales.	Length Reaction time Temperature in degrees Kelvin (where there is an absolute 0) Amount of money earned

* Considerable debate exists regarding whether Likert-type items should be treated as ordinal or interval when analyzing data.

rather than "how much." In other words, nominal data can be examined by looking at frequencies of occurrences in different categories. A nominal classification would include any sort of measurement that involves categories that differ from one another in kind, but not in any sort of quantitative sense. For example, if you are tallying votes for different political parties (Democrat, Republican, Libertarian, Green), then you might assign a 1 to Democrats, a 2 to Republicans, and so on. This allows you to count the number of people who respond either Democrat or Republican, but the actual numerical values of 1 and 2 are arbitrary.

Ordinal Scale.   The second type of measurement is an **ordinal scale**, which has the properties of identity and magnitude. Each value is unique and has an ordered relationship to the other values on the scale. What distinguishes an ordinal scale from other, more powerful, scales is that the numbering of values reflects information only about rank—it does not tell you anything about the value of the distance between ranks. In other words, the distance between each rank may differ from point to point. Consider an ordinal scale of measurement where you ask a preschool teacher to rank her students from the most to the least aggressive. When the teacher ranks Johnny as the most aggressive, Samantha as second, and Emma as third, we cannot assume that the "distance" between Johnny and Samantha and that between Samantha and Emma is uniform. Johnny may be much more aggressive than any other student in the class, and there might be a big drop-off between Johnny's and Samantha's aggression. Further, it could be that Samantha and Emma are almost equal in their aggression, with Samantha having only a slight edge. The rank orders tell us nothing about the distance from one rank to the next. Another familiar example is class rank for high school students. The distances between the ranks of valedictorian, salutatorian, third in the class, and so forth may be variable.

Ordinal scale A scale possessing the property of identity and magnitude such that each value is unique and has an ordered relationship to the other values on the scale.

Interval Scale.   Like the ordinal scale, the **interval scale** contains rank order information, but it also has the property of equal intervals between points. What this means is that a score of 4 is a single unit greater than a score of 3, and the size of the interval between 4 and 3 is the same as the size of the interval between 3 and 2. Treating measurements as interval scales is common in psychological research. A well-known example is the IQ score, where each point on the scale is an equivalent unit (i.e., the distance between 100 and 110 is the same as the distance between 90 and 100).

Interval scale A scale containing rank order information, as well as the property of equal intervals between points; the most common scale in psychological research.

Ratio Scale.   Finally, the **ratio scale** contains the most quantitative information. It shares all the properties of an interval scale, but it also contains a meaningful absolute zero point, where zero represents the absence of the thing that is being measured. Whereas most psychological constructs that we choose to measure do not contain such an absolute zero point (as in the example of IQ, there is no "0," representing the absence of intelligence), a variety of basic measurements are, in fact, ratio scale. Examples include measurements of

Ratio scale A scale sharing all the properties of an interval scale (rank order information and equal interval), but also containing a meaningful absolute zero point, where zero represents the absence of the thing that is being measured.

time, speed, and length, that is, the length of 0 on a ruler represents the absence of any length. A ratio scale allows you to compare measurements in terms of ratios. For example, if you were measuring how long two different groups needed to complete a task, you could note that participants in group 1 responded, on average, twice as quickly as participants in group 2.

Select Your Scale

The big question you should ask yourself in choosing your scale is, "How will I statistically think about the data I collect?" The form in which you collect the data will determine how—and even *whether*—you will be able to use certain statistical approaches to analyze your data. In the worst-case scenario, the data you collect may turn out to be unanalyzable. Your answer to the above question will help you make the right choice and avoid excruciating headaches down the road.

When analyzing data, researchers often have a choice between various parametric and nonparametric tests. **Parametric tests** require that the measurement scale be interval or ratio and make strong assumptions about the distribution of measurements in your population. **Nonparametric tests** make few assumptions about the population distribution and may be applied to nominal (names or categories) and ordinal (order) measurements. We discuss both types of test at greater length in Chapter 14. But, the truth is that researchers try to select measures that enable parametric analyses (interval and ratio data) whenever possible. Of course, some research will dictate the measurement scale you can use, and it is not possible to measure everything using interval/ratio measures. Certain information is inherently categorical and must be scaled that way. For instance, if we conduct a study of different types of psychotherapy and count the number of people who comply with treatment for the different types, then the type of therapy (e.g., cognitive-behavioral, psychodynamic, humanistic) is a categorical variable.

There is some controversy about whether a common type of measurement in psychological research, called **Likert-type ratings** of attitudes, can, in fact, be considered an interval scale. An example of a Likert-type item would be, "I feel anxious when I am going to speak in front of a group of people." Participants respond on something like a 1-to-5 scale, with 1 representing "strongly disagree" and 5 representing "strongly agree." Critics such as Jamieson (2004) have argued that we abuse Likert-scale ratings when we treat them as intervals, because we cannot, in fact, assume that the intervals between the values are equal (i.e., that the distance between "strongly disagree" and "disagree" is the same as the distance between "agree" and "strongly agree"). These critics contend that we should instead be treating Likert-type data as ordinal. Although we cannot resolve this controversy here (and most researchers do treat such measures as interval), it is important to be aware of the debate surrounding this issue.

Reliability and Validity

A final, crucial consideration in selecting your measures brings us back to our discussion of reliability and validity in Chapter 5. Ideally, any measures you use should be high in both

---

Parametric test
A statistical test that requires that the measurement scale of your data be interval or ratio and makes strong assumptions about the distribution of measurements in your population.

Nonparametric test
A statistical test that makes few assumptions about the population distribution and may be applied to nominal and ordinal measurements.

Likert-type ratings
Items that ask participants to rate their attitudes or behavior using a predetermined set of responses that are quantified (that are often treated as an interval scale). An example would be a 5-point rating scale that asks about level of agreement from 1 (strongly disagree) to 5 (strongly agree).

validity and reliability, meaning they should capture what they are intended to measure (validity), and they should yield consistent results (reliability). The best measures do both well, although there is often an interesting interplay between reliability and validity.

Some steps intended to make a measure more valid, so that it represents the "real thing" as closely as possible, might harm its reliability and vice versa. For example, if you wanted to measure a complex construct such as creativity, you might assume you could find a fairly reliable measure—such as counting the number of solutions that a participant generated in response to a particular problem. The difficulty with this measure, however, is that the definition of creativity as fluency of ideas in problem solving is likely only a piece of the true construct. A more valid measure might involve an evaluation of the novelty of each individual solution. Although this would be a valid way to measure creativity, reliably measuring novelty is challenging.

Again, you do not need to reinvent the wheel. A search through the literature can yield a treasure trove of previously established measures that are both reliable and valid (see Chapter 6). Developing such measures from scratch requires considerable work, and you can benefit from the efforts of others.

CONDUCT A POWER ANALYSIS

Once you have determined your sample and your measures, two more important steps remain in developing your protocol: conducting a power analysis and formulating an analysis plan. Researchers are inclined to cut corners in these steps, frequently bypassing them altogether. In fact, conducting a power analysis has become a regular practice in psychological research only within the past couple of decades, although it has become a required component of most federal grant submissions.

The primary reason that researchers skip these steps is simple: you cannot begin your study without a sample and a set of measures, but you can always go back after completing your study to determine your level of power and to design an analysis plan. We argue that although you *can* perform research without conducting a power analysis and designing an analysis plan up front, researchers who follow best practices (and hence generate the best research) make these steps a part of the planning process.

Prospective versus Retrospective Power Analysis

What exactly does it mean to conduct a power analysis? **Statistical power** refers to the probability that your study will be able to detect an effect in your research (such as a difference between groups or a relationship between two variables), if such an effect exists. The latter point is important—that power refers *only* to your ability to detect effects that are actually present. If your study does not elicit the hypothesized effect, no amount of statistical power can help you. Power is typically reported as a coefficient that represents the probability of being able to detect the effect. So, a power of .6 means that you have a 60% chance of detecting an effect of a given size, assuming that one exists.

Statistical power
The probability that your study will be able to detect an effect in your research, if such an effect exists.

Prospective power analysis A series of computations that help you to determine the number of participants that you will need to successfully detect an effect in your research.

Effect size The magnitude of the primary measure you use to test your hypothesis (such as a difference of means or a relationship between two variables).

Retrospective power analysis A series of computations that help you determine how much power you had in a study after the fact.

There are two primary ways to go about a power analysis: prospectively (a priori) and retrospectively (post hoc). We prefer a **prospective power analysis,** because it suggests that you are thinking about the issue of power as you design your study. A prospective analysis involves a computation that helps you to determine the number of participants that you will need to successfully detect an effect in your research. Although there is no hard and fast rule about what your power should be, psychology researchers should strive for a power of .8 (80% chance of detecting a real effect of a given size).

One challenge in doing a prospective power analysis is that it requires that you know the effect size of the phenomenon that is being studied before you conduct the research. **Effect size,** as the name suggests, measures the magnitude of a particular effect. To determine the power needed to detect an effect, you must know the size of that theoretical effect. As you might expect, a small or moderate-size effect will require a larger sample size to get adequate statistical power, whereas a larger effect requires a relatively smaller sample, because the effect itself is easier to detect.

When researchers do not know the magnitude of an effect before conducting their research, they will rely instead on a **retrospective power analysis**, where they can report how much power they had in their study after the fact. Thus, although it is preferable in principle to take the a priori approach, doing so requires that you are either studying an effect where previous research has already established an effect size or you have firm theoretical grounding to make an educated guess about the likely effect size. If you are dealing with an entirely new area, you always have the option to do a pilot study first to get a handle on the effect size. Ultimately, however, these extra steps lead some researchers to give up on prospective power analysis altogether. Chapter 13 includes a more in-depth discussion of statistical power.

Why Is Power Often Underemphasized?

The practice of conducting power analyses, although it is not new, has only become a regular practice of researchers in psychology in recent years. Critics of psychological research have long chastised researchers for their lack of attention to power analyses. The first high-profile attention to this issue dates back more than 50 years, when Cohen (1962) surveyed articles from *The Journal of Abnormal and Social Psychology* (a major journal at the time) and determined that the average power of research in those reports was 53%. This meant that the research he surveyed was underpowered and likely to be missing effects in many cases (47% of the time). A follow-up more than 25 years later by Sedlmeier and Gigerenzer (1989) concluded that work in the same journal (now titled the *Journal of Abnormal Psychology*) was even slightly lower in power than had been found in Cohen's original 1962 work.

More recently, Maxwell (2004) noted that underpowered studies persist in psychological literature. He speculated that psychological researchers largely continue to skirt the issue because they structure their studies with multiple hypotheses, meaning that even if the statistical power is inadequate to detect effects for any single hypothesis, a researcher is likely to obtain at least some statistically significant findings across several different hypotheses. He argued that this effectively allows them to ignore the charge that their studies are underpowered because they can ultimately report some effects. In other words, the issue of power can be evaded by having many analyses where at least some findings are likely to emerge as significant.

Whatever the reasons, the underemphasis on power and effect size speaks to another bias in psychological research that has likely contributed to the problem—an emphasis on obtaining statistical significance to the exclusion of everything else. **Statistical significance** refers to the probability of obtaining an effect size as large as (or larger than) the one you actually obtained; the standard probability used in most psychological research is 5%. Researchers in the field have traditionally worried about achieving statistical significance, often to the point of neglecting other issues, because it is an almost certain prerequisite for having your research published.

Statistical significance
An indicator of the probability of obtaining an effect size as large as (or larger than) the one you obtained.

Why Does Power Matter?

Although this issue of having enough power may seem esoteric, it is worth considering the real-world implications of underpowered research that might fail to detect meaningful effects. Imagine, for example, that you are conducting research on a new psychotherapeutic intervention for panic disorder. An underpowered study that fails to detect whether your treatment approach is effective could prevent individuals and therapists from hearing about a highly effective treatment. For individuals struggling with panic disorder and for the therapists who work with them, this would be a tangible and tragic consequence of this frequent oversight in psychological research methods.

FORMULATE AN ANALYSIS PLAN

The final step of developing your protocol is a particularly interesting topic to end with, because it is rife with disagreement about best practices. Formulating an analysis plan requires a specific strategy for what sorts of analyses you will conduct. For example, if you plan to examine differences in performance between two groups, then you will need to apply one type of statistical analysis. However, if you want to look at the relationship between two variables, you must use a different statistical technique (see Chapters 13 and 14). Your analysis plan should be laid out before collecting data. Almost all researchers plan their selection of sample and measures (although admittedly to varying degrees), and most would agree on the wisdom of conducting a power analysis, even if many do not do it. In contrast, not all researchers would agree they should formulate their analysis plan at the beginning of the research process *and then stick to it.*

The argument in favor of including an analysis plan in your protocol design is that it may help to keep "false positives" in your research findings to a minimum. What does this mean? You want your hypothesis—*not* the significant statistical results you may gather—to drive your research and analyses. As we mentioned before, because statistical significance is central to being able to report your research findings, the temptation to maximize your chances of reaching statistical significance in your analyses is considerable. Holding yourself to an analysis plan is one way to combat this temptation.

In contrast, is there anything wrong with data exploration? Should researchers really constrain themselves from looking at analyses that had not been conceptualized at the beginning of the process after the fact? What you think of the issue even shapes how you refer to the practice. Consider, for example, the terms *data mining* or *data fishing* as opposed to *data exploration*. Exploration sounds like a full, worthwhile (and even noble) undertaking, whereas mining and fishing sound a bit suspect and imply some rule breaking.

Although we cannot resolve this debate for you here (because ultimately there is no single correct answer), we can offer some general (and less controversial) recommendations. First, it is a good idea to have an analysis plan as you formulate your research protocol, even if you do not intend to stick to that plan strictly throughout your research. Thinking carefully about how you will analyze your data will lead to a more thorough study design. It may help you realize that you should collect different data or that you do not actually need some of the data you are collecting. Considering the type of data your study will generate and how you will answer your questions with particular statistical techniques can only lead to more carefully constructed research.

Second, be aware that if you decide to explore your data for potentially statistically significant findings *after* your study is completed, you are leaving yourself open to the appearance of "*p*-Hacking"—the process of deliberately manipulating factors in your research to maximize your chance of uncovering a statistically significant finding ($p < .05$). *p*-Hacking can include a variety of actions, such as dropping groups, specific cases, or variables from an analysis or adding analyses that were not part of an initial plan.

p-Hacking The process of deliberately manipulating factors in your research to maximize your chance of uncovering a statistically significant finding ($p < .05$).

Simmons, Nelson, and Simonsohn (2011) argue that whatever steps you take, you should aim for transparency (i.e., letting the scientific community know what you have done so that your work can be fairly evaluated). They do not suggest that *p*-Hacking is acceptable as long as you talk about it; rather, they contend that you must disclose fully any steps you undertake that may either intentionally or unintentionally enhance your chances of uncovering statistically significant findings. They also suggest that the burden to show that results did not emerge out of "arbitrary analytic decisions" (Simmons et al., 2011, p. 1363) lies with the researcher. The greater your ability to show that your analysis plan was well considered at the outset of your research, the more defensible your findings will be in the end.

THE ART OF JUGGLING CHOICES

In a perfect world, you could always choose the best research design and participant population to address your research question. However, researchers rarely operate in such a world. When conducting research, you are always faced with making difficult choices, making compromises, and trying to come up with the best solutions for less-than-optimal situations. Sometimes recruiting your desired participant population will be difficult or nearly impossible. Often your research will be constrained by time and resources.

Participant Recruitment Issues

Many research studies require a particular participant population to address the research question of interest. The more specialized the population, the more difficult recruiting participants will be. What do you do if you cannot find the desired number of participants (or anyone) to participate in your study? First, you can offer some type of incentive. Many researchers today routinely pay participants to participate in research. This often leads to greater participation rates and fewer "no shows" and also helps with recruiting a more diverse sample. The payment should be approved by the institutional review board (see Chapter 3) and should not be so large as to be viewed as coercive. Many researchers offer a raffle for a gift card or some other prize to keep overall costs of the study down.

Another approach is to go where the participants are. If you are interested in children, go to day-care centers or the homes of children that you know or have contacts with. If you are interested in individuals with Parkinson's disease, find support groups that focus on that disease. If feasible, consider "moving" the laboratory to a place that is convenient or easily accessible for the participant population you are interested in. We know several researchers who study older adults and set up satellite laboratories in malls, as well as others who have gone to retirement communities. If none of these approaches works, it is time to rethink your research question, design, or participant population.

Time Constraints

A few different types of time constraints exist. If you are a college senior collecting data for your senior thesis, you may have only three to six months to collect your data. You may have to alter your participant population or methods so that you can finish on time. Experienced researchers also confront time constraints. Some research, such as on seasonal affective disorder, is best done during the winter months when the disorder is prevalent. Other research that uses undergraduates is best done during the academic year. Thus, researchers working on a particular problem or using a particular participant population must time their research appropriately. If you cannot meet the time constraints, you may need to rethink your research question, design, or participant population.

Amy Bohnert:

"When I was an undergrad I worked on a study that looked at friendships between children with traumatic brain injuries. I coordinated a team of undergrads and we had to recruit people for the study. We had to make a lot of phone calls, drive up to an hour all over southern Michigan, and also deal with the intensive nature of data collection, which was going into people's houses as an undergrad and giving them questionnaires. Getting it all done in time was a big challenge. Looking back I don't know how I did it. The study was eventually published in Developmental Neuropsychology and is still cited."

Money Constraints

Research can cost a lot of money, including payment to research participants, travel expenses for participants or experimenters, and the cost of materials or stimulus preparation. These costs can add up quickly, especially if you require a large sample. You can keep participant costs down by offering participants a chance to win money or a gift card in a raffle, but this approach might not be as successful as paying each participant individually for recruiting the number of participants you need.

More and more researchers are using online approaches to obtain relatively large samples at a relatively small cost. For example, Amazon's MTurk (discussed earlier in this chapter) is an online crowdsourcing resource where researchers can pay a relatively small amount of money to individuals willing to complete surveys online for funds they can then use on Amazon. Although this route potentially offers a lot of data, it may not include much information about the people completing the survey.

Because of the growing trend of researchers copyrighting their measures, you may need to purchase copies of questionnaires or established measures. Once a measure has been copyrighted, other researchers generally cannot use that measure without paying a fee. You are faced with the choice of coming up with your own measure, one that is potentially less desirable and less well established, or finding some way to pay for the copyrighted material. Again, if you cannot meet the monetary constraints, you may need to rethink your research question, design, or participant population.

Equipment Constraints

Some researchers love to use high-tech data collection and coding techniques that can be very costly. For example, researchers using the sophisticated technique of functional magnetic resonance imaging may need to pay up to $400 per hour for machine time to collect data. Researchers studying brain activity using event-related potentials often require systems costing a few hundred thousand dollars. Obviously, the cost of this equipment is well beyond that of a beginning researcher, but most research will require at least a computer for generation of materials, data storage, and data analysis. Most, if not all, research requires some equipment. What if you cannot afford it? Or what if you are collecting data in a remote location and cannot transport the desired equipment? Once again, you are faced with choices that pit the optimal with the obtainable.

Make the Best Choices

How does one juggle these different constraints to design and implement the best research study possible? It is difficult. But remember that there is no perfect study. Do the best you can with the resources that you have. Often your constraints stimulate creative, low-cost, and low-tech solutions that are more reliable and valid than expensive, high-tech solutions. Just do not forget about reliability and validity in the decision-making process.

Another option to consider is collecting converging evidence using a variety of different methods. This approach may help you get around some of the constraints and ultimately provide better data. For example, if you decide to run your survey on MTurk to collect a large number of participants at a relatively low cost, consider a companion survey with another sample population that may cost more to collect but that will provide more information about participants' demographics and other potentially important characteristics.

PRACTICAL TIPS

Practical Tips for Developing Your Research Protocol

1. Be sure to leave yourself adequate time to recruit your sample.

2. Clearly define your population of interest, giving thought to the criteria for inclusion and exclusion.

3. Consider the ways in which your sample needs to be representative (or not), and select your sampling methodology accordingly.

4. Determine payment for your participants, being sure to consider potential benefits and problems with compensation.

5. Choose your measurements, keeping in mind both the scale of those measurements and the issues of validity and reliability. Do not reinvent the wheel—you can use existing measures.

6. Consider conducting a prospective power analysis to determine how many participants you need in your study before you begin collecting data.

7. Formulate a general analysis plan before you begin collecting data.

CHAPTER SUMMARY

With research question and hypotheses in hand, you have moved on to the task of designing your research protocol, which will keep you in good stead when it comes time to launch your study. The protocol process begins with the challenge of obtaining representative participant samples, so that you can create valid conclusions that will apply to broad groups of people.

Approximations of random sampling—considered the gold standard for gathering participants—have grown easier in recent years thanks to online systems such as MTurk, which offer a low-cost, large pool of participants. You may also choose from alternative methods, such as stratified random sampling, oversampling, and snowball sampling.

Next, you must select a scale of measurement—nominal, ordinal, interval, or ratio—depending on the complexity of information your study requires. Above all, your measure should gather data that are both valid (well founded and reflecting the real world) and reliable (consistent).

Conducting a power analysis will tell you the probability that your research will be able to detect an effect. Researchers complete a power analysis either before or after designing the study (although preferably before).

The final step in your design should be formulating an analysis plan. This is a specific strategy for what sorts of analyses you will conduct.

Up for Discussion

1. The issue of obtaining a representative sample, that is, a sample that accurately represents your population of interest, presents substantial challenges for researchers. As important as this issue may be for some research studies and topics, it may not be an issue for all psychological research. As a prospective researcher, what criteria would you use to determine whether a representative sample is necessary for a given study?

2. Likert-type ratings are popular in survey methodology, which is widely used in social science research. How much should researchers worry about the controversy over whether these scales should be treated as ordinal or interval data? If such ratings should really be treated as ordinal, does it matter that researchers tend to use them as interval instead? Why or why not?

3. The importance of formulating an analysis plan (and sticking to it) at the outset of research is widely debated. Some have argued that this is essential in reducing the temptation to "fish" for significant findings in one's data; whereas, others argue that the freedom to explore within a dataset is important to the process of scientific inquiry. Where do you fall in this debate? Justify your position.

Key Terms

Convenience sampling, p. 130

Effect size, p. 138

Interval scale, p. 135

Likert-type ratings, p. 136

Measurement error, p. 133

Nominal scale, p. 134

Nonparametric test, p. 136

Nonprobability sample, p. 130

Ordinal scale, p. 135

Oversampling, p. 129

Parametric test, p. 136

p-Hacking, p. 140

Population, p. 122

Prospective power analysis, p. 138

Random sampling, p. 128

Ratio scale, p. 135

Representative sample, p. 123

Retrospective power analysis, p. 138

Sample, p. 123

Self-selection, p. 131

Snowball sampling, p. 130

Statistical power, p. 137

Statistical significance, p. 139

Stratified random sampling, p. 129

Survey and Interview Approaches

INSIDE RESEARCH: JOHN SCHULENBERG

Professor of Developmental
Psychology, Department of
Psychology, and Research Professor,
Institute for Social Research,
University of Michigan

I'm trying to understand adolescent drug and alcohol use—the dark
side of adolescence, when things go wrong. A lot of what I do is figuring out how adolescents get into trouble and then the consequences. For instance, to what extent does it matter if people get
involved in risky and unhealthy behavior in the short term or the
long term? We know that the longer drug and alcohol use can be
delayed, the better. A lot of behaviors in adolescence are experimental. They're done without a lot of thought, and people might not
mean to get so far into something. Then they might pull back, and

as long as they don't hurt themselves or anyone else, no harm done. Others are not so lucky. So what causes someone to go off the deep end? What makes someone turn it around? These questions have kept me going for a couple of decades.

The kind of surveys I use are self-report, which is a very useful research method for the questions we have. I ask people to tell me the sort of risky things they're doing. Because of that I need for them to trust me. I want to know how they see the positive and negative aspects of their risky behaviors, so we ask them, "Why do you see this as a good thing?" or "Why do you see it as a bad thing?"

In our national samples, we have used mostly mail questionnaires to follow young people as they make the transition to adulthood, but recently we started to use online surveys, which we think will help with response rate and confidentiality concerns. We first contact subjects when they are high school seniors. Our survey administrators visit the schools and tell them about the study and how we keep the data confidential. We keep the teacher out of the way to help protect confidentiality. By then they trust or they don't. If they trust us, they give us valid information. Then we stay in contact with them and provide them with incentives to stay in the study. We conduct these long-term studies over decades, which I've always found to be the most exciting. We get to find out what happens with people from adolescence to late in adulthood.

There is so much heterogeneity within my sample population in terms of what might be a risk factor for alcohol and drug use. Risk factors are individual and contextual characteristics that increase the chance of engaging in substance use, and we find that they vary across people and time. We're starting to find out that it matters when the risk factor occurs; there are times in life that are sensitive periods when risk factors are especially powerful.

It's very complicated, but that's what makes our work so interesting. I'm trying to look at this in many different ways to try to tame the complexity. Instead of avoiding it, we try to embrace the complexity and then figure out how to tame it with statistical modeling. We're not always successful, but the field is getting much better at understanding how, when, and for whom risk factors are most powerful.

John Schulenberg relies on survey methods to research the psychosocial development of adolescents and young adults. A fellow of the American Psychological Association, he has co-authored several books and dozens of journal articles. His research includes nationwide studies on neurodevelopmental pathways in adolescent health risk behavior and developmental models of high-risk alcohol use and social roles in young adulthood.

Research Focus: Drug and alcohol use across adolescence and the transition to adulthood and the impact of developmental transitions on trajectories of health and well-being

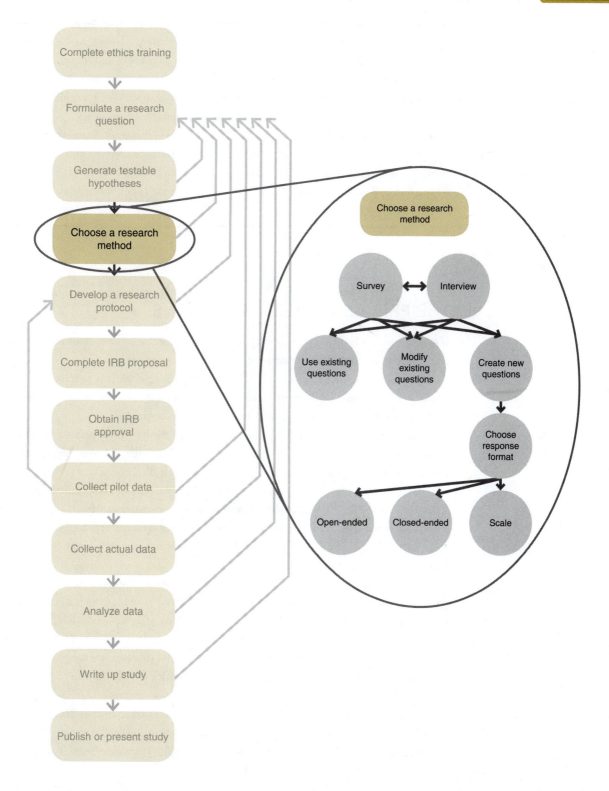

Chapter Abstract

This chapter focuses on the design and construction of surveys and interviews, highlighting key issues that you should consider in creating a survey or interview, choosing a survey method, and obtaining the desired sample population. We first explain the factors you should consider when evaluating results reported for surveys, which have grown increasingly popular with the advent of online technology. Then, we help you decide whether to use an existing survey, modify an existing survey, or create your own survey from scratch. Finally, we provide you with some guidance on how to design and write your own questions and figure out which response types will best suit your research goals.

THE PERVASIVENESS OF SURVEYS

If you still have a landline phone, you have probably received more than one call from a telemarketer, and now many telemarketers know how to reach you on your cell phone. During campaign season, especially presidential campaigns, people may be inundated with opinion polls asking about various issues and candidates. But even outside the realm of politics, surveys and marketing are part of the fabric of everyday life.

Survey results bombard us daily. They appear in all media—from print to television, from radio to Internet blogs—and report on an incredible range of topics. Survey studies reported in the media include the going rate of a tooth for the Tooth Fairy (Pisani, 2013), whether men or women cheat more on their partners (Schonfeld, 2013), who believes in God (Newport, 2013), and who should be president (*Polling Center*, 2012). Topics range from the sublime, such as those listing travelers' recommendations for the best destinations (*Best Travel Destinations*, 2016), to the ridiculous, such as a survey examining the most absurd reasons for missing work (Gillie, 2013).

A central issue with all these surveys lies in the trustworthiness of the data. Should you believe the results of surveys that rank your school as one of the best colleges or universities ("Best College Rankings and Lists," 2016) or as a party school ("Top 20 Party Schools for 2015," 2015)? Does the Tooth Fairy really shell out $50 a tooth? In other words, how can we tell whether the survey is valid (measures what it is designed to measure) and reliable (provides consistent results across similar contexts or situations)?

The answer depends, in part, on knowing the questions asked in the survey, how the questions were asked, and who was asked the questions in the first place. For example, in the Tooth Fairy poll discussed in "Media Matters: The Profligate Tooth Fairy," what

The Profligate Tooth Fairy

The Tooth Fairy has gone on a spending spree, tucking as much as $50 for a tooth underneath children's pillows at night, according to an online survey conducted in 2013.

The survey reports that only about 2% of all children receive that hefty sum, and children now receive an average of $3.70 per tooth. That figure is 23% higher than in 2012 and 42% more than in 2011. About 6% of children found $20 replacing lost teeth when they awoke in 2013.

These survey results were so remarkable that they garnered coverage in several mainstream media outlets, including the *Chicago Tribune*, *Reuters*, and *ABC News*.

All the reports speculated on possible causes of the Tooth Fairy's extravagance.

"I think the Tooth Fairy is suffering from irrational exuberance," said Jason Alderman, director of global financial education at Visa, which conducted the study. He attributed the increase to the improving economy and parental reluctance to say no to their children, particularly in a small area where they feel they can be generous. ("Inflation Remains in Check," 2013).

Neale Godfrey, author and chair of the Children's Financial Network, pointed to parental remorse. "I think the amounts have gone up because we feel guilty about our parenting. . . . We are not spending as much time with our children as we would like, and so we substitute money for time" ("Inflation Remains in Check," 2013).

Other sources explained the increase as a result of parents' age-old desire to keep up with the Joneses and spare their children's feelings. "A kid who got a quarter would wonder why their tooth was worth less than the kid who got $5," says Kit Yarrow, a consumer psychologist and professor at Golden Gate University (Pisani, 2013).

ABC News reported that the amount kids receive from the Tooth Fairy depends on where they live. Kids in the Northeast get the most, at $4.10 per tooth. In the West and South, kids received $3.70 and $3.60 per tooth, respectively. Midwestern kids received the least, at $3.30 a tooth. About a third of all parents surveyed say the Tooth Fairy left a dollar or less (Pisani, 2013).

But parents (or the Tooth Fairy) can finally determine an appropriate amount to leave children. As part of the company's personal finance education program, Visa offers a downloadable Tooth Fairy Calculator app that tells users how much parents in their age group, income bracket, and education level are giving their kids, Alderman says. The newly updated app is available for iPhones and iPads on iTunes, and the calculator is available on the Facebook apps page (Pisani, 2013).

Although the reports ruminated on all the complexities, possible causes, and solutions to the Tooth Fairy's spendthrift ways, none of them examined the confusing, questionable survey methods that lay behind Visa's claims. Maybe the survey itself should have been the story.

questions were parents asked and how were the parents recruited to complete the survey?

In this instance, the survey that garnered mainstream media attention appeared on a website titled *Practical Money Skills for Life* (Visa, 2013). Under the heading

"Financial Literacy for Everyone" was listed a long series of questions about personal finances, three of which concerned the Tooth Fairy. The first was, "How much did the Tooth Fairy leave your kids in 2013?" Participants could choose from four responses:

1. More than $4.
2. $2–$3.
3. $1 exactly.
4. Less than $1.

If you checked the results in October 2013, you would find that there were only 643 votes; 28.8% responded $1 exactly, 27.5% responded more than $4, 23.2% responded less than $1, and 20.5% responded between $2 and $3.

It is not clear how these responses were averaged to obtain a single value, because the website includes no information about how averaging was done. For example, is the response "less than $1" coded as $1, 50 cents, or nothing? Are responses of "more than $4" coded as $4 or some other value? As you can see, it is difficult to understand how the sponsor of the study calculated an average of $3.70 per tooth from the responses given.

A subsequent question asked, "Parents, how much does the Tooth Fairy give your child for each lost tooth?" This time participants were given a different set of choices:

1. Nothing.
2. Less than $2.
3. $2 to $5.
4. More than $5.

The same problem of how to map these values onto the averages plagues this question. And how are the answers to this question combined with those from the previous question, especially given that this one attracted fewer respondents ($n = 624$)?

Another question later in the survey asked, "How much does the Tooth Fairy leave your kids?" Response choices were as follows:

1. Nothing.
2. Less than $1.
3. $1 exactly.
4. $2.
5. $5.
6. More than $5.

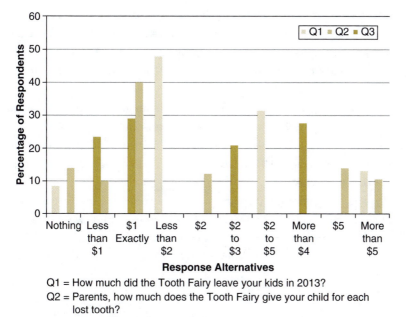

Q1 = How much did the Tooth Fairy leave your kids in 2013?
Q2 = Parents, how much does the Tooth Fairy give your child for each lost tooth?
Q3 = How much does the Tooth Fairy leave your kids?

FIGURE 7.1.   Percentage of respondents providing different responses to the Tooth Fairy question.

This question actually drew 1,130 respondents, with 40% picking "c," or $1 exactly. Determining which data led to various media reports of children getting an average of $3.70 per tooth in 2013 (when 2013 had not even ended) is extremely difficult. What we *can* see is that these three questions result in different patterns of responses. As Figure 7.1 shows, the reliability and validity of this particular survey appear questionable. Different forms of the questions frame the issue in a variety of ways (a possible threat to validity), and different response categories clearly lead to a different pattern of responses (a possible threat to reliability).

SURVEYS VERSUS INTERVIEWS

Although the terms "survey" and "interview" are often used interchangeably, they differ in format. With **surveys**, researchers present questions on paper or online for participants to complete on their own. With **interviews**, researchers ask participants questions orally—in person or on the phone.

Questionnaires are made up of a set of questions that let participants respond freely or choose from a preselected set of options. They can be presented in either a survey or an interview format. Questionnaires usually have a relatively narrow focus. Although the terms

Survey A set of questions administered to a group of respondents, usually via paper or online, to learn about attitudes and behavior.

Interview A data collection technique in which researchers ask participants questions orally, either in person or over the phone.

Questionnaire A set of questions that may be part of a survey or interview.

"questionnaire" and "survey" may be used interchangeably, the term "survey" is often reserved for measures that contain more than one questionnaire or that include interview methods. Individual questionnaires used in a survey will often have been developed by other researchers and have been shown to be valid, reliable measures of some topic in past research.

In some cases, researchers copyright a particular survey or questionnaire and then charge researchers for use of the measure. In other cases, researchers collaborate with organizations such as the National Institutes of Health to create and validate a number of standard measures, such as the NIH Toolbox (http://www.nihtoolbox.org/), that are free and available to any researcher.

Surveys and interviews are likely the most widely used methods in psychology and related fields. The use of surveys in particular has grown rapidly with the ease of conducting online research. Although both approaches possess a number of advantages, the research question—not just convenience—should always drive the choice of method.

THE PROS AND CONS OF SURVEYS

John Schulenberg:

"We try to make our participants feel part of a bigger project. When someone takes part in our study, they represent 10,000 people, so we try to let them know how important their involvement is and that we really need them to continue on. We send them updates and newsletters to keep them connected and also try to make the survey as interesting as possible to keep it engaging."

When John Schulenberg's (see "Inside Research") survey administrators ask students to participate in the longitudinal part of study, they offer participants a small sum of money and a University of Michigan pencil, along with an appeal to make a difference. Because of their potential ability to engage participants, surveys are popular, and they have a number of advantages compared with other research methods.

Advantages of Surveys

Surveys are widely used by researchers because they are efficient and economical and because they enable the collection of large samples in a relatively short time frame. They also allow for greater anonymity for participants and greater flexibility than some other methods.

Efficient and Economical.   Researchers can use surveys to collect a large amount of data in a relatively short time. For example, researchers can collect data from hundreds of students in an introductory psychology class within a single class period. With online surveys, researchers can contact thousands of potential participants in locations all over the world relatively quickly. We know of one online survey called the Personality Project that has collected information from 260,000 respondents to explore current personality theory and research (http://www.personality-project.org/revelle.html/).

Large Sample Sizes.   When working with survey data, researchers can use more sophisticated statistical approaches for data analysis, often requiring large sample sizes that may be difficult (if not impossible) to collect using interviews or an experimental design. The cost in time and money of these other approaches often makes obtaining large samples impractical, whereas survey approaches offer a large sample, often readily within reach. If you collect a large sample, you can run statistical analyses on randomly selected portions of the data. This allows you to determine whether the statistical results can be reproduced within the same overall data set.

Allure of Anonymity.   Yet another advantage of survey methods is that researchers can use them to obtain information that a participant might not be willing to share in a face-to-face interview, especially if the information requested concerns sensitive or illegal behavior. Questions about sexual behavior, illicit drug or alcohol use, attitudes about racial or gender issues or religious beliefs, or questions about immigration status are some of the many topics that individuals might be unwilling to discuss openly with an interviewer, but may be willing to answer on a survey as long as anonymity is ensured. Surprisingly, even telephone interviews provide a greater level of anonymity than face-to-face interviews. For example, there is evidence to suggest that surveys on the thorny topic of substance abuse, when conducted by telephone, can yield relatively accurate prevalence estimates (McAuliffe, Geller, LaBrie, Paletz, & Fournier, 1998).

Flexibility.   Surveys also have a number of other attributes that make them desirable. They can be used to investigate a large number of different research questions, they can be adapted to a participant's responses, and they can be completed at the convenience of the respondent.

With the use of computers and specialized software, surveys can be flexibly modified to present different sets of questions based on initial responses. This approach can provide a more efficient means of collecting the data because only those questions relevant to a participant will be asked. For example, a survey investigating sexual harassment in the federal workplace (see Erdreich, Slavet, & Amador, 1994) might provide a different set of questions to men and women. It is also easy to quickly modify your study if you discover a problem with some questions, realize you left out some important questions, or decide that an altogether different set of questions is needed.

A customized survey places less of a burden on participants because they need to respond only to questions that pertain to their circumstances. There is also evidence that, despite fears to the contrary, computer-based surveys that people complete independently provide data that are just as valid as that obtained from surveys given in a supervised location (Carlsmith & Chabot, 1997).

John Schulenberg:
"If I set up my study correctly and make it clear how we protect respondent confidentiality, the individual will share private information with me and will be comfortable that I won't share it with any authority. If I can do it right, people will tell me about all sorts of potentially embarrassing or illegal activities, including how much heroin they use."

A related, substantial advantage is that participants may choose to complete the survey when they have the time and motivation to respond. This is not without its own risks, however, because we have been told that students sometimes complete surveys assessing the quality of an instructor or class late at night in a less-than-sober state of mind.

Disadvantages of Surveys

Despite the many advantages that surveys offer, they do have some downsides, including potential biases and fraud. Identifying and eliminating biases in a particular survey sample can be difficult, and researchers must acknowledge this as a potential limitation in their designs.

Selection Bias. Participants may differ from nonparticipants because of issues with the sampling methodology or because they have different motivational issues or time constraints. The method for contacting potential respondents may induce a particular type of undesirable **selection bias**. In the past, when surveys were completed over the phone, potential respondents were often randomly selected from phone directories. This approach tended to miss relatively poor people (who could not afford to pay for a phone line), people who intentionally opted out of being listed in the phone directory, or people who moved repeatedly.

Today, researchers commonly collect data using online surveys, which are effective for recruiting participants who have an e-mail address and online access. But again, this approach likely misses a large number of individuals who do not have regular online access (e.g., low-income people or older adults who may not be technologically savvy).

The description of the survey in the Tooth Fairy "Media Matters" feature does not provide information about who responded to the survey. All we know is that individuals who completed the survey accessed it on a website designed by Visa to provide information about "practical money matters." This site likely draws people who have money, likely more money than the average person in the United States. But we have no idea how representative the sample is. See Figure 7.2 for an example of selection bias.

> **Selection bias** Bias resulting from a selected sample not being representative of the population of interest. This may come about because of under- or oversampling of particular types of respondents, respondent self-selection, or respondent nonresponse.

FIGURE 7.2. An example of selection bias. The people participating in the poll are selected in such a way as to ensure they are not representative of the population of interest.

Participation Biases.   Individuals may have different reasons for choosing to complete a survey. These reasons introduce a number of different forms of **participation bias**, three of which are nonresponse, self-selection, and motivated respondent.

Nonresponse Bias.   **Nonresponse bias** occurs when individuals who were contacted and chose to complete the survey differ in some ways from others who were contacted but chose not to take the survey. Individuals may have many reasons for not completing a survey, but a common reason is that they simply lack time. In some cases, this factor might skew or bias the sample in important ways. Suppose you are trying to conduct a survey of new parents. Those who are juggling work and family might not want to take the time to complete your survey. Thus, families who have more time to respond to surveys—for example, those with fewer children or those with one family member at home to care for the children—may be overrepresented in your sample. Depending on your research question, the sample of participants who choose to respond may bias your results in a particular direction. In the Tooth Fairy example, parents with fewer children may pay more per tooth than parents with more children. But without more information it is difficult to determine who has chosen to complete the survey.

Self-selection Bias.   The **self-selection bias** occurs when individuals are free to choose to complete a survey, which may be problematic when the choice to participate relates in some way to the research topic. For example, when people watching a television channel that has a particular political bias are asked to call in or complete an online survey to rate politicians or issues, the individuals who respond are likely to have views similar to those of the channel. Therefore, the results will likely show the same bias.

Motivated Respondent Bias.   A particular kind of participant bias occurs in situations where people are highly motivated to complete a survey in hopes of changing public opinion. In one example of **motivated respondent bias**, Wells, Cavanaugh, Bouffard, and Nobles (2012) examined data on attitudes about carrying concealed handguns. They compared responses from college students who completed a survey in their classroom with those of students who were given the option to complete the survey online. Students who responded to the web survey were systematically more extreme in their responses and attitudes than the in-class sample. This suggests that for some topics, the most motivated respondents may be those with the most extreme views and may not represent the larger population.

Experimenter Bias.   Yet another source of bias for survey design is the experimenter. **Experimenter bias** is not unique to survey methodology; it can occur in all aspects of the research process (design, analysis, interpretation). But the way it usually plays out is in the construction of the survey questions or items. The Pew Research Center for the People and

Participation biases
Biases resulting from potential respondents choosing to participate in the survey or not. These include nonresponse bias, self-selection bias, and motivated respondent bias.

Nonresponse bias
Bias that occurs when individuals who are contacted and choose to complete a survey differ in some ways from others who are contacted but choose not to participate.

Self-selection bias
Bias that may occur when it is completely up to potential respondents whether they participate in a survey.

Motivated respondent bias Bias that occurs in situations where people are highly motivated to complete a survey for the purpose of affecting public opinion.

Experimenter bias
In survey/interview research, bias introduced by the way in which experimenters ask questions (related to framing effects).

the Press provides an excellent example of how subtle—and perhaps unintentional—differences in survey wording can dramatically affect results. In a 2005 Pew Research survey, 51% of respondents favored "making it legal for doctors to give terminally ill patients the means to end their lives," but only 44% favored "making it legal for doctors to assist terminally ill patients in committing suicide" (Pew Research Center, n.d.). You might imagine that researchers could unconsciously select one of these statements, depending on their own views. This is another example of a framing effect (see Chapter 1), which is also important to consider when constructing surveys.

Fatigue Effects and Attrition.   Although surveys can be amazingly efficient in gathering information, they also risk fatiguing participants, so that the data that are eventually collected are not valid. Longer surveys are more susceptible to **fatigue effects**, so it is important to examine the data to see whether the pattern of responses indicates genuine participation. It is not uncommon in a longer survey for earlier responses to be valid (and appropriately variable), but then later answers to fall into a **response set**, which is the tendency to respond with a consistent pattern of responses regardless of the question being asked (e.g., answering "strongly agree" to a long string of questions).

A related problem to fatigue is **attrition**, in which participants begin the survey but decide to drop out after completing only a portion of it. Some participants may stop if they tire of your survey, whereas others may lose interest for various idiosyncratic reasons. Procedures for dealing with missing data may involve the removal of cases with any missing values, application of special techniques for analyzing data with missing values, or using relationships among variables in the data set to provide best guesses as to what those missing values might be. How you deal with incomplete data, however, depends on a range of methodological and statistical issues beyond the scope of our discussion here. (For more information, see Enders, 2010.) As with survey responses that are compromised by fatigue, you will need to make decisions about what to do with partial responses.

Social Desirability Bias.   Another potential hazard in survey methodology is the issue of social desirability. **Social desirability**—also referred to as **evaluation apprehension**—effects arise when you question participants about behaviors or attitudes that might not be viewed as acceptable in society. The work of John Schulenberg is an excellent example of survey research that must attend to social desirability, especially since his work asks about illegal behavior (underage alcohol and drug use).

Although there is no easy fix for the problem of social desirability, some research instruments that ask about undesirable behaviors approach the topic with enough subtlety that participants may be more comfortable sharing otherwise stigmatized behaviors. For example, the Conflict Tactics Scale (Straus, 1979; Straus, Hamby, Boney-McCoy, & Sugarman, 1996) is a self-report measure widely used by researchers interested in domestic violence. The measure examines the use of reasoning, verbal aggression, and violence within the

Fatigue effects Negative effects on survey responses or completion resulting from subjects tiring of the survey.

Response set The tendency for a participant to respond to survey items with a consistent pattern of responses regardless of the question being asked (e.g., answering "strongly agree" to a long string of questions).

Attrition The loss of research participants prior to completion of a study.

Social desirability bias (also **evaluation apprehension**) The tendency of respondents to provide answers that will be viewed favorably by others.

family. Because the survey asks about a full range of behaviors in a way that presents them all as normative ways of resolving conflict, participants may be more comfortable disclosing otherwise socially undesirable behaviors. For example, the negotiation scale items, presented in order of social acceptability, range from "Discussed an item calmly" at the low end of the scale to "Used a knife or gun" at the high end.

Potential Threats to Validity and Possible Solutions.

You can never be sure that respondents are giving accurate, honest answers. Many of the factors that make surveys attractive to use (anonymity, ease of responding) potentially increase the rate of invalid responses and responders. There are at least four potential threats to validity: respondents who do not understand questions, respondents who answer fraudulently, respondents with an agenda, and careless respondents. Although it is not possible to completely protect your survey from all malicious behavior, you can take a few steps to minimize the impact of potential fraud.

Respondents Who Do Not Understand Questions.

The first potential threat arises when an individual does not understand the questions; this may be a result of language or vocabulary issues or intellectual disabilities. In this case, the individual may produce invalid responses by answering in a random fashion. You may see response patterns that do not make sense (e.g., all of one type of response or a truly random pattern). Such a pattern would indicate that you should not use the data.

Respondents Who Answer Fraudulently.

A second potential threat may arise when an individual fraudulently completes a survey. Individuals may complete the survey as quickly as possible to receive compensation or attempt to complete the survey repeatedly to receive additional rewards. You can detect this threat through nonsensical response patterns, as in the first threat. You can also use various techniques to identify outliers in your data (see Hodge & Austin, 2004, for a more extensive discussion of methodologies that identify outliers in data). With online surveys it is also possible to collect the IP addresses of the computers used to submit the survey responses and allow only a single submission from any one IP address. This restricts your sample to only one member of a household or to one participant from any public computer, for example, those in university computer labs or public libraries, but it is better than having multiple responses from a single respondent.

Another way researchers have reduced multiple responses is to prescreen participants. Researchers can collect certain demographic data in the prescreening (name, telephone number, address) that they can use later to double check against survey responses. For example, researchers may check to see whether the same identifying information appears in multiple surveys. If it does, one or both surveys are likely invalid. As long as the prescreening data are kept separate from the actual data, most institutional review boards will approve the approach. After individuals have completed the prescreening, they are usually given a separate link to the actual survey. This process ensures the confidentiality of the respondent.

Another way to detect fraudulent responses is to add similar (or even the same) questions in a long survey to see whether participants give similar responses. Divergent responses to similar items suggest that a participant is not taking the survey seriously and give you a reason for potentially dropping the data from that respondent. As a way of decreasing the incentive for fraud in the first place, it is important to consider the issue of compensation when deciding how you will select and recruit potential participants. By keeping the compensation level relatively low, or using a raffle, for example, where only 1 of 100 participants is compensated, you can minimize incentives for completing the survey multiple times. A related strategy with online surveys involves breaking up the survey so that it takes time to respond to different sections, thereby dissuading those who may not want to invest the time.

Respondents with an Agenda.   Related to the motivated respondent bias discussed previously, a third potential threat to the validity of your survey is posed by respondents who are motivated to deliberately bias the results or invalidate the study once they have already agreed to participate. In this case, participants who have a vested interest in a particular program might respond in a way that is likely to characterize the program positively (e.g., provide more extreme values than they really think are warranted). This type of threat can be addressed through the use of a "**lie scale**," a set of items that are written to check that participants are taking the task seriously and not just answering questions to present themselves in the best possible light. A typical lie scale item used by researchers is "I never get angry." Everyone gets angry sometimes, so participants who respond that they never get angry are likely not providing valid responses. If respondents answer too many items on the lie scale in a way that indicates that they are not honestly engaging with the task, then you can consider their responses as invalid.

One of the best-known personality tests, the Minnesota Multiphasic Personality Inventory (Butcher, 2005) uses a lie scale, termed the "L scale," which assesses participants' willingness to acknowledge difficulties or problems. A high score on the L scale in the Minnesota Multiphasic Personality Inventory indicates that test-takers are trying to represent themselves in an unrealistically favorable light, and their results may not be valid. Adding prescreening questions may also reduce the threat posed by motivated respondents.

Careless Respondents.   A final potential threat to validity is posed by **careless responding (CR)**, where participants want to complete the survey as quickly as possible. CR is a particular risk when participants are required to complete a survey either for their

Lie scale A set of survey items used to determine whether participants are taking the task seriously and not simply responding in such a way as to present themselves in the best possible light.

Careless responding (CR) Lack of careful attention to one's own responses in a survey because of disinterest or the desire to complete the survey as quickly as possible.

job or for class credit (as is common in introductory psychology classes). Some have argued that CR is a particular problem in Internet-based research, where there is no direct connection between researcher and participant (Ward, 2015).

To address CR, you can use several approaches that overlap some of the suggestions for dealing with fraud and motivated respondents. One is to include "CR indicators" and exclude participants who fall below a particular cutoff score. Similar to the lie scale, it involves at least four different strategies.

1. Include "instructed response" questions such as, "Please select slightly disagree for this item," to ensure that your participants are, in fact, reading the questions.
2. Look for even–odd consistency, where participants' responses to items measuring similar variables are checked for consistency. For example, if you strongly agree with the statement, "This textbook is riveting," then you should not slightly disagree with the statement, "This textbook has interesting content."
3. Use a strategy termed "LongString," which involves looking for response patterns where respondents repeatedly choose the same response option.
4. Include self-report items that directly ask participants whether their responses were accurate and of high quality (Ward, 2015).

Another approach for dealing with CR, also from Ward (2015), involves trying to prevent such responding before it occurs by creating perceived interaction between participants and researchers. For example, some online surveys warn participants of particular consequences of CR, whereas other surveys ask participants to identify themselves on each page (i.e., type out their name on each page). Another approach is to notify participants that they will receive feedback on the quality and utility of their responses, to give them a greater sense of connection to the information they provide. In addition, some researchers introduce a "virtual human" into the survey by having the virtual figure occupy a small part of the screen.

Although all of these challenges to ensuring valid data should not discourage you from capitalizing on survey methodology's many strengths, it is worth noting that, by themselves, surveys are only one methodology for reaching a definitive conclusion. As with all the techniques we discuss, an approach that uses multiple methods will yield the most conclusive results.

THE PROS AND CONS OF INTERVIEWS

Interviews that involve the researcher talking with the respondent over the phone, in person, or through technologies such as FaceTime or Skype offer several advantages. However, although the issues related to threats to validity are often less likely to be a problem with interviews, they still exist.

Advantages of Interviews

Interviews can provide a rich source of data and enable the researcher to judge whether any threats to validity occur. In particular, researchers conducting interviews can often confirm that participants understand the questions and can also detect CR.

Rich Data.   Interviews permit a researcher to collect much richer data than is possible with surveys alone. With the right kinds of questions and follow-up probes, a researcher can delve deeply into a participant's thoughts, attitudes, values, and behavior. Interview responses can help explain the results of more limited questions posed in a survey because the reviewer can explicitly ask why a participant responded in a particular way. Interviewers can also develop a rapport with participants that may help the participants to be more honest or provide more detailed responses. In these ways, interviews can provide compelling information that can be used in presentations and manuscripts to "bring the data to life."

Confirmation of Participant Understanding.   Rich data are only useful if they accurately reflect participants' thoughts and feelings. To that end, it is important that participants understand what they are being asked. This is something that researchers must check for when they interview young children, individuals who may not understand the language, or individuals with cognitive impairments.

In the case of interviews with young children, researchers may provide a few pretest or warm-up questions designed to determine whether children understand the nature of the interview. In the case of individuals who might be cognitively impaired, researchers may provide a quick screening to assess cognitive function. One such instrument is the Mini-Mental State Examination, which provides a simple, quick assessment of cognitive functioning in older adults (Folstein, Folstein, & McHugh, 1975). If performance on this test falls below a certain score (typically 20 on the 30-point scale), then the respondent likely has some form of cognitive impairment. In general, if a respondent appears to have trouble understanding or has cognitive impairments, you must determine whether the main interview should proceed. Even if you continue with the interview, the data are likely to be invalid and should not be used in any subsequent analyses.

Detecting Careless Interview Responding.   A clear advantage of interviews over surveys is that you can often detect CR as it occurs (rather than after data collection is complete, as is often the case in survey research) and take steps to remedy the situation. Signs of CR in interviews with young children include excessive laughing or a particular response set, for instance, a consistent "yes" to every question without regard to content. Sometimes merely asking children to provide their best answer can help focus them. In interviews with children under age 5, any indication of lack of understanding or CR is grounds for assuming the interview is not producing valid data. With adult interviewees, facial expressions (e.g., smirks) and a cavalier attitude may indicate CR. In these cases, you can politely ask the respondent to take the survey seriously, but again, these types of responses indicate that the data will likely be invalid.

Disadvantages of Interviews

Although interviews enable researchers to confirm that participants understand the questions and can ultimately provide rich data, they do have a number of drawbacks. These include lack of efficiency, potential interviewer effects, response biases, and issues of standardization.

Inefficient Use of Time and Resources.   Interviews can be very time-consuming. Unlike online surveys that can reach hundreds or thousands of participants in a relatively short time and require little or no labor during the data collection phase, face-to-face interviews require an experimenter to meet in person with the participant. Even greater time and financial demands are required if the experimenter must travel to interview the participants. New technologies such as FaceTime and Skype enable researchers to conduct interviews without traveling. However, our own experience with these technologies is that they work best when you are communicating with people you already know. We would not recommend these technologies for initial interviews with participants, because the interaction is just different enough from actual face-to face interactions (e.g., lack of eye contact, occurrence of delays in the transmission, etc.) that the interview might not go as well as it would in person.

Interviewer Effects.   Another disadvantage of interviews is the potential influence of the interviewer, known as **interviewer effects**. The way the interviewer asks questions and responds to the participant's answers may influence the way the respondent answers questions. Participants may interpret slight changes in the interviewer's tone, inflection, facial expressions (e.g., the raising of an eyebrow), or posture (e.g., a nod of the head or crossing of arms) as positive or negative evaluations of their responses. Over the course of the interview, these interpretations may lead participants to alter their answers. Interviewers should be trained to provide neutral responses, but even the most highly trained interviewer may inadvertently provide subtle cues that may influence the participant.

Interviewer effects Influences that the interviewer may have on responses, including the way in which he/she asks and responds to questions, tone of voice, or facial expressions. All of these may be interpreted by the interviewee as positive or negative evaluations of their responses and may lead the respondent to alter his/her answers.

A famous example of this phenomenon is the case of "Clever Hans" (Pfungst, 1911). Hans was a horse who appeared to be able to do simple math. But on investigation, it was determined that the horse was responding to the subtle cues of his handler rather than performing any arithmetic. The handler was completely unaware that he was providing these cues and was convinced of the brilliance of Hans. A more recent case of this has been reported with drug-sniffing hounds that apparently respond to unintended signals from their handlers and produce many more false alarms in controlled tests than should occur if they were actually sniffing out the drugs (Lit, Schweitzer, & Oberbauer, 2011).

Interviewers must be conscious that their own characteristics (e.g., age, gender, ethnicity) and behavior, including the way they dress and present themselves, may influence participants in various, sometimes subtle ways.

Response Bias.   Threats to validity, which are present in surveys, can also arise in face-to-face situations. Participants being interviewed in a face-to-face situation may exhibit a number of **response biases**. One common form of response bias occurs when individuals respond in a way that they think the interviewer wants them to respond. Not usually done with malicious intent, response bias results from the participant consciously or unconsciously wanting to help or gain favor with the interviewer. Another type of response bias occurs when participants are unwilling to provide potentially sensitive or illegal information during face-to-face interviews. A related problem is an **acquiescence bias**, where a respondent will respond affirmatively to answer any question when in doubt. These problems of response bias are not limited to interviews and may also arise with surveys.

Standardization.   To effectively quantify the responses of a group of participants, it is important to standardize interview questions. **Standardization** refers to the idea that all respondents answer the same set of questions. Complete standardization can be difficult with in-person interviews because participants often respond freely or an interviewer may ask follow-up questions to clarify a response. These free responses can be difficult to code and analyze using quantitative approaches because participants may each focus on different issues in their responses. If standardization is crucial to your research question, it may be better to use a standard questionnaire or survey, rather than an interview.

THE VALUE OF COLLECTING DATA ON SOCIOECONOMIC STATUS

SES stands for socioeconomic status. Although SES can be defined, measured, and interpreted in many different ways, it is a useful measure of several economic and sociological factors that interact in a complex manner. Generally, measurement of SES includes some assessment of family income, parental education, and parental occupation (Jeynes, 2002). The dimensions of SES have also been viewed more abstractly (Oakes & Rossie, 2003) as material (e.g., money), human (e.g., level of education), and social capital (e.g., social status in your community). These factors or dimensions are generally used to assess the *relative* status of participants or their families with respect to the larger population. SES is used in psychological and related research as either a principal measure (e.g., how health behavior varies as a function of SES; Adler, Epel, Castellazzo, & Ickovics, 2000; Goodman, 1999) or a control variable in the examination of another variable of interest (e.g., how SES influences the effects of divorce on children; Amato & Keith, 1991). A **control variable** is either

---

Response bias Bias introduced into participants' responses to interview or survey questions because of such considerations as a desire to respond with responses one believes the researcher would want, an unwillingness to provide sensitive information, or a tendency to always respond positively when unsure about a question.

Acquiescence bias A form of bias where the participant responds affirmatively to every question or to every question where they are unsure of the correct response.

Standardization The designing of interview questions such that they are used in a consistent manner by all interviewers.

Control variable A variable that is either held at a constant value or is accounted for statistically in an analysis. The purpose of controlling for a variable is to remove (or statistically account for) any effect it might have on the dependent variable.

kept constant or "controlled for" in statistical analyses. Controlling for a variable in a statistical analysis means that you use techniques to remove the effects of this variable from the overall analysis. Researchers use these procedures if they believe that a variable likely influences the variable of interest, but does not directly relate to the research question being addressed.

When investigating a question such as, "What are the effects of divorce on children?" researchers want to know whether the effects are a result of divorce or some other factor, such as SES. Thus, researchers will include measures of SES to "control" for the influence of this variable on the main variable. In practice, many variables are highly correlated with SES, including measures of intelligence (Tate & Gibson, 1980), academic achievement (Sirin, 2005), executive function (Sarsour et al., 2011), and weight and obesity in children (Keane, Layte, Harrington, Kearny, & Perry, 2012). For this reason, many researchers in the social sciences routinely collect SES data even when it is not the main focus of their research.

USING AN EXISTING SURVEY VERSUS CREATING A NEW ONE

Before you come up with questions to include in your survey, it is important to revisit your research question or questions. What do you want to find out from the survey? Also, can you use questions or questionnaires constructed by other researchers to address your research question? Many researchers will argue that you should start with existing measures and only create your own if there are no valid or reliable measures in your research area. We believe, however, that you can learn a great deal about surveys and interviews by constructing your own survey.

Researchers use preexisting surveys or questionnaires for a number of reasons. First, using an existing survey is more efficient than constructing a new one. Creating a survey from scratch can involve countless hours of writing, revising, and pretesting. Writing a good question is not easy, and even if you have a lot of expertise and practice, it may be challenging. For example, how should you assess social class? Should you ask about income? Only income? Should you ask the subjects to report their yearly income (which many people are unwilling to do)? Or should you use some other measure of social standing? These are not simple issues, and many researchers have spent a lot of time thinking about and conducting research on this issue (e.g., Oakes & Rossi, 2003).

Second, researchers have determined the validity and reliability of many existing survey instruments. That is, researchers have assessed how well the survey measures what it is designed to measure and how well it compares with other existing instruments, as well as how reliable the measure is when used over repeated assessments (see Chapter 5). Unfortunately, constructs such as SES have been measured using a variety of instruments, and widespread agreement on which measure is best to use for your own research is rare. Look for information on the validity and reliability of particular measures related to your research question and whether the existing studies were conducted on a population similar to the one you are planning to study. You might also choose a couple of different established measures to obtain converging information. Again, the choice of a particular instrument should be closely related to your overriding research question.

A final benefit of using an existing survey instrument is that it facilitates comparisons between studies that use similar measures. When researchers use established surveys—or adapt a series of items from existing instruments—they are better able to compare their results with other findings that have been previously reported. Making this kind of comparison can be especially valuable if you are doing research on a population that differs from those that have been already studied.

MacArthur Scale of Subjective Social Status A measure of subjective social standing, obtained by having respondents place themselves on a socioeconomic "ladder."

For example, the **MacArthur Scale of Subjective Social Status** (Goodman et al., 2001) was developed to account for people's perceptions of how they fit within the social hierarchy. The assumption behind this measure is that people's *perceptions* of social standing may be a more valid measure of their social standing than their *actual* income, education, or occupation (Adler et al., 2000). One problem with objective measures of actual income is that many individuals are uncomfortable or unwilling to provide information about how much they earn. The MacArthur Scale asks respondents to place themselves on a ladder (see Figure 7.3) that represents people who have the most money, highest level of education, and highly respected jobs at the top and people who have the least money, little or no education, and no job or a job that is not respected at the bottom. This assessment tool uses a standard question format and includes published information about its reliability (Goodman et al., 2001) and validity (Cundiff, Smith, Uchino, & Berg, 2013).

As you decide whether to write your own questionnaire/survey or use an existing one, spend some time examining the literature in your area of interest. If well-established survey instruments with information on their reliability and validity already exist, strongly consider using them. However, if existing questionnaires do not really address the issue you are interested in, consider how you might modify some or all of the questions to be useful for your research.

Even established measures may require some modification if your study will include participants of different ages, groups, or cultures than were included in past research. For example, responses to the MacArthur Scale appear to vary by race/ethnicity (Wolff, Acevedo-Garcia, Subramanian, Weber, & Kawachi, 2010), so this measure may

Imagine that this ladder shows how your society is set up.
- At the top of the ladder are the people who are the best off—they have the most money, the highest amount of schooling, and the jobs that bring the most respect.
- At the bottom are people who are the worst off—they have the least money, little or no education, no jobs or jobs that no one wants or respects.

Now think about your family. Please tell us where you think your family would be on this ladder. **Place an 'X' on the rung that best represents where your family would be on this ladder.**

FIGURE 7.3. The MacArthur ladder for measuring subjective social status.

not capture the same information for different racial/ethnic groups. That said, you should also be cautious about modifications. Once an instrument has been modified, the information on reliability and validity may no longer be valid, and you may need to pretest your questions or assess the instrument's reliability/validity.

In some cases, it is entirely appropriate to develop your own survey or questionnaire. Obviously, if your topic has rarely or never been studied, then you will need to write your own questions. Also, if no reliable or valid surveys or questionnaires exist or the validity or reliability of existing questionnaires or surveys is questionable, then it is appropriate to design a new measure. Additionally, if your research involves a different sample than the original instrument was developed for, then you may need to modify an existing instrument or create a new one.

Finally, you may have empirical or theoretical reasons for creating a new measure. For example, researchers created the MacArthur Scale on both empirical and theoretical grounds. Empirically, some researchers found that the measure they used did not successfully predict outcomes of interest. Many people do not feel comfortable reporting their income; they may under- or overreport how much they earn. For this reason, measures of social status that take income into account are likely to be inaccurate. From a theoretical perspective, researchers argued that an individual's *perception* of social status, rather than social status measured by objective measures of income or education, was a more valid indicator of social status.

STEPS TO BUILDING YOUR OWN QUESTIONNAIRE

If you decide not to use an existing questionnaire, be aware that generating valid and reliable instruments requires a number of steps and can take substantial time and resources. In fact, there is an entire field of psychology—called psychometrics—devoted to test construction and validation. If you do make the decision to create your own survey, this section includes some critical steps in the process.

Question Wording

Whether you create a new survey or modify an existing one, writing a *good* survey is challenging. The way you ask questions will strongly influence the responses that you are likely to receive. If your questions are too complicated, you will probably confuse your participants and not obtain good data. Likewise, you must be careful about wording questions so as not to bias participants' responses. The overall goal of survey design is to create questions that are valid and reliable. It is also important to remember what type of response you want from your participants (free response, multiple choice, rating scale, etc.), which we will address after considering issues relevant to the form and content of the survey questions.

Simplicity Is Good!   Simple, straightforward questions are the best way to ask for information. Avoid long, multiclause questions or compound questions. You should also avoid terms or phrases that may not be understood by everyone (Fowler, 2002). Acronyms are abundant on college campuses, but unless students encounter them regularly, they may easily forget them. In one instance on our campus, two different committees had the same acronym (URGC). One stood for the *Undergraduate Research Grant Committee*, which funded undergraduate research proposals, and the other represented the *University Research Grant Committee*, which funded faculty research proposals. Asking questions about the URGC might lead to different responses depending on what contact a participant has had with these committees. In any case, avoid acronyms in your questions when possible, but if you must use them, make sure to spell them out at least once.

Write Questions at the Appropriate Reading Level.   The average reading level in the United States is generally around the eighth- or ninth-grade level (Kirsch, Jungeblut, Jenkins, & Kolstad, 1993). The institutional review board may request that your survey be written at this reading level to ensure that respondents clearly understand what they are being asked. Of course, if the grade level of your participants is lower than eighth or ninth grade (e.g., you have a sample comprising fourth graders), then you would need to adjust the reading level accordingly. Commonly used word processing programs enable you to check the "readability" or "reading level" of your questions.

Double-barreled question A question that refers to more than one issue but requires or expects only one response. Also known as a **compound question**.

Compound question Question that attempts to ask about more than one issue in the same question. Also known as a **double-barreled question**.

Avoid Double-barreled Questions.   **Double-barreled** or **compound questions** refer to more than one issue but require or expect only one response. Consider the following examples:

- "Do you think your introductory psychology class was interesting, and was the instructor engaging?"
- "Do you like the president of the United States, and do you think the president is doing a good job?"
- "Do you agree or disagree with the following statement: 'Psychology majors are the most creative and interesting students'?"

In each of these examples, participants might have two different responses for the distinct parts of the question, but joining the issues in a single question does not enable the researcher to determine which part of the question is being answered. It is better to address each issue separately. For example,

- "Was your introductory psychology class interesting?" and "Was the instructor for the class engaging?"
- "Do you like the president of the United States?" and "Do you think that the president of the United States is doing a good job?"
- "Do you agree or disagree with the following statement: 'Psychology majors are the most creative students'?" and "Do you agree or disagree with the following statement: 'Psychology majors are the most interesting students'?"

Avoid Loaded Questions.   A **loaded question** presupposes information or biases the potential response. That is, the question includes an assumption that might not be justified. A classic example is the following question: "Have you stopped beating your spouse?" The question both assumes that you have a spouse *and* that you have been beating him or her. You cannot answer this question without implying that either you used to beat your spouse and have now stopped (the "yes" response) or that you are still beating your spouse (the "no" response). Less egregious examples include questions such as, "Research Methods is a difficult course because it requires a lot of reading, statistics, and papers. How difficult did you find the class?" This question assumes that the Research Methods course is difficult and potentially biases the respondent to answer in a particular way. A better approach would be to simply ask, "Did you find the Research Methods course to be difficult?" or to use some form of rating scale to assess the level of difficulty.

> **Loaded question**
> A question that presupposes information or potentially biases a response by including an assumption that may not be justified.

Some surveys may also be designed to skew responses in a particular direction (e.g., partisan political polls), but good social science researchers understand that data obtained from such methods are neither reliable nor valid. Consider the following question: "Most people agree that gun violence is out of control in our society; do you favor gun control measures as a way of reducing unnecessary killings?" In this case, the statement "Most people agree that gun violence is out of control" assumes that the respondent will share this view and likely advocate for more gun control. The way the question is constructed indicates a clear bias in favor of gun control. Although such a question may satisfy a particular political viewpoint, you would be hard-pressed to argue that it will yield objective, fair responses. A better question would be simply to ask, "Do you favor gun control?" (See Figure 7.4 for an example of a loaded question.)

Be Positive!   In general, it is better to word questions in a positive or neutral manner than in a negative one. For example, "On a scale of 1 (not at all) to 5 (a lot), how much did you *like* your introductory psychology class?" is better than "On a scale of 1 (not at all) to 5 (a lot), how much did you *dislike* your introductory psychology class?" That being said, there is some place for negatively worded questions as a way of ensuring that your participants are, in fact, paying attention as they answer questions. A participant who answers a positively worded and a negatively worded question in contradictory ways may not be providing you with valid responses.

FIGURE 7.4.
An example of a loaded question. In the third panel, the question is worded in such a way as to suggest that a smart person would not be in favor of the current mayor.

Also, avoid double negatives, which are confusing and unlikely to yield valid, reliable data. Consider the question, "Which of the following is not an example of a method that you have not encountered in your research methods class—experiment, correlational study, or observational study?" The use of the word "not" twice may lead different participants to interpret the question in different ways. A better question would ask, "Which of the following methods have you encountered in your research methods class—experiment, correlational study, or observational study?"

Response Types

A key question in designing a survey is, How should the participant respond? We do not mean the actual content of the response, but the form the response will take. Surveys can present a large number of response types, including open ended, closed ended, true/false, Likert scales of various lengths, multiple choice, fill in the blank, and many, many more. In picking your response type, it is important to consider how you will analyze the data collected from your survey. We present more detailed information about statistical analysis in Chapters 13 and 14.

Open-ended versus Closed-ended Responses. Most surveys that you encounter in your everyday life likely involve **closed-ended response** types, which require you to choose among a variety of responses predetermined by the survey's author. Their popularity rests on the fact that they are simpler and easier than open-ended responses to quantify and analyze statistically, and they are more efficient for the participant to complete than questions that are open ended, making them more likely to be answered. An **open-ended question** is one in which participants are free to answer in any way they like. However, as we saw in the Tooth Fairy example earlier in the chapter, merely providing closed-ended responses will not guarantee a well-constructed question. Think carefully about your overarching research question and how you plan to use the responses to address that question when determining the most appropriate question type. If your goal is not to quantify but to conduct a more qualitative study, then open-ended responses may be most appropriate.

Closed-ended response item A survey item/question that requires respondents to choose from a number of predetermined responses.

Open-ended response A survey item/question in which respondents are free to respond in any way they want.

Many researchers avoid open-ended responses because of the potential problem of interpreting participants' answers, difficulty in summarizing and quantifying responses across participants, and the constraints that open-ended responses place on potential statistical analyses. However, open-ended responses can be helpful in early stages of research and in providing a richer framework for interpreting responses to some closed-ended questions. Such responses can even be part of the strategy for developing and piloting survey items, which we discuss in the next section.

It is also possible to quantify open-ended responses, although it requires more steps in the analysis process. You must first reliably classify the responses into different types that can be quantified (i.e., develop a coding scheme). For example, in a study concerning parent–adolescent communication about sex, Jerman and Constantine (2010) included the open-ended question, "What is the most difficult part for you in talking to your child about sex and relationships?" Responses to this question were assigned to categories such as "difficulties related to embarrassment or discomfort" (e.g, "I think that it is just a comfort level that you feel, because it is a topic we are not in the habit of discussing"); "difficulties related to knowledge and self-efficacy" (e.g., "It is difficult for me to talk with her; I fear that I may explain something poorly to her or give her incorrect information"); and "cultural and social influences or issues" (e.g., "I think that sexual relations are a very delicate subject due to our culture"; p. 1169). Once responses were coded in this way, the researchers were able to assess which types of responses occurred most frequently and to evaluate how response frequencies differed with variables such as sex of the parent and age of the child.

Using open-ended questions during a pilot test of your ideas can also help you develop better, more informed closed-ended questions for the actual survey. Open-ended questions can provide anecdotes that serve to highlight an interesting aspect of the results from closed-ended responses. For example, if you are surveying fathers about the ways in which they are involved in the lives of their young children, you could use a standard closed-ended measure that quantifies degrees of involvement. In addition, you could also ask men to describe what they most value about their parenting experience as a way of getting a deeper understanding of what drives their involvement. In this example, open-ended responses enrich and deepen the closed-ended responses (Gorvine, 2002), giving the best of both worlds.

Likert Scales and Response Format.   One of the most common survey item response types is the Likert response format, which was developed by Renis Likert in 1932 for his dissertation at Columbia University (Likert, 1932). A **Likert response format** includes an ordered range and is often used to measure particular attitudes or values. Response options usually include between three and seven choices that vary from "strongly agree" to "strongly disagree." Questions using a Likert response format generally start with a declarative statement (e.g., "I like rutabagas"), followed by an ordered continuum of response categories (e.g., "agree," "neither agree nor disagree," "disagree"). In this format it is important to balance the number of positive and negative options and provide descriptive labels for each category. A numeric value is usually provided for each category (Carifio & Perla, 2007).

Many researchers have modified the original Likert response format to assess frequency ("never," "once," "2–3 times," "4 or more times") or amount ("0," "$1," "$2," "$3+"), as in the Tooth Fairy example. Others use a ruler on which respondents have to mark a continuous scale (as in the SES ladder shown in Figure 7.3) or a "slider" for respondents to record their responses online (these are termed "visual analogue" scales). The latter approaches yield interval data that are more appropriate for parametric statistical techniques. These statistical techniques make assumptions about the parameters or defining properties of the population distribution from which one's data are drawn (see Chapter 14 for a discussion of these issues).

> **Likert response format** An ordered range of responses used to measure particular attitudes or values. Response options usually include three to seven options that vary from "strongly disagree" to "strongly agree."

If you decide to use a scale, you will need to consider several issues. First, how many different responses should you provide on your scale—3, 5, 7, or 21? Although there is no simple rule for deciding how many categories is appropriate, 5 is the norm. As you have probably guessed, this choice (as with all choices in research) should be driven by your research question. How many categories make sense with respect to your question? Are you able to provide a distinct label for each category? Are your participants likely to use the full range of responses given the question you are asking? The choice of how many response categories to use may also depend on whether the survey is administered online or via a paper survey, where it is easier to present more category options, or administered verbally, such as over the telephone, where presenting more response options may be cumbersome for the interviewer and taxing to the memory of the respondent.

Midpoint The center value of a scale with an odd number of response possibilities. An example of a midpoint on a scale of agreement is "neither agree nor disagree."

A second issue is whether you should provide a **midpoint**, the "neither agree nor disagree" option. Again, this depends on your research question, but using a midpoint and an odd number of categories ("agree"/"neither agree nor disagree"/"disagree") may yield different results than using an even number of responses with no midpoint ("agree"/"disagree"; Carifio & Perla, 2007). Some researchers, however, have found only negligible differences with particular measures when comparing the use of even and odd numbers of responses in Likert scales (Adelson & McCoach, 2010; Armstrong, 1987). If the question has a true midpoint from a conceptual standpoint, that is, if there is meaningful information to be gleaned from a "neither agree nor disagree" sort of response, then use a midpoint.

Endpoint A point or value that marks one end of a line segment or interval.

Anchor (or **endpoint**) A point or value that marks one end of a line segment or interval.

A third issue involves using **endpoints** or **anchors**—either of two points or values that mark the ends of an interval—to scales. Many respondents hesitate to use endpoints in their responses, which may effectively reduce a 7-point scale to a 5-point scale. Many researchers advocate for the use of a longer scale format for this reason. Leung (2011), who uses different Likert-scale structures with a well-known psychological self-esteem measure, argues that longer-scale formats reduce skew and provide a more normal distribution of scores. Providing clear examples of the endpoints, ones that are meaningful for your participants, can also be helpful. A good example can be found in medical situations that assess pain using a 10-point scale. Women who have experienced childbirth often rate the pain during delivery as a "10." This is problematic when doctors ask these women to rate chest pains related to possible heart attacks. Comparing the pain with that of childbirth, women may rate their chest pains lower than men in the same situation. This lower rating potentially leads doctors to not treat women with chest pain as aggressively as men.

It is always a good idea to examine the distribution of your data to see whether respondents are avoiding the endpoints or clustering in the middle. If you discover either in the next stage, your pilot test, you might consider rewording your questions to provide a more differentiated response pattern. You should also be sensitive to different subject populations (especially those from different cultures), who may view the scales and end-points quite differently. A careful examination of the data, pilot testing, and sensitivity to group differences will help you determine an appropriate way to handle this particular issue.

A fourth issue regarding Likert and Likert-like response formats concerns data analysis. Many researchers treat the terms Likert scale and Likert response formats as equivalent (Carifio & Perla, 2007). However, the Likert response format refers *only* to how the responses are set up for a survey question. The sum of responses to multiple questions intended to measure the same variable form a **Likert scale** (Likert & Hayes, 1957).

Although many researchers analyze the data from single questions that use a Likert response format, statisticians disapprove of this approach (Carifio & Perla, 2007; Gardner, Cummings, Dunham, & Pierce, 1998). As Carifio and Perla (2007) argue, would you ever try to use a single item on an IQ test to evaluate differences between groups? You should not! However, it is appropriate to examine responses to a single question as part of an item analysis or exploratory process as you develop your survey.

Likert scale The sum of responses to multiple questions intended to measure the same variable using the Likert response format.

Evaluating Your Survey

Once you have completed a draft of your survey, it is crucial that you spend some time assessing its accuracy. Following are some tried-and-true ways of making sure your survey will accomplish what you want it to and ultimately address your research question.

Obtain Feedback.   Established researchers may run their questions by a panel of experts to garner feedback. These experts may consider whether the questions measure what they are supposed to measure (external validity) and whether subsets of questions sensibly group together to form coherent scales (internal validity). They may also make suggestions for modifying the items. Students or novice researchers working on their first research project may want to do their own version of this by running their questions by a group of peers.

Conduct Pilot Testing.   The next step involves conducting a **pilot study** to collect data to assess the instrument or try out a methodology. It is generally useful to obtain a relatively large sample for your pilot data. The exact number of participants you will need in your pilot study depends on a number of factors, including the number of items in your survey, the difficulty of obtaining samples from your target population (i.e., if you are studying a relatively hard to get group of subjects, such as individuals with a rare disorder, you may not want to use members of this group in your pilot study); time and resources; and your overall goal. For some researchers, the piloting process may involve conducting interviews and asking open-ended questions to develop the more tightly worded items that will make up the final survey.

Pilot study
A "prestudy" conducted before your actual study to assess your survey/interview instrument or test a methodology.

Assess Instrument Reliability.

Recalling the concept of reliability from Chapter 5, a survey instrument is reliable to the extent that it yields similar results under similar conditions. There are three general types of reliability that may be relevant as you construct your survey: test–retest reliability, parallel-forms reliability, and internal consistency.

Test–retest reliability
A measure of survey reliability that examines the consistency of responses of respondents who complete the same survey on two separate occasions.

Test–retest Reliability.

Test–retest reliability entails asking participants to complete your survey and then complete the same survey again at a later time. You then examine whether responses are consistent across the two surveys. You may do this for individual questions and for overall scores, if your survey is such that you combine items to arrive at a single score. Unfortunately, the test–retest approach suffers from the fact that participants may remember how they responded the first time, potentially leading to overestimates of reliability.

Parallel-forms (or alternate-forms) reliability A measure of survey reliability that examines the consistency of responses of respondents across two versions of a survey, with items in both surveys having been designed to probe the same variables.

Parallel-forms Reliability.

Parallel-forms or **alternate-forms reliability** involves creating two different versions of the survey, with items in both surveys designed to probe the same variables. Standardized tests such as the SAT, ACT, and GRE use parallel forms: not everybody takes the exact same version of the test. As with test–retest reliability, participants' memories of their responses in one version of the survey may affect their responses on the second version, although the questions are not strictly identical. In addition, you may find a lack of consistency if the parallel items do not truly address the same variables.

Internal consistency
A survey is internally consistent to the extent that items intended to measure the same variable yield similar responses.

Internal Consistency.

If your survey uses multiple questions to measure a single variable, then you want to ensure that you have **internal consistency** in your instrument. A survey is internally consistent to the extent that items that are intended to measure the same variable yield similar responses. For example, suppose your survey has three Likert items that are meant to measure extraversion. If you find that participants who agree with one item tend to also agree with the other two, whereas participants who disagree with one tend to disagree with the other two, then these items are internally consistent.

Split-half reliability
A measure of internal consistency assessed by dividing survey items intended to measure the same variable into two sets and examining how well responses to those two sets of items agree with one another.

Split-half reliability is one measure of internal consistency. This type of reliability is assessed by splitting survey items that are intended to measure the same variable into two sets and examining how well responses to those two sets of questions agree with one another.

Cronbach's alpha
(α) A measure of the internal consistency of a set of scale items.

Cronbach's alpha (α) is a common statistical measure used to assess internal consistency, taking into account how well all of the items that relate to a single variable agree with one another (Cronbach, 1951). α has an upper bound of 1.0, with the higher scores indicating better internal consistency of the items. Many statistical packages allow you to examine the impact of deleting one or more items on the overall α. Depending on the outcome of this analysis, you may choose to remove or modify items to increase internal consistency.

Use Factor Analysis for Advanced Scale Construction.   Distinct parts of a larger instrument that measure different aspects of a variable are referred to as subscales. These **subscales** may be derived in a similar way to the overall instrument, based on expert evaluation, conceptual groupings, or theoretical motivations. Researchers may use more sophisticated statistical approaches, such as **factor analysis** (Floyd & Widaman, 1995), a technique that examines the relation between items in a scale. Factor analysis is useful for determining whether your scale measures a single variable (or factor) or multiple ones. For example, in constructing a spirituality questionnaire, Parsian and Dunning (2009) used factor analysis to assign items such as "I am satisfied with who I am" and "I have a number of good qualities" to a self-awareness subscale and items such as "I try to find answers to the mysteries of life" and "I am searching for a purpose in life" to a spiritual needs subscale.

Subscales Distinct parts of a larger instrument that measure different aspects of a variable.

Factor analysis A statistical technique that examines the relationships between items in a scale. This approach is useful for determining whether a scale measures a single variable or multiple ones.

Practical Tips for Survey and Interview Approaches

1. Understand the strengths and limitations of surveys and interviews.

2. Be aware of the various biases (selection, choice, experiment, social desirability) and, as much as possible, design your instruments to minimize these biases.

3. Minimize opportunities for fraud, and inspect your data for signs of fraud.

4. Consider using an already-existing survey instrument that has been subjected to tests of validity and reliability.

5. If you construct your own survey, be sure your questions are simple, written at the appropriate reading level, and, in general, expressed in positive terms. Avoid double-barreled and loaded questions.

6. It is always a good idea to pilot your survey or interview before formally collecting data.

7. Carefully consider the purposes for which you might use closed-ended and open-ended items. You must consider the analyses that you will perform as you choose the items.

8. When constructing a new instrument, be sure to subject it to tests of validity and reliability. Pilot studies are a critical part of this process.

9. If you are conducting an interview, make sure your interviewers are trained and have practiced the interview multiple times.

CHAPTER SUMMARY

Surveys and interviews provide powerful tools with which to conduct your research. They come with a host of advantages: they are economical and efficient; they provide the opportunity to conduct sophisticated statistical analyses because of their potentially large sample sizes; and they can ensure the anonymity of your subjects. It is important to remember, however, that your surveys or interviews must serve your research question. You must also be vigilant of the range of potential biases that lurk in surveys and interviews, including choice and sampling biases. And although online surveys enable greater speed, efficiency, and numbers of participants, they also open up a greater potential for fraud.

As you start to generate your survey, first look for an existing measurement instrument that has been shown to be reliable and valid for your proposed sample population. If one exists, consider using it. You may need to modify an existing instrument to address your particular research question or apply it to your specific population of interest. If no such instruments exist, start developing your own questions, simultaneously considering the response format you plan to use and the data analysis approach you plan to employ. Pilot test your questions. Check for readability, understanding, and meaningfulness to the potential participants.

Up for Discussion

1. The ease of conducting surveys has increased with the ease of online methodologies for collecting data. The resulting proliferation of surveys and survey results has created many challenges for evaluating the quality of information that is "in the ether." What are the most important factors to consider in evaluating the utility of survey findings? What red flags may signal especially poor or potentially invalid survey results?

2. Some experts assert that, because survey writing is such a complex and challenging task, novice researchers should be discouraged from designing their own survey instruments and should instead default to using existing measures. Given the difficulty of writing good survey questions, do you agree with this advice? Why or why not? Under what circumstances, if any, might a novice design a survey?

3. Researchers often debate the benefits and drawbacks of closed-ended versus open-ended questions in their survey instruments. In trying to decide which way to go in designing a survey (or whether to use a combination of question types), what aspects do you consider most important?

Key Terms

Acquiescence bias, p. 162

Anchor (or endpoint), p. 170

Attrition, p. 156

Careless responding (CR), p. 158

Closed-ended response item, p. 168

Compound question, p. 166

Control variable, p. 162

Cronbach's alpha (α), p. 172

Double-barreled question, p. 166

Endpoint, p. 170

Experimenter bias, p. 155

Factor analysis, p. 173

Fatigue effects, p. 156

Internal consistency, p. 172

Interview, p. 151

Interviewer effects, p. 161

Lie scale, p. 158

Likert response format, p. 169

Likert scale, p. 171

Loaded question, p. 167

MacArthur Scale of Subjective Social Status, p. 164

Midpoint, p. 170

Motivated respondent bias, p. 155

Nonresponse bias, p. 155

Open-ended response, p. 168

Parallel-forms (or alternate-forms) reliability, p. 172

Participation biases, p. 155

Pilot study, p. 171

Questionnaire, p. 151

Response bias, p. 162

Response set, p. 156

Selection bias, p. 154

Self-selection bias, p. 155

Social desirability bias (also evaluation apprehension), p. 156

Split-half reliability, p. 172

Standardization, p. 162

Subscales, p. 173

Survey, p. 151

Test–retest reliability, p. 172

Experimental Designs

INSIDE RESEARCH: TRAVIS SEYMOUR

Director, Cognitive Modeling
Laboratory, Psychology Department,
University of California, Santa Cruz

I did my first psychology experiment in high school. I was fascinated by the relationship between Circadian rhythms and performance. I read in a psychology textbook that when the sun is at its peak in the middle of the day, it marks a shift in your performance and afterwards you don't perform as well. The book said it had to do with Circadian rhythms, which was something I didn't believe. I thought, "You know, lunch also happens around then and I bet it has more to do with lunch than where the sun is at noon." At my school in Georgia there were nearly 1,000 people, so lunch had to be staggered for several time periods. I was allowed to give people math tests before and after lunch period; one happened to be around noon, and another occurred around 10:30. As a control, I tested one group before and after early morning periods. The data showed that without lunch, post-test scores were the same or better than before, but when straddling lunch, post-test scores were worse. However, the results were the same for late morning and noon lunch periods, suggesting that the sun's peak was not a major influence. Since then, I've learned many things about methodology that I wish I knew at 16. For example, I should have compared the pre-noon lunch data to data from a post-noon group to see if the size of the lunch-related decrement increases after noon. I've also learned many things about human memory that makes me wonder if my recollection of this study from 25 years ago is accurate.

Doing that experiment was life changing for me. It was my first experience with understanding something about what's going on in the brain just by doing simple behavioral analysis and a little bit of math. That's when I decided I wanted to be a psychologist. You get access to something you otherwise wouldn't have access to simply by asking people controlled questions and analyzing their responses in a certain way. People take that for granted today, but at the turn of the 20th century that was huge news.

I went on to study psychology first at Northwestern University and then in graduate school at the University of Michigan. My first research project at Michigan studied the degree to which you can control the way your body manifests familiarity or recognition. If you recognize something, it's an automatic process that you can't control. But can you control whether or not your body reacts to that? That was fun because we started to think about how we could prove that, and what the implications were. Eventually this led me to research a lie detector test that I call the "concealed knowledge test," which is much more accurate than the traditional polygraph test. Today, I use a huge variety of experimental methods.

Travis Seymour is an expert in a wide range of experimental methods, from basic designs to highly sophisticated computer models he creates himself. He has used these methods to develop a lie detector test that surpasses the efficacy of the polygraph and to study many issues related to multitasking and attention.

Research Focus: Theoretical and empirical investigations in the role of memory in human performance

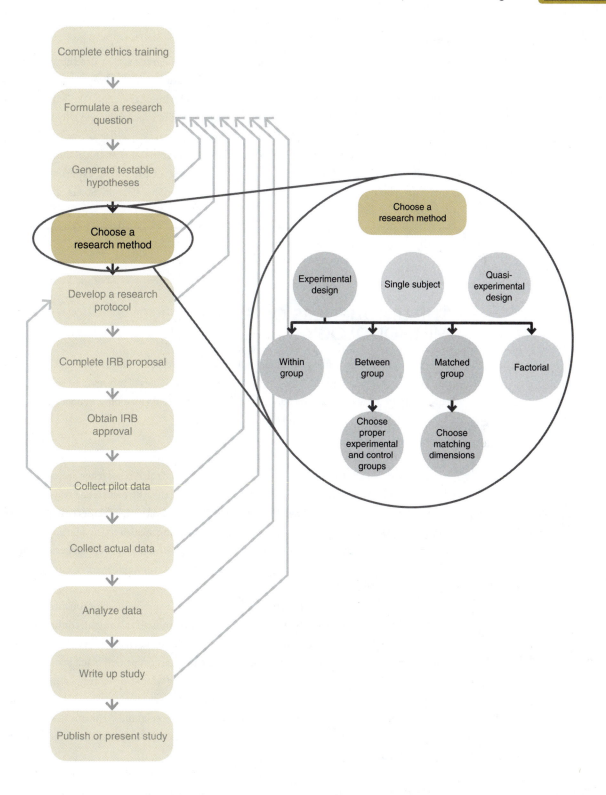

Chapter Abstract

Over the past two chapters, we have discussed some of the most widely used approaches in psychological research—observational methods, case studies, and survey designs. We now turn to the gold standard for scientific study: the experimental design. We will consider why it has been championed as the optimal way to conduct research (and why that is not always the case), as well as its advantages and disadvantages. We will examine the key constructs that underlie experimental designs and address some of the ethical concerns that such designs may raise. We will also walk through one of the classic experiments from social psychology, a groundbreaking study conducted by Claude Steele and Joshua Aronson.

THE UNIQUENESS OF EXPERIMENTAL METHODOLOGY

Experimental designs offer two crucial and closely related advantages that set them apart from other available methods. The first is control over variables of interest and the second is the ability to draw conclusions about causality. Experiments also offer benefits and drawbacks with respect to internal and external validity.

Experimental Control

Independent variable A variable manipulated by the researcher to observe its effect on a dependent variable.

Dependent variable The factor of interest being measured in the study that changes in response to manipulation of the independent variable.

Stereotype threat The prompt of a stereotypical belief that leads an individual to fulfill the expectations of that stereotype.

The hallmark of experimental designs is experimental control. A researcher exercises direct control over a variable (or variables) of interest. Specifically, the researcher systematically manipulates an **independent variable**. The researcher holds all other factors constant to see whether the **dependent variable**, the factor of interest being measured in the study, changes in response to manipulation of the independent variable. The goal is to construct a situation in which the independent variable is the only explanation for any observed change in the dependent variable.

The work of Steele and Aronson (1995) provides an example of experimental control. They wanted to demonstrate that, in certain contexts, individuals might confirm a commonly held stereotype about their own group. Steele and Aronson predicted that activating a stereotype in a test-taking situation—in this case the stereotype that black people are less intelligent—would lead a black individual to perform worse on a test of intellectual ability—a phenomenon known as **stereotype threat**.

Like many published experimental studies, the full Steele and Aronson (1995) paper comprises multiple experiments, each of which clarifies a different aspect of their theory. Here, we focus on the initial study.

Steele and Aronson obtained their experimental control through a carefully manipulated independent variable, which consisted of two possible **conditions** (sometimes termed **levels** of the experimental variable). In the "threat" condition, students were told that the test was diagnostic of intellectual ability, thereby potentially invoking a stereotype threat. In the "nonthreat" condition, students were told that the test was a laboratory problem-solving task that did not indicate ability. The dependent variable was performance on a difficult set of GRE verbal items. The only difference between the groups of participants was whether the task was presented as testing intellectual ability. Steele and Aronson hypothesized that if the stereotype threat operated as expected, black participants in the threat group would perform more poorly than black participants in the nonthreat group. They did not expect this difference for the white participants.

We should note here that in the original Steele and Aronson study, the researchers employed three different conditions: a diagnostic condition (which we refer to as the "threat" condition), a nondiagnostic condition (our "non-threat" condition), and a third condition, called the challenge condition, which we have omitted for our discussion.

Determination of Causality

The second hallmark of experimental design—and arguably its most important advantage—is that it enables researchers to draw causal conclusions. Recall that a major constraint of observational and survey research is that they provide correlational data, meaning that however tempting it might be, you cannot draw cause-and-effect conclusions. The designs merely show that some variable is somehow related to another variable. In contrast, an experiment enables the researcher to isolate the variables of interest and control the temporal ordering (ensuring that the independent variable occurs *prior* to the dependent variable), so that causal conclusions are justified. In addition, the ability to randomly assign your participants to different conditions (i.e., different levels of your independent variable) enables you to assume that the only difference between your groups is caused by that independent variable.

Recent advances in research methods and statistics have enabled additional paths to determining causality. These cutting-edge approaches, which can be used to infer and even test causality (e.g., structural equation modeling), require sophisticated statistical methods that are covered in depth elsewhere (e.g., Pearl, 2009).

Christensen (2012) succinctly summarizes the key elements of an experimental design that allow you to assert causality. He notes that the experimental plan must control overall aspects of the study, including the assignment of participants to different groups, determination of who ends up receiving which treatment and in which order, and the amount of treatment that each individual receives. Choosing the amount or level of treatment is not an easy decision—arriving at the proper "dose" often

Condition The intervention or treatment in an experiment given to a particular group of participants.

Level A possible condition in the experimental variable.

requires considerable study, pretesting, and even some luck. Many experiments that were not effective because of the level of the dose or intervention languish in file drawers.

All of the participants in Steele and Aronson's (1995) study completed the same set of GRE questions and were randomly assigned to the threat and nonthreat conditions, which differed only in how the task was described. Researchers could conclude that disparities in performance between the two groups were likely *caused* by the independent variable—the threat or nonthreat description of the task. Of course, this would be true only if they could be sure that other uncontrolled variables were not also in play.

Internal versus External Validity

Internal validity
An assessment of whether a particular variable is the actual cause of a particular outcome.

Another advantage of a well-designed experimental method is its high level of **internal validity**. A design that has high internal validity allows you to conclude that a particular variable is the direct cause of a particular outcome. In Chapter 5, we discussed how to evaluate whether *Baby Einstein* videos actually boost young children's intelligence. A well-designed study to evaluate this claim, that is, a study that is high in internal validity, would combine experimental control, temporal ordering of variables, and random assignment. It would enable you to determine whether the videos themselves cause an increase in intelligence or whether the parents who provide the videos for their children are doing other things that lead to the increase (e.g., reading to their children, engaging them intellectually in other ways).

External validity
A measure of the degree to which the conclusions drawn from a particular set of results can be generalized to other samples or situations.

In contrast, external validity is often seen as a challenge for experimental work. **External validity** is the degree to which conclusions drawn from a particular set of results can be generalized to other samples and situations. The sample in a particular experiment may not represent the larger population of interest, and the experimental situation may not resemble the real-world context that it is designed to model because of its artificiality. The concern around artificiality is controversial and not shared by everyone who does psychological research. For example, Stanovich (2013) has argued, "the artificiality of scientific experimentation is not a weakness but actually the very thing that gives the scientific method its unique power to yield explanations about the nature of the world" (p. 105). In essence, Stanovich insists that the very ability to isolate variables in the experimental paradigm is what makes it such a potent tool. He further notes the double standard for different sciences in this regard, pointing out that fields like physics are not criticized for using the experimental method, but psychological researchers often are.

As with many of the debates in psychology today, we cannot tell you what to conclude about external validity. The truth is, it depends. External validity of experimental designs may matter more for some issues that you might study than others. In Steele and Aronson's (1995) study, for instance, does it matter that participants completed the GRE questions while being given different prompts about the task in an experimental situation? On the one hand, if the study demonstrates effects of the threat condition even in an artificial experimental test situation, you could argue that the results (and the effect) are likely to be valid. You might even predict that an effect found in a relatively stress-free experimental setting would be magnified in a stressful real-world situation. On the other hand, because an experimental paradigm cannot truly replicate the pressures of a high-stakes testing situation, you could argue that it is impossible to be sure that stereotype threat—even if it does operate in the experiment—would occur in a genuine testing situation. Such different perspectives on external validity reinforce the advantage of using multiple methods to examine a research question. How better to demonstrate both the internal and the external validity of your work than to replicate your findings across different methodologies?

KEY CONSTRUCTS OF EXPERIMENTAL METHODS

Now that we have explored some of the unique features of experimental methods—experimental control, the ability to determine causality, and a tradeoff between internal and external validity—we investigate the concepts that are crucial to understanding how experimental methods work, again using the study of Steele and Aronson (1995) as an example.

Independent and Dependent Variables

Independent and dependent variables, which we identified earlier, are central to experimental designs. It is worth noting that experimenters do not always manipulate independent variables. For example, an independent variable might be a preexisting characteristic of the participant that cannot be altered and to which one cannot be randomly assigned, such as sex, age, or ethnicity. We refer to such variables as **quasi-independent variables**.

In Steele and Aronson's (1995) study, the independent variable was the description of the task: the threat condition (being told that the test was diagnostic of intellectual ability) and the nonthreat condition (being told that the test was a laboratory problem-solving task that did not indicate ability). The dependent variable was performance on the GRE questions. In addition, the ethnicity of the participants (black versus white) served as a quasi-independent variable. The researchers hoped to show that the threat condition would lead to poorer performance on the GRE items than the nonthreat condition and that this detrimental effect of the stereotype threat would apply only to black participants.

Experimental and Control Groups

Another key characteristic of experimental design is the assignment of participants to different groups. The ability to compare outcomes across these groups is essential to the logic of the experimental method. In most classic experimental designs, researchers compare at least two groups—an experimental group and a control group. The

Travis Seymour:

"Because of the human performance and memory work I do, most of my analyses are standard repeated measures that you might find in your first-year advanced stats class. But I have used a huge variety of methodologies. Getting a range of research experiences and really geeking out about why the rules of research methods are the way they are—what exactly they are protecting against—gave me a sense of methodology that I didn't have before."

Quasi-independent variable A preexisting characteristic (e.g., sex, age or race) to which a participant cannot be randomly assigned.

Experimental group
Participants who receive the intervention or treatment, for example, a dose of the independent variable.

Control group
Participants who serve as a direct comparison for the experimental group and receive either an inert version of the treatment or no treatment at all.

experimental group receives the intervention or treatment, that is, a dose of the independent variable. The **control group** serves as a direct comparison for the experimental group and receives either an inert version of the treatment or no treatment at all. The most familiar example of this design comes from drug studies in medical research, in which a treatment group receives the medication that is being tested and a control group receives a placebo ("sugar pill"). The belief is that, all other things being equal, if the treatment group does better than the control group on the relevant dependent variable (whatever the drug is designed to treat), there is evidence for the effectiveness of the medication.

This sort of design, however, does pose an obvious difficulty. To conclude that your treatment or intervention is responsible for any change that occurs, you must ensure that your control group receives everything that the experimental group receives, with the exception of the "active ingredient." Researchers who are testing a pill can accomplish this fairly easily by having the control group simply receive an inert version of the pill. But most psychological research involves a more complex intervention. For example, imagine we are studying the effectiveness of a particular form of group therapy for reducing anxiety. What do we do with our control group? Do they simply sit at home while those in the experimental group receive the group therapy sessions?

Attention control group A type of control in which participants receive everything the experimental group receives (e.g., the same amount of time and attention), with the exception of the "active ingredient" of the intervention or treatment.

A particular type of control group addresses this concern. Called an **attention control group**, it provides an experience as similar to that of the experimental group as possible (e.g., the attention control group receives the same amount of time and attention as the experimental group), with the only difference being the active ingredient of the experiment. In our study on group therapy for anxiety, an attention control group would also attend a weekly group meeting, but it might be a generic support group instead of one specifically for anxiety.

Steele and Aronson's (1995) work has clear experimental and control groups: participants in the experimental group were assigned to the threat condition, whereas the control group received the nonthreat condition. These two groups were otherwise identical and were given the same GRE questions; by design, the only difference remaining between the groups was the experimental manipulation—whether the task was framed as a (potential) threat or not.

Placebo Effect

Placebo effect A result of treatment that can be attributed to participants' expectations from the treatment rather than any property of the treatment itself.

An effect of treatment that can be attributed to participants' expectations from the treatment rather than any property of the treatment itself is called a **placebo effect**. In studies designed to test the beneficial effects of an intervention, the comparison between an experimental and placebo control group is essential, so that you can determine whether your treatment is more effective than a placebo alone. In drug trials, placebo control groups are given sugar pills, which should have no therapeutic effect. Even in such cases, participants often report beneficial effects, which is why researchers must be able to show that the effects of their interventions exceed those of the placebo alone.

A recent example of a classic experimental/control group design that demonstrates the power of the placebo effect appeared in the *New England Journal of Medicine* (Sihvonen et al., 2013). The study was designed to evaluate the effects of surgery for a group of patients with degenerative wear and tear of the meniscus, which is part of the knee (Sihvonen et al., 2013; see "Media Matters: The 'Sugar Pill' Knee Surgery"). The study compared a type of arthroscopic knee surgery with "sham" knee surgery. The sham knee surgery served as the placebo in this case, and individuals in this condition received an incision in the knee, but nothing was done to the meniscus. At a one-year follow up, there was no difference in reported knee pain between the two groups.

It is important to note that you should not think of placebo effects as fake effects. The benefits of placebos are real and measurable. Patients in both the arthroscopic meniscectomy and the sham groups reported reduced pain, thereby experiencing a real benefit.

In a high-profile meta-analysis, Kirsch and Sapirstein (1998) reported a similarly compelling power of the placebo in which they concluded that much of the benefit attributed to widely marketed antidepressant medications like Prozac could actually be the result of a placebo response. Again, the placebo response here was real—patients reported measurable improvement in their depressive symptoms, suggesting that such effects have true neurobiological underpinnings. We do not mean to suggest that interventions should not seek to provide benefits beyond placebo, but rather propose that placebo effects in and of themselves can provide therapeutic benefits. Contemporary researchers consider the placebo effect much more than inert physical content; rather, they recognize it as "the overall simulation of a therapeutic intervention" (Price, Finniss, & Benedetti, 2008, p. 565).

Random Assignment

Other than experimental control itself, the most notable hallmark of an experimental design is **random assignment**—the procedure by which researchers place participants in different experimental groups (i.e., assign them to different levels of the independent variable) using chance procedures. Any given individual has an equal probability of being assigned to each group in the experiment. For example, in the knee surgery study, each patient had an equal probability of being assigned to the real surgery group or the sham surgery group. In Steele and Aronson's (1995) work, participants were likewise randomly assigned to the threat or nonthreat testing conditions.

Why bother with random assignment? The major benefit is that a random assignment procedure presumably balances out unwanted variation between the different groups (Dehue, 2001). From a conceptual standpoint, if unwanted variation (resulting from

Random assignment
The procedure by which researchers place participants in different experimental groups using chance procedures, so that any individual has an equal probability of being assigned to any of the groups in the experiment.

The "Sugar Pill" Knee Surgery

Medical researchers have long recognized the strength of the placebo effect in studies on medical treatments. One recent groundbreaking study again confirmed its power and has led the medical community to question the most common orthopedic procedure in the United States: a surgery called arthroscopic meniscectomy intended to relieve knee pain. Approximately 700,000 patients undergo the procedure annually.

The study, published in the *New England Journal of Medicine* (Sihvonen et al., 2013) and conducted by researchers in Finland, tracked 146 patients between 35 and 65 years of age with symptoms of degenerative wear and tear of the meniscus, a piece of cartilage that cushions the shinbone and thighbone (Hellerman, 2013). They assigned patients to two groups: the first group underwent arthroscopic meniscectomy, a procedure in which a surgeon inserted a blade through an incision in the knee and trimmed the worn edges of the meniscus, whereas the second group received only a "sham" surgery, in which an incision was made in the knee, but nothing was done to the meniscus.

Neither the participants nor the researchers who evaluated the results knew whether a particular patient had received the real or sham surgery. The surgeons clearly knew but did not communicate who received what treatment until the results were being analyzed. Both groups spent the same length of time in recovery and received the same walking aids, instructions for recovery, and directions for over-the-counter painkillers (Jaslow, 2013), making excellent use of an attention control group.

One year later, patients in both groups reported the same rate of recovery and pain relief. About two-thirds of each group said they were satisfied with the treatment and would undergo it again (Hellerman, 2013). "These results argue against the current practice of performing arthroscopic partial meniscectomy in patients with a degenerative meniscal tear," the study's authors concluded (Sihvonen et al., 2013).

Given the popularity of the surgery in the United States, not to mention the $4 billion in its direct costs to consumers, the study garnered considerable attention in the mainstream media as well as its share of controversy. Not surprisingly, some medical professionals were displeased with the findings. Dr. Frederick Azar, the vice president of the American Academy of Orthopaedic Surgeons, warned that the patients in the study were atypical because only 1 percent of his patients have a degenerative meniscus tear and no evidence of arthritis. He also expressed concern that the study would scare away patients who could be helped. "This is a very useful low-cost intervention, with a short recovery time and good results in most patients" (Hellerman, 2013). Yet, experiencing relief without the risks of surgery is an undeniably positive outcome.

Despite such intriguing results that attest to the potency of the placebo effect, exactly how and why it works remains unclear. One thing is for certain: Tapping into the mind's ability to cure disease and alleviate pain is an exciting, ongoing research opportunity.

individual differences and the randomness of the world) is eliminated, then what remains is the variation of interest caused by the experimental manipulation itself.

Random assignment usually works effectively to equalize the many other factors that the experimental and control group might differ on besides the experimental assignment to groups. However, a truly random assignment is most likely to occur only when the groups are relatively large. In a relatively small study that comprises only a few participants per group, the likelihood of the experimental and control group differing on some dimension increases. For example, imagine you were running a small study with a pool of participants with equal numbers of men and women. You hoped to have 16 participants in the experimental group and 16 participants in an attention control group. You decide to flip a coin to randomly assign participants to groups: when the coin comes up "heads" you put a participant in the experimental group and when it comes up "tails" you place the participant in the control group. Just by chance, you might end up with a sample distribution of 11 women and 5 men in the experimental group and 5 women and 11 men in the control group. At the end of the study, it might be hard to rule out that any significant results were not caused by the unequal distribution of women and men. In a case such as this, with a smaller group of participants, you might choose to do a **quasi-random assignment** where you assign equal numbers of men and women across the experimental and control conditions.

Quasi-random assignment The researcher assigns equal numbers of participants with key characteristics (e.g., sex, age, or race) across the experimental and control conditions.

TYPES OF EXPERIMENTAL DESIGNS

In an experiment researchers can choose between two basic designs: between subjects and within subjects. They may also use a third design—matched group—which contains elements of both between-subjects and within-subjects designs. All three of these designs have advantages and disadvantages, which we discuss in the sections that follow.

Between-subjects Designs

In a **between-subjects design** (also called **between-groups design**), researchers expose two (or more) groups of individuals to different conditions and then measure and compare differences between groups on the variable(s) of interest. In such a design, the researcher is looking for differences *between* individual participants or groups of participants, with each group exposed to a separate condition. Both Steele and Aronson's (1995) stereotype threat work and Sihvonen et al.'s (2013) sham knee surgery study are examples of between-subjects design, with different groups being exposed to different conditions (threat vs. nonthreat, real surgery vs. sham surgery). Figure 8.1 illustrates a between-subjects design. Note that the initial pool of participants is randomly assigned to different conditions and each group of participants is distinct from the others.

Between-subjects (or between-groups) design A type of experimental design in which the researcher assigns individual participants or groups of participants to one of several conditions to detect differences *between* groups of participants, with each group exposed to a separate condition.

Advantages of Between-subjects Designs.
Major advantages of between-subjects designs include simplicity of setup, their intuitive structure, and the relative ease

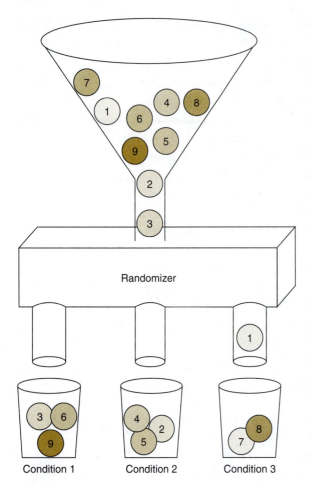

FIGURE 8.1.   Randomization in a between-subjects research design.

of statistical analyses that they permit. As Keppel and Wickens (2004) note, the number of statistical assumptions required for a between-subjects design is smaller than that for other designs. Between-subjects designs are straightforward in their construction and interpretation.

Disadvantages of Between-subjects Designs. Between-subjects designs have two notable disadvantages. One is cost. Because these designs require a separate set of participants for *each* condition, the resources required to gather a sample can be considerable depending on the numbers of conditions and participants.

The second disadvantage relates to variability. When looking at differences between groups, the individual differences that exist between your participants are a major source of variability. Dealing with this variability, in addition to the variability that really interests you (i.e., the variability caused by your treatment/experiment/intervention), makes for a less powerful design in terms of successfully detecting treatment effects. With smaller samples, the between-subjects variability may be particularly problematic.

For example, suppose you are evaluating two different teaching methods. Method 1 is, in reality, more effective than Method 2, raising test scores about 5 points on average. However, students vary greatly in their knowledge and testing abilities, so individual test scores can range from the 50's and 60's to the high 90's. Such a range of individual differences may swamp the 5-point advantage of Method 1 over Method 2, requiring quite a large number of participants to reveal this advantage with any statistical confidence.

Within-subjects (or **within-group** or **repeated measures**) **design** A type of experimental design in which the researcher assigns each participant to all possible conditions.

Within-subjects Designs

A **within-subjects design** (also called **within-group** or **repeated measures design**) assigns each participant to all possible conditions. For example, imagine you want to study the effects of caffeine on performance on a memory task. In your study you have three conditions: a "caffeine-free" condition in which participants are given a cup of decaffeinated herbal tea before performing the memory task, a "moderate-caffeine condition" in which participants are given a cup of green tea before the task, and a "high-caffeine condition" in which participants are given a triple shot of coffee before the task. In a within-subjects design, the same group of participants would take part in all three conditions (presumably on different days). In contrast, in a between-subjects design, separate groups of partici- pants would take part in each condi-

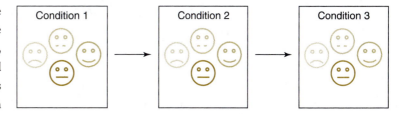

FIGURE 8.2. Example of a within-subjects design where the same four individuals are presented with three different conditions.

tion. Figure 8.2 illustrates a within-subjects design, showing that the same group of participants repeats participation in each condition.

Another example of a well-designed within-subjects study comes from the work of Master et al. (2009). Prior research had shown that social support is associated with re- duced pain. Master et al. were interested in the ways in which social support would impact the experience of pain in a group of participants. In particular, they wondered whether the simple presence of a romantic partner's photograph might provide the social support neces- sary to lessen pain.

To examine this hypothesis, Master et al. (2009) recruited 28 women in long-term rela- tionships (greater than six months). Participants received a series of "thermal stimulations" (applications of heat) that were tailored to their particular level of moderate discomfort based on a pretest. These thermal stimulations were given to each participant across seven different conditions:

- Holding her partner's hand (with the partner sitting behind a curtain);
- Holding the hand of a male stranger (also sitting behind a curtain);
- Holding a squeeze ball;
- Viewing photographs of her partner;
- Viewing photographs of a male stranger;
- Viewing photographs of an object (a chair); or
- Viewing a simple crosshair (i.e., no image).

During these conditions, participants rated their level of discomfort. As hypothesized, the researchers found that holding a partner's hand lessened pain more than did holding an object or a stranger's hand. Similarly, viewing a partner's photograph lessened pain more than viewing photographs of an object or a stranger. This study was considered a within-subjects design because the women in the study participated in all seven condi- tions, rather than having seven separate groups of women participate in a single condition.

Advantages of Within-subjects Designs.   The major benefits of within-subjects designs are twofold. First, relative cost—a disadvantage of between-subjects designs—is lower. You need fewer participants than in a between-subjects design because each individual participates in all the conditions. From the standpoint of recruiting your sample, this is a more economical option.

A second advantage is that you do not have to worry about variability resulting from unwanted individual differences among your participants. Because you use the same participants repeatedly, you can proceed with the assumption that the variability is caused by the real factor of interest—the differing experimental conditions. In effect, your participants serve as their own controls. This results in greater statistical power or, in other words, a greater probability of being able to detect an effect that is present, as discussed in Chapter 6.

Disadvantages of Within-subjects Designs.

Despite these laudable advantages, the drawbacks of within-subjects designs are also substantial. First, they require a more complex set of statistical assumptions (Keppel & Wickens, 2004). You cannot assume that measurements made under different conditions are completely independent because they come from the same participants. This notion of independence of participants is a crucial assumption of a number of statistical techniques. Measurements made on the same person under different conditions are clearly related in some ways. Thus, the assumption of independence between conditions does not hold, and you will need to use different statistical procedures.

Second, within-subjects designs have several potential side effects, called **order effects** because the order in which participants receive different experimental conditions may influence the outcome. There are several types of order effects: simple, fatigue, and carryover are the most common.

A **simple order effect** occurs when the particular order of the conditions influences the results. Consider a simple within-subjects design in which participants are given the control condition (A) first, followed by the experimental condition (B). To test for an order effect you would need to have a second group that received the experimental condition (B) first, followed by the control condition (A). If the results in the experimental condition differ between participants in the AB group compared with the BA group, then the order of presentation matters.

As a result of repeated exposure to experimental conditions in a within-subjects design, participants may show a **fatigue** (or **boredom**) **effect** and begin to perform more poorly as the experiment goes on. This may occur even if you vary the order systematically across participants. For example, in our caffeine–memory study described previously, it is easy to imagine that participants might grow weary of the memory task by the second or third session, even if the task were varied in some way. The resulting lowered motivation could skew results.

An additional potential consequence of within-subjects designs is the **carryover effect** (sometimes described as a learning or practice effect). As with a simple order effect, this

Order effect
A potential effect of a within-subjects design in which the order that participants receive different experimental conditions may influence the outcome.

Simple order effect
The particular order of the experimental conditions influences the results.

Fatigue (boredom) effect Participants begin to perform more poorly as the experiment goes on as a consequence of repeated exposure to experimental conditions in a within-subjects design.

Carryover effect The result of a participant's performance in one experimental condition affecting his or her performance in a subsequent condition.

occurs because a participant's performance under one experimental condition inevitably affects his or her performance under a subsequent condition. In our caffeine–memory study, a participant who becomes accustomed to the memory task and therefore more proficient at it exhibits a carryover effect. This would complicate the ability of the researcher to ensure that any differences between the conditions were caused by the true variable of interest, caffeine dosage. Carryover effects may also occur because a particular experimental manipulation lasts beyond the experimental condition. Specifically, some drugs may alter behavior even after they have left the body. In this situation it may be useful to measure the baseline behavior and then wait to move on to the next condition until participants have returned to baseline levels.

In some cases, order and carryover effects will rule out the use of a within-subjects design. For example, you would be hard-pressed to conduct Steele and Aronson's (1995) stereotype threat study using a within-subjects design, because if you gave a participant the verbal GRE task with the two different frames (threat and nonthreat), the manipulation might not work. Whatever frame was provided first might influence the impact of the second frame.

Matched-group Designs

An important alternative approach to between-subjects or within-subjects designs is a **matched-group design**, which contains elements of both. A matched-group design has separate groups of participants in each condition and involves "twinning" a participant in each group with a participant in another group.

For example, imagine that you want to conduct the sham knee surgery study as a matched-group rather than between-subjects design. Although you would still have two groups of patients—one that received the real surgery and another that received the sham surgery—you would also match each patient in one group with a patient in the other group *on dimensions that are critically related to the dependent variable.* This point is crucial. Matched designs work only if the matching is on dimensions relevant to what is being measured. In the knee surgery study, matching would need to occur on the aspects of patients' medical history and background that relate to the nature of their injury (e.g., background playing soccer) and their prognosis for recovery. If matching were done on some irrelevant aspect of the patient's background (such as eye color or cholesterol level), then you would not be able to assert you had a true matched-group design.

Figure 8.3 illustrates a matched-group design. Imagine that the creatures in the figure are participants in a study comparing two different training programs designed to improve running speed. Suppose that you know that two aspects of these creatures' anatomy most impact their innate running ability: foot shape and tail shape. In a matched-group design, you would pair each creature with another creature that has identical dimensions of foot and tail shape. Note that the creatures are not literal twins, that is, they still differ on many other dimensions (eye shape, ears, nose, etc.).

Matched-group design A type of experimental design in which researchers assign separate groups of participants in each condition and "twin" a participant in each group with a participant in another group. It contains elements of both between-subjects and within-subjects designs.

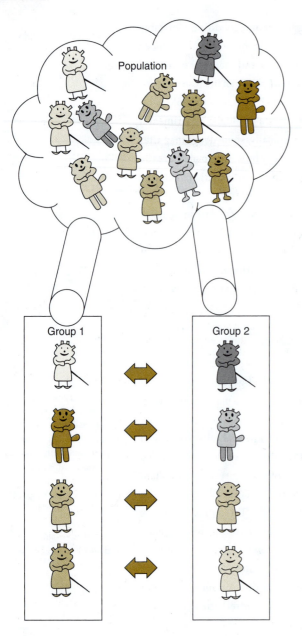

FIGURE 8.3. Example of a matched-group design.

A matched-group design also offers you the option to conduct a study so that you match on more than one variable for the purpose of multiple analyses—especially if matching on different variables has different theoretical and practical implications. One area where matched designs are often used is in the study of individuals with various delays and disorders. Using a matching design allows you to examine whether any finding is caused by the disorder, delay, or some other factor such as mental age.

Joffe and Varlokosta (2007) studied the development of language syntax in a group of children with Down syndrome and another group with Williams syndrome (a genetic disorder that results in developmental delays that occur with relatively high verbal abilities). They decided to match their participants on three different dimensions: chronological age, mental age, and performance IQ (a subset of IQ test items that tap various aspects of nonverbal intelligence). Having a design that matched participants in three different ways for separate sets of analyses enabled the researchers to tease out which dimensions (chronological age, mental age, or performance IQ) could provide the best basis of comparison for children with these differing disorders.

Although this example highlights how matching might be used, the study does not include a true experimental design because participants were not randomly assigned to different experimental conditions. An experimental design using a matched sample could be designed to investigate whether a new intervention might boost the acquisition of language skills in children with Down syndrome. The researcher could use a matched sample to cancel out age and IQ differences as factors that might "interfere" with the intervention in this population. To do this, a researcher would pair children with Down syndrome on chronological age and performance IQ and then randomly assign one member of the pair to an intervention group and the other to a control condition.

Advantages of Matched-group Designs. Although you are using different participants across your conditions, as long as you have matched participants properly on dimensions of relevance to the dependent variable, you do not need to worry about the unwanted variability of individual differences. As was the case in the within-subjects design, participants in a matched-group design serve as their own controls. This results in greater statistical power or, in other words, a greater probability of being able to detect an effect that is present, as discussed in Chapter 6.

Additionally, order and carryover effects (both substantial limitations of a within-subjects design) are *not* a concern in a matched-group design. As we mentioned previously, the latter design involves separate participant samples that are only paired for the purpose of data analysis.

Disadvantages of Matched-group Designs.

As appealing as matched-group designs may be, they do have disadvantages. First, as is the case with within-subjects designs, matched-group designs require a more complex set of statistical assumptions (Keppel & Wickens, 2004).

Second, the process of matching can prove difficult. It can be hard to know on which dimensions you should match your participants, and if you cannot identify those dimensions correctly, your matching will be ineffective. Researchers must be knowledgeable on the key variables. Matching in the knee surgery study required researchers with expertise on the medical issues involved in this sort of knee injury. Participants were placed in different groups and were matched on age, sex, and the presence or absence of minor degenerative changes detected on a radiograph.

Third, recruiting matched samples may be difficult and expensive. Finding matches for a large set of participants with many matching dimensions poses challenges. Imagine that one type of creature in Figure 8.3 was relatively rare or that you lived in a community with a relatively small population. In these cases, you would have to devote considerable resources to finding the right match, such as traveling a long way to obtain your desired sample.

CONFOUNDING FACTORS AND EXTRANEOUS VARIABLES

Any discussion of experimental methodology must include the important concepts of confounding factors and extraneous variables. **Confounds**, also known as **extraneous variables,** are uncontrolled variables that vary along with the independent variable in your experimental design and could account for effects that you find. In other words, confounds may affect the outcome of your study, although they are not the primary variables of interest. These effects could occur either in lieu of or in addition to an effect of the independent variable. When an experimenter fails to account for confounds, the validity of the findings comes into question.

For example, suppose you are comparing two different reading fluency training programs with a group of second graders. The teacher presenting technique A is more

Confounds (or **extraneous variables**) Uncontrolled variables that change with the independent variable(s) in your experimental design and could account for effects that you find.

Extraneous variables (or **confounds**) Uncontrolled variables that vary with the independent variable(s) in your experimental design and could account for effects that you find.

"I had a professor who said that one of the biggest things you learn after you do a study is what you should have done. I thought at the time that it wasn't true, because you could just be more careful. But since then I've found that it's inevitable that participants' behavior is either smaller than the range you believe or greater than the range you believed. . . . If you completed a series of experiments and you still felt like you didn't know what was going on, then that's a design problem. But to conduct one experiment and feel that it doesn't capture all of what's interesting, that's pretty normal."

Hawthorne (or observer effect) Participants in a study modify their behavior as a result of knowing they are being observed.

charismatic and engaging than the teacher presenting technique B, so the teacher's personal characteristics may be a confounding factor in your study. If you found that technique A was significantly more effective than technique B, you would be unable to conclude whether the difference was a result of the programs themselves or the greater effectiveness of the more appealing teacher. It could also be that technique A is more effective *and* the teacher's appeal is an additional variable influencing the results, but it would be impossible to separate out which of these variables accounts for what portion of the effect. Researchers must account for several different types of confounds. First, we will discuss the different types of confounds; second, we will discuss the various strategies for addressing confounds in your experimental design.

Participant Characteristics

The first confounding variable that you must address concerns characteristics of participants in the study. The astonishing variability among human beings is what makes studying them equal parts fascinating and challenging. Because your goal is to isolate and measure the variability resulting from your design, you want to minimize or eliminate other variability that will confuse the issue, and variation in the characteristics of your participants may overshadow the variability that you are trying to investigate.

Of particular concern for researchers is the possibility that experimental groups may differ systematically in their participant characteristics. What if the group assigned to the nonthreat condition in Steele and Aronson's (1995) study on stereotype threat actually performed more favorably on the GRE test items because they had greater verbal skill than the threat group? That would call into question any interpretation of the findings around stereotype threat generating an effect on performance. In fact, Steele and Aronson were concerned enough about this potential problem that although they used random assignment, they still collected students' verbal SAT scores and used them in their statistical analyses.

Provided you have a large enough sample, randomization is likely to be effective in minimizing group differences. It is also an effective strategy when you do not know on which dimensions to match; in effect, randomization is the equivalent of matching on all possible dimensions.

The Hawthorne Effect

Another confounding factor relates to a potential effect of the experiment simply being an experiment. Aside from the various order and carryover effects we have discussed, you should also think about the impact of participants' awareness that they are in an experiment, which can change their actions. This is often referred to as the **Hawthorne effect** or **observer effect**, which acknowledges that the act of observation can alter the behavior being observed.

The effect was first described by Landsberger (1958), who analyzed data from the Haw-thorne Works factory, an electrical plant outside of Chicago. Landsberger intended to ex-amine whether higher or lower levels of light would affect worker productivity, but his analyses revealed that worker productivity increased as a function of the interest shown by the researchers and declined once the observation was over. Although controversy exists about what really drives the Hawthorne effect, the important lesson for researchers is that participants' expectations, which are an unavoidable part of the research process, may sometimes drive effects in unanticipated ways.

Demand Characteristics

Another major set of potential confounding factors in experimental design is referred to as **demand characteristics**. Demand characteristics are features of the experimental design itself that lead participants to make certain conclusions about the purpose of the experi-ment and then adjust their behavior accordingly, either consciously or unconsciously. Demand characteristics can be a function of comments that participants have heard about the study before participating or may simply be based on what participants believe to be the goals of the research—even if you tell them otherwise.

An example of a demand characteristic familiar to virtually all researchers who study cognitive development involves parental expectations. When parents bring their children into a laboratory setting for any study around cognitive developmental topics, researchers have a hard time convincing them that they are *not* studying their child's intelligence, even when that is truly not the focus of their study. As a result, some parents try to influence their child's answers to make the child look as intelligent as possible. In grappling with the chal-lenge posed by such characteristics, Orne (1962) argued that any participant must be rec-ognized as an active participant in the experiment and, as such, the possibility of demand characteristics should always be considered.

Demand characteristics Features of the experimental design itself that lead participants to make certain conclusions about the purpose of the experiment and then adjust their behavior accordingly, either consciously or unconsciously.

Other Confounds

There are so many possible confounds for any given experimental design that no researcher can be expected to anticipate them all. It is not surprising, then, that you may eventually uncover a confounding variable you had not initially considered.

Anderson and Revelle (1994) and Revelle, Humphreys, Simon, and Gilliland (1980) encountered an unanticipated confounding factor in their studies examining the complex interaction of personality (such as introversion–extraversion) with impulsivity, arousal level, and caffeine intake. For some time, Revelle and his colleagues were puzzled by difficul-ties in replicating a particular finding related to impulsivity and caffeine intake. After con-siderable discussion, they realized that their results varied depending on what time of day the data were collected. After further analysis, they found that the effects of impulsivity in con-junction with caffeine intake varied by time of day (Anderson & Revelle, 1994).

For example, individuals low on impulsivity were more aroused in the morning and less aroused in the evening than were individuals with high impulsivity. By discovering this unforeseen confounding variable (time of day), the authors were able to explain some of their discrepant results. The point is, you should consider all dimensions that may affect an experimental design—even something that initially seems insignificant (like time of day).

Strategies for Dealing with Confounds

A carefully designed experiment anticipates possible confounds and ensures that the design either eliminates those confounds altogether or deals with them in other ways. The following five strategies will help you address confounds.

Hold Potential Confounding Variables Constant.   The first strategy works to minimize the influence of potential confounds. In the example of reading fluency training, a well-designed study would standardize the presentation of the two approaches as much as possible so that the only substantial difference between the technique A and technique B conditions would be the techniques themselves. Key characteristics of how the teachers administer the training would be held constant to reduce the impact of the teachers' personalities.

Vary Test Items and Tasks.   This strategy applies only to within-subjects designs. If carryover effects are a concern, then the design should include a range of tests or tasks that vary enough such that practice alone would not lead to improvement. Participants might still benefit from repetition of testing in a broad sense (even if the details differ), but varying the items on the test would minimize this as a confound. For the related issue of fatigue effects, building rest into the design would be the best remedy. In our reading fluency example, for a within-subjects design you would need to employ different tests of fluency (with the same level of difficulty) across the different conditions. To reduce the effects of fatigue, you would need to ensure that the fluency tests are not overly long.

Use Blind and Double-blind Designs.   These strategies address the Hawthorne effect. In a **blind** or **blinded design**, the experimenter measuring the behavior of interest does not know what intervention (if any) the individuals being observed have received. A contemporary example of how a blinded study minimizes the Hawthorne effect can be seen in Rapport, Orban, Kofler, and Friedman (2013), which reviewed programs that aim to train children with attention deficit hyperactivity disorder to improve their working memory and other cognitive functions. In this study, the experimenters assessing memory and cognitive function did not know what program the children were in. When studies used unblinded raters to assess the effectiveness of training, they reported substantially larger benefits than did blinded raters. In other words, raters who knew that they were

Blind or **blinded design** The experimenter measuring the behavior of interest does not know what intervention (if any) the individuals being observed have received.

evaluating children who had received intervention expected and recorded a higher level of benefit than raters who did not know whether the children they were observing had received the intervention (Rapport et al., 2013).

In many experiments, either experimenters or participants are unaware of the experimental condition they are in. If only one of these groups is "blind" to the intervention, then the study is said to have a **single-blind design**. It is more common for researchers to keep participants blind to the hypotheses than it is for experimenters to be blinded. Part of this reasoning is because of the pragmatics of conducting research; if all the experimenters are blind to the hypotheses, it becomes difficult to do the actual research.

In a **double-blind design**, which is often considered the gold standard because it most rigorously implements a blinded design, you would ensure that both the experimenter doing the rating *and* the participant receiving the intervention do not know to which condition they have been assigned. This was the case in the sham knee surgery example— neither the researchers nor the patients knew which surgery the participants had received.

Statistically Control for Variables That Cannot Be Experimentally Controlled.

A fourth strategy for dealing with confounds is through **statistical control**. In analyzing your study results, you can make a statistical adjustment that will account for the influence of a specified third variable and allow you to analyze the results with the influence of that third variable eliminated. Statistical control requires you to know what your confound is, to measure it systematically, and to include these measurements in your statistical analysis. Statistical control is often applied in situations where matched-group designs would be difficult to implement. As noted earlier, Steele and Aronson (1995) collected verbal SAT scores from their participants and statistically controlled for these scores in their analysis.

In our reading study example, say that you suspect that students' reading fluency prior to the interventions will have a substantial impact on their response to the different techniques. (Perhaps the students who were better readers to start with will reap larger benefits from the techniques.) As long as you measure reading fluency at the beginning of the study, you would be able to statistically control for the prestudy fluency and ensure that you were only measuring change resulting from the independent variable of interest, the interventions themselves.

Use Randomization and Counterbalancing.

This strategy consists of two closely related sets of techniques. Both specifically address confounds that may be caused by the particular order in which you present conditions in your experiment. The problem of order effects is especially relevant in within-subjects designs where the same individuals are exposed to multiple conditions in your study, which leads to concerns about carryover effects. In **randomization**, you simply randomize the order of the presentation of conditions/stimuli for each participant so that you can assume that, across all of your participants, no one particular order influenced the results.

Single-blind design
Either the participants or the experimenters collecting the data are unaware of the condition to which participants have been assigned.

Double-blind design
Both participants and experimenters collecting the data are unaware of the condition to which participants have been assigned.

Statistical control
In analyzing study results, the researcher makes a statistical adjustment that accounts for the influence of a specified third variable and allows for the analysis of results with the influence of that third variable eliminated.

Randomization
The researcher arranges the presentation of conditions or stimuli for each participant in a random way to ensure that no one particular order influences the results.

	Condition 1	Condition 2	Condition 3	Condition 4
P1	A	B	C	D
P2	C	D	A	B
P3	B	A	D	C
P4	D	C	B	A

FIGURE 8.4.   Example of a Latin square design.

Counterbalancing
A strategy that ensures control for the order of experimental interventions. The researcher calculates all the possible orders of interventions and confirms even distribution of the different order combinations across participants.

Latin square A type of counterbalancing technique in which each participant receives different experimental conditions in a systematically different order.

Ceiling effect This occurs when a bounded response measurement results in scores that cluster at the upper end (the "ceiling") of the measurement scale because of a constraint in the measure itself.

Floor effect This occurs when a bounded response measurement results in scores that cluster at the lower end (the "floor") of the measurement scale because of a constraint in the measure itself.

An alternative approach to randomization is **counterbalancing**, a more intentional process that ensures control for the order of your experimental interventions. You calculate all the possible orders of your interventions and confirm that you evenly distribute the different order combinations across your participants. This can be safer than pure randomization, especially if you are dealing with a relatively small number of participants where randomization may still result in a skewed distribution of different order combinations.

A particularly well-known type of counterbalancing is a **Latin square** (see Figure 8.4). In this example, each of the four participants receives the four different experimental conditions in a systematically different order. If we wanted to conduct our reading fluency study as a within-subjects design in which each participant was exposed to all the different fluency interventions, a Latin square would ensure that the order in which the interventions were presented would not be a factor. It could not, however, ensure that practice might not have an effect, which could be a larger concern that would lead you to rule out this design. Latin square designs allow you to either control for or test for order effects without implementing every possible order.

Ceiling and Floor Effects

Although they are not considered confounding factors per se, ceiling and floor effects have the potential to derail your experimental design. Both occur when your instrument for data measurement (the measure of your dependent variable) has a constraint such that you end up with a cluster of scores at either end of the instrument's measurement scale. The former, called a **ceiling effect**, occurs when the scores cluster at the upper end of the measurement scale, whereas the latter, a **floor effect**, occurs when the scores cluster at the lower end.

Although ceiling and floor effects are of concern in many areas of research, they frequently occur when developmental researchers use measures that are not appropriate for the given population. Consider the following pair of examples: Gorvine, who teaches college-level statistics, gives his final exam to his daughter's fourth grade class. What is likely to happen? Conversely, what would happen if he gave his college students the elementary math exam from his daughter's class? In the first example, the likely result would be a floor effect (see Figure 8.5), whereas in the second example, the likely result would be a ceiling effect (see Figure 8.6).

Ceiling and floor effects remind researchers that, as much as you need to carefully construct your design to minimize confounds, your measurement tools also must be appropriately sensitive for the purposes for which you will use them.

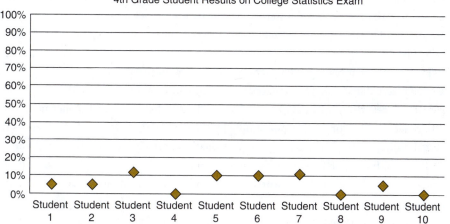

FIGURE 8.5.   Example of a floor effect. All participants perform relatively poorly on the exam, suggesting that the exam was too hard for the students.

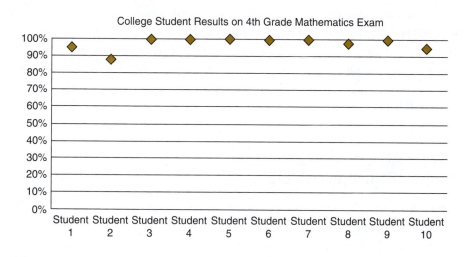

FIGURE 8.6.   Example of a ceiling effect. In this example, all participants performed well, suggesting that the exam was too easy.

WHAT STEELE AND ARONSON FOUND

Throughout this chapter, we have used the classic work of Steele and Aronson (1995) on stereotype threat to demonstrate various aspects of experimental design. We would be remiss in using this example without telling you what the research on stereotype threat found.

Steele and Aronson (1995) aimed to demonstrate that individuals would be at risk to self-confirm a commonly held stereotype about their own group if that stereotype was activated. Steele and Aronson predicted that the creation of a self-evaluative threat in a test-taking situation would disrupt an individual's actual performance on that test. In the 1995 study (the first of many on stereotype threat), they hypothesized that the invocation of a stereotype about intellectual ability would disrupt the performance of black students in particular.

They found that black participants did, in fact, underperform on a set of challenging GRE verbal items when compared with their white counterparts in the threat condition, whereas the nonthreat condition showed no such difference. Furthermore, this difference could not be explained simply by the potential confound of differences in verbal ability because their analysis statistically controlled for participants' verbal SAT scores. Black participants who had done just as well as their white counterparts on the SAT still performed worse on the verbal GRE items under the threat condition.

Work on stereotype threat in recent years has provided additional validation for the concept and has expanded our understanding of the so-called achievement gap in standardized testing. Indeed, evidence in this area suggests that stigmatized groups may suffer in their performance as a function of the stereotypes alone. A meta-analysis confirmed the robustness of the effect with a range of minority groups and women (Nguyen & Ryan, 2008), and a separate meta-analysis showed that advantaged groups can even experience a "stereotype lift" as a consequence of comparisons with a denigrated group (Walton & Cohen, 2003). This work not only illustrates principles of experimental design, but also serves as an excellent example of the applicability of findings from the laboratory to real-world contexts.

ETHICAL CONSIDERATIONS IN EXPERIMENTAL DESIGN

Although we offer a much more extended discussion of ethics in Chapter 2, it is worth noting that experimental designs evoke two specific ethical issues. One involves the placebo/control group and denial of treatment; the other entails the use of confederates and deceit in experimental design.

Placebo/Control Group and Denial of Treatment

Use of a placebo or control group in a study becomes problematic when there is reason to believe that your treatment group will receive some therapeutic benefit. Researchers must grapple with the ethical concerns of denying treatment to the placebo/control group. This is an obvious challenge in research on medications for serious illnesses (e.g., a new cancer drug), but it can also arise in other contexts more directly relevant to psychological research, such as a study focusing on a particular educational technique or a new psychotherapy approach.

In some cases, the ethical challenge of denying the control group the therapeutic benefit can be met by a waitlist approach. Once the initial evaluation has been made, the control group receives the treatment on a delayed schedule, if the intervention proves to be effective. However, in other cases—especially if time is short (i.e., if a patient may not survive the delay)—a waitlist approach may not be sufficient. This concern arose in a study by Zannad et al. (2012), which investigated the development of therapeutic approaches for heart failure. One controversial option is for researchers to stop a clinical trial early for therapeutic benefit. In the example of the heart failure treatment, an investigation of the medication eplerenone for patients with mild heart failure symptoms was halted early after several interim data analyses revealed substantial clinical benefits for those in the treatment group over those in the placebo group (lower incidence of cardiovascular death or hospitalization for heart failure).

There is no singular answer as to how to proceed in such situations, and there is a tension between scientific rigor (which may suggest completing the study on the designated timeline) and the rights of trial participants to receive potentially beneficial treatments, as well as the broader public good of disseminating information about therapeutic benefits as quickly as possible. This tension is succinctly summarized by Zannad et al. (2012): "Maintaining the integrity of the trial and obtaining precise final results must be balanced against the risks for patients who are randomly assigned to an apparently inferior treatment and the need to rapidly disseminate evidence supporting a treatment benefit to the broader community" (p. 300).

In a compelling *New York Times* account that documents the human toll of this debate, Harmon (2010) recounts the story of two cousins, both of whom had a form of lethal skin cancer. One cousin received an experimental drug treatment as part of a clinical trial, and the other received the control treatment (a chemotherapy drug that had been shown to be generally ineffectual). In the end, the cousin who received the experimental drug survived, whereas the cousin in the control treatment succumbed to the cancer.

Concerns about the ethics of experimental research that may have therapeutic benefits—especially in the field of medicine—are hardly new. Indeed, Lewis's (1925) classic novel *Arrowsmith* grappled with concerns that are still the focus of research ethicists. The novel's protagonist, the physician Martin Arrowsmith, struggles with the tension between the medical researchers' desire for fame and the importance of conducting rigorous controlled experiments on the one hand and the ultimate obligations of physicians and researchers for the well-being of their patients on the other.

Confederates and Deceit

Confederate A person who is part of an experiment and plays a specific role in setting up the experimental situation.

The second ethical issue, the use of confederates in experimental studies, relates more broadly to questions around deception of research participants. A **confederate** refers to an actor who is part of an experiment (i.e., they are "in on it") and plays a specific role in setting up the experimental situation. Participants are generally unaware of the role of the confederate, believing the individual to be another participant in the study.

Studies by Stanley Milgram and Seymour Asch provide two classic examples of the use of confederates. In the Milgram study (1963), discussed in more detail in Chapter 2, the confederate pretended to be shocked when the participant flipped switches on a shock generator, going so far as to scream in pain and beg the participant to stop the study. In the Asch (1951) study, the participant was the only real subject in a room full of confederates (seven confederates took part in the original study). Asch was interested in whether an individual would conform to the opinion of the majority, even when the majority was clearly wrong. In the original study, the participant was presented with a card showing three lines of different lengths and asked to choose one that matched a line on another card. After a warm-up period during which the confederates responded accurately, Asch had all of the confederates make a clearly wrong choice prior to the participant's turn to choose. The participant was then asked to state his or her choice. Seventy-five percent of participants provided the inaccurate, conforming response.

Cohen and colleagues (Cohen, Nisbett, Bowdle, & Schwarz, 1996; see Dov Cohen's caption for a *New Yorker* cartoon in Chapter 4) conducted a study in which a confederate pretended to be bumped by the participant and responded with a curse. The researchers were interested in how the participant would respond to the insult and whether this varied by whether the participant grew up in the North or in the South. They found that Southern participants were much more likely than their Northern counterparts to respond aggressively.

This study highlights the risk of such experiments. Participants may be upset or angry about having been deceived and may even behave aggressively toward the confederate and researcher. It is important to consider not only the safety of the participant and research team, but also the impact of deception on the participant's self-worth. For example, tricking participants into acting in a shameful way may have a negative impact on their self-image. When you engage in deception, you are ethically obligated to consider the benefits and risks of the deception and to properly debrief the participant subsequent to the study to ensure that they are left physically and emotionally intact. Most institutional review boards require that you demonstrate that your study cannot be completed without the use of deception.

Practical Tips for Experimental Designs

1. Carefully consider the different conditions for your experimental design and choose the levels of your independent variable with experimental control in mind.

2. In designing your experiment, consider the temporal ordering of your variables (i.e., the hypothesized cause must precede the hypothesized effect).

3. To simplify your analyses and interpretation, consider designing a few discrete experiments that build on one another, rather than conducting a single large experiment with many factors.

4. Ensure the internal validity of your design through random assignment of participants to your different experimental conditions. If you have a small sample size, quasi-random assignment to guarantee distribution of participants across key characteristics may be necessary.

5. Ensure that any control group in your design is equivalent to the intervention group on all possible dimensions other than the intervention itself.

6. Assess whether your topic can be best examined through a between-group or within-group design. Make your decision based on both pragmatic considerations and what is likely to give you the most accurate results.

7. Consider the confounds that may be present in your design. When you can, use strategies to control for these confounds as part of the design or account for them in analyzing your results.

8. Weigh the ethical issues that may be presented by your design, especially if your control group is being denied a potentially beneficial treatment or intervention. Develop a plan to address those ethical limitations and protect the rights of all of your participants.

CHAPTER SUMMARY

Experimental designs offer a potent tool for testing your hypothesis, giving you control over your variables of interest and enabling you to draw conclusions concerning causality. Although experimental designs rate high in internal validity, they sometimes do not fare as well in external validity and, therefore, may not generalize to populations beyond your specific sample of participants. Whether you choose within-subjects, between-subjects, or matched-group designs, it is better to design a few discrete experiments that build on one another than to conduct a large experiment with many factors. Increasing the number of factors that you include in an experiment increases the complexity of the statistical analyses and can make the interpretation of your results more difficult. In our next chapter, we discuss more complicated experimental designs, including factorial designs.

Up for Discussion

1. It is often said that experimental methodology is the "gold standard" approach in psychological research. Why are experimental methods often given such a prized status? Is this status deserved? Are there any circumstances under which you might argue that experimental methods are not the gold standard?

2. One of the major critiques of experimental methods is the assertion that such methods may struggle to achieve high levels of external validity, that is, generalizability of the results to real-world settings. This criticism is rooted in the idea that the artificiality of the experimental setting may mean that findings observed in such a setting do not apply to the rest of the world. Do you agree that this is a weakness of experimental methods? Or do you side more with theorists like Stanovich who have argued that the power to isolate variables is the very strength of experimental methods and that concerns about artificiality are overblown? Are there some circumstances or topics where the artificiality/external validity critique might be of more concern than in others?

3. In experimental research in psychology, between-subjects designs are much more common than within-subjects or matched-group designs. Given some of the substantial methodological and statistical advantages of within-subject and matched-group designs, why do you think that such designs are less frequently used? What are the major barriers to setting up a within-subject or matched-group study? Do you think that the extra effort needed to use these methodological approaches is worth it, given the advantages?

Key Terms

Attention control group, p. 184

Between-subjects (or between-groups) design, p. 187

Blind (blinded) design, p. 196

Carryover effect, p. 190

Ceiling effect, p. 198

Condition, p. 181

Confederate, p. 202

Confounds (or extraneous variables), p. 193

Control group, p. 184

Counterbalancing, p. 198

Demand characteristics, p. 195

Dependent variable, p. 180

Double-blind design, p. 197

Experimental group, p. 184

External validity, p. 182

Extraneous variables (or confounds), p. 193

Fatigue (boredom) effect, p. 190

Floor effect, p. 198

Hawthorne (or observer effect), p. 194

Independent variable, p. 180

Internal validity, p. 182

Latin square, p. 198

Level, p. 181

Matched-group design, p. 191

Observer (or Hawthorne) effect, p. 194

Order effect, p. 190

Placebo effect, p. 184

Quasi-independent variable, p. 183

Quasi-random assignment, p. 187

Random assignment, p. 185

Randomization, p. 197

Repeated-measures (or within-subjects) design, p. 188

Simple order effect, p. 190

Single-blind design, p. 197

Statistical control, p. 197

Stereotype threat, p. 180

Within-subjects (or within-group or repeated measures) design, p. 188

Variations on Experimental Designs

INSIDE RESEARCH: STEVEN ASHER

Professor, Psychology and
Neuroscience, Duke University

My first research project was with children, which was pretty unusual at the time. I was very interested in children and schools, and really wanted to do research in a real-world context. I conducted a study on children's racial preferences in which I tried to replicate one of the famous "Doll Test" studies by Kenneth Clark and Mamie Clark in the 1940s (Clark & Clark, 1947). In 1967, when I collected my thesis data, that study hadn't been replicated. No one had checked again, even after the civil rights movement.

I replicated Clark and Clark's study with black and white middle- and lower-class kids. I was interested in where things had changed since the 1940s. I asked, "Were things better?" and the answer was no. I used puppets and the children were still picking the white puppets. The study was published in the *Journal of Social Issues* (Asher & Allen, 1969).

In my research I've used a variety of methods, including experimental, correlational, and longitudinal. One experimental study I conducted with Sherri Oden (Oden & Asher, 1977) embodied why I went into psychology—to help kids who were really hurting, who lacked friends. We tested our hypothesis that if we could help kids improve their social competence, we could help them make friends. We coached third- and fourth-grade socially isolated children in social skills, whom we placed in one of three separate experimental conditions for four weeks. Children in the first condition received support and instructions in making friends from an adult, played games with peers to practice social skills, and had a post-play review session with an adult. Children in the second condition, called peer-pairing, played the same games with the same peers, but did not receive verbal instruction or review. Those in the third condition (control) were taken out of the classroom with the same peers but played solitary games and did not interact or receive verbal instruction or review. At the end of the four weeks, the first group rated significantly higher on a sociometric rating than the peer-pairing or control groups. This was a study that allowed you to test a hypothesis and run a true experiment on a problem that was important.

The method I choose depends on the question I'm trying to answer. If we were interested in children's thoughts about social situations, then we would typically use some kind of interview method, where we give kids imaginary situations and ask them what they would do in that situation. If we want to study social rejection in students' everyday life in school, we go to the school and observe interactions.

This is what I tell my students about research: Find the topics you're most excited about and pursue those. Make sure you're not doing what someone else wants you to do.

Steven Asher studies social development in childhood, early adolescence, and the college years. In particular, he focuses on how children and college students respond to interpersonal conflict, how social relationships influence feelings of loneliness and belonging, and how dysfunctional beliefs about friendship play a role in college students' adjustment. He recently completed a four-year longitudinal study at Duke University on the connections among social relationships, alcohol use, academic engagement, and feelings of well-being in college.

Research Focus: Peer relations and social competence in childhood and adolescence

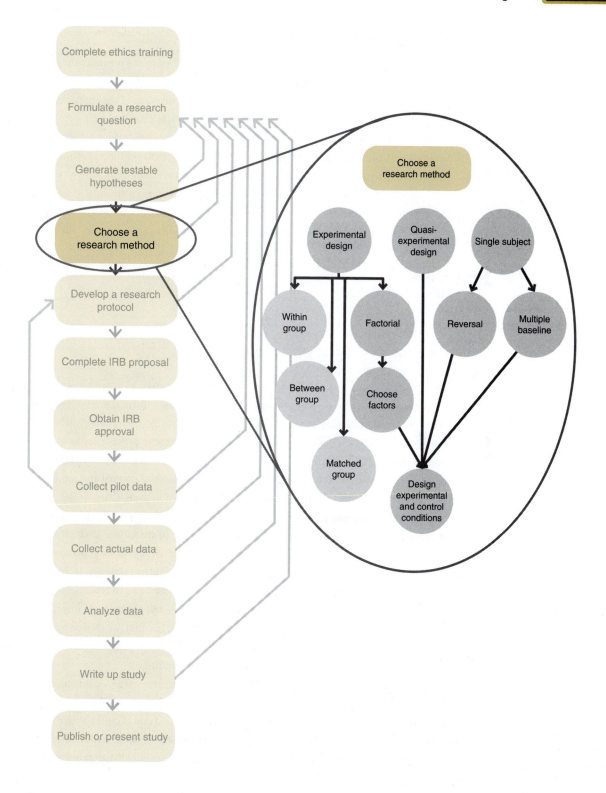

Chapter Abstract

Although the classic experimental design that we described in the previous chapter is often seen as the gold standard in research methodology, a number of variations on such designs also merit attention and discussion. These variations retain some of the core components of experimental methodology, but differ in important ways. We begin the chapter with an investigation of single-case experimental and quasi-experimental designs, which have modifications that allow researchers to preserve some of the benefits of full experimental design while dealing with practical issues. Next, we examine factorial designs, which are modifications of the classic experiment design that enable researchers to consider complex effects that may involve more than a single independent variable. Then, we move on to a discussion of higher-order factorial designs, which permit researchers to consider three or more factors.

SINGLE-CASE EXPERIMENTAL DESIGNS

Single-case experimental design
A design in which experimental methodology (e.g., implementing experimental and control conditions) is applied to a single subject.

The first modification of experimental design is also a variation of within-groups design (see Chapter 8). **Single-case experimental design** uses experimental methodology to focus on only one subject. This design is distinct from case study methodology, which also focuses on one individual, because it uses the same systematic procedures as other experimental designs. Case studies, although they yield rich, useful information that can guide subsequent research, do not have the benefits of experimental control and tend to provide idiosyncratic (i.e., not highly generalizable) information (see Chapter 10). Although single-case experimental designs are not widely used in many areas of psychology, they are still often used in research in clinical psychology and in medicine. Understanding how these designs work provides a good analogue for research design more generally.

Two key characteristics ensure that a single-case experimental design is, in fact, an experiment. First, the researcher sets up the study to manipulate an independent variable (or variables) and to measure how a dependent variable—the measure of interest in your study—responds to changes in the independent variable. Second, this design has the experimental benefit of a controlled comparison, insofar as the individual subject actually serves as his or her own control by participating in all of the conditions.

Building on the authors' well-established obsession with caffeine, imagine that your roommate has struggled with insomnia for the past several months. Observant and considerate roomie that you are, you notice that she often drinks a cup of coffee with dinner at the dining hall. (Assume that you and your roommate always eat dinner around the same time each day, 6:00 p.m.) It occurs to you that her late-day dose of caffeine may be driving her insomnia. You decide to devise an experiment to gather evidence about whether caffeine is, in fact, the cause of her sleep difficulties.

A single-case design gives you a couple of options to examine this situation. The most basic would be a **reversal design**, in which you start by measuring the individual's behavior of interest (the dependent variable) at baseline, that is, before implementing any intervention. You then implement your intervention (the independent variable) and measure the behavior of interest again. Finally, you withdraw the intervention and measure the behavior of interest again.

In the case of your roommate, the dependent variable (the variable you hope to change) is sleep. Although there are several ways to operationalize your friend's insomnia, we will settle on how long it takes her to fall asleep at night. Imagine that the intervention is to have your friend switch from caffeinated to decaf coffee for several weeks. It would be a good idea to not tell your friend when she is drinking caffeinated versus decaf so that she would be blind to the experimental condition (and less likely to have her expectations shape the results, as with a placebo effect).

If the amount of time your friend requires to fall asleep decreases from baseline A, when she drinks regular coffee, to intervention B, when she drinks decaf, and then reverts back to baseline A after she resumes drinking regular coffee, then you have evidence that the intervention worked (see Figure 9.1).

This sort of reversal design is sometimes referred to as an **ABA design**, which underscores the importance of the particular order of baseline–intervention–baseline. Knowing the baseline *first* is crucial for identifying meaningful change. Returning to baseline A is just as critical. Without it, determining the efficacy of the intervention would be impossible. In a sense, the final A of the ABA design serves as a placebo group in a traditional experimental design. If the behavior of interest differs in the final A condition from the initial A condition it may suggest that there is some carryover effect from the intervention.

Figure 9.2 shows hypothetical results of an ABA design for our caffeine study. Following baseline measurements for five days (first A), we see a drop in the amount of time to fall asleep when we remove caffeine (B) and then a rise when we once again have the participant drink caffeinated coffee (second A).

Reversal design (or ABA design) A type of single-case experimental design in which baseline measurements are initially taken (A), a treatment/intervention is then implemented and measurements are taken (B), and finally the treatment/intervention is removed and measurements are taken one last time (A).

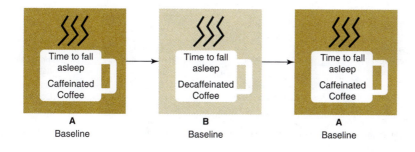

FIGURE 9.1. Example of a reversal design to examine the influence of caffeine consumption on time to fall asleep.

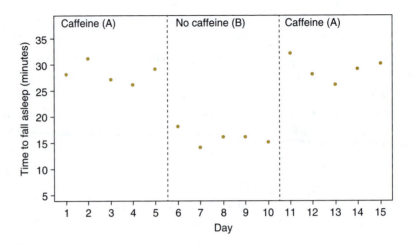

FIGURE 9.2. Hypothetical results for a caffeine study with an ABA design.

ABAB design A type of single-case experimental design that involves a baseline measurement (A), a treatment/intervention measurement (B), a measurement following removal of the treatment/intervention (A), and finally a second treatment/intervention measurement (B).

A second, superior option for the insomnia study would be an **ABAB design**. This design offers the same benefits as a reversal design, but involves more than one iteration of the intervention. Instead, you have at least two rounds of baseline and intervention (hence, ABAB), or as many repetitions as you want. Going beyond a single reversal provides more data (and consequently greater certainty) to establish a difference between the baseline and intervention state—and it ensures that the change from baseline to intervention is not just part of a normal pattern of variation. If your friend takes less time to fall asleep during the intervention phase of the experiment (decaf coffee) the first time around, then you can feel pretty good about the effectiveness of your approach. If your friend takes less time to fall asleep during the decaf coffee intervention for several rounds, then you have even stronger evidence to support your hypothesis that coffee is the culprit (see Figure 9.3).

Figure 9.4 shows what happens when the intervention of decaffeinated coffee is applied a second time (the final B phase). We once again see a drop in the amount of time it takes our participant to fall asleep. These results provide further evidence for the effect of our intervention of administering decaffeinated rather than caffeinated coffee.

An alternative option to either a reversal design or an ABAB design is a **multiple baseline design.** In a reversal or ABAB design, a researcher cannot be certain that the application and/or the amount of intervention is truly the agent for change, but the multiple baseline

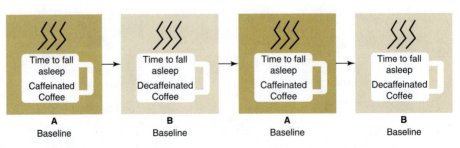

FIGURE 9.3. Example of an ABAB design to examine the influence of caffeine on time to fall asleep.

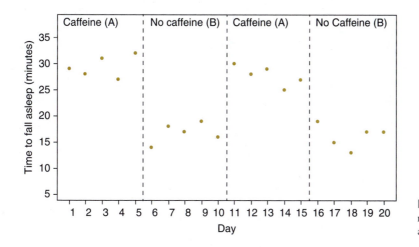

FIGURE 9.4. Hypothetical results for a caffeine study with an ABAB design.

approach uses a varying time schedule that helps determine whether the treatment itself (as opposed to just the passage of time) is actually leading to the change. In our caffeine study, a multiple baseline approach would involve several different variations in the amount of time between the consumption of coffee and your roommate's bedtime; it might also involve different dosages of coffee (both caffeinated and decaffeinated). Systematically looking at the timing and dosage this way would help you to be sure that your roommate's insomnia was not driven by the mere passage of time between coffee consumption and bedtime.

Figure 9.5 shows two sets of hypothetical results for a multiple baseline design in which the first two phases (the first AB pairing) each have a duration of five days and the last two phases each have durations of three days. In Scenario 1, on the one hand, we see a drop in the amount of time to fall asleep each time we switch to no caffeine, regardless of whether the baseline continued for five or three days. In Scenario 2, on the other hand, the drop in amount of time to fall asleep appears to have more to do with the passage of five days' time than with the intervention. That is, we see a drop in times after five days regardless of when the intervention occurs.

Multiple baseline design An approach that uses a varying time schedule to help determine whether the treatment itself is actually leading to the change (as opposed to just the passage of time). In this design, measurements are made at baseline, then after an intervention or treatment, and then again when the intervention is completed or the treatment withdrawn (return to baseline).

Advantages of Single-case Experimental Designs

Single-case designs have a number of benefits. First, a "true" single-case design requires studying only one individual, which is obviously easier and more convenient than assembling a large group of participants. However, if a researcher wishes to go beyond a single individual but still use this type of design, replicating the impact of an experimental manipulation over a number of subjects with repeated single-case designs enhances the validity of the research (Dallery, Cassidy, & Raiff, 2013). In fact, most single-case experimental studies use the design repeatedly, with as many as 20 or more subjects (Dallery, Glenn, & Raiff, 2007; Silverman et al., 1996). The single case also may refer to an individual, a group, or organization depending on the research question.

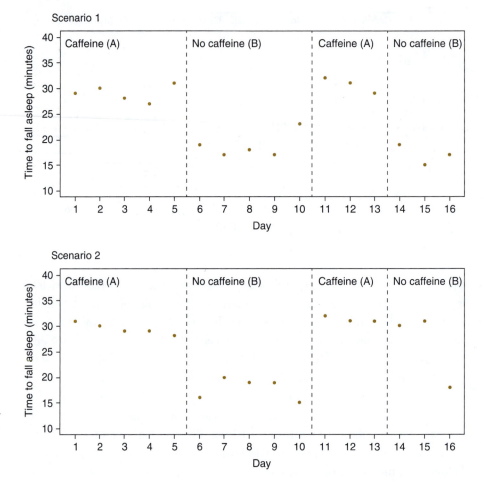

FIGURE 9.5. Hypothetical results for a caffeine study with a multiple baseline design.

This type of design also retains the powerful advantage of experimental control, allowing you to collect evidence to determine causal relationships. For instance, being able to determine the cause of your friend's insomnia (or at least rule out the noncauses) would be enormously useful. Single-case designs are also useful for establishing the preliminary efficacy of specific interventions. Researchers have used these designs to evaluate new technology-based health interventions on the Internet (Dallery et al., 2003) and to provide relatively low-cost, efficient alternatives to randomized clinical trials that evaluate treatments for behaviors such as suicide and self-injury (Rizvi & Nock, 2008).

Disadvantages of Single-case Experimental Designs

Although it is often assumed that single-case experimental designs have limited utility in terms of the generalizability of their findings, this is true mainly of studies that have only a single subject. Because they focus on a single subject, it is difficult (if not impossible) to draw any conclusions about a larger population. However, by replicating the study over a number of subjects, it is possible to produce generalizable research (Raiff & Dallery, 2010). Generalizability is often not the goal of a single-case design, however. As with your insomniac roommate, you would be less interested in broad data supporting the hypothesis that caffeinated coffee contributes to sleep difficulties than in solving your individual friend's sleep problems.

A second disadvantage of single-case experimental designs is that multiple observations and exposures to the intervention itself may affect the responses of your participant, similar to the carryover effect of within-group designs. How much you should be concerned about it depends on what you are studying. Returning to our caffeine example, you probably would not be especially concerned with carryover effects (because it is unlikely that repeated exposure and withdrawal from caffeine itself would create a problem for your findings). But if you were conducting a single-case design on the effects of an antidepressant medication for a single patient, you would be much more concerned. There is the potential for real-life consequences (and some ethical challenges) in having an individual alternate between taking a potentially efficacious medication and then withdrawing from that medication for some increment of time.

Relatedly, a final drawback to these designs relates to ethics. In particular, what are the ethics of withdrawing treatment, which is required to measure the benefits of the treatment approach? If your friend is able to fall asleep more readily after the introduction of decaf coffee, is it problematic to reintroduce caffeinated coffee, knowing that this will likely lead your friend's insomnia to return? Ultimately, the justification for the design is the certainty of the answers that it can provide. In other words, although your friend may temporarily return to her unhappy sleepless state, the benefit of being sure that caffeinated coffee is the culprit exceeds the risk posed by the discomfort.

QUASI-EXPERIMENTAL DESIGNS

Other types of designs possess some elements of experimental control without being full-fledged experiments. A **quasi-experimental design** is partially experimental; in effect, it is a category for a design that does not fit neatly into any other single category. A study can be quasi-experimental when it manipulates an independent variable but perhaps does not have a full set of other experimental controls (such as random assignment). Conversely, a study can be quasi-experimental if it has some experimental controls but does not fully manipulate an independent variable.

A good example of a quasi-experimental design can be found in research from DeLoache, Uttal, and Rosengren (2004), who studied a group of 18- to 30-month-old children to examine a behavior they labeled "scale errors," that is, the failure to correctly use visual information about size when interacting with objects (Figure 9.6). (An example would be a child trying to sit in a dollhouse-size chair.) They speculated that such errors, originally observed

Quasi-experimental design A design that includes some elements of experimental control without being a true experiment.

FIGURE 9.6.
Examples of young children performing scale errors. (a) A 21-month-old attempting to slide down a miniature slide. (b) A 24-month-old attempting to get in a miniature car. (c) A 28-month-old attempting to sit on a miniature chair.

anecdotally, were a result of the combination of a lack of ability to suppress an action that is inappropriate for a given situation and a lack of integration of visual information used to identify objects and to guide actions.

Experimenters brought children into a laboratory playroom with large versions of objects (an indoor slide, a child-size chair, and a toy car). The children were allowed to play freely in the room, although the experimenter made sure they interacted with the large toys at least a couple of times. Children were then taken to an adjacent room to complete a different task. Once the child left the room, the experimenter replaced the large toys with miniature versions, and then the child was returned to the original room and allowed to play. In the second round of play, children were not compelled to play with the miniature objects, but the experimenter did draw the children's attention to the toys if they did not spontaneously interact with them. Researchers then analyzed video data of the play sessions for scale errors to identify when children tried to interact with the miniature toys in the same way they had interacted with the larger versions. Twenty-five of the 54 children committed scale errors on the miniature objects, attempting to slide down the miniature slide, sit in the miniature chair, or climb in the miniature car.

Note that some elements of the study are clearly experimental. For example, children came to a laboratory environment with a standardized collection of toys and objects, and they played in the laboratory playroom for a standardized amount of time. Experimenters interacted with children in a minimal and standardized manner. There was a fair amount of control over the situation, as is typical of an experimental design. Yet, the study lacked other elements of a classic experimental design. For example, there was no random assignment of participants to different conditions (rather, the design was within-subjects, with children exposed to both full-size and miniature furniture conditions) and no explicit manipulation of the independent variable. Instead, children were exposed to different stimuli in a loose sort of fashion. The study was a hybrid of a full-fledged experimental design and an observational design.

Advantages of Quasi-experimental Designs

The primary advantage of a quasi-experimental design is flexibility. Because quasi-experimental methodology does not have as many requirements as a full experimental design, researchers have greater freedom, both in how they set up their methods and in the topics they choose to study. In fact, quasi-experimental research designs offer good options for studying a number of topics that pose practical or ethical constraints preventing full-fledged experimental studies. For example, we may be interested in studying the effects of teacher:student ratio on cognitive gains in elementary school classrooms. Although we would probably not have the opportunity to randomly assign students to classrooms or schools with differing teacher:student ratios (and it would be unscrupulous to do so), we can take advantage of naturally occurring groups to study the effects of the differing ratios. In such a study we might still be able to exercise some elements of experimental control (e.g., standardizing the curriculum and/or the approach of the classroom teachers), while living with the practical constraint of not being able to use true random assignment.

Disadvantages of Quasi-experimental Designs

Although flexibility is a boon, the trade-off in using a quasi-experimental design, rather than a true experimental design, is clear: quasi-experimental designs will not provide as much clarity about cause-and-effect relations as full experimental designs. In fact, the line between a quasi-experimental study and a correlational study can be fuzzy. In the case where a quasi-experimental design has a naturally occurring independent variable, it may even be indistinguishable from a correlational design. However, when quasi-experimental designs involve at least some experimental control, they still allow researchers to reach powerful conclusions.

FACTORIAL DESIGNS

Another set of research designs examines issues that are so complex that they require more than a single independent variable. A **factorial design** refers to any experimental design that has more than one independent variable (also known as a **factor**, i.e., an independent variable manipulated by the researcher).

Before we delve into the particulars, it is worth asking: Why would anyone want to examine more than one independent variable in a single design? A factorial approach offers some major benefits. First, because a factorial design examines multiple independent variables simultaneously, it gives you the ability to look not only at the effects of single variables in isolation, but also at the effects of combinations of variables (i.e., different variables working in tandem). The second, perhaps more compelling reason is the way factorial designs allow us to examine the complexity of the real world in an experimental paradigm. Many of the most interesting questions and hypotheses may involve different variables influencing one another, and if we are really interested in designing experiments with good external validity (i.e., that represent the nuances of the outside world), then factorial designs may give us the best chance of representing this complexity.

Steven Asher:

"You shouldn't confuse or mistake experiments with lab research; you can conduct experiments in a natural environment with description and observation. There have always been people who could understand that you can do experiments in the lab and field, that you can cross boundaries, that you don't have to be wedded to the idea of lab and experiments."

Factorial design An experimental design that has more than one independent variable.

Factor A variable manipulated by the experimenter.

As an example, we might be interested in the extent to which a therapist is directive (provides specific prompts and guidance) versus nondirective and whether one of these therapeutic styles is more likely to generate positive change for clients. In a single-factor design, the independent variable would be therapeutic style (whether the therapist is directive or nondirective) and the dependent variable would be a measure of client change. This could undoubtedly yield interesting findings. Suppose you had reason to believe that the question of when a therapeutic style is most effective depends on certain characteristics of the client, such as openness to the therapeutic process. To examine that question, you would need a factorial design, where one factor would be the therapeutic style and the second factor would be client openness to therapy. In this example, we would want clients who were low or high on openness to therapy. Participants would be randomly assigned to the therapeutic styles in a manner that balanced the number of participants who were high or low on openness to therapy in each of the therapeutic conditions. We will return to this example when we discuss the types of results factorial designs can yield.

Basic Factorial Designs: The 2 × 2

The most basic example of a factorial design is the 2 × 2. But what do we mean when we say "2 × 2"? First, each number refers to a factor, or independent variable. In a 2 × 2 design, we would examine two factors. In a 2 × 2 × 2 design, we would examine three factors (see "Media Matters: Almighty Avatars" for an example of a study that includes a 2 × 2 × 2 design).

Levels The values taken on by an independent variable or factor. For example, in a drug effectiveness study, you may have a factor of "treatment," which has levels of "placebo" and "drug."

Second, each number tells you how many **levels** each factor has. A level refers to a condition within the factor, so that a two-level factor has two possible conditions. In our therapy example, the two levels of the therapeutic style factor would be directive versus nondirective.

To make referencing the factors more convenient, we often assign a letter to each factor. In the 2 × 2 design, we would refer to the first factor (therapeutic style) as factor A and to the second factor (openness to therapy) as factor B.

Cell A combination of one level from each factor in the experiment. The number of cells in a factorial design equals the number of levels of the different factors multiplied by each other. For example, a 2 × 2 design would have 4 cells, whereas a 3 × 4 design would have 12 cells.

The number of conditions in a factorial design—or all the possible combinations of your independent variables—can be easily computed by multiplying the numbers of levels of your different factors. A 2 × 2 design has four possible conditions, computed by multiplying the number of levels of factor A (two) by the number of levels of factor B (two). A 2 × 3 design would have six possible conditions, whereas a 2 × 2 × 2 would have eight. Each condition (often referred to as a **cell**) represents a unique combination of the levels of the independent variables. In the therapeutic style (directive/nondirective) and openness of the client (high/low) example, there are four possible combinations: directive therapy with a high-openness client, directive therapy with a low-openness client, nondirective therapy with a high-openness client, and nondirective therapy with a low-openness client (see Table 9.1).

MEDIA MATTERS

Almighty Avatars

If you had to choose between the fearsome villain Lord Voldemort and the legendary hero Superman as your avatar in a video game, which would you pick? What if someone told you that your choice could potentially affect your behavior in the real world? You might think, "How could that be true? It's just a game!"

Yet, researchers at the University of Illinois, Urbana–Champaign, found that participants who took on the persona of a villain in a video game were more likely to make questionable moral decisions in real life. Those who chose the role of hero were more likely to act in an altruistic way when they were not playing the game (Yoon & Vargas, 2014).

Gunwoo Yoon and Patrick Vargas used factorial design in the study, titled "Know Thy Avatar: The Unintended Effect of Virtual-Self Representation on Behavior," which comprised two experiments. In the first experiment, which was a 3 × 2 design, participants were told they would take two unrelated tests, the first on game usability and the second a blind taste test. The experimenters did not tell them the true nature of the study. They randomly assigned each participant to one of the three avatars of Superman, Voldemort, and a neutral circle. Participants played the video game for five minutes and then answered questions designed to measure their identification with their avatar (Yoon & Vargas, 2014). This is the first factor with three levels.

Next, participants were asked to taste either (delicious) chocolate or (scorching) hot chili sauce and then to determine how much of the food they tasted would be given to another, unknown volunteer (Yoon & Vargas, 2014). This is the second factor with two conditions. The researchers anticipated that participants who played the video game as Superman would be more likely to pick chocolate to give to others, and the Voldemorts would tend to pick hot chili for the unsuspecting volunteers. They were right—heroes were twice as likely to act heroically and the villains villainously (Herbert, 2014). This was after *only five minutes* of playing the game.

In the second experiment, Yoon and Vargas wanted to rule out alternative interpretations of the results (Herbert, 2014). They compared the tendency among those who actually played the game (players) to act like their avatars with those who were asked merely to put themselves in the shoes of Superman or Voldemort, but did not play the game (observers). They found again that playing the game caused participants to act in ways consistent with their avatars and that these effects were stronger in players than in observers (Yoon & Vargas, 2014).

Yoon and Vargas theorized that playing video games results in an "arousal" that incites action in real life and that violent video games could lead players to behave violently in real life. Yoon said he was surprised that participants continued to act in the real world in ways consistent with their avatars' characters even if they said they did not closely identify with them (Channelling Superman, 2014). Yoon and Vargas suggested that creating more heroic avatars for gamers could promote prosocial behavior in general (Vincent, 2014).

The avatar study received a sizeable amount of media attention from outlets such as the *Economist*, the *Harvard Business Review*, Reuters, *Huffington Post*, and the *Independent*, as well as mentions in several psychology blogs (Herbert, 2014; Raven, 2014; Vincent, 2014). The coverage the study received was good; every story correctly cited the researchers' names, the institution where the research took place, and the facts. In addition, reporters refrained from overstating the study's implications, such as proclaiming that people who play violent video games are likely to commit crimes. The *Independent* went the extra step of placing the study in the context of previous research on gamers (Vincent, 2014), which showed that people who play a lot of video games report game images appearing offscreen. The line between "virtual" and "real" grows more blurry by the study.

Table 9.1.   Example of a 2 × 2 factorial design with an independent variable and a participant variable

Factor A	Factor B	
Therapeutic style (independent variable)	Openness to therapy (participant variable)	
	Low openness	High openness
Nondirective	Low openness Clients receive nondirective therapy	High openness Clients receive nondirective therapy
Directive	Low openness Clients receive directive therapy	High openness Clients receive directive therapy

Experimental Independent Variables versus Participant Variables.   It is important to note that each factor can be either a traditional independent variable (i.e., an experimental condition that is systematically varied across participants) or a participant variable (i.e., a characteristic that varies across participants but is not manipulated by the experimenters).

For example, we might have a 2 × 2 design where one independent variable is the therapeutic style (directive versus nondirective) and the second independent variable is the participant's gender. Our first variable (therapeutic style) is a traditional independent variable in the sense that the experimenter manipulates it, whereas the second variable (gender) cannot be assigned experimentally, but is a set characteristic of your participants. Likewise, the openness of the client to therapy might be considered a participant variable (i.e., it is a preexisting characteristic that is not subject to experimental manipulation). Table 9.1

presents a factorial design that contains both an experimental independent variable as one factor (therapeutic style: directive versus nondirective) and a participant variable (openness to therapy: high or low) as a second factor.

Main Effects and Interactions.   A factorial design allows you to look for two different types of effects. The first, called a **main effect**, refers to the effect of a single independent variable—acting alone—on a dependent variable. (This can also be examined in a single-factor experimental design.) If we want to see whether directive or nondirective therapy is more effective in terms of eventual client outcome, we will look at the main effect of therapy style. If we want to see whether high-openness or low-openness individuals do better in therapy, then we will look at the main effect of client openness.

The other type of effect that you can examine is the **interaction**—arguably the raison d'être for factorial methodology. An interaction refers to the joint effect of multiple independent variables considered in combination, or in tandem. Another way of thinking about interaction is that the effect of the factors that interact is more than a simple cumulative effect of those factors. To get past this simple additive notion, looking at an interaction allows a researcher to examine whether the effects of one variable (the first independent variable) on another variable (the dependent variable) are conditional on the other remaining variables.

In our 2×2 therapy study, the interaction question would be whether the effectiveness of therapy type is contingent on the level of openness of the client. (It is not simply that therapy type matters and client openness matters as two separate effects.) Although such an interaction might play out in several different ways, one possibility is that a particular style of therapy works better for one type of client than for another. The combination of directive therapy and low openness, or nondirective therapy and high openness, might yield the best therapeutic outcomes. Examining only main effects in this example would miss the important way in which these two factors operate jointly.

Figure 9.7 illustrates an interaction effect for our hypothetical therapy study. When using directive therapy, there is no difference in the effectiveness of the therapy between high-openness and low-openness individuals. In contrast, when using nondirective therapy, the therapy is considerably more effective for high-openness individuals. Because the effectiveness of the therapies depends on the openness of the client, we say that there is an interaction between therapy and openness with respect to therapeutic effectiveness.

Main effects and interactions can occur in a number of combinations. You can have multiple main effects *and* an interaction; you can have only main effects (or a single main effect) and no interaction; or you can have no main effects but still have an interaction. Consider the five **interaction charts** displayed in Figure 9.8. They represent different combinations of the presence or absence of main and interaction effects, and they are just a sampling of the types of patterns you might see with a 2×2 design. The key takeaway point, however, is that interactions will lead to nonparallel line segments.

Main effect The overall effect of a single factor on the dependent variable, ignoring the effects of or averaging over the levels of all other factors.

Interaction A situation that arises when the effect of one factor (independent variable) on the dependent variable is contingent on the levels of at least one other factor.

Interaction chart A diagram that represents different combinations of the presence or absence of main and interaction effects.

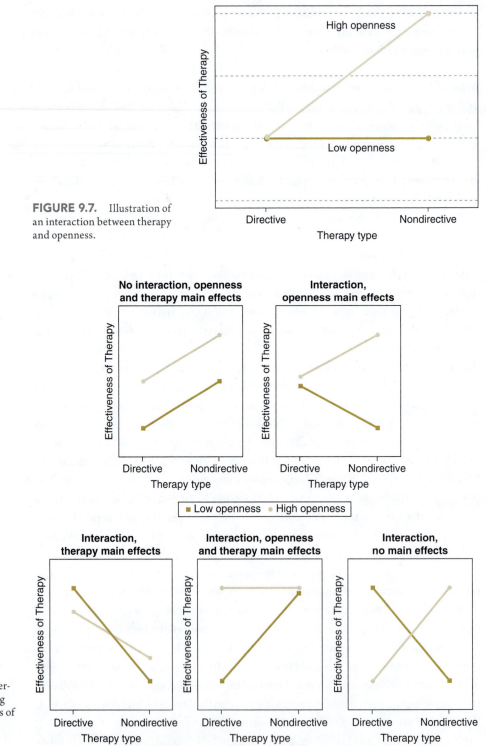

FIGURE 9.7. Illustration of an interaction between therapy and openness.

FIGURE 9.8. Interaction charts showing various combinations of main effects and interactions.

When significant interactions are present, they substantially modify how one might frame (or think about) the importance of the main effect. In our therapy example, a finding of a main effect for client openness would not be particularly meaningful by itself if there was a significant interaction between type of therapy and client openness. An interaction effect (for example, that clients who are more open would do better in nondirective therapy) would tell the more important story. In the next sections, we provide examples of between-subjects, within-subjects, and mixed factorial designs, including a detailed discussion of factorial analyses.

An Example of a Between-subjects Factorial Design. You might recall the classic work of Michelene Chi (1978), originally introduced in Chapter 4. Chi's work serves as an excellent illustration of a between-subjects factorial design. Chi was interested in determining whether age or knowledge (expertise) was the central driving force for cognitive development in the area of memory recall. To determine which was more important, she pitted child chess experts against college-age novices in a task to recall either pieces on a chessboard or a list of numbers. Her study is an example of a 2 × 2 between-subjects factorial design: the first factor, memory task, had two levels—either chess pieces or the number list. The second factor, maturation/expertise, also had two levels—either child expert or adult novice. (You might argue that the second factor is two different factors—age and expertise combined into one.)

Chi's findings indicated that child experts performed at a superior level to adult novices when completing the chessboard task, but adult novices outperformed child experts on the number list task. The findings serve as an elegant example of an interaction, in this case, between type of memory task and age/expertise, such that the memory task that evoked expertise (the chessboard) was enhanced more by the presence of expert knowledge (the young chess experts), whereas the memory task that evoked pure retention (the number list) was enhanced more by the more advanced cognitive development of the older (novice) participants (see Figure 9.9). Chi's work also illustrates both types of independent variables defined previously: an experimental variable (memory task) and a participant variable (maturation/expertise).

An Example of a Within-subjects Factorial Design. In contrast to the between-subjects factorial design, within-subjects factorial designs involve conditions where the groups for each level of a factor are not independent of each other, but rather each group is exposed to each level of the factor. The term "repeated measures" reflects the idea that groups are repeatedly exposed to the different levels of the factor(s). Imagine that you are interested in the effects of caffeine dosage (high or low) on two different memory tasks—a visual recall task (where participants are shown a list of words and then asked to recall as many of them as possible after a set increment of time) and an auditory recall task (where participants are read a list of words and are then asked to recall as many as possible). This

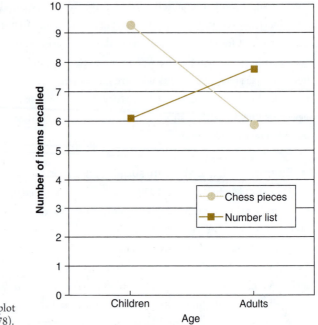

FIGURE 9.9.   Interaction plot of data adapted from Chi (1978).

could be set up as a 2 (high versus low caffeine dosage) × 2 (visual versus auditory memory task) within-subjects design, so that your research subjects participate in both the auditory and the visual recall tasks (probably on different days) and are given both high and low dosages of caffeine in combination with the recall tasks.

An Example of a Mixed Factorial Design.   Given the range of advantages and disadvantages for between-subjects and within-subjects designs, some researchers opt to maximize the benefits of both approaches in a **mixed factorial design** (also called a **mixed design**), an intentional hybrid. In the most basic version of a mixed design, one independent variable is set up as between-subjects and another is set up as within-subjects. In the simplest mixed design (a 2 × 2), participants would be randomly assigned to one of the two conditions of the first independent variable (the between-subjects independent variable), and each participant would then be exposed to both conditions of the second independent variable (the within-subjects independent variable).

Suppose you were interested in studying exposure therapy versus traditional supportive therapy (the "aspirin" of psychotherapy) to treat coulrophobia, the fear of clowns. Exposure therapy is a popular technique for treating phobias; it operates on the premise that exposing someone to a feared stimulus, coupled with techniques for relaxation (deep breathing, imagery, progressive muscle relaxation), can break the association between the stimulus and the fear response (Nowakowski, Rogojanski, & Antony, 2014).

Mixed factorial design (or mixed design) A design that includes both within- and between-subjects factors.

In a mixed design, you would recruit a group of coulrophobic participants and then, as a pretest, measure their level of anxiety during exposure to a clown. After completing the pretest, you would randomly assign your participants to one of two groups: the exposure therapy condition or the supportive psychotherapy condition. Participants would undergo therapy for a predetermined period of time and then would again be measured in a posttest for their level of anxiety during exposure to a clown.

How exactly is this a mixed design? When you look at your two factors, you will note that one (anxiety pre- and posttest) is a within-subjects factor because the subjects participate in all levels (the pre- and posttest levels of anxiety). The other (type of therapy) is a between-subjects factor because the subjects are assigned either to exposure therapy or to supportive psychotherapy. As a researcher, you get the benefits of a "within" comparison (being able look at the change in anxiety within particular individuals) and the benefits of a "between" comparison (being able to compare two different therapies without worrying about the problems of carryover effects). In some ways these designs give you the best of both worlds: they allow for generalization because they are repeated over the randomized groups levels and they also reduce error resulting from individual differences.

Higher-order Factorial Designs

Complexity is an issue that permeates all factorial research designs. In addition to the two-factor designs we have reviewed, researchers may also choose **higher-order factorial designs** (i.e., designs with three or more factors that are considered simultaneously).

Imagine that you are a memory researcher looking at the most effective strategies for short-term retention of a list of nouns. A higher-order factorial design with three independent variables could involve one experimental variable (one of two different memory strategies that participants are asked to use, say either rote rehearsal or imagery) and two different participant variables, gender (male or female) and age (high school, college, middle age).

In this 2 (strategy) × 2 (gender) × 3 (age) design, you would be able to examine a number of research questions, including whether one memory strategy works better than the other, whether one gender has superior memory to the other, and whether one age group does better than the others in terms of memory. Although they all would be valuable main effect questions, the real benefit of the higher-level design is that you could also look at the complex interplay between two, or even all three, of your factors.

For example, a possible two-way interaction between gender and strategy might reveal that imagery is an effective strategy for both men and women, but it gives women in particular a large boost in performance. A possible three-way interaction (gender × strategy × age) could be the enhanced effectiveness of the imagery strategy when used with women, but only for high school and college-age women, with middle-age women showing no benefit of imagery beyond the benefits for men.

Many of the most interesting questions that we want to ask in social science are not univariate sorts of questions—they are not about single causes and single effects. A higher-level

Higher-order factorial design A design that includes more than two independent variables. For example, a 2 × 2 × 2 design, with three factors, two levels for each factor, and eight cells or conditions.

factorial design is best suited to capture the complexity of the world that we live in. As you might recall from Chapter 5, external validity depends on ensuring that your research design captures the reality of your topic. Higher-order factorial designs may be used to increase the external validity of your study.

The downside of such complexity often appears at the level of interpretation. Consider the description of the three-way interaction between strategy, gender, and age as just described—and then imagine adding a fourth or fifth factor into the mix. Conceptualizing a two- or three-factor interaction is challenging enough, and the more complexity you add, the greater the challenge becomes.

PRACTICAL TIPS

Practical Tips for Variations on Experimental Designs

1. Remember that your research design and methods should be determined by your research question and not the fancy, high-tech equipment you might have access to.

2. Carefully consider whether a traditional experimental design can be used to conduct your study and whether a variation from the traditional design is necessary.

3. Learn to recognize and evaluate main effects and interactions in factorial designs.

4. Be wary of using complex factorial designs that result in numerous main effects and interactions. Evaluating more than a three-way interaction effect can be quite difficult.

5. Consider the other tips we provided in Chapter 8 for experimental designs in general.

CHAPTER SUMMARY

After reading this chapter you should have an understanding of the range of variations of experimental designs available to researchers today. Single-case experimental designs often used to evaluate interventions focus on one subject and measure how a dependent variable responds to changes in the independent variable. The most basic single-case design is a reversal, which measures a baseline of behavior before the implementation of any intervention and follows an ABA pattern. An ABAB pattern is an extension of the reversal design because it repeats the intervention, whereas a multiple baseline design examines interventions across varying time intervals. Quasi-experimental designs contain some elements of experimental control but are not completely experimental; in essence, they do not fit into any other category.

Factorial designs require more than a single independent variable. They permit researchers to study the effects of combinations of variables and examine the complexity of the real world in an experimental model. Examples of factorial designs include the basic 2 × 2, mixed, between-subjects, and within-subjects designs. All of these enable researchers to look for a main effect and an interaction among multiple independent variables. In higher-order factorial designs, researchers can simultaneously consider three or more factors.

Up for Discussion

1. In this chapter, we discussed within-subject designs and gave an example in which each participant takes part in "caffeine-free," "moderate-caffeine," and "high-caffeine" conditions. In such a design, we would look at differences among the three conditions on memory task performance. A single-subject experiment also uses a type of within-subjects design, but rather than the "group" effect, we are interested in the effects on individuals. Under what type of situation might the single-subject design provide insights not revealed by a group-level analysis?

2. Suppose you are interested in the effectiveness of a particular teaching method on algebra test scores. You select two algebra classes in which average test scores and the distributions of test scores have been about the same across several tests. You implement the new teaching method in one of these classes and keep the old method in the other class (the control group). You then look at scores for the next two tests to see whether the teaching method leads to increases in scores relative to the control group. This is a quasi-experimental design. What characteristic(s) does it share with a true experimental design? What characteristic(s) keep it from being experimental? What challenges would you face in interpreting the results?

3. Look back at the interaction charts in Figure 9.8. How would you describe the results presented in each of the charts? For example, we described Figure 9.7 as follows:

   When using directive therapy, there is no difference in the effectiveness of the therapy between high-openness and low-openness individuals. In contrast, when using nondirective therapy, the therapy is considerably more effective for high-openness individuals.

Key Terms

ABA design (reversal design), p. 209
ABAB design, p. 210
Cell, p. 216
Factor, p. 215
Factorial design, p. 215
Higher-order factorial design, p. 223

Interaction, p. 219
Interaction charts, p. 219
Levels, p. 216
Main effect, p. 219
Mixed factorial design (mixed design), p. 222
Multiple baseline design, pp. 210, 211

Quasi-experimental design, p. 213
Reversal design (ABA design), p. 209
Single-case experimental design, p. 208

Observation, Case Studies, Archival Research, and Meta-analysis

INSIDE RESEARCH: DAN MCADAMS

Henry Wade Rogers Professor of Psychology, Professor of Human Development and Social Policy, Northwestern University

Psychology is a field that gets at human nature, something I've been interested in forever. It's what I find the most fascinating, and my interest first came from literature. I like fiction, particularly novels—contemporary novels, Victorian novels. They offer great insights across the board. But what psychology does as a science is what fiction can't do—subject characters to empirical tests. Literature can make pronouncements and have great insights about human nature, but to see how relevant and true those pronouncements are you can't beat some sort of research test.

People in their teenage years and 20s are figuring out who they are in life. This has been a big issue in psychology for 100 years. Erik Erikson wrote about it in the most powerful ways. One answer in my work is that people create their identities by constructing broad

227

narratives about themselves that make a coherent identity and a sense of purpose. So I study how life stories create identity for people. Another subject I studied that comes from Erikson is the concept of generativity—adults' concern for promoting the well-being of generations. I developed questionnaires and other measures to assess generativity in midlife, which I highlighted in *The Redemptive Self* (McAdams, 2013).

I use interviews a lot. Most researchers don't because they're labor intensive and have a lot of potential problems. But the main concept I'm researching—a person's life story—is difficult to get at unless you interview somebody. We all have stories of our lives in our minds. My students and I devised a standard life-story interview method in which we ask a set of particular questions. We begin by asking the person to think about his or her life as if it were a book and to divide their life into chapters. Then we zero in on particular scenes in your story—we ask for a high point, low point, and turning point. So people say, "This was the greatest thing that ever happened in my life." They describe in great detail how the event played out, what it meant. At the end, we ask the person to recap, to discern a theme or message. All these questions in the interview require about an hour and a half to two hours to complete. They are recorded and transcribed. We devised methods to analyze the data. We use various rating schemes to assess particular psychological ideas that play out in people's narratives. It's called content analysis.

One of the biggest challenges with this method is getting interrater reliability. Independent raters have to find agreement, but sometimes different coders see it very differently. If you have to rate a person's low point or the extent to which they feel agency—how much control they have in a particular situation—you have to train encoders to look at it the same way.

In my research we're looking for some psychological independent variable and comparing people on that variable, but we do not manipulate that variable. So we don't try to make them depressed or make them feel psychologically healthy and then study them. What we do well is standardize these methods in rigorous ways and develop psychological coding procedures for content analysis.

Dan McAdams explores how individuals use personal life stories to create a sense of identity, unity, and purpose. In *George W. Bush and the Redemptive Dream: A Psychological Portrait* (2011), McAdams applied his narrative psychological approach in a case study of the former president. McAdams has also garnered significant attention for his book *The Redemptive Self: Stories Americans Live By* (2006), which examines the theme in American culture of people who have overcome suffering and pain to lead successful, fulfilling lives.

Research Focus: Narrative psychology, the development of a life-story model of human identity, generativity, and adult development

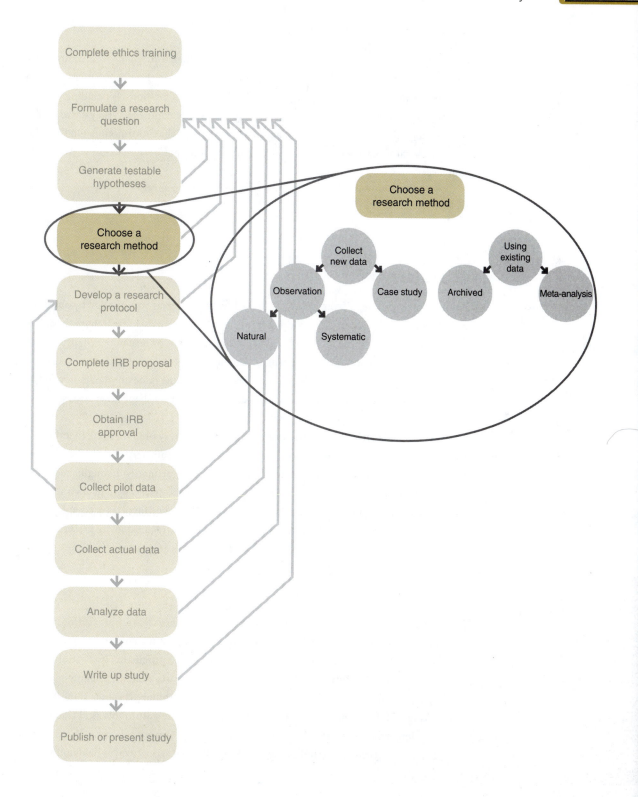

Chapter Abstract

In this chapter, we delve into how to select and use particular methods by examining the strengths and limitations of each one. The designs discussed in this chapter go beyond the pure experimental method. On the one hand, observational methods—including naturalistic and systematic—and case studies involve observing phenomena as they occur. Often, researchers using these two methods systematically record that information. On the other hand, archival research and meta-analysis—two additional designs—use existing data sources.

OBSERVATIONAL METHODS

Observational methods A class of research techniques that involve gathering information by observing phenomena as they occur.

As the name suggests, **observational methods** involve gathering information by observing phenomena as they occur. But what distinguishes observation as a research methodology from just "looking around"? Observational methods, as used by researchers in psychology and other social sciences, are more formal than most people's casual understanding of observation. Observational research methods focus on a specific issue or set of issues and are organized around a specific goal. Particular rules and structures shape how the observation is constructed, depending on the type of technique.

Observational methods can be described in a number of ways, but we think that the most useful distinction involves two broad categories: naturalistic and structured. The boundaries between these categories may seem blurry, but they are primarily distinguished by the extent to which the researcher manipulates the setting. Each comes with its own set of advantages and disadvantages, and choosing one over the other involves a complex set of trade-offs. To illustrate the strengths and challenges of each technique, we present several studies that serve as excellent examples of how researchers can examine the same question with different methods.

Naturalistic Observation

Naturalistic observation Looking at phenomena as they occur (naturally) in the environment.

Considered the most basic type of observational method, **naturalistic observation** involves watching and studying phenomena as they naturally occur in the environment. Although the researcher may be interested in specific behaviors, in naturalistic observation the researcher does little to control the setting. A researcher seeks to describe phenomena by recording them through a variety of techniques, most commonly through some form of note-taking or transcribing. This method has its roots in the anthropological tradition in which an impartial observer or, in those cases where an outsider does not have access, someone who participates in the setting ("participant observation") takes field notes.

Although it is clearly associated with anthropology, naturalistic observations also have their place within psychological research. For example, Piaget's theory of cognitive development (1926, 1952) was based in part on natural observations of his own and other children. He watched his infant son, Laurent, as he moved his body and interacted with the environment, leading Piaget to the concept of the sensorimotor stage of development. "At 0:1 Laurent in his crib with hunger. He is lifted to an almost vertical position. His behavior goes through four sequential phases quite distinct from one another. He begins by calming himself and tries to suck while turning his head from left to right and back again while his hands flourish without direction. Then (second phase) the arms, instead of describing movements of maximum breadth, seem to approach his mouth. Several times each hands brushes his lips; the right hand presses against the child's cheek and clamps it for a few seconds" (Piaget, 1952, pp. 51–52).

Many people assume that researchers conduct naturalistic observation by going into a setting of interest and waiting for something to emerge. There is some merit to this approach because it takes time to become a good observer of behavior. Indeed, William Charlesworth, an ethologist (ethology is the study of animal behavior) who studied child behavior, argued that a new investigator should devote at least 1,000 hours to merely observing children in their natural environments before conducting any formal research. This type of naturalistic observation, if done thoughtfully and carefully, may help researchers better understand how a behavior is influenced by a particular context and more effectively generate ideas for future research. Yet, outside of a few researchers interested in human behavior (Blurton Jones, 1972; Charlesworth, 1986; Eibl-Eibesfeldt, 1967), most current researchers do not devote this much time to developing the skills of broad observation because of constraints on time and resources.

Most naturalistic observations start with a relatively focused area of interest. The researcher's background and theoretical orientation often constrain the focus of the research. For example, a developmental psychologist interested in gender differences may look generally at the activity levels of boys and girls in a playground setting. In contrast, a researcher interested in aggression might focus only on aggressive acts between boys on a playground.

It is important to note that naturalistic observation may involve ethical considerations. For example, if you observe parenting behavior in a grocery store that is verging on abusive, do you maintain your status as impartial observer, or do you have obligations to report the behavior or intervene for the protection of the child? There are no simple formulas for answering this question, but as with other areas of research, ethical dilemmas can arise.

Advantages of Naturalistic Observation.   The benefits of a naturalistic approach are perhaps obvious—and significant. First, naturalistic observation may be the only practical way to study certain topics. Second, by its very definition, naturalistic observation is high in external validity. You may recall from our discussion of validity in Chapter 5 that external validity reflects the extent to which your findings can be generalized to other settings. Because naturalistic observation involves gathering data directly in the settings of interest, we can assume that its external validity is high. This means it may be especially useful for complex, novel settings that would be hard to simulate in a laboratory.

Imagine, for example, that you were interested in observing parenting practices in a grocery store (Fortner-Wood & Henderson, 1997; O'Dougherty, Story, & Stang, 2006), the behavior of parent spectators at youth sport events (Arthur-Banning, Wells, Baker, & Hegreness, 2009; Shields, Bredemeier, LaVoi, & Power, 2005), or family interactions at the dinner table (Messer & Gross, 1995; Moens, Braet, & Soetens, 2007). It is hard to envision any methodology other than direct observation for understanding behavior in these contexts. Similarly, many studies in environmental psychology rely heavily on naturalistic research because they seek to answer questions about how people use physical spaces such as parks or plazas (Kaczynski, Potwarka, & Saelens, 2008; Shores & West, 2010).

Disadvantages of Naturalistic Observation. As powerful as naturalistic observation can be in complicated, unique settings, clearly defined research questions and hypotheses may justify a structured or even experimental approach. In particular, the lack of control in naturalistic observation that is an asset when you are still developing your questions becomes more problematic if you have already defined them. In such cases, something that started as a naturalistic observation may become more structured as definitions become clearer.

A second limitation of naturalistic observation has to do with the timing and frequency of the event(s) that you examine. In the example of prosocial behavior on the playground, you can imagine that you will witness several examples of children helping each other during a single recess if you are patient. In contrast, if you want to observe accidents on the playground and how children react, you may have to spend a lot of time gathering enough data. Natural observation, then, may not be the best choice for studying relatively infrequent behaviors.

A third limitation of naturalistic observation is the problem of bias. When you ask participants to observe within their own context (for instance, parents to observe their own children), you may imagine that they would find being objective difficult. For example, parents may interpret a babbling sound made by a young infant as an actual word that a trained observer would conclude has no meaning. Because this lack of objectivity has no absolute remedy, the best way to address participant observation is to acknowledge this inherent limitation and to provide training and as many guidelines as possible for observers to minimize bias. Depending on your research question, the participant observer may still be the best source of information.

The final challenge with naturalistic observation is embedded in the methodology itself. **Reactivity** occurs when the individuals being observed know they are being watched and, as a result, change their behavior. Although researchers who use observational methods

Reactivity A shift in an observed individual's normal behavior as a result of the knowledge that he/she is being observed.

seem to worry more about this problem than those who use experimental methods, in reality, reactivity is *always* a concern when people in any setting know their behavior is being studied.

There are two imperfect strategies for dealing with reactivity. The first, **concealment,** means exactly what the word suggests: the observer finds some credible way to prevent subjects from knowing they are being watched. Some situations are less challenging than others. For example, if you conduct an observation at a laboratory child-care center (found at many universities) in which classrooms have observation rooms behind one-way mirrors, concealment is a nonissue. But if you are in the open classroom, the challenge to be nonintrusive is much greater. The observer must also contend with the ethics of concealment and gain the consent of the observed. Generally speaking, researchers may observe only public behavior unless they have the consent of participants.

The second strategy for dealing with reactivity is waiting it out. Researchers who regularly conduct naturalistic observations often spend a lot of time in the environment before beginning the formal observation, so that those being observed become used to their presence. This strategy takes advantage of **habituation**, meaning that individuals become accustomed to a novel stimulus in the environment (see Chapter 4), in this case, the experimenter.

Although we can never be certain that observing behavior in a natural setting does not at least subtly change behavior, some research over the years has concluded that reactivity does not always pose a significant threat to the validity of observational research (Christensen & Hazzard, 1983; Jacob, Tennenbaum, Seilhamer, Bargiel, & Sharon, 1994). In fact, recording behavior with technology alone (i.e., a video-recording device) or with a live observer using technology may not affect the level of reactivity (Johnson & Bolstad, 1975). Ultimately, we may have to live with the uncertainty suggested by Craig Gilbert, the producer of the 1973 PBS series, *An American Family*, the first true reality show (see "Media Matters: *An American Family*"). In summing up the effect of filming on the family, Gilbert states, "There is no question that the presence of our camera crews and equipment had an effect on the Louds, one which is impossible to evaluate" (PBS Video, 2013). Although we still have no definitive answers about how being observed affects human behavior, it is interesting to speculate how contemporary reality television culture has shifted our expectations and perceptions of the scrutiny of others.

Example of Naturalistic Observation: Parent and Child Sportsmanship Behavior.

In a study using naturalistic observation, Arthur-Banning et al. (2009) examined the relationship between adult behaviors and the behaviors of third- through sixth-grade athletes in a community basketball league. Trained observers recorded all examples of positive and negative sportsmanship behaviors of parents, coaches, and athletes during 142 games. They worked with a list of examples of positive sportsmanship (e.g., cheering on opponents, checking on an injured player) and negative sportsmanship

Concealment
A strategy for handling participant reactivity by keeping observers or recording equipment hidden from participants.

Habituation
Diminished response to a stimulus that comes about through repeated exposure to that stimulus.

An American Family

Before Snookie, before the *Real Housewives*, before the Kardashians, there was *An American Family*, the first-ever reality television show. Although most people today have never heard of it, the series debuted more than 40 years ago on PBS and drew more than 10 million viewers (Maerz, 2011).

The show broke new ground by televising the daily lives of the Louds, an upper-middle-class family in Santa Barbara, California. Camera crews followed Bill and Pat Loud and their children—Lance, Delilah, Grant, Kevin, and Michele—for seven months, filming 300 hours from May 30 to December 31, 1971. Conceived and directed by the television producer Craig Gilbert, the series debuted in 1973 and consisted of 12 one-hour episodes. The show was shot in cinema vérité, a naturalistic style of filmmaking that has no host, no interviews, and very little voice-over narration. In fact, by today's standards, *An American Family* resembles an exercise in naturalistic observation with its slow pacing, long takes, and lack of background music. As Lance put it later, the footage could be "draggy" (Heffernan, 2011).

This is not to say that the Louds were free of drama. Although early episodes depicted self-conscious conversations around the breakfast table, later episodes eventually revealed—and perhaps exacerbated—painful tensions that ripped the family apart. After 20 years of marriage, Pat asked for a separation from Bill, who had been unfaithful for years. Lance, the eldest, was the first person to announce that he was gay on national television, and the show included scenes from his life in New York. When the show concluded, Bill and Pat divorced, although they reunited in 2001 after Lance died from AIDS-related complications (Galanes, 2013).

Immediately after the series had aired, the Loud children appeared on the Dick Cavett show and discussed the issue of their reactivity to the cameras (*The Dick Cavett Show*, 1973). "I felt that I was pressed for something to say when there was no action or anything, and we'd just be sitting there talking to friends," Delilah said. "Viewing yourself, you think, 'Oh God, say something intelligent, don't just sit there. Because if you're just sitting there and they're filming you, there's nothing you can say, except try to strike up anything, like 'Hey, how was school?'"

Cavett responded, "So you said a lot of stuff just because you need to say something?"

"Yes, you felt pressed for something to say," Delilah agreed.

The Louds and Gilbert were shocked by viewer reaction to the show. Critics attacked the Loud family as "affluent zombies," and many viewers blamed Bill and Pat for seeking publicity and failing to keep their family together. The family has largely kept out of the public eye since, although they did allow the filmmakers of the original series to record Lance's last days, at his insistence.

After *An American Family* aired and Gilbert saw what happened to the Louds, he became deeply depressed for many years. He recalled receiving phone calls from Pat, who was hysterical over the attacks on her family. "That, right there, was the beginning of my own confusion. What have I done? What do I do? I've never resolved it. I didn't know what I had wrought. I still don't" (Winer, 2011).

Gilbert never produced another television show, but reality television has lived on.

(e.g., taunting opponents, yelling at referees, acts of excessive aggression). Prior to data collection, observers received training that involved viewing video examples of sportsmanship behaviors, rating those behaviors, and reaching agreement with other trained observers.

Using this methodology, the researchers found some expected associations: positive spectator and coach behaviors served as predictors of positive athlete behavior, whereas negative spectator behaviors predicted negative athlete behavior. Being able to directly link adult behavior to child athlete behavior has obvious implications for how youth leagues might set policies to maximize sportsmanlike conduct among athletes.

Example of Naturalistic Observation: Child-Care Quality.   One major hurdle in naturalistic observation is that for your data to be meaningful and valid, you must develop a comprehensive coding system to narrow the questions and variables *beforehand*. Benjamin Gorvine's experience with naturalistic observation as part of the National Institute of Child Health and Human Development (NICHD) Study of Early Child Care in the mid-1990s illustrates this challenge.

The NICHD study was an ambitious project designed to examine short- and long-term outcomes for young children in different care arrangements (home day care, center day care, parental care, etc.). A major task for this study was to figure out ways to use observation to systematically measure the characteristics of care being received by children. This was accomplished through a carefully constructed checklist called the Observational Record of Classroom Environment (ORCE). The ORCE listed caregivers' behaviors that had been identified in the research literature as facilitating positive cognitive or socioemotional development in infants and young children (NICHD Early Child Care Research Network, 2003).

Gorvine, who worked as a research assistant on the study, and the other observers received training in both live settings and via video recordings and had to demonstrate a high level of reliability before engaging in actual data collection. This means they had to accurately identify and record behaviors based on the ORCE, and the observations had to match a set of "master codes" with a high level of consistency. Observers were retested every three

Time sampling
The taking of measurements at different time intervals; these intervals may be of fixed length or determined randomly.

to four months to ensure that their observations had not drifted from the original system. The NICHD observers conducted **time sampling**, alternating observation and recording (in 30-second intervals) for a specific time period (in this case 44-minute segments), with the goal of capturing as many caregiving behaviors on the lengthy checklist as possible. ORCE training carefully operationalized and exhaustively illustrated all of the behaviors on the checklist. For example, positive categories of caregiver behavior included "positive physical contact," "responds to vocalization," "asks questions," and "shared positive affect," whereas negative categories included items such as "restricts infant's activities," "uses negative physical actions," and "restricts in physical container" (NICHD Early Child Care Network, 1996).

In Gorvine's experience, reaching adequate proficiency and accuracy in completing observations with this measure involved many months of difficult, often tedious training. As shown in Figure 10.1, observations were focused exclusively on specific, carefully defined caregiver behaviors. In addition, the behaviors of interest were clearly informed by both previous research and theory about what behaviors facilitated (or discouraged) successful development. Although thoughtfully designed naturalistic observations can yield useful data, creating a workable observational scheme and training researchers to use that scheme reliably require a substantial investment of time and effort.

Example of Naturalistic Observation: Scale Errors.   The work of Rosengren, Guitiérrez, Schein, and Anderson (2009) on scale errors provides a final example of the naturalistic observational approach. Recall from Chapter 9 that scale errors are behaviors where children attempt to act on objects that are much too small to accommodate their actions. In their 2009 study, Rosengren, Guitiérrez et al. (2009) recruited a group of mothers of 13- to 21-month-old children and asked the mothers to record scale errors they observed in their children over a 6-month period.

Event sampling
The recording of each occurrence of a particular behavior or event.

This project involved a data collection method called **event sampling,** where researchers count each occurrence of a particular behavior or event. Event sampling is effective when behavior can be easily categorized and when the researcher wishes to record a relatively small number of events.

Participant observation Looking at a behavior of interest by an individual who is part of the environment (for example, a parent making observations of a child during their normal interactions).

The design used by Rosengren, Guitiérrez et al. (2009) is best described as **participant observation,** where an individual who is part of the environment (in this case, a parent) observes the behavior of interest (in this case, scale errors by their children). To address potential observer bias, parents attended a 40-minute training session where experimenters gave a clear definition of scale errors and showed videos of different scale error types. Parents were also asked to rate the occurrences on a scale from "Definitely pretending" to "Definitely serious" and to record details of the child's reactions to their unsuccessful actions. Experimenters discussed the ratings and observations with parents during training to make sure that they understood what was being asked of them and then provided forms and a notebook so parents could record their children's behaviors. Experimenters checked

Form |___| of |___|

ID# |___|___|___|___|___|___|___|

Interviewer ID # |___|___|___|___|

CHILD-CAREGIVER OBSERVATION SYSTEM
CHILD-FOCUSED
OBSERVATION FORM

EXHIBIT 1

CODING PERIOD: *START:* |___|___|:|___|___| AM/PM   END: |___|___|:|___|___| AM/PM   CHILD'S AGE: ____ Years ____ Months

CHECK ALL THAT APPLY	1	2	3	4	5	6	7	8	9	10
A. TYPE OF CAREGIVER TALK (ALL CODES IN "A" ARE FC/FC GROUP EXCEPT RESPONDS)										
Responds to FOCUS CHILD (FC) Talk (CODE TYPE BELOW)										
Language or Communication Requested										
Action Requested										
Reading										
Other Talk/Singing										
B. FC TALKS TO...										
Self or Unknown										
Other Child(ren)										
Direct Provider										
Other Caregivers										
C. FC INTERACTION WITH OR ATTENDING TO...										
Other Child(ren) or Group										
Caregiver										
Material (Played with or explored)										
Television or Video										
None: Wondering/Unoccupied										
D. FC WAS...										
Smiling/Laughing										
Upset/Crying										
Being Hit/Bit/Bothered by Other Child										
Hitting/Biting/Bothered Other Child										
E. THE MAIN CAREGIVER INTERACTING OR ATTEMPTING TO INTERACT WITH FC WAS... CHECK ONE ONLY										
Direct Provider of Care										
Other Caregiver										
All Caregivers Roughly Equal										
No Interaction										

FIGURE 10.1.   Example of time sampling coding form from Boller, Sprachman, and the Early Head Start Research Consortium (1998).

in with parents monthly to ensure they were continuing their observations and to see whether they had any questions.

The study yielded useful observational data indicating that children did, in fact, commit scale errors in their everyday lives, with parents reporting an average of 3.2 scale errors per child over the 6-month period. Parents reported that their children tried to sit in tiny chairs, slide down tiny slides, and lie down on tiny beds. Keep this finding in mind, because we will return to another example of scale error research that shows the value of using converging evidence across observational methods to study an issue.

Structured Observation

In contrast to the open-ended context of naturalistic observations, researchers use more **structured observation** when they are ready to exert greater control over the setting in which the observation occurs. In the example of parent and child sportsmanship discussed previously, there was no attempt to control the setting (youth basketball games) in which the behavior was observed. A study of sportsmanship that observed youth behavior in two different leagues with systemically different rules and policies about parent and athlete behaviors could be termed a structured observation since an element of control over the setting (the rules and norms of the leagues) has now been introduced.

Structured observations are often more useful when you have already identified and carefully defined the phenomenon of interest based on theory, prior research, or some combination of the two and you have some particular ideas about how the phenomenon might vary based on specific factors in the environment. Contrast this with a naturalistic observation approach where a researcher might take notes or otherwise code all occurrences of the behavior(s) of interest without exerting any control over the environment.

Advantages of Structured Observation.   The structured approach can allow for discoveries that would not be possible in naturalistic studies. For example, structured observations can reveal the ways in which specific factors influence the context of interest in your research. If more stringent policies and norms for how parents must behave in a youth league relate to higher levels of athlete sportsmanship, then there is practical information that can be useful for commissioners of youth leagues going forward.

Because well-designed structured observations involve a process of carefully defining the variables of interest and controlling the environment in which these variables occur, they have the potential for *both* high external and construct validity. Construct validity, which refers to the degree to which a variable captures the behavior it is intended to measure, is often a strength of good observational research generally. Structured observations also offer the benefit of high external validity, which refers to the extent to which findings can be generalized to other settings.

Disadvantages of Structured Observation.   The primary disadvantage of structured observation lies within the idea of the structure itself. To effectively use and benefit from the structured observational approach, you must be able to specify the dimensions where the structure will be applied. In the youth sport example, the idea of creating different rule structures is an obvious approach, but depending on what you are observing, it may not be obvious where control should be applied.

Structured observation
In contrast to the open-ended context of naturalistic observations, an approach where researchers exert greater control over the setting in which the observation is occurring.

Example of Structured Observation: Scale Errors. We previously described a naturalistic observational study of scale errors in young children. Rosengren and his colleagues used a more structured observational approach in a different study of the same phenomenon. Rosengren, Schein, and Gutiérrez (2010) observed 24 children between 18 and 29 months of age who attended a laboratory preschool. In contrast to the naturalistic design, in which parents recorded scale errors as they occurred over a period of months, this structured observational design was intended to increase the likelihood of observing scale errors by placing miniature replica toys in the preschool classroom during predetermined observational periods.

Although the findings showed that most young children do, in fact, perform scale errors, the systematic approach in this study revealed substantial individual differences in frequency and persistence of committing scale errors. This study also found that the frequency of such errors decreased during the 10-week observation period. These discoveries would not have been possible in the naturalistic parent report method used previously. This demonstrates that multiple approaches can provide converging evidence, different perspectives, and complementary data on the same issue.

Video Recording

Many observational approaches involve video recordings. Video recording has been used for several decades, and recent technological advances have made it easier and less expensive than ever before. Still, you should consider a number of issues when you record subjects as part of an observational approach.

The first obvious issue is reactivity. The visible presence of recording equipment may increase the artificiality of the observational situation (e.g., participants "acting" for the camera). As we have mentioned, there is no "magic bullet" solution for reactivity. Concealment of the observer or recording device and habituation by the subject to the observational situation are often the best solutions available. Ultimately, as researchers we must wrestle with the uncomfortable truth that we can never truly know the impact of our observation on those being observed.

A second issue relates to the ethics of research. Advances in technology have made concealment easier and more convenient, but privacy concerns are a serious issue (see Figure 10.2). As a general principle, you can record without the consent of those being recorded only if you are observing in a public setting; other types of recording require the explicit consent of those being observed

FIGURE 10.2. Google Glass enables users to covertly film anywhere without other people knowing. However, a number of businesses banned them from their premises because of privacy concerns (Stenovec, 2013), leading Google to scale back on their marketing of this device. Although the privacy issue is serious, tools such as these glasses may someday be useful, allowing observational researchers to effectively capture a wide range of behavior while simultaneously inputting coded data.

(ruling out concealment as an option). In some cases, state and local laws may trump that general principle. For example, the state of Illinois allows for the recording and photography of people in most public places, but not in areas such as restrooms and locker rooms (Illinois Criminal Code, 2012).

Despite the challenges posed by ethics and reactivity, recording equipment offers researchers substantial advantages, including more narrow, focused, and tightly operationalized constructs and variables. In addition, recorded video data can be viewed repeatedly, which diminishes the possibility of missing a key event or behavior. Recording data also facilitates the use of multiple raters to assess levels of agreement on the coding of behaviors. If you code an observation for a child's aggressive act on the playground, you can check that multiple observers also noted and recorded it.

Coding of Observational Data

Coding The process whereby data are categorized to facilitate analysis.

As previously mentioned, video recording offers the possibility of capturing large amounts of information, which can then be coded and examined quantitatively. **Coding** is the broad term referring to the process whereby data are categorized to facilitate analysis. In the context of observations, coding typically refers to taking the rich, qualitative information that is gathered and distilling it into a form that is more readily amenable to statistical examination. Although coding is often discussed in the context of video recording (especially since such recording has become virtually ubiquitous in modern social science research), it is worth noting here that coding more generally refers to a process, which can be applied to any form of observational data.

Specimen record An observation approach where all of the behaviors in a given time period are recorded.

There are three broad types of sampling that relate to the process of coding: specimen record, event sampling, and time sampling. In a **specimen record** approach, all of the behaviors in a given time period are recorded. In this approach, it is essential to have access to technology such as video recording to ensure that nothing that occurs is missed. A specimen record approach when observing children on a playground would mean recording all of the observed behaviors. A somewhat more focused type of approach is reflected in event sampling, where all instances of a specific behavior in a given time period are recorded (previously described in Rosengren et al., 2009). An event sampling approach on that same playground might involve recording all the instances of aggressive behavior between children that occur during a recess period. In a final approach, time sampling (previously described with the ORCE and the NICHD Child Care study), the observer records whether certain behaviors occur during a sample of short time intervals. So, returning to our playground, you might record all instances of aggressive behavior that occur within a predetermined series of 30-second intervals (or note if no such behaviors occur during those intervals).

Regardless of the type of sampling implemented to gather your data, developing a good coding system to deal with those data involves creating a careful set of categories that are both valid and reliable. They must be valid in the sense that they should reflect the concept you are trying to capture, and they must be reliable in that different observers seeing the same thing would agree on the category to use within your coding system. In our playground aggression example, it would be important to develop a clear list of behaviors that would be coded as aggressive (e.g., pushing, hitting, biting), while also making decisions about how coders should define an aggressive act. This can include a complex—but arguably important—set of decisions. For example, should an "accidental" act of aggression still be counted as aggression (e.g., one child absent-mindedly bumps another child), or does the child's behavior need to be intentional? How will verbal aggression be coded? What counts as a discrete act of aggression? If a child punches another child three times in rapid succession, is that three acts of aggression or just one? There are many possible "right" ways to answer these questions in a coding system, but the most important thing for any system is that the answers are clear and well reasoned so that, in the end, you can make the case that your coding system really did capture the behavior(s) of interest and that it did so in a way that was clear and reliable.

CASE STUDIES

Although observational methods make up a substantial proportion of nonexperimental research, another major category for nonexperimental design is the **case study**, a detailed examination of a single individual over a period of time (not to be confused with single-case experimental designs, discussed in Chapter 9). Case studies are most useful for studying rare phenomena and are often the only way to do so. Because they are limited to one person, their primary strength is also their weakness; a case study can provide rich data about that unique circumstance, but it cannot provide information that can necessarily be generalized to other situations or individuals.

Although this lack of generalizability constrains the broad application of findings from case studies, it does not mean that the case study methodology cannot yield useful information. Indeed, case studies can suggest themes and directions for future systematic study. One area in which case studies have been used frequently is in the field of neuropsychology. Case studies in this field have been used to provide new insights into the working of the brain and how particular brain injuries yield changes in specific psychological functions and behaviors (Martin & Allen, 2012). We now turn to two case studies—Nadia, and H.M.—that provide excellent examples of how remarkable individuals or idiosyncratic events can yield amazingly rich, useful case study information.

Drawing Insight from the Exceptional Drawing of Nadia

A well-known case study involves Nadia, a young girl with autism, who at the age of 3½ began to create highly realistic drawings well beyond the ability of most children her age (Selfe, 1977). Lorna Selfe studied Nadia extensively over several years and published her

Dan McAdams:

"We don't manipulate variables. We simply tell people— certain kinds of people, for instance, if we're interested in studying people who have experienced depression, we pre-screen them for those who have scored especially high on tests for depression—to tell their stories. We're looking for some psychological independent variable and comparing people on that variable, but we do not manipulate that variable. So we don't try to make them depressed or make them feel psychologically healthy and then study them."

Case study A detailed examination of a single individual over a period of time.

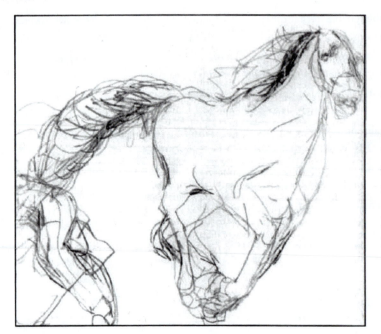

FIGURE 10.3.   Drawing of a horse by Nadia at age 5 (Henley, 1989).

drawings in *Nadia: A Case of Extraordinary Drawing Ability in an Autistic Child.*

What was so intriguing about Nadia was her ability to capture motion and perspective on par with that of gifted artists (see Figure 10.3). Yet, in terms of language and cognitive function, Nadia was severely impaired. At 6½ Nadia could produce two-word utterances (e.g., "good girl," "bed time"), but not longer ones. Because many cognitive evaluations rely heavily on verbal abilities, assessments of her cognitive function are difficult to interpret; however, based on her performance on the Wechsler Intelligence Scale for Children, Nadia was considered below average (Selfe, 1977).

Many researchers have used the case of Nadia and others like hers to examine the relation between autism and giftedness (Drake & Winner, 2011; Henley, 1989; Mottron, Limoges, & Jelenic, 2003; Pariser & Zimmerman, 2004; Selfe, 1977, 2011) and even the neuropsychology of artistic production (Chatterjee, 2004; Ramachandran, 2002). When evaluating case reports such as these, you should consider whether the inferences are based on actual studies of the individual or drawn from reports of the original case study. As in the old game of telephone, data can be transformed in secondary reports.

The Memorable Case of H.M.

One of the most famous (if not *the* most famous) case studies in psychology and neuroscience is that of the patient H.M. (Ogden & Corkin, 1991). At age 10, this individual began suffering minor seizures, which developed into major seizures by the time he was 16. The seizures became so severe that he had difficulty with daily functioning and was unable to work. When H.M. was 27, he and his family agreed to an experimental surgery that they hoped would reduce or eliminate the debilitating seizures. The effects of the surgery were much more dramatic than expected. In addition to effectively reducing the frequency and severity of the seizures, the surgery had the side effect of rendering him unable to remember any recent events (Scoville & Milner, 1957).

Until his death in 2008, when his name was finally revealed, Henry Molaison had likely been studied by every prominent memory researcher and neuroscientist in the world. The many case studies of H.M. were instrumental in determining the hippocampus's role in memory (Scoville & Milner, 1957); the impact of amnesia on everyday functioning (Corkin, 1984, 2002); and the relationship between memory and language processing (MacKay, James, Taylor, & Marian, 2007).

A number of films have captured the challenges faced by H.M. *Memento* (2001) is a psychological thriller involving a killer with anterograde amnesia (similar to that of H.M.) that makes it difficult for him to remember new events. The romantic comedy *50 First Dates* (2004) portrays the difficulty of having a relationship with an individual who has a form of anterograde amnesia. As was the case with H.M., the main character has great trouble remembering new information. Unlike H.M., the movie has a Hollywood ending.

Advantages of Case Studies

If case studies are detailed and extensive, they provide incredibly rich data sets that can address interesting theoretical or applied research questions. Many neuropsychologists have used case studies of individuals with particular lesions or intriguing characteristics to explore different theories of brain function and brain–behavior linkages. In many circumstances, insights obtained from case studies (such as those of Nadia and H.M.) would not likely have been obtained using other types of research methods.

Disadvantages of Case Studies

Although case studies can provide a wealth of data, you must be careful about generalizing too far from any one case study. For example, any brain injury is unique to that individual. Because of the plasticity of the brain and changes in brain structure and function over development, the diversity of experiences pre- and postinjury and any subsequent recovery are also likely unique to that individual (von Hofsten, 1993). In fact, individuals with brain injuries are a more diverse group than individuals without brain injuries. Drawing inferences from a case study to the more general population may not be valid.

Case studies can also include both accurate and inaccurate information, and it may not be easy to determine what information is the most accurate. In the case of Nadia, reports differ greatly on when and why she apparently stopped drawing (at age 8, Pariser & Zimmerman, 2004; or at age 12, Carter, 1999) and whether she lost her exceptional ability or merely the desire to express herself in drawings. Some imply that as she gained language skills, she lost her ability to create the highly realistic drawings that led her to be labeled gifted (Selfe, 2011). Others posit that Nadia lost her ability to produce remarkable drawings because of a combination of therapy, loss of her mother, and aging (Henley, 1989). However, over a number of sessions, Henley (1989) was able to coax more skilled drawings from an older Nadia, who no longer spontaneously produced extraordinary art.

In historical cases or cases studied by only a few researchers, such as Nadia, you should consider both the validity and the reliability of the reports, because they may be incomplete or biased by the researcher's expertise. Although this is arguably the case for all research reports, it is of particular concern for case studies where there is only one observer reporting at a time and only one subject of observation. In the case of Nadia, a cognitive psychologist (Selfe, 2011) drew different conclusions than an art therapist (Henley, 1989).

ARCHIVAL RESEARCH

Archival research
The study of data that have been previously collected.

Archival research refers to studies of data that have been previously collected. Although some institutional review boards will require approval to analyze these records, many place this type of research in the exempt category, meaning that you do not need to obtain institutional review board approval.

Many archival databases are available for use by any researcher interested in analyzing the data. Probably the best-known archival database is the U.S. Census, which provides online tools that enable researchers (or anyone) to examine data from a variety of social, economic, and housing categories. For example, the American Community Survey provides access to data collected on a number of variables, including educational attainment, housing, employment, commuting, language spoken at home, and ancestry (http://www.census.gov/programs-surveys/acs/).

Dan McAdams:

"My research methods are really retro compared to cutting-edge methodologies such as [functional magnetic resonance imaging]. But what we do well is standardize these methods in rigorous ways and develop innovative psychological coding procedures for content analysis. We found new ways to use these old methods."

More relevant to researchers in psychology is the General Social Survey (http://www3.norc.org/GSS+Website/), which contains demographic and attitudinal data. One study published using data from the General Social Survey (Oishi, Kesebir, & Diener, 2011) explored the relation between income inequality and happiness. The researchers tracked levels of average happiness from 1972 to 2008 and found that Americans reported being happier in years when there was less national income inequality than in years with greater inequality.

A more specific database is the Child Language Data Exchange System (http://childes.psy.cmu.edu/), which enables investigators to examine particular research questions that involve everyday language and communication. The website includes an extensive reference list of publications based on this database. For example, Bloom and Wynn (1997) used this database to explore linguistic cues that might aid children in acquiring number words.

Dan McAdams (see "Inside Research" at the start of the chapter) uses existing data to address specific research questions. McAdams has used published writings and mass communication records to create a psychological portrait of the former president, George W.

Bush (McAdams, 2011). Although this type of research may seem simple, conducting it properly requires the creation of detailed coding schemes and long hours poring over transcripts and other existing materials.

Advantages of Archival Research

Using archival or existing data offers several clear advantages. First, researchers do not need to collect the data themselves, which saves substantial time and money. Second, many archives include a large amount of data on a large number of respondents. The nature of the data, if collected and analyzed appropriately, enables the researcher to obtain a relatively large, representative sample. The previously mentioned study by Oishi et al. (2011) reported data on 53,043 respondents ranging in age from 18 to 89 years. Large samples such as this enable investigators to use complex, sophisticated statistical approaches to test different models or theories against one another.

Some databases enable researchers to access data that would be difficult and costly to collect on their own and might be beyond the scope of what an individual researcher could collect in a reasonable amount of time. For instance, the Child Language Data Exchange System includes examples of natural language and communication between children and their parents collected over many years. Although researchers could collect similar data on their own, the pooling of natural language into a database allows access to a much greater amount of data.

Disadvantages of Archival Research

The biggest problem with using existing databases is that they limit your research questions to the specific data that have been collected. The database might not include variables that you want, may include items worded differently than you like (see Chapter 7 on survey construction), or may have been collected on populations that differ from those you wish to study. Databases do add or subtract questions and generally improve the quality of the data they contain over time. However, databases that were established some time ago may contain questions that are no longer viewed as valid assessments of the constructs you are most interested in.

META-ANALYSIS

Meta-analysis is a statistical technique that permits researchers to compare results across a number of studies (Cooper, 2010; Valentine, 2012). Imagine that you were interested in determining whether various personality traits, such as introversion and extroversion, remain relatively stable across the life span. Although you could conduct a longitudinal study that examines this issue in a group of adults, many studies have already examined this topic. For example, Roberts, Walton, and Viechtbauer (2006) report

Meta-analysis
A statistical technique that combines results across a number of studies.

on 92 studies that examined whether personality traits changed with age. Rather than using precious resources to replicate the existing work, a more efficient and effective approach might be to summarize and synthesize this past research. But how would you go about this?

You could evaluate the past research in a number of ways. First, you could read the entire body of research and write a review paper that captures the overall conclusions from the individual reports. This type of review paper is common and can be useful for uncovering gaps in our knowledge and providing directions for new research. However, these reviews often represent the particular bias of the writer and may lack systematic comparison across different studies. For example, the author may emphasize certain results or articles more than others if they fit better with the proposed theory or model.

Second, you could count the studies that show one outcome, the studies that show the opposite outcome, and the studies that are inconclusive. By comparing counts across these three categories, you could argue that past research supports a particular outcome. However, this approach could treat a study examining the stability of the Big 5 personality traits (openness, conscientiousness, extraversion, agreeableness, and neuroticism) among 25 participants as having the same evidentiary power as a study of one or two of these traits among 500 participants.

Effect size Refers to the strength of the relationship between or magnitude of the difference of two variables.

Finally, you could opt for a third and more effective method by conducting a meta-analysis that compares the effect sizes across different studies. The term **effect size** most often refers to the strength of the relationship between or magnitude of the difference of two variables. You can assess effect sizes (Borenstein, 2012) based on a single study or single measure (nonstandardized) or based on converted measures that can be used to compare across studies or measures (standardized).

The correlation coefficient (r) is one type of standardized measure of effect size. Another common measure of effect size used in meta-analyses is the standardized mean difference, which is often labeled as Cohen's d, the d-index, or d (Valentine, 2012). You can obtain this measure by calculating the difference between two means and dividing by the standard deviation of either one of the means or a pooled estimate of the standard deviation. The nature of the research question and the data will determine your choice. (We discuss effect size, the correlation coefficient, and Cohen's d in greater detail in Chapter 13.)

Conducting a meta-analysis requires several key steps. Researchers first must devise a method for locating studies, ideally by casting as wide a net as possible. Roberts et al. (2006) report six methods for locating relevant studies:

1. Review references from earlier meta-analytic studies (Roberts & DelVecchio, 2000).
2. Review additional literature databases created by other authors (Roberts, Robins, Caspi, & Trzesniewski, 2003).

3. Search the PsychLIT and Dissertation Abstracts using relevant keywords (e.g., normative personality change).
4. Review current issues of relevant journals.
5. Create a preliminary list of studies and review the citation lists from each of them.
6. Ask knowledgeable colleagues to review the list for studies that might have been overlooked.

This search approach is logical, extensive, and reported fully in the method section of the paper (Roberts et al., 2006). Depending on your research question and your expertise in a particular field, you may find other methods appropriate. For example, you may want to search more medically oriented articles for some topics by using PubMED rather than PsychLit to find relevant studies.

Finding articles is only the beginning. Next, you must establish some criteria for including particular studies in your meta-analysis. Some articles may be too tangential to your main research question, or the research may not be of sufficiently high quality to include in the analysis. Roberts et al. (2006), in their study of whether personality traits change with age, required that studies meet the following five criteria for inclusion in their meta-analysis:

1. Include dispositional or trait variables, which are relatively consistent across different situations.
2. Measure variables more than once using test–retest intervals of one year or longer.
3. Report information on mean-level change, sample size, and age of participants.
4. Focus on nonclinical samples.
5. Focus on fairly narrow age ranges because one of the study questions addressed the impact of age on personality development.

The approach described here yielded 92 studies; however, some of the articles reported on more than one sample. Thus, the researchers included 113 different samples with a total of more than 50,000 participants. It is important to note that these five criteria were based on the research question. Different research questions will warrant different selection criteria and will yield different numbers of studies.

The next step, which can be done simultaneously with the development of the selection criteria, is selection of variables to be examined. Because Roberts et al. (2006) were interested in the stability of personality traits over the life span, participant age was one of their key variables. Again, they used established criteria to focus their sample, only including studies of subjects over the age of 10. They also made decisions regarding how to group ages into different categories.

Because the research mainly focused on the stability of personality across the life span, the variables of interest were the Big 5 personality traits. Two independent judges categorized the scales used in the individual studies in terms of the Big 5. Roberts et al. (2006) also identified a number of moderators. As you may recall from Chapter 5,

Moderating variable
A variable that influences (but does not causally explain) the direction and/or strength of relationship between two other variables.

moderating variables influence the direction or strength of the relationship between independent and dependent variables. For example, Roberts et al. (2006) identified the sex of the sample (all male, all female, or both) as one moderating variable, because they expected that the stability of personality might vary in these different samples as a function of having only male participants, only female participants, or both. Other potential moderators include ethnicity, education, and socioeconomic status.

In most cases, researchers conducting a meta-analysis will need to make a number of choices about the variables they are examining. For example, researchers must determine how to classify and combine data from different scales that assess either similar or somewhat different variables, how to code data into meaningful categories that can be used in the analysis, and what to do with low-quality or missing data.

Once researchers have coded all the studies, they compute a standardized effect size for each study, which can be done in a variety of ways. Roberts et al. (2006) calculated a standardized effect size by subtracting the mean of the trait scores at the second time point (Time 2) from those obtained at the initial time point (Time 1). They divided the mean value by the standard deviation of the raw scores at the first time point to create a standardized effect size for each study. Then they used the values in a variety of statistical analyses, similar to those involved in analysis of variance and regression analyses (Valentine, 2012; see Chapter 14), to examine the main research question and explore the influence of various moderating variables. Overall, Roberts et al. (2006) found that as people age, they show an increase in measures of social dominance (an aspect of extroversion), conscientiousness, and emotional stability. They did not find that sex had much effect on the relationship between personality traits and development, so there was minimal moderating influence.

Advantages of Meta-analysis

As with archival research, you do not need to collect data to conduct a meta-analysis. Depending on the area of study, you can also obtain a relatively large sample of studies (and participants) in a relatively short period of time. Likely the greatest advantage of meta-analysis is that it provides an objective way to compare findings across many studies, even those that have very different sample sizes or use different types of scales or measures. Also, meta-analysis assigns more weight to studies with larger samples, so they have a greater influence on the overall analysis than studies with relatively small samples. By standardizing effect sizes across different scales or assessments, they provide a measure of the overall effect.

Meta-analysis also enables researchers to examine particular claims to determine whether the overall evidence supports the effectiveness of an intervention or whether personality traits or behaviors change over the life course. Researchers can sift through a large number of studies to determine an overall effect that, without the use of meta-analysis, might have remained unknown because of the variety of results reported in multiple studies.

Disadvantages of Meta-analysis

The quality of a meta-analysis depends on finding high-quality research reports, which may simply be lacking in some areas of interest. In addition, only studies that find statistically significant effects tend to be published. This is known as the **file-drawer problem**, because studies with nonsignificant findings are often tossed into a file and never published. An example of how this problem has led to biased reports in the scientific literature comes from work on bilingualism.

De Bruin, Treccani, and Della Sala (2015) document such a publication bias favoring studies with positive results over those with null results, showing that bilingual individuals have an advantage over monolingual individuals in cognitive "executive control tasks"—those involving memory, attention, planning, monitoring, etc. Through a systematic examination of the research literature, particularly conference presentations (where data are often presented before being submitted for publication), they were able to document that studies showing a bilingual advantage, followed by studies showing mixed results, were more likely to be published than those with null findings (i.e., no differences between bilinguals versus monolinguals). This systematic bias means that if you were conducting research on whether bilingual individuals possessed this cognitive advantage, you would be likely to conclude more of a scientific consensus than actually exists.

One example of a remedy to this problem is a clinical trial registry, such as the registry maintained in the United States at ClinicalTrials.gov, where a comprehensive record of all initiated clinical trials is maintained by the U.S. government. The goal of such a registry is to ensure that all results—not just the positive ones—become part of the public scientific record.

A second remedy is available to you as a conscientious researcher who wishes to minimize the effects of this problem: you can look at the Dissertation Abstracts (http://www.proquest.com/products-services/dissertations/find-a-dissertation.html), a database of all PhD theses, many of which never result in a formal publication. These unpublished sources of data can help researchers estimate the frequency of nonsignificant findings and correct for this in their analysis. Researchers can also use statistical approaches to examine the pattern of data in existing studies to estimate the rate of nonsignificant findings.

Another disadvantage of meta-analysis is that it is time-consuming to search for studies, code each study, and conduct the analysis. Each of these steps requires some expertise and experience with the content area and methods used in meta-analysis, which can make this approach relatively challenging for the beginning researcher.

File-drawer problem
Bias in published research resulting from the issue that studies that do not exhibit statistical significance are less likely to be published (or even submitted for publication) than findings that do exhibit statistical significance.

Practical Tips for Observation, Case Studies, Archival Research, and Meta-analysis

1. Be aware of participant reactivity and techniques for managing it, such as concealment and habituation.

2. Carefully choose a system for coding observational data, taking into account the need for both reliability and validity.

3. Consider using a case study if you come across an individual with an interesting set of behavioral characteristics.

4. Consider archival research if you are looking for a more efficient and more economical approach to answering your research question.

5. Be aware of the file drawer problem; null findings on a particular phenomenon may be underreported.

6. As part of a literature review, consider using meta-analysis to combine and analyze results across multiple studies.

CHAPTER SUMMARY

Depending on your research question, it may be appropriate to use a nonexperimental design, which does not involve experimental controls. You may choose from one of four types: observational, case study, archival research, or meta-analysis. An observational study, whether naturalistic or systematic, offers the widest range of methods. Naturalistic observation will be optimal if you plan to delve into a new area of research, whereas systematic observation will be more effective if you have already operationalized key variables of interest. A case study focuses on an unusual individual and is most common in neuropsychology.

Archival research involves studies of data that have already been collected, particularly large databases such as the U.S. Census. This method provides a ready-made, relatively large, representative sample, but it may limit the scope of your question. Meta-analysis also uses preexisting data and allows you to compare results across studies. It requires locating studies, determining criteria for inclusion into your study, selecting variables, and finding the standardized effect size.

Up for Discussion

1. Suppose you want to study the ways in which people at different job levels interact within a company. How might you use naturalistic observation in your research? How might you use systematic observation? What are the advantages and disadvantages of each observational method?

2. In this chapter, we discussed the case studies of Nadia and H.M. What characteristics of these particular cases allow researchers to make observations and draw conclusions that make valuable contributions to the understanding of human behavior? What characteristics might result in a case study having little or no value in studying behavior?

3. If you are interested in the effects of caffeine on short-term memory, how might you use naturalistic observation, systematic observation, case studies, archival research, and meta-analysis to research these effects?

Key Terms

Archival research, p. 244

Case study, p. 241

Coding, p. 240

Concealment, p. 233

Effect size, p. 246

Event sampling, p. 236

File-drawer problem, p. 249

Habituation, p. 233

Meta-analysis, p. 245

Moderating variable, p. 248

Naturalistic observation, p. 230

Observational methods, p. 230

Participant observation, p. 236

Reactivity, p. 232

Specimen record, p. 240

Structured observation, p. 238

Time sampling, p. 236

Neuroscience Methods

INSIDE RESEARCH: MARIE T. BANICH

Professor, Department of Psychology, and Director, Institute of Cognitive Science, University of Colorado, Boulder

I ended up becoming a psychologist because of my mother's left-handedness. A lot of people in her family are left-handed, and I'm right-handed, and my relatives were always saying things like, "Left-handed people are special and Leonardo da Vinci was a leftie and left-handed people are more creative." I had planned on being a physician, but in college I took several courses in psychology. Even though I went through premed, eventually I decided to pursue a career in psychology and found out that the brains of left-handers are, in fact, different than right-handers. (Basically the division of labor between the two halves of the brain is less severe in left-handed people.) It was in this intersection of biological and psychological issues that I became so interested.

In my research I use functional magnetic resonance imaging (fMRI) and behavioral methods to study the brain. My research has two prongs. One is theoretical, or basic, science. I attempt to understand how brain systems work to support executive function. My other focus is to use that information to try to understand disorders in clinical populations, such as individuals with attention-deficit/hyperactivity disorder and adolescents with severe substance and conduct problems. I like collaboration; a lot of my work is multidisciplinary.

There has been a huge, huge shift in technology from when I went to grad school to where things are today. In the 1980s, researchers were still using x-ray techniques that had been used in World War II to identify brain injuries in soldiers. Doctors could see roughly where the brain damage was and they had to try to correlate that with behavioral symptoms.

That was the state of the world until the early 1990s, when neuroimaging came to the fore. Now we can actually look at the functioning of a normal brain, not a disordered or diseased brain, and look at what parts of the brain are active. Unlike CAT scans or PET scans, MRI techniques don't involve ionizing radiation, so they are safer. I got involved with MRI because Paul Lauterbur, the creator of the MRI, was at the University of Illinois where I was teaching at the time, and other faculty members knew people at the National Institutes of Health who were using this technique. We said, "Wow this is amazing. We have the guy who invented the technique here, and let's start to use it."

Using the MRI totally changed the way I did science. It has been revolutionary. Instead of just collecting data on time and how accurately people do tasks, my research became more technically complicated. It required new knowledge about stats and new computer skills, because analysis of data is very intensive. It was a huge switch and required huge retraining.

Marie T. Banich specializes in the use of brain-imaging techniques to better understand how our brains allow us to direct our attention and actions so that we can prioritize, organize, and target our behavior in a goal-oriented manner—abilities often referred to as executive function. She investigates these issues in normal individuals as well as clinical populations, such as people with attention deficit hyperactivity disorder and adolescents with severe substance and conduct problems. Her studies lie at the vanguard of experimental psychological research.

Research Focus: Using brain-imaging techniques to understand the neural systems that enable us to prioritize, organize, and target our behavior in a goal-oriented manner (i.e., executive functioning)

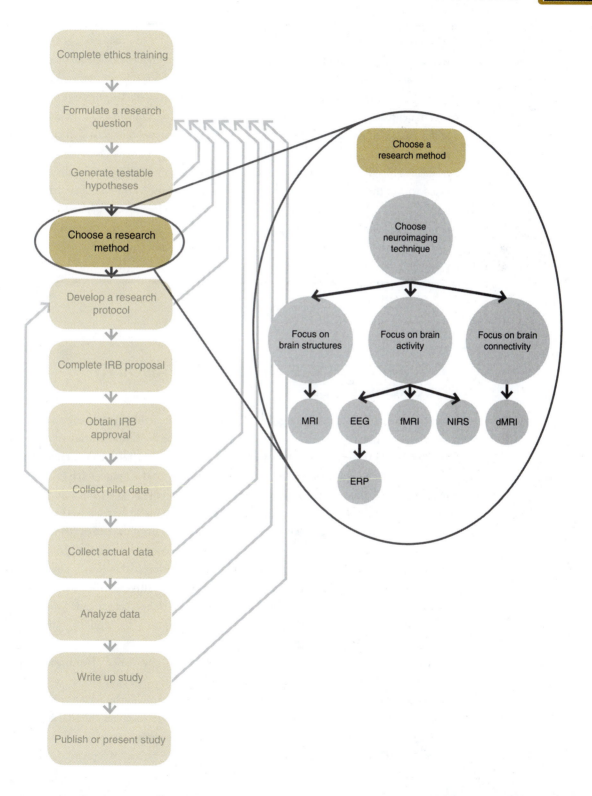

Chapter Abstract

In this chapter, we examine a number of neuroscience techniques that create images of the brain, allowing researchers to conduct studies that were unimaginable only a few decades ago. We present an archival search of PsycINFO that shows a striking upsurge in the mention of neuroscience terms in scholarly journals, reflecting an increase in the use of these techniques. We provide definitions of the techniques most commonly used in psychology: electroencephalography (EEG), magnetic resonance imaging (MRI), functional magnetic resonance imaging (fMRI), and near-infrared spectroscopy (NIRS). Each definition appears within the context of an experimental study to show how researchers harness the power of data obtained through these techniques. We explore several papers whose text is dense with technical language and images, but wading through the information is well worth the struggle. We end with a discussion of ethical concerns in this emerging area of psychological research.

THE IMPORTANCE OF UNDERSTANDING NEUROSCIENCE

Neuropsychology
A term generally used to refer to studies of individuals with brain damage.

Cognitive neuroscience
Research with the goal of furthering a brain-based understanding of mind.

Neuroscience plays an increasingly influential role in the field of psychology. One quick way to assess the impact of neuroscience is to search for the term "neuropsychology" in the PsycINFO database, an extensive online bibliographic database maintained by the American Psychological Association. An older term that is used to refer to studies of brain-damaged patients, **neuropsychology** can be understood as a clinical precursor to the modern study of the brain. Figure 11.1 shows the dramatic increase in the use of the term "neuropsychology" in PsycINFO records from 1980 until the end of 2014.

In the past few years there has also been a growing interest in expanding our understanding of the brain beyond brain-damaged individuals. The effort to develop a brain-based understanding of the mind is more generally referred to as **cognitive neuroscience**. Cognitive neuroscience has not supplanted neuropsychology, but rather has expanded the areas of inquiry. Figure 11.1 shows the dramatic increase in mentions of the term "cognitive neuroscience" in PsycINFO from 1980 to 2015.

If we extend our search to include the terms "fMRI" and "EEG" (two brain-imaging techniques we will discuss later in this chapter) either in the title or anywhere in the text of sources cited in PsycINFO, we see another measure of the growing importance of neuroscience in psychology. Figure 11.2 shows that EEG appeared in either the title or the text about 500 times or more in the years 1980 to 1984 and then rose sharply after the year 2000. In contrast, fMRI was not mentioned in either the title or the text of sources in PsycINFO

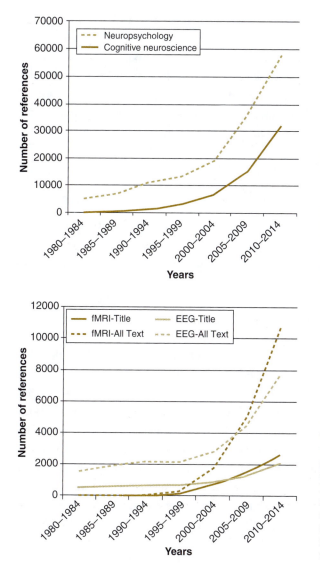

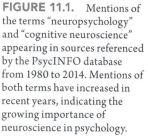

FIGURE 11.1. Mentions of the terms "neuropsychology" and "cognitive neuroscience" appearing in sources referenced by the PsycINFO database from 1980 to 2014. Mentions of both terms have increased in recent years, indicating the growing importance of neuroscience in psychology.

FIGURE 11.2. Mention of the terms "fMRI" or "EEG" in the title or in any text in sources referenced by the PsycINFO database from 1980 to 2014. Mentions of both terms have increased in recent years, with fMRI overtaking EEG, further indicating the growing importance of neuroscience techniques in psychology.

until 1990. However, use of the term increased rapidly after the year 2000; from 2010 to 2014 there were more than 10,000 references to fMRI. References to fMRI begin to surpass those of EEG somewhere around 2005, suggesting that use of this imaging technique was adopted at a faster rate.

Taken together, the data shown in Figures 11.1 and 11.2 suggest that cognitive neuroscience has assumed a major role in the field of psychology. Further evidence of the growing use of imaging can be found in a 2008 paper in *Current Directions in Psychological Science* titled "Neuroimaging as a New Tool in the Toolbox of Psychological Science" (Cacioppo, Berntson, & Nussbaum, 2008).

Understanding basic cognitive neuroscience research methods will help you evaluate claims made by researchers and those found in the mainstream media. Do not assume, however, that just because researchers use expensive, fancy equipment to examine brain function that all neuroscience research is valid and reliable. Unfortunately, individuals without expertise may be more likely to rate explanations that rely on neuroscience data as more satisfying than explanations without any neuroscience data—even when the neuroscience is completely irrelevant to the explanation (Weisberg, Keil, Goodstein, Rawson, & Gray, 2008).

NEUROIMAGING TECHNIQUES

Techniques that provide images of brain structures and measure neural activation rely on a range of technologies, from powerful magnets, to electrical sensors, to optical fibers. Table 11.1 lists a number of different technologies used in cognitive neuroscience with brief descriptions of how they work and some advantages and disadvantages of each method. Neuroscience technologies give researchers unprecedented views into the functioning of the human brain, but they are expensive, require specialized equipment, and result in large amounts of complex data that can be challenging to analyze.

We focus on EEG, MRI, fMRI, diffusion MRI, and NIRS because these are the most commonly used neuroimaging techniques in psychology. Few of these techniques are used alone, however; many are used to provide complementary information collected with other methods. For example, researchers may use **transcranial magnetic stimulation (TMS)**, a method that causes a small group of neurons to fire in a particular region of the brain, along with EEG, a technique that enables researchers to measure brain activity (see Casarotto et al., 2010). In addition, researchers often combine various neuroscience techniques with the collection of behavioral data. Our goal in providing an overview of these neuroimaging methods is to help you interpret studies and media reports of studies that use various forms of neuroimaging.

Electroencephalography

Researchers use **electroencephalography (EEG)** to measure the electrical activity of the brain. This noninvasive technique involves placing a net of sensors (electrodes) on a participant's head, corresponding to approximate anatomical landmarks (see Figure 11.3). The net is easy to place and remove (generally taking just a few minutes) and permits recording of the brain's electrical activity from more than 100 locations.

EEG data are presented over time so they resemble a set of wave patterns, with each wave representing electrical signals captured from different locations of the scalp. Figure 11.4a shows the location of the electrode array used in one study (Mai et al., 2014). Brain activity is categorized in terms of wave frequency and pattern into five general types: alpha, beta, gamma, theta, and delta (see Figure 11.5). Alpha waves exhibit a regular rhythm at a

Transcranial magnetic stimulation (TMS) A method that uses a strong magnet to cause a small group of neurons to fire in the brain. Used in concert with other neuroimaging techniques, researchers can study the impact of the activation on cognitive function.

Electroencephalography (EEG) A noninvasive technique for measuring brain activity that involves attaching electrodes to a participant's scalp and recording ongoing electrical signals from the brain.

Table 11.1. An overview of techniques used in cognitive neuroscience

Technique	Full Name	Method	Advantages	Disadvantages
EEG	Electroencephalography	Measures electrical activity of the brain	Relatively inexpensive/noninvasive High temporal resolution Subject can move a little Can detect changes at millisecond level	Must attach electrodes to scalp Poor spatial resolution Influenced by intervening tissue
ERP	Event-related potentials	Same as EEG but examines response to single events	(same as above)	(same as above)
MEG	Magnetoencephalography	Measures magnetic fields produced by electrical activity of the brain	Good temporal and spatial resolution Can be used to assess both structure and function/noninvasive Not influenced by intervening tissue	Expensive Subject should not move
CT scans	Computed tomography (also known as CAT, computerized axial tomography)	Uses x-rays to assess structures in brain	Good for examining brain structures Good for detecting lesions/tumors/blood clots	Uses x-rays Does not provide high resolution Not useful for examining ongoing activity
PET scans	Positron emission tomography	Trace amounts of radioactive material are ingested As material decays, positrons are emitted that indicate brain activity	Good for diagnosis Subject can move a little	Expensive Uses radioactive material Poor temporal resolution
MRI	Magnetic resonance imaging (structural)	Large magnet with changing orientations is used to measure neural activity	No radiation Provides details about structures Good for detecting lesions/tumors Mostly used in clinical settings	Expensive Not useful for examining brain activity Subject should not move

(continued)

Table 11.1.   An overview of techniques used in cognitive neuroscience   *(continued)*

Technique	Full Name	Method	Advantages	Disadvantages
Functional	Functional magnetic resonance imaging	Measures changes in blood oxygenation and flow that occur in response to neural activity	Can provide highly detailed activation maps of the brain Good spatial resolution	Expensive/poor temporal resolution Subject should not move Very noisy
Diffusion MRI	Diffusion magnetic resonance imaging	Measures motion of water protons throughout the brain	Useful for early detection and assessment of stroke, tumor, and neurodegenerative disease Provides information about connectivity within and between brain regions	Expensive Subject should not move Very noisy
NIRS	Near-infrared spectroscopy	Near-infrared light shined through the skull—Light diffraction pattern is used to measure blood oxygenation levels	Participants can move, sit, or stand	Influenced by intervening tissue
TMS	Transcranial magnetic stimulation	Large magnetic coil placed against head—creates weak electrical currents that stimulate targeted brain region	Can be used to measure both activity and function of specific brain regions High spatial and temporal resolution Stimulate reversible lesions in intact brains Can link activation and behavior	Has caused seizures in patients but not normal volunteers Noisy Only regions on the cortical surface can be stimulated

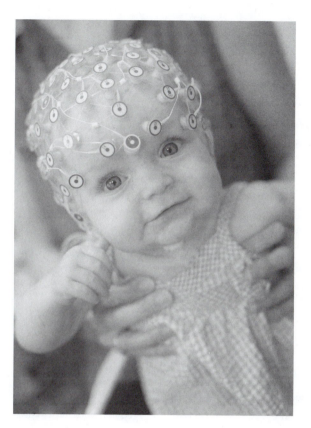

FIGURE 11.3. A child with electrodes attached to measure EEG. This is a noninvasive technique; the electrodes are attached to an elastic net that is placed on the infant's head.

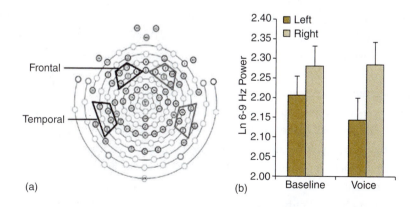
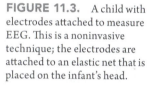

FIGURE 11.4. (a) Layout of electrode array and (b) mean electrical activity at baseline and when infants were hearing a voice. *Reduced* power actually indicates *increased* cortical activity, so in (b), the lower bar for the voice condition indicates higher cortical activity. From Mai et al. (2014).

EEG and States of Arousal

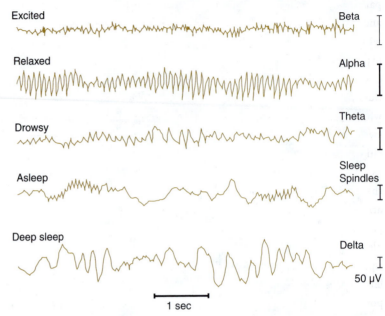

FIGURE 11.5. An example of the different brain waveforms. Alpha waves occur when adults are awake but not actively engaged in mental processing. Beta waves occur when individuals are awake and engaged in conscious processing. Gamma waves are thought to be involved in abstract reasoning. Theta waves are most common in children and young adults and often appear during daydreaming and sleep. Delta waves occur mostly in young children during sleep.

frequency of 8 to 12 cycles per second. In adults this type of activity occurs when an individual who is awake closes his or her eyes and is not actively engaged in mental processing. Figure 11.4b shows data that indicate increased frontal alpha activity compared with baseline (brain activity during a quiet, restful state) when young infants hear human voices (Mai et al., 2014).

Beta waves are high-frequency (greater than 13 cycles per second) patterns that occur when individuals are awake and engaged in conscious processing. Gamma waves exhibit even higher frequencies (more than 40 cycles per second) and are thought to be involved in higher cognitive functioning, such as abstract reasoning. Theta waves are most common in children and young adults and occur in the frequency range of 4 to 7 cycles per second; they often appear during daydreaming and sleep (Figure 11.5).

Delta waves occur at about 0.5 to 3.5 cycles per second, mostly in young children during sleep. The overall pattern of EEG activity and the five different waveforms change as a function of behavioral state (e.g., asleep, awake), age, cognitive activity (e.g., meditation, active processing), mood, and other factors (e.g., the presence of various drugs such as stimulants). Individual EEG waveforms are quite "noisy," meaning that a consistent pattern is obtained only after many trials are collected and averaged; researchers generally report grand averages, that is, averages across all trials and all subjects.

Although researchers often use EEG to detect abnormal brain activity (indicated by unusual spikes in the waveforms), they also use EEG to monitor changes in response to particular stimuli in what is called the **event-related potential**. With this methodology, participants are shown a stimulus, such as a happy face in a study of reactions to emotions, and the EEG pattern following the event is monitored and compared with a baseline or with the pattern of brain activity following a control event, such as a face with a neutral expression.

One example of a research study using event-related potential is shown by Hillman, Buck, Themanson, Pontifex, and Castelli (2009). These researchers were interested in whether aerobic fitness influences how well children plan, problem solve, reason, and switch between tasks—aspects of **executive control**. They conducted EEG analysis on children who were in good shape (high-fit) and those who were in poor shape (low-fit), as the children performed what is called a **flanker task**. A flanker task is a task that asks the participant to focus on a particular stimulus in the center of a display, such as an arrow or animal facing in one direction, and to ignore other surrounding stimuli. The participant presses a key to indicate the direction the arrow or animal faces. For example, if the target is a cow facing toward the right, the participant should press a key on the right side of the keyboard. If the target faces left, the participant should press a key on the left. In some trials, called **"congruent,"** the target is surrounded by similar items all pointing in the same direction (<<< < <<<). In **"incongruent" trials**, the target is surrounded by similar items facing in the opposite direction (>>> < > >>). Individuals generally respond with longer reaction times and exhibit a different EEG pattern in the incongruent compared with the congruent trials. That is, participants take longer to press the correct key and make more errors (e.g., pressing the wrong key) in incongruent than in congruent trials.

Figure 11.6 shows a typical EEG pattern comparing the brain activity at one scalp location (Fz) for the high- and low-fit children in the Hillman et al. (2009) study. As Figure 11.6 illustrates, the amplitude of the EEG signal was generally higher for the high-fit children. Overall, the results of this study imply that higher levels of physical fitness are associated with better executive control in children.

Event-related potential Brain activity measured in response to a particular stimulus or event using electroencephalography.

Executive control The management of cognitive processes involved in planning, problem solving, reasoning, and switching between tasks.

Flanker task A test that measures attention and inhibitory control by asking the participant to focus on a particular stimulus (<) while ignoring other stimuli surrounding it (>>>> < > >>>>).

Congruent trials In a flanker task, trials where the target and distractor items face in the same direction (<<< < <<<).

Incongruent trials In a flanker task, trials where the target and distractor items face in a different direction (<<< > <<<).

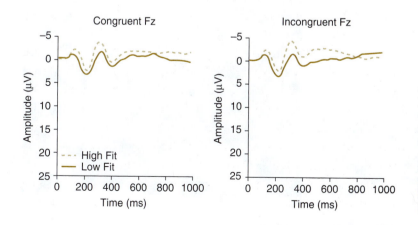

FIGURE 11.6. Examples of ERP data from Hillman, Buck, Themanson, Pontifex, and Castelli (2009) examining brain activity in response to congruent or incongruent trials of the flanker task for high-fit and low-fit children. The amplitude of the EEG signal was generally higher for the high-fit children, implying that higher levels of fitness are associated with better executive control in children.

Magnetic Resonance Imaging

Magnetic resonance imaging (MRI) techniques use powerful magnets to create images of the brain. Although these techniques use the same basic MRI machine, they obtain information related to brain structure, function, or connectivity in different ways.

The most basic type of neuroimaging is structural MRI. You can think of MRI as taking a static image of the brain, much as x-rays are used to take images of bones. Figure 11.7 shows an MRI machine and a typical image of the brain obtained from this technology. The strength of the magnetic field produced by an MRI machine is measured in **Tesla (T)**, with higher numbers indicating a stronger magnet. Most MRI machines used for brain imaging and research in cognitive neuroscience vary in strength from 1 T to 3 T.

MRI technology is based on the magnetic properties of protons in the nuclei of hydrogen atoms that are found throughout the body. These protons can be thought of as tiny magnets that align with strong magnetic fields. In their normal state in the brain (and other parts of the body), protons are spinning in a variety of random orientations. MRI produces a steady magnetic field that causes the protons to align in one direction.

During an MRI scan, the machine produces a **radiofrequency pulse**—a high-wavelength, low-energy electromagnetic wave—that pushes the protons out of alignment. When the pulse stops, the protons return to their steady-state alignment. The return in orientation to

Magnetic resonance imaging (MRI) A neuroimaging technique that uses powerful magnets to create images of anatomical structures in the brain.

Tesla (T) A measure of the strength of a magnetic field produced by a magnet. Higher numbers indicate a stronger magnetic field.

Radiofrequency pulse A short burst of a high-wavelength, low-energy electromagnetic wave that is produced by radiofrequency coils in a magnetic resonance imaging machine to alter the alignment of protons.

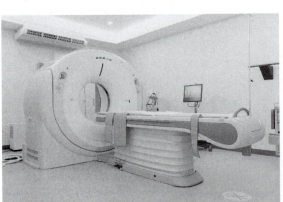

FIGURE 11.7. An MRI scanner and T1-weighted image of the brain.

the steady state following the pulse is referred to as **relaxation. Radiofrequency coils** in the MRI machine create the pulses and also measure energy that is given off as the protons relax. Tissue in different regions of the brain has varying levels of density (and thus the density of hydrogen protons), which influences the rate of relaxation and orientation of the protons (Kulkarni, 2009).

Two basic images can be obtained from MRI: T1-weighted images and T2-weighted images. A **T1-weighted image** is produced when energy is emitted as the protons recover their original magnetization. The T1-weighted image is used to assess anatomical structures in the brain: tissues with high fat-content, such as the white matter of the brain, appear bright, whereas sections of the brain filled with water appear dark. The right panel of Figure 11.7 shows a T1-weighted image. **T2-weighted images** capture energy emitted as excessive spin (rather than magnetization) induced by the radiofrequency pulse returns to the steady state. These images have the opposite contrast to T1 images. Specifically, tissues with high fat content look dark, whereas areas with high water content appear light in shading.

Although MRI is often used to investigate structural problems, such as lesions or other brain abnormalities related to cognitive and behavioral problems, researchers increasingly use this technology to examine changes in brain structures over the life span (Giedd et al., 2015) and to look for structure–function correlations that explain individual differences in performance (Maguire, Woollett, & Spiers, 2006). Figure 11.8 shows developmental patterns for the volume of different regions in the brain; there is considerable variability in the measures across individuals and over age.

Psychology researchers have found fascinating and creative uses for MRI. For example, Van Horn et al. (2012) used MRI to reconstruct the anatomical damage suffered by Phineas Gage, perhaps the most famous brain injury victim in the history of science. Gage's unfortunate fame began when he survived a rock-blasting accident that occurred during his work as a railroad construction foreman in Vermont when he was 25. On September 13, 1848, a tamping iron (3 feet 8 inches long, with a diameter of 1.25 inches) shot completely through his skull, destroying much of his left frontal lobe. Gage survived and recovered so quickly that his original physician, John Harlow, submitted a report to the *Boston Medical and Surgical Journal* (Harlow, 1848) that was met with great skepticism. No one thought anyone could survive such an injury.

Two years later, Henry Bigelow, a professor of surgery at Harvard University, published another report (Bigelow, 1850). Although Bigelow asserted that Gage had "quite recovered" from the accident and had few lasting symptoms, Gage's friends and family noted dramatic changes to his personality (Macmillan, 2000). Gage's case is significant because it was one of the first instances where an accident that had impacted psychological function (in this case, dramatic personality changes) gained national attention. In many ways, this horrible incident made psychological research of greater interest to the general public.

As discussed in Chapter 10, case studies can include both accurate and inaccurate information. In the case of Phineas Gage, newspapers, physicians, and clinicians

Relaxation A measure used with magnetic resonance imaging that assesses the time it takes for protons to return to their original state following a radiofrequency pulse that altered their alignment.

Radiofrequency coils Part of the magnetic resonance imaging machine that is used to produce radiofrequency pulses. These coils are also used to measure the energy given off by protons as they return to the state they were in prior to the radiofrequency pulse.

T1-weighted image A weighted magnetic resonance image that is produced as energy is emitted from the protons as they recover their original magnetization. In these images, tissues with high fat-content, such as the white matter of the brain, appear bright and sections of the brain filled with water appear dark.

T2-weighted image A weighted magnetic resonance image that captures energy emitted as excessive spin induced by the radiofrequency pulse returns to the steady state. In these images, tissues with high fat content look dark, and those areas with high water content appear light in shading.

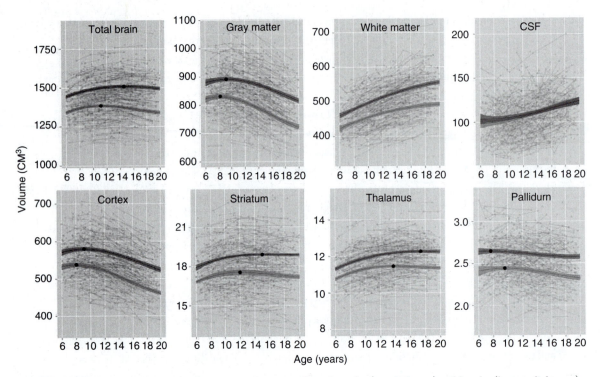

FIGURE 11.8. Raw and best-fit models of the overall pattern of data for males (top, dark gray) and females (bottom, light gray). Bolded dots represent the peak volume achieved for each brain region during ages 6 to 20 years. Data are from Giedd et al. (2015).

Marie Banich:

"I use magnetic resonance imaging in a number of different approaches. I have looked at what part of the brain is involved when people do specific tasks. We have been able to discern that when people are at rest, the parts of the brain that talk to each other when they're doing something also talk to each other even when they're at rest."

provided different accounts about the level of impairment and recovery from the injury (Macmillan, 2000), suggesting some facts were misrepresented or even entirely fabricated. For example, some reports noted that Gage mistreated his wife and children subsequent to the accident (although he was unmarried and did not have any children), whereas other unsubstantiated accounts stated that he engaged in inappropriate sexual behavior or that he liked to show off his wound. Modern neuroscience can shed light on the accuracy of these accounts by pinpointing the regions of the brain that might have been damaged by the rod.

Since Gage's accident, neuropsychologists have often speculated on which regions of his brain were injured or destroyed and how these regions might be responsible for the dramatic changes in his personality that occurred as a result of the accident. When Gage died in 1860, his skull and the iron rod ended up in the Warren Anatomical Museum at the Harvard University School of Medicine. This donation, in combination with two imaging techniques, has enabled neuroscientists to create detailed three-dimensional images of Gage's injury.

First, researchers conducted a computed tomography scan (see Table 11.1) of the skull, which enabled them to reconstruct the extent of damage to bone (Ratiu, Talos, Haker, Liberman, & Everett, 2004). More recently, researchers used this information to create a best-fit trajectory of where the iron rod passed through the skull (Van Horn et al., 2012). These neuroscientists then used MRI data of typical brains to create detailed three-dimensional images of Gage's injury, identifying particular regions likely impacted by the accident (see Figure 11.9). The actual colors of this image are not captured on the page, but the full-color image is available online at http://global.oup .com/us/companion.websites/gorvine.

These models enabled the researchers to infer the brain location of the damage and, in conjunction with knowledge from modern neuroscience, infer subsequent changes in inhibition, planning, and memory that Gage likely experienced (Damasio, Grabowski, Frank, Galaburda, & Damasio, 1994; Van Horn et al., 2012). These later studies provide rich sources of data that allow researchers to compare the case study of Gage with other data sets, enabling even more precise inferences to be drawn from the experiences of a single individual. You can find more information on the unfortunate case of Phineas Gage in books by Macmillan (2000) and Fleischman (2004) and empirical articles by Damasio et al. (1994), Ratiu et al. (2004), and Van Horn et al. (2012).

Functional Magnetic Resonance Imaging

In contrast with MRI, **functional magnetic resonance imaging (fMRI)** enables researchers to obtain images of the brain while the brain is processing information. Using an MRI scanner, this technique measures changes in blood flow—referred to as the **hemodynamic response**—to regions of the brain. In fMRI studies, researchers measure the amount of activation in **voxels**, which are the standard unit of brain volume in three-dimensional displays of the brain. Increased blood flow to particular regions of the brain is associated with increased activity in those locations. Researchers look at a measure known as the **BOLD response** (blood oxygen level dependent). Blood that is oxygenated has different magnetic properties than blood that is deoxygenated. Higher levels of oxygenated blood are found in active brain regions (see "Media Matters: Helping the Blind to See" on page 271).

Although the same scanner used in MRI is used to collect fMRI data, the images produced by this technology are usually colorful, because different colors are used to indicate different levels of activation. Often researchers will contrast participants' activation patterns during different types of cognitive or emotional processing or compare activation

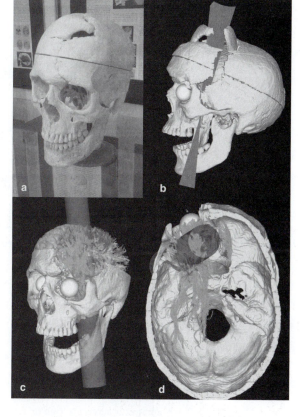

FIGURE 11.9. Three-dimensional modeling of the injury to Phineas Gage. (a) A reconstructed model of Gage's skull, (b) a three-dimensional image based on modeling of the trajectory of the iron rod, and (c) and (d) images of the inserted tissue damages derived from the 3-D modeling (Van Horn et al., 2012). (See Companion Website for color image: http://global .oup.com/us/companion.websites/gorvine).

Functional magnetic resonance imaging (fMRI) A neuroimaging technique that, by measuring changes in blood flow, enables researchers to obtain images of the brain while the brain processes information.

Hemodynamic response
Changes in blood flow in the brain. Increased blood flow to regions of the brain is associated with increased activity in that brain region.

Voxels In functional magnetic resonance imaging, the smallest volume for which it is possible to compute a blood oxygen level–dependent response.

BOLD response
Blood oxygen level–dependent response. Oxygenated blood has different magnetic properties than blood that is deoxygenated. Higher levels of oxygenated blood compared with deoxygenated blood are found in brain regions that are active.

Motion artifacts
Data that are caused by the movement of the participant rather than a response to the stimuli of interest.

patterns while participants perform a cognitive task with patterns observed during a baseline scan.

Although participants must remain quite still during the scan, researchers have developed a visual apparatus that enables participants to view stimuli while in the scanner and respond to stimuli using key presses or a joystick. As long as small movements of the fingers and hand do not result in movement of the participant's head, clear images can be obtained. At this point, any movements in the participant's head lead to blurred images. Researchers, however, have been working on different statistical techniques to identify and "remove" **motion artifacts,** data that are caused by the movement of the participant rather than a response to the stimuli of interest.

Combining a simple behavioral response with brain imaging is one example of a clever design that permits researchers to collect both brain-imaging and behavioral data simultaneously. By designing studies that encourage participants to process particular information, researchers can explore whether particular regions of the brain become activated. The fMRI images show relative degrees of activation compared with some other task, because the brain is always active. Classical fMRI only shows whether a given region is more or less active during one task compared with some other task. Researchers will often compare activation during a task to activation during "rest" periods between tasks; however, there is a whole network of brain areas that is active during rest.

Figure 11.10 shows an fMRI scan obtained by researchers investigating whether social exclusion leads to changes in brain activation (Eisenberger, Lieberman, & Williams, 2003). During this study, participants played a virtual ball-tossing task (Cyberball) while in the scanner. This task involves using a button press or joystick move to "toss" a virtual ball on a computer screen to one or more "other players." These other players are computer generated, but the participant is often told that he or she is playing with other people in a virtual environment. Researchers can manipulate to whom the other players toss the ball. In studies of social exclusion, the other players rarely or never toss the ball to the participant.

Using fMRI in their study of social isolation, Eisenberger and colleagues found that the **anterior cingulate,** a part of the brain associated with a variety of autonomic functions

FIGURE 11.10.
(a) fMRI scan showing increased activity in the anterior cingulate cortex during social exclusion relative to inclusion and (b) scatterplot showing a significant correlation between activation and self-reported social distress (adapted from Eisenberger, Lieberman, & Williams, 2003). (See Companion Website for color image: http://global .oup.com/us/companion .websites/gorvine).

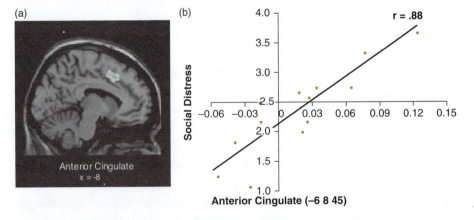

including heart rate and blood pressure, was more active in participants when they were excluded in the ball-tossing game than when they were included. The anterior cingulate is one of the most studied regions of the brain in cognitive neuroscience and has been found to be involved in processing any kind of aversive state. For example, it is active when people make errors, when they experience pain, and when they exert hard mental effort.

The light spot in the left panel of Figure 11.10 is a **data map**, which shows regions where the BOLD response is correlated with social distress. The response appears to be localized in the anterior cingulate. These researchers also obtained a measure of self-reported distress after completing the procedure. The right panel of Figure 11.10 shows the correlation between the activation of the anterior cingulate shown on the left and self-reported social distress. In this study, levels of activation in the anterior cingulate cortex were positively related to participants' reports of distress. Studies such as this one indicate that the anterior cingulate cortex appears to play an important role in emotion regulation.

Diffusion-weighted Imaging

Diffusion-weighted magnetic resonance imaging, also referred to as **diffusion-weighted imaging (DWI),** provides researchers with information about the connections within and across different brain regions. These images are obtained using the same MRI machine used for MRI and fMRI scans; however, DWI is based on the motion of water molecules through tissues in the brain. This water motion is referred to as diffusion, and rates of diffusion differ as a function of the type of brain tissue involved.

DWI enables researchers to measure diffusion in any direction in three-dimensional space. To capture movement, researchers must conduct repeated scans. The data from these repeated scans are then combined to produce a single image that displays the overall pattern of diffusion (Schaefer, Grant, & Gonzales, 2000). Because of differences in tissue density, water diffuses more easily along—rather than through—white matter pathways. Researchers have developed computational techniques that follow the paths of water diffusion and can be used to infer connections in the brain (Allen, Spiegel, Thompson, Pestilli, & Rokers, 2015). Prior to the development of DWI, examining the structure and integrity of neural pathways in the brain was difficult or impossible.

Figure 11.11 shows the steps involved in processing and analyzing diffusion data used by Allen et al. (2015) in an investigation of visual white matter pathways in a group of adults with amblyopia. **Amblyopia** is a developmental visual disorder that arises in young infants and children when inputs to the two eyes are poor or poorly coordinated. Amblyopia leads to impairments in the neural processing of visual information from the affected eye even when the original cause of the poor input is successfully treated. For example, if an infant or young child has a cataract in one eye that disrupts vision, the information from that eye might be suppressed. Even after the cataract is removed, the brain may continue to suppress information from that eye.

Although the steps involved in obtaining information about brain pathways from DWI are quite complex, the overall process shown in Figure 11.12 can be described in a general

Anterior cingulate A region of the brain involved in processing any kind of aversive state—for example, it is active when people make errors, when they experience pain, and when they exert hard mental effort.

Data map A region in an fMRI image that shows BOLD changes correlated with changes in activation pattern.

Diffusion-weighted magnetic resonance imaging (or diffusion-weighted imaging (DWI)) An imaging technique that uses an MRI machine to measure the diffusion of water molecules in different brain regions. Combined with anatomical images and three-dimensional modeling researchers are able to identify pathways in the brain.

Amblyopia A developmental visual disorder that arises when the inputs to the two eyes are not well correlated in young infants and children.

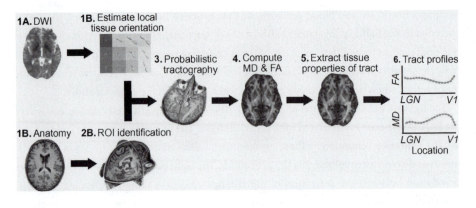

FIGURE 11.11. The diffusion-weighted image is shown in (a) and the T1-weighted image is shown in (b). ROI, region of interest. MD, mean diffusion. FA, fractional anisotropy. LGN, lateral geniculate nucleus in the brain. V1, a visual region in the brain. Adapted from Allen, Spiegel, Thompson, Pestilli, & Rokers (2015). (See Companion Website for color image: http://global.oup .com/us/companion.websites/gorvine).

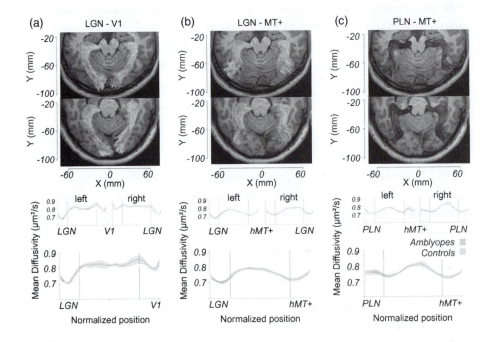

FIGURE 11.12. Visual pathways for an adult with amblyopia (bottom image in a, b, and c) and an age- and gender-matched control (top images in a, b, c). (a) Visualization of the path between the lateral geniculate nucleus (LGN) and vision region (V1); (b) Visualization of path between the lateral geniculate nucleus (LGN) and brain area hMT+; and (c) Visualization of path between the pulvinar nucleus (PLN) region and brain area hMT+. The figures at the bottom indicate that individuals with amblyopia exhibit higher rates of diffusion than control participants, indicating less dense connections between regions of the brains in adults with amblyopia compared with adults without this visual disorder. Adapted from Allen, Spiegel, Thompson, Pestilli, & Rokers (2015). (See Companion Website for color image: http://global.oup.com/us/companion.websites/ gorvine).

Helping the Blind to See

Since the 1990s neuroimaging has allowed psychologists to research a huge range of topics—from the human brain falling in love to how interracial contact affects people's executive functioning (Carey, 2005; Richeson et al., 2003). One of the most fascinating research areas relates to showing how blind people might be able to learn to "see."

Researchers at the Brain and Mind Institute at the University of Western Ontario used fMRI to study four male participants (Thaler, Arnott, & Goodale, 2011). Two of the men were blind and considered experts at echolocation—an ability similar to that of bats and dolphins that enables people to navigate their environments (Chung, 2011). By clicking their tongues or clapping their hands, the two experts at echolocation could create sound waves that bounce off objects and return to their ears, giving them a "picture" of the objects around them. The other two participants were sighted and were included as sex- and age-matched fMRI controls; they did not use echolocation.

Because fMRI requires participants to lie down in a noisy MRI machine, the participants were not able to move and had to wear headphones to protect their ears. This posed a challenge to the researchers, because studying echolocation is not possible while participants are in the MRI machine. To get around this, the researchers used what is called a "passive listening paradigm," which involves capturing sounds just as they were produced in a normal situation. The sounds were captured during a behavioral study done outside of the MRI, where the participants were asked to judge the location of a nearby pole, whether it was convex or concave, and whether it was stationary or moving. The researchers were amazed at the details the echolocators could discern from their environment. "They can tell a

flat thing from convex. They can tell a bush from a wall, a car from a lamp post," Melvyn Goodale, one of the study's authors and the director of the institute, told *CBC News* (Chung, 2011).

To obtain the stimuli used in the fMRI study, the researchers had participants make echolocation clicks and recorded both the clicks and their echoes in the listener's ears. The sounds were collected with special microphones placed in the participants' ears, so that when a participant lay in the MRI machine he would hear the exact same sounds coming through his earphones. This approach enabled the researchers to study how the brains of the two blind echolocators and the matched controls responded to the sounds.

The results revealed how the brains of the two blind echolocators activated the occipital cortex, an area normally involved in vision, to process sound (Lin, 2012). This result suggests that the brains of the blind individuals were organized differently than the control participants. Specifically, regions of the brain devoted to vision in normally sighted individuals were activated by these two echolocators to process auditory information related to spatial environment.

The results, which were published in the journal *PLoS ONE* in 2011, received significant attention from media outlets, including *Men's Journal*, the *New York Times*, the Invisibilia podcast on *National Public Radio*, and *Science* magazine (Finkel, 2011; Lin, 2012; Miller & Spiegel, 2015; Underwood, 2014). Most of the stories focused on one of the echolocators, a man named Daniel Kish who has been blind since he was 13 months old. Kish taught himself how to echolocate as a toddler and has lived his life essentially as an adventurous sighted person—exploring the wilderness alone, biking trails along steep cliffs, climbing trees (Finkel,

2012). The other blind participant, a younger man whom Kish had trained to echolocate, did not lose his sight until he was 14.

The research article includes several fMRI scans of the participants (Thaler et al., 2011). Like most brain scans, they are both striking in appearance and difficult for a nonneuroscientist to understand fully. Herein lies the challenge posed by neuroimaging studies: they are cutting edge and technical, demanding strong attention to detail and often extensive background knowledge of neuroscience to be evaluated. In addition, you must know how the data were collected, like any old-fashioned study.

With the exception of the excessive focus on one participant (fascinating though Kish may be), the media reports seemed generally fair and accurate. The main issue is the generalizability of these results, given the very small number of participants. We do not really know to what extent the majority of blind people would be able to use echolocation to locate and identify objects in the environment. Some readers, however, may assume that all blind people know how to echolocate—or are at least capable of learning how—when that might not be the case. The bottom line: this study holds promise for a potentially transformative new technique; yet, it is still important to view these results with healthy skepticism.

Tractography
A three-dimensional modeling technique used to visualize the neural pathways.

Mean diffusion
A measure of how fast water molecules move, or diffuse, through brain regions.

Fractional anisotropy
A measure of the spatial pattern of diffusion. Basically, it describes whether diffusion is occurring equally in all directions or is greater in one direction or another.

Near-infrared spectroscopy (NIRS)
A neuroimaging technique for assessing brain function; a near-infrared light is shone through the scalp using optical fibers that are placed in a cap and reflected back to detectors in the cap.

way. The top part of Figure 11.12 shows how information from DWI provides information about the orientation of tissue in the brain. This information is combined with anatomical information shown in a T1-weighted image in the lower part of Figure 11.12. The structural information is used to identify regions of interest that are combined with the DWI image.

Tractography, a three-dimensional modeling technique, is then used to identify the neural pathways. Within these pathways, measures of **mean diffusion** rate—how fast water molecules move through the brain regions—and **fractional anisotropy** are obtained. Fractional anisotropy is a measure of the spatial pattern of diffusion. Basically, it describes whether diffusion occurs equally in all directions or is greater in one direction or another. Mean diffusion and fractional anisotropy data enable researchers to map the structural integrity of pathways in the brain. The denser the tissue, the slower the diffusion rates. For example, diffusion rates in healthy white matter are slower than in diseased or underdeveloped white matter.

Figure 11.12 shows the resulting images of the white matter pathways identified by Allen et al. (2015). In the study, adults with amblyopia were compared with a group of adults matched on age and gender, and participants in the control group had normal or corrected-to-normal vision with no history of visual disorders. Results of the analysis of tract profiles suggest that individuals with amblyopia exhibited greater diffusion (higher mean diffusion values) in three of the six visual pathways investigated, as shown in Figure 11.13. The authors suggest that higher rates of diffusion are related to a lower density of axons, less myelination, and less organization of the white matter axons. Overall, the results suggest that early visual problems resulting in amblyopia are related to structural changes in connections in the brain.

Near-infrared Spectroscopy

Although not as common as MRI or fMRI, **near-infrared spectroscopy (NIRS)** is another technique for assessing brain function (Aslin, 2012). Near-infrared light (light that is

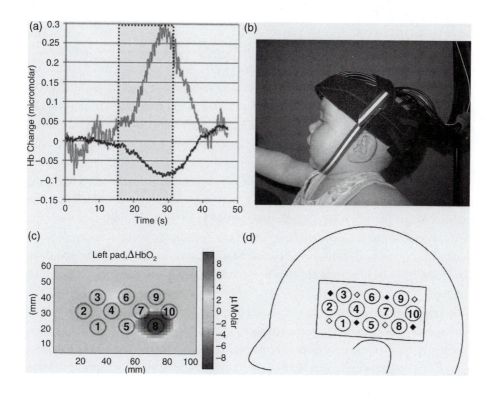

FIGURE 11.13. An overview of near-infrared spectroscopy. The typical hemodynamic response is shown in (a). The upper line shows an increase in oxygenated blood in response to an event and the lower line shows a decrease in deoxygenated blood in response to the event. An infant wearing a cap with optical fibers for projecting near-infrared light into the infant's scalp (b). The highest level of activation in this instance is found in location 8, indicated by the dark smudge in (c). The location of the scalp where the detectors are placed (d). Adapted from Lloyd-Fox, Blasi, & Elwell (2010). (See Companion Website for color image: http://global.oup.com/us/companion.websites/gorvine).

closest to the visible light spectrum) is shone through the scalp using optical fibers that are placed in a cap, and the light is reflected back to detectors in the cap (see Figure 11.13). The detectors measure the amount of light absorbed by oxygenated and deoxygenated blood. When a part of the brain is active, blood flows to that region and can be measured. For example, if an infant is presented with some sort of event that activates his or her brain regions, there is an increase in oxygenated blood and a decrease in deoxygenated blood that occurs in the activated cortical region. NIRS basically measures the same information that fMRI does, but NIRS systems are considerably cheaper. An additional advantage of NIRS is that, unlike fMRI, the participant does not need to keep his or her head perfectly still during the assessment.

ETHICAL ISSUES IN NEUROPSYCHOLOGY

Ethical issues, such as concern for the safety and well-being of participants, are not distinct to the field of neuroscience. However, the rapidly changing technology and information generated provide a number of unique challenges to researchers using neuroimaging techniques. In this section, we discuss three ethical issues related to neuroscience research: safety concerns, the potential discovery of brain anomalies, and subject selection issues.

Safety Concerns

Earlier techniques that enabled researchers to "look" inside participants' heads, such as computed tomography scans, involved the use of x-rays, which exposed participants to radiation. Other techniques, such as positron emission tomography, involved the injection of radioactive glucose, although the radiation levels used in this technique are quite low. In fact, people are exposed to higher levels of radiation every time they fly in a plane. As researchers developed noninvasive techniques for investigating the brain, however, additional safety issues arose.

The debut of MRI, fMRI, and TMS initially raised concerns about the safety of placing participants in magnetic fields and scanning them repeatedly (Farar, 2002). Today, the majority of institutional review boards consider MRI and fMRI of minimal to moderate risk, although at many campuses the review of protocols involving these technologies is handled by biomedical institutional review boards rather than social-behavioral ones. Generally, these technologies are considered safe for use in research, even with young children.

Several cognitive neuroscience techniques (e.g., MRI, fMRI), however, involve powerful magnets. These magnets have the strength to pull all sorts of objects into the magnet, potentially endangering a participant or damaging the equipment. Figure 11.14 shows a patient on a hospital gurney that has been sucked into an MRI machine (see http://www.simplyphysics.com/flying_objects.html for other examples of what an MRI machine can draw in).

Because of the risk of injury by the strong magnetic pull of the MRI machine, it is *very* important that participants be carefully screened for any metal that might be contained in their bodies or on their clothing. Any ferromagnetic materials (containing iron, cobalt, and nickel) can be attracted by the magnets in an MRI and can potentially injure the

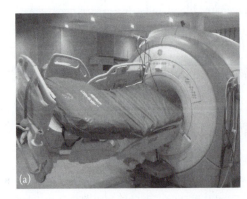

FIGURE 11.14. Magnetic resonance imaging (MRI) machines contain powerful magnets that can attract metal objects including a hospital gurney (a) and scaffolding used in construction (b). Patients and hospital workers have been seriously injured by accidents involving MRIs and their strong magnets.

participant. Although not of ethical concern, other metals may lead to a distortion of the image quality.

MRI and fMRI also require participants to be placed in a confined space, hold their heads still, and endure loud noises. For young children or individuals with claustrophobia, this can be scary and uncomfortable. Researchers will often use a model of the actual machine to familiarize children and potentially anxious individuals with the equipment and procedures.

Finding Incidental Brain Abnormalities

One way that brain imaging differs from other behavioral research is that during a routine scan of a participant, the image may reveal an abnormality, such as a tumor, lesion, or aneurysm. Although many fMRI studies involve patient populations with known issues, an increasing number of individuals without any known problem are being scanned as neuroimaging techniques grow in popularity.

Research suggests that as many as 15% of study participants who have no prior symptoms of anything wrong with their brains have some kind of brain abnormality that is revealed during a routine scan. A significant number of these individuals have anomalies that may impact their health (Illes, 2006). The possibility of this type of discovery raises a number of questions. What should be done about the abnormal scan? Should the participant be told about the abnormality? Does the experimenter have the expertise to make an accurate and valid diagnosis? One way to deal with this issue is to provide information on the consent form that describes the possibility of an abnormality, outlines the procedure for reporting the abnormality to the participant, and provides appropriate referral information for the participant to follow up on. The consent form and the protocol should be worked out with your local institutional review board (see Chapter 3).

Bias in Participant Selection

As we discussed in Chapter 7, selection bias can influence the data that are collected and the overall interpretation of results in any research study. In neuroimaging, selection bias may occur when researchers include only those individuals who are not bothered by the procedures involved in data collection. For example, in the case of research using fMRI, there might be a bias to select people who are not upset by loud noises and confined spaces. This might lead to a researcher studying children who are compliant or patient populations who are relatively high functioning. By choosing to limit the study to these individuals, the researcher may not collect data that generalize to the larger population of interest or are even valid for noncompliant children or lower-functioning individuals.

Another potential selection bias occurs when neuroscience researchers use selection criteria designed to reduce variability in their sample and, consequently, in their data. For example, it is not uncommon for researchers to include only males or only females in their study with the assumption that including both males and females increases the overall variability in the data. However, this approach of restricting the sample to only males or females may make it difficult to generalize the results to the population as a whole. Likewise, as we discussed, many researchers have included only right-handed participants. However, some researchers argue that it is better to include left-handers in the proportion found in the general population, because left-handedness is part of normal human diversity that should be included in research (Willems, Van der Haergen, Fisher, & Francks, 2014).

Marie T. Banich:

"The amount of data we're getting is enormous. We have faster computers and better mathematical models of how to extract information from that data. I'm convinced these methods are going to enhance how we extract information and the questions we ask."

USING NEUROSCIENCE IN CONJUNCTION WITH OTHER METHODS

All of the techniques listed in Table 11.1 enable the collection of massive amounts of data. Data acquisition and analysis for these neuroscience approaches require sophisticated software and statistical procedures that take considerable training to master. Standards for the measurement and analysis of these data continue to evolve as the technology itself improves. For this reason, a consistent set of standards for acquiring and analyzing data across different neuroscience research studies has yet to be established.

Many studies collect a variety of behavioral measures in addition to the brain images. These measures may include reaction times, forced choice responses, a variety of key presses that indicate some aspect of cognition or emotion, or various physiological responses (e.g., heart rate, blood pressure). These behavioral measures serve to enhance interpretation of and validate information obtained from any neuroimages. Without these behavioral measures, the brain images resulting from the technologies are not very useful for psychology, although they might be useful for clinical purposes. Interesting psychological research occurs when neural measurements help to explain or provide results that are found with behavioral measurements.

> ### PRACTICAL TIPS
>
> ## Practical Tips for Using Neuroscience Methods
>
> 1. Remember that your research design and methods should be determined by your research question and not the fancy, high-tech equipment you might have access to.
>
> 2. Carefully consider whether a traditional experimental design can be used to conduct your study and whether use of advanced technologies is necessary.
>
> 3. Become familiar with the basic techniques in neuroscience because they are helpful in interpreting and evaluating research in this growing area of psychology.
>
> 4. Be aware of ethical and safety concerns involved with using MRI machines.

CHAPTER SUMMARY

After reading this chapter you should have an understanding of some of the basic neuroimaging techniques available to researchers today. The field has changed dramatically since the early 1990s, when the advent of neuroimaging techniques—including MRI, fMRI, positron emission tomography scans, and computed tomography scans—created a vast new world of possibilities for psychological research. We have focused on the tools most commonly used in psychological research: EEG, MRI, fMRI, diffusion MRI, and NIRS.

EEG measures electrical impulses coming from different regions of the brain to provide data over time that appear in wave patterns, which are categorized as alpha, beta, gamma, theta, and delta. MRI uses a machine with powerful magnets to align protons in the nuclei of hydrogen atoms that are found throughout the body; it creates static, black-and-white images of the brain. The capability of MRI to image healthy as well as diseased brains is, as Marie Banich noted, nothing short of revolutionary.

The technique of fMRI also uses an MRI machine, but it measures changes in blood flow to regions of the brain in units called voxels; fMRI produces images that can be very colorful. DWI also uses the MRI machine to give researchers information about the connections within and across different brain regions, but it measures the motion of water molecules through brain tissue. NIRS assesses brain function by shining near-infrared light (light that is closest to the visible-light spectrum) through the scalp using optical fibers that are placed in a cap; the light is reflected back to detectors in the cap.

These high-tech tools can be used in conjunction with more traditional methods that measure behaviors, opening a new frontier in psychological research. Although neuroscience research can be intimidating, it is producing some of the most compelling findings in psychology today.

Up for Discussion

1. Researchers have found that people without any expertise in neuroscience perceive explanations containing some information about the brain and its functioning as more compelling—even when the neuroscience information is completely irrelevant to the explanation—than explanations that do not contain such information. This finding is troubling because it suggests that people give more weight to neuroscience information and potentially ignore important details in an explanation. As an ethical neuroscientist, what steps would you take to ensure that those reading the research results give the neuroscience information the weight that it deserves—not more or less?

2. In this chapter, we discussed different techniques for imaging the brain. What factors do you think are the most important for choosing between one technique versus another? When should behavioral measures be included along with neuroimaging in a research study?

3. How might participation bias and selection bias influence the results obtained in studies using fMRI?

4. What are some of the potential consequences of using selection criteria designed to reduce the variability in the sample? Do you think it is appropriate to restrict a research sample to only men? Or only women? Or only right-handed men or women? To what extent might these selection criteria be based on underlying assumptions about the brain and its function?

Key Terms

Amblyopia, p. 269

Anterior cingulate, pp. 268, 269

BOLD response, pp. 267, 268

Cognitive neuroscience, p. 256

Congruent trials, p. 263

Data map, p. 269

Diffusion-weighted magnetic resonance imaging (DWI), p. 269

Electroencephalography (EEG), p. 258

Event-related potential, p. 263

Executive control, p. 263

Flanker task, p. 263

Fractional anisotropy, p. 272

Functional magnetic resonance imaging (fMRI), p. 267

Hemodynamic response, pp. 267, 268

Incongruent trials, p. 263

Magnetic resonance imaging (MRI), p. 264

Mean diffusion, p. 272

Motion artifacts, p. 268

Near-infrared spectroscopy (NIRS), p. 272

Neuropsychology, p. 256

Radiofrequency coils, p. 265

Radiofrequency pulse, p. 264

Relaxation, p. 265

T1-weighted image, p. 265

T2-weighted image, p. 265

Tesla (T), p. 264

Tractography, p. 272

Transcranial magnetic stimulation (TMS), p. 258

Voxels, pp. 267, 268

Research over Age and Time

INSIDE RESEARCH: ERIKA HOFF

Director, Language Development Lab, and Professor of Psychology, Florida Atlantic University

I started out with a purely intellectual interest in how children figure out language and with the very ordinary observation that the language children hear has something to do with their language acquisition.

But of course children's language skills have very important practical consequences for the children. So my research has become more applied. The question of what is the normal course of development for bilingual children is particularly important. We don't yet know the answer to that question, although I'm working on it. When you start to look at children in bilingual environments, you have a whole new set of properties of language experiences that can influence language development. And again, it's intellectually interesting, but it's also of great practical consequence to know the potential targets of intervention for children who are having trouble acquiring language. Children may experience difficulty because they have some impairment or because their environments don't provide them with the inputs they need to acquire language.

What I do now is mostly longitudinal work. I use a within-subjects design to investigate the effect of input, because some bilingual children hear more English and less Spanish, while other children hear more Spanish and less English. You can look at the effects of input by comparing bilingual children's learning in the language they hear more to the language they hear less.

One thing I have discovered to my surprise is that bilingual children are slower in language development than monolingual children, if you consider just one language in a bilingual child. It's important to point out that if you consider bilingual children's total language knowledge they are not slower, but in single language comparisons, bilingual children lag behind monolingual children.

That's not what the literature said when I first started studying this topic, but I have demonstrated clearly that it does take longer to acquire two languages than one, even for children. It's quite clear to me from my data that the reason it takes longer for bilingual children to acquire each of their languages is that they get less input in each language. If input is divided between two languages, you must hear less of each, on average. It shouldn't be surprising, but it's not what people thought.

The widely held view that children are better than adults in language learning is true in the sense that children will ultimately be more successful at a language learned early than at a language learned later in life. But that doesn't mean children will learn a second language at the same rate as if they were acquiring only that language and no other language.

Erika Hoff, a developmental psychologist, first gained national attention for a groundbreaking study that showed how differences in children's language skills, related to the socioeconomic status of their mothers, arise from differences in how the mothers talk to their children (Hoff, 2003). Since then, Hoff has conducted several longitudinal studies, the most recent of which focuses on how bilingual children acquire language skills.

Research Focus: The effects of language input on children's language development

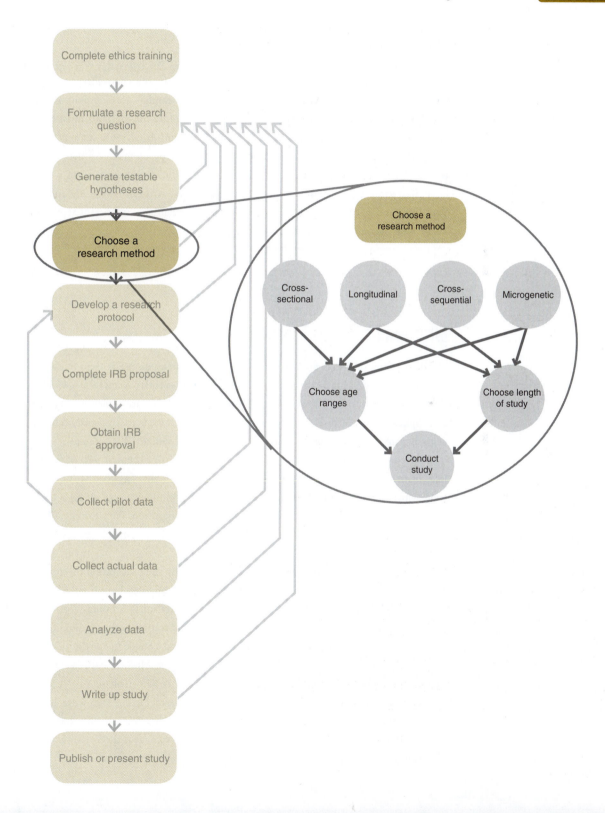

Chapter Abstract

In this chapter, we discuss a variety of designs to study the behaviors and psychological processes of human beings over time and throughout the life span. First, we define the terms commonly used in this type of psychological research—development, maturation, aging, and change over time. Then, we present and explore the methods most commonly used to examine these phenomena: cross-sectional, longitudinal, cross-sequential, and microgenetic studies. We include a discussion of issues and problems that must be addressed with each of these designs, as well as their strengths and weaknesses. Last, we examine large, well-known longitudinal studies, such as the Harvard Growth Study and the New York Longitudinal Study, and the controversial yet undeniably important study of Lewis Terman on the outcomes of gifted children.

DEFINING DEVELOPMENTAL TERMS

Development
Changes that occur over the first part of the life span (e.g., from conception to adulthood), which are often thought of as positive, unidirectional (operating in a single direction), and cumulative. This term is often used to describe advances in such areas as motor skills, language, and cognition.

Maturation Growth and other changes in the body and brain that are associated with underlying genetic information.

Although many scientists use the word **development** as an umbrella term to describe any research that studies humans over time, it is only one of several relevant terms, which include aging, change over time, maturation, and learning. Each differs in subtle yet important ways and applies to specific research designs. Because these terms actually signify different concepts, it is important to move past use of the term "development" as a catch-all.

Development primarily refers to changes that occur over the first part of the life span (e.g., from conception to adulthood), which are often thought of as positive, unidirectional (operating in a single direction), and cumulative. Development is often used to describe advances in such areas as motor skills, language, and cognition. For example, the work of Erika Hoff (see "Inside Research") focuses on the development of language in children (e.g., Parra, Hoff, & Core, 2011).

Although some scientists use the terms development and maturation interchangeably, **maturation** refers to growth and other changes in the body and brain that are associated with underlying genetic information. In this sense, maturation is "automatic" and related to genes. In contrast, development encompasses both maturation *and* an individual's life experiences. As we have gained increasingly sophisticated knowledge of the interaction of genes and experiences (Caspi, Hariri, Holmes, Uher, & Moffitt, 2010; Champagne & Mashoodh, 2009; Manuck & McCaffery, 2014; Taylor & Kim-Cohen, 2007), researchers have come to realize that maturation and experience interact in complex ways, influencing one another and leading to psychological and behavioral changes. Indeed, Champagne and Mashoodh (2009) argue that a critical feature of development is the dynamic interaction between genes and environments.

Aging, in contrast to development, refers to changes associated over the latter part of the life span (e.g., from adulthood to death). Although these changes can be both positive and negative, the term aging is often linked with loss of function in the areas of motor skills, language, and cognition. For example, researchers have studied declines in language function in older adults (e.g., Burke & Shafto, 2004). However, an increasing number of researchers are studying the potential benefits of aging, with considerable work being done on "resilient aging" (Aldwin & Igarashi, 2015; see "Media Matters: An Aging and Able Workforce"), as well as variables that may ameliorate some of the negative impacts of aging. Considerable research has shown that speaking more than one language may improve cognition and delay the onset of dementia in older adults (Bak, Nissan, Allerhand, & Deary, 2014; Bialystok, Craik, & Freedman, 2007). Other researchers have examined the positive impact of activity and exercise on the cognitive function of older adults (e.g., Colcombe & Kramer, 2003). Like development, aging also implies a complex interaction of genetic and environmental factors.

Change over time is a more general way to capture temporal changes, particularly changes brought about by learning and experience. Although psychologists have long debated how to distinguish development from learning (Piaget, 1964/1997; Vygotsky, 1978; and many more), the term **learning** is often restricted to changes tied to specific instruction or experiences over relatively short periods of time. Development and aging, in contrast, are thought to be universal processes impacting all members of a species.

DESIGNS TO STUDY CHANGE OVER AGE AND TIME

Determining the causes of underlying differences between individuals of different ages, or in the same individuals assessed at different points over their life spans, makes developmental research both interesting and challenging. These challenges have led to the creation of a number of specific research designs: cross-sectional, longitudinal, cross-sequential, and microgenetic.

Cross-sectional Designs

Cross-sectional research designs are the most common types of studies across age and time and involve simultaneously assessing two or more different age groups. Suppose you wanted to conduct an educational research study to assess third- and ninth-grade students in reading and mathematics (see Figure 12.1). Before determining which age groups to study and the spacing between the ages, you should consider results from past research, theoretical arguments about the timing and process of developmental change, and your specific research question. In other words, you should choose the ages for your design based on specific questions that you are trying to address about those particular ages. In any written report of your research you will need to justify your choice of age groups.

Aging Changes both positive and negative, associated over the latter part of the life span (e.g., from adulthood to death).

Change over time A general way to capture temporal changes, particularly changes brought about by learning and experience.

Learning Changes tied to specific instruction or experiences over relatively short periods of time.

Cross-sectional research designs The most common types of studies across age and time, involving simultaneously assessing a number of different age groups.

An Aging and Able Workforce

Although millions of baby boomers turned 65 in 2011—the first members of that iconic generation to move into retirement age—many of them have no intention of stopping work anytime soon. For one thing, the Great Recession of 2008 disproportionately affected older Americans who were in their prime earning years, plunging many of them into long-term unemployment and damaging their financial prospects for retirement (Tugend, 2013; Winerip, 2013). For another, many boomers are healthier and more active than previous generations, and they want to continue working through their sixties and beyond.

Negative stereotypes about aging workers in a youth-oriented culture certainly do not help their chances as they vie for coveted jobs in a global marketplace. Television shows, movies, and advertising are full of jokes and messages about older workers as cognitively and physically slower, technophobic, and resistant to change (Scheve & Venzon, 2015). According to Jacquelyn James, the director of research at the Sloan Center on Aging and Work at Boston College, "We know age discrimination is widespread. Age discrimination lawsuits have been increasing over the last five years, and those are just the people who decide to take legal action" (Tarkan, 2012).

New developmental research, however, is upending some of those assumptions and revealing the benefits of aging to the workplace. It turns out that some traits actually improve with age. According to Susan Fiske, a psychology professor at Princeton University, older workers tend to be more knowledgeable, reliable, and emotionally stable than younger employees and can "stand back and see the big picture" (Sleek, 2013).

In addition, researchers at the Max Planck Institute for Human Development in Berlin have shown that the work of older adults may be more consistent than that of their younger counterparts (Sleek, 2013). The researchers tested more than 200 adults who fell into two groups—those ages 20–31 and those ages 65–80—on 12 separate tasks, including perceptual speed, episodic memory, and working memory (Schmiedek, Lövdén, & Lindenberger, 2013). They repeated the tasks over 100 days to determine learning improvements and daily fluctuations in performance. Nine of the 12 tasks were cognitive, and in these tasks the older group showed more consistent performance from day to day and had high performance compared with the younger group. This result did not change when researchers took into account differences in average performance favoring the young group (Sleek, 2013).

"Further analyses indicate that the older adults' higher consistency is due to learned strategies to solve the task, a constantly high motivation level, as well as a balanced daily routine and stable mood," explained Florian Schmiedek, one of the Planck researchers (Sleek, 2013). Despite its groundbreaking findings, the study did not garner widespread media attention.

Those results matched those of another, larger study called the Midlife in the United States, or Midus, which was launched in the mid-1990s and continues to track the physical and emotional growth of more than 7,000 people ages 25–74 years old (Cohen, 2012). The design of this study enables researchers to track the same person over a long period of time.

The good news for people in middle age and beyond is that they show higher levels of "crystallized" intelligence (as opposed to "fluid" intelligence, which peaks in the twenties). People acquire crystallized intelligence through experience and education and improve in areas such as verbal ability, inductive reasoning, and judgment. Rather than a direct product of genetics, crystallized intelligence depends more on factors such as personality, motivation, opportunity, and culture (Cohen, 2012).

FIGURE 12.1. An example of a cross-sectional design. In this example, researchers might compare the performance of children in two separate classrooms, studied at the same point in time, on reading and math skills.

Advantages of Cross-sectional Designs. Cross-sectional designs enable researchers to gather information about different age groups in a short period of time. For instance, researchers conducting cross-sectional studies in schools may be able to collect all the data in a single day, with participants from different grades completing a survey. This approach uses fewer resources and results in lower overall costs.

Cross-sectional research also offers an excellent way to discover and document the age-related differences associated with certain behaviors. In a relatively short period of time, you can potentially identify ages at which an important change in behavior occurs (e.g., a toddler saying her first word) or document the increase or decrease in a behavior of interest (e.g., an improvement or decline in a cognitive skill). For this reason, cross-sectional designs are often useful for determining transition points in development, identifying standard behavior at certain ages, and tracking trends in development or aging. Determining standard or normative levels of behaviors is also essential for developing assessments that can help to determine how a child performs compared with peers of the same age.

Disadvantages of Cross-sectional Designs. Although cross-sectional designs are excellent for revealing differences among different age groups, in general they do not identify the underlying causes of differences. For example, imagine we find that fifth graders perform significantly higher than third graders on a mathematics test. We cannot tell what is causing this difference: age, maturation, specific learning experiences, or a combination of all of these. It could also be a **cohort effect**, the result of experiences that impact an entire group of individuals. An example of a cohort effect is the start of compulsory education or the invention of smartphones. Individuals who lived through these events will think or behave differently from those who were born at some other time. In the mathematics test

Cohort effect Effects that generate change as a result of experiences that impact an entire group of individuals.

example, we might expect a cohort difference for first and fourth graders growing up in the age of smartphones, all of which have built-in calculators, when compared with first and fourth graders from an earlier generation who did not have access to smartphones with embedded calculators.

Another difficulty posed by cross-sectional designs is verifying that the methods are equally good at measuring the behavior of interest for the different age groups in the sample, also known as **equivalent measures** (to be discussed at greater length later in this chapter). For many standardized measures of cognitive or language behavior, the assessments are pretested (normed) to be appropriate for use with individuals in a particular age range. Use of the assessment outside of that range is likely to lead to floor or ceiling effects (see Chapter 8).

Finally, cross-sectional designs tend to underestimate variability within an age group, which can be quite large, to characterize differences between groups. By focusing on differences between age groups, achievements obtained at specific ages gain greater status than they likely deserve. Examples are motor milestones such as crawling and walking, which are often displayed in developmental textbooks as happening at 9 months and 12 months, respectively. This leads the reader to assume that this is the normal pattern of development, but it ignores or obscures the large amount of variability found between children of the same age in both the timing and the pattern of crawling or walking.

Longitudinal Research Designs

Longitudinal research designs track groups of participants over a period of time with two or more assessments of the same individuals at different times. Figure 12.2 shows an example of five different individuals studied at three different time points. Longitudinal studies can be of any length. Researchers often use short-term longitudinal studies to study young infants, who undergo rapid changes in a short time (e.g., weeks or months). However, most longitudinal studies cover longer time periods, often several years or, in rare cases, even decades. Although it was not a formal academic study, the highly acclaimed 2014 film *Boyhood* took this longitudinal approach in telling the story of Mason. Filming began when the actor was 6 years old and continued at intervals over the next 12 years.

The longest-running longitudinal study was started in 1922 by Lewis Terman (Terman, 1925, 1930, 1947). Terman advocated eugenics, which was a movement in the early part of the 20th century that claimed certain people were genetically superior to others. Eugenics sought to improve humans through selective breeding and refinement of the gene pool. For this reason, Terman's work is highly controversial, although the longitudinal nature of his data still has great value.

Terman's goal was to examine the development of highly gifted individuals over their entire life spans in the hope of dispelling a belief that was common at the time, namely, that

Equivalent measures Methods that are equally good at measuring a behavior of interest for different age groups in a sample.

Longitudinal research designs Designs that track groups of participants over a period of time with two or more assessments of the same individuals at different times.

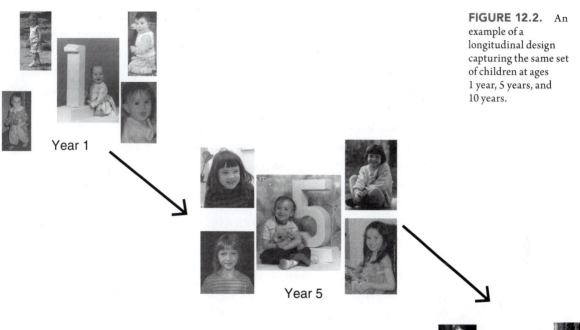

Year 1

Year 5

Year 10

gifted children were less healthy than their nongifted counterparts. He collected data from more than 1,500 children between 8 and 16 years old living in California who scored 135 or higher on his intelligence test (the Stanford–Binet intelligence test). Every 5 to 10 years, Terman collected a massive amount of data from participants, including surveys completed by parents, teachers, the participants, and their spouses; one-on-one interviews; a battery of IQ tests; assessments of health and physical and emotional development; and home, family, school, and employment histories. Access to the actual data collected from 1922 to 1986 and a number of publications stemming from the data can be obtained from the National Archive of Computerized Data on Aging (http://www.icpsr.umich.edu/icpsrweb/ICPSR/studies/8092).

Although Terman's study helped convince the general public that intelligent children could be healthy and happy, it did not find that high intelligence leads directly to success

(Leslie, 2000). Two-thirds of the participants (whom he affectionately called "Termites") earned bachelor's degrees, which was 10 times the national average at the time. They were also more likely to complete graduate degrees than the general population: 97 earned PhDs, 57 earned MDs, and 92 became attorneys. But in other aspects, participants appeared vulnerable to the same troubles afflicting their peers. They committed suicide, became alcoholics, and got divorced at the same rates as non-Termites. One participant went to prison and a few were arrested (Leslie, 2000).

Other notable longitudinal studies include the Harvard Growth Study (Dearborn, Rothney, & Shuttleworth, 1938) and the New York Longitudinal Study (Chess & Thomas, 1996; Thomas & Chess, 1977; Thomas, Chess, Birch, Hertzig, & Korn, 1963). The Harvard Growth Study began in 1922 with an initial sample of 3,650 first graders. The primary goal was to track physical growth and maturation (e.g., height, weight, body dimensions, onset of puberty) from first grade until the participants graduated or left high school, although the researchers also collected data on cognitive function (e.g., intelligence, achievement). The original study was completed in 1935, but researchers continued to follow up on surviving participants (Must, Jacques, Dallal, Bajema, & Dietz, 1992; Scott & Bajema, 1982). One study, for example, found that overweight teenagers were at much greater risk for a number of negative health outcomes (e.g., coronary heart disease, some cancers, early mortality) than lean teenagers (Must et al., 1992).

The New York Longitudinal Study sought to investigate the development of personality. It began in 1956 with a sample of 133 white, middle-class infants (66 male, 67 female). The study researchers originally planned to examine the children in the first two years of life, but they ended up collecting extensive data from participants and their families until 1988: measures of childhood temperament, health and physical development, cognitive development, academic achievement, family function, parent–child relations, sexuality, drug use and abuse, and vocational interests and career development. This longitudinal data set and publications stemming from it can be accessed at the Henry A. Murray Research Archive at Harvard University.

Advantages of Longitudinal Designs.   Researchers studying change over time often argue that more longitudinal research should be done. They say that longitudinal research provides the only way to truly understand the process of change in individuals, because they track change within the same individuals over a period of time. Cross-sectional designs, although they are convenient, can only infer such change based on comparisons of different groups of individuals.

Another advantage of this method is that it can yield a considerable amount of data that enable researchers to explore a wide variety of different research questions—even ones that were not part of the original study. For example, the Terman study led to more than 100 journal articles and many books on numerous topics. Similarly, the well-known

Minnesota Twin Family Study (Iacono & McGue, 2002) was originally designed to examine the relative contributions of genetics and environment on a range of psychological traits. It has spawned a number of related projects, including studies of adult development and sibling interaction.

Disadvantages of Longitudinal Designs.   Longitudinal designs pose a number of challenges. Probably the biggest obstacle for using a longitudinal design is the cost in time and resources. A longitudinal study is much more expensive and takes longer to conduct than a cross-sectional study with the same number of participants and a similar target age range.

A second issue that arises from many designs used to examine changes associated with age, maturation, or learning is the impact of repeated testing. If you study a group of children over time, as in a longitudinal design, you must assess participants at more than one point in time. Taking similar forms of an exam or assessment on several occasions can lead to changes in performance solely because of repeated testing. Individuals may learn from repeated assessments how they are to perform and improve on later assessments, or they may become bored and less motivated with later assessments if they are too similar to the previous ones. This problem of repeated testing relates to the issue of potential order effects faced by experimental researchers (see Chapter 8). The best approach to dealing with the impact of repeated testing is to use different versions of your assessment and to explicitly test for order effects.

A third issue facing researchers conducting longitudinal research is **subject attrition**, which occurs when participants drop out of the study after the first assessment and are unavailable for later assessments. Participants drop out for all sorts of reasons— losing interest, moving, illness, and even death, particularly if the study involves older adults.

Subject attrition
When some participants drop out of a study after the first assessment and are unavailable for later assessments.

Subject attrition poses two problems for researchers studying participants over time. First, attrition can lead to an insufficient number of participants at the end of the study, which may mean not having the appropriate statistical power to conduct desired analyses. To avoid this issue, most researchers oversample; that is, they collect more participants at the start of the study than they will need at the end. It is common to expect a 10% loss in participants over the course of a multiassessment study, but this percentage is influenced by the nature of the study, the time between assessments, the overall length of the study, and characteristics of your sample. Attrition rates will likely be higher for studies that require participants to do a lot (high subject burden), have longer time intervals between assessments, and go on for longer time periods.

The second problem posed by attrition is that it may result in significant changes to the study over the course of multiple assessments. Imagine that you want to study how language changes over years 2 to 5 in a sample of young children. You start your study with

50 2-year-olds, half male and half female, who come from diverse socioeconomic backgrounds. You attempt to collect additional data from your participants at age 3½ and then again at 5. At the 3½-year-old assessment you find that you have lost 10% of your sample (5 children), and at age 5 you find that you have lost an additional 10% of your sample (another 5 children), leaving a final sample of 40 children. You want your sample characteristics at the end of the study to match those you started with. In this case, you hope to end with 50% females (20 females, 20 males) and maintain the socioeconomic diversity of your sample.

In actuality, however, most researchers' final samples rarely match their initial one, and they end up with a more skewed distribution (e.g., only 40% of the final survey is female or most of the participants of higher socioeconomic status have dropped out). If your sample is large enough and you have collected sufficient demographic information about your initial and final samples, you can assess the impact of attrition statistically to determine whether it influences your final results.

Although some attrition is inevitable, researchers can take steps to minimize the potential impact. Researchers using multiple assessments in their research often send updates, newsletters, and even birthday cards to participants; provide incentives for participation (usually money or gift cards); provide greater incentives for completing all the assessments; and devote a substantial amount of resources to recruitment and retention of participants. Many institutional review boards want to know details of the procedures researchers will use to retain participants. The review board's main concern is whether continued participation is clearly voluntary and whether retention procedures are potentially overzealous. When researchers study populations that are difficult to contact or ambivalent about staying in the research (e.g., poor families who move frequently or individuals with mental disorders), researchers may make many attempts to maintain contact with participants, including home visits or contacting their friends and family. In these cases, loss of confidentiality may result, and repeated attempts to contact participants may be viewed as harassment by those who are reluctant or uninterested in continued participation.

A fourth disadvantage of longitudinal studies is maintaining the research personnel over time. In some cases, the study can outlive the original researchers. Terman directed the study until 1954, when he was replaced by Dr. Robert Sears, who directed it until his death in 1987. At that point, Dr. Al Hastorf took over the study. Although changing directors can be relatively problem free, maintaining a consistent, well-trained staff can be difficult. Given the complexity of longitudinal research, having a staff that maintains high standards in research activities in the face of inevitable change is no small feat. In addition, turnover in the research team can affect long-term relationships with participants.

A fifth problem with longitudinal studies is determining whether the outcomes observed are the result of developmental processes or the timing of data collection. For example,

Erika Hoff:

"I always want to have as representative a sample as possible, and that's very, very difficult to do. It's much harder to get lower [socioeconomic status] families. We can do it, but we have to work much harder. We find them through neighbors, nursery schools, and community centers. We go to playgrounds. Once we get going and one family knows another family that knows another family, we're okay. It's like getting out the vote. It's legwork."

certain outcomes in the Terman study may have been a result of the fact that the sample contained only gifted individuals. However, the results might also have been influenced by the point in history when the study began. The period from 1920 until 1980 was a time of rapid change, encompassing the Great Depression, World War II, increases in industrialization, and changing attitudes about sex and sex roles. The absence of a control group that was tracked at the same time makes it even more difficult to tease apart the factors of "giftedness" and experiences particular to this cohort.

One final issue arises in long-running studies: the quality of the overall study depends above all on the initial sample and the quality of measures and data collection used in the earliest assessments. Although sampling is, of course, an issue with all studies, it takes on extra weight in a longitudinal study where researchers are "stuck" with their original samples for an extended period of time. If the sample is not representative enough, then it is harder to generalize the results. For example, Terman's original sample comprised children who scored 135 or higher on his intelligence test. Over the years, a wide range of data were collected on these individuals. However, it is not clear whether the results regarding career satisfaction, marital history, and other variables can be generalized to the population as a whole or whether it is valid only for individuals with a relatively high IQ. With an extensive longitudinal data set, this sort of challenge arises—even when it may not have been the goal of the original study to generalize to the population—because there are so few longitudinal data to speak to some of the key questions.

Over the course of a longitudinal study, new technologies may lead to significant advances in research methodology. These may include the creation of new assessment tools with greater validity and reliability than those used at the beginning of the study. Unfortunately, researchers do not have the luxury of replacing measures with newly developed, better ones in the middle of a study. This makes it imperative for researchers to carefully consider which measures will provide the best data over time.

Cross-sequential Designs

Cross-sequential research designs refer to research approaches that combine aspects of both cross-sectional and longitudinal designs. These have a variety of different labels, including "sequential," "mixed," and "accelerated longitudinal designs." Each refers to a study design where multiple age groups or cohorts are studied over time. Figure 12.3 provides a simplified version of this design. The original cross-section comprises four groups (2-, 4-, 6-, and 8-year-olds); each of these groups is measured three times, with a two-year interval between assessments, which are labeled Time 2 and Time 3. Sometimes researchers add samples during later assessment to (1) increase their sample size and (2) study the effects of time on the same-age children—to see, for example, whether children of a particular age (e.g., preschoolers) look similar to one another even if they were born a few years apart. In Figure 12.3, additional groups of 2-year-olds are brought in at Time 2 and Time 3 (Groups 1A and 1B). These repeated periods of data collection

Erika Hoff:

"When I did my dissertation I transcribed by hand, I wrote things on huge pieces of paper, and I counted the length of the utterances by hand. Nobody does that any more. You still have to transcribe, but there are computer-based programs for analyzing what you have typed in transcripts to generate counts of different words and the lengths of utterances, and pretty much anything that you want to code. So you can handle much, much more data than you could."

Cross-sequential research design An approach that combines aspects of both cross-sectional and longitudinal designs where multiple age groups or cohorts are studied over time. Sometimes also referred to as "sequential," "mixed," and "accelerated longitudinal designs."

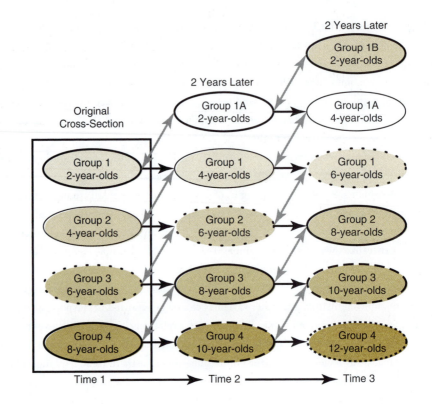

FIGURE 12.3.
Example of a cross-sequential design. Black lines and shapes indicate the same groups of children over time. Gray double-sided arrows and similar outlines around the ovals indicate comparisons of same-age children at two or more different time periods to explore possible cohort effects. Columns represent cross-sections collected at a single time point.

Waves Repeated periods of data collection in a cross-sequential design.

are often referred to as **waves.** At Time 3, the original 2-year-olds are now 6, and the 8-year-olds are now 12. Over four years (Time 1 to Time 3), the researchers collected data on children from ages 2 to 12.

Advantages of Cross-sequential Designs. Mixing cross-sectional and longitudinal designs in a single study enables the researcher to study a wider age range in a shorter time period than traditional longitudinal designs. The additional groups of children enable researchers to examine whether children of the same age provide similar data even when the data are collected at different time points. If you trace up the gray diagonal lines in Figure 12.3, you will see that at each wave of data there is a group of 2-year-olds, as well as groups of 4-, 6-, and 8-year-olds. If the data collected from one age group differ from that collected for the same age group at a different wave, it suggests that the different cohorts of the same age are distinctive, and the research may need to explore these distinctions. Ideally, researchers hope that measurements from the same age group collected at different points in time are similar, so that they can be potentially combined in some of the data analyses. In this way, researchers can explicitly test for cohort effects, something that is not possible in a traditional longitudinal design.

Disadvantages of Cross-sequential Designs.   Cross-sequential designs share many of the same disadvantages as longitudinal designs with respect to issues of repeated testing, equivalent measures, and susceptibility to subject attrition. They are also costly to conduct in terms of time and resources. Yet, they usually cost less than a longitudinal study covering the same age range. In addition, most researchers would argue that, when they are possible to implement, the advantages of mixed designs far outweigh the disadvantages.

Microgenetic Designs

The final research design pertinent to change over time is referred to as the **microgenetic design** (Siegler, 2006: Siegler & Crowley, 1991). The overall goal of this design is to capture changes as they occur and attempt to understand the mechanisms involved in any observed changes. The major aspects of the microgenetic design include focusing on a key **transition point** or dramatic shift in the behavior of interest (Granott & Parziale, 2002). In developmental research, transition points could focus on behaviors such as the shift from crawling to walking (Karasik, Tamis-LeMonda, & Adolph, 2011); acquisition of the first few words (MacWhinney, 1987); or attainment of new strategies for adding or subtracting numbers (Siegler & Jenkins, 1989).

Researchers employing a microgenetic design conduct a large number of closely spaced observations that begin prior to the transition point and then continue until the behavior has stabilized after the transition point. For example, a researcher interested in the transition from crawling to walking would start with determining the possible transition point. In this case, because past researchers have documented the timing of key motor milestones, the researcher could merely consult an earlier study of this transition. The World Health Organization has been collecting these data as part of a Multicentre Growth Reference Study (WHO Multicentre Growth Reference Study Group, 2006). This particular transition point occurs at approximately one year of age. The researchers then define a time window around this point, starting at an age where no child being observed is yet walking and ending at an age where all the children being observed are walking. The Multicentre Growth Reference Study (2006) suggests that the window of walking independently occurs between 8 and 18 months. In this time window, the researcher would conduct frequent observations of motor behavior that might be related to the start of independent walking. Adolph and Robinson (2011) advocate for a sampling frequency as often as once a day, although this is rarely feasible for any study involving a relatively large time window.

Seigler and Crowley (1991) suggest that three characteristics define the microgenetic approach: (1) a focus on a key transition in behavior, (2) densely packed observations that follow the behavior from one stable state through the transition to another (different) stable state, and (3) a focused analysis of the behavior in terms of change from one observation to the next.

Microgenetic design An approach that attempts to capture changes as they occur and to understand the mechanisms involved in any observed changes by focusing on a key transition point or dramatic shift in the behavior of interest.

Transition point The point in development where key changes occur, often the focus of microgenetic designs.

Advantages of Microgenetic Methods. A key advantage of the microgenetic approach is that it can provide new and important insights about the processes that lead to change. This in turn can provide information that may be used to accelerate transitions (e.g., the acquisition of new addition strategies), identify behaviors that indicate the transition is imminent, and specify places where interventions can be implemented for individuals having difficulty making the transition. A growing number of researchers (Adolph & Robinson, 2011; Siegler, 2006) suggest that the microgenetic approach offers the best way of capturing both quantitative and qualitative aspects of behavioral change.

A second advantage of this approach is that it enables researchers to examine transitions that occur infrequently in detail. For example, children make the transition to walking only once, acquire their first word once, and learn to ride a bicycle once. Over the normal life course, these behaviors are not forgotten. Capturing these transitions can only really be done using microgenetic methods.

Disadvantages of Microgenetic Methods. Microgenetic studies share some of the same disadvantages as longitudinal and cross-sequential designs with respect to the issues of repeated testing and susceptibility to subject attrition. In addition, microgenetic methods are difficult and time-consuming to conduct (Siegler & Crowley, 1991). Determining precise transition points in many behaviors is also challenging. Even with the transition to walking, the age range during which children achieve independent walking is quite large, and this and most other behaviors exhibit considerable variability in onset (Rosengren, 2002; Siegler, 2007). Thus, a researcher wanting to be sure that he or she captures the transition point and stable periods before the transition might need to start collecting data around 6 months of age and continue to as long as 19 or 20 months of age.

Most microgenetic studies involve a relatively small number of participants. This is primarily because of the limitations of making a larger number of observations in a relatively small time period. However, using relatively small samples means that the sample may not be representative of the larger population of children. Thus, another disadvantage is that microgenetic research may not be generalizable. Researchers using this approach generally focus on behaviors that are more or less universal (e.g., transition to walking, acquisition of first words) so that their findings are likely to be relevant and meaningful. The relatively small sample size also affects how the data can be analyzed. In particular, the small sample and densely packed observations can make it difficult to use traditional statistical approaches.

ADDITIONAL CHALLENGES TO CONSIDER IN DEVELOPMENTAL DESIGNS

The research designs used to study change over time are more challenging than some of the other designs discussed in this book, in part because of the problems that researchers must consider as they design their research study. Although we have discussed a number of issues related to specific designs, several other issues are relevant for all of the designs discussed in this chapter. These include (1) determining the cause of any observed changes, (2) determining whether measures used at different times or for different ages are equivalent, and (3) determining the appropriate sample interval.

Determining the Underlying Cause of Changes

One of the main reasons that researchers examine changes in behavior over time is to uncover what factors play the most important role in causing observed changes. Unfortunately, this is not an easy task because changes can be a result of age, maturation, learning, specific experiences, and cohort effects. Many of these factors also interact in a complex manner, as discussed previously with respect to interactions between genes and the environment.

Developmental changes are thought to be driven by underlying genetic factors that operate at both the species and the individual levels. For example, genes guide the universal emergence of crawling, walking, and running in developing humans, but individual factors and the specific environments in which the child grows up influence when and how these changes happen (Berger & Adolph, 2007). For example, in some cultures infants walk at earlier or later ages because of differences in parenting practices (Dennis, 1940; Hess, Kashigawa, Price, & Dickinson, 1980). Other researchers have shown that infants learn through specific experiences exploring the environment, such as finding the most efficient manner of getting from one place to another (Adolph, Robinson, Young, & Gill-Alvarez, 2008). It can be highly challenging to tease apart age, maturation, or learning as the causes of change. Researchers who succeed in separating these influences do so using complex (cross-sequential) designs and sophisticated statistics and by collecting the right kinds of data.

One additional factor that may lead to differences between individuals of different ages is the cohort effect. Experiencing the first generation of smartphones (or, in the case of your authors, the very first video game) is a different and more striking event than growing up in a generation that has never experienced life without them. Cohort differences are also associated with different generations such as baby boomers, generation Xers, or millennials. Again, the idea is that members of these different cohorts have shared a set of universal experiences that make them think and behave differently from members of other generations.

Finding Equivalent Measures

It would be ideal if developmental researchers could use a single assessment to measure a behavior of individuals of different ages. But a particular assessment that works best for toddlers may not work so well for teenagers. Young children cannot perform well on tasks that require language skills, whereas older children find tasks designed for younger children too easy. This problem resembles the floor and ceiling effects discussed in Chapter 8. Tasks that are at the correct level for one age group are often too easy (ceiling effect) or too difficult (floor effect) for another age group. One solution for this challenge is to test measures across different ages to find those that provide a reasonable assessment across all different ages. The National Institutes of Health have created a set of assessments or toolboxes that can be used to study various behaviors over the age range of 3 to 85 years (Zelazo & Bauer, 2013).

A tangible example of creating developmentally appropriate assessments can be found in the work of Rovee-Collier (1999). In her work on memory in young children, she begins with a task for 3-month old infants involving a mobile in a crib; the task makes use of classical conditioning to measure memory at this very young age. However, to trace the development of memory from infancy to toddlerhood, Rovee-Collier develops a parallel but different memory task to acknowledge the limitation that toddlers are no longer stimulated by mobiles. Her older (toddler) participants instead learn how to operate a train by pressing a button. The mobile and train tasks are equivalent measures of memory, but they are attuned to the developmental skills and interests of the participants at different ages.

Determining the Appropriate Sampling Interval

A final issue confronting researchers examining change over time is choosing an appropriate **sampling interval.** By its very nature, research on development and aging requires that sampling occur at different ages or different time points, but how frequent should these sampling periods be? As Adolph and Robinson (2011) discuss, most researchers opt for relatively large spacing between ages or repeated assessments.

Sampling interval
The amount of time elapsed between different data collection points in a developmental study.

The risk of inadequate sampling is that the pattern of change over time may be mischaracterized, leading to theories built on faulty data (Adolph & Robinson, 2011). As Adolph and Robinson point out, large sampling intervals can make uncovering important relationships difficult (Boker & Nesselroade, 2002), can lead researchers to miss important events or transitions (Collins & Graham, 2002), and can lead researchers to underestimate variability in the behavior of interest (Siegler, 2006). Large gaps in sampled participants' ages can also make modeling the pattern of change or distinguishing between a variety of different potential trajectories of change difficult (Adolph et al., 2008). For example, if you are studying the development of theory of mind (how children come to understand that other people have thoughts and feelings that differ from their own) and you wait an entire year between measurements, you might be left with the impression that children's theory of mind dramatically emerges, like flipping on a light switch. Theory of mind actually seems to emerge for most children sometime between the ages of 3 and 4. Longitudinal study that involves multiple measurements between the ages of 3 and 4 is more likely to reveal a pattern of change that shows subtle, incremental shifts, rather than a single dramatic jump.

Adolph and Robinson (2011) advocate frequent longitudinal sampling, arguing for a default sampling rate involving daily summaries for each 24-hour period. The appropriateness of this technique depends on the particular age of the participant (it may be most useful for studying periods of rapid change, such as those found in infancy) and the particular behavior of interest.

They base this decision on a study (Adolph et al., 2008) that collected summaries of 32 motor skills—including rolling, crawling, sitting, and walking—in young infants. They tracked 11 infants from birth until 17 months. They were able to use the data to examine how patterns of development would look if they had used different sampling rates (daily, every other day, every third day, etc.). They found that the patterns across and within children were highly variable and that the daily summary approach yielded the best characterization of the data. Frequent sampling is expensive, but it yields a lot of data.

SUMMARY OF RESEARCH INVESTIGATING CHANGE OVER TIME

Although research studying change over time can be difficult to conduct, the designs discussed in this chapter can be useful for addressing research questions that focus on changes over the life span and processes that may cause these changes. Table 12.1 highlights the four designs discussed in this chapter—cross-sectional, longitudinal, cross-sequential, and microgenetic—providing a summary of some of the advantages and disadvantages of each approach.

Table 12.1. Advantages, disadvantages, and relative cost in time and money of different designs to measure change

	Advantages		Disadvantages				Cost
Design	Good for Documenting Normative Differences	Good for Documenting Factors Influencing Change	Problem of Determining Underlying Cause of Differences between Time 1 and Time 2	Problem of Repeated Testing	Problem of Equivalent Measures	Problem of Subject Attrition	Time/$
Cross-Sectional	X		XX		X		Fast/ Low $
Longitudinal		X		X	X	X	Slow/ High $
Cross-Sequential	X	X		X	X	X	Slow/ High $
Microgenetic		X		XX		X	Fast/ High $

Practical Tips for Doing Research over Age and Time

1. In the study of change over age and time, be clear on whether you are studying development, maturation, aging, or some combination of the three.

2. Weigh the benefits and drawbacks of different research designs: cross-sectional, longitudinal, cross-sequential, and microgenetic. When time and resources allow, consider combinations of these different methods.

3. When assessing underlying causes of change, be sure to consider all possible sources: age, maturation, learning, specific experiences, and cohort effects.

4. Explicitly test for order effects and use different versions of your assessment to combat the negative impact of repeated testing.

5. Be attentive to the problem of finding equivalent measures for different ages. Test measures across different ages.

6. Consider strategies to reduce subject attrition in longitudinal studies by devoting a substantial amount of research resources to recruitment and retention of participants.

7. Be thoughtful in choosing an appropriate sample interval in your study of change over age and time. The choice of spacing between ages or repeated assessments should be dictated by the research question and appropriate use of theory.

CHAPTER SUMMARY

Psychological research over age and time is a far richer, more rewarding, and more challenging area than its more commonly used name—developmental psychology—suggests. Research over age and time encompasses the study of the complex processes of maturation, learning, change over time, and aging. Researchers can choose from four methods to investigate questions in this area: cross-sectional, longitudinal, cross-sequential, and microgenetic designs.

Cross-sectional studies are the most popular because they enable researchers to simultaneously assess several different age groups and, in doing so, discover and document age-related differences in behavior. Longitudinal studies track participants over a period of time, assessing individuals at least twice at different times. Data from previous longitudinal studies, such as the Harvard Growth Study, can serve as a tremendous resource for researchers trying to answer new questions. Cross-sequential or mixed designs combine aspects of cross-sectional and longitudinal designs. They enable researchers to study a wider age range in a shorter amount of time than traditional longitudinal designs. Researchers using microgenetic studies capture changes as they occur by conducting many closely spaced observations on key transition points, for example, as infants shift from crawling to walking.

Because of its complexity, research over age and time presents some challenges, most notably determining the underlying cause of observed changes, assessing the impact of repeated testing on participants' response, determining equivalent measures, controlling subject attrition, and choosing an appropriate sample interval. In Chapter 13, we will turn our attention to statistics, specifically, how to transform raw data into understandable conclusions.

Up for Discussion

1. At the beginning of the chapter, the considerable debate about the meaning and boundaries of the terms "development," "maturation," "aging," "change over time," and "learning" is discussed. Is this debate about more than just semantics? Are there particular reasons why these terms should be clearly differentiated and used in a consistent and precise fashion by theorists and researchers?

2. Developmental researchers can select from a range of methodologies: cross-sectional, longitudinal, cross-sequential, and microgenetic. What sorts of factors should be considered when choosing from these different broad approaches in a developmental research design? Of these approaches, do you think that some produce more valid and reliable findings than others? Considering Table 12.1, which set of advantages or disadvantages would you most heavily weigh in your decision about what methodologies to use?

3. Do you agree with the argument put forth in this chapter that developmental research designs may face special challenges that go beyond other research designs (e.g., determining underlying causes of change, finding equivalent measures, determining the appropriate sample interval)? What sort of impact do you think these unique challenges have on researchers interested in studying development?

Key Terms

Aging, p. 283

Change over time, p. 283

Cohort effect, p. 285

Cross-sectional research designs, p. 283

Cross-sequential research design, p. 291

Development, p. 282

Equivalent measures, p. 286

Learning, p. 283

Longitudinal research designs, p. 286

Maturation, p. 282

Microgenetic design, p. 293

Sampling interval, p. 296

Subject attrition, p. 289

Transition point, p. 293

Waves, p. 292

Analyzing Your Data I: An Overview

INSIDE RESEARCH: LAWRENCE HUBERT

Lyle H. Lanier Professor of
Psychology, Emeritus, University of
Illinois at Urbana–Champaign

I got into statistical methods because of Sputnik, the first satellite
that went into space in 1957, the year I was in the 8th grade. The
Soviet Union had caught the world off guard, and the launch
caused mass panic in the United States. People thought we would
be overrun by the Russians. The U.S. government said, "We have
to do something," and invested an enormous amount of money in
testing and training students in math and science. I had planned
on going in a vocational direction and thought that I might
become an electrician. But immediately after Sputnik every
junior-high-school student was assessed in math and science. I did
well and attended a two-week program at St. Olaf College, where
we were given an intensive college-level introduction to physics,
chemistry, biology, and mathematics. After 10th grade I went

back to St. Olaf for the whole summer, paid for by the National Science Foundation. This changed my perspective about my capabilities and what I could do with my life. I subsequently went to Carleton College and majored in mathematics. From there I went to Harvard and then to Stanford for my PhD, where I studied statistics and applications in the behavioral sciences. I didn't have to pay a penny for my education. It was a very different time.

As I see it, one of the payoffs for taking a statistics course is to obtain a basic grasp of probabilistic reasoning. We live in an uncertain world; things can apparently happen for mostly random and/or unknown reasons. But if you have an understanding of the probability principles that underlie statistical methods, you can begin to separate the signal from the obscuring noise.

Lawrence Hubert has taught the graduate statistics sequence for doctoral students from all areas of psychology (in addition to teaching other multivariate analysis courses at more advanced levels) for more than 40 years, most recently at the University of Illinois. He has contributed to more than a dozen books on statistical methods. He is currently interested in the interface of ethics and statistics, which is the topic of his recent book, *A Statistical Guide for the Ethically Perplexed* (2013), with co-author Howard Wainer.

Research Focus: Data analysis methods in psychology with an emphasis on representation techniques

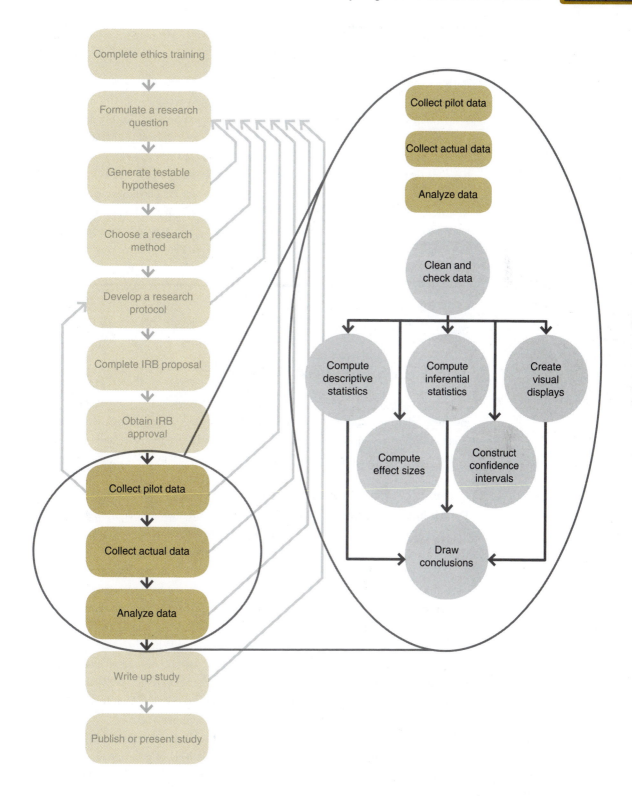

Chapter Abstract

In this chapter, we provide an overview of data analysis, discuss a variety of descriptive statistics and visual displays that will help you understand your data, describe the rationale for traditional inferential statistics, and examine issues related to performing analyses. With a well-designed study, you should know before you begin collecting data how your analysis will proceed. Your research question, the characteristics of your study design, and the type of data you collect will inform the type of analysis you will perform. This chapter is not meant to replace a more formal statistics class, but instead to serve as a review of statistical issues that are important for researchers to consider. As Travis Seymour (see "Inside Research," Chapter 8) observed, "If you are limited in terms of your knowledge of statistics, you miss opportunities in your own data, or you end up having to rely on people who know more about statistics than you. You're giving away power. People are making decisions that you should be making."

THE STEPS OF DATA ANALYSIS

The process of transforming raw, unprocessed data into conclusions consists of the following steps: checking and cleaning your data, computing descriptive statistics including effect sizes, creating visual displays, constructing confidence intervals, and computing inferential statistics to apply inferential tests.

Checking and Cleaning Data

Data cleaning The process of checking that your measurements are complete and accurate prior to any analysis.

Data cleaning is the process of checking that your measurements are complete and accurate prior to any analysis. Although it is not the most exciting or engaging part of analyzing data, it is a critical step. If your data values are inaccurate, the results of your data analysis will be inaccurate and potentially misleading. As the saying goes, "Garbage in, garbage out."

Incorrect computations and the failure to check data can have catastrophic results. In 1999, rocket scientists failed to convert data from English units to the metric system, leading them to overestimate the distance to Mars, and the $125 million Mars Orbiter crashed (Lloyd, 1999). In another example, known as the "London Whale" venture, financial analysts at JPMorgan Chase & Co. mistakenly divided by a sum instead of an average when modeling data. This mistake led to wildly wrong predictions (Kwak, 2013) and ultimately trading losses of more than $2 billion for JPMorgan Chase & Co. Finally, a graduate student at the University of Massachusetts uncovered a number of errors—including a relatively simple Excel coding mistake—made by the Harvard economists Carmen Reinhart and Kenneth Rogoff in their paper on the acceptable level of government indebtedness (Krugman, 2013). Although the monetary impact of their error is more difficult to quantify, the paper was widely used to influence economic policy. The lesson is that although it is boring, *check your data and your calculations and have someone else check them too!*

If responses are entered manually, it is *always* a good idea to have more than one person review the entered data for accuracy. One strategy is to have two different people enter the values and then have each check the other's work or have other people check the values. Data entry, particularly for larger data sets, can be tedious and mistakes are common.

When checking data, look for values that fall outside the allowed responses. For example, suppose you asked participants to respond to a series of questions using scale responses ranging from 1 to 7. Values less than 1 or greater than 7 would be invalid.

Visual displays, such as graphs and other figures that show numerical data, can help in identifying unusual data points. Extreme values or values that do not match the pattern of the rest of your data are known as **outliers**. Outliers may be valid, but they may also arise as a result of data entry errors.

Computing Descriptive Statistics

Descriptive statistics tell us about our samples. They are numerical values that summarize the data and give a sense of the shape and spread of the data or the extent to which two variables are related to one another. We distinguish between **univariate statistics**, which are computed for one variable at a time, and **bivariate statistics**, which characterize the relationship between two variables.

Univariate descriptive statistics fall into the categories of central tendency, dispersion, or shape. Measures of **central tendency**—including **mean**, **median**, and **mode**—let us know the typical or average values of our data. **Dispersion** refers to how spread out or variable data values are in our sample. **Shape** refers to whether the data values are normally distributed, have a flat or sharp peak, or are **skewed** to one end or the other of the data **range**. Bivariate statistics measure the degree to which two variables vary with one another, for example, whether higher verbal SAT scores tend to be accompanied by higher math SAT scores. Table 13.1 presents the most common descriptive statistics.

The three hypothetical data sets displayed in Table 13.2 will be used to illustrate the common univariate descriptive statistics and their associated visual displays. The first two sets of data show hours of television watched per week for 30 students at each of two different schools. The third shows response times in a timed task for 20 individuals.

Table 13.3 presents descriptive statistics for the three sets of data. The means and medians give us a sense of the "centers" of the data sets, about 20 for both television-watching samples and 1,000 for the response-time data. The **standard deviations** tell us how much, on average, the sample values tend to deviate from the mean values. We also see that the samples from the two schools have identical means and standard deviations, but diverge somewhat with respect to the median, percentiles, and **kurtosis**. These summary values start to give us a feel for the data, but it is difficult to get a full understanding from these numbers alone.

Outliers Extreme values that do not match the pattern of the rest of the data.

Descriptive statistics Numerical values that summarize the data and give a sense of the shape and spread of the data or the extent to which two variables are related to one another.

Univariate statistics Numerical values that summarize one variable at a time.

Bivariate statistics Numerical values that characterize the relationship between two variables.

Central tendency A description of the typical or average values of our data.

Mean (or arithmetic average) A measure of central tendency that is calculated by summing all of the values in a data set and then dividing by the number of values in the data set.

Median A measure of central tendency that is the middle value of all the data points; 50% of the values are below the median and 50% are above.

Table 13.1. Common univariate and bivariate descriptive statistics

UNIVARIATE DESCRIPTIVE STATISTICS
Central tendency
Mean—arithmetic average—sum of values divided by the number of values
Median—the middle value (or average of the two middle values for an even number of values)—50% of the values are below the median and 50% are above
Mode—the most common value
Dispersion/spread
Range—the maximum value minus the minimum value
Quantiles/percentiles—the Nth percentile is the value below which N% of the values fall; the median is the 50th percentile
Interquartile range—the range of values between the 25th and 75th percentiles
Variance—the average squared deviation of values from the mean value
Standard deviation—the square root of the variance
Shape
Skewness—a measure of how asymmetric a distribution of values is
Kurtosis—a measure of how flat or peaked a distribution is relative to the normal distribution
BIVARIATE DESCRIPTIVE STATISTICS
Association
Pearson correlation—measure of the strength of *linear* relationship between two interval or ratio variables
Spearman correlation—measure of the strength of relationship between two sets of ranks (ordinal data)
Phi (φ) coefficient and Cramer's V—correlation-like measures for the relationship between two categorical (nominal) variables

Mode A measure of central tendency; the most common value in the data set.

Dispersion Refers to how spread out or variable data values are in a sample.

Shape Refers to whether the data values are normally distributed, have a flat or sharp peak, or are skewed to one end or the other of the data range.

Skewness A measure of how asymmetric a distribution of values is.

Range The maximum value minus the minimum value in a data set.

Standard deviation A measure of the dispersion of a data set calculated by taking the square root of the variance.

Kurtosis A measure of the shape of a distribution that assesses how flat or peaked the distribution is relative to the normal distribution.

Creating Visual Displays for Univariate Descriptive Statistics

Presenting your data graphically can be extremely useful in helping you understand your data set and the story it tells. Commonly used graphical displays include stem-and-leaf plots, histograms, and box-and-whisker plots. These displays are particularly useful for helping you to understand any interval- or ratio-level variables in your data set. (See Table 6.1 in Chapter 6 to review the four measurement scales.)

Table 13.2. Sample data sets to illustrate descriptive statistics and visual displays

HOURS OF TELEVISION WATCHED PER WEEK						RESPONSE TIMES (MILLISECONDS)	
School 1			School 2				
21	35	24	16	30	15	763	861
31	19	25	14	15	29	690	881
12	29	33	10	13	17	2511	1100
17	16	11	28	12	22	1813	833
30	6	26	7	11	29	541	632
21	22	27	29	24	0	1045	891
18	22	21	13	26	30	1039	1133
3	0	22	28	8	35	999	941
10	27	13	14	19	14	772	750
19	17	8	20	26	31	962	1197

Table 13.3. Descriptive statistics for the three data sets in Table 13.2

	HOURS OF TELEVISION WATCHED PER WEEK		RESPONSE TIMES (MILLISECONDS)
	School 1	School 2	
Number of participants	30	30	20
Mean	19.5	19.5	1,017.7
Median	21	18	916
Minimum	0	0	541
Maximum	35	35	2,511
Range	35	35	1,970
Variance	77.3	77.3	194,679
Standard deviation	8.8	8.8	441.2
25th percentile	13.75	13.25	770
75th percentile	25.75	28	1,059
Skewness	-0.38	-0.11	2.4
Kurtosis	-0.31	-0.86	6.9

Stem-and-leaf plot
A simple way to display data for small to moderately sized data sets that involves using columns and numbers to represent the data. For example, the "stems" of the plots could be represented by a column of numbers in the tens places and the "leaves" could be captured by the ones places.

Unimodal A data set with a single peak in the distribution of data.

Bimodal A data set with two distinct peaks in the distribution of data.

Histogram A visual display of data that shows how many responses on a variable fall within predefined ranges of values with these counts being represented by bars in a chart.

Stem-and-leaf Plots.   **Stem-and-leaf plots** display data for small to moderately sized data sets in a simple yet informative way; they are less useful when counts are very small or large. Figure 13.1 shows stem-and-leaf plots for the two television-watching samples of Table 13.2. In this example, the "stems" of the plots are the tens places of the data values and are positioned to the left of the vertical lines. The "leaves" are the ones places and appear to the right of the vertical lines. The school 1 row of 2 | 56779, then, represents the five measurements for school 1 of 25, 26, 27, 27, and 29.

We learned from the descriptive statistics in Table 13.3 that the mean, range, and standard deviations for these two school data sets are identical. The stem-and-leaf plots, however, reveal that the shapes of the two samples are quite different. The sample for school 1 shows a single peak—i.e., it is **unimodal**—with more values in the lower 20's than anywhere else. In contrast, the school 2 values show two distinct peaks—**bimodal**—one in the lower teens and the other in the upper 20's. This relatively simple method of displaying data clearly tells us something about the samples we could not immediately see from the descriptive statistics alone.

Stem-and-leaf plots can be constructed easily by hand and give a good sense of the shape and spread of your data set. In addition, if no rounding is involved, stem-and-leaf plots completely preserve the data such that the precise data values can be recovered from the display.

Histograms.   **Histograms** show how many responses on a variable fall within predefined ranges of values with these counts being represented by bars in a chart. Figure 13.2 presents histograms for the two television-watching samples. The heights of the bars in the two histograms are identical to the numbers of leaves on each of the rows of the stem-and-leaf displays. For example, the bar representing 10-14 in the school 2 sample has a height of 8, which corresponds to the eight leaves of the 10-14 row in the school 2 stem-and-leaf display in Figure 13.1.

In essence, the stem-and-leaf plot is itself a kind of histogram because each row represents a range of values, and the number of leaves determines the length of the bar. Histograms, however, are more practical than stem-and-leaf plots as sample sizes increase. Larger data sets that might yield unwieldy stem-and-leaf plots can easily be represented in histograms.

Box-and-whisker Plot.   **Box-and-whisker plots** (often simply called **box plots**) display a number of descriptive statistics in graphical form. Two slightly different variations of box-and-whisker plots are shown in Figure 13.3 for the response time data of Table 13.2.

In the plot on the left, the minimum and maximum values are represented by the shorter horizontal bars (the "whiskers"), the median

Stems	Leaves		Stems	Leaves
0	03		0	0
0	68		0	78
1	0123		1	01233444
1	677899		1	55679
2	1112224		2	024
*2	56779		2	6688999
3	013		3	001
3	5		3	5
	School 1			School 2

*Represents the values of 25, 26, 27, 27, and 29.

FIGURE 13.1.   Stem-and-leaf displays for television-watching data of Table 13.2.

is represented by the heavy horizontal bar inside the box, and the box itself represents the **interquartile range**, meaning the range of values from the 25th percentile (the bottom of the box) to the 75th percentile (the top of the box). Although it is not always included, it is also instructive to include the mean, represented by the small filled squares in the plots.

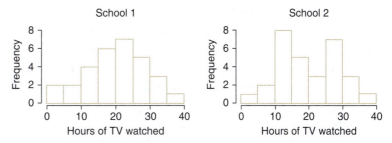

FIGURE 13.2.   Histograms for television-watching data.

The box-and-whisker plot on the left of Figure 13.3 reveals that the most extreme response times are not distributed symmetrically around the mean or median, with the maximum value being much farther than the minimum from the center. A slightly different version of this box-and-whisker plot is shown on the right of Figure 13.3. This version illustrates that the large spread of values above the central box in the plot on the left is caused by just two outliers. Rather than representing the absolute minimum and maximum values in this figure, the whiskers represent the most extreme values that fall within 1.5 times the interquartile range from the top and bottom of the box. Any values outside those limits are plotted as small circles. In this example, the interquartile range is $1{,}059 - 770 = 289$. Our new range for constructing whiskers, then, is from $770 - 1.5 \times 289$ to $1{,}059 + 1.5 \times 289$, or 336.5 to 1,492.5. The minimum data value of 541 does fall within this range, so the bottom whisker is identical in both plots. In contrast, the two largest values of 1,813 and 2,511 do not fall within this range, so they are represented by the open circles.

The box-and-whisker plot allows you to see whether the data set is symmetric about the mean, in what direction nonsymmetric data are skewed, how spread out the values are, how close the median and mean are to each other, and whether there are potential outliers in your data. Because of the amount of information conveyed in these plots, it is always a good idea to construct box-and-whisker plots for interval- or ratio-level variables (see Chapter 6 for a discussion of different measurement scales).

Box-and-whisker plots (or box plots) Visual display for presenting a number of descriptive statistics in graphical form. The box might be used to represent the interquartile range and the whiskers to represent the minimum and maximum of the data set.

Interquartile range The range of values from the 25th percentile to 75th percentile; the middle 50% of values.

Computing Bivariate Descriptive Statistics and Creating Visual Displays

Often, we are interested not only in describing single variables, but also in understanding how two variables are associated with one another. For example, if we collect high school and college grade point averages (GPA)

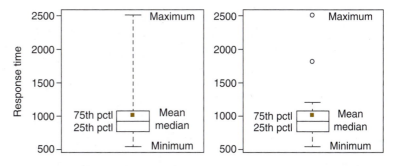

FIGURE 13.3.   Box-and-whisker plots for response-time data.

Pearson's r (or Pearson product-moment correlation) A bivariate statistic that measures the extent of the linear relationship between two interval- or ratio-level variables and ranges from −1 to 1.

Spearman's rho (ρ) (or Spearman rank-order correlation coefficient) A bivariate statistic used to measure the association between two ordinal/rank-order variables. This statistic varies from −1 to 1 and is typically used when data show a generally increasing (or decreasing) relationship between two variables, but one that is clearly not linear.

Categorical data Information captured by discrete groups or categories.

Contingency table (or cross tabulation) A tabular display for representing categorical or nominal level data.

for a sample of college seniors, we might be interested in knowing whether high school GPA is a strong predictor of college GPA or whether college GPA is only weakly related to high school GPA. Similarly, we might want to know how responses to different attitudinal questions on a survey about social and political issues are related to one another.

A common bivariate statistic for interval/ratio data is the Pearson product-moment correlation coefficient (often simply called **Pearson's r**). Pearson's r measures the extent of the linear relationship between two interval- or ratio-level variables and ranges from −1 to 1. A positive correlation indicates that larger values on one variable tend to be associated with larger values on the other (similarly for smaller values). A negative correlation indicates that larger values on one variable tend to be associated with smaller values on the other variable. A zero correlation indicates no linear relationship between the two variables.

The Spearman-rank order correlation coefficient (**Spearman's rho (ρ)**) is often used to measure the association between two ordinal/rank-order variables. Like Pearson's r, this statistic also varies from −1 to 1. Spearman's ρ is typically used when your data show a generally increasing (or decreasing) relationship between two variables, but one that is clearly not linear.

Categorical data, information captured by discrete groups or categories, are typically represented in a **contingency table**, which is not, strictly speaking, a descriptive statistic, but rather a tabular display. The correlation-like measures φ (**phi**) and **Cramer's V** are used to summarize data in contingency tables. For 2 × 2 contingency tables (for example, if we had two groups of participants and only two possible responses such as "yes"/"no," the φ coefficient may be computed as a measure of association between group membership and response). For contingency tables with more than two categories for either variable, Cramer's V may be used. Like Pearson's r, φ ranges from −1 to 1, whereas Cramer's V ranges from 0 to 1.

To illustrate the meaning of various values of φ, suppose you ask 60 people whether they prefer chocolate to vanilla ice cream and whether they prefer dogs to cats. Different sets of response are presented in the four different scenarios below.

	Scenario 1		Scenario 2		Scenario 3		Scenario 4	
	Prefer dogs?		Prefer dogs?		Prefer dogs?		Prefer dogs?	
Prefer chocolate?	No	Yes	No	Yes	No	Yes	No	Yes
No	8	16	24	0	0	24	18	6
Yes	12	24	0	36	36	0	11	25
	φ = 0.0		φ = 1.0		φ = -1.0		φ = 0.44	

In scenario 1, knowing whether a person prefers chocolate to vanilla ice cream tells you nothing about whether he/she prefers dogs to cats ($\varphi = 0.0$, indicating no relationship). Overall, there is a 40/60 or 2/3 chance that a person prefers dogs. If a person prefers chocolate, then there is still a 2/3 chance (24/36) he/she also prefers dogs. If a person does not prefer chocolate to vanilla, there is, again, a 2/3 chance (16/24) he or she also prefers dogs to cats. Knowing ice cream preference gives you no additional information about pet preference.

In scenario 2, if you know that a person prefers chocolate to vanilla, then you also know, with certainty, that he or she also prefers dogs to cats, so $\varphi = 1.0$, indicating a perfect positive relationship. In scenario 3, if you know a person prefers chocolate to vanilla, then you also know he or she does *not* prefer dogs to cats, indicating a perfect negative relationship between chocolate preference and dog preference ($\varphi = -1.0$). Finally, in scenario 4, if a person prefers chocolate to vanilla, he or she is more likely than not to prefer dogs to cats, but the relationship is not perfect. In this case, $\varphi = 0.44$.

Cramer's V extends the concept of φ when there are more than two options for one or both of the variables. Suppose we ask our 60 people whether they prefer strawberry, vanilla, or chocolate ice cream and whether they prefer snakes, cats, or dogs. Three possible sets of responses are considered below.

	Scenario 1			Scenario 2			Scenario 3		
	Snakes	Cats	Dogs	Snakes	Cats	Dogs	Snakes	Cats	Dogs
Strawberry	2	3	5	10	0	0	7	2	1
Vanilla	4	6	10	0	20	0	4	14	2
Chocolate	6	9	15	0	0	30	4	5	21
	Cramer's $V = 0$			Cramer's $V = 1$			Cramer's $V = 0.53$		

In scenario 1, knowing ice cream preference does not help you at all in determining pet preference, so Cramer's V equals 0 (no relationship). In scenario 2, if you know the ice cream preference, you know with certainty the pet preference, so Cramer's V is 1 (perfect relationship). Finally, in scenario 3, knowing ice cream preference gives you some (but not perfect) information about pet preference and in this case Cramer's V is 0.53.

Scatterplots.   A **scatterplot** simultaneously displays the values for two (or more) variables and is useful for investigating the relationship(s) between those variables. The values for hypothetical pairs of variables are displayed in the scatterplots in Figure 13.4, along with Pearson's r. Plot A presents two variables that are positively correlated with one another and the corresponding Pearson's r is 0.80, indicating a relatively strong positive relationship. Plot B illustrates a negative relationship between the two variables, with a Pearson's r of -0.80. Note that for both A and B, the relationships appear to be relatively linear.

Phi (φ) A correlation-like measure used to summarize data in 2×2 contingency tables.

Cramer's V A correlation-like measure used to summarize data in contingency tables.

Scatterplot A method for simultaneously displaying the values for two or more variables that is useful for investigating the relationship between those variables.

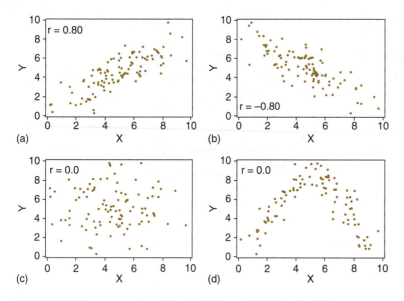

FIGURE 13.4.   Scatterplots showing (a) positive, (b) negative, (c) no, and (d) non-linear relationships between pairs of variables.

Plot C of Figure 13.4 displays two variables with a correlation of 0, indicating no relationship between them. In such a case, knowing whether X takes on a large or small value tells you nothing about whether the Y value is likely to be large or small.

Finally, the two variables represented in plot D also exhibit a Pearson correlation of 0.0. There is clearly a relationship between the variables, although not a linear one; rather, it is an inverted U relationship. A finding such as this underscores the importance of examining scatterplots to determine whether a relationship might exist between two variables that the Pearson correlation (a measure of linear association) might not reveal. Such nonlinear relationships may be modeled with more sophisticated techniques.

Contingency Tables.   When we have measurements on each of two categorical/nominal-level variables for a set of respondents, we can construct what is known as a contingency table or **cross-tabulation**. Suppose you sample 200 registered voters from city 1 and 150 from city 2 and ask them who they are likely to vote for in an upcoming presidential election. You might construct something like Table 13.4, in which each value in the table indicates the number of respondents who fall into the corresponding table cell. Of the 200 respondents in city 1, 75 intend to vote for candidate A and 105 for candidate B. Similarly, 75 of the City 2 respondents intend to vote for candidate A, but only 50 for candidate B.

In addition to the actual counts, it is also instructive to include percentages in the table. This is especially true when the row (or column) totals are unequal. In this example, we have included row percentages (the percentage of respondents in each row who fall into the given cell). However, depending on your design and purpose, column percentages may also be appropriate.

Although the visual displays previously described are among the most common for presenting data collected in behavioral research, there are many other types of displays that may prove helpful depending on what you hope to learn or convey. As researchers have struggled to understand large, complex data sets, new ways of visualizing data for both analysis and presentation have been developed. Useful resources include Cleveland (1993, 1994), Few (2006), Jacoby (1997, 1998), Harris (1999), and Tufte (1983). In addition,

Cross-tabulation (or contingency table)
A tabular display for representing categorical or nominal-level data.

Table 13.4. Contingency table for hypothetical voter study

NUMBER AND PERCENTAGE OF VOTERS PREFERRING EACH CANDIDATE					
	Candidate A	Candidate B	Someone else	Undecided	Total
City 1	75	105	5	15	200
	37.5%	52.5%	2.5%	7.5%	100%
City 2	75	50	13	12	150
	50%	33.3%	8.7%	8%	100%

Tukey (1977) presents a classic treatment of both graphical and nongraphical methods for exploratory data analysis.

Computing Effect Sizes

An important category of descriptive statistic is effect size, which we introduced in the section on power analysis in Chapter 6. According to Cohen (1990), "Effect-size measures include mean differences (raw or standardized), correlations and squared correlation of all kinds, odds ratios, kappas—whatever conveys the magnitude of the phenomenon of interest appropriate to the research context" (p. 1310). Cumming (2012) pithily describes an effect size as "simply the amount of something that might be of interest" (p. 34). An effect, then, is the primary measurement that you use to test your hypothesis, and effect size is simply the magnitude of that effect. There are three general classes of effect size: raw effects, standardized effects, and correlation-like effects.

Raw Effects. **Raw effects** (also called **unstandardized effects**) include common, straightforward measures such as the difference in the means for two samples. For example, if you observed the mean IQ scores for two different groups of respondents to be 101 and 113, the size of the raw effect of the difference of means would be 12. Raw effects are not adjusted based on measures of variability such as the standard deviation.

Standardized Effects. **Standardized effects** (also called *d* type effects) adjust the raw effect based on the amount of variability in your data. For example, a common measure of effect size for the independent-samples *t* test is **Cohen's *d*,** which is defined as the difference in the means for the two samples divided by a combined standard deviation for both samples. For example, if we continue with the IQ example and find that the standard deviation for our data values is 15, then Cohen's *d* would be the raw effect of 12 divided by the standard deviation of 15 to give a standardized effect size of 0.8.

Raw effects (or unstandardized effects) Common, straightforward measures of effect size such as the difference in the means for two samples.

Standardized effect (or *d* type effects) Adjusts the raw effect based on the amount of variability in the data.

Cohen's *d* A standardized effect size that is defined as the raw effect divided by its standard deviation.

Standardized effects have two main advantages over raw effects. The first is that they can readily be compared across studies even when the specific measures used are on different scales. For example, Cohen's d computed on data using a measurement scale ranging from 0 to 20 can be meaningfully compared with Cohen's d computed on data from a 0 to 100 scale. This comparison would not make sense using raw effects. The second advantage of standardized effects is that they can be interpreted with respect to the standard deviation. For example, the effect size of 0.8 for our IQ example tells us that the two groups differ in mean IQ scores by a little less than one standard deviation.

Table 13.5 illustrates the difference between raw and standardized effect sizes. The mean scores for groups A and B are identical in the two scenarios, but the standard deviations are twice as large in scenario 2. The raw effect size of the difference between mean scores is 12 in both scenarios, but the standardized effect, which we compute by dividing the raw effect by the standard deviation, is twice as large in scenario 1 as in scenario 2.

Correlation-like Effects.   These effects measure the association between two variables. Pearson's r and Spearman's ρ fall into this category. We can also compute a **point-biserial correlation**—the correlation between a binary variable (one that takes on only two values such as "yes" or "no") and a continuous variable—as an effect size when comparing the means of two independent samples. To continue with our IQ example, if we assign a numerical value of 0 to all respondents in the first of our two groups and a 1 to all respondents in the second group, then the Pearson correlation of this 0/1 group variable with the continuous IQ score variable is a point-biserial correlation.

Correlation-like measures such as eta squared (η^2) and omega squared (ω^2) may be computed with analysis of variance designs, where we have multiple factors or more than two levels on a single factor. Although showing how these effect sizes are computed is beyond the scope of this chapter, they are part of the standard output of many statistical packages. The relationships between pairs of variables in contingency tables are often quantified using φ for 2 × 2 tables and Cramer's V for tables with more than two categories on either

Point-biserial correlation A measure that describes the degree to which a binary variable (e.g., yes/no) relates to a continuous variable.

	SCENARIO 1		SCENARIO 2	
Table 13.5. Illustration of the difference between raw and standardized effects				
	Group A	Group B	Group A	Group B
Mean IQ score	101	113	101	113
Std. deviation	15	15	30	30
Raw effect	12		12	
Standardized effect (Cohen's d)	0.80		0.40	

variable. We will present several of
these effect sizes for the examples
discussed in Chapter 14 with specific
inferential tests.

Confidence Intervals

Whereas effect size indicates the magnitude of a finding, confidence intervals give a sense of the precision of
your estimate of the effect. A **confidence interval** is a range of values
around the effect size obtained in your
sample that is likely to contain the
true population effect size with a given
level of plausibility or confidence.

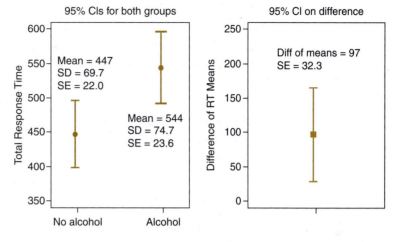

FIGURE 13.5.   Confidence intervals for means and difference of means.

Confidence interval
A range of values
around the effect size
obtained in a sample
that is likely to contain
the true population
effect size with a given
level of plausibility or
confidence.

Most commonly, we use 90% or 95% confidence intervals in behavioral research. A 95%
confidence interval is constructed so that if we were able to identify the true population
value of our measure of interest (e.g., a difference of two group means), there is a 95% chance
that our confidence interval would contain that true value. The size of a confidence interval
depends on both the variability in your data and your sample size.

Figure 13.5 presents confidence intervals for a hypothetical study examining the effects
of alcohol on speed of response in a timed task. The plot on the left shows 95% confidence
intervals for the means for each of the two experimental conditions (alcohol vs. no alcohol).
The lower and upper bounds of a confidence interval are obtained by multiplying the critical t value by the standard error and then adding that resulting value to and subtracting it
from the mean to obtain the upper and lower 95% confidence bounds, respectively. The plot
on the right shows the 95% confidence interval for the difference of the two means.

INFERENTIAL STATISTICS AND NULL HYPOTHESIS
SIGNIFICANCE TESTING

To this point we have presented methods for describing and displaying collected data. Depending on the details of your study, you have computed such statistics as means, medians,
standard deviations, correlations, frequencies, and proportions, and you have displayed
your data and/or summary statistics using box-and-whisker plots, stem-and-leaf plots, histograms, scatterplots, or contingency tables. Where appropriate, you have also computed
effect sizes and confidence intervals.

One might argue that once all of these steps have been completed, you have done all you
need to in terms of analysis and all that remains is interpretation. Most behavioral researchers,
however, have traditionally followed one additional step: applying **inferential statistical tests**,

**Inferential statistical
tests** Statistical
methods such as t tests
or χ^2 tests that help
researchers draw
conclusions about data.

that is, statistical methods such as t tests or chi-square (χ^2) tests that help you in drawing conclusions about your data. Furthermore, they typically apply these tests in the context of what has become known as **null hypothesis significance testing (NHST).**

NHST generally comprises the following steps:

1. Specify a **null hypothesis** (usually denoted H_0). This is typically (but not necessarily) a hypothesis of "no effect," meaning, for example, no difference between mean responses for different experimental conditions or zero statistical correlation between two variables. An alternative hypothesis (denoted H_1 or H_A) of "not H_0" is usually implied. For example, there *is* a difference in mean responses or there *is* a linear relationship between two variables.

2. Choose a **statistical significance level**, denoted by the Greek letter alpha (α), typically 0.05 or 0.01.

3. Compute your **test statistics** (e.g., t, F, χ^2) and their associated **probability (p) values**. This p value indicates how likely you were to see results at least as extreme as those you observed under the assumption that the null hypothesis is true.

4. If the computed value of p is smaller than the significance level chosen in Step 2, then reject H_0. If $p > \alpha$, then we fail to reject the null hypothesis and treat the test results as statistically nonsignificant. We might be tempted to use the less convoluted phrase of "accept the null hypothesis" rather than "fail to reject the null hypothesis," but the former implies that we have proven that the null hypothesis is, in fact, true, and this is not the case.

Example 1: Assessing the Fairness of a Coin

To illustrate the steps and logic of NHST, we start with a simple example of determining whether a coin is fair by flipping it 20 times. If the coin is fair, we would expect to get somewhere in the neighborhood of 10 heads and 10 tails. How far from an equal split of heads and tails, however, would lead us to conclude the coin is unfair?

We know that we cannot necessarily expect to get exactly 10 heads and 10 tails in 20 flips. In any process that involves uncertainty, we anticipate fluctuations from the expected value just by chance. This chance deviation is known as **sampling error**. Note that the term "error" in this context does not indicate any kind of mistake, but a difference between what we observe in the sample and what we would expect from the population.

Referring back to step 1 of NHST, we will specify a null hypothesis (H_0). In this case, our null hypothesis is that the coin is fair—in other words, that the probability of getting a head on any given flip is exactly 0.5, as is the probability of getting a tail, that is, $\text{prob}(H) = \text{prob}(T) = 0.5$. The alternative hypothesis (H_A) is that the coin is not fair.

With these two hypotheses, consider the possibilities outlined in Table 13.6 regarding the true state of the coin and what we might conclude about it after we conduct our experiment of flipping the coin 20 times.

Two of the cells represent a correct decision and two represent errors. If the coin is fair and we do not reject the null hypothesis of a fair coin, then we have made a correct decision.

Null hypothesis significance testing (NHST) A traditional approach to inferential statistical tests that attempts to determine whether a specific hypothesis (the null hypothesis) can be rejected at a given probability level.

Null hypothesis Typically, a statement of "no effect" in your results. For example, a null hypothesis might suggest no difference in mean responses for different experimental conditions or zero correlation between two variables.

Statistical significance level A conventional value, usually 0.05 or 0.01, used to assess whether the null hypothesis in NHST should be rejected.

Test statistics Computed values associated with particular approaches designed to test hypotheses.

Probability value (or p value) Indicates how likely it would be to see results at least as extreme as those observed under the assumption that the null hypothesis is true.

Table 13.6.   Illustration of Type I and Type II error in coin-flipping example

	WHAT DO WE CONCLUDE AFTER FLIPPING THE COIN 20 TIMES?	
What is the true state of the coin?	Fail to reject null hypothesis that coin is fair	Reject null hypothesis that coin is fair
Coin is fair (H_0) Prob(H) = Prob(T) = 0.5	Correct decision	Type I error
Coin is unfair (H_A) Prob(H) ≠ 0.5; Prob(T) ≠ 0.5	Type II error	Correct decision

Similarly, if the coin is unfair and we reject the null hypothesis of a fair coin, this is also a correct decision. A **type I error** occurs if you conclude the coin is unfair—that is, you reject the null hypothesis—when, in fact, the null hypothesis is true. In this example, a type I error would occur if we conclude that the coin is unfair when it is actually fair. The probability of a type I error is the same as the value of α noted in step 2 above.

A **type II error** occurs when you fail to reject a null hypothesis when it is, in fact, false. Here we would fail to reject the null hypothesis of a fair coin when the coin is actually unfair. The probability of a type II error is typically denoted by the Greek letter beta (β). Another way to say this is that β represents the probability of failing to identify an experimental effect when such an effect actually does exist. Recall that in Chapter 6 we discussed the concept of the power of your experimental design. The quantity 1 – β is known as the power of the test and tells you, in essence, how likely you are to detect a real effect of a certain magnitude given your sample size. A power of 0.80 has traditionally been considered a reasonable level to shoot for, although the powers of studies frequently fall well below this mark (Cohen, 1962; Maxwell, 2004; Mone, Mueller, & Mauland, 1996; Rossi, 1990; Sedlmeier & Gigerenzer, 1989).

For step 2 of NHST, the traditional approach is to set the probability of a type I error sufficiently low, so that if you performed your experiment over and over, you would commit a type I error, on average, only 1 time in 20. In other words, the probability of a type I error, α, is 1/20 = 0.05. Another often-used α level is 0.01 (or 1/100), but for our coin-flipping experiment, we will use an α level of 0.05.

The key to using NHST to draw conclusions about our data comes in step 3, in which we compute test statistics and p values based on certain assumptions about the data. With our coin-flipping example, we do not need to compute a test statistic but can directly compute a p value using rules of probability theory. Suppose we flip the coin 20 times and obtain 15 heads and 5 tails. For a fair coin, the probabilities of obtaining 0 through 20 heads on 20 flips are presented in Table 13.7.

Sampling error Chance fluctuations between the measurements observed in a data set and what would be expected from the population values.

Type I error Occurs if a researcher rejects the null hypothesis when, in fact, the null hypothesis is true.

Type II error Occurs if a researcher fails to reject the null hypothesis when, in fact, it is false.

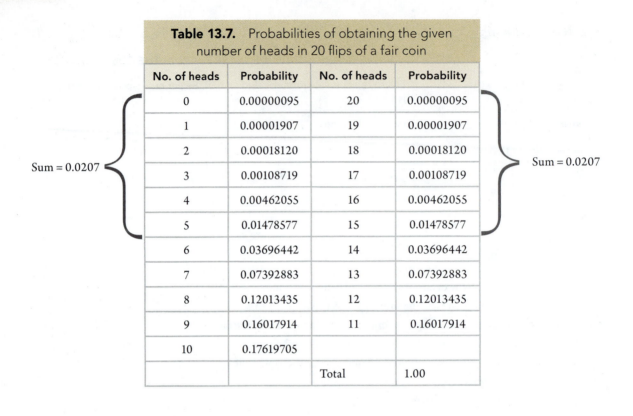

Table 13.7.   Probabilities of obtaining the given number of heads in 20 flips of a fair coin

No. of heads	Probability	No. of heads	Probability
0	0.00000095	20	0.00000095
1	0.00001907	19	0.00001907
2	0.00018120	18	0.00018120
3	0.00108719	17	0.00108719
4	0.00462055	16	0.00462055
5	0.01478577	15	0.01478577
6	0.03696442	14	0.03696442
7	0.07392883	13	0.07392883
8	0.12013435	12	0.12013435
9	0.16017914	11	0.16017914
10	0.17619705		
		Total	1.00

Sum = 0.0207

Sum = 0.0207

When we compute a p value for an inferential test, what we are computing is the probability of obtaining a result *at least as extreme* as the one we obtained *given that the null hypothesis is true*. With 15 heads on 20 flips, we would add up the probabilities of obtaining 15 heads, 16 heads, and so on up to 20 heads. This gives a total probability of 0.0207. We are not done computing the p value of interest, however, because we also need to consider that the coin might be biased toward tails. A result of 15, 16, ..., or 20 tails would be just as extreme a result as 15, 16, ..., or 20 heads, so when we add up all the values, we obtain a p value of $0.0207 + 0.0207 \approx 0.041$.

Finally, we apply step 4 of NHST. We had set an α level of 0.05 and we computed a p value of 0.041. Because 0.041 is less than 0.05, we reject the null hypothesis of a fair coin in favor of the hypothesis of an unfair coin.

Example 2: Comparison of Two Means

To understand the logic of statistical inference for situations more complex than coin-flipping, for example, comparing the mean responses across different experimental conditions, we need to review four statistical concepts: the normal distribution, sampling distributions, standard error, and the central limit theorem.

The Normal Distribution. The **normal distribution** is central to the traditional approach to statistical inference, and a number of statistical tests for means include an assumption of normally distributed populations. Figure 13.6A displays the histogram for a hypothetical population of normally distributed values with a mean of 100 and standard deviation

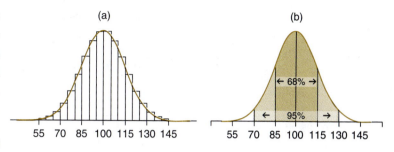

FIGURE 13.6. Histograms for a hypothetical population of normally distributed values.

of 15. The smooth curve overlay takes the shape of the classic bell curve of the normal distribution.

The normal distribution has several important features. It is symmetric about its mean, median, and mode, all of which are equivalent. Furthermore, as shown in Figure 13.6B, 68% of the values fall within one standard deviation on either side of the mean, and 95% of the values fall within 1.96 standard deviations on either side of the mean.

Sampling Distributions.   When we collect data and compare the responses for different groups or experimental conditions, we generally do not compare individual responses across the groups, but instead compare summary statistics—such as means or proportions—from each sample. Sampling distributions describe the distributions of values for these summary statistics.

Suppose we take a random sample of 20 men from a large population of men, measure their heights, and compute the mean of those 20 heights. Then we take a second random sample of 20 men and compute their mean height. We continue to do this many times computing mean heights for each sample of 20 men. Now, in addition to the original distribution of individual heights in the population, we have a distribution of means based on these many samples of size 20. This distribution of means is the **sampling distribution of the mean** for a sample size of 20. If we had used repeated samples of, say, 30, we would have a different sampling distribution.

Sampling distributions are not limited to means. In theory, they may be constructed for any summary statistic such as medians, standard deviations, ranges, and even differences in means for pairs of samples (this latter is the sampling distribution used for the independent groups t test). In practice, we are rarely able to draw large numbers of samples from our population of interest, so we are not able to construct a sampling distribution based on repeated sampling from that population. Instead we *estimate* the sampling distribution based on the relatively few samples we do collect.

The top row of Figure 13.7 displays sampling distributions of the mean for sample sizes of 1, 5, and 10. The bottom row displays sampling distributions for the difference obtained

Normal distribution
A unimodal pattern of data, with the mode occurring in the center of the distribution, with values dropping off sharply in a symmetrical pattern on both sides of the mean. The traditional approach to statistical inferences assumes that the data in a sample are normally distributed.

Sampling distribution of the mean The pattern of mean values obtained when drawing many random samples of a given size from a population and computing the mean for each sample.

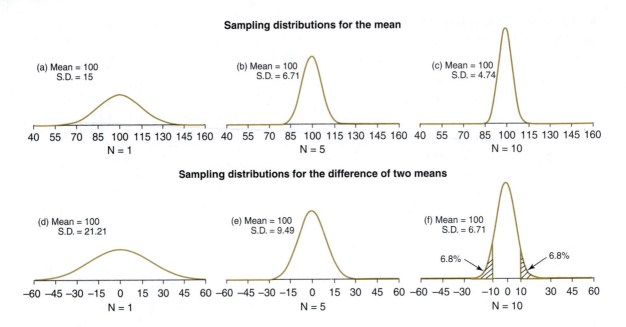

FIGURE 13.7. Sampling distributions of the mean and difference of pairs of means for samples sizes of 1, 5, and 10.

by repeatedly drawing pairs of samples, each of the given sample size, and computing the difference between each pair of means. These are all based on an original "population" of values that are normally distributed with a mean of 100 and standard deviation of 15. Note that a sampling distribution for a sample size of one simply reflects the original distribution of values.

To see how the sampling distribution informs inferences about our data, we will focus on the plot in Figure 13.7f. Suppose we collect information for two groups of 10 participants and we find that the mean score for group 2 is 10 points higher than that for group 1. Suppose we make the simplifying assumption that the standard deviation of the population is 15. Then we have the situation illustrated in Figure 13.7f. The two shaded regions represent differences in pairs of means of 10 or more. We see that these two regions account for 13.6% of all values. Given the assumptions of a normally distributed population with a standard deviation of 15, if both samples were drawn from this same population, we would expect a difference in means of 10 or more 13.6% of the time, or with a probability of 0.136. In reality, we rarely, if ever, know the true standard deviations of the populations we are studying, so we must estimate them from our samples. In such cases, we use the *t* distribution, rather than the normal distribution, to compute the probabilities, but the same logic holds true.

As illustrated in Figure 13.7, an important property of sampling distributions is that as sample size increases, the variability (**variance**, standard deviation) of the sampling distribution decreases. This leads us to the concept of standard error.

Standard Error.   A **standard error** is the standard deviation of a sampling distribution. In Figures 13.7a–c, the variability in the distributions reflects the standard errors of the mean for sample sizes of 1, 5, and 10. In Figures 13.7d–f, the variability reflects the standard error of the *difference* of pairs of sample means for sample sizes of 1, 5, and 10. The standard error decreases as sample size increases in a very regular way: the standard error of the sampling distribution equals the standard deviation of the original distribution divided by the square root of the sample size, that is:

$$\text{Standard error} = \text{Standard deviation}/\sqrt{N}.$$

As a result, the larger the sample size, the greater precision in our estimates and the smaller our p value will be. The standard error of the mean plays an important role in the computation of both confidence intervals and test statistics, such as the t value for a t test.

Central Limit Theorem.   In Figure 13.7, we can see that the sampling distributions of both means and differences of means when sampling from a normal distribution appear to be normally distributed themselves, and this is, in fact, true. Figure 13.8 displays two distributions that deviate substantially from a normal distribution, one being bimodal and the other being heavily skewed. Also presented are sampling distributions of means and differences of pairs of means for samples sizes of 2, 5, and 10. Remarkably, despite the marked nonnormality in the populations, the sampling distributions appear to take on the familiar normal curve shape with increasing sample size.

The **central limit theorem** confirms this observation and tells us that even with populations having dramatically nonnormal distributions, the sampling distribution of the mean will be increasingly normal in shape as sample sizes increase. This allows us to make use of the many attractive properties of the normal distribution, even when underlying distributions may not themselves be normal.

NHST has been the dominant approach for drawing inferences about data for a long time. Arbuthnot (1710) introduced it in an essay arguing for the existence of God, based on the fact that if one studied birth records over time there always seemed to be a relatively equal number of boys and girls. Techniques developed by R.A. Fisher, J. Neyman, E. Pearson, and others instrumental to the creation of modern statistics have been used to apply NHST in a wide variety of situations (Robinson & Wainer, 2001). Although much of psychological research has been based on applications of NHST, criticisms of this approach have increased over the past several decades. In this next section we explore these criticisms to emphasize that researchers should always be thoughtful about the decisions they make in the design and analysis of their research.

Variance A measure of the dispersion of a data set; the average squared deviation of values from the mean value.

Standard error The standard deviation of a sampling distribution. This value is calculated by dividing the standard deviation by the square root of the sample size.

Central limit theorem Theorem that says with a large sample size, the sampling distribution of the mean will be normal or nearly normal in shape.

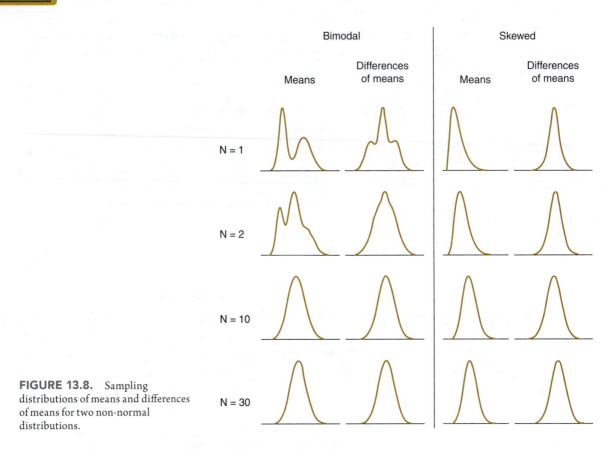

FIGURE 13.8. Sampling distributions of means and differences of means for two non-normal distributions.

CRITICISMS OF NHST

Although behavioral researchers have relied heavily on NHST to analyze and interpret data, criticisms of NHST have appeared regularly (Carver, 1978, 1993; Gigerenzer, 2004; Hubbard & Lindsay, 2008; Krueger, 2001; Loftus, 1996; Rozeboom, 1960). Although some support of NHST continues (Hagen, 1997; Harris, 1997; Wainer, 1999), many arguments in its favor have been refuted (Schmidt & Hunter, 1997), leading to demands for modifications to or the outright abandonment of NHST in a variety of fields. As criticisms mount, it is clear that the traditional NHST approach has serious limitations, some of which are based on misunderstanding and misapplication of the process and others on NHST's inherent weaknesses as a tool in the scientific endeavor. Common issues surrounding the use of NHST are (1) the misuse of p as an indicator of effect size or importance, (2) the arbitrary nature of a reject/fail-to-reject decision based on p, (3) the various misinterpretations of what p actually tells us, and (4) the overemphasis on α and type I errors leading to underpowered research studies.

Misuse of *p* as an Indicator of Importance

Unfortunately, some researchers misinterpret statistical significance as a measure of the size of an effect or as a measure of the meaningfulness of a result. The word "significance" in NHST refers only to *statistical* significance and to neither the magnitude of the effect (e.g., the value of a correlation or the difference between two means) nor the substantive importance of the result (i.e., how meaningful the result is). The *p* value used to evaluate statistical significance depends on three things: the size of the experimental effect, the sample size, and the variation in sample values. We will focus on sample size to show why *p* is a poor indicator of effect size or importance.

Consider Table 13.8, which presents the results of six hypothetical studies evaluating the effectiveness of two teaching methods. Each study includes two independent groups of students, one experiencing method 1 and the other experiencing method 2, with the measurement being student scores on an exam of 100 possible points. Both study 1 and study 2 show method 2 having an eight-point advantage over method 1; that is, the magnitude of the raw effect in both studies is identical. Yet, because of the difference in sample size, the *p* value resulting from an independent samples *t* test for study 2 is 0.016 (statistically significant by the α = 0.05 criterion), whereas the *p* value for study 1 is 0.09 (not statistically significant). Although we have the same raw effect in both studies, NHST leads us to reject the null hypothesis of no difference for study 1, but fail to reject the null hypothesis for study 2.

Now consider studies 3 and 4. For both studies, method 2 enjoys a two-point advantage over method 1. Again, however, a difference in sample sizes leads to different *p* values (in this case, substantially different) and conflicting decisions on whether to reject or fail to reject the null hypothesis.

The other piece of information the *p* value does not carry is the theoretical importance of the result. Study 4 yields a statistically significant *p*, but to what extent is a two-point

Lawrence Hubert: *"Any good methodologist has not pushed NHST for 60 years. You do effect sizes and confidence intervals, and NHST isn't relevant at all. It's just not where it's at. In the era of Big Data we can find out so many things but we don't know whether they're chance happenings or real results. One of the most important things we need to do is talk about methods in a way that visualizes data and helps students get a sense of random processes."*

Table 13.8. Results of six hypothetical studies to illustrate problems with the *p* value

	N of each group	Mean test scores		Difference of means	Std. dev. in each group	*p*
		Method 1	Method 2			
Study 1	10	70	78	8	10	0.090
Study 2	20	70	78	8	10	0.016
Study 3	30	70	72	2	10	0.44
Study 4	200	70	72	2	10	0.046
Study 5	13	70	78	8	10	0.053
Study 6	14	70	78	8	10	0.044

increase on test scores an important finding? In contrast, study 1 yields a larger p value than study 4, but the eight-point advantage (nearly a whole letter grade) of method 2 over method 1 in study 1 might well be considered a meaningful result.

It is clear from these examples that p is a poor surrogate for effect size, yet effect size is one of the findings we should most care about. It is, therefore, recommended that effect sizes be included in the presentation of any research results (see Wilkinson et al., 1999), and many journal editors now require this information to be included in any publication. The practical importance of a finding can only be determined in the context of the particular phenomenon under investigation (e.g., a small effect may be quite important in medicine), but it should be clear that gauging importance should not rely so heavily on the magnitude of p.

Arbitrary Nature of Reject/Fail-to-Reject Decisions

As we saw in the steps outlining the NHST process, once we have computed our test statistic and p value, we either reject the null hypothesis if our computed p is below our prespecified cutoff value of (usually) 0.05 or 0.01, or we fail to reject the null hypothesis if p is too large. Does such a dichotomous decision to either reject or fail to reject the null hypothesis make sense?

Consider studies 5 and 6 in the final two rows of Table 13.8. A strict adherence to NHST and a critical p value of 0.05 would lead us to reject the null hypothesis of no difference between the two methods for study 6. However, we would fail to reject the same null hypothesis in study 5, although the mean difference in both studies is identical and the sample sizes differ only by one case. It seems preferable to use a process in which we treat the evidence for or against our experimental hypothesis in a more continuous rather than all-or-none manner, for example, through the use of confidence intervals.

Misinterpretation of the *p* Value

Inverse probability fallacy Refers to researchers interpreting the p value as a measure of the probability of the null hypothesis being true given the results observed, when this value is dependent on a number of other assumptions, such as the prior probability of the null hypothesis and the alternative hypothesis being true.

As we have noted, the p value computed in statistical tests has a specific and somewhat limiting interpretation: *it is the probability of obtaining a result at least as extreme as the one you observe given that the null hypothesis is true.* Said differently, if you repeated your experiment a large number of times using the same population and sample size, you would expect to obtain results at least as extreme as the ones you observed $100 \times p$ percent of the time.

Researchers have misunderstood and misinterpreted the p value in a variety of ways. Goodman (2008) identified "a dirty dozen" of such misconceptions. One is the **inverse probability fallacy** (Carver, 1978), which refers to researchers interpreting the p value as *a measure of the probability of the null hypothesis being true given the results we observed.* Although it would be tremendously useful to know this probability, it depends on several assumptions about other probabilities (e.g., the prior probability of H_0 being true and the prior probability of H_A being true).

A second misinterpretation is the **replication fallacy** (Carver, 1978), which points to the assumption that the value of $1 - p$ refers to the probability that we would obtain a statistically significant result if we replicated the experiment. It is tempting to believe, for example, that a p value of 0.05 means we have a 0.95 (or 95%) chance of obtaining a statistically significant result in a replication, but this is not the case.

A third fallacy is known as the **odds-against-chance fallacy** (Carver, 1978). In this misconception, p is interpreted as the probability that the obtained result occurred by chance. For example, a p of 0.01 would suggest that there is a probability of only 1 in 100 that the results are due to chance and a probability of 99 in 100 that the observed effect is real. In fact, the p value is computed based on the premise that the results were 100% due to chance, that is, caused by sampling error. If the sample means in a study with two samples are identical, there is no need to carry out the statistical test. If the sample means are different then, under the assumption of a true null hypothesis, this difference must be due to chance.

> **Replication fallacy**
> The assumption that the value of $1 - p$ refers to the probability of obtaining a statistically significant result if the experiment were to be replicated.

> **Odds-against-chance fallacy** A misconception where p is interpreted as the probability that the obtained result occurred by chance.

A Culture of Low-Power Studies

Earlier in this chapter we described type I and type II errors and revisited the concept of statistical power from Chapter 6. Recall that a test is powerful to the extent that it is able to detect an effect of a certain size. If, for example, we consistently designed studies to achieve statistical power of 0.8 for medium-size effects, then over the course of many such experiments, we would expect to detect an effect 80% of the time.

Figure 13.9 demonstrates how statistical power increases with sample size when comparing means from two independent samples (where the independent-samples t test is typically applied). This relationship is shown for three different values of Cohen's d, a commonly used measure of effect size. The values of 0.2, 0.5, and 0.8 for small, medium, and large effect sizes were suggested by Cohen (1988), although the relative importance of an effect of a given size will very much depend on the specific context.

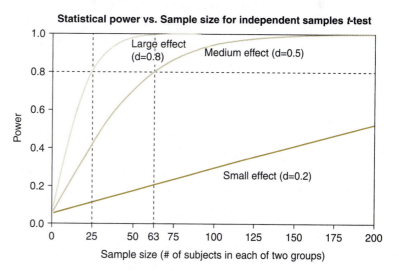

FIGURE 13.9. Statistical power as a function of sample size when comparing the means from two independent groups.

The dashed horizontal line in Figure 13.9 corresponds to the widely accepted benchmark of 0.8 at which a study is deemed to have adequate power. To achieve such power in the presence of a large effect, 25 participants (the leftmost dotted vertical line) would be required for each of the two groups. For a study with a medium effect size, samples sizes of 63 (the rightmost dotted vertical line) are required to achieve a power of 0.8. Finally, the point at which the "small effect" curve meets the 0.8 power line reaches well beyond the extent of the chart and, in fact, 393 participants would be required in each of the two samples.

A number of researchers have examined statistical power across many published studies and found that the average power to detect small or even medium effects is often below 0.5 (Cohen, 1962: Fraley & Vazire, 2014; Rossi, 1990; Sedlmeier & Gigerenzer, 1989). A power of 0.5 means that in half the studies in which a real, medium effect exists, the null hypothesis will *not* be rejected. Low power can lead to an increase in type II error, leading a researcher to potentially equate failure to reject H_0 with no effect. In turn, this may lead to the researcher deciding not to submit the statistically nonsignificant findings to a journal, contributing to the file-drawer problem described in Chapter 10 (i.e., the research report is not accepted for publication, contributing to a bias in published studies; see "Media Matters: Publication Bias and a Possible Solution").

GOING BEYOND NHST: EFFECT SIZE AND CONFIDENCE INTERVALS

Given the limitations of NHST, how can we improve on the analysis and interpretation of data? We recommend using effect sizes, confidence intervals, replication, and meta-analysis as tools to augment (and perhaps replace) NHST in the investigation and analysis of data.

1. Perform a power analysis as part of the design of your study. In doing so, you will be forced to think about effect size (see Step 3) and will have a much better sense of what your sample size should be.
2. After checking data and performing any necessary cleaning, compute descriptive statistics and construct visual displays.
3. Compute—and place more focus on—effect sizes.
4. Construct and visually present confidence intervals around effect size measures such as means, differences in means, and correlations.
5. Carry out your inferential tests and compute p values, but do not let p be the main driver for the presentation and interpretation of results.
6. As part of any continuing research program (in contrast to a single experiment or two), incorporate replication and meta-analysis as part of the cumulative scientific endeavor.

MEDIA MATTERS

Publication Bias and a Possible Solution

Editors at top scientific journals have traditionally shown bias when selecting from the hundreds of new research papers coming out every year. They tend to look for studies that have produced positive and innovative results, the kind that make readers (and reporters) sit up and take notice and help launch younger researchers' careers. They also tend to shun so-called negative findings, those that declare a theory is unsupported or discount a relationship between two things.

As a result, the editorial process motivates some researchers to manipulate their methods or comb through their data until they come upon a positive finding. This practice has come to be known as "p-Hacking" because it stems from a desire to the make statistical significance stronger and hence the findings more believable.

This environment has also discouraged researchers from attempting replication of previous studies, which, as a *Slate* article put it, "is science's most basic way of verifying correctness" (Meyer & Chabris, 2014). This has led many to declare a "replication crisis" in scientific research, including psychology. A 2012 survey of the top 100 psychology journals discovered that a scant 1% of papers published since 1990 were true attempts at reproducing previous findings (Meyer & Chabris, 2014).

These problems have prompted distress in the scientific community for years. One widely cited 2005 paper by the Stanford epidemiologist John Ioannidis asserted,

The high rate of nonreplication of research discoveries is a consequence of the convenient, ill-founded strategy of claiming conclusive research findings solely on the basis of a single study assessed by formal statistical significance, typically for a *p* value less than 0.05. Research is not most appropriately represented and summarized by *p* values, but unfortunately, there is a widespread notion that medical research articles should be interpreted based only on *p* values. (Ioannidis, 2005)

Recently, mainstream media have begun to weigh in on the matter. *The Guardian* ran a story about Registered Replication Reports, a project launched by three psychologists seeking to raise the standard of psychological research (Gage, 2013). The journal *Perspectives on Psychological Science* has begun publishing a new article type, the Registered Replication Report, which consists of multilaboratory, high-quality replications of important experiments in psychological science along with comments by the authors of the original studies.

The *New York Times* reported that the federal government was soliciting public comment "on how [it could] 'leverage its role as a significant funder of scientific research to most effectively address' the replication crisis" (Nyhan, 2014). The writer, an assistant professor of government at Dartmouth College, suggests that journal editors and peer reviewers study designs and analysis plans and pledge to publish the results if the researchers conduct and report the study in a professional manner (Nyhan, 2014). That approach, Nyhan argues, will motivate authors and reviewers to develop the strongest possible designs and discourage them from finding or emphasizing significant results after the fact. Nyhan ends his article optimistically, noting that several journals across the social and natural sciences have adopted a new scientific format titled Registered Reports, which uses this approach. If federal funding rewarded publications that used Registered Reports, top scientists would respond accordingly, and publication bias would decrease (Nyhan, 2014).

Focus on Effect Size

There are a number of reasons to emphasize effect size rather than simply using the p value as a decision-making criterion:

- In nearly all cases, we are (or should be) interested in the actual size of the effect and not simply whether we have enough evidence to reject the null hypothesis of no effect.
- Effect sizes are not dependent on sample size in the way that p is. As we increase our sample size, the effect size will start to converge to the actual population value. In contrast, the p value approaches 0 with increasing sample size.
- Computations of power require the specification of an effect size (albeit prior to collecting your data).
- Effect sizes (particularly of the d and r types) can be meaningfully compared with one another. This can be useful when performing a meta-analysis (see Chapter 10).
- We can place confidence intervals around effect sizes to get a sense of the precision of our findings.

Use Confidence Intervals

Like p values, confidence intervals depend on the variability in your sample values and on the sample size. All other things being equal, confidence intervals narrow as your sample size increases. Like p values, confidence intervals may be used to draw the types of inferences (e.g., reject/fail to reject) common with NHST. In fact, confidence intervals on a single mean or on a difference of two means may be used to reject/fail to reject the null hypothesis of no difference with precisely the same results as the p value.

Similar to p values, confidence intervals are subject to misinterpretation. When we construct a 95% confidence interval, this does *not* mean that there is a 95% chance that the population mean falls within the boundaries of that interval. The population mean has a specific value and it either does or does not fall within our interval range. The correct interpretation is that if we knew the population mean, there is a 95% chance that our interval would include that mean (Savory, 2008). Said differently, in the long run, we would expect 19 of 20 of the 95% confidence intervals we construct to contain the true population mean (Savory, 2008).

Given the many shared characteristics of p values and confidence intervals, why would we recommend confidence intervals in addition to or even in lieu of p values? Confidence intervals give you a sense of the precision of your results; that is, they provide a range of values for your effect that might be considered reasonable given your data. By doing so, they also lead you to focus on effect size as opposed to only the p value, which, as described previously, tells you nothing of substance about your effect.

Practical Tips for Analyzing Your Data

1. Plan your data analysis before you collect your data.

2. Be sure to check and double-check your data.

3. As the first part of your analysis, always compute descriptive statistics and create visual displays of your data.

4. Be sure your statistical tests are appropriate for your data.

5. Be sure to check all calculations.

CHAPTER SUMMARY

All data analysis should begin with a thorough checking of your data, ideally with the help of someone else, so that you know your analysis will be accurate. Once you have completed that task, using descriptive statistics and visual displays will give you a deeper understanding of the numerical values in your data and the story they tell about your samples.

Data for individual variables may be displayed in stem-and-leaf plots, histograms, and box-and-whisker plots. For examining the relationship between two variables, data may be displayed in scatterplots or contingency tables. The Pearson product-moment and Spearman rank-order correlations measure the strength of the relationship between two variables.

An effect size communicates the magnitude of your phenomenon of interest. Effect size comprises three general classes: raw effects, standardized effects, and correlation-like effects.

Whereas effect size indicates the magnitude of a finding, confidence intervals give a sense of the precision of your estimate of the effect. Confidence intervals are computed for either traditional statistics such as means and differences of means or standardized effect sizes.

NHST is a traditional data analysis tool used by behavioral researchers that has come under heavy criticism over the past several decades. Researchers who rely solely on NHST commonly misinterpret the p value and tend to produce low-power studies. Effect sizes, confidence intervals, replication, and meta-analysis can all be used to augment or even replace NHST in the investigation and analysis of data.

Up for Discussion

1. Suppose you are interested in the impact of different types of background noise on performance in a memory task. You randomly assign participants to one of three groups, which differ in the type of noise presented. Once you have collected your data, the first thing you do is compute the mean scores on the memory task for each group and find that they are nearly identical. At this point, should you simply conclude that there were no differences among the three groups and move on to another study? If not, what are some things you might want to do with the data?

2. We compute statistical power to determine how likely we are to detect an experimental effect of a given size. What it means to "detect" an effect relies on the concept of the p value. For example, when designing an experiment in which we compare an experimental group with a control group, we might say something like "given a standardized effect size of 0.5 and 40 participants in each group, the power to detect this effect at the $p = 0.05$ level is 0.61." Given the many problems with using the p value for statistical inference, do you think statistical power is still useful? Why or why not?

3. Suppose you run an experiment to examine the effects of alcohol consumption on speed of response in a timed task. Participants in one group consume no alcohol, whereas those in the second group consume a moderate amount of alcohol. What types of information do each of the following give you to help you understand your data or draw conclusions about your results?

   (a) Descriptive statistics for the response times in each group (mean, standard deviation, etc.).

   (b) Box-and-whisker plots of response times for each group.

   (c) Confidence intervals for mean response times in each group.

   (d) A confidence interval for the difference in mean response time between the two groups.

   (e) Cohen's d for the difference of means.

   (f) The p value from the t test on the difference of means.

Key Terms

Bimodal, p. 308

Bivariate statistics, p. 305

Box-and-whisker plots (or box plots), pp. 308, 309

Categorical data, p. 310

Central limit theorem, p. 321

Central tendency, p. 305

Cohen's d, p. 313

Confidence interval, p. 315

Contingency table, p. 310

Cramer's V, pp. 310, 311

Cross-tabulation, p. 312

Data cleaning, p. 304

Descriptive statistics, p. 305

Dispersion, pp. 305, 306

Histogram, p. 308

Inferential statistical tests, p. 315

Interquartile range, p. 309

Inverse probability fallacy, p. 324

Kurtosis, pp. 305, 306

Mean (or arithmetic average), p. 305

Median, p. 305

Mode, pp. 305, 306

Normal distribution, p. 319

Null hypothesis, p. 316

Null hypothesis significance testing (NHST), p. 316

Odds-against-chance fallacy, p. 325

Outliers, p. 305

Pearson's r (or Pearson product-moment correlation), p. 310

Phi (φ), pp. 310, 311

Point-biserial correlation, p. 314

Probability value (or p value), p. 316

Range, pp. 305, 306

Raw effects (or unstandardized effects), p. 313

Analyzing Your Data II: Specific Approaches

INSIDE RESEARCH: YING ("ALISON") CHENG

Associate Professor of Psychology,
University of Notre Dame

As an undergraduate in China I majored in English and electrical engineering, and I earned a master's degree in statistics from the University of Illinois Urbana–Champaign. With the help of my mentors, Hua-Hua Chang and Lawrence Hubert (see "Inside Research," Chapter 13), I was able to further develop my interest in quantitative psychology, which is basically psychology interfacing with statistics. I obtained my Ph.D. in quantitative psychology in 2008.

Eventually I began to focus on computerized adaptive testing, or CAT, which uses item selection algorithms. Very large testing programs, such as the GRE and GMAT, use adaptive testing to make their tests more efficient. Essentially, CAT adjusts the level of questions in response to the estimated ability of the person taking the test, so that the test will not present very difficult questions to someone who is not performing well, or very easy questions to someone who is getting them all correct. This makes the testing experience more efficient, because it saves time and maintains measurement precision.

Most recently, I have been exploring the problem of examinees who are unduly penalized for inadvertently making mistakes early in the test because they were warming up or thinking too much. This is actually a common phenomenon that has been observed by test preparation companies. They tell their students, "Make sure you get the first bunch of questions correct if you're taking an adaptive test. If you get them wrong, then the test's estimate of your ability will be so low that you can never get a good score on the test."

At first people assumed this was a myth that was spread word-of-mouth. But in 2009, researchers started to look at this and found that it was true and that there were statistical reasons behind it. Recently I published a paper that shows having a parameter to account for such behavior can help, so that test-takers will not be sent to such low extremes that they can never recover, even if they made mistakes on the early questions.

A famous and highly influential statistician named John Tukey said, "The best thing about being a statistician is that you get to play in everyone's backyard." I feel the same being a quantitative psychologist, because we deal with all sorts of data from psychologists. For example, I get to work with developmental psychologists and help them plan their data collection scheme and design experiments and interventions. I also work with health psychologists and help them design clinical trials at multiple sites all over the country. The contributions of quantitative psychologists are highly valued and it is fun to be able to see how various subdisciplines within psychology benefit from our expertise and experience.

Ying ("Alison") Cheng uses advanced statistics in her research on educational and psychological testing. She has won a number of awards for her research, recently the 2012 Jason Millman Promising Scholar Award, which is given by the National Council on Measurement in Education, for her investigations into computerized adaptive testing to assess performance in schools.

Research Focus: Psychological and educational measurement, in particular item response theory, including computerized adaptive testing and equity across ethnicity and gender groups

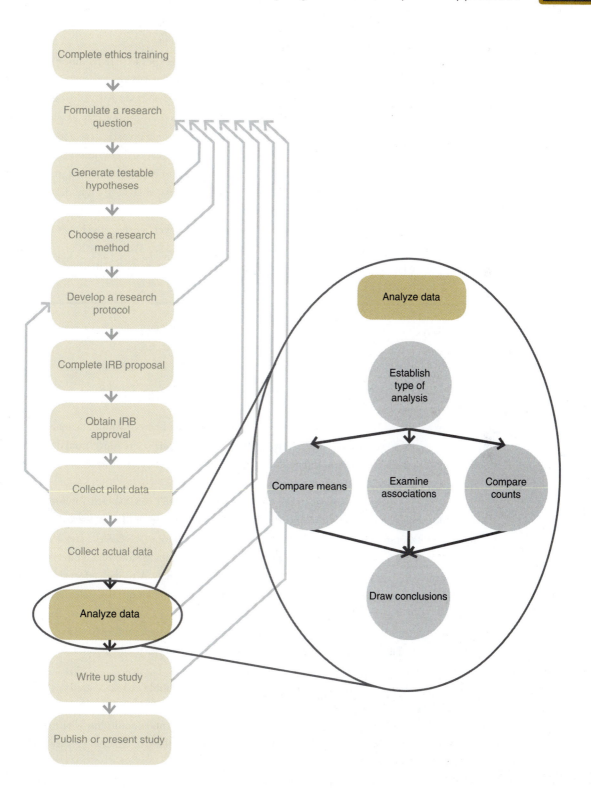

Ying "Alison" Cheng:

"NHST is widely used in virtually every discipline that involves using data to justify or falsify a statistical hypothesis. However, it has been subject to criticism for several reasons. One is that statistical significance does not equal practical significance. Any effect size can turn statistically significant provided a large enough sample size. Some journals have taken a serious stance on this issue. For example, Psychological Science recommends the use of the "new statistics" (e.g., effect sizes, confidence intervals). The journal Basic and Applied Social Psychology even published an editorial asking authors to remove all statistics of NHST prior to publication."

Chapter Abstract

In this chapter, we present analysis techniques for the types of data commonly encountered in behavioral research. At the core of your analysis plan you should consider how best to answer the research question you have designed your study to address. It is also important to realize that few, if any, research studies turn out exactly as planned. To understand your results, you will probably have to do some investigative data sleuthing. We begin the chapter with a general approach to data analysis, providing flowcharts to help you choose your path of analysis depending on your experimental design, the scales of your measures, and whether you are comparing means, analyzing count data, or investigating associations among variables. We also emphasize the use of visual displays to help you understand and interpret your results. Moreover, we describe how to use effect sizes and confidence intervals as you work with your data. We end with brief introductions to two modern sets of tools for data analysis, robust statistical methods and Bayesian data analysis.

GENERAL APPROACH TO DATA ANALYSIS

In Chapter 13, we identified a number of steps to take as part of your data analysis. These steps include computing descriptive statistics and effect sizes, creating visual displays, and constructing confidence intervals. In this chapter we will describe each of these steps in detail for a variety of different types of data analysis.

Although we presented a number of criticisms of NHST in Chapter 13 and recommend deemphasizing inferential tests in drawing conclusions from your data, we do include such tests throughout this chapter (e.g., t test, analysis of variance (ANOVA), χ^2 test). At present, NHST still represents the dominant approach in psychology and related disciplines and remains the approach expected by many academic journals. Although effect sizes and confidence intervals are increasingly required to be reported in journal articles, the emphasis remains on test statistics and their associated p values (see "Media Matters: The Power of the p Value"). In addition, many decades' worth of published studies have used NHST to analyze data, and you must be familiar with inferential tests to understand the interpretation of results in these studies.

As we have emphasized throughout this book, you should choose a statistical approach *as you develop your research question and plan your study*. You should know whether you will be comparing mean responses across various experimental conditions, whether you will compute measures of association between pairs of variables, or whether you are interested

The Power of the *p* Value

Many researchers have questioned the soundness of the traditional NHST approach for decades. The continued power of *p* values in current research, however, cannot be denied. No one knows this better than W. Scott Harkonen, a physician who was prosecuted and sentenced to six months of home confinement in 2013 for his interpretation of *p* values in medical research. Specifically, what landed Harkonen in hot water was a two-sentence press release based on that interpretation.

Harkonen had been the chief executive officer of InterMune, a publicly traded biotechnology company that manufactured a drug called interferon-γ-1b (marketed as Actimmune) to help patients suffering from idiopathic pulmonary fibrosis (IPF), a terminal lung disease (Brown, 2013). In hopes of gaining U.S. Food and Drug Administration approval for Actimmune in the treatment of IPF, InterMune launched a clinical trial in 2000 that randomly assigned 330 patients in 58 hospitals around the world to receive either interferon-γ-1b or placebo injections (Brown, 2013). Of the patients receiving the placebo, 52% worsened or died, whereas only 46% of those receiving Actimmune had the same outcomes. The trial's results had a *p* value of 0.08, which is larger than 0.05, the conventionally accepted level of significance (Brown, 2013). Within the traditional NHST approach to statistical hypothesis testing, this $p = 0.08$ value would not allow the researcher to conclude that the drug was effective.

Yet, Harkonen remained hopeful about proving the drug's efficacy. After examining the data more closely, Harkonen found that more patients with mild to moderate cases of IPF survived than the original participant group as a whole (Briggs, 2013). When InterMune's statisticians ran the numbers again within that subset, they found that only 5% of those patients died, as opposed to 16% of the original group. These percentages yielded a *p* value of 0.04, a value that suggests the drug was effective. Excited by the new interpretation, Harkonen issued the following press release: "InterMune Announces Phase III Data Demonstrating Survival Benefit of Actimmune in IPF. Reduces Mortality by 70% in Patients with Mild to Moderate Disease" (Brown, 2013).

Harkonen's statement was technically true, which is what makes this case so strange. But someone (in fact, another statistician, by the name of Thomas Fleming) took issue with Harkonen's methodology (Briggs, 2013). The U.S. government agreed and filed a lawsuit, alleging that Harkonen drew "improper conclusions" from the data and that he did so for financial gain (Brown, 2013). He was convicted of fraud, a decision that was upheld by the 9th Circuit Court of Appeals.

According to Allan Gordus, a lawyer in the Justice Department's office of consumer litigation, "The government has always agreed that there was no falsification of data here. Whether there was falsification of the conclusions that could be drawn from the data—that was what the trial was all about" (Brown, 2013).

Goodman put Harkonen's conviction in another context in an article that appeared in *Nature*: "This would be a lot like throwing weathermen in jail if they predicted a 40% chance of rain, and it rained" (Callaway, 2013).

Although this case did not draw much media attention apart from an article in the *Washington Post*, it alarmed the drug industry and countless researchers who rely on *p* values to establish statistical significance. "If you applied this rule to scientists, a sizable proportion of them might be in jail today," said Steven N. Goodman, a pediatrician and biostatistician at Stanford University who submitted a statement supporting Harkonen's appeal (Brown, 2013).

Harkonen asked the U.S. Supreme Court to review his case, but he was denied in December 2013

(Walsh, 2013). He served his home incarceration and paid a fine of $20,000. In addition, he was banned by the U.S. Department of Health and Human Services from working for virtually all medical institutions until 2016 and barred by the U.S. Food and Drug Administration from employment by any company seeking the agency's approval for a product (Brown, 2013).

in differences in the frequencies of certain types of responses. Figures 14.1 and 14.2 are meant to help you determine the steps that should be part of your data analysis.

Figure 14.1 outlines the decisions you must make to compare means. To the left in Figure 14.1 is the decision tree to consider if your comparisons involve a between-subjects design, and to the right is the decision tree for determining what kind of analysis to

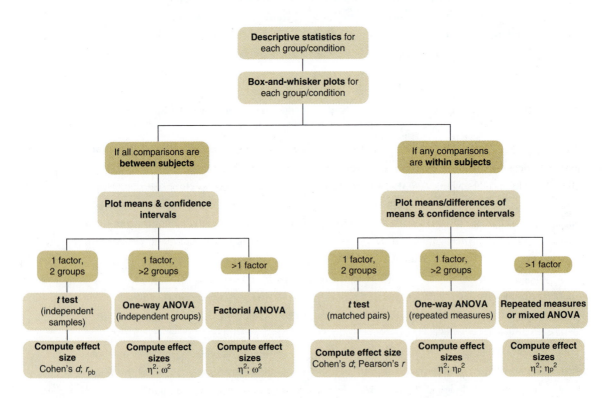

FIGURE 14.1. Data analysis flowchart for comparing means.

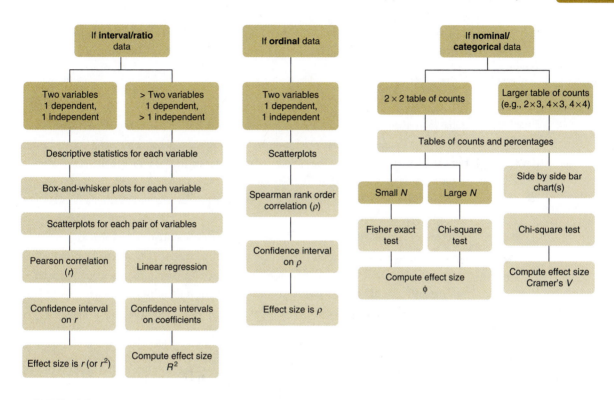

FIGURE 14.2. Data analysis flowchart for examining relationships among variables.

conduct for within-subjects or mixed designs. The second row from the bottom lists particular statistical tests that can be done (e.g., *t* test, one-way ANOVA, factorial ANOVA). At the top, middle, and bottom of Figure 14.1 are reminders to calculate descriptive statistics, visually display your means and confidence intervals, and compute effect sizes. The decision trees in the figure address questions about whether you have a between- or within-subjects design and whether you are examining one or more factors or one or more groups of participants.

Not all research questions, however, require comparisons of means. Many research studies explore the relationships between two or more variables. Figure 14.2 provides a data analysis flowchart for deciding what type of analysis to use to explore a research question involving such relationships. The top row of Figure 14.2 presents different types of data (e.g., interval/ratio, ordinal, nominal/categorical) and the second row displays the steps or decisions that must be made depending on the number of variables and the size of your sample. As with the comparison of means, the bottom row advocates for the calculation of effect sizes.

In the next section, we provide a review of the methods for comparing two or more means. We then review statistical approaches to examining the association between variables.

COMPARING MEANS

Behavioral researchers are commonly interested in looking at patterns of means across conditions. The standard approach to the mean for a single sample or comparing the means for two samples is to use *t* tests. The approach for comparing means for more than two samples or for more than one factor is called an **analysis of variance (ANOVA)**. Both of these approaches include variations depending on whether the researcher has used a between- or within-subjects design.

A *t* test or an ANOVA test is an example of a **parametric statistical test** that assumes data are interval or ratio level and the distribution of data values is normally distributed. **Nonparametric statistical tests** do not make such strong assumptions and can be used to analyze ordinal and nominal data and data sets that deviate substantially from normality. With each parametric test below, we also list a nonparametric alternative.

One-Sample *t* Test

The **one-sample *t* test** is used to compare the mean of a single sample with some criterion or "standard." The assumptions of this test are as follows:

Assumptions:

1. Interval- or ratio-level data.
2. Observations/cases are *randomly sampled* from the population of interest.
3. Observations/cases are *independent* of one another.
4. The values in the population from which we are sampling are *normally distributed*.

Nonparametric alternative: one-sample **Wilcoxon signed-rank test**

When the data are either ordinal or nonnormally distributed, the one-sample Wilcoxon signed-rank test may be used as a nonparametric alternative.

As an example, we revisit the school 1 data set introduced in Table 13.2. The stem-and-leaf plot, box-and-whisker plot, and frequency histogram for these data are reproduced in Figure 14.3. Suppose you want to know whether students in school 1 watch more hours of television per week than a reported national average of 22 hours. Hence, 22 is the value that we will compare our sample mean against. These 30 values have a mean of 19.5, a median of 21, a range of 35, and a standard deviation of 8.79. From Figure 14.3, the data look to be relatively symmetric about the mean, perhaps with a slight *negative skew* (there is a longer tail to the left than to the right), but none of these displays suggests that the data values deviate seriously from normality or that there are problematic outliers (see the section on assumption violations later in this chapter for more formal methods of assessing normality).

Analysis of variance (ANOVA) A statistical technique to test for differences among means. (See also **one-way ANOVA, repeated-measures one-way ANOVA, two-way ANOVA.**)

Parametric statistical test A statistical test that requires data to be interval or ratio level and makes strong assumptions about the distribution of measurements in the population. Such distributions have parameters such as the mean and standard deviation.

Nonparametric statistical tests A statistical test that makes few assumptions about the distribution of measurements in the population and does not require data to be interval or ratio level. Some nonparametric tests are appropriate for ordinal-level data and others require only nominal-level data.

t test, one sample A statistical test for comparing the mean of a single sample to a specified value.

Wilcoxon signed-rank test A nonparametric alternative to the one-sample or matched-pairs *t* tests.

Our raw effect size is simply the sample mean of 19.5 minus the hypothesized value of 22, which gives −2.5. We can also compute a standardized (*d*-type) effect size such as Cohen's *d*, which is simply the difference of −2.5 divided by the sample standard deviation of 8.79, giving a *d* value of −0.28 (which would likely be considered a "small" effect). There is no *r*-type effect size in the one-sample case, since such effects measure the strength of relationship between two (or more) variables.

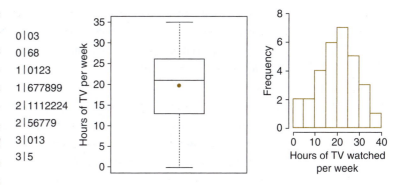

```
0 | 03
0 | 68
1 | 0123
1 | 677899
2 | 1112224
2 | 56779
3 | 013
3 | 5
```

FIGURE 14.3.   Stem-and-leaf display, box-and-whisker plot, and histogram for the school 1 data in Table 13.2.

Confidence intervals on the mean are computed as follows:

$$\bar{X} \pm t_{crit} * SE$$

$\bar{X}$ is the sample mean, SE is the standard error of the mean, and t_{crit} is the critical *t* value that depends on the prespecified α level and sample size. The t_{crit} can be obtained from a table of critical values for the *t* distribution often found in statistics books or online (merely search online for *t* distribution critical values). For a 95% confidence interval with a sample size of 30, the critical value of *t* is 2.045, so the confidence interval is 19.5 ± 3.28 or the range 16.22 to 22.78. This confidence interval includes the national average of 22 hours, so we are unlikely to conclude that students of school 1 watch statistically fewer hours of television than the national average. We can also construct the confidence interval around the difference of -2.5, giving us the range of -5.78 to 0.78. Here, we see that a difference of 0 is included within the confidence interval, so again we are unlikely to conclude that the students of school 1 watch statistically fewer hours of television than the national average.

Finally, we compute our test statistic *t* using the following formula:

$$t = \frac{(\bar{X} - \mu_0)}{s / \sqrt{N}}, df = N - 1$$

In the formula, $\bar{X}$ is the sample mean, μ_0 is the value to which you want to compare the sample mean, s is the sample standard deviation, and *n* is the sample size. The term in the denominator, $s / \sqrt{N}$, is the SE of the mean, the same SE value used in constructing our 95% confidence interval. The number of **degrees of freedom (df)** is the number of values that are free to vary in the computation of a statistic. For example, if you know the mean

Degrees of freedom (df) The number of values that are free to vary in the computation of a statistic.

of 10 values, once you have identified 9 of those values, the 10th can be readily determined. Therefore, in this case there are 9 values that are free to vary, so the number of degrees of freedom is 9. It is important to understand that for different statistical tests, the degrees of freedom will depend on the sample size and/or the number of groups being studied.

For a one-sample t test, there are $n - 1$ degrees of freedom, so in this example, $t = -1.558$ with $df = 30 - 1 = 29$. This t value is associated with a p value of 0.13. Since 0.13 is greater than our α value of 0.05, we fail to reject H_0 and cannot conclude that the average number of hours of television watched in this classroom differs from the national average.

Independent-Samples t Test

t test, independent samples A statistical test for comparing the means of two independent samples.

An **independent-samples t test** is used to compare the means of two independent samples. Assumptions of the test and alternative tests follow. Regarding the fourth assumption, the impact of unequal variances is less when your two samples are the same size, so it is a good practice to try to obtain the same number of participants per group (Mewhort, Kelly, & Johns, 2009).

Assumptions:

1. Interval- or ratio-level data.
2. Random sampling and independence of observations/cases.
3. The values in the two populations from which the samples are drawn are normally distributed.
4. The two populations from which the samples were drawn have equal variances.

Welch's t test
A version of the independent-samples t test that takes into account unequal variances between the two groups.

Alternative test when variances cannot be assumed to be equal: **Welch's t test**

Nonparametric alternative: **Mann–Whitney U test/Wilcoxon rank-sum test**

Mann–Whitney U test (or Wilcoxon rank-sum test) A nonparametric alternative to the independent-samples t test.

The values in Table 14.1 represent total response times across 10 trials for 20 hypothetical participants participating in a Stroop interference task (see Chapter 1). In the interference condition, respondents had to name the color of the ink for color words where the ink color disagreed with the color named by the word, for example, the word "red" printed in blue ink. In the no-interference condition, color-neutral words were used with the same color-naming task, for example, the word "cat" printed in blue ink. Each participant took part in only one of the conditions.

Table 14.2 presents descriptive statistics for these two samples and Figure 14.4 displays box-and-whisker plots and histograms. The visual displays do not reveal any severe outliers or obvious deviations from normality. The variance for the interference group is larger than that for the no-interference group by a factor of about 2.5, but this is still within a reasonable range. We also see a good degree of separation between the two groups, both in the box-and-whisker plot and in the histogram, suggesting a fairly strong effect.

Table 14.1. Total response times across 10 trials for 20 participants, half assigned to each of two conditions in a Stroop task

TOTAL RESPONSE TIME (SEC) FOR 10 TRIALS	
No interference	Interference
3.27	4.08
3.35	5.46
2.07	3.89
2.62	5.13
2.51	2.58
3.63	3.12
3.45	3.51
4.28	4.37
3.91	6.11
2.64	4.87

Table 14.2. Descriptive statistics for Stroop data of Table 14.1

	No Interference	Interference
Mean	3.17	4.31
Median	3.31	4.23
Std. dev.	0.69	1.10
Variance	0.48	1.20
N	10	10

Effect sizes can be calculated a number of different ways, and some variation exists in how different statistical packages calculate effect size. For this data set, we find that when we calculate the effect size using the difference of means (effect size = 1.14), Cohen's d (effect size = 1.24), or a point-biserial correlation ($r_{pb} = 0.55$), each of these measures suggests a large effect.

Just as in the one-sample case, confidence intervals may be constructed for each of the two groups by computing the standard errors (standard deviation divided by the square root of N) and finding the critical value of $t = 2.26$ for a 95% confidence interval with

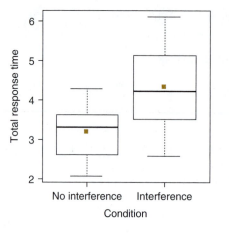
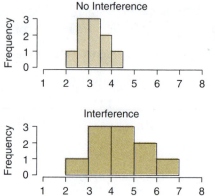

FIGURE 14.4. Box-and-whisker plots and histograms for data in Table 14.1.

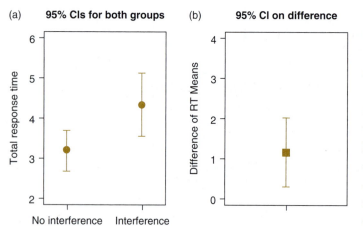
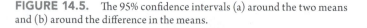

FIGURE 14.5. The 95% confidence intervals (a) around the two means and (b) around the difference in the means.

$10 - 1 = 9$ degrees of freedom. This gives 95% confidence intervals ranging from 2.68 to 3.67 and 3.53 to 5.10 for the no-interference and interference groups, respectively. These are plotted on the left of Figure 14.5. Note that the confidence intervals for the two conditions overlap just a little. The overlap in confidence intervals does not necessarily suggest that the difference is statistically nonsignificant, so it is useful to construct the 95% confidence interval for the difference of the two means. Doing so gives us 1.14 ± 0.86, or a range from 0.28 to 2.00. This confidence interval does not span 0, so we are on solid ground in concluding that the means for the two groups are not equal to one another. The confidence interval for the difference of the means is displayed on the right side of Figure 14.5.

Applying the independent-samples t test gives us $t(18) = 2.77$, $p = 0.013$. Our p value is less than 0.05, so we reject the null hypothesis of no difference between the means. Note that for the independent-samples t test, $df = N - 2$ where N is the total count for both samples.

Matched-Pairs t Test

A **matched-pairs t test** compares means of the same participants on two different measures. Test assumptions and an alternative test are shown here:

Assumptions:

1. Interval- or ratio-level data.
2. Random sampling.

t test, matched pairs A statistical test for comparing the means of two matched samples. The samples may represent two different measurements from the same participants or may represent different participants matched on some criteria (e.g., academic achievement).

3. Independence of observations (between cases, not within).
4. Difference scores are normally distributed.

  Nonparametric alternative: Wilcoxon signed-rank test

  Suppose you want to determine whether juniors at a particular high school score higher on the math portion of a standardized test than on the verbal portion. You randomly select 10 juniors, administer the tests, and collect the test scores as shown in Table 14.3.

  Since the same individuals are participating in both conditions, our two conditions are not independent of one another, and we should not use the independent-samples t test. The matched-pairs t test operates on the differences of the matched scores, that is, the differences between the math scores and verbal scores, computed for each individual. The mean difference between the math and verbal scores is 8.1, and the 95% confidence interval for this mean ranges from 1.30 to 14.90. Since the confidence interval does not include 0, we would conclude that the juniors in the school do score differently on the two portions of the standardized test. To determine the size of the effect, we could calculate the effect size using the difference of means (effect size = 8.1), Cohen's d ($d = 0.85$), or a Pearson correlation ($r = 0.72$), all of which indicate a large effect.

  Application of the matched-pairs t test gives $t(9) = 2.70, p = 0.025$, and we would reject the null hypothesis of no difference between the two sets of test scores. Note, again, how the

Table 14.3. Verbal and math test scores for 10 students

Student	VERBAL Score	MATH Score	DIFFERENCE (math–verbal)
1	43	52	9
2	54	76	22
3	56	70	14
4	65	75	10
5	72	69	-3
6	72	71	-1
7	73	80	7
8	79	71	-8
9	79	96	17
10	81	95	14
Mean	67.4	75.5	8.1
Standard deviation	12.6	12.9	9.5

p value leads to the same conclusion of rejecting the null hypothesis as the 95% confidence interval, but that the confidence interval combined with the mean value gives us important information about the size of the difference and the precision of our estimate.

COMPARISONS OF MORE THAN TWO MEANS: ANOVA

One-way analysis of variance (ANOVA)
A statistical technique to test for differences of means on a single factor.

Often we want to consider the means from more than just two groups, samples, or conditions. If we wish to compare the means for three or more samples on a single factor, then we employ **one-way analysis of variance (ANOVA)**. Just as with *t* tests in the two group case, the analysis proceeds differently depending on whether we have used a between-subjects design (independent groups) or a within-subjects design (repeated measures).

Independent-Groups One-Way ANOVA (Between Subjects)

A one-way ANOVA is used to compare two or more independent samples. The assumptions for independent-groups one-way ANOVA are identical to those of the independent-samples *t* test:

Assumptions:

1. Interval- or ratio-level data.
2. Random sampling and independence of observations.
3. The values in the *k* populations from which the samples are drawn are normally distributed (*k* = # of groups or factor levels).
4. The *k* populations have equal variances (homogeneity of variance).

Kruskal–Wallis test
A nonparametric alternative to one-way analysis of variance.

Nonparametric alternative: **Kruskal–Wallis test**

Consider a specific example using the hypothetical caffeine experiment described in Chapter 8, where we tested the effects of caffeine on performance in a memory task. We will first start with a between-subjects version of this experiment and later consider a within-subjects version when we discuss repeated-measures ANOVA below.

Each of 30 participants is randomly assigned to one of three conditions: a "caffeine-free" condition, where participants are given a cup of herbal tea before performing the memory task; a "moderate-caffeine condition," where participants are given a cup of green tea before the task; and a "high-caffeine condition," where participants are given three shots of strong coffee before the task. The memory task scores for each participant, along with means, medians, standard deviations, and standard errors, are shown in Table 14.4. Box-and-whisker plots and 95% confidence interval plots are shown in Figure 14.6.

The plots in Figure 14.6 strongly suggest a difference between the moderate caffeine group and the other two groups. On the one hand, there is a small amount of overlap between the moderate- and high-caffeine confidence intervals and somewhat more overlap for the moderate- and no-caffeine groups. The high- and no-caffeine groups, on the other hand, have similar means and nearly completely overlapping confidence intervals.

Table 14.4. Data and descriptive statistics for memory task for 30 participants, each assigned to one of three conditions

	No caffeine	Moderate caffeine	High caffeine
	88	78	85
	82	82	84
	79	93	64
	90	91	66
	68	94	87
	70	69	74
	61	90	82
	65	76	77
	91	96	59
	75	88	69
Mean	76.9	85.7	74.7
Median	77.0	89.0	75.5
Standard dev.	10.8	9.0	9.8
Standard error	3.4	2.8	3.1

ANOVA table A table used to organize and display the results of analysis of variance.

Sums of squares Mathematical quantities that measure the amount of variability in data. These include between-subjects, within-subjects, and total sums of squares.

The **ANOVA table** for these data is presented in Table 14.5. Three types of **sums of squares**, all of which measure the amount of variability in the data, are displayed. The between-subjects sum of squares shows the extent to which the group means deviate from the overall mean. The within-subjects sum of squares indicates the extent to which each data point deviates from its group mean. Adding the between- and within-subjects values gives the total sum of squares that indicates the extent to which the data values deviate from the overall mean. Each mean square value, which is computed by dividing the corresponding sum of squares by its associated degrees of freedom, is an estimate of the population variance. If the between-subjects mean square is considerably larger

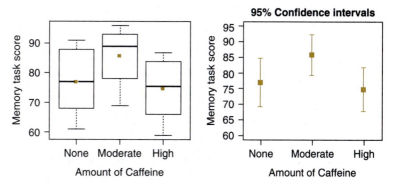

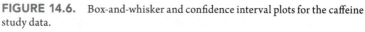

FIGURE 14.6. Box-and-whisker and confidence interval plots for the caffeine study data.

Table 14.5. One-way analysis of variance table for between-subjects caffeine study

	Sum of squares	df	Mean square	F	p
Between subjects	677.6	2	338.8	3.46	0.046
Within subjects (error)	2,647.1	27	98.0		
Total	3,324.7	29			

than the within-subjects mean square, this is evidence that the population means differ from one another.

Omnibus null hypothesis In analysis of variance, the null hypothesis that all group means are equal.

The **omnibus null hypothesis** tested by one-way ANOVA is that the population means for all the groups are equal. In this example, the null hypothesis is as follows:

$$H_0: \mu_{moderate\_caffeine} = \mu_{high\_caffeine} = \mu_{no\_caffeine}$$

According to the ANOVA table, the p value associated with this null hypothesis for the caffeine experiment is 0.046. This is smaller than our standard α level of 0.05, so we would reject the null hypothesis and conclude that the three population means are not equal.

Eta squared (η^2) An effect size measure for one-way analysis of variance.

A common effect size for a one-way ANOVA is **eta squared** (η^2), which is defined as

$$\eta^2 = \frac{SS_{between}}{SS_{total}}$$

The value of η^2 ranges from 0 to 1. For the caffeine data, $\eta^2 = 0.20$. According to Cohen (1988), an effect size of 0.20 is considered small, 0.50 medium, and 0.80 or higher large. For this example we have obtained a relatively small effect.

Multiple Comparisons

As described above, the F test and its associated p value for the caffeine experiment led us to conclude that the means for the three populations under consideration are not identical. Beyond that, we concluded nothing else about where the differences lie. We do not know, for example, whether the moderate caffeine mean differs from the other two while the other two means may not statistically differ from one another. We need something to go beyond the omnibus test.

This takes us into an area that has not been without controversy and that will require even more careful consideration as researchers move away from the traditional NHST approach to analyzing data. To understand the issues, we must revisit the notion of type I error from Chapter 13. Recall that we set the α level of a test to 0.05 so that, in the long run, we reject the null hypothesis when it is actually true only 5% of the time. But what happens when we run multiple tests on our data and, for each test, we set the α level to 0.05? For instance, in our caffeine example, there are three pairwise comparisons we could make: no caffeine versus moderate caffeine, no caffeine versus high caffeine, and moderate caffeine versus high caffeine. If we had four instead of three conditions, the number of pairwise comparisons would increase to six. If we applied t tests with the normal α value of 0.05 to each pairwise comparison, then we have a 5% change of committing a type I error for each test. Our probability of committing at least one type I error across all three tests—called the **familywise error rate**—is now greater than 5%.

A number of tests and/or correction factors have been developed to help with this issue. We will not cover them here, but which test to use depends on whether your comparisons were planned prior to collecting your data or whether they were unplanned (*post hoc*). They also vary in their conservativeness, that is, how they trade off type I and type II errors, as well as whether they apply to simple pairwise comparisons or more complex comparisons. Some of the more common **multiple comparison tests** include the Bonferroni–Dunn test, Tukey's HSD test, the Newman–Keuls method, Dunnett's test, and the Scheffé method.

Repeated Measures One-Way ANOVA (Within Subjects)

Recall from our discussion of the t test that when respondents provide measures for both variables under study, we are able to apply the matched-pairs t test. The advantage of a matched-pairs design is that this helps control for the variability across participants. In a similar way, **repeated-measures one-way ANOVA** incorporates the same kind of control when we are investigating more than two groups/conditions. Assumptions for this test are as follows:

Assumptions:

1. Interval- or ratio-level data.
2. Random sampling and independence of subjects (but not the k observations within a subject).
3. The values in the k populations from which the samples are drawn are normally distributed.
4. The k populations exhibit sphericity, which is an extension of the homogeneity of variance assumption.

Nonparametric alternative: **Friedman test**

Sphericity means that if you compute differences between all pairs of experimental groups, the variances of those differences should be approximately equal. Many statistical packages include diagnostic tests for sphericity, and violations of the sphericity assumption may call into question the results of your ANOVA.

Consider a repeated-measures (or within-subjects) variation of our caffeine experiment as displayed in Table 14.6. In this case, rather than having each of 30 participants take part in only one of the three caffeine conditions, each of 10 participants took part in all three conditions (presumably with enough intervening time and in different orders to control for some of the potential hazards of within-subjects designs described in Chapter 8).

Table 14.6.   Data for repeated-measures version of caffeine study

Participant	No caffeine	Moderate caffeine	High caffeine
1	72	73	67
2	69	81	67
3	66	68	71
4	88	91	73
5	67	79	74
6	78	87	75
7	80	88	78
8	81	92	88
9	91	82	88
10	90	93	89
Mean	78.2	83.4	77.0

Table 14.7.   Analysis of variance table for repeated-measures analysis of data in Table 14.6

	Sum of squares	df	Mean square	F	p
Caffeine condition	231.5	2	115.7	4.9	0.020
Participant	1,668.1	9	185.3		
Error	421.9	18	23.4		
Total	2,321.5	29			

The values in Table 14.6 have been ordered in such a way that you can easily see that respondents who scored relatively low on one of the memory tests also tended to score relatively low on the others, whereas those who scored high on one tended to score relatively high on all tests. This might reflect the fact that some people tend to have better memories, in general, than others. By controlling for this variation across participants, we can increase the power of our ANOVA test.

A repeated-measures analysis estimates the variation due to respondents and removes this estimate from the SS_{error} term. The ANOVA table for this analysis is shown in Table 14.7.

Now we see that the test for condition (between groups) gives $F(2,18) = 4.9$, $p = 0.020$. In this case, we reject the null hypothesis of equal means across the three conditions. For a one-way repeated-measures design, effect size is commonly measured by partial η^2, defined as SS condition$/(SS$ total $- SS$ participant). For our example, partial $\eta^2 = 0.354$.

Two-Way ANOVA

Researchers frequently collect information on more than one factor, as we discussed in Chapter 9. For example, in our hypothetical caffeine study, suppose we want to investigate not only the effects of caffeine, but also the effects of amount of sleep. In this case, we might use a **two-way ANOVA** to analyze our results. As with one-way ANOVA, we can have between-subject and within-subject measurements. We will focus here on a two-way between-subjects example. The assumptions are the same as those for the independent-groups t test and between-subjects one-way ANOVA, with the addition of the assumption that all cells have the same number of observations.

Consider the data in Table 14.8. We have added a second factor to our study examining the effects of caffeine on performance in the memory task, namely the amount of sleep (4–5 hours or 7–8 hours) the previous night. Each of 30 participants took part in a single combination of the two factors. The combination of three caffeine levels and two sleep levels gives a total of six experimental cells with five participants per cell.

Means and standard deviations for each of the six groups are shown in Table 14.9, and the 95% confidence intervals around the means are shown in Figure 14.7.

We note several things from the descriptive statistics and the confidence intervals. The low-sleep means (4–5 hours) all fall below the high-sleep means (7–8 hours), although there is

Two-way ANOVA
A statistical technique for comparing means when the experimental design includes two factors.

Table 14.8. Memory task scores for 30 participants with two between-subject factors

Amount of sleep	No caffeine	Moderate caffeine	High caffeine
4–5 hours	61	74	59
4–5 hours	67	83	53
4–5 hours	71	75	63
4–5 hours	78	89	71
4–5 hours	83	89	64
7–8 hours	72	80	85
7–8 hours	79	92	76
7–8 hours	82	87	93
7–8 hours	86	95	89
7–8 hours	91	96	87

Table 14.9. Means and standard deviations for each of the six groups in the 2 × 3 caffeine study

	AMOUNT OF CAFFEINE			
Amount of sleep	None	Moderate	High	Overall
Low (4–5 hours)	Mean = 72	82	62	72
	(SD = 8.72)	(7.28)	(6.63)	(10.99)
High (7–8 hours)	82	90	86	86
	(7.18)	(6.60)	(6.32)	(7.07)
Overall	77	86	74	79
	(9.19)	(7.79)	(14.05)	(11.54)

Main effect
The pattern of means across the different levels of a single factor in an analysis of variance design, averaging over any other factors. (See also **interaction effect**.)

Interaction effect
A measure of the extent to which the effect of one factor depends on the levels of the other factor. It is common to test for interaction effects in multifactor analysis of variance designs.

significant overlap in confidence intervals for the no- and moderate-caffeine levels. There is a large difference in the means for the two sleep levels at the high-caffeine level. Moreover, the mean scores for the moderate-caffeine groups are consistently larger than those for the no-caffeine and high-caffeine groups. The ANOVA table for this data set is shown in Table 14.10.

Look at the rows labeled Caffeine and Sleep. The results represented in these rows are for **main effects**, and they tell us the effect (the pattern of responses across the different levels) of each factor separately. We observe values of $p < 0.05$ for both main effects. Within the NHST framework, then, we would reject the null hypotheses of (1) no difference in means for the three levels of caffeine and (2) no difference in means for the two levels of sleep. We see from Table 14.10 and Figure 14.7 that the overall mean memory score for the moderate-caffeine group (86) is notably larger than the scores for the no-caffeine (77) and high-caffeine (74) groups. We also see that the mean score for the high-sleep group (86) is higher than that for the low-sleep group (72).

The third row of the ANOVA table shows us the caffeine × sleep **interaction effect**. As we discussed in Chapter 9, the interaction effect tells us the extent to which the effect of one factor depends on the levels of the other factor. An examination of Figure 14.7 should make this clear. We see that the difference between the low-sleep participants and the

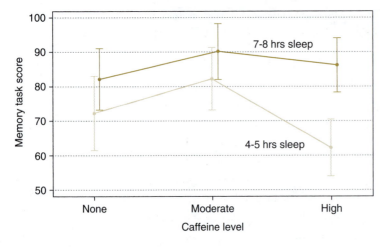

FIGURE 14.7. 95% confidence intervals for each of the six groups in the 2 × 3 memory task study.

Table 14.10. Analysis of variance table for memory task experiment with between-subject sleep and caffeine factors

	Sum of squares	df	Mean square	F	p
Caffeine	780	2	390.0	7.6	0.003
Sleep	1,470	1	1,470.0	28.6	0.00002
Caffeine × sleep	380	2	190.0	3.7	0.04
Residual (error)	1,232	24	51.3		
Total	3,862	29			

Table 14.11. Effect sizes for the caffeine and sleep example

	η^2	Partial η^2	ω^2
Caffeine	0.20	0.39	0.17
Sleep	0.38	0.54	0.36
Caffeine × sleep	0.10	0.24	0.07

high-sleep participants is considerably larger for the high-caffeine group than for either of the no-caffeine or the moderate-caffeine groups; that is, the gap between the means is considerably larger for the high-caffeine group. In Table 14.10, the p value of 0.04 for the caffeine × sleep interaction leads us to reject the null hypothesis of no interaction.

Since we are investigating three different effects (two main effects and one interaction effect), we compute an effect size for each. As with between-subjects one-way ANOVA, we may use η^2 as a measure of effect size, although we may also use partial η^2 and ω^2. These effect sizes are shown in Table 14.11 and suggest small to moderate effects (Cohen, 1988).

Interactions.   Because the concept of interactions can be difficult to grasp, we want to say just a little more about them here. As we noted earlier, we observe an interaction when the strength of the effect of one of our factors (e.g., amount of caffeine) depends on the level of the other factor (e.g., amount of sleep). As we saw in Figure 14.7, the difference between the low-sleep and high-sleep groups is much greater in the high-caffeine condition than in the other two conditions. This suggests an interaction between caffeine level and sleep level. Figure 14.7, in which we plotted the means for all six groups and then connected the means within each of the sleep levels, gives an example of an interaction chart. The nonparallel lines suggest the presence of an interaction effect.

As part of the interpretation of an interaction chart, you should consider confidence intervals in conjunction with the patterns of means. In Figure 14.8a, the large separation of the confidence

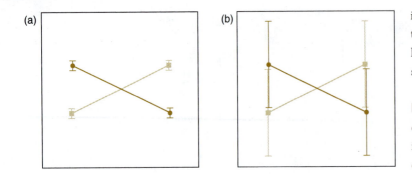

FIGURE 14.8.   Interaction charts with confidence intervals: (a) large separation of confidence intervals and (b) large overlap of confidence intervals.

intervals strongly suggests an interaction effect. In contrast, the large overlaps in Figure 14.8b do not provide support for an interaction effect.

Multiple Comparisons.   As with one-way ANOVA, various methods for investigating the multiple comparisons can be made among the different groups/cells in the experimental design. The appropriate method will depend on whether your comparisons are planned or post hoc and the trade-offs you are willing to make between type I and type II errors (i.e., whether the test tends to be conservative or liberal). Typically these comparisons will not be examined unless at least one of your effects is statistically significant.

COMPARING COUNTS/FREQUENCIES

So far in this chapter, we have focused on statistical tests for data that are on interval or ratio scales. But suppose you are interested in whether men and women differ in their preferences for two political candidates. This yields a different type of data and requires different statistical approaches. For example, imagine that you randomly sample 90 men and 100 women and ask them to choose between candidate A and candidate B (for this example, assume that no one is undecided). Consider the hypothetical results in Table 14.12 showing the number of men and women who prefer each candidate. Rather than examining differences among mean responses as we did when considering *t* tests and ANOVA, we are now interested in whether there is a difference in the patterns of counts or frequencies between men and women with respect to their candidate preferences. The two variables (sex and preferred candidate) are both nominal/categorical, and we are interested in whether there is an *association* between the two variables.

Table 14.12.   Number of men and women preferring each of two candidates

	PREFERRED CANDIDATE		
	A	B	Total count
Men	57	33	90
Women	48	52	100
Total	105	85	190

Table 14.13.   Row percentages for candidate preference data

| | PREFERRED CANDIDATE | | |
	A	B	Total
Men (%)	63	37	100
Women (%)	48	52	100

Table 14.14.   Cell labels for computing the odds ratio

| | VARIABLE 1 | |
Variable 2	Category 1	Category 2
Category 1	a	b
Category 2	c	d

We will first consider a 2 × 2 table as in Table 14.12. Then, we will move on to tables with more than two levels on at least one of the variables/factors.

2 × 2 Tables

To better understand what the data tell us, we will first transform the counts to percentages. In this case, we are more interested in the percentage of each sex who prefer each candidate (rather than the percentage of those who prefer each candidate who are men or women), so we will compute row percentages as shown in Table 14.13.

The results suggest an association between sex and preferred candidate, with men more likely than women to prefer candidate A over candidate B. For 2 × 2 contingency tables, the most common measure of effect size is the coefficient φ. Like a correlation, φ ranges from -1 to 1. For the data in Table 14.12, $\varphi = 0.15$. Another measure of effect size for 2 × 2 contingency tables is simply the difference in proportions. If we focus on preference for candidate A, then the proportion of respondents who prefer candidate A is 0.63 for men and 0.48 for women. The difference in these proportions, then, is $0.63 - 0.48 = 0.15$.

Confidence intervals are not as straightforward with categorical data as with interval/ratio data, but we can compute confidence intervals for a quantity known as the **odds ratio**. Labeling the four cells as in Table 14.14, the odds ratio is computed as ad/bc and is 1.87 for the data in Table 14.12. An odds ratio of 1 would indicate that men and women are equally likely to prefer candidate A to candidate B. The confidence interval on the odds ratio in this example is $[1.05, 3.35]$. This confidence interval does not include 1, so we have good evidence of an association between the variables of gender and preferred candidate.

Odds ratio A measure of association between two variables, each of which has only two possible values.

The χ^2 test is commonly applied to contingency tables. Assumptions for this test are shown here:

Assumptions:
1. Random sampling and independence of observations.
2. For 2 × 2 tables, all expected frequencies should be at least 5.
3. For larger tables, 80% of expected cell frequencies should be at least 5, and none should be 0 (Yates, Moore, & McCabe, 1999, p. 734).

For the current example, this test yields $\chi^2 = 4.50$, $df = 1$, $p = 0.034$. The standard χ^2 test is most appropriate with larger sample sizes. For smaller samples, Campbell (2007) recommends test statistics to use for 2 × 2 tables under various conditions.

χ^2 Test of Independence for *R* × *C* Contingency Tables

When we have more than two levels on either of the factors, we typically use a χ^2 test for independence to determine whether the distribution of responses on one variable is independent of the distribution of responses on the second variable. Table 14.15 shows the number of men and women who prefer each of four candidates.

Table 14.16 allows us to more easily detect potential differences between men and women with respect to their voting preferences. For example, we see that the differences between the percentages is largest for candidate A and smallest for candidate C.

When we have more than two categories for either variable, it can be instructive to graph the data as in Figure 14.9. In addition to the absolute differences that we were able to observe in Table 14.16, the bar plot highlights the relative differences; for example, the percentage of women preferring candidate D is more than double the percentage for men.

The disparities between the bars on the left (for men) and the bars on the right (for women) certainly suggest a difference in candidate preferences between men and women. A common effect size measure for *R* × *C* contingency tables is Cramer's *V* (also called Cramer's φ_c), which ranges from 0 to 1. For the current example, Cramer's *V* is 0.21, a small effect (Cohen, 1988).

Table 14.15. Number of men and women preferring each of four candidates

	Preferred candidate				
	A	B	C	D	Total
Men	54	26	30	10	120
Women	38	39	29	24	130
Total	92	65	59	34	250

Finally, the χ^2 test gives us $\chi^2 = 10.78$, $df = 3$, $p = 0.013$. With an α of 0.05, we would reject the null hypothesis that the proportions of respondents who prefer each candidate are the same for men and women. As with ANOVA, it is possible (and usually desirable) to perform additional tests to determine where the differences lie, perhaps a series of 2×2 analyses. As with ANOVA, however, multiple tests increase the probability of a type I error, and adjustments to test statistics and/or p values may be necessary.

Tests of Association: Correlation and Regression

As we discussed in the section on bivariate descriptive statistics in Chapter 13, the most common measure of the association between two interval- or ratio-level variables is the Pearson product-moment correlation (Pearson's r). Next, we provide an example with confidence intervals and describe the Spearman rank-order correlation (Spearman's ρ) and linear regression.

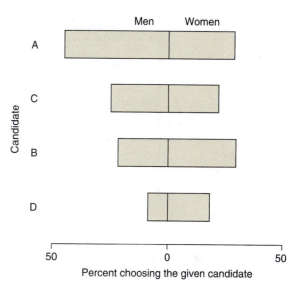

FIGURE 14.9. Bar plot of voting preference by sex.

Pearson's r.   Pearson correlations are used when you want to determine the degree of linear association between two interval- or ratio-level variables. This approach assumes that the two populations are normally distributed and that the relationship between the variables is linear.

Hypothetical math and verbal standardized test scores for 12 students are shown in Table 14.17, and a scatterplot of these scores is shown in Figure 14.10. The plot suggests that, on average, higher math scores are associated with higher verbal scores. In addition, there does not seem to be an obvious nonlinear relationship that we need to be aware of.

The Pearson r is 0.60 (this is also the effect size) and the 95% confidence interval is from 0.039 to 0.873. The p value for testing the null hypothesis of $r = 0$ is 0.039, so we would reject

Table 14.16.   Row percentages for candidate preference data of Table 14.15

	Preferred candidate				
	A	B	C	D	Total
Men (%)	45.0	21.7	25.0	8.3	100
Women (%)	29.2	30.0	22.3	18.5	100

Table 14.17. Math and verbal test scores for 12 students

Student	Math score	Verbal score
1	62	55
2	41	30
3	65	34
4	95	54
5	66	80
6	35	35
7	90	96
8	72	64
9	35	58
10	48	53
11	71	89
12	95	76

Linear regression
A statistical technique for determining the joint impact/effect of one or more independent variables on a single dependent variable.

this null hypothesis of zero correlation. The very wide confidence interval (which is not unexpected with such a small N), however, provides a sense of just how imprecise our estimate of the population correlation really is. Computing Spearman's ρ rather than Pearson's r may be more appropriate when (1) your measurement scale is ordinal, (2) your data set violates the assumption of normality, or (3) your two variables are not linearly related. When you have a small sample size and a number of outliers in your data, Spearman's ρ is generally a more conservative approach.

Linear Regression. **Linear regression** is used to determine the joint impact/effect of one or more independent variables on a single dependent variable. The assumptions for linear regression are as follows:

Assumptions:
1. The dependent variable is interval or ratio level.
2. The relationship between the dependent variable and the independent variables is linear.

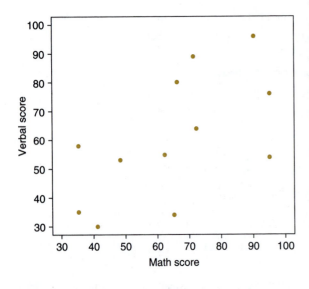

FIGURE 14.10. Scatterplot of math and verbal test scores.

3. The residuals (differences between predicted and actual dependent variable values) are independent.
4. The residuals have equal variance across all independent variable values.
5. The residuals are normally distributed.

Let's return to the math and verbal test scores in Table 14.17. Pearson's r for those two variables was 0.60. Regression analysis provides us with additional information about that relationship. If we treat the math score as the independent variable and the verbal score as the dependent variable, we obtain the following **regression equation**:

$$estimated\ verbal\ score = 0.596 * math\ score + 21.9$$

The equation tells us that we estimate the verbal score of a student by multiplying that student's math score by 0.596 and then adding 21.9. As depicted in Figure 14.11, the regression equation represents *the best-fitting straight line* through the points of the scatterplot.

The value of 0.596 is a **regression coefficient**, which indicates how the independent variable changes with changes in the dependent variable. In this example, 0.596 tells us that, on average, for a one-point increase in the math score, we would expect an increase of 0.596 points on the verbal score. The **y-intercept value** of 21.9 tells us where the regression line intersects the y-axis (in this case, the verbal score axis).

A key measure of how accurately the regression equation predicts or estimates the true verbal scores is R^2, the squared multiple correlation. When there is a single predictor or independent variable, R^2 is identical to the square of Pearson's r and, for this example, equal to 0.36 (which is the square of our Pearson's r of 0.6). R^2 represents the percentage of variance in the verbal scores accounted for by the math scores.

The real utility of regression is that it is applicable when you have more than one independent variable. Suppose we want to predict students' grade point averages their freshman year in college (FYGPA) from their high school GPAs (HSGPA) and a standardized test score (TEST). We could look at the Pearson correlations between FYGPA and each of the other two measures, but we are also interested in whether there is any kind of additive effect such that the two measures together more accurately predict FYGPA than either by itself. For example, we might find that the correlations of HSGPA and TEST with FYGPA are 0.45 ($r^2 = 0.20$) and 0.35 ($r^2 = 0.12$), respectively, but that a regression analysis that includes both predictors results in an equation such

Regression equation
A mathematical equation that expresses a linear relationship between a dependent variable and one or more independent variables.

Regression coefficient
A quantity in a linear regression equation that indicates the change in a dependent variable associated with a unit change in the independent variable.

y-intercept value
The point at which a regression line intersects the y-axis.

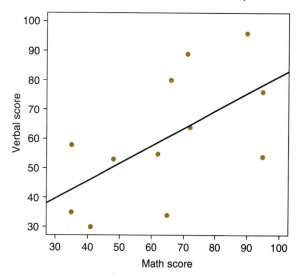

FIGURE 14.11. Scatterplot with regression line superimposed.

as $FYGPA = 0.38 * HSGPA + 0.0077 * TEST + 1.3$ and a multiple R^2 of 0.25. Regression allows us to look at the joint effect of multiple predictors on a dependent variable.

The details of regression are beyond the scope of this chapter, but here are a few things to keep in mind:

1. Regression analysis will produce p values for the multiple correlation R and for each of the coefficients in the regression equation, and confidence intervals may (and should) be constructed for each of these values.
2. R (or R^2) serves as an effect size.
3. Both ANOVA and regression fall under a more general statistical model known as the general linear model. Because of this, regression may be used to analyze the data in complex ANOVA designs.
4. Regression is particularly useful in situations where you want to include variables that cannot be experimentally manipulated (e.g., income, socioeconomic status).

TESTS ON ORDINAL DATA

In behavioral research, the response measure is often a rating on a scale (satisfaction, strength of preference, liberalness vs. conservativeness, etc.) of a relatively small number of values (5, 7, 11). Some controversy surrounds the use of parametric statistical tests such as t tests or ANOVA to analyze such data. These tests are meant to apply to interval- or ratio-level data, and such rating scales almost surely do not meet the necessary criteria. On one side are arguments that such data should be analyzed using techniques appropriate for ordinal data (see, for example, Jamieson, 2004). On the other side are those who argue that parametric tests, at least for relatively simple designs, are robust and may safely be applied to such ratings scales (e.g., Norman, 2010).

In any case, ordinal tests are worth knowing about, and we present an example using the Mann–Whitney U test. The data in Table 14.18 are from a hypothetical study in which 10 men and 10 women were asked to rate an episode of *The Three Stooges* using a 7-point scale, ranging from 1 = extremely unfunny to 7 = extremely funny. A side-by-side stem-and-leaf plot of the data is shown in Figure 14.12. Since the stem is "0" for every observation, it is omitted for clarity. The stem-and-leaf plot certainly suggests that men tend to rate the Stooges higher than do women.

The Mann–Whitney test is concerned with whether the values in one group tend to be higher than those in the other group. When the *shapes* of the two distributions are roughly the same, the Mann–Whitney test can be treated as a test of the equivalence of the medians of the two samples.

In this example, we compute the U statistic as 17.5. A U value of 17.5 with two sample sizes of 10 gives a p value of 0.013, so we would reject the null hypothesis of equal medians. If we divide U by the product of the sample sizes, in this case $17.5/(10 * 10) = 0.175$, it gives

```
Women  Men
   11|
   22|
   33|3
    4|44
   55|55
    6|666
     |77
```

FIGURE 14.12.
Stem-and-leaf plots for data of Table 14.18.

Table 14.18. Funniness ratings on 7-Point scale

FUNNINESS RATING	
Women	Men
4	5
1	7
3	4
2	6
6	3
2	6
5	4
1	7
5	6
3	5

us the probability of a woman's rating exceeding a man's rating if we consider all possible pairings of the women's scores with the men's scores. This value is considerably smaller than the 0.5 we would expect from the null hypothesis.

ASSUMPTION VIOLATIONS

Throughout this chapter, we have provided lists of assumptions for the various statistical tests because performing a statistical test when its assumptions are violated may affect the accuracy of confidence intervals, p values, and your estimates of quantities such as means and standard deviations, as well as increasing the probabilities of type I or type II errors. Early in the analysis phase, you should examine your data for obvious assumption violations. Unfortunately, there is considerable disagreement about which violations are the most potentially damaging and how to assess and address these violations (Hoekstra, Kiers, & Johnson, 2012; Norman, 2010). Despite this lack of agreement, however, it is still important to be familiar with the main concerns and possible solutions. In the remainder of this section, we briefly review a number of potential assumption violations and point to diagnostic tools and potential aids for analyzing data in the presence of those violations.

Random Sampling and Independence of Observations

Random sampling and independence of observations are key assumptions for nearly any common statistical test. We discussed random sampling in detail in Chapter 6 and how

Independence of observations A measurement obtained on an observation (e.g., from a participant) in the experiment does not depend on the measurements obtained on other observations (e.g., from other participants). The responses are *independent* of one another.

deviations from random sampling affect your ability to generalize your results. **Independence of observations** means that a measurement you obtain, say, from one participant in your experiment does not depend on the measurements you obtained from other participants: their responses are *independent* of one another. In general, random sampling and independence of observations are elements of the experimental design process as opposed to assumptions you evaluate after collecting your data.

Nonnormal Distributions

A number of statistical methods include the assumption of normally distributed population values. Since we rarely, if ever, are able to determine the actual distribution of values in the population, we rely on inspection of the values in our samples and evaluate the extent to which the sample data may violate normality. Here, we will consider two of the more worrisome deviations from normality: distributions with outliers and strongly skewed distributions.

Outliers.   Outliers (extreme value or values that deviate dramatically from the overall pattern of your data) represent one of the more serious problems you may encounter with your data. They can dramatically affect your estimates of means, standard deviations, and effect size measures, as well as confidence intervals, test statistics, p values, and the probabilities of type I and type II errors. Because of their potential effects on your results, you should always check your data for outliers.

Histograms and box-and-whisker plots are very helpful for identifying outliers for individual variables, whereas scatterplots can help identify outliers when you examine bivariate relationships. In more complex designs such as linear regression or ANOVA, **leverage values**, **Cook's distance**, or **residuals** may be used to identify outliers. Whichever method you use to identify outliers, it is important to understand that if you drop outliers from your analysis, you must explicitly state that you have done so, offer a rationale for dropping the value(s), and show how your analysis differs with and without the outliers.

Leverage value A measure used to detect outliers in a data set.

Cook's distance A measure used to detect outliers in a data set.

Residuals Differences between actual values and predicted values in linear regression or ANOVA.

QQ plot (or normal quantile–quantile plot) A graphical technique to identify deviations from normality in a data set.

Skewed Distributions.   You may have a data set that does not have values that would be considered outliers, but is still nonnormal by being skewed either to the left or right (see Figure 13.8). Histograms and stem-and-leaf displays are useful for rough visual assessments of normality, for example, you look for a pattern similar to the bell shape of the normal curve. Another visual tool is the **QQ plot** (or **normal quantile–quantile plot**), two examples of which are displayed in Figure 14.13. Our school 1 data are reproduced in the stem-and-leaf display in the top left of Figure 14.13. In a QQ plot, normality is indicated by points falling along a relatively straight line. This certainly seems to be the case in the school 1 QQ plot at the bottom left of Figure 14.13. In contrast, the stem-and-leaf display in the upper right of Figure 14.13 represents an obviously skewed, quite asymmetric data set. The S-shape distribution of the points in the corresponding QQ plot strongly suggests a nonnormal distribution of data values.

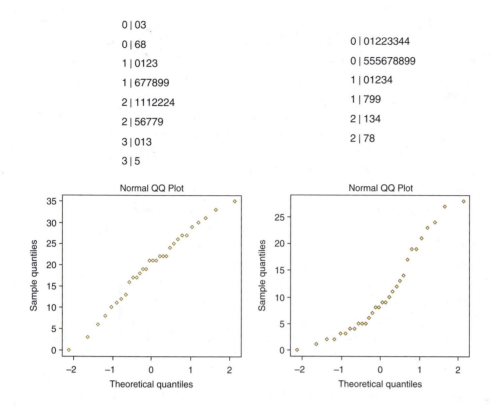

```
0 | 03              0 | 01223344
0 | 68              0 | 555678899
1 | 0123            1 | 01234
1 | 677899          1 | 799
2 | 1112224         2 | 134
2 | 56779           2 | 78
3 | 013
3 | 5
```

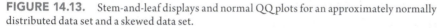

FIGURE 14.13.   Stem-and-leaf displays and normal QQ plots for an approximately normally distributed data set and a skewed data set.

In addition to graphical techniques, there are also a number of statistical tests that may be performed to determine whether data deviate from normality. These include the **Shapiro–Wilk test** and the **Kolmogorov–Smirnov test** (see Ghasemi & Zahediasl, 2012).

There are a few things to keep in mind concerning statistical tests for checking assumptions. They are hypothesis tests in the same sense that a *t* test or ANOVA is a hypothesis test, so they receive the same types of NHST criticisms. A common criticism of assumption tests is that low power for small sample sizes may prevent them from identifying sizeable assumption violations even if they actually exist, whereas for large sample sizes, they will suggest a normality problem with your data, even for quite small violations (Micceri, 1989; Razali & Wah, 2011). In addition, if you use the results of an assumption violation hypothesis test to determine which subsequent hypothesis test you then apply to your data (e.g., a *t* test vs. a Mann–Whitney test), you run the risk of increasing the probability of a type I error (Schucany & Ng, 2006).

Data transformations are sometimes useful for converting a skewed distribution of data values into one that is more normal in shape. These include logarithmic and square root or cube root transformations. It is important to note, however, that when you transform data

Shapiro–Wilk test
A statistical test of whether a set of data values is normally distributed.

Kolmogorov–Smirnov test A statistical test of whether a set of data values is normally distributed.

and run hypothesis tests on the transformed data, your conclusions apply to the transformed data rather than the original data, which may make interpretation of your results more difficult.

Unequal Variances

Statistical tests like the independent-samples *t* test and ANOVA tests have the assumption of equal variances across the different groups. With equal group sizes, the impact of unequal variances may be minor, but you should always inspect your data to look for large differences in groups variances. Examining descriptive statistics and side-by-side graphical displays such as box-and-whisker plots and histograms for each group will give you a very good sense of how variances differ across groups. Statistical tests of equality of variances such as **Levene's test** or the **F test of equality of variances** may also be applied (subject to the caveats we noted earlier for tests of assumptions). As with nonnormality, transforming your data using logarithms or square roots may also help equalize variances.

Levene's test A test of the equality of two variances.

F test of equality of variances A test of the equality of two variances.

Unequal Cell Sizes in Factorial ANOVA Designs

To the extent that it is possible, you should strive for equal numbers of respondents across all groups in factorial ANOVA designs. Unequal group counts are problematic because they can lead to confounding of experimental effects; that is, one cannot completely separate the effects of the different experimental factors. Analyzing such data requires the computation of a different type of sum of squares than appears in the standard ANOVA table and can complicate the interpretation and presentation of your results.

Lack of Sphericity with Repeated Measures

Recall that the condition of sphericity in a repeated-measures ANOVA design means that if you compute the differences between all pairs of groups on a within-subjects factor, the variances of those differences should be approximately equal. Violations of sphericity may increase the probability of a type I error. You can look for sphericity violations by examining the variances of the differences between groups or by applying a test such as **Mauchly's test of sphericity**. In the face of sphericity violations, you may analyze your data by applying statistical adjustments such as the **Greenhouse–Geisser correction**.

Mauchly's test of sphericity A test of the sphericity assumption in repeated-measures analysis of variance.

Greenhouse–Geisser correction A statistical adjustment to account for violation of sphericity in repeated measures analysis of variance.

With the use of descriptive statistics, visual displays, and various diagnostics offered by statistical programs, you should have a good sense of whether your data exhibit worrisome violations of assumptions. With this information, you can determine whether to proceed with the originally planned tests, perhaps after removing outliers or transforming your data, or whether a different approach is required, such as those presented in the section that follows on robust statistical methods.

You should also be aware, however, that the presence of such violations might be of substantive interest, for example, if you have groups with distributions that deviate strongly from normality or from each other. Ask yourself why this might be and what it might be telling you. The same holds true if groups show great differences in variability. Although such characteristics of the data may make the computation of confidence intervals and p values less straightforward or require transformations of the data or the altering of your original analysis plan, they may also provide additional insights into your research endeavor.

Before we end this chapter, we address two current trends in analyzing behavioral research data. The first is the use of robust statistical methods, which involves the application of techniques that may provide more accurate test statistics, p values, and estimates of effect sizes and confidence intervals when assumptions are violated. Although such methods may still fall within the domain of NHST, they are often more appropriate than traditional tests. The second trend, which represents a quite different approach than traditional NHST methods, sees a growing number of researchers adopting a Bayesian approach to statistics that emphasizes probability distributions rather than test statistics and p values. In the next two sections, we briefly examine robust statistical methods and Bayesian data analysis; we believe that understanding these approaches will be useful for researchers and individuals evaluating research.

ROBUST STATISTICAL METHODS

We have already alluded to **robust statistical methods** by listing nonparametric versions of statistical tests and in our use of the Mann–Whitney U test to analyze rank-order data. Given the increasing availability of robust techniques available in statistical packages such as SPSS, SAS, and R, as well as criticisms regularly leveled against the blind application of classic parametric statistical tests (e.g., t tests and ANOVA), it is worth saying just a few more words about robust statistics.

Statistics (such as means, standard deviations, or medians) and statistical tests are robust to the extent that they are not greatly affected by conditions that violate the assumptions of standard parametric tests, for example, the presence of outliers, skewed distributions, or unequal variances. Robust statistical tests may be either nonparametric or parametric. Classic nonparametric tests include those we listed earlier as alternatives to parametric tests, such as the Wilcoxon signed-rank test, the Wilcoxon rank-sum test, the Mann–Whitney U test, and the Kruskal–Wallis test. These methods are applicable to relatively simple experimental designs, such as those that might otherwise be analyzed using simple t tests or one-way ANOVA. More sophisticated (and considerably more complicated) rank-based techniques, however, have been developed as analogs to factorial ANOVA and linear regression analyses.

Robust tests may also be parametric. Welch's t test is a parametric test that is robust under violations of the equal variance assumption for the independent-groups t test. Additional parametric techniques involve using **trimmed means**, in which some percentage (usually 10 or 20%) of the largest and smallest data values are removed from your data set,

Robust statistical methods Statistical tests that are not greatly affected by conditions that violate the assumptions of standard parametric tests, for example, the assumption that population values are normally distributed.

Trimmed mean A mean computed after removing some fixed percentage (often 10% or 20%) of the largest and smallest values in a data set.

Bayesian data analysis An approach to data analysis in which a prior distribution concerning a hypothesis is combined with experimental data to construct a posterior distribution for the hypothesis.

Prior distribution In Bayesian data analysis, information the experimenter has concerning a statistic or effect prior to running the experiment. Such prior information may come from previous experiments or a meta-analysis of the relevant literature.

Objective prior (or **minimally informative prior**) In Bayesian data analysis, a prior distribution that reflects relative ignorance concerning the value of an experiment effect.

Posterior distribution In Bayesian data analysis, the distribution around a statistic (e.g., mean, difference of means, standard deviation) that incorporates both prior information and experimental data.

or various methods in which data values are removed based on their identification as outliers. It is important to understand that although these approaches are parametric, they estimate specialized parameters, such as a difference in *trimmed* means rather than the traditional difference in means, and that they require special procedures for computing important values such as standard errors and confidence intervals. More information on robust statistical techniques may be found in Wilcox and Keselman (2003); Erceg-Hurn and Mirosevich (2008); Erceg-Hurn, Wilcox, and Keselman (2013); Hoaglin, Mosteller, and Tukey (2000); and Wilcox (1998, 2012).

BAYESIAN DATA ANALYSIS

An alternative approach to NHST is offered by **Bayesian data analysis**. There are three main conceptual components to such an analysis. We will illustrate these components using a Bayesian approach to analyzing the Stroop task data from Table 14.1.

In a Bayesian analysis, one first specifies a **prior distribution** concerning the hypothesis of interest. For the Stroop task, our hypothesis focuses on the difference in mean response times between participants in the interference condition and those in the no-interference condition. A prior distribution will incorporate any information that we already have before collecting our data, perhaps based on previous experiments or a meta-analysis of the relevant literature. For example, we may have good reason to believe that the difference in mean response times between the interference group and the no-interference group is relatively likely to be between 0.5 and 2.0 seconds, somewhat less likely to be between −0.05 and 0.5 seconds or 2.0 and 2.5 seconds, and quite unlikely to be less than −0.5 seconds or greater than 2.5 seconds. By attaching actual numbers to "relatively likely," "somewhat less likely," and "quite unlikely," we can specify a prior distribution that incorporates our prior knowledge. If, in contrast, we have little idea of what the difference in mean response times might be, we can use what is known as an **objective prior** or **minimally informative prior** (the terms uninformative prior and noninformative prior are also used, but they are misleading because any prior distribution provides *some* information). In our example, we might use a prior distribution in which any value of the difference in means from −30 seconds to 30 seconds is considered equally likely.

The second component for a Bayesian analysis is the actual collected data, in this case the response times represented in Table 14.1. In this data set we can compute sample characteristics such as the means and standard deviations of each group and, most relevant to our current analysis, the difference in means between the two groups.

The final component is the **posterior distribution**, which is computed by combining the prior distribution with the sample data. The posterior distribution gives us the relative likelihood of different values of the difference in means. For example, given our prior distribution and our data, how likely is it that the actual difference in means is 2 versus 1 versus 0 and so on? This posterior distribution also leads naturally to the construction of

credible intervals, which are similar to confidence intervals but with a more intuitive interpretation.

The posterior distributions shown in Figure 14.14 were constructed using the BEST (Bayesian Estimation Supersedes the *t* Test) package in the R statistical computing program. A minimally informative prior distribution was used. Figure 14.14a shows the distribution of values of the difference of mean responses times. The mean of the posterior distribution is 1.14, which is identical to the sample difference of means of 1.14. With a minimally informative prior, we expect a very close match between the posterior distribution mean and the sample mean. The 95% credible interval ranges from 0.136 to 2.13. The nice thing about a credible interval is that, unlike confidence intervals, the 95% credible interval tells us that, based on our prior distribution (in this case, a minimally informative one) and our collected data, there is a 95% chance that the actual difference of means in the population falls between 0.136 and 2.13. We also see in Figure 14.14a that only 1.5% of the values in the posterior distribution fall below 0 (the value that would represent our null hypothesis in NHST).

Figure 14.14b shows the posterior distribution for the difference in standard deviations of the two groups. The mean value of this difference is 0.451 and the 95% credible interval ranges from -0.409 to 1.39. Moreover, 12.3% of the values in the distribution fall below 0. In contrast to Figure 14.14a, which provides us with substantial evidence of a difference between the two means, the evidence for a difference between the two standard deviations is clearly not as strong.

Advantages of Bayesian Approaches

Bayesian approaches to data analysis offer a number of advantages over traditional NHST approaches. First, the interpretation of the posterior distribution and credible intervals is more intuitive than the interpretation of *p* values and confidence intervals. Second, a Bayesian approach allows for the explicit inclusion of prior knowledge and expertise in the specification of the prior distribution. Finally, the Bayesian approach does not assume underlying normal distributions, so it can robustly handle skewed or otherwise nonnormal distributions that may cause problems for classical statistical tests.

Credible interval
In Bayesian data analysis, a range of values from the posterior distribution of a given quantity (e.g., mean, difference of means) for which you have a given level of credibility (e.g., 95%) concerning the true value of the quantity.

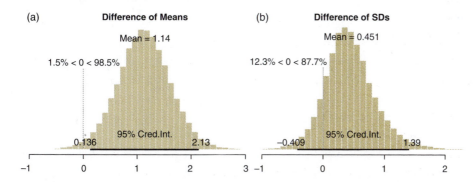

FIGURE 14.14.
Posterior distributions for difference of means and difference of standard deviations for Stroop task example.

Disadvantages of Bayesian Approaches

A primary concern with Bayesian methods is with the specification of the prior distribution. Trying to select what prior distribution to use may seem like a daunting task, particularly to those inexperienced with Bayesian approaches. Even minimally informative priors do provide some information, so choosing to express ignorance about a hypothesis still requires some careful thought. In addition, there may be concern that, under the guise of informed knowledge, researchers might select prior distributions for the explicit purpose of supporting their hypotheses. The clear lesson is that if you analyze your data with Bayesian methods, you must be very explicit in reporting the exact form of your prior distributions and your reasons for using those priors.

The computations involved with Bayesian data analysis are also considerably more complex than those associated with, say, classic t tests or ANOVAs. They rely on computer-intensive sampling techniques and cannot be summarized by simple formulas. This complexity and the relative absence of techniques from standard statistical software likely serve as barriers to learning and using Bayesian approaches. Fortunately, there are a number of strong resources for learning these techniques (Gelman et al., 2013; Jackman, 2009; Kruschke, 2013, 2014; Lynch, 2007; van de Schoot et al., 2014), and specialized software is readily available through the R statistical programming environment.

PRACTICAL TIPS

Practical Tips for Specific Approaches to Data Analysis

1. Prior to gathering your data, understand the type of data you will collect (e.g., means, counts) and what statistical methods are appropriate (e.g., t test, χ^2 test).

2. As the first part of your analysis, always compute descriptive statistics and create visual displays of your data.

3. Check the assumptions of your statistical tests and, in particular, identify values that might be considered outliers.

4. Compute effect sizes and, when appropriate, confidence intervals.

5. If appropriate, consider using nonparametric tests or robust parametric tests.

CHAPTER SUMMARY

In this chapter, we examined a variety of statistical methods that you have at your disposal when conducting research. As you conduct your analysis, you should inspect descriptive statistics and plot data in different ways, compute effect sizes, and use confidence intervals and inferential statistical tests to help you draw conclusions. Although you should have a good sense of how your data analysis will proceed prior to even collecting your data, do not apply statistical tests rigidly.

The specific statistical test you choose depends on your research question and measurement type. To examine patterns of means, you will typically use *t* tests, one-way ANOVA, or factorial ANOVA. To examine the relationships between variables measured on interval or ratio scales, you will most often use correlations or regression analysis. When inspecting counts or frequencies for categorical data, you will typically use a χ^2 test. Finally, the Mann–Whitney *U* test is commonly used for examining ordinal data.

Once you have completed your data analysis, it is a good idea to develop a clear, concise summary of what you have found. A good place to start is to create visual displays that capture any of your key results. This process should help you understand what your results mean and help you interpret why your results may or may not have come out as you had expected. This is also a good time to write a formal paragraph that captures the design of your analyses and results, so that you can see the big picture that has emerged. In the next chapter, we lead you through the process of writing up your results in a way that conveys a narrative of your research most effectively.

Up for Discussion

1. You are interested in whether the difference in siblings' ages is indicative of how well they get along. You collect information from 20 pairs of siblings in each of four age-difference categories (13–24 months, 25–36 months, 37–48 months, and 49–60 months). You have siblings provide ratings of how much they like each other on an 11-point scale ranging from 0 to 10. How might you analyze your data? What statistics, visual displays, etc., would you like to see to help you understand and interpret your results?

2. Referring back to question 1, suppose that instead of numerical ratings, you have siblings simply indicate whether they like each other "not at all," "a little bit," "somewhat," or "a lot." How might you analyze your data? What statistics, visual displays, etc., would you like to see to help you understand and interpret your results?

3. Revisiting an example from Chapter 9, suppose you are interested in the effectiveness of directed versus nondirected therapy for patients who exhibit either high or low openness to therapy. Shown below are descriptive statistics, box-and-whisker plots, and an ANOVA table for hypothetical data, where the dependent variable is effectiveness of therapy measured on a scale from 0 to 100. How would you interpret these results? What other information would you like to see to help in your interpretation?

DESCRIPTIVE STATISTICS				
	Directive High openness	Nondirective High openness	Directive Low openness	Nondirective Low openness
Count	10	10	10	10
Mean	43.2	57.8	38.7	40.3
Median	43.0	58.0	41.5	40.5
Standard deviation	7.50	11.92	14.22	7.45

ANALYSIS OF VARIANCE TABLE					
	Sum of squares	df	Mean square	F	p
Therapy	656.1	1	656.1	5.75	0.022
Openness	1,210.0	1	1,210.0	10.61	0.0025
Therapy × openness	422.5	1	422.5	3.71	0.062
Residual	4,105.4	36	114.0		

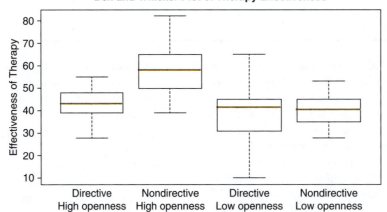

Box-and-Whisker Plot of Therapy Effectiveness

Key Terms

Analysis of variance (ANOVA),
   p. 340

ANOVA table, p. 347

Bayesian data analysis, p. 366

Cook's distance, p. 362

Credible interval, p. 367

Degrees of freedom (*df*), p. 341

Eta squared (η^2), p. 348

F test of equality of variances,
   p. 364

Familywise error rate, p. 349

Friedman test, p. 349

Greenhouse–Geisser correction,
   p. 364

Independence of observations,
   p. 362

Interaction effect, p. 352

Kolmogorov–Smirnov
   test, p. 363

Kruskal–Wallis test, p. 346

Levene's test, p. 364

Leverage value, p. 362

Linear regression, p. 358

Main effect, p. 352

Mann–Whitney *U* test, p. 342

Mauchly's test of sphericity,
   p. 364

Multiple comparison tests, p. 349

Nonparametric statistical test,
   p. 340

Objective prior (or minimally
   informative prior), p. 366

Odds ratio, p. 355

Omnibus null hypothesis, p. 348

One-way analysis of variance
   (ANOVA), p. 346

Parametric statistical test, p. 340

Posterior distribution, p. 366

Prior distribution, p. 366

QQ plot (or normal quantile–
   quantile plot), p. 362

Regression coefficient, p. 359

Regression equation, p. 359

Repeated-measures one-way
   ANOVA, p. 349

Residuals, p. 362

Robust statistical methods,
   p. 365

Shapiro–Wilk test, p. 363

Sphericity, p. 349

Sums of squares, p. 347

t test, independent samples,
   p. 342

t test, matched pairs, p. 344

t test, one sample, p. 340

Trimmed mean, p. 365

Two-way ANOVA, p. 351

Welch's *t* test, p. 342

Wilcoxon rank-sum test, p. 342

Wilcoxon signed-rank
   test, p. 340

y-intercept value, p. 359

Writing Up Your Results

INSIDE RESEARCH: STELLA CHRISTIE

Assistant Professor, Cognition and Development Lab, Department of Psychology, Swarthmore College

As an undergraduate at Harvard, I co-authored a paper that studied how gravity affects people's ability to mentally rotate objects (Mast, Ganis, Christie, & Kosslyn, 2003). I participated in writing up the methods as well as other sections of the paper. The most challenging part of it for me was explaining the experiment to my parents, my peers, and my friends. It took a lot of practice for me to tell other people why the research question was interesting and worth pursuing. This is something I see a lot when I work with undergraduates.

I went on to focus on learning mechanisms—studying how human beings learn. I work mostly with infants and toddlers ages

18 months to 4 years. Part of what I do is look at the mutual influence between language learning and conceptual development. I ask, "How does language influence one to acquire knowledge?" and also "How does knowledge influence language development?" In my studies I use a variety of behavioral methods. For example, we measure infants' looking times to see if infants notice any changes between events during habituation and at test. I often use a reaching paradigm where we give infants and toddlers several options and observe which objects they reach for first. In some spatial studies, I have used a kind of hide-and-seek game in which the experimenter hides an object at a certain location and notes where and how children search for that object.

Explaining your research to other people—especially those who are not psychologists—is always an interesting experience. But it's a good way to evaluate whether or not you really know what you're doing. Even though starting to write up my results is still a little hard for me, by the time I get to the middle of it I come to enjoy it. If you can explain your question and the logic of your experiment well, you can write it well. That is very fun.

Stella Christie won the Editor's Choice Award for Best Article from the *Journal of Cognition and Development* in 2010 for a paper she wrote with Dedre Gentner, a psychology professor and her mentor at Northwestern University.

Research Focus: How infants and children acquire concepts and language; how language development shapes children's learning about the world

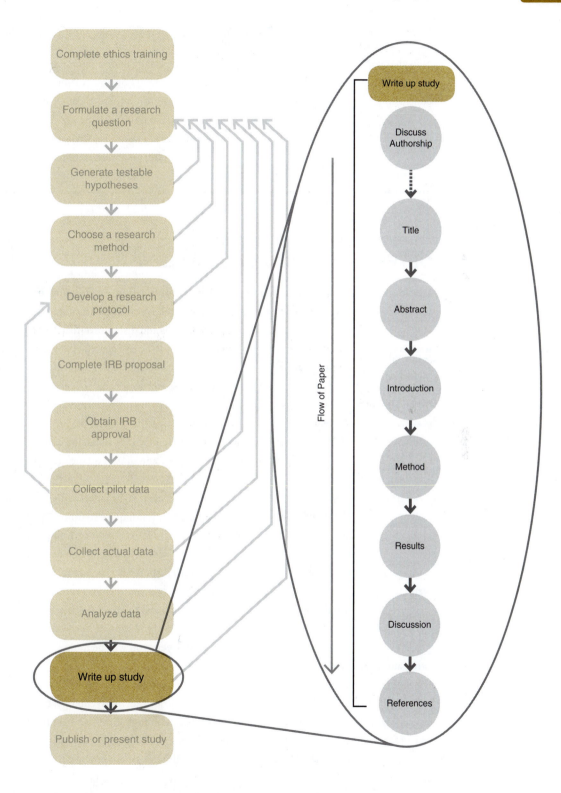

Chapter Abstract

Now that you have completed your study, you face the task of communicating your work to others. This involves crafting your hypotheses, experiments or observations, results, and conclusions into a readable article. In this chapter, we direct you through this process, which, as Stella Christie says, can be daunting but ultimately exhilarating. You will learn how to identify your target audience and how best to reach them. Finally, you will discover the key elements of good scientific writing, as well as additional resources to help you with structure and style.

DETERMINING YOUR AUDIENCE

Writing a research report is different from other kinds of writing, but, like any form of writing, it is a skill that can be improved with practice. Effective communication of research is a valuable skill that is transferable to many different fields and disciplines. Much of our advice in this chapter applies to scientific writing in general, although specific conventions differ by academic journal and field. Regardless, high-quality scientific writing requires knowing your audience and what readers expect to see in a research report.

One of the first questions you must answer when writing up your research is: Who will you write for? Will you write for individuals interested in general science, researchers within the broad discipline of psychology, or researchers within a specific area of psychology? The answer depends in part on you as a researcher and in part on the quality and originality of your research.

High-quality research with novel results will interest a broader audience (Gray & Wegner, 2013), whereas the best audience for work that is not quite so innovative might be readers of a journal focused on a subdiscipline of psychology. Most beginning researchers write for the latter group, which often includes both seasoned and novice researchers and perhaps a few interested nonresearchers and journalists from the general public. If you write for a subdiscipline journal, you will want to target seasoned researchers. Although they may be hard to please because of their experience and relatively high expectations for what the report should (and should not) include, they read reports because they want to gain new knowledge. On the bright side, if you succeed, you will be more likely to satisfy other audiences as well.

Although research reports can take several forms, in this chapter we focus primarily on writing up the results of a single study for an academic journal in psychology, because most beginning researchers start with this kind of paper. Although it is often best to write your report for the requirements of a specific journal, once you have collected the basic information and outlined the structure, it is usually not difficult to adapt the paper for another journal. You might consider using a paper that was recently published in a scientific journal you are considering for your own work as a model. You can also find example scientific papers in *The APA Publication Manual* and on many websites. A number of colleges and universities provide online writing resources that will help you as you craft your paper. For example, Purdue University's Online Writing Lab (Purdue Owl) is available for anyone to use. This website presents information about how to write experimental papers in APA format, principles to guide your writing, and a sample paper.

ELEMENTS OF GOOD SCIENTIFIC WRITING

The primary goal of scientific writing is to communicate. Scientific writing is designed to show why your research is interesting and important, why you conducted the particular study, what you did in the study, what you discovered, and implications that can be drawn from your results. Scientific reports are not meant to entertain or provide wild conjecture, but to provide the facts in a clear, concise, and relatively structured fashion. They are also meant to provide enough detail about the methods that a researcher working in another laboratory would be able to replicate your research (see Chapter 5).

Clear

Clarity is important to scientific writing because, first and foremost, scientists want other people to understand their work. The APA offers a number of tips in its sixth edition of the *Publication Manual of the American Psychological Association* (American Psychological Association, 2010, sections 3.09 and 3.11) for improving clarity in writing research reports. These include, among others, being precise in your word choice, avoiding colloquial expressions, avoiding scientific jargon, making sure that pronouns have clear antecedents, and avoiding the third person when describing methodology or procedure. We also suggest the following tips: (1) avoid artsy or flowery language (as in the APA's tip on jargon); (2) at the same time, avoid being dry and boring; and (3) write in readable, succinct sentences. Readers of scientific writing do not want to spend time and energy unpacking the meaning of long, complex sentences. Shorter, more direct sentences are best; there is no need to impress your audience with your extensive vocabulary. Also, be sure to define your terms and use them in a consistent manner throughout the manuscript.

Concise

Most researchers read a lot of research articles. They want to be able to grasp the gist of your article quickly and relatively easily. If you take 10 pages to say what you could say in 5, you will lose many readers. Gray and Wegner (2013) suggest that you should strive to be "clear, concise, and direct" (p. 552).

Brevity is also practical because it relates to the cost of publishing. Scientific journals are not produced to make money. They often have relatively limited readership and circulation, and members of the scholarly organization that publishes the journal must bear production costs—often through member dues. An increasing number of journals, therefore, require authors to pay for the cost of printing their articles (Kolata, 2013). These printing costs can range from $80 to $400 per page, with additional costs for printing color figures ranging from $160 to $1,000 per page. The longer the article, the higher the cost—either to the publisher or to you. A rising industry of "open access" publications (some of questionable quality) is accelerating the trend of authors paying for publication, but it also reflects a facet of the economics of publication.

Avoiding redundancy will help you to stay concise. Undoubtedly, you will have to mention some aspects of your research in different sections of the report. What you write in later parts of the report, however, should build on what you have already said, not merely restate it. Also, journal editors frown on duplication of information provided in the text, tables, and figures, even if the information is provided in somewhat different formats.

Compelling

Narrative A description of your research that flows from highly structured and organized ideas.

One of the most important aspects of good scientific writing is to provide a compelling **narrative** about your research—a description that flows from highly structured and organized ideas. Sternberg (1992) argues that high-quality scientific writing should "emphasize logical flow and organization" (p. 13). He also posits that a research article tells a story, and "like a story, it should capture readers' interest" (p.13). We prefer the word "narrative" to "story" because the latter term can imply a form of creativity that does not belong in scientific writing. The goal is not to make up details, as Diederik Stapel did (see Chapter 1), but to state the facts in as unbiased a way as possible. We base many of the following suggestions on Sternberg's article, "How to Win Acceptances by Psychology Journals: 21 Tips for Better Writing," which appeared in the APS *Observer* in 1993 and provides valuable insights about scientific writing.

Be Interesting.   Spell out clearly why the work is noteworthy and how it is novel, without being grandiose. As Sternberg (1992) suggests, "Tell readers why they should be interested" (p. 12). Also, without overstating the contribution or scope of your work, describe how your research fits with and builds on past work and moves our understanding of your topic forward. In addition, it is helpful to provide some concrete examples that highlight key concepts. But with each example, ask yourself: "Does the example clarify the concept?" and "Does it make my narrative more compelling?"

Use Logical, Evidence-based Reasoning.   You should base your research and write-up on logical, evidence-based reasoning. The ideas you developed in the introduction should build on past research, which you should cite appropriately, meaning you must provide a citation to any ideas or research that are not your own. Your hypotheses, study design, analysis, results, and discussion should flow logically.

Start and End Strong.   The three most important parts of your research report are the abstract, the first paragraph, and the last paragraph. This is because readers usually use these three elements to determine whether they want to know more about your study. Gray and Wegner (2013) argue, "With writing, as with life, first impressions matter" (p. 551). Spend extra time drafting and redrafting these sections. Indeed, Gray and Wegner (2013) advocate that you "should spend hours and hours to make [the] first few sentences sing" (p. 552). But the end should "sing" too, so spend equal time drafting the last paragraph.

Use Active Voice.   One persistent misconception about scientific writing holds that researchers should write in the passive voice to emphasize objectivity. This misconception likely stemmed from a desire to deemphasize the individual conducting the research. However, we wholeheartedly encourage you to reject the notion that the identity of researchers must be obscured behind awkward phrasing. Your high school English teacher would be happy to know that the most recent (sixth) edition of the APA publication manual explicitly directs writers to avoid passive voice in favor of more active phrasing and to use personal pronouns rather than the third person when describing researchers' methodology.

Write Multiple Drafts and Proofread.   Good writing takes time, energy, and a lot of rewriting. Some researchers complete as many as 10 drafts before sending a paper off for review. Just like faculty members who are annoyed by students who submit assignments with typos, grammatical errors, and missing sections, reviewers are annoyed by researchers who submit papers with these same issues. A research report that has many of these problems will likely receive negative reviews. Many seasoned researchers will ask a colleague to read over their papers before submitting them to a scientific journal. They want to make sure their arguments are convincing and that they have not missed an important detail. An unbiased reader or a new set of eyes will more easily catch flaws in logic or typos not caught by spell-checking software (e.g., "their" instead of "there").

OVERALL MANUSCRIPT FLOW AND ORGANIZATION

In this chapter, we focus on writing up quantitative research, in part because this perspective dominates contemporary psychology. Quantitative reports generally follow a similar, rather rigid template in contrast to qualitative reports, which follow a more narrative structure and have less strict guidelines regarding organization, flow, and content. Although it is important to create a compelling narrative in quantitative reports, this format generally has distinct subsections that are required by specific journals. Regardless of the type of research you conduct, however, when it comes to writing up that research, you must ensure that you have organized your paper in a logical, intuitive way and that you have included the right level of detail.

Hourglass Organization

The best way to envision the flow of the manuscript is to think of an hourglass. The wide top of the hourglass is your introduction—the place to present your general ideas and situate your work in the broader context of past research. Many beginning researchers start too broadly or reach too far back in time. How far back in time you need to go depends on the topic and how rapidly the information related to that topic has changed. Most of your readers will know the deep history of the topic, so cite it only if you can make an explicit, direct link to your current research. For example, if you are writing an experimental research paper, there is no need to cite Wilhelm Wundt as the first individual to have created an experimental psychology laboratory. The introduction should taper like an hourglass, ending with a set of precise hypotheses or goals.

The narrowest part of the hourglass represents the section that should contain the most specific details. These include a description of your method and procedures, followed by the analysis and results. This section tends to be less speculative and more cut and dried.

Finally, just as the hourglass begins to flare and then widens at the bottom, the discussion section should delve into specific results in detail and then broaden the scope of the discussion to include larger implications. As in the introduction, you want to avoid overreaching—the vast majority of studies do not produce earth-shattering results.

The Right Level of Detail

How much detail is necessary? Capturing the correct level of detail in a research report is a skill that takes practice. Your goal should be to provide enough detail that an independent researcher (i.e., someone from a different laboratory) could read the article and use the information to satisfactorily replicate your research. One question to consider as you are writing and revising is, "Does the reader need to know this?"

You will find that almost all articles, even the simplest of studies, miss some important detail regarding participant selection, methods, measures, or data analyses. If you have been using the same type of methods repeatedly, you might mistakenly assume that certain aspects are "understood" by other researchers and not even consider describing them in your report. This is why a second set of objective eyes can be so important before submitting a paper for review. A good practice, then, is to ask a colleague to read your "final" draft for clarity, logic, and appropriate level of detail.

Some beginning writers provide far too much information about the cited author or authors and their institutions. We have encountered numerous write-ups that contain sentences such as the following: "Professor Benjamin Franklin of the Department of Psychology at the University of Philadelphia in 1776 wrote a paper titled 'Psychological effects of getting struck by lightning' published in the *Journal of Early American Psychology*."

What's wrong with that sentence? Much of the detail is unimportant for readers to know, can be said more concisely, or belongs in other places, like the reference section. In addition, generally you should only use the last names of researchers. A more appropriate sentence is: "Franklin (1776) examined the impact of getting struck by lightning on a number of psychological processes including. . . ." You would then include details about Franklin's paper in the reference section.

BASIC SECTIONS OF A QUANTITATIVE RESEARCH PAPER

Quantitative research reports have a highly formulaic structure. You should be able to open any psychology journal and quickly determine whether the article is a report of empirical research, a review paper, or a commentary (see Chapter 4). Although this structure may seem constraining to a novice research report writer, it helps readers and reviewers find the important details quickly and efficiently.

Most empirical articles published in psychology journals will contain the following key elements: title page, abstract, introduction, methods and procedures, results and analysis, general discussion, and references. Here, we discuss each of these using sections of Stella Christie's award-winning article as an example (Christie & Gentner, 2010). We use a published paper as an example for a number of reasons. First, it should be the goal of any research project, even one conducted by an undergraduate, to produce high-quality research that could be published in an academic journal. Second, highlighting a published article provides another opportunity to discuss the reading of and thinking about research articles (see Chapter 4). Keep in mind that different journals—and even individual editors—may have slightly different preferences about the structure of manuscripts submitted to their journals.

Title Page

Although it may seem obvious, we like to start with the title page when we write a research report. The title informs the reader of the content of the report. Many journals have specific word or character limits for titles. Some editors and journals want clear, direct, informative titles, such as "Low self-control promotes the willingness to sacrifice in close relationships" (Righetti, Finenaur, & Finkel, 2013), whereas others encourage cute or humorous titles, such as, "Rising stars and sinking ships: Consequences of status momentum" (Pettit, Sivanathan, Gladstone, & Marr, 2013). Think carefully about the title and how others will perceive it. Many journals request that a short list of key words be included on the title page. It is a good strategy to include one or more of these key words in the title to make it easier for other researchers to find your published article through literature searches. When choosing your key words, think about how you would conduct a reference search to find a paper like your own. We often start with a "working title," or even a couple of alternative titles, and modify it as we write our paper. Like the rest of the paper, it is not a bad thing to revise, rethink, and rewrite titles to arrive at one that is clear and effective.

Stella Christie:

"We determine the order of authorship just like we determine ownership of data: the person who thought up the research question has primary ownership of the collected data and should be the primary author. Anyone else who works on the project is a secondary author. For example, students who worked on the project but who didn't come up with the original question—or anybody else who has done sufficient work—will be on the paper. But the one who came up with the research idea should be primary."

The title page includes the authors' names and their professional affiliations. Sometimes journals want both the department and the college or university affiliation, whereas others want only the latter. The title page should also list contact information for the corresponding author—the individual who submits the manuscript to a journal and who is responsible for all communication with the journal editor. For most multiple-author research projects, the corresponding author is the most senior author, who is most likely to be at the same institution through the review and publication process. However, in the case of articles based on a senior thesis or dissertation, which sometimes include multiple authors, the student may be the most appropriate corresponding author. In multiple-author papers it is customary—but not required—to list the corresponding author first or last.

The title page for multiple-author papers also provides an opportunity to discuss each author's contribution and the order of authors of the paper. The convention in psychology is to list the individual who did the most work on the paper first and then the other authors, in order of decreasing contribution to the paper. In contrast, in some other disciplines, such as engineering, the convention is to name the senior author or individual who made the largest contribution last.

Before deciding the order of authors, it is important to determine who should be considered an author at all. The APA offers a number of resources about what constitutes a contribution substantial enough to be listed as an author on a paper (Graf et al., 2007). These include making significant conceptual or intellectual contributions to the paper, playing a role in the design of methods, conducting the primary data analyses, and writing substantial aspects of the paper. Scheduling participants, collecting data, and entering data are not considered intellectual contributions that warrant authorship. Many journals now require the contribution of each author to be explicitly stated when the manuscript is submitted for consideration. Some journals also publish this information along with the actual paper.

In our view, determining authorship and order of authors is rarely straightforward. People often overestimate their own contributions and underestimate those of their colleagues. We advocate open, frank conversations about authorship beginning with the initial planning of the project. Over time, these discussions should be repeated with all members of the research team to discuss changes in individual effort that might warrant adding or subtracting authors or changing the order of authorship.

Abstract

The abstract provides a brief summary of the research. Although different journals specify different lengths, most abstracts range from about 150 to 250 words. Stay within the limits. The abstract for single research study reports should state the following:

- The purpose of the research: one or two sentences;
- Why the research is important: one or two sentences;

- Who the participants were: usually one sentence;
- What the participants did: about three sentences;
- What the results revealed: one or two sentences;
- An interpretation of the results: one or two sentences; and
- Any implications that can be drawn from the study: one or two sentences.

Not all abstracts will contain all of these points, especially abstracts for articles that contain more than one study, because it may be difficult to fit in all the details of the research. It may be easy for some studies to combine aspects of the research, such as the participant population and what the participants did, in a short phrase (e.g., "Young adults completed a 20-minute survey assessing happiness.").

Many readers will read only the abstract, so you want it to be succinct and interesting and to capture the essence of your study. Many researchers will write the abstract last, after they have completed the rest of the paper, because it is often easier to do after the entire narrative has been spelled out.

Figure 15.1 shows the abstract written by Stella Christie and Dedre Gentner for their article that explores how preschoolers' learning changes when they compare different spatial representations of objects and animals.

In just 158 words comprising seven sentences, Christie and Gentner effectively describe the goal of their experiments, their participants, the methods they used, the results, and their interpretation. They use simple language and the first person. A few terms in this abstract may stand out to nonexperts as jargon: "exemplar" and "structural alignment processes," which refer, respectively, to specific examples and the cognitive process where an

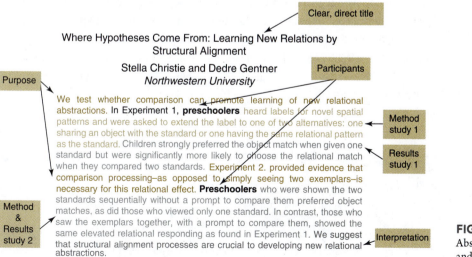

FIGURE 15.1.
Abstract from Christie and Gentner (2010).

individual might make comparisons in an analogy. Although it is best to avoid jargon as much as possible, sometimes you will have to use standard terms. Overall, this abstract promises readers interested in this field an investigation into the cognitive mechanisms that preschoolers use to form hypotheses.

Some journals, especially those in more medically oriented areas of psychology, will require highly structured abstracts that contain a number of specific sections corresponding to the aspects of the paper, such as the objective, the design, the participants, the outcome measures, the results, and the conclusion. Again, if the journal requires this format, you should follow it or the editors may reject your paper without ever sending it out for review.

Spend time on the abstract. Think of it as your chance to convince casual readers that they want to learn more about your research. If people never read beyond your abstract, you are not doing an effective job of describing your work, and ultimately your work will not have the impact you would like.

Introduction

Your introduction should accomplish three main goals. First, it should clearly articulate the purpose of your research.

In the first paragraph of their introduction, Christie and Gentner set the stage by asserting the significance of their topic—relational abstractions—and then move quickly to their overall goal of studying the process by which children learn it (see Figure 15.2).

Second, the introduction should make clear to readers why they should be interested in your research. In the following paragraph a few pages into the introduction, Christie and Gentner put their research into a larger context to help readers understand its relevance (see Figure 15.3).

Christie and Gentner back up each of their points in this paragraph with citations to other research. Although the citations make the paragraph more difficult to read, they provide important information for other researchers reading the article. Some journals may limit the number of references you have in your paper, in which case you need to cite only the most relevant ones. Some journals may not allow you to cite work that is "in press," as is the case for the last citation. The "in press" label indicates that a manuscript

Why topic is important

Learning relational abstractions is fundamental to the development of knowledge. Children must learn to categorize and reason over functional relations (X is edible), biological causal relations (X needs water to grow), mechanical causal relations (X can move things), and spatial relations such as those that underlie the meanings of prepositions and many verbs (X is moving upwards–*ascending*–or X is located *above* another object.) A critical question is how children achieve this learning.

Specific goal

FIGURE 15.2. First paragraph from Christie and Gentner (2010).

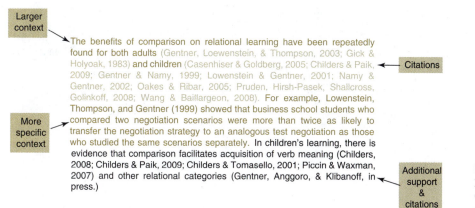

Larger context

The benefits of comparison on relational learning have been repeatedly found for both adults (Gentner, Loewenstein, & Thompson, 2003; Gick & Holyoak, 1983) and children (Casenhiser & Goldberg, 2005; Childers & Paik, 2009; Gentner & Namy, 1999; Lowenstein & Gentner, 2001; Namy & Gentner, 2002; Oakes & Ribar, 2005; Pruden, Hirsh-Pasek, Shallcross, Golinkoff, 2008; Wang & Baillargeon, 2008). For example, Lowenstein, Thompson, and Gentner (1999) showed that business school students who compared two negotiation scenarios were more than twice as likely to transfer the negotiation strategy to an analogous test negotiation as those who studied the same scenarios separately. In children's learning, there is evidence that comparison facilitates acquisition of verb meaning (Childers, 2008; Childers & Paik, 2009; Childers & Tomasello, 2001; Piccin & Waxman, 2007) and other relational categories (Gentner, Anggoro, & Klibanoff, in press.)

Citations

More specific context

Additional support & citations

FIGURE 15.3.
Paragraph from Christie and Gentner (2010).

has undergone peer review and been accepted for publication, but it has not yet been formally published. These journals want citations to research that has been formally published.

The third goal for your introduction is to situate your research in the context of past studies and current trends in your *specific* research area. For most empirical papers, it is not necessary to write an exhaustive history of the field (that level of depth and breadth belongs in a major review paper). Rather, you want to get to the issues relatively quickly, providing summaries of the methods and conclusions most relevant to your own research (Sternberg, 1992). Your literature review should also articulate how your research builds on past research, complements that work, and moves beyond it in important ways. Figure 15.4 illustrates how Christie and Gentner highlight past research and set up additional questions the research raises to be examined in the current study.

In a study that relates to the present work, Gentner and Namy (1999) taught 4-year-olds a new name for a pictured object (e.g., a bicycle) and asked them to choose another with the same name. The alternatives were a perceptually distinct match from the same category (e.g., a skateboard) or a perceptually similar object from a different category (e.g., eyeglasses), thus pitting perceptual similarity against conceptual commonalities. When children saw a single standard, they tended to choose the perceptually similar alternative, consistent with prior studies (Baldwin, 1989; Imai, Gentner, & Uchida, 1994; Landau, Smith, & Jones, 1988). In contrast, children who initially compared two standards (e.g., bicycle and tricycle) showed a greater preference for the conceptual match. This was a striking result, because the two standards always shared the same properties with each other as they did with the perceptual alternative, so on a feature-overlap account, comparison should have led to *more* perceptual responding rather than less. Gentner and Namy concluded that structural alignment between the two standards fostered noticing common (hitherto implicit) relational structure (such as "both can be ridden"; "both stay in the garage," etc.) and thus pointed the children toward the category choice.

Highlighting a past study directly relevant to current one

Highlighting a striking finding that leads to current study

Presenting a hypothesis from previous work to be examined in current study

FIGURE 15.4.
Paragraph highlighting past research directly relevant to the current study and setting up arguments for the current research from Christie and Gentner (2010).

Children were given a word extension task on a triad of pictures. To ensure children's interest, the pictures were made up of animals. The standard was labeled with a novel noun, and children were asked to extend the label to one of two choices: a relational match (new animals in the same configuration) or an object match (same animal[s] in different configuration). We included the object match to provide a viable nonrelational choice, because previous studies have found that young children attend strongly to object similarity (Gentner, 1988; Gentner & Rattermann, 1991; Gentner & Toupin, 1986; Halford, 1987; Landau, Smith, & Jones, 1998; Paik & Mix, 2006; Richland, Morrison, & Holyoak, 2006). As in the Gentner and Namy (1999) studies, half the children were given one standard (the solo condition), and the other half were given two standards and asked to compare them (the comparison condition). We predicted that the comparison group would be more likely to choose the relational match than the solo group.

What the researchers did in Experiment 1

Support for method

Prediction

FIGURE 15.5.
Introductory paragraph to the first experiment from Christie and Gentner (2010).

In papers focusing on a single study or experiment, the introduction will often end with a brief paragraph that outlines the specific hypotheses investigated in the research. Papers that contain multiple experiments will often introduce each separate experiment with a brief paragraph that presents issues specific to that experiment. Christie and Gentner present two studies in their 2010 paper. The first study is introduced in a separate section with a new heading (see Figure 15.5). Careful reading of this paragraph along with the introduction will indicate some redundancy across sections. Although you should generally avoid repetition, sometimes it is necessary to repeat information across sections to ensure clarity.

Methods and Procedures

In principle, the main goal of the methods and procedures section is to provide enough information so that your study could be replicated—a description of participants, materials used, and procedures followed. As described earlier, exact replication is likely impossible for a variety of reasons, unless it is done in the same laboratory with the same experimenters. However, if that level of replication is necessary to produce the psychological effect of interest, then it is time to worry about the generalizability of your findings.

Participants.   You should provide details about how you recruited participants and their age, sex, racial, or ethnic background. These details aid the reader in considering how well the results might generalize beyond the participant population studied. It is also important to provide details about any compensation provided to participants. Compensation can aid in recruiting a more diverse sample or ensure a higher retention rate, and if another researcher attempts to replicate your work, the amount of compensation could be an important factor.

Christie and Gentner described their participants in Experiment 1 in the paragraph shown in Figure 15.6.

This description of participants contains a few details specific to the *Journal of Cognition and Development,* in which the article appeared. First, the specification of ages, such as "3-year-olds ($M = 3;8$, range = $3;6-4;2$)," is a convention indicating that the average or mean age of the children is three years and eight months with a range of ages from three

Participants. Twenty-six 3-year-olds (M = 3;8, range = 3;6—4;2) and thirty 4-year-olds (M = 4;8, range = 4;5—5;1) participated. The children were from predominately white middle- to upper-middle-class families in the greater Chicago area.

FIGURE 15.6.
Participant section from Christie and Gentner (2010).

years and six months to four years and two months. Conventions such as this may vary somewhat from journal to journal, so be sure to follow the "Author Guidelines" or "Instructions to Authors," which are often found on the front or back covers of print versions of journals or online at the journal submission website. Second, the description of participants as "white middle- to upper-middle-class families in the greater Chicago area" tells the readers important details about the participant population. One detail missing from this participant description is the breakdown by sex, specifically how many boys or girls participated in the study. Even if there is no reason to expect that the results would differ for males or females, it is a good idea to include this information, broken down by any subgroups (e.g., age, condition) that are used in the study.

Another detail to include is the rate of participation—the number of individuals who agree to participate versus those who were initially contacted. Participation rates are influenced by a number of factors, including the research focus, the time commitment required by the study, and whether the researcher provides some type of incentive for participation. Related to rates of participation is the attrition rate, the number of participants who started the study but for some reason eventually dropped out. This is mostly an issue with longitudinal research, but information about the number of participants who began the study and the number who complete it should be included in your write-up. On the one hand, high dropout rates may indicate potential problems with recruiting or result in a final sample that is not representative. On the other hand, low dropout rates may indicate a successful recruiting strategy or potential fraud.

In a study such as Christie and Gentner's (2010) that involves relatively old preschool children, it is likely that all children whose parents had provided consent and who were approached by the experiments agreed to participate and completed the study. In many areas of psychology, including developmental psychology, participation rates are not commonly reported. However, in areas where attrition is common, such as with research with young infants, researchers should provide information about the drop rate. For example, it is not uncommon in studies of infants to have "dropout" because they become hungry or fussy or fall asleep.

Researchers conducting studies involving highly technical equipment may also drop some participants because of "equipment malfunction" or "experimental error." You should report this information. Finally, participation rates are also commonly reported in survey research where many people may be contacted but only a subset of them agree to participate. For example, an experimenter may send out 200 surveys, but receive only 45 completed surveys.

Participation rates that were much higher than those found in similar research ultimately led to researchers uncovering fraud in a widely reported study in *Science* that found that views of gay marriage could be changed through door-to-door canvassing (http://www .npr.org/2015/05/24/409210207/author-says-researcher-faked-gay-marriage-opinon-study). The fraud was revealed in part because a researcher from another laboratory was surprised at the reported participation rate and asked the original investigator how he had been so successful. Attempts to replicate the recruiting strategy failed to yield similar rates, and as the researchers delved more deeply into the study, they eventually found convincing evidence of fraud. The paper was ultimately retracted.

Materials.   You will need to describe any materials used in your study, including any apparatus that presents stimuli, the stimuli themselves, and any questionnaires and surveys. If you are using standard equipment, surveys, or questionnaires that are commonly used by researchers and have been described in other published works, you can cite those studies and provide a brief description that is tailored to and relevant to your own research. If you have developed new materials, then you must describe them in detail.

As shown in the paragraph in Figure 15.7, Christie and Gentner constructed their own stimuli for use in their study and described the stimuli in a clear fashion; they also provided a figure (see Figure 15.8, corresponding to Figure 2 in the original article) in the manuscript to clearly show how they presented stimuli to the children.

The materials section is also the place to include any available information about surveys or questionnaires about the validity and reliability of your measures. Again, the level of detail in the materials section should be sufficient for another researcher to recreate your study.

FIGURE 15.7.
Description of materials used from Christie and Gentner (2010).

Materials. There were eight sets of colored animal pictures, each consisting of two standards, plus an object match and a relational match. Each picture depicted two or three animals configured in a novel spatial relation (e.g., a black cat directly above an otherwise identical white cat). The second standard within a given set showed different animals in the same spatial configuration (e.g., a black dog above a white dog). The object match contained an exact animal match from each standard but in a different relational pattern (e.g., a black dog diagonally above a black dog). The relational match was composed of new animals in the same relational configuration as the two standards (e.g., a black bird directly above a white bird; Figure 2). Children were randomly assigned to either the solo condition (single standard) or the comparison condition (two standards presented together, as shown in Figure 2). Within the solo condition, which standard children saw was counterbalanced.

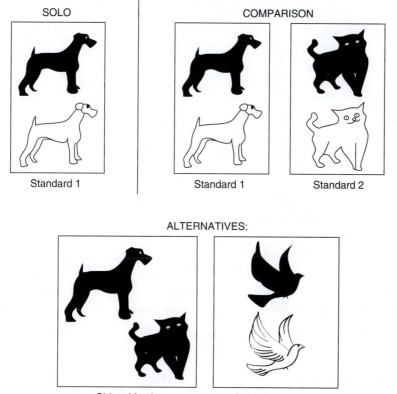

FIGURE 15.8.
Stimuli in experiment 1 from Christie and Gentner (2010).

Procedures. The final part of the methods and procedures section describes the actual procedures completed by participants (see Figure 15.9). Specifically, describe what the participants did, the order of any tasks or conditions, and why you used that particular order. It is also important to clearly state your variables and how they were operationalized. Christie and Gentner provide the exact wording of the questions that the children were asked and explicitly describe the different steps of the experimental procedure, providing a level of detail that should make it relatively easy for other researchers to understand what was done and potentially replicate the methods.

Note that the researchers refer to a previous study (Gentner & Namy, 1999) to justify some of their procedures. Although it is entirely appropriate, and often necessary, to explain why you chose particular procedures, you can also refer to previous research for more details about particular methods and procedures; this approach can help keep the procedure section relatively short and concise. A growing number of journals are also asking authors to make many of the details of methods and procedures available as online resources connected to a particular journal.

Procedure. Children were seated across from the experimenter. In the solo condition, the experimenter laid out a single standard and labeled it with a novel count noun: "Look, this is a jiggy! Can you say jiggy?" The experimenter then placed the two alternatives side by side below the standard and asked the child, "Can you tell me which of these two is a jiggy?" After the child made a choice, the experimenter continued with a new standard from a new set.

The comparison condition began in the same way: The experimenter presented and labeled the first standard. Then the experimenter placed the second standard near the first one. Half the standard pairs were laid out horizontally (side by side), the other half vertically. The experimenter named the second standard with the same label as the first and encouraged the child to repeat the word and to compare the two standards: "Can you see why these are both jiggies?" (As in Gentner and Namy's (1999) studies, no answer was required; the idea was to invite children to think about it.) Then the two alternatives were presented as in the solo condition.

Eight different novel labels were used, one for each relational pattern. The order of novel words and the item order were varied in four semi-random orders, counterbalanced within each condition. Left-right placement of the two alternatives was also counterbalanced.

FIGURE 15.9.
Procedure section from Christie and Gentner (2010).

Results

You may find the results section one of the most difficult sections to write well. The difficulty arises from the problem of providing clear, logically organized prose about sometimes dry and complex statistical analyses. Three strategies can enhance readability of the results section: (1) divide the analyses into sections addressing particular hypotheses or issues; (2) provide brief explanations throughout the results section to clarify statistical statements (which often look more like math text), but save interpretation of the results for the discussion; and (3) consider placing some of the key results in tables and/or figures to reduce the density of the text (number of sentences) in the results section.

Many researchers begin their results section with a brief, descriptive overview of the data before starting on a more specific discussion of the statistical analyses used. The start of a results section might include a report of overall means between groups to give a summary of the data obtained.

The results section should provide sufficient detail about the statistical tests you conducted. Remember that your goal in a research report is to provide a narrative; in general, you should include statistical analyses that directly address your goals or hypotheses, as well as any statistical tests that could be done to rule out potential alternative hypotheses. Some reviewers may demand an exhaustive set of analyses that explore factors that may not be at all relevant to your main hypothesis. In our view (and that of others, e.g., Cohen, 1990), this approach is unwarranted. Yet, you should report both tests that revealed statistically significant results and those that did not result in significant findings, especially if these results go against your stated hypotheses and predictions.

The beginning of Christie and Gentner's results section states, "Figure 3 shows the mean proportion of relational matches selected by 3- and 4-year-olds in the solo and comparison conditions." This statement effectively orients the reader to the figure (shown here as Figure 15.10), and the figure provides a clear and effective overview of the results.

As Christie and Gentner make clear in the caption, the figure presents data from two different experiments. Often researchers will include data from two or more studies in a figure to facilitate comparison of the results across related studies. It may be better to present the results of the initial study in a figure and then provide the comparison in a second figure that comes later in the paper. In the example presented in Figure 15.10, readers will not understand the statement "with two intervening fillers" until they have read the

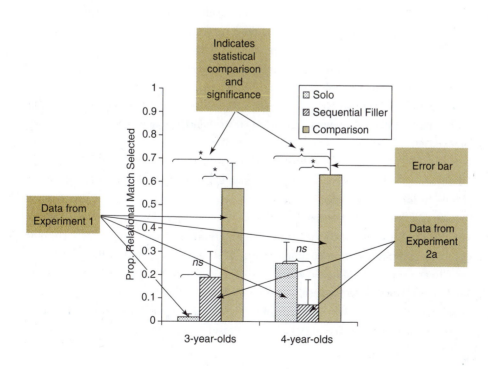

Stella Christie: *"I was very lucky to be drawn into a research project as an undergraduate, and worked with my professor and two post-doctoral fellows. I actually participated in the write-up of the methods section. As an undergrad it was obviously too challenging for me to write the results section. But the other authors were very good mentors and they said, "Why don't you write up the methods section? You really know how." And they included me as an author. It was a thrilling moment!"*

FIGURE 15.10.
Figure reproduced from Christie and Gentner (2010). Providing the "mean proportion of relational responses in solo and comparison (Experiment 1) and in the sequential—with two intervening fillers—condition (Experiment 2a). *$p < 0.05$."

procedures reported in experiment 2a. When deciding whether to combine data across studies in a single figure, think about the narrative you are telling. Does this approach help clarify the results or does it make the results section more confusing?

Christie and Gentner also provide information about statistically different means in a noncluttered way by providing "*" and "ns" labels. The "*" indicates that the means are statistically different at $p < 0.05$ level (as mentioned in the caption). The "ns" label stands for nonsignificant, indicating that the means that are bracketed with that label do not statistically differ from one another. These are common conventions used to indicate when means are similar or different from one another. Another common convention is to provide **error bars** that depict the amount of variability in the sample. Figure 15.10 contains error bars, but the authors do not provide information about whether the error bars indicate the standard deviation or standard error of the means. This information should be provided.

After the introductory sentence of the results described earlier, Christie and Gentner provide the following sentence: "A 2 (condition: solo and comparison) × 2 (age: 3-year-olds and 4-year-olds) analysis of variance (ANOVA) revealed a significant main effect of condition, $F(1, 52) = 23.83$, $p < 0.001$, $\eta^2 = 0.30$."

This statement tells the reader that the researchers included two factors (condition and age) in the analysis, evaluated potential differences between conditions using an ANOVA, and found that the main effect of the condition was statistically significant. The "η^2" refers to the effect size, a measure of the strength of the effect. The effect size reported by the authors falls between a small (0.20) and medium (0.50) effect size (Cohen, 1988). As described in Chapter 13, effect sizes provide an indication of the magnitude of the difference between groups. According to Christie and Gentner, the analysis revealed they did not find a significant main effect of the age factor and they did not find a significant interaction between their two factors. Although the authors then describe their results in more detail, this initial analysis successfully tests their key hypotheses involving condition and age.

Sternberg (1992) argues that you should briefly explain what the results mean rather than leaving the interpretation up to the reader. Christie and Gentner (2010) do exactly this in the following sentence in their results section: "the fact that children in the comparison condition chose relational matches more than twice as often as those in the solo condition is consistent with the claim that structural alignment is an effective way to induce children to focus on common relational structure" (p. 363). Although you will need to present a more detailed analysis of your results in the discussion section, these brief explanations make the results section more readable and improve readers' understanding of the findings. One way to organize these explanations is to refer the reader back to your hypotheses by indicating which of your results support (or fail to support) specific hypotheses.

Error bar A graphical representation of the amount of variability of a sample statistic, such as a mean.

Discussion

The discussion section is analogous to the bottom of the hourglass. Start with a review of your most important and specific results and then present the general implications of your research. Many researchers end the discussion with ideas about what kinds of future research are needed or with more practical applications of the research findings.

The discussion section provides an opportunity to include secondary findings that relate peripherally to your main findings. Although we advocate presenting alternative explanations in the results section, in some cases you can consider them in the discussion section. When you do this, however, tell readers why these alternative explanations fall short of your primary explanation. Christie and Gentner do this in their discussion, stating, "A key question here was whether our results could be explained by cross situational learning, without invoking comparison, by assuming that children formed a set of hypotheses when they saw the initial standard and then used the other standard to filter these guesses. Contrary to this account, children showed relational insight only when they saw the standards simultaneously and were invited to compare them" (Christie & Gentner, 2010, p. 369). If the results are equivocal, you should be honest, but if you do not take a stand in your discussion, your work will never be published.

Remember, the goal is to tell a compelling, accurate narrative of your study. This narrative should provide the facts, an interpretation of what the facts mean, an acknowledgment of problems or limitations, an explanation of why these limitations do not undermine the overall conclusion, and a statement about the direction the research should take in the future.

Christie and Gentner discuss their findings and suggest areas for future research in the paragraph shown in Figure 15.11. This paragraph effectively states their main finding ("that relational abstraction requires structural alignment"), defines the scope of the finding, situates their research in the context of other research with adults and children, provides

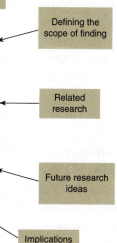

FIGURE 15.11.

Section of discussion section from Christie and Gentner (2010).

suggestions about how a researcher might further explore this area of research, and provides implications of predicted findings.

An important issue to consider is that authors cannot always control how the popular press and other researchers will interpret their work. Providing a clear, objective interpretation of your own results, however, improves the chances that others will capture your work accurately. In addition, if you do not plainly define your participant categories up front, you can leave your work open to wild misreading. This happened to the researcher profiled in "Media Matters: When Research Is Misrepresented."

As with the overall paper, you should start and end strong. The first and last paragraphs of the discussion section are two of the paper's most important paragraphs. Spend time on them. Make sure they are clear and convey why your work is interesting and important. Highlighting the importance of your final paragraph, Gray and Wegner (2013) write, "The conclusion should not be a restatement of the results but instead a grander statement, one that ideally takes the reader back to the first paragraph or the opening quote or one that links the findings to some famous idea" (p. 552). As they note, based on the work of Kahneman and colleagues (Kahneman, Frederickson, Schreiber, & Redelmeier, 1993), people tend to form the strongest memories of the last part of a narrative they encounter. Make it sing like your introductory paragraph.

References

All articles cited in the text should appear in the reference section, and all articles listed in the reference section should be cited in the main text. Reviewers will often go back and forth between the text and the references to learn more about the area that you are studying. In fact, one of the reasons for being a reviewer is to keep up on the latest research in a particular area, and reviewers will look up references of which they were not aware. As a reviewer, it is frustrating to get excited about an idea discussed in a citation, but then be unable to find the paper in the reference section.

The reference section should follow the format dictated by the journal and the discipline. For most psychology journals this means following APA format guidelines (as outlined in the *APA Publication Manual*), although non-APA journals vary in requiring this format. You can usually find guidelines regarding references on the journal website. If you do not follow these guidelines, do not bother submitting your work, because it will most likely be rejected without being sent out for review.

Figures and Tables

As you decide which tables and figures to include in your article, you should always ask yourself the following questions: Are they necessary? Do they replicate information in the text? Do they capture the data in a compelling and interesting way that magnifies the results? Or, do they state the obvious and really add nothing to information in the text? The *APA Publication Manual* has advice about how best to present information in both figure

When Research Is Misrepresented

Any serious researcher knows the importance of writing up research results honestly, without distortion, overreaching inferences, or false claims. Yet, even the most experienced researchers cannot always predict how the media will react to their papers, sometimes *even before they are officially published.*

Consider the example of David Figlio, a professor of education, social policy, and economics at Northwestern University. He watched in astonishment at the intense and mistaken media reaction to his working paper, which appeared on the website of the National Bureau of Economic Research (NBER), a nonprofit organization that publishes working papers by premier economists.

The paper, *Are Tenure Track Professors Better Teachers?*, examined differences in teaching effectiveness between Northwestern's tenure-track professors and non-tenure-line lecturers among first-term freshmen (Figlio, Schapiro, & Soter, 2013). The paper's conclusion stated that non-tenure-track faculty at Northwestern "not only induced students to take more classes in a given subject than do tenure line professors, but also lead the students to do better in subsequent coursework than do their tenure track/tenured colleagues."

The problem arose when two magazines specializing in higher education misrepresented the study. *Inside Higher Ed* (Jaschik, 2013) and the *Chronicle of Higher Education* (Berrett, 2013) reported incorrectly that Figlio's study focused on adjunct professors, who comprise a wide range of full- and part-time faculty at many different kinds of universities and colleges. Many adjuncts earn meager salaries and are forced to cobble together various jobs; their status on campuses across the country has become a hotly debated issue.

However, Figlio says, "There is nothing in the paper that suggests we are talking about part-time adjuncts.

We studied full-time, long-term designated teaching faculty. . . . We were really careful not to say anything about policy or make major policy recommendations."

Within days, several major media outlets, including the *New York Times*, *The Wall Street Journal*, *USA Today*, and the *Atlantic*, picked up the story and in most cases failed to mention that the nontenure faculty members were long-term, full-time instructors. In fact, these instructors are hired and rehired based on their teaching prowess. Perhaps most egregious was the *Atlantic*'s original headline, which read "Study: Tenured Professors Make Worse Teachers" (Weissman, 2013a). These stories created much controversy in academia and fed some suspicion that the study was a politically motivated attack (Kazarian, 2013).

"It surprised me that the paper received so much attention given the way it was released as an NBER working paper," Figlio says. "There was no PR. It was a prepublication communication by economists for economists. The level of coverage that this working paper received was unprecedented."

Figlio wrote a few letters to editors, and he was gratified by the response of the *Atlantic* writer, who followed up with a literature review and a mea culpa that his original article contributed to misinformation (Weissman, 2013b).

When asked what advice he would give to beginning researchers, Figlio says, "I think it's very important not to make outlandish claims, because there are already people who will take whatever you find and intentionally distort it one way or another, or misinterpret it. The author has a sacred duty not to draw inferences that are way outside what they actually say or what they can actually study."

and table formats. Do not try to do too much in any one figure or table. Too much information can appear cluttered and overwhelm the reader. Well-formatted tables and figures can effectively simplify a section of otherwise dense text (as noted earlier in the results section), but use them judiciously.

COMMON ISSUES TO CONSIDER

Beginning researchers tend to make a number of mistakes in their write-ups. Here, we present few additional guidelines for avoiding some of the most common mistakes.

Avoid Using the Word "Prove."   One of the most common mistakes is to include a statement to the effect that the results prove something. No single research study or collection of studies can actually prove anything, so avoid using that word. "The results indicate that . . ." or, "The results suggest that . . ." are better ways to present your findings.

Do Not Anthropomorphize.   It is not uncommon for authors to state that "The research found . . ." or "The data revealed . . . ," suggesting that research or data are real actors in the world. It is better to say "The researchers found . . ." or "Our inspection of the data revealed . . ." Give credit where credit is due.

Round to the Nearest Decimal That Captures the Accuracy of the Measurement Tool.   When writing a description of your data and data analysis, report the data based on the accuracy of your measurement tools rather than to all the decimals that might be generated by a calculator or statistical program. With modern statistical programs it is possible to report values to many decimal places, but this level of accuracy is rarely meaningful.

Number of significant figures The number of digits that you can report about your measurement that you know are correct.

Generally, it is important to understand the **number of significant figures** that your measurement tool allows. The number of significant figures refers to the number of digits that you can report about your measurement that you know are correct. The convention is that this number also includes one estimated digit. For example, if you are comparing means on two different versions of a test that goes from 0 to 100 with only whole number values (e.g., 85, 96, 98), then it is appropriate to report the mean scores to one decimal place (e.g., $M = 93.7$), not to many decimal places (e.g., $M = 93.7521$). This latter value is not meaningful because the precision of your measurements does not justify reporting the result to four decimal places.

Report Data in a Meaningful Manner.   We have encountered papers where students have coded male and females as 1's and 2's in the data file and report a mean for this variable of 1.7. Although a statistical package will easily calculate a mean for this category, calculating means for categorical data is not appropriate. Consider whether your data are categorical or continuous and report the data appropriately.

Be Careful How You Report Your Statistics.   Statistical programs will spew out p values and other statistics to four or more decimals, but be careful about reporting these "exact" values. These values are only as accurate as your overall measurement tools. Too many researchers become infatuated with small p values, assuming that smaller p values imply greater significance (Cohen, 1990). However, p values are greatly influenced by sample size. For this reason, it is important to consider whether the difference is meaningful, even if the statistical tests show significant results. Many journals now require researchers to provide information about effect sizes or statistical power (see Chapters 6 and 13). We also advocate rounding the values that you report for various other statistics (t, F, or r) to values that are meaningful, as well as rounding p values to the nearest conventional level ($p < 0.05, 0.01, 0.001$).

Provide Enough Detail about the Statistical Test Used to Examine the Data.   Another common mistake is not providing enough detail about the statistical test used to examine the data. This is particularly true in students' reporting of their use of ANOVA. Rather than merely stating, "An ANOVA was conducted to examine difference between groups," you should provide details about the ANOVA: How many groups or conditions did you use? Was it a one-way ANOVA or a multivariate ANOVA? Did you have any covariates? Did you repeat any measures? Did you examine within- and between-subjects effects?

Keep the Statistics Simple.   Gray and Wegner (2013) argue that you should keep the statistics simple because complicated, sophisticated statistics can confuse the findings. In addition, the use of novel, sophisticated analyses will require space for explanation, detracting from your main narrative. It is better to advocate for the use of such a technique in a separate methodology paper. However, be cognizant that to successfully examine some data sets you may need to employ complex and/or sophisticated approaches. If you do use novel or complex statistics to examine your data, take the time and space in your write-up to adequately explain the statistics and the results that are derived from them.

Discuss Hypotheses and Limitations.   Sternberg (1992) encourages researchers to consider alternative interpretations of the data and results in the results section. This is not only a highly effective way to convince your audience of the value of your research, but also fair and ethical because it acknowledges that no single study in psychology definitively establishes a key finding as fact. If you bring up an alternative interpretation of the data in the results section, then it is appropriate to examine and potentially rule out that alternative using appropriate statistical procedures. If you bring up alternative interpretations in the discussion section, then be sure to explain why they may or may not be plausible.

All research studies have limitations, and many journals require authors to state a study's limitations in the final section of the written report. Some journals may even have a special section or sections where limitations must be listed. Although it is appropriate and, for many journals, necessary to list limitations, do not stop with merely listing them. Rather, discuss how the limitations might have influenced the results obtained and conclusions drawn from the research. Yet, remember that you must advocate for your research, so be sure to discuss the limitations in ways that do not undermine the value of the research you have just completed. In some cases, it might be appropriate to point out how potential limitations might be addressed in future research.

VARIATIONS FROM A SINGLE-EXPERIMENT PAPER

Empirical research reports are not the only types of articles produced by psychologists and other social scientists. Here, we briefly describe multiple-experiment papers and qualitative research reports because they are the most common for beginning researchers to write.

Multiple-experiment Papers

Multiple-experiment papers are common in psychology, and the more prestigious journals will rarely accept a single-experiment paper. However, the preference for single or multiple experiments varies by journal and the discipline of psychology. In fact, many journals have begun to publish rapid reports of only one study or experiment in addition to more traditional, longer, multiple-experiment papers.

The organization and structure of a multiple-experiment paper is similar to that of a single-experiment paper. The main difference is that there is generally a separate brief introduction to each study or experiment, with each study followed by a brief discussion. The manuscript then ends with a final discussion that summarizes and integrates the findings from all of the research reported in the manuscript.

For more experienced researchers, deciding whether to "package" experiments together or submitting one or more rapid research reports can take considerable thought and deliberation with co-authors. Although it is not ethical to divide up a study solely for the purpose of publishing more than one paper, often the narrative works better in either a short report or a multiple-experiment paper. The narrative that you want to tell should ultimately drive this decision.

Qualitative Research Reports

Although a quantitative research report is by far the most common form of article in psychology, a significant number of qualitative researchers in psychology write up their research in a completely different manner. These two approaches differ not only in how they are written, but also in their research designs (see Chapter 5).

As with quantitative reports, qualitative reports should strive to be clear, direct, and accurate (Kirkman, 1992; Strong, 1991). A number of excellent sources provide detailed guidance in conducting and writing up qualitative research (e.g., Denzin & Lincoln, 1998a, 1998b; Flyvbjerg, 2006; Holliday, 2001; Kidder & Fine, 1997; Robson, 2002: Willig, 2008), so we will provide only a brief description of a qualitative research report here.

Qualitative research reports vary to a much greater extent than quantitative research reports in terms of structure and style. For this reason, it is important to determine before you start writing who you want your audience to be. Then, you can tailor your writing for that audience (and the specific journal that will reach that audience).

Generally, the difference between a qualitative and a quantitative report can be found as soon as you look at the title. Whereas few quantitative reports will use the term "quantitative" in the title, because this is the default assumption, it is not uncommon for qualitative reports to include the term "qualitative" or some other related term (e.g., "narrative," "personal meanings," "social construction") that distinguishes the report as qualitative in nature.

In terms of the actual content, qualitative reports rarely, if ever, report any type of statistical analysis, which is at the heart of most quantitative reports. Instead, many qualitative reports include relatively lengthy narrative accounts of interviews or observations. In addition, direct quotes from participant interviews will generally be interspersed throughout. This is in contrast to quantitative reports that rarely include quotes, except in the final discussion to highlight an important finding.

We could present only a brief overview of qualitative reports here. If your real interest is in qualitative research and methods, you should explore some of the many books and articles devoted to this topic (e.g., Denzin & Lincoln, 2005; Fischer, 2006; Forrester, 2010).

PRACTICAL TIPS

Practical Tips for Writing Up Your Results

1. Write clearly and concisely.

2. Be sure to cite research that your work builds on.

3. Cite other researchers for any ideas that are not your own.

4. Avoid repetition. Avoid repetition.

5. Never think that a first draft is sufficient. Revise, edit, and rewrite often.

6. Find someone who can read and comment on your final draft. This person can help you make sure that your narrative flows logically, that you have not left out steps in an argument, and that your writing is clear and concise.

7. Writing well takes effort and practice. Try to schedule time for writing into every workday.

CHAPTER SUMMARY

Although writing your first research report can be intimidating, remembering the rules for good scientific prose will keep you in good stead. Tell the narrative of your research in language that is clear, concise, and engaging. Be careful to organize your information into appropriate sections, particularly for quantitative papers: title page, abstract, introduction, methods and procedures, results, discussion, and references. Above all, adhere to the requirements of the journal to which you are submitting. Now, you should be ready to tackle the final stage of your research—submitting your article for presentation at a conference or in the pages of a journal (Chapter 16).

Up for Discussion

1. This chapter primarily focuses on writing up results for an academic journal in psychology, often the "first stop" for research findings for both novice and experienced researchers. Imagine that you have just successfully published your first peer-reviewed article that demonstrates a promising new intervention to boost reading fluency in young children. The local press catches wind of your research and wants to run a story on your findings. What should be the primary considerations in terms of how much detail you provide to the reporter about your research? What are the benefits of a more detailed (and technical) press report? What are the hazards? How would you think about striking the right balance between technical details and accessibility to your audience?

2. You are an undergraduate student who has just completed your honors thesis after an arduous year of work. As you prepare to apply to graduate school, you seek to publish a manuscript based on a portion of your dissertation. As you ready your submission, your former advisor insists that he be listed as the first author on the manuscript, noting that the research was entirely funded by a multimillion-dollar grant that he had secured and that all of the equipment used in the study was also from his laboratory. You also used several survey instruments authored by your advisor, but you wrote the entire manuscript. What are the considerations in determining authorship? Does your advisor have a valid claim to first authorship? To any authorship at all?

3. Given the story of the media's misrepresentation of David Figlio's research regarding the effectiveness of teaching faculty versus tenure-line faculty (see "Media Matters: When Research Is Misrepresented"), what measures do you think researchers should take to minimize the risk of their research being misrepresented? Figlio suggests that researchers should not make outlandish claims, but since he did not do so in the case of his research and his work was *still* misreported, are there any further measures to be taken?

Key Terms

Error bar, p. 392

Narrative, p. 378

Number of significant figures, p. 396

Publishing Your Research

INSIDE RESEARCH: HAZEL ROSE MARKUS

Davis-Brack Professor in the
Behavioral Sciences,
Department of Psychology,
Stanford University

The main psychological issue I've always thought about is exploring the form and function of the self in a social world. The self is at the center of experience. It integrates, it organizes, it puts the "you" of yesterday with the self of today—the person who went to bed last night is the same one who wakes up in the future. Your self reflects the various social contexts you've been a part of. That's where the self gets content.

Because I'm interested in the self and culture, I rely a lot on self-report. But I also believe that studies are best when they use a variety of methods. I think people can tell you things about their experience that no one else can, but sometimes what they're saying doesn't match what they're thinking or feeling. For example, I did a study with East Asians and European Americans that examined how cultural values and individual preferences for uniqueness or conformity influenced each other (Kim & Markus, 1999). We asked individuals to fill out questionnaires and as a thank you gift for participating we showed them a group of pens, four orange and one green, and said, "Please choose one." We found that Americans—always seeking their uniqueness—chose the green pen about 70% of the time, while the East Asians would invariably choose an orange pen, because from their perspective being unique has to do with standing out and being vulnerable, not something desirable. But when we asked people why they chose the pen, everybody said, "I just liked the color of that pen."

My research has been misrepresented in the media, but I don't think that's the media's fault. Journalists today don't have much time to read anything; they just call up. They can't know and read everything. As researchers we need to be much more media savvy.

Hazel Rose Markus is the author of four books and dozens of influential journal articles. She is a renowned social psychologist and trailblazer in the field of cultural psychology. In her most recent book, *Clash! 8 Cultural Conflicts That Make Us Who We Are*, Markus and her co-author, Alana Conner, explore how the qualities of independence and interdependence permeate individuals' sense of self and influence everything from governments to parenting.

Research Focus: The sociocultural shaping of the mind and self

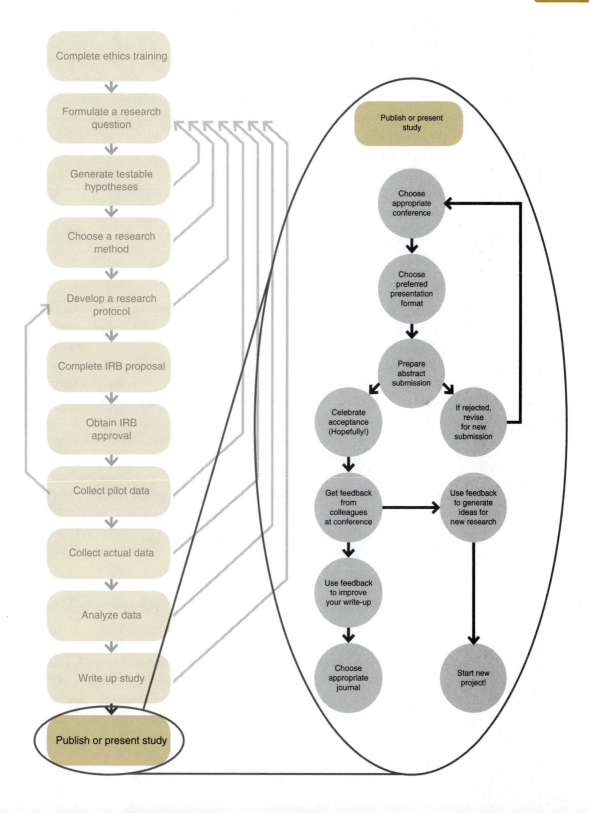

Chapter Abstract

This chapter focuses on how to report your results in various ways to the wider scientific community. We begin with a discussion about presenting work at conferences, which is often the initial forum for introducing research. Then, we provide recommendations for the process of how to publish your research in a journal. Finally, we guide you through the crucial peer review process, which can be as challenging as it is worthwhile. Gaining acceptance of your work is one of the most important aspects of the research process and is considered by many researchers the most rewarding.

THE PAPER IS DONE! NOW WHAT?

As we have detailed throughout this book, conducting research is an iterative process that involves continually returning to your research question, revising your ideas and protocols, and testing a variety of different approaches. This process does not end when you have collected or even analyzed all your data. Rather, it continues as you determine how to best present your results and incorporate feedback from reviewers, who may suggest alternative ways to frame your research question, analyze your data, or interpret your results.

Traditionally, many students have approached undergraduate research projects, as well as senior honors projects, as a way to develop research skills independent of formal classroom instruction. Few students consider presenting their results at a conference or attempting to publish their work in an academic journal, unless directed by their mentor. For better or worse, however, it has become increasingly important for students applying to PhD programs to have research experience and even a publication or two. So how do you get your work published? The first step is to present your research findings at a conference.

PRESENTING RESEARCH AT CONFERENCES

Generally, you should present your work to a conference only after you have collected the majority of your data, conducted sufficient preliminary analyses to provide a clear pattern of results, and crafted a brief, lucid narrative based on your understanding of the results. Most conference submissions go through a review process. Generally, you cannot submit the same data to more than one conference, and most reviewers will not accept submissions that look like rough drafts or are poorly prepared. They look for work that is interesting, novel, and compelling to the majority of the researchers most likely to attend the conference.

You must consider the timing of the completion of your project and submission deadlines. Many seasoned researchers have a number of studies in different stages of completion, so it is fairly easy for them to find data to present at conferences. However, for beginning researchers, completion of data collection and analyses may not coincide with the conference at which they hope to present. In this situation, researchers may attempt to submit preliminary results with the hope they will be accepted (and that the final results will match the preliminary results). Alternatively, they may choose to wait and submit to a different conference when they have collected and analyzed the complete data set.

Types of Conferences

Every academic discipline offers many types of conferences. Most conferences fall into two main categories: general and specialized. **General conferences** cover many areas within a particular subject, such as psychology. **Specialized conferences** focus on a particular branch, such as social or developmental psychology, or even on particular research or statistical methodologies, such as methods for analyzing longitudinal data (see Chapter 12).

Two important general psychology conferences are the annual meetings of the American Psychological Association (APA) and the Association for Psychological Science (APS). APA is the largest, drawing approximately 20,000 researchers and clinicians every summer (usually in late July or early August). Like many conferences, APA offers workshops and continuing education sessions in addition to research presentations.

APS was founded in 1988 mainly out of concern that clinicians were dominating the APA and that the field of psychology needed an organization focused on advancing science. Although the APS has more than 20,000 members, the conference, which takes place in May, draws about 6,000 researchers.

In addition to APA and APS, numerous smaller, more focused conferences meet every year or two. For example, developmental psychologists may choose to attend conferences focusing on infancy (Biennial Conference of the International Society of Infant Studies), cognitive development (Biennial Meeting of the Cognitive Developmental Society), or development more broadly (Biennial Meeting of the Society for Research in Child Development). Social psychologists may present their research at annual meetings of the Society for Personality and Social Psychology or the Society of Experimental Social Psychology.

The APA and other organizations, such as the Eastern Psychological Association, the Midwestern Psychological Association, and the Western Psychological Association, also sponsor regional meetings. These smaller conferences range in size from a few hundred to a

---

Hazel Markus:

"It behooves investigators to be thinking from the beginning: 'What is this problem about? Why would this matter? Who would care?' That's the advice I'm trying to give students these days, because when it comes time to submit your paper to a journal or talk to the media, that's not the time to think about it. We need to be thinking about it all along, and how to say things in a clear way."

General conference A professional meeting that covers many areas within a particular subject, such as psychology.

Specialized conference A professional meeting that focuses on a particular branch of a discipline, such as social or developmental psychology, or on particular research or statistical methodologies, such as methods for analyzing longitudinal data.

few thousand participants, and they are often organized around a particular theme that varies from year to year or by a particular branch of psychology.

A number of conferences—often hosted by universities—are geared especially for undergraduate research presentations. Some are open only to students attending the institution. These meetings tend to be broad, covering undergraduate research and creative work across most of the disciplines represented at the university. However, others are discipline specific and recruit undergraduate researchers from the entire country, such as the Stanford Undergraduate Psychology Conference and the UCLA Psychology Undergraduate Research Conference. In addition, groups of colleges and universities co-host specialized regional conferences, such as the Western Pennsylvania Undergraduate Psychology Conference and the Mid-America Undergraduate Psychology Research Conference. Many national psychology conferences also offer sessions devoted to undergraduate research posters and presentations.

Choosing the Right Conference

A number of factors influence researchers' choices of conferences. These include the conference audience, the status of the conference, the size of the conference, and the conference location.

Audience.   Most important, you must match your area of research and the expected audience at a particular conference. Consider your data and results and your ideal audience. If your research examines stereotype threat in a college population, do not try to present your work at a conference devoted to developmental psychology unless your research is in some way relevant for developmental psychologists. Choose a conference where your work will be presented alongside related work. This can occur in a small, focused conference or in the more specialized sessions of a larger conference.

Status.   The status of the conference also influences which researchers it will attract. Status is determined in part by who presents at the conference (more famous researchers = higher status) and how difficult it is for work to be accepted at the conference (higher rejection rate = higher status). Submit to the highest-status conference for which you think your work is suited. Generally, conferences that focus only on undergraduate research are not considered high status because they have few, if any, renowned researchers presenting (other than perhaps a keynote address) and high levels of acceptance. Despite this issue of status, conferences devoted to undergraduate research can still provide invaluable experience to novices.

Size.   Another important factor is the size of the conference. Whereas some researchers love the excitement and diversity of very large conferences (such as APA), others prefer smaller conferences that enable them to focus on research that relates to their own work in a more intimate setting. Smaller conferences generally stimulate more discussion and feedback about your research. As you will discover after attending a conference or two, networking with other researchers in both formal and informal sessions is an important aspect of attending conferences.

Location.   A final consideration that affects submissions is the conference's location. Most conferences move around from city to city or, if they draw an international audience, from country to country. This can benefit attendees, because the cost of travel to the same conference for researchers from different locations will even out over time. Additionally, attendance and submissions increase for conferences that take place in locations that people would like to visit.

Presentation Formats

There are not only many different conferences, but also many different types of presentations. The most common form is a poster format, but several other types exist, including oral presentations, symposia, podium talks, data blitzes, and even hybrid formats.

Poster Presentations.   Most conferences use a similar format and present posters in special sessions that range from a dozen posters in a small room to hundreds of posters in a large conference hall. Posters are generally four feet wide and three feet tall, but the exact dimensions vary with different conferences. Although the author or authors decide on a particular design and style, most posters include all the sections found in a formal paper—an abstract, introduction or background, methods and procedures, results, and conclusion (see Figure 16.1). Researchers vary in whether they include a reference section.

Generally, for a poster presentation it is better to present the information in figures and tables as much as possible, rather than with detailed text. Other researchers want to be able to determine quickly whether your poster is of interest. Most conferences will provide specific information about the poster, as well as tips on how to present your work.

Researchers usually have between 30 and 90 minutes to present their poster, and they are expected to discuss their findings and answer questions for some, if not all, of that time period. Presenters should prepare a few different versions of their poster talk.

The shortest version should be a few sentences that communicate the overall purpose of the research—in other words, the version you would give to an acquaintance who wants to know what you do, but is not particularly interested. The goal is to inform and spark interest in the longer version.

The intermediate version is a five-minute presentation that provides more details about the background, importance, methods, and results. This version is sometimes called an "elevator talk" because the information should be able to fit into the time it takes to wait for an elevator or ride between floors.

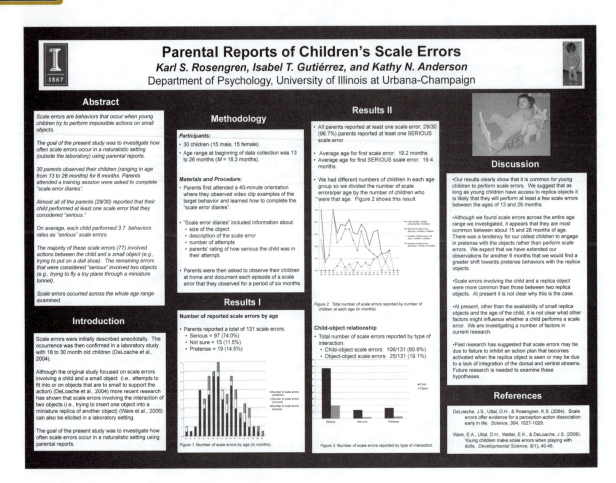

FIGURE 16.1.   Example of a poster presentation.

Finally, a longer 10- to 15-minute presentation should "walk" listeners through the entire poster. If you are presenting a poster, do not be shy: when people start reading the poster, ask whether they would like to be walked through or given the short version.

Oral Presentations.   Conferences generally include a variety of oral presentations, with some given by famous people. The head or president of the hosting society or organization often provides a **presidential address**, which generally deals with the collective body of research to be found at the conference, often including a historical context as well as ideas for future research. Conferences typically have one or more **keynote addresses** delivered by important researchers who may be from a closely related discipline. Keynotes are designed to inform attendees of the hottest new research and ideas in the field and to inspire them to think about extending their own research in interesting directions. These

Presidential address A speech given at a conference by the head or president of the hosting society or organization, who discusses the collective body of research to be found at the conference within a historical context and presents ideas for future research.

presentations often are placed in a prominent location and time in the conference program so that all can attend. Other established researchers or up-and-coming stars in the field may also give **invited talks**, of which there are usually several. These talks range in length from 60 to 90 minutes.

Symposia.   Conferences often group together three to five shorter talks that contain an overlapping theme. These **symposia** talks usually last approximately 20 minutes and focus on a particular research study or studies. The symposia are generally concluded by someone who summarizes and critiques the talks, focusing on overarching issues. They are also more prestigious than poster presentations. In addition, a variety of blended versions of talks and posters can be found at conferences. These include **poster symposia**, which present thematically linked posters along with a moderated discussion among the presenters.

Podium Talks.   Also more prestigious than poster presentations, **podium talks** are oral presentations that last from 10 to 20 minutes and report the results of a single study. They generally include the purpose, background, methods, results, and conclusions in abbreviated form. Some conferences have mostly symposia and others mostly podium talks.

Data Blitzes.   A **data blitz** involves a very short oral presentation with one or two slides that convey the essence of research and data in a fast, clear way. This format continues to grow in popularity, especially at smaller, more specialized conferences. Data blitzes can be as short as 1 minute or as long as 5 or 10 minutes. They are sometimes presented as part of a larger poster session where individuals who find your data blitz interesting can learn more about your research from your poster.

For data blitzes in particular, you must focus on what you want to convey and how to convey it. As with all talks and presentations, we recommend practicing beforehand, because conference organizers will not tolerate speakers going over the time limit. For a 1-minute presentation, you must zone in on the main point—and only the main point. Limit text to a couple of bullet points or phrases and the number of figures or graphs on your slide to two. Never try to cram 20 minutes of data into a 1- or 5-minute talk. If you overload people, they will not be interested in talking to you later.

Choosing the Right Presentation Format

Unless you present your work at an undergraduate conference or a smaller regional or topic-oriented conference, you probably will not have much choice of format. Your only real option as a beginning researcher will most likely be to submit your work as a poster. However, posters are an excellent way to start learning how to present your work. Poster sessions are relatively free-form, with people walking around looking at posters and asking authors about their work. For most researchers, this means that presenting a poster is a fun and less stressful experience than a more formal oral presentation.

Keynote address
A speech delivered at a conference by an important researcher who presents groundbreaking research and ideas to inspire attendees to think about how they can extend their own research in interesting directions.

Invited talks
Discussions lasting between 60 and 90 minutes that are led by established researchers or up-and-coming stars at a conference.

Symposia Twenty-minute talks given by researchers at a conference that contain an overlapping theme and focus on a particular research study or studies.

Poster symposia A meeting at a conference in which researchers present thematically linked posters and take part in a moderated discussion.

Podium talk A 10- to 20-minute oral presentation given at a conference that provides an abbreviated report of the results of a single study, including its purpose, background, methods, results, and conclusions.

Data blitz A 1- to 10-minute oral presentation that uses one or two slides to convey the essence of research and data in a fast, clear way at a conference.

As you gain experience presenting your research, try an oral format. This format is generally considered more prestigious because the focus is on a single presenter rather than a room full of posters; many conferences reserve oral presentations for high-quality research that is likely to appeal to a wide audience of attendees.

WRITING UP RESEARCH FOR PUBLICATION

Research requires a large commitment of time and energy, and we believe you should launch your research project with the goal of presenting your findings at a conference and ultimately publishing them. In thinking about presenting your work to a larger audience, it is important to consider both the small, ordinary details of research and the broader context in which your research is situated. This involves determining how your research fits in the larger context of related research and how your work extends beyond that work to break new ground.

After you have taken the important first step of submitting and presenting your research at a conference, you will likely leave the conference filled with new ideas about how to effectively present your work. Conferences are excellent places to get ideas for new directions to take your research and learn about alternative ways to examine your data and frame your research. Following are some resources that provide all the details you will need to write your research report.

The APA-Style Manuscript

Most, if not all, journals in psychology and related disciplines require a particular format for the contents of the submission. Most editors will not even consider your research for publication if you ignore the formatting instructions; they will reject it without sending it out for review.

The sixth edition of the *Publication Manual of the American Psychological Association* (American Psychological Association, 2009) provides extensive information about the formatting, organization of content, reference citations, and writing style required by APA journals. Most psychology journals follow the APA style of formatting even if they are not associated with the APA.

The APA manual provides specific details for all the sections required in an empirical research report or review article, as well as examples of manuscripts in the proper format. Although many of the guidelines may seem picky and somewhat arbitrary, you should follow them as meticulously as possible because they make reviewers' jobs much easier. The consistent format across articles and different journals enables experts to efficiently extract the important details of a study without reading the entire article. Remember, most researchers rarely read a paper from start to finish. Rather, they jump from section to section, pulling out details that interest them (see Chapter 4).

A number of excellent online resources also provide tips and guidelines that help with APA formatting. The online writing lab at Purdue University is one of the best and most extensive websites on APA-style writing (APA Formatting and Style Guide, 2016). Many other colleges and universities provide similar, but often less detailed, information about formatting and writing papers in APA style.

Types of Journals

Whereas you can apply to many different conferences to present your research, you can submit your research to an even greater number of journals. Consider a number of criteria before deciding where to send your manuscript, including the journal's audience and status.

First, consider the match between your research topic and the journal's audience. Your work will most likely not be published in a journal that focuses on an area unrelated to your own research. Look at the journals that published the research that you cite in your own paper; publication in those journals virtually guarantees that you will reach an audience that appreciates your work.

Another factor to consider is the status of the journal, because journals vary greatly in prestige. Prestige is determined both by how hard it is to have your work accepted by the journal and by how often the research reported in the journal is cited. Generally, journals that reject the most papers and whose papers are cited most frequently enjoy the highest status. One measure of status is the **journal impact factor**.

The journal impact factor measures how often other researchers cite papers published in a particular journal. Journals with high impact factors are considered more prestigious than those with lower values. However, this measure is only valid for comparison with other journals within a particular field because fields vary in both size and scope. For example, in 2014 the journal with the most citations (and the highest impact factor) was the *New England Journal of Medicine*, followed by *Chemical Reviews*—not a publication in which most (if any) psychologists would publish. However, the top 10 most cited journals included *Nature* and *The Lancet*—both of which publish research by psychologists (National Institutes of Health, 2014). Papers appearing in these journals are cited often. According to *Science Watch*, an open Web resource for science metrics and research performance analysis, the average citation impact from 2000 to 2010 for psychiatry and psychology papers published in *Nature* was 80.3 and in *Science*, 91.1. To put these numbers in perspective, many specialized psychology journals have impact factors around 1.0, with the top-cited journals in psychology ranging from 4.8 to 22.

However, publishing in these high-status journals is very difficult. Some of the most pre-eminent scholars in a field never publish in *Nature* or *Science* (see "Media Matters: Q & A with *Economist* science writer Matt Kaplan"). These journals are widely read, which means

Journal impact factor A measure of how often other researchers cite papers published in a particular journal.

Hazel Markus:

"Young people are becoming more media savvy because they spend so much time on social media. They also need to think about their science and how they can communicate it more effectively. We should encourage partnerships with journalists. If you talk to journalists, and they know what you're doing and follow what you're doing and they get some expertise in your field, that would help our work be better represented."

Q & A with *Economist* Science Writer Matt Kaplan

The journalist Matt Kaplan writes about science and technology for *The Economist* and is the author of *The Science of Monsters*. His articles also appear in *National Geographic*, *Scientific American*, *Science*, and *New Scientist*.

As the science correspondent for *The Economist*, how do you decide which scientific studies to cover?

I do a lot of reading. Every week I go through about 40 journals. They are not the best known, but they come up with interesting science. I usually find between 20 and 30 papers that I will read abstracts for. I note which ones I think show promise and later that day read between 7 and 15 papers—not the whole paper, only the intro and the methods section to determine whether or not the work is statistically significant. Then I summarize 4 or 5 of them and pitch them to my editor. The editor comes back and says he'd like one, or some, but never none. Then I spend two days writing.

What do you think of the state of reporting on psychological research?

A lot of science in psychology is not done right and that harms the field. . . . One of the greatest challenges that young psychologists face is the media. It's important for them to get the message out, especially if they're getting funding from someplace like the National Science Foundation. But journalists can so easily spin psychology in the wrong direction; you've got to be really careful how your findings are communicated.

How can science journalists do a better job?

A lot of journalists read press releases off science news services or read newspapers, and they don't remember that they are part of a larger peer-review process. We have a responsibility to think about what we are reading and ask ourselves, "Is this good science?" You can't trust the journals alone—that's just part of the process. You have to remember that you and your editor are part of a larger peer and review system.

What advice would you give new psychology researchers?

Be aware that most science journalists are not scientists. Be aware that they had to digest someone's research that they conducted over years in less than two days. Be aware that there is a culture of not quote- or fact-checking with scientists, and that is a shame, because it means that journalists who could get things right don't, and that they are misinformed.

that their readers are interested in science in general and may not have specialized training to evaluate the key issues in your own field. Writing for these impact journals is also different from writing for a more specialized journal, in part because you are writing for a more general, yet highly educated audience. Many of these high-status journals also require the authors to write clear but short papers. Summarizing an exciting finding in a thousand words, as is sometimes required by these journals, is quite challenging. Refrain from submitting to these journals unless you have a groundbreaking finding that has implications well beyond your own field of inquiry.

Table 16.1 lists the top 25 psychology journals based on **journal citation reports**. These reports are similar to impact factors but provide a ranking that takes into account journals indexed in the **Web of Science**, an online academic citation index published by Thomson Reuters. Journal impact factors are calculated by taking the number of citations that articles in a particular journal receive and dividing that number by the number of articles published in that journal in the same year. These journal impact factors are calculated on a yearly basis and can be easily found at a number of different websites by simply searching for the "top XX psychology journals."

Impact factors vary from year to year and are influenced by how specialized the journal is, the average number of authors per paper, the type of journal, and the size of the journal (Amin & Mabe, 2000). More specialized and applied journals generally have lower impact factors than more general journals. For example, *Science* had an impact factor of 31.36 in 2010, significantly higher than that of the highest ranked psychology journal (*Behavioral and Brain Sciences* at 21.95). Impact factors in a subject area also tend to increase as the average number of authors per paper increases. Journals that specialize in review articles (e.g., *Psychological Review, Developmental Review*) generally have higher impact factors than journals that focus on more empirical articles. Smaller journals, which publish fewer articles per year, tend to show more variability in the impact factor from year to year than larger journals.

If you look at multiple sites, you will find that the overall ranking varies somewhat. Part of this is because rankings can include both psychology and psychiatry journals, be based on different years of data, or incorporate averages over different time periods. Rankings should serve as a general guide to help you choose where to submit your work, but do not think of them as absolutes that are carved in stone.

Choosing the Proper Home for Your Research

How should you decide where to send your manuscript? Again, the most important factor is matching your research topic with the scope of the journal. Spend some time looking at different journals, reading the descriptions of the journals, and determining who is on the

Journal citation report A ranking of journals provided in the Web of Science, an online academic citation index published by Thomson Reuters.

Web of Science An online resource for researchers hosted by Thomson Reuters that provides search and analysis tools in a variety of fields. Examples of resources available on this site are citation reports and journal impact factors.

Table 16.1. The Top 25 psychology journals in 2015, ranked by impact factor

Rank	Journal	Impact factor
1	*Behavioral and Brain Sciences*	20.415
2	*Psychological Science in the Public Interest*	19.286
3	*Annual Review of Psychology*	19.085
4	*Trends in Cognitive Science*	17.850
5	*Psychological Bulletin*	14.839
6	*Annual Review of Clinical Psychology*	12.214
7	*Health Psychology Review*	8.976
8	*Clinical Psychology Review*	8.146
9	*Perspectives on Psychological Science*	7.658
10	*Psychological Review*	7.581
11	*Personality and Social Psychology Review*	7.571
12	*Journal of the American Academy of Child and Adolescent Psychiatry*	7.182
13	*Psychological Inquiry*	6.714
14	*Journal of Child Psychology and Psychiatry*	6.615
15	*Advances in Experimental Social Psychology*	6.150
16	*Neuropsychology Review*	6.061
17	*Journal of Managerial Psychology*	6.051
18	*Journal of Educational Psychology*	5.688
19	*Current Directions in Psychological Science*	5.545
20	*Journal of Abnormal Psychology*	5.538
21	*Psychological Medicine*	5.491
22	*Psychological Science*	5.476
23	*American Psychologist*	5.454
24	*Journal of Clinical Psychiatry*	5.408
25	*Journal of Memory and Language*	5.218

Source: (http://ipscience-help.thomsonreuters.com/incitesLiveJCR/JCRGroup/howtoCiteJCR.html)

editorial boards. An **editorial board** comprises researchers who cover the scope of a journal's focus and who ultimately decide what is published. A journal with editorial board members who conduct research in the area on which your paper focuses will likely prove a good match for your work.

    If a number of journals look like good matches, then consider the impact factor. Generally, it is best to shoot high. Top-tier journals usually have a more extensive review process, which means that even if they reject your paper, you will receive high-quality feedback that you can use to improve your paper before submitting it to another journal.

Editorial board A group of researchers who make decisions about what a specific journal will publish.

THE REVIEW PROCESS

Once you decide on a journal to which you will send your paper, you enter what is known as the review process. This multistep experience may involve rigorous appraisal by members of the journal editorial board as well as peer researchers in your field, with the goal of producing the best possible paper. The steps of the review process generally include submission of your paper, editorial review, revisions, and, sometimes, acceptance for publication.

Paper Submission

The first step in the submission process is to write a brief cover letter to the editor of the journal (when required; not all journals require such a letter). Journals that require such a letter usually specify what the contents should be. Generally, the letter should include the title of your paper, your name and the name of any co-authors, a brief description of your research, why your research is important, and why the journal is a good fit. The cover letter should also include a statement that your paper has not been submitted simultaneously to any other journal, that none of the material in the paper has been published previously, and that the institutional review board approved the research described in the paper (see Chapter 3, "Negotiating the Institutional Review Board Process").

    Most journals now use an online submission process in which you upload your manuscript either as a single document or in stages (i.e., cover letter, abstract, main paper, figures, tables). Ensure that everything uploads correctly. Reviewers hate to read poorly formatted papers or papers missing sections (see Chapter 15). It is your job to ensure that your paper conforms to all of the journal's requirements. After double-checking and formally submitting the manuscript, you will receive an e-mail notification with information about the review process and the assignment of a manuscript number to your paper. You can use this information to track the progress of your paper and should reference this number in any correspondence you have with the editor.

Editorial Review

Once you have submitted your paper, the editor or members of the editorial board will look over the manuscript and, in most cases, quickly make a decision about whether to send your paper out for review. In reality, editors at journals such as *Science* and *Nature* will reject most papers without sending them out for review. The higher the number of submissions to a particular journal, the more likely this "triaging" of papers will occur. Editors make triage decisions based on the match of your paper with the journal's focus and their judgments of the importance and novelty of your research findings. Because editors evaluate your submission quickly in this initial review, you should write the cover letter with care and make the abstract, introduction, and discussion sections interesting and compelling.

Soliciting Reviewer Feedback.   If you have found a good match for your paper and editors agree that it lies within the journal's focus, they are likely to send it out for review. Journals and editors vary in how many reviewers they will ask to comment on your paper. The most prestigious journals may request four or more reviews of your paper, whereas other journals will ask only two reviewers. Generally, the more reviewers, the harder it is to please everyone and the more likely your paper will be rejected or that you will be asked to revise your paper substantially.

Although editors instruct reviewers to provide constructive feedback on your paper, not all reviewers adhere to this request, and some reviews can be overly critical or even hostile. We believe it is the editor's duty to rein in hostile reviewers. The review process should improve the science of psychology, not take shots at researchers.

The review process takes time, the length of which varies with both the type of journal and the type of manuscript you have submitted. Although many journals strive for a two- or three-month turnaround, most take closer to six months. Unfortunately, some journals take much longer—up to a year or more—to decide on the status of your paper, so the length of the review cycle can be another factor in determining where you send your paper.

Receiving Reviewer Feedback.   Once the editor has received all the reviews, he or she will read them and then reread your paper. The reviewers usually write comments for the author(s) and a set of confidential comments for the editor. Comments to the author(s) should not include a decision about the paper—that is reserved for the confidential comments. This approach provides the editor with some leeway in either rejecting a paper that most reviewers thought favorably of or accepting a paper that some of the reviewers felt quite negative toward. Editors may make these decisions because they have expertise in the area of your research or because they find your work interesting and feel that publication will advance the field in important ways.

Most journals ask reviewers to judge whether the paper should be (1) accepted with minor revisions, (2) accepted with major revisions, (3) revised and resubmitted for further consideration, or (4) rejected. After making a decision, the editor writes a one- or two-page letter that gives an overall evaluation of the paper. If the editor makes the decision to ask for any revisions, he or she will usually provide some suggestions to you for how best to revise your paper. The editor will also send along the individual reviews, which typically run between one and three pages each.

Rejection letters tend to be much shorter, often only half a page in length, and supply just the facts, especially if your paper has been triaged by the editor (i.e., we thank you for submitting your paper but we do not want to publish it). Some editorial letters for rejected manuscripts, however, can be detailed and informative. Rejections occur for a number of reasons, including lack of fit with the journal, lack of originality, poor experimental design, problems with the materials or stimuli, inadequate theoretical framing, failure to cite other important works in the area, inadequate statistical analyses, and poor writing. Many of these issues are ones that should have been dealt with prior to submission. That is, if you spend the time and energy beforehand thinking about your audience and writing and rewriting your paper before submission, you will be more likely to receive a "revise-and-resubmit" decision. If you receive a revise-and-resubmit letter, do not view it as a negative outcome. This editorial decision is a positive outcome that enables you to significantly improve your paper.

Revising.   Most papers require substantial revision prior to being accepted for publication. Higher-status journals often insist that papers undergo at least two revisions before being formally accepted. Although not all feedback is equally helpful, in general reviewers tend to supply mostly interesting, constructive, and valuable feedback. You can increase your chances of acceptance by taking all of the feedback seriously.

One of the best ways to demonstrate your commitment to publication is to draft a cover letter for your revision that addresses each of the comments made by the editor and the reviewers, point by point. It is difficult for an editor or reviewer to reject a revision if you have effectively outlined how you have addressed each of the criticisms. You do not have to agree with all the requested changes or suggestions, but you must provide a convincing argument for why you did not make some of the requested changes. The more detailed and complete your response, the greater the chance your revision will be accepted.

Even if you ultimately decide to send the revision to another journal, you should still take the reviewer feedback seriously because you are likely to run into at least some of the same reviewers again in the future. There is nothing more irritating to a reviewer than an author who ignores his or her comments and resubmits the paper without making any changes.

The Imperfect Review Process.   The review process depends greatly on skilled, experienced researchers in the field taking time to carefully evaluate your work. Most academics are short on time, so reviewers often work on a relatively tight deadline, which means they may sometimes miss an important detail or two. If this happens, you may *politely* bring the oversight to their attention in a revision letter without creating ill will.

The review process also requires editors who have a broad and deep perspective on the field, keep up to date on current issues and trends, and have many contacts in the field who might serve as reviewers. If an editor selects poor reviewers, you may end up with disparate reviews. One reviewer may state that your work is creative and novel and should be published, whereas another may assert that your finding has been known for years. This can be frustrating, but as long as you have the opportunity to revise your paper, you can address both sides. And you *always* have the opportunity to revise your paper—it just might be for a different journal.

An unfortunate way in which some of the imperfections of reviewing come to light is with the issue of fraud. When scientific fraud occurs—as in the well-publicized cases of Diederik Stapel and Marc Hauser, discussed in Chapter 1—reporters often ask why the fraud was not uncovered during the review process (Bhattacharjee, 2013). This brings to the forefront some of the inherent flaws in peer reviewing.

Fraud is difficult to uncover for a number of reasons. First, reviewers generally do not have access to the raw data used in the analyses. In Stapel's case, he made up the data, so there were no raw data to examine. In fact, collaborators confirmed his fraud when they asked to see the raw data so they could run analyses, and he failed to produce the data. But reviewers generally trust researchers to behave ethically. Indeed, much of the scientific process relies on trust, even when that trust might not be warranted. More and more professional organizations and journals require researchers to make their data sets publicly available to anyone who might want to examine them. If researchers are behaving ethically, they should not hesitate to share their data. Such sharing requires proper data storage and management, a good practice in general (see Chapter 3).

But not all problems with data stem from fraud; sometimes they are a result of errors in data entry or management. These errors can have a huge impact, as highlighted in "Media Matters: The Rise in Retractions," so always check and double-check your data. Do this all the time—not just when your results contradict your predictions.

Publication

The review and publication process is long and challenging. You must develop a thick skin and not take reviews personally. This can be hard, even for accomplished researchers. In a sense, publishing your work is a lot like learning to ride a bike—you will fall, but if you keep trying you will succeed. As Robert J. Sternberg (whom we mentioned in Chapter 15) notes, the only sure way to avoid rejection is to never submit anything. All researchers receive rejection letters. The successful ones take the feedback, respond quickly, and submit a revision. It feels great when a journal accepts your first paper, and then your second one. Take time to celebrate this achievement.

The Rise in Retractions

According to a 2011 study in the *Wall Street Journal*, retractions in research journals have increased 15-fold since 2001, an astounding rate (Naik, 2011). Although some retractions reflect human error, others point to deliberate fraud. The *Wall Street Journal* study found that between 2004 and 2009, retractions caused by error doubled; those involving fraud rose sevenfold (Naik, 2011).

The study proposed several reasons for the dramatic rise. Some scientists claim that retractions are easier to find because journal archives are now online and more accessible to all researchers. Editors may also have become better at detecting errors. Furthermore, they have the advantage of recently developed plagiarism detection software that catches scientists who duplicate their own work or steal someone else's work.

But others blame a more competitive atmosphere in which rising numbers of scientific researchers seek to publish their articles in prestigious journals. "The stakes are so high," said Richard Horton, editor of *The Lancet*, the leading peer-reviewed general medical journal. "A single paper in *Lancet* and you get your chair and you get your money. It's a passport to success" (Naik, 2011).

Ideally, researchers would stop citing a study whose findings have been refuted by an editor or another researcher (who may have tried to replicate the study without success; see Chapter 1). But that has not been the case. In 2011, a study by researchers at the University of Washington (Banobi et al., 2011) published in the journal *Ecosphere* showed that 95% of retracted articles continued to be cited as if their results had gone unchallenged. The authors strongly advocated changes to the journal publishing process so that rebuttals would be prominently linked to the original articles.

The blog *Retraction Watch*, which was launched in 2010 by the medical reporters Ivan Oransky and Adam Marcus, has tried to publicize retractions (Gladstone, 2013). They post retractions from science journals, particularly life science journals, and keep running tabs of researchers whose findings spur shockingly high numbers of retractions. As of 2013, the record-holder was a researcher named Yoshitaka Fujii, who had reached 183 retractions (*Retraction Watch*, 2013).

Of course, not all retractions involve deception. In 2013, *Retraction Watch* praised the preemptive actions of Laurie Santos, an associate professor of psychology at Yale University (and, coincidentally, a former student of Marc Hauser at Harvard), who voluntarily retracted two papers after discovering problems with her data (Oransky, 2013). The study, which focused on in-group bias in monkeys, had appeared in *Developmental Science* and *Journal of Personality and Social Psychology*. Santos wrote of her experience:

Having to retract papers is a scientist's worst nightmare. Especially in the current climate in psychology right now (e.g., Hausergate, Stapelgate, etc.), this is pretty much the most awful thing that could happen to a [principal investigator]. But I also hope that this awful situation can—at least in some sense—serve as a positive example of correcting the scientific record. We would have never caught the coding error without replicating the initial JPSP effects. . . . And as soon as we found the problems, we immediately went back and checked all the other datasets too. I'm obviously embarrassed that we didn't catch all this earlier, but I'm still glad that we caught it when we did.

Another important effort to strengthen the peer review process is the Registered Replication Report (RRR), an initiative started in 2013 by the APS journal *Perspectives on Psychological Science* to encourage high-quality, multicenter replications of significant psychological findings (Drew, 2013). The first RRR project attracted 30 laboratories from all over the world in attempting to replicate an important 1990 study on a finding related to verbal memory. Once all the data have been collected, the psychology researcher Daniel Simons (see Chapter 4, "Inside Research") and two other researchers will compile it in a meta-analysis to estimate the study's true effect.

Page proofs Copies of the accepted paper that include questions from the copy editors for the authors to address.

Once a paper has been accepted, expect to wait between six months and a year before the paper is published. These days many articles first appear online before being printed a few months later. In addition, the number of online-only journals is increasing. The basic process for online journals is similar to that of print versions. Prior to publication, authors receive **page proofs**, which are versions of the paper that include questions from the copy editor. This is the time to proofread the paper carefully for errors or typos and to update any references that have changed. This is not the time for extensive rewriting of the manuscript. If you do make extensive changes, you will be charged for them. Once the paper formally publishes, it is time once again to celebrate your achievement.

PRACTICAL TIPS

Practical Tips for Publishing Your Research

1. Spend time looking for conferences and journals that are a good match for your research.

2. Proofread your submissions and make sure that they read clearly and logically.

3. Try to catch all of the small things (e.g., typos, unclear sentences) that might irritate a reviewer.

4. Follow all the guidelines for submission provided by the journal.

5. Do not get discouraged by rejections—even experienced researchers have their work rejected from time to time.

6. Take the editors' and reviewers' comments seriously. Respond to all comments and suggestions to the best of your ability.

7. Revise and resubmit rejected papers in a timely fashion.

8. Celebrate your successes! Enjoy seeing your name in print!

CHAPTER SUMMARY

Once you have collected the majority of your data, conducted preliminary analyses to show a clear pattern of results, and created a short narrative based on your understanding of the results, you are ready to present your research at a conference. You can apply to present at either a general or a specialized conference; most important, you should try to reach the audience that will be most receptive to your research. As a student, you will likely be asked to present your findings in an informal poster format, but as you gain experience you may participate in data blitzes, symposia, podium talks, and more formal oral presentations.

Presenting your findings at a conference should give you plenty of ideas for framing your research, which will help you immeasurably as you write up your research report and submit it for publication. As you decide where to send your manuscript, it is vital that you find a journal whose audience is a good match for your research. A great place to start is the list of journals that published the papers you cite in your own research. It is also important to consider the status of the journal, which you can determine from the journal impact factor. Once you have decided on an appropriate journal, you will begin the review process, which consists of submission, editorial review, revisions, and, sometimes, acceptance for publication. Do not lose hope if your submission is initially rejected; persistence will pay off.

Introducing your research at a conference and seeing it in the pages of a journal provide the ultimate reward for all your hard work. You will have made your debut into the wider scientific community, where you will meet others with similar interests, discover new facets of your field, and encounter new, exciting ideas. We hope you have found it a gratifying, enlightening journey.

Up for Discussion

1. You have just completed a study that you believe is potentially groundbreaking, with some novel findings about ways to reduce prejudicial attitudes among young children. Although the findings are not ready for publication, a conference is likely your first stop for these results. The next conference is a small meeting of social psychologists in just a couple of months, but the next major meeting of a national psychological association is a full 10 months away. In the service of presenting your findings to a community of peers as quickly as possible, should you present at the small conference, knowing that your study will reach a much smaller audience? Or should you wait for the larger national conference, which would assure that your research would make a bigger "splash"? Why?

2. Researchers from the University of Washington (Banobi, Branch, & Hilborn, 2011) questioned the impact of rebuttals of previously published findings, saying, "For those convinced that science is self-correcting, and progresses in a forward direction over time, we offer only discouragement" (p. 8). Do you agree or disagree with the pessimistic outlook of this statement regarding the nature of scientific progress? Are the increasing retractions in psychology and in other fields a good thing or something about which we should be concerned? Why or why not?

3. In this chapter, we suggest that if you are committed to publishing your work in a particular journal and you receive a request to "revise and resubmit," the best way to respond to the editor/reviewer

feedback is to draft a cover letter for your revision that addresses each of the comments, point by point. Although this approach maximizes your chance of publication, what would you do if you knew that a particular response—although being the most honest in terms of your research—was likely to be dismissed by the editor as insufficient? Would you be willing to change your response to something that was "less true" to your original research to increase your chances of acceptance and publication? Why or why not?

Key Terms

Data blitz, p. 409

Editorial board, p. 415

General conference, p. 405

Invited talks, p. 409

Journal citation report, p. 413

Journal impact factor, p. 411

Keynote address, pp. 408, 409

Page proofs, p. 420

Podium talk, p. 409

Poster symposia, p. 409

Presidential address, p. 408

Specialized conference, p. 405

Symposia, p. 409

Web of Science, p. 413

Appendix

READING A RESEARCH ARTICLE—KEY QUESTIONS

[As discussed in Chapter 4, you may want to use this document to take notes on the key points as you read a research article.]

Introduction

1. What are the problem areas—both broad and specific—that have led the researchers to study this problem and generate hypotheses? Why does the topic matter?
2. What are the central research questions?
3. What is the research hypothesis (or hypotheses)?

Method

1. Who is being studied (sample size and demographics)?
2. What are the key variables that were measured in the research? If the study is experimental, you should also be able to identify the independent and dependent variables.
3. How have the researchers operationalized those variables (i.e., defined them in measurable terms)?
4. What methods are used to collect the data, and what sorts of controls are in place to deal with potential error and false variables? How do the methods allow for distinguishing among various possibilities?

Results

1. What are the methods of data analysis (broadly speaking)—qualitative, quantitative, or both?
2. Based on the analyses, what did the researchers find with reference to each of their hypotheses? Were their hypotheses supported?

Discussion

1. What are the major conclusions of the authors? What are the implications for this area of research?
2. Are the conclusions reasonable and well grounded in the actual findings?
3. What are the caveats and major limitations of the research?

Glossary

ABA design (reversal design) A type of single-case experimental design in which baseline measurements are initially taken (A), a treatment/intervention is then implemented and measurements are taken (B), and finally the treatment/intervention is removed and measurements are taken one last time (A).

ABAB design A type of single-case experimental design that involves a baseline measurement (A), a treatment/intervention measurement (B), a measurement following removal of the treatment/intervention (A), and finally a second treatment/intervention measurement (B).

Abstract A brief summary of a research article's purpose, methods, and major findings. Abstracts are typically about 150 to 300 words in length.

Accommodation A concept of Piaget's (a cognitive developmental psychologist) that refers to a process where internal mental structures change as a function of maturation and taking in new information (assimilation).

Acquiescence bias A form of bias where the participant responds affirmatively to every question or to every question where they are unsure of the correct response.

Active deception The giving of false information to study participants.

Aging Changes, both positive and negative, associated over the latter part of the life span (e.g., from adulthood to death).

Amblyopia A developmental visual disorder that arises when the inputs to the two eyes are not well correlated in young infants and children.

Analysis of variance (ANOVA) A statistical technique to test for differences among means. (See also **one-way ANOVA, repeated-measures one-way ANOVA, two-way ANOVA**.)

Anchor (or endpoint) A point or value that marks one end of a line segment or interval.

Anchoring A heuristic that leads individuals to use a particular value as a base for estimating an unknown quantity and adjust their estimate based on that quantity, even if the value given is entirely arbitrary.

ANOVA table A table used to organize and display the results of analysis of variance.

Anterior cingulate A region of the brain involved in processing any kind of aversive state—for example, it is active when people make errors, when they experience pain, and when they exert hard mental effort.

Applied research Research that generally seeks to address a practical issue or problem.

Archival research The study of data that have been previously collected.

Assimilation A concept of Piaget's (a cognitive developmental psychologist) that refers to a process where internal mental structures take in new information and fit it in with existing structures (schemas).

Atheoretical research The idea that a given approach is not driven by an underlying theory or set of assumptions.

Attention control group A type of control in which participants receive everything the experimental group receives (e.g., the same amount of time and attention), with the exception of the "active ingredient" of the intervention or treatment.

Attrition The loss of research participants prior to completion of a study.

Availability heuristic A cognitive process that leads individuals to overestimate the likelihood of events that come easily to mind.

Basic research Research that strives to advance knowledge within a particular area of science.

Bayesian data analysis An approach to data analysis in which a prior distribution concerning a hypothesis is combined with experimental data to construct a posterior distribution for the hypothesis.

Belief perseverance bias A cognitive bias that leads individuals to maintain a belief or theory even when confronted with considerable counterevidence.

Belmont Report Developed in 1976, it is a series of basic ethical principles to guide researchers as they perform studies with human subjects.

Between-subjects (or between-groups) design A type of experimental design in which the researcher assigns individual participants or groups of participants to one of several conditions to detect differences *between* groups of participants, with each group exposed to a separate condition.

Bimodal A data set with two distinct peaks in the distribution of data.

Bivariate statistics Numerical values that characterize the relationship between two variables.

Blind (blinded) design The experimenter measuring the behavior of interest does not know what intervention (if any) the individuals being observed have received.

BOLD response Blood oxygen level–dependent response. Oxygenated blood has different magnetic properties than blood that is deoxygenated. Higher levels of oxygenated blood compared with deoxygenated blood are found in brain regions that are active.

Bottom-up approach The idea that the data should drive the formation of theory.

Box-and-whisker plots (or box plots) Visual display for presenting a number of descriptive statistics in graphical form. The box might be used to represent the interquartile range and the whiskers to represent the minimum and maximum of the data set.

Careless responding (CR) Lack of careful attention to one's own responses in a survey because of disinterest or the desire to complete the survey as quickly as possible.

Carryover effect The result of a participant's performance in one experimental condition affecting his or her performance in a subsequent condition.

Case study A detailed examination of a single individual over a period of time.

Categorical data Information captured by discrete groups or categories.

Causal design A research method designed to understand what causes or explains a certain phenomenon.

Causality bias The tendency to assume that two events are causally related because of proximity of time and place, when in fact no such causal relation exists.

Ceiling effect This occurs when a bounded response measurement results in scores that cluster at the upper end (the "ceiling") of the measurement scale because of a constraint in the measure itself.

Cell A combination of one level from each factor in the experiment. The number of cells in a factorial design equals the number of levels of the different factors multiplied by each other. For example, a 2×2 design would have 4 cells, whereas a 3×4 design would have 12 cells.

Central limit theorem A theorem that says with a large sample size, the sampling distribution of the mean will be normal or nearly normal in shape.

Central tendency A description of the typical or average values of our data.

Change blindness A phenomenon in which people fail to notice significant changes in a visual scene or within their own environment. Research has shown that people often do not realize when large details of a visual scene have been changed.

Change over time A general way to capture temporal changes, particularly changes brought about by learning and experience.

Clinical psychology The area of psychology that integrates science, theory, and practice to treat patients' psychologically based distress.

Clinical Research Committee A group of scientists given the power to approve or modify experiments, originally created by administrators at the National Institutes of Health. It is the prototype for today's institutional review boards.

Closed-ended response item A survey item/question that requires respondents to choose from a number of predetermined responses.

Coding The process whereby data are categorized to facilitate analysis.

Coercion The act of taking away someone's voluntary choice to participate through either negative or positive means.

Cognitive bias Approach to thinking about a situation that may lead you to respond in a particular manner that may be flawed.

Cognitive dissonance The idea that we are uncomfortable holding conflicting thoughts simultaneously and that we are motivated to reduce this discomfort (or "dissonance") by changing our existing thoughts to bring about a more consistent belief system.

Cognitive miser model A cognitive bias that leads individuals to attend to only a small amount of information to preserve mental energy.

Cognitive neuroscience Research with the goal of furthering a brain-based understanding of mind.

Cohen's d A standardized effect size that is defined as the raw effect divided by its standard deviation.

Cohort effect Effects that generate change as a result of experiences that impact an entire group of individuals.

Collaborative Institutional Training Initiative (CITI) An educational program that provides training in human subjects research at more than 1,100 participating institutions.

Collaborative research Research conducted by scholars at different institutions (generally all of the affiliated institutions will need to approve the research from an ethics perspective).

Common-sense theory (*see also* **naive theory**) An implicit, everyday belief that influences how individuals reason about events.

Compound question Question that attempts to ask about more than one issue in the same question. Also known as a double-barreled question.

Concealment A strategy for handling participant reactivity by keeping observers or recording equipment hidden from participants.

Conclusion validity An assessment of the degree to which the inferences drawn from a study are reasonable (valid or justified).

Condition The intervention or treatment in an experiment given to a particular group of participants.

Confederate A person (accomplice) who is part of an experiment or study (but unknown to the participants) and plays a specific role in setting up the experimental situation.

Confidence interval A range of values around the effect size obtained in a sample that is likely to contain the true population effect size with a given level of plausibility or confidence.

Confirmation bias The tendency to give the most weight to information that supports your theory, potentially discounting or ignoring data that go against your strongly held theoretical bias.

Conflict of interest A situation in which financial or other considerations may compromise or appear to compromise a researcher's judgment in conducting or reporting research.

Confounds (or extraneous variables) Uncontrolled variables that change with the independent variable(s) in your experimental design and could account for effects that you find.

Congruent trials In a flanker task, trials where the target and distractor items face in the same direction (<<< < <<<).

Construct validity A measure of the extent to which a particular variable or measure actually captures what it is meant to capture.

Contingency table (or cross tabulation) A tabular display for representing categorical or nominal level data.

Control group In an experimental design, the set of participants who do not receive the experimental treatment (or who receive an inert version). This group is compared with the experimental group.

Control variable A variable that is either held at a constant value or is accounted for statistically in an analysis. The purpose of controlling for a variable is to remove (or statistically account for) any effect it might have on the dependent variable.

Convenience sampling A method of sampling that makes use of the most readily available group of participants.

Converging evidence Results from multiple research investigations that provide similar findings.

Cook's distance A measure used to detect outliers in a data set.

Correlational design A research method that is designed to uncover underlying causes related to certain phenomena, but that attempts to understand how different variables are related to one another.

Counterbalancing A strategy that ensures control for the order of experimental interventions. The researcher calculates all the possible orders of interventions and confirms even distribution of the different order combinations across participants.

Cramer's *V* A correlation-like measure used to summarize data in contingency tables.

Credible interval In Bayesian data analysis, a range of values from the posterior distribution of a given quantity (e.g., mean, difference of means) for which you have a given level of credibility (e.g., 95%) concerning the true value of the quantity.

Cronbach's alpha (α) A measure of the internal consistency of a set of scale items.

Cross-cultural research Research that occurs in countries with different ethical rules and regulations, often with few or no standing institutional review board committees.

Cross-sectional research design The most common types of studies across age and time, involving simultaneously assessing a number of different age groups.

Cross-sequential research design An approach that combines aspects of both cross-sectional and longitudinal designs where multiple age groups or cohorts are studied over time. Sometimes also referred to as "sequential," "mixed," and "accelerated longitudinal designs."

Cross-tabulation (or contingency table) A tabular display for representing categorical or nominal-level data.

Data blitz A 1- to 10-minute oral presentation that uses one or two slides to convey the essence of research and data in a fast, clear way at a conference.

Data cleaning The process of checking that your measurements are complete and accurate prior to any analysis.

Data map A region in an fMRI image that shows BOLD changes correlated with changes in activation pattern.

Data mining The use of advanced statistical techniques to search large data sets for meaningful patterns.

Debrief To give participants study information that was initially withheld and the reasons that information was withheld.

Decision fatigue A phenomenon that occurs when the quality of decision making declines as an individual is required to make a large number of decisions in a short period of time.

Declaration of Helsinki Formalized in 1964, this international proclamation broadened the Nuremberg Code guidelines from 1947, stating, "It is the mission of the doctor to safeguard the health of the people."

Degrees of freedom (*df*) The number of values that are free to vary in the computation of a statistic.

Dehoax To make participants fully aware of any deception to prevent potential harm.

Deidentified data Data for which any information that may be used to identify participants (e.g., name, address, phone number) has been removed.

Demand characteristics Features of the experimental design itself that lead participants to make certain conclusions about the purpose of the experiment and then adjust their behavior accordingly, either consciously or unconsciously.

Dependent variable The factor of interest being measured in the study that changes in response to manipulation of the independent variable.

Descriptive statistics Numerical values that summarize the data and give a sense of the shape and spread of the data or the extent to which two variables are related to one another.

Development Changes that occur over the first part of the life span (e.g., from conception to adulthood), which are often thought of as positive, unidirectional (operating in a single direction), and cumulative. This term is often used to describe advances in such areas as motor skills, language, and cognition.

Developmental psychopathology A subfield of psychology that looks at when children (and older individuals) deviate from the normal pathway of development.

Diffusion-weighted magnetic resonance imaging (also referred to as **diffusion-weighted imaging (DWI)**) An imaging technique that uses an MRI machine to measure the diffusion of water molecules in different brain regions. Combined with anatomical images and three-dimensional modeling researchers are able to identify pathways in the brain.

Discounting base-rate information A cognitive bias that leads individuals to favor anecdotal evidence over more detailed information that is available.

Dispersion Refers to how spread out or variable data values are in a sample.

Domain specific The idea that knowledge and/or expertise in different areas is not based on an underlying general capability, but rather determined by particular capabilities or experiences within an area.

Double-barreled question A question that refers to more than one issue but requires or expects only one response. Also known as a compound question.

Double-blind design Both participants and experimenters collecting the data are unaware of the condition to which participants have been assigned.

Editorial board A group of researchers who make decisions about what a specific journal will publish.

Effect size The magnitude of the primary measure used to test a hypothesis, such as a difference of means or the correlation between two variables.

Electroencephalography (EEG) A noninvasive technique for measuring brain activity that involves attaching electrodes to a participant's scalp and recording ongoing electrical signals from the brain.

Empirical Based on observations or experience that can be verified.

Endpoint A point or value that marks one end of a line segment or interval.

Equivalent forms reliability When two different versions of a scale or assessment are used and result in similar levels of performance.

Equivalent measures Methods that are equally good at measuring a behavior of interest for different age groups in a sample.

Error bar A graphical representation of the amount of variability of a sample statistic, such as a mean.

Essentialism Scientific claim that there exist certain fundamental (or essential) properties.

Eta squared (η^2) An effect size measure for one-way analysis of variance.

Ethics Conduct in research that reflects the social responsibility that the researcher has toward society at large.

Event sampling The recording of each occurrence of a particular behavior or event.

Event-related potential Brain activity measured in response to a particular stimulus or event using electroencephalography.

Executive control The management of cognitive processes involved in planning, problem solving, reasoning, and switching between tasks.

Exempt research Research that does not require institutional review board review.

Expedited research Research that may be reviewed by the institutional review board through accelerated procedures.

Experimental group In an experimental design, the set of participants that receives the intervention or treatment (e.g., a dose of the independent variable) with the goal of determining whether the treatment impacts the outcome.

Experimenter bias In survey/interview research, bias introduced by the way in which experimenters ask questions (related to framing effects).

External validity A measure of the degree to which the conclusions drawn from a particular set of results can be generalized to other samples or situations.

Extraneous variables (or confounds) Uncontrolled variables that vary with the independent variable(s) in your experimental design and could account for effects that you find.

F test of equality of variances A test of the equality of two variances.

Factor A variable manipulated by the experimenter.

Factor analysis A statistical technique that examines the relationships between items in a scale. This approach is useful for determining whether a scale measures a single variable or multiple ones.

Factorial design An experimental design that has more than one independent variable.

Falsifiable The concept that researchers can test whether the hypothesis or claim can be proven wrong.

Familywise error rate The probability of committing at least one type I error across multiple significance tests.

Fatigue (boredom) effect Participants begin to perform more poorly as the experiment goes on as a consequence of repeated exposure to experimental conditions in a within-subjects design.

Fatigue effects Negative effects on survey responses or completion resulting from subjects tiring of the survey.

File-drawer problem Bias in published research resulting from the issue that studies that do not exhibit statistical significance are less likely to be published (or even submitted for publication) than findings that do exhibit statistical significance.

Flanker task A test that measures attention and inhibitory control by asking the participant to focus on a particular stimulus (<) while ignoring other stimuli surrounding it (>>>> < >>>>>).

Floor effect This occurs when a bounded response measurement results in scores that cluster at the lower end (the "floor") of the measurement scale because of a constraint in the measure itself.

Formal scientific theory A belief grounded in a body of empirical research, as opposed to a common-sense or naive theory.

Fractional anisotropy A measure of the spatial pattern of diffusion. Basically, it describes whether diffusion is occurring equally in all directions or is greater in one direction or another.

Framework theory A formal explanation that provides a broad perspective and set of assumptions about an area of inquiry. These assumptions are not likely to be falsifiable.

Framing effect A cognitive bias caused by seemingly inconsequential differences in wording in a question or problem that lead respondents to vary their choices.

Friedman test A nonparametric alternative to repeated measures one-way analysis of variance.

Functional magnetic resonance imaging (fMRI) A neuroimaging technique that, by measuring changes in blood flow, enables researchers to obtain images of the brain while the brain processes information.

General conference A professional meeting that covers many areas within a particular subject, such as psychology.

Generalizable knowledge Refers to a variety of information: conclusions drawn from data gathered in a study; principles of historical or social development; underlying principles or laws of nature that have predictive value and can be applied to other circumstances for the purpose of controlling outcomes; explanations about past study results; and predictions of future results. Such knowledge defines the boundaries of research that is regulated by institutional review boards.

Greater than minimal risk research Research that may pose substantial risk to participants and requires a full institutional review board review.

Greenhouse–Geisser correction A statistical adjustment to account for violation of sphericity in repeated measures analysis of variance.

Grounded theory An explanatory framework that assumes researchers should allow themes to emerge from the data and adopt a more atheoretical approach.

Habituation Diminished response to a stimulus that comes about through repeated exposure to that stimulus.

Hawthorne (or observer effect) Participants in a study modify their behavior as a result of knowing they are being observed.

Hemodynamic response Changes in blood flow in the brain. Increased blood flow to regions of the brain is associated with increased activity in that brain region.

Heuristic Simple procedure that assists people in finding adequate but often imperfect solutions to difficult problems.

Higher-order factorial design A design that includes more than two independent variables. For example, a $2 \times 2 \times 2$ design, with three factors, two levels for each factor, and eight cells or conditions.

Histogram A visual display of data that shows how many responses on a variable fall within predefined ranges of values with these counts being represented by bars in a chart.

Hypotheticodeductive method A view of scientific methodology that uses quantitative data to teach a particular hypothesis or theory.

Implicit Association Test A test of implicit cognition that measures participants' reaction time to investigate the strength of association between people's mental representations.

Inattentional blindness An error of perception where people do not pay attention to an unexpected object (e.g., a gorilla walking across a basketball court).

Incongruent trials In a flanker task, trials where the target and distractor items face in a different direction (<<< > <<<).

Independence of observations A measurement obtained on an observation (e.g., from a participant) in the experiment does not depend on the measurements obtained on other observations (e.g., from other participants). The responses are *independent* of one another.

Independent variable A variable manipulated by the researcher to observe its effect on a dependent variable.

Induction A process where novel ideas and concepts emerge from exploration of data.

Inferential statistical tests Statistical methods such as t tests or χ^2 tests that help researchers draw conclusions about data.

Informed consent Agreement of a participant to take part in a study, having been made aware of the potential risks.

In-group bias A cognitive bias to view members of your own social group more positively than members outside of your social group.

Institutional Animal Care and Use Committee (IACUC) Review committee responsible for protecting the health and well-being of nonhuman animals involved in research. These committees are the equivalent of institutional review boards, but for researchers who involve animals in their investigations.

Institutional review board (IRB) A committee that is active in almost every U.S. hospital, university, and organization that supports research. These boards are responsible for protecting the health and well-being of research participants, and they are liable for the research they approve.

Interaction A situation that arises when the effect of one factor (independent variable) on the dependent variable is contingent on the levels of at least one other factor.

Interaction chart A diagram that represents different combinations of the presence or absence of main and interaction effects.

Interaction effect A measure of the extent to which the effect of one factor depends on the levels of the other factor. It is common to test for interaction effects in multifactor analysis of variance designs.

Internal consistency The degree to which items within an assessment are measures of the same thing. A survey is internally consistent to the extent that items intended to measure the same variable yield similar responses.

Internal validity An assessment of whether a particular variable is the actual cause of a particular outcome.

Interquartile range The range of values from the 25th percentile to 75th percentile; the middle 50% of values.

Interval scale A scale containing rank order information, as well as the property of equal intervals between points; the most common scale in psychological research.

Interview A data collection technique in which researchers ask participants questions orally, either in person or over the phone.

Interviewer effects Influences that the interviewer may have on responses, including the way in which he/she asks and responds to questions, tone of voice, or facial expressions. All of these may be interpreted by the interviewee as positive or negative evaluations of their responses and may lead the respondent to alter his/her answers.

Inverse probability fallacy Refers to researchers interpreting the *p* value as a measure of the probability of the null hypothesis being true given the results observed, when this value is dependent on a number of other assumptions, such as the prior probability of the null hypothesis and the alternative hypothesis being true.

Invited talks Discussions lasting between 60 and 90 minutes that are led by established researchers or up-and-coming stars at a conference.

Journal citation report A ranking of journals provided in the Web of Science, an online academic citation index published by Thomson Reuters.

Journal impact factor A measure of how often other researchers cite papers published in a particular journal.

Keynote address A speech delivered at a conference by an important researcher who presents groundbreaking research and ideas to inspire attendees to think about how they can extend their own research in interesting directions.

Kolmogorov–Smirnov test A statistical test of whether a set of data values is normally distributed.

Kruskal–Wallis test A nonparametric alternative to one-way analysis of variance.

Kurtosis A measure of the shape of a distribution that assesses how flat or peaked the distribution is relative to the normal distribution.

Laboratory Animal Welfare Act Legislation that stipulates guiding principles for the treatment of animals in research.

Language acquisition device Noam Chomsky's hypothetical construct within the human mind that explains the innate capacity for acquiring language.

Latin square A type of counterbalancing technique in which each participant receives different experimental conditions in a systematically different order.

Learning Changes tied to specific instruction or experiences over relatively short periods of time.

Level A possible condition in the experimental variable.

Levels The values taken on by an independent variable or factor. For example, in a drug effectiveness study, you may have a factor of "treatment," which has levels of "placebo" and "drug."

Levene's test A test of the equality of two variances.

Leverage value A measure used to detect outliers in a data set.

Lie scale A set of survey items used to determine whether participants are taking the task seriously and not simply responding in such a way as to present themselves in the best possible light.

Likert response format An ordered range of responses used to measure particular attitudes or values. Response options usually include three to seven options that vary from "strongly disagree" to "strongly agree."

Likert scale The sum of responses to multiple questions intended to measure the same variable using the Likert response format.

Likert-type ratings Items that ask participants to rate their attitudes or behavior using a predetermined set of responses that are quantified (that are often treated as an interval scale). An example would be a 5-point rating scale that asks about level of agreement from 1 (strongly disagree) to 5 (strongly agree).

Linear regression A statistical technique for determining the joint impact/effect of one or more independent variables on a single dependent variable.

Literature review A summary of previous research that has been done on the topic, typically located in the introduction of the paper.

Loaded question A question that presupposes information or potentially biases a response by including an assumption that may not be justified.

Longitudinal research design Designs that track groups of participants over a period of time with two or more assessments of the same individuals at different times.

MacArthur Scale of Subjective Social Status A measure of subjective social standing, obtained by having respondents place themselves on a socioeconomic "ladder."

Magnetic resonance imaging (MRI) A neuroimaging technique that uses powerful magnets to create images of anatomical structures in the brain.

Main effect The overall effect of a single factor on the dependent variable, averaging over the levels of all other factors. (See also **interaction effect**.)

Mandated reporters Individuals who, by virtue of their role, possess a legal obligation to report incidents such as elder or child abuse to the authorities.

Mann–Whitney U test (or **Wilcoxon rank sum test**) A nonparametric alternative to the independent-samples t test.

Matched-group design A type of experimental design in which researchers assign separate groups of participants in each condition and "twin" a participant in each group with a participant in another group. It contains elements of both between-subjects and within-subjects designs.

Maturation Growth and other changes in the body and brain that are associated with underlying genetic information.

Mauchly's test of sphericity A test of the sphericity assumption in repeated-measures analysis of variance.

Mean (or arithmetic average) A measure of central tendency that is calculated by summing all of the values in a data set and then dividing by the number of values in the data set.

Mean diffusion A measure of how fast water molecules move, or diffuse, through brain regions.

Measurement error The difference between the actual or true value of what you are measuring and the result obtained using the measurement instrument.

Median A measure of central tendency that is the middle value of all the data points; 50% of the values are below the median and 50% are above.

Mediating variable A variable that explains the relation between two other variables.

Meta-analysis A statistical technique that combines results across a number of studies.

Methodology The body of practice, procedures, and rules that regulate a discipline.

Microgenetic design An approach that attempts to capture changes as they occur and to understand the mechanisms involved in any observed changes by focusing on a key transition point or dramatic shift in the behavior of interest.

Midpoint The center value of a scale with an odd number of response possibilities. An example of a midpoint on a scale of agreement is "neither agree nor disagree."

Mission creep The problem of the expansion of institutional review board oversight to include areas unrelated to the protection of human subjects.

Mixed factorial design (mixed design) A design that includes both within- and between-subjects factors.

Mode A measure of central tendency; the most common value in the data set.

Moderating variable A variable that influences (but does not causally explain) the direction and/or strength of relationship between two other variables (e.g., socioeconomic status).

Mood effect Influence on decision making that occurs because of either a positive or a negative mood state.

Motion artifacts Data that are caused by the movement of the participant rather than a response to the stimuli of interest.

Motivated respondent bias Bias that occurs in situations where people are highly motivated to complete a survey for the purpose of affecting public opinion.

Multiple baseline design An approach that uses a varying time schedule to help determine whether the treatment itself is actually leading to the change (as opposed to just the passage of time). In this design, measurements are made at baseline, then after an intervention or treatment, and then again when the intervention is completed or the treatment withdrawn (return to baseline).

Multiple comparison tests Statistical tests for controlling type I error rate when multiple significance tests are applied to the same data set, for example, comparing multiple pairs of means in a larger analysis of variance design. Examples of such tests include the Bonferroni–Dunn test, Tukey's HSD test, the Newman–Keuls method, Dunnett's test, and the Scheffe method.

Naive theory (*see also* **common-sense theory**) An implicit, everyday belief that influences how individuals reason about events.

Narrative A description of your research that flows from highly structured and organized ideas.

National Institutes of Health (NIH) The U.S. government agency primarily responsible for biomedical and health-related research.

Naturalistic observation Looking at phenomena as they occur (naturally) in the environment.

Near-infrared spectroscopy (NIRS) A neuroimaging technique for assessing brain function; a near-infrared light is shone through the scalp using optical fibers that are placed in a cap and reflected back to detectors in the cap.

Neuropsychology A term generally used to refer to studies of individuals with brain damage.

Nominal scale The most basic measurement, when scale points are defined by categories.

Nonexperimental methods A group of research approaches that do not attempt to manipulate or control the environment, but rather involve the researcher using a systematic technique to examine what is already occurring.

Nonparametric statistical test A statistical test that makes few assumptions about the distribution of measurements in the population and does not require data to be interval or ratio level. Some parametric tests are appropriate for ordinal-level data and others require only nominal-level data.

Nonparametric test A statistical test that makes few assumptions about the population distribution and may be applied to nominal and ordinal measurements.

Nonprobability sample A sample in which members of the population are not all given an equal chance of being selected.

Nonresponse bias Bias that occurs when individuals who are contacted and choose to complete a survey differ in some ways from others who are contacted but choose not to participate.

Normal distribution A unimodal pattern of data, with the mode occurring in the center of the distribution, with values dropping off sharply in a symmetrical pattern on both sides of the mean. The traditional approach to statistical inferences assumes that the data in a sample are normally distributed.

Null hypothesis Typically, a statement of "no effect" in your results. For example, a null hypothesis might suggest no difference in mean responses for different experimental conditions or zero correlation between two variables.

Null hypothesis significance testing (NHST) A traditional approach to inferential statistical tests that attempts to determine whether a specific hypothesis (the null hypothesis) can be rejected at a given probability level.

Number of significant figures The number of digits that you can report about your measurement that you know are correct.

Nuremberg Code of 1947 A group of 10 standards that guide ethical research involving human beings.

Objective prior (or **minimally informative prior**) In Bayesian data analysis, a prior distribution that reflects relative ignorance concerning the value of an experiment effect.

Objectivity Approaching knowledge as a quest for the truth, rather than as an attempt to find results that support one's own beliefs or theory.

Observational methods A class of research techniques that involve gathering information by observing phenomena as they occur.

Observer (or Hawthorne) effect Participants in a study modify their behavior as a result of knowing they are being observed.

Odds ratio A measure of association between two variables, each of which has only two possible values.

Odds-against-chance fallacy A misconception where p is interpreted as the probability that the obtained result occurred by chance.

Omnibus null hypothesis In analysis of variance, the null hypothesis that all group means are equal.

One-way analysis of variance (ANOVA) A statistical technique to test for differences of means on a single factor.

Open-ended response A survey item/question in which respondents are free to respond in any way they want.

Operationalizing The process by which a researcher strives to define variables by putting them in measurable terms.

Operationism The idea that scientific concepts must be observable and measurable. It is related to operationalizing one's variable.

Order effect A potential effect of a within-subjects design in which the order that participants receive different experimental conditions may influence the outcome.

Ordinal scale A scale possessing the property of identity and magnitude such that each value is unique and has an ordered relationship to the other values on the scale.

Outliers Extreme values that do not match the pattern of the rest of the data.

Overconfidence bias A cognitive bias where an individual is highly sure of his or her response or decision, although that choice has little relation to the correctness of the choice or decision.

Oversampling The intentional overrecruitment of underrepresented groups into a sample to ensure that there will be enough representation of those groups to make valid research conclusions.

Page proofs Copies of the accepted paper that include questions from the copy editors for the authors to address.

Parallel-forms (or alternate-forms) reliability A measure of survey reliability that examines the consistency of responses of respondents across two versions of a survey, with items in both surveys having been designed to probe the same variables.

Parametric statistical test A statistical test that requires that the measurement scale of your data be interval or ratio and makes strong assumptions about the distribution of measurements in your population. Such distributions have parameters such as the mean and standard deviation.

Participant observation Looking at a behavior of interest by an individual who is part of the environment (for example, a parent making observations of a child during their normal interactions).

Participation biases Biases resulting from potential respondents choosing to participate in the survey or not. These include nonresponse bias, self-selection bias, and motivated respondent bias.

Passive deception The withholding of some study details from participants.

Pearson's r (or Pearson product-moment correlation) A bivariate statistic that measures the extent of the linear relationship between two interval- or ratio-level variables and ranges from −1 to 1.

Peer-reviewed journals Scholarly journals whose editors send any submitted article out to be evaluated by knowledgeable researchers or scholars in the same field.

p-Hacking The process of deliberately manipulating factors in your research to maximize your chance of uncovering a statistically significant finding ($p < 0.05$).

Phi (φ) A correlation-like measure used to summarize data in 2×2 contingency tables.

Pilot study A "prestudy" conducted before your actual study to assess your survey/interview instrument or test a methodology.

Placebo effect A result of treatment that can be attributed to participants' expectations from the treatment rather than any property of the treatment itself.

Podium talk A 10- to 20-minute oral presentation given at a conference that provides an abbreviated report of the results of a single study, including its purpose, background, methods, results, and conclusions.

Point-biserial correlation A measure that describes the degree to which a binary variable (e.g., yes/no) relates to a continuous variable.

Population The entire group of individuals relevant to your research.

Positive psychology An area of psychology that focuses on studying the strengths and virtues that enable individuals and communities to thrive.

Poster symposia A meeting at a conference in which researchers present thematically linked posters and take part in a moderated discussion.

Posterior distribution In Bayesian data analysis, the distribution around a statistic (e.g., mean, difference of means, standard deviation) that incorporates both prior information and experimental data.

Presidential address A speech given at a conference by the head or president of the hosting society or organization, who discusses the collective body of research to be found at the conference within a historical context and presents ideas for future research.

Priming The presentation of cues to push thinking in a certain direction.

Prior distribution In Bayesian data analysis, information the experimenter has concerning a statistic or effect prior to running the experiment. Such prior information may come from previous experiments or a meta-analysis of the relevant literature.

Probability value (or p value) Indicates how likely it would be to see results at least as extreme as those observed under the assumption that the null hypothesis is true.

Prospective power analysis A series of computations that help you to determine the number of participants that you will need to successfully detect an effect in your research.

Protocol document A document that summarizes an intended research project, including the specific aims, background and importance, participants, methods, and predicted results.

Pseudoscience Explanation that is presented with the veneer of science, but does not fundamentally conform to valid scientific methods.

PsycINFO A database specific to psychology journals and related references.

QQ plot (or normal quantile–quantile plot) A graphical technique to identify deviations from normality in a data set.

Qualitative research The use of open-ended and exploratory methodology, which focuses on gathering in-depth information on topics of interest.

Quantitative research The use of numerical data and statistical techniques to examine questions of interest. Or, research that results in data that can be numerically measured.

Quasi-experimental design A design that includes some elements of experimental control without being a true experiment.

Quasi-independent variable A preexisting characteristic (e.g., sex, age or race) to which a participant cannot be randomly assigned.

Quasi-random assignment The researcher assigns equal numbers of participants with key characteristics (e.g., sex, age, or race) across the experimental and control conditions.

Questionnaire A set of questions that may be part of a survey or interview.

Radiofrequency coils Part of the magnetic resonance imaging machine that is used to produce radiofrequency pulses. These coils are also used to measure the energy given off by protons as they return to the state they were in prior to the radiofrequency pulse.

Radiofrequency pulse A short burst of a high-wavelength, low-energy electromagnetic wave that is produced by radiofrequency coils in a magnetic resonance imaging machine to alter the alignment of protons.

Random assignment The procedure by which researchers place participants in different experimental groups using chance procedures, so that any individual has an equal probability of being assigned to any of the groups in the experiment.

Random sampling A method in which every member of a given population has an equal chance of being selected into a sample.

Randomization The researcher arranges the presentation of conditions or stimuli for each participant in a random way to ensure that no one particular order influences the results.

Range The maximum value minus the minimum value in a data set.

Ratio scale A scale sharing all the properties of an interval scale (rank order information and equal interval), but also containing a meaningful absolute zero point, where zero represents the absence of the thing that is being measured.

Raw effects (or unstandardized effects) Common, straightforward measures of effect size such as the difference in the means for two samples.

Reactivity A shift in an observed individual's normal behavior as a result of the knowledge that he/she is being observed.

Regression coefficient A quantity in a linear regression equation that indicates the change in a dependent variable associated with a unit change in the independent variable.

Regression equation A mathematical equation that expresses a linear relationship between a dependent variable and one or more independent variables.

Relativist perspective The focus by qualitative researchers on how participants construct meaning from a particular event or experience.

Relaxation A measure used with magnetic resonance imaging that assesses the time it takes for protons to return to their original state following a radiofrequency pulse that altered their alignment.

Reliability The idea that an investigation or measurement tool should yield consistent findings if researchers use the same procedures and methods repeatedly.

Repeated measures one-way ANOVA A statistical technique for testing differences of means across a single factor in which the same participants provide measurements for each level of the factor.

Repeated-measures (or within-subjects) design A type of experimental design in which the researcher assigns each participant to all possible conditions.

Replication The process through which either the original researcher or the researchers from an independent laboratory repeat the investigation and obtain the same or highly similar results.

Replication fallacy The assumption that the value of $1 - p$ refers to the probability of obtaining a statistically significant result if the experiment were to be replicated.

Representative sample A sample that shares the essential characteristics of the population from which it was drawn.

Residuals Differences between actual values and predicted values in linear regression or ANOVA.

Response bias Bias introduced into participants' responses to interview or survey questions because of such considerations as a desire to respond with responses one believes the researcher would want, an unwillingness to provide sensitive information, or a tendency to always respond positively when unsure about a question.

Response set The tendency for a participant to respond to survey items with a consistent pattern of responses regardless of the question being asked (e.g., answering "strongly agree" to a long string of questions).

Retrospective power analysis A series of computations that help you determine how much power you had in a study after the fact.

Reversal design (ABA design) A type of single-case experimental design in which baseline measurements are initially taken (A), a treatment/intervention is then implemented and measurements are taken (B), and finally the treatment/intervention is removed and measurements are taken one last time (A).

Robust statistical methods Statistical tests that are not greatly affected by conditions that violate the assumptions of standard parametric tests, for example, the assumption that population values are normally distributed.

Sample A subset of individuals drawn from the population of interest.

Sampling distribution of the mean The pattern of mean values obtained when drawing many random samples of a given size from a population and computing the mean for each sample.

Sampling error Chance fluctuations between the measurements observed in a data set and what would be expected from the population values.

Sampling interval The amount of time elapsed between different data collection points in a developmental study.

Scatterplot A method for simultaneously displaying the values for two or more variables that is useful for investigating the relationship between those variables.

Schema A concept of Piaget's (a cognitive developmental psychologist) that refers to internal mental structures.

Scientific method An approach that seeks to generate explanations for observable phenomena with an emphasis on objectivity and verifiable evidence.

Secondary source An article or reference in which the author describes research that has previously been published.

Selection bias Bias resulting from a selected sample not being representative of the population of interest. This may come about because of under- or oversampling of particular types of respondents, respondent self-selection, or respondent nonresponse.

Self-efficacy Situation specific self-confidence.

Self-selection An instance where participants electively place themselves into a particular sample (or they opt out of participation).

Self-selection bias Bias that may occur when it is completely up to potential respondents whether they participate in a survey.

Self-serving bias A cognitive bias that leads to the tendency to perceive or favor your own views and beliefs over those of others.

Shape Refers to whether the data values are normally distributed, have a flat or sharp peak, or are skewed to one end or the other of the data range.

Shapiro–Wilk test A statistical test of whether a set of data values is normally distributed.

Simple order effect The particular order of the experimental conditions influences the results.

Single-blind design Either the participants or the experimenters collecting the data are unaware of the condition to which participants have been assigned.

Single-case experimental design A design in which experimental methodology (e.g., implementing experimental and control conditions) is applied to a single subject.

Skewness A measure of how asymmetric a distribution of values is.

Snowball sampling A method of sampling in which participants are asked to help recruit additional participants.

Social desirability bias (also evaluation apprehension) The tendency of respondents to provide answers that will be viewed favorably by others.

Spearman's rho (ρ) (or Spearman rank-order correlation coefficient) A bivariate statistic used to measure the association between two ordinal/rank-order variables. This statistic varies from −1 to 1 and is typically used when data show a generally increasing (or decreasing) relationship between two variables, but one that is clearly not linear.

Specialized conference A professional meeting that focuses on a particular branch of a discipline, such as social or developmental psychology, or on particular research or statistical methodologies, such as methods for analyzing longitudinal data.

Specific theory A more focused explanation and set of assumptions that deal with a particular area of inquiry.

Specimen record An observation approach where all of the behaviors in a given time period are recorded.

Sphericity An assumption for repeated-measures analysis of variance that requires that the variances of the differences between all pairs of groups be approximately equal.

Split-half reliability A measure of internal consistency assessed by dividing survey items intended to measure the same variable into two sets and examining how well responses to those two sets of items agree with one another.

Standard deviation A measure of the dispersion of a data set calculated by taking the square root of the variance.

Standard error The standard deviation of a sampling distribution. This value is calculated by dividing the standard deviation by the square root of the sample size.

Standardization The designing of interview questions such that they are used in a consistent manner by all interviewers.

Standardized effect (or d type effects) Adjusts the raw effect based on the amount of variability in the data.

Statistical control In analyzing study results, the researcher makes a statistical adjustment that accounts for the influence of a specified third variable and allows for the analysis of results with the influence of that third variable eliminated.

Statistical power The probability that your study will be able to detect an effect in your research, if such an effect exists.

Statistical significance An indicator of the probability of obtaining an effect size as large as (or larger than) the one you obtained.

Statistical significance level A conventional value, usually 0.05 or 0.01, used to assess whether the null hypothesis in NHST should be rejected.

Stem-and-leaf plot A simple way to display data for small to moderately sized data sets that involves using columns and numbers to represent the data. For example, the "stems" of the plots could be represented by a column of numbers in the tens places and the "leaves" could be captured by the ones places.

Stereotype threat The activation of a negative belief about a particular group that influences members of that group to underperform in certain situations.

Stratified random sampling A technique whereby a population is divided into homogeneous groups along some key dimension (for example, race/ethnicity), and then random samples are drawn from within each of the subgroups.

Stroop effect A specific cognitive bias influenced by knowledge, where reaction time slows when you print a color word in an ink color that differs from the actual word.

Structured observation In contrast to the open-ended context of naturalistic observations, an approach where researchers exert greater control over the setting in which the observation is occurring.

Subject attrition When some participants drop out of a study after the first assessment and are unavailable for later assessments.

Subjectivity Approaching knowledge from the standpoint of an individual's own beliefs, experiences, and interpretations.

Subscales Distinct parts of a larger instrument that measure different aspects of a variable.

Summer Research Opportunity Program A summer research program designed to provide individuals from diverse backgrounds with research experience in a laboratory. Many schools have these programs.

Sums of squares Mathematical quantities that measure the amount of variability in data. These include between-subjects, within-subjects, and total sums of squares.

Survey A set of questions administered to a group of respondents, usually via paper or online, to learn about attitudes and behavior.

Symposia Twenty-minute talks given by researchers at a conference that contain an overlapping theme and focus on a particular research study or studies.

t **test** A statistical approach that compares the difference between the means and variance between two groups.

t **test, independent samples** A statistical test for comparing the means of two independent samples.

t **test, matched pairs** A statistical test for comparing the means of two matched samples. The samples may represent two different measurements from the same participants or may represent different participants matched on some criteria (e.g., academic achievement).

t **test, one sample** A statistical test for comparing the mean of a single sample to a specified value.

T1-weighted image A weighted magnetic resonance image that is produced as energy is emitted from the protons as they recover their original magnetization. In these images, tissues with high fat-content, such as the white matter of the brain, appear bright and sections of the brain filled with water appear dark.

T2-weighted image A weighted magnetic resonance image that captures energy emitted as excessive spin induced by the radiofrequency pulse returns to the steady state. In these images, tissues with high fat content look dark, and those areas with high water content appear light in shading.

Tesla (T) A measure of the strength of a magnetic field produced by a magnet. Higher numbers indicate a stronger magnetic field.

Test statistics Computed values associated with particular approaches designed to test hypotheses.

Testable hypothesis A claim that makes a specific prediction that can be supported or refuted through the collection of relevant data or information.

Test–retest reliability A measure of survey reliability that examines the consistency of responses of respondents who complete the same survey on two separate occasions.

Time sampling The taking of measurements at different time intervals; these intervals may be of fixed length or determined randomly.

Top-down approach The view that theory constrains the manner in which data or information are interpreted.

Tractography A three-dimensional modeling technique used to visualize the neural pathways.

Transcranial magnetic stimulation (TMS) A method that uses a strong magnet to cause a small group of neurons to fire in the brain. Used in concert with other neuroimaging techniques, researchers can study the impact of the activation on cognitive function.

Transition point The point in development where key changes occur, often the focus of microgenetic designs.

Trimmed mean A mean computed after removing some fixed percentage (often 10% or 20%) of the largest and smallest values in a data set.

Two-way ANOVA A statistical technique for comparing means when the experimental design includes two factors.

Type I error Occurs if a researcher rejects the null hypothesis when, in fact, the null hypothesis is true.

Type II error Occurs if a researcher fails to reject the null hypothesis when, in fact, it is false.

Unimodal A data set with a single peak in the distribution of data.

Univariate statistics Numerical values that summarize one variable at a time.

Validity Overall, this concept refers to the idea that your measurements and methodology allow you to capture what you think you are trying to measure or study. There are a number of different types of validity.

Variance A measure of the dispersion of a data set; the average squared deviation of values from the mean value.

Voxels In functional magnetic resonance imaging, the smallest volume for which it is possible to compute a blood oxygen level–dependent response.

Waves Repeated periods of data collection in a cross-sequential design.

Web of Science An online resource for researchers hosted by Thomson Reuters that provides search and analysis tools in a variety of fields. Examples of resources available on this site are citation reports and journal impact factors.

Welch's *t* test A version of the independent-samples *t* test that takes into account unequal variances between the two groups.

Wilcoxon rank-sum test A nonparametric alternative to the independent-samples *t* test.

Wilcoxon signed-rank test A nonparametric alternative to the one-sample or matched-pairs *t* tests.

Within-subjects (or within-group or repeated measures) design A type of experimental design in which the researcher assigns each participant to all possible conditions.

***y*-intercept value** The point at which a regression line intersects the *y*-axis.

References

Adelson, J. L., & McCoach, D. B. (2010). Measuring the mathematical attitudes of elementary students: The effects of a 4-point or 5-point Likert-type scale. *Educational and Psychological Measurement, 70,* 796–807.

Adler, N. E., Epel, E. S., Castellazzo, G., & Ickovics, J. R. (2000). Relationship of subjective and objective social status with psychological and physiological functioning: Preliminary data in healthy white women. *Health Psychology, 19,* 586–592.

Adolph, K. E., & Robinson, S. R. (2011). Sampling development. *Journal of Cognition and Development, 12,* 411–423.

Adolph, K. E., Robinson, S. R., Young, J. W., & Gill-Alvarez, F. (2008). What is the shape of developmental change? *Psychological Review, 115,* 527–543.

Akins, C. K., & Panicker, S. (2012). Ethics and regulation of research with nonhuman animals. In H. Cooper, P. M. Camic, D. L. Long, A. T. Panter, D. Rindskopf, & K. J. Sher (Eds.), *APA handbook of research methods in psychology: Vol 1, Foundations, planning, measures, and psychometrics* (pp. 75–82). Washington, DC: American Psychological Association.

Alam, Q. G., & Srivastava, R. (1977). Influence of culture in perception of Müller–Lyer illusion. *Indian Journal of Behaviour, 1,* 22–23.

Aldhous, P. (2011, November 2). Psychologist admits faking data in dozens of studies. *NewScientist.* Retrieved from http://www.newscientist.com/article/dn21118-psychologist-admits-faking-data-in-dozens-of-studies.html/

Aldwin, C. M., & Igarashi, H. (2015). Successful, optimal, and resilient aging: A psychosocial perspective. In P. A. Lichtenberg & B. T. Mast (Eds.), *APA handbook of clinical geropsychology, Vol. 1 History and status of the field and perspectives on aging.* Washington, DC: American Psychological Association.

Allen, B., Speigel, D. P., Thompson, B., Pestilli, F., & Rokers, B. (2015) Altered white matter in early visual pathways of humans with amblyopia. *Vision Research, 114,* 48–55. doi:10.1016/j.visres.2014.12.021

Amato, P. R., & Keith, B. (1991). Parental divorce and adult well-being: A meta-analysis. *Journal of Marriage and Family, 53,* 43–58.

American Psychological Association. (2009). *Publication manual of the American Psychological Association* (6th ed.). Washington, DC: Author.

———. (2010). *Publication manual of the American Psychological Association* (6th ed.). Mountain View, CA: Mayfield.

———. (2015, August 7). APA's council bans psychologist participation in national security interrogations. Retrieved from http://www.apa.org/news/press/releases/2015/08/psychologist-interrogations.aspx/

———. Committee on Animal Research and Ethics. (2012). Guidelines for ethical conduct in the care and use of animals. Retrieved from http://www.apa.org/science/leadership/care/guidelines.aspx/

Amin, M., & Mabe, M. (2000). Impact factors: Use and abuse. *Perspectives in Publishing, 1*(2), 1–6.

Anderson, K. J., & Revelle, W. (1994). Impulsivity and time of day: Is rate of change in arousal a function of impulsivity? *Journal of Personality and Social Psychology, 67,* 334–344.

APA Formatting and Style Guide. (2016). Purdue Online Writing Guide. Retrieved from https://owl.english.purdue.edu/owl/resource/560/01/

Arbuthnot, J. (1710). An argument for divine providence taken from the constant regularity in the births of both sexes. *Philosophical Transactions of the Royal Society, 27,* 186–190.

Armstrong, K., Schwartz, J. S., Fitzgerald, G., Putt, M., & Ubel, P. A. (2002). Effect of framing as gain versus loss on understanding and hypothetical treatment choices: Survival and mortality curves. *Medical Decision Making, 22,* 76–83.

Armstrong, R. L. (1987). The midpoint on a five-point Likert-type scale. *Perceptual and Motor Skills, 64,* 359–362.

Arthur-Banning, S., Wells, M. S., Baker, B. L., & Hegreness, R. (2009). Parents behaving badly? The relationship between the sportsmanship behavior of adults and athletes in youth basketball games. *Journal of Sport Behavior, 32,* 3–18.

Asch, S. E. (1951). Effects of group pressure on the modification and distortion of judgments. In H. Guetzkow (Ed.), *Groups, leadership and men* (pp. 177–190). Pittsburgh, PA: Carnegie Press.

Asher, S., & Allen, V. (1969). Racial preference and social comparison processes. *Journal of Social Issues, 25*(1), 157–166.

Ashman, K. M., & Barringer, P. S. (2001). *After the science wars.* London, UK: Routledge.

Aslin, R. N. (2012). Questioning the questions that have asked about the infant brain using near-infrared spectroscopy. *Cognitive Neuropsychology, 29,* 7–23.

Bak, T. H., Nissan, J. J., Allerhand, M. M., & Deary, I. J. (2014). Does bilingualism influence cognitive aging? *Annals of Neurology, 75,* 959–963. doi:10.1002/ana.24158

Bandura, A. (1977). Self-efficacy: Toward a unifying theory of behavioral change. *Psychological Review, 84,* 191–215.

Banobi, J., Branch, T., & Hilborn, R. (2011). Do rebuttals affect future science? *Ecosphere, 2*(3), 37. Retrieved from http://onlinelibrary.wiley.com/store/10.1890/ES10-00142.1/asset/ecs210001421.pdf?v=1&t=isj0vnsb&s=5254fab42c9213d49fc 43446496028478290bb71&system

Baron, R. M., & Kenny, D. A. (1986). The moderator–mediator variable distinction in social psychological research: Conceptual, strategic, and statistical consideration. *Journal of Personality and Social Psychology, 51,* 1173–1182.

Baumeister, R. F. (2003). The psychology of irrationality: Why people make foolish, self-defeating choices. In I. Brocas & J. D. Carrillo (Eds.), *The psychology of economic decisions, Volume 1: Rationality and well-being* (pp. 3–16). Oxford, UK: Oxford University Press.

Baumrind, D. (1964). Some thoughts on ethics of research: After reading Milgram's "Behavioral Study of Obedience." *American Psychologist, 19,* 421–423.

BBC Horizon. (2005). Dr. Money and the boy with no penis. Retrieved from http://www.bbc.co.uk/sn/tvradio/programmes/horizon/dr_money_prog_summary.shtml/

Beauchet, O., Allali, G., Annweiler, C., Berrut, G., Maarouf, N., Herrmann, F. R., & Dubost, V. (2008). Does change in gait while counting backward predict the occurrence of a first fall in older adults? *Gerontology, 54*(4), 217–223.

Beck, A. T., Steer, R. A., & Brown, G. K. (1996). *Manual for the Beck Depression Inventory-II.* San Antonio, TX: Psychological Corporation.

Beck, A. T., Ward, C. H., Mendelson, M., Mock, J., & Erbaugh, J. (1961). An inventory for measuring depression. *Archives of General Psychiatry, 4,* 561–571.

Beecher, H. K. (1966). Ethics and clinical research. *The New England Journal of Medicine, 274,* 1354–1360.

Bellazzi, R., & Zupan, B. (2008). Predictive data mining in clinical medicine: Current issues and guidelines. *International Journal of Medical Informatics, 77,* 81–97.

Bem, D. J. (2011). Feeling the future: Experimental evidence for anomalous retroactive influences on cognition and affect. *Journal of Personality and Social Psychology, 100,* 407–425.

Bentley, J. P., & Thacker, P. G. (2004). The influence of risk and monetary payment on the research participant decision making process. *J. Medical Ethics, 30,* 293–298.

Berger, S. E., & Adolph, K. E. (2007). Learning and development in infant locomotion. *Progress in Brain Research, 164,* 237–255.

Berrett, D. (2013, September 9). Adjuncts are better teachers than tenured professors, study finds. *The Chronicle of Higher Education.* Retrieved from http://chronicle.com/article/Ad-juncts-Are-Bet-ter/141523/

Beskow, L. M., Grady, C., Iltis, A. S., Sadler, J. Z., & Wilfond, B. S. (2009). Points to consider: The research ethics consultation service and the IRB. *IRB: Ethics & Human Research, 31*(6), 1–9.

Best College Rankings and Lists. (2016). *U.S. News & World Report.* Retrieved from http://colleges.usnews.rankingsandreviews.com/best-colleges/rankings/

Best Travel Destinations. (2016). Traveleye.com. Retrieved from http://traveleye.com/travel-guide/top/top-100-travel-destinations/

Bhattacharjee, Y. (2013, April). The mind of a con man. *The New York Times Magazine.*

Bialystok, E., Craik, F. I., & Freedman, M. (2007). Bilingualism as a protection against the onset of symptoms of dementia. *Neuropsychologia, 45,* 459–464.

Bigelow, H. J. (1850). Dr. Harlow's case of recovery from the passage of an iron bar through the head. *The American Journal of Medical Sciences, 20,* 13–22.

Bloom, P., & Wynn, K. (1997). Linguistic cues in the acquisition of number words. *Journal of Child Language, 24,* 511–533.

Blurton Jones, N. (1972). *Ethological studies of child behavior.* New York, NY: Cambridge University Press.

Bohnert, A. M., Parker, J. G., & Warschausky, S. A. (1997). Friendship and social adjustment of children following a traumatic brain injury: An exploratory investigation. *Developmental Neuropsychology, 13,* 477–486.

Boker, S. M., & Nesselroade, J. R. (2002). A method for modeling the intrinsic dynamics of intraindividual variability: Recovering the parameters of simulated oscillators in multiwave panel data. *Multivariate Behavioral Research, 37,* 137–160.

Boller, Sprachman, and the Early Head Start Research Consortium. (1998.) Time-sampling coding form. *The NICHD Study of Early Child Care and Youth Development.* Retrieved from https://www.nichd.nih.gov/publications/pubs/documents/seccyd_06.pdf

Bonner, S. E., & Sprinkle, G. B. (2002). The effects of monetary incentives on effort and task performance: Theories, evidence, and a framework for research. *Accounting, Organizations and Society, 27,* 303–345.

Bootsma, van der Wiel, A., Gussekloo, J., de Craen, A. J. M., van Exel, E., Bloem, B. R., & Westerndorp, R. G. J. (2003). Walking and talking as predictors of falls in the general population: The Leiden 85-Plus Study. *Journal of the American Geriatric Society, 51*(10), 1466–1471.

Borenstein, M. (2012). Effect size estimation. In H. Cooper (Editor in Chief), *APA handbook of research methods in psychology: Vol. 3. Data analysis and research publication* (pp. 131–146). Washington, DC: American Psychological Association.

Bornstein, M. H., Mash, C., Arterberry, M. E., & Manian, N. (2012). Object perception in 5-month-old infants of clinically depressed and nondepressed mothers. *Infant Behavior & Development, 35,* 105–157.

Brice, S. R., Jarosz, B. S., Ames, R. A., Baglin, J., & Da Costa, C. (2011). The effect of close proximity holographic wristbands on human balance and limits of stability: A randomised, placebo-controlled trial. *Journal of Bodywork and Movement Therapies, 15,* 298–303.

Briggs, M. (2013, October 1). Use the wrong *p*-value, go to jail: Not a joke. [Web log comment]. Retrieved from http://wmbriggs.com/blog/?p=9308/

British Broadcasting Corporation. (2001). The BBC prison study. Retrieved from http://www.bbcprisonstudy.org/

Brody, J. (2012, June 25). Having your coffee and enjoying it too. *The New York Times.* Retrieved from http://well.blogs.nytimes.com/2012/06/25/having-your-coffee-and-enjoying-it-too/

Brookshire, B. (2013, May 8). Psychology is WEIRD. *Slate magazine.* Retrieved from http://www.slate.com/articles/health_and_science/science/2013/05/weird_psychology_social_science_researchers_rely_too_much_on_western_college.html/

Brown, D. (2013, September 23). The press release conviction of a biotech and its impact on scientific research. *Washington Post.* Retrieved from http://www.washingtonpost.com/national/health-science/the-press-release-crime-of-a-biotech-ceo-and-its-impact-on-scientific-research/2013/09/23/9b4a1a32-007a-11e3-9a3e-916de805f65d_story.html/

Buhrmester, M., Kwang, T., & Gosling, S. D. (2011). Amazon's Mechanical Turk: A new source of inexpensive, yet high-quality, data? *Perspectives on Psychological Science, 6,* 3–5.

Burger, J. M. (2009). Replicating Milgram: Would people still obey today? *American Psychologist, 64,* 1–11.

Burke, D. M., & Shafto, M. A. (2004). Aging and language production. *Current Directions in Psychological Science, 13,* 21–24. doi:10.1111/j.0963-7214.2004.01301006.x

Burman, R. (1997). *Deconstructing feminist psychology.* New York, NY: Sage.

Butcher, J. N. (2005). *The MMPI-2: A beginner's guide* (2nd ed.). Washington, DC: American Psychological Association.

Butzlaff, R. L., & Hooley, J. M. (1998). Expressed emotion and psychiatric relapse: A meta-analysis. *Archives of General Psychiatry, 55,* 547–552.

CCFC press release. (2007, December 6). "Disney no longer marketing Baby Einstein videos as educational." Retrieved from http://www.commercialfreechildhood.org/blog/disney-no-longer-marketing-baby-einstein-videos-educational/

Cacioppo, J. T., Berntson, G. G., & Nussbaum, H. C. (2008). Neuroimaging as a new tool in the toolbox of psychological science. *Current Directions in Psychological Science, 17,* 62–67.

Callaway, E. (2013, October 2). Uncertainty on trial. *Nature.* Retrieved from http://www.nature.com/news/uncertainty-on-trial-1.13868/

Camerer, C. F., & Hogarth, R. M. (1999). The effects of financial incentives in experiments: A review and capital-labor-production framework. *Journal of Risk and Uncertainty, 19,* 1–3, 7–42.

Campbell, I. (2007). Chi-squared and Fisher–Irwin tests of two-by-two tables with small sample recommendations. *Statistics in Medicine, 26,* 3661–3675.

Carey, B. (2005, May 31). Watching new love as it sears the brain. *New York Times.* Retrieved from http://www.nytimes.com/2005/05/31/health/psychology/watching-new-love-as-it-sears-the-brain.html?_r=0

————. (2006, July 11). John William Money, 84, sexual identity researcher, dies. *New York Times.* Retrieved from http://www.nytimes.com/2006/07/11/us/11money.html

Carifio, J., & Perla, R. J. (2007). Ten common misunderstandings, misconceptions, persistent myths and urban legends about Likert scales and Likert response formats and their antidotes. *Journal of Social Sciences, 3*(3), 106–116.

Carlo, W., Feiner, N., Walsh, M., Rich, W., Gantz, M., Laptook, A. R., . . . Higgins, R. D. (2010). Target ranges of oxygen saturation in extremely preterm infants. *The New England Journal of Medicine, 362,* 1959–1969.

Carlsmith, K. M., & Chabot, H. F. (1997). A review of computer-based survey methodology. *Journal of Psychological Practice, 3,* 20–26.

Carpenter, S. (2012, September 6). Harvard psychology researchers committed fraud, U.S. investigation concludes. *Science.* Retrieved from http://www.sciencemag.org/news/2012/09/harvard-psychology-researcher-committed-fraud-us-investigation-concludes/

Carter, R. (1999). Artistic savants tune in and tune off. *New Scientist, 2207,* 30–34.

Carver, R. P. (1978). The case against statistical significance testing. *Harvard Educational Review, 48,* 378–399.

————. (1993). The case against statistical significance testing, revisited. *Journal of Experimental Education, 61,* 287–292.

Casarotto, S., Lauro, L. J. R., Bellina, V., Casali. A. G., Rosanova, M., Pigorini, S., . . . Massimini, M. (2010). EEG responses to TMS are sensitive to changes in the perturbation parameters and repeatable over time. *PLoS One, 5*(4), e10281. doi:10.1371/journal.pone.0010281

Caspi, A., Hariri, A. R., Holmes, A., Uher, R., & Moffitt, T. E. (2010). Genetic sensitivity to the environment: The case of the serotonin transporter gene and its implications for studying complex diseases and traits. *American Journal of Psychiatry, 167,* 509–527.

Chabris, C., & Simons, D. (2010). *The invisible gorilla: And other ways our intuitions deceive us.* New York, NY: Crown/Random House.

_____ (2015, February 10). Don't be the next Brian Williams: 10 ways to avoid false memories. *Slate*. Retrieved from http://www.slate.com/articles/health_and_science/science/2015/02/false_memories_of_brian_williams_memory_experts_chabris_and_simons_tips_.2.html/

Champagne, F. A., & Mashoodh, R. (2009). Gene–environment interplay and the origins of individual differences in behavior. *Current Directions in Psychological Science, 18*(3), 127–131.

Chang, K., Karchemskiy, A., Kelley, R., Howe, M., Garrett, A., Adelman, N., & Reiss, A. (2009). Effect of Divalproex on brain morphometry, chemistry, and function in youth at high-risk for bipolar disorder: A pilot study. *Journal of Child and Adolescent Psychopharmacology, 19*, 51–59.

Channelling Superman: Avatars and real-world behaviour. (2014, February 5). *The Economist*. Retrieved from http://www.economist.com/blogs/babbage/2014/02/avatars-and-real-world-behaviour/

Charlesworth, W. R. (1986). Darwin and developmental psychology: 100 years later. *Human Development, 29*, 1–35.

Chatterjee, A. (2004). The neuropsychology of visual artistic production. *Neuropsychologia, 42*, 1568–1583.

Chess, S., & Thomas, A. (1996). *Temperament*. New York, NY: Routledge.

Chi, M. T. H. (1978). Knowledge structure and memory development. In R. Siegler (Ed.), *Children's thinking: What develops?* (pp. 73–96). Hillsdale, NJ: Erlbaum.

Chinn, C. A., & Brewer, W. F. (2000). Knowledge change in response to data in science, religion, and magic. In K. S. Rosengren, C. N. Johnson, & P. L. Harris (Eds.), *Imagining the impossible: Magical, scientific, and religious thinking in children* (pp. 334–371). Cambridge, UK: Cambridge University Press.

Christensen, A., & Hazzard, A. (1983). Reactive effects during naturalistic observation of families. *Behavioral Assessment, 5*, 349–362.

Christensen, L. (2012). Types of designs using random assignment. In C. Harris, P. M. Camic, D. L. Long, & A. T. Panter (Eds.), *APA handbook of research methods in psychology, Vol. 2* (pp. 469–488). Washington, DC: American Psychological Association.

Christie, S., & Gentner, D. (2010). Where hypotheses come from: Learning new relations by structural assignment. *Journal of Cognition and Development, 11*, 356–373.

Chung, E. (2011, May 25). Blind people echolocate with visual part of brain. *CBC News*. Retrieved from http://www.cbc.ca/news/technology/blind-people-echolocate-with-visual-part-of-brain-1.1012642/

Clark, K. B., & Clark, M. P. (1947). "Racial identification and preference among negro children." In E. L. Hartley (Ed.), *Readings in social psychology*. New York, NY: Holt, Rinehart, and Winston.

Clarke, A. C. (1962). *Profiles of the future: An inquiry into the limits of the possible*. New York, NY: Holt.

Cleveland, W. S. (1993). *Visualizing data*. Summit, NJ: Hobart Press.

_____. (1994). *The elements of graphing data*. Summit, NJ: Hobart Press.

Cohen, D., Nisbett, R. E., Bowdle, B., & Schwarz, N. (1996). Insult, aggression, and the southern culture of honor. *Journal of Personality and Social Psychology, 70*, 945–960.

Cohen, J. (1962). The statistical power of abnormal social psychological research: A review. *Journal of Abnormal and Social Psychology, 65*, 145–153.

_____. (1988). *Statistical power analysis for the behavioral sciences* (2nd ed.). Hillsdale, NJ: Erlbaum.

_____. (1990). Things I have learned (so far). *American Psychologist, 45*, 1304–1312.

Cohen, P. (2012, January 19). A sharper mind, middle age and beyond. *New York Times*. Retrieved from http://www.nytimes.com/2012/01/22/education/edlife/a-sharper-mind-middle-age-and-beyond.html/

Colapinto, J. (2000). *As nature made him: The boy who was raised as a girl*. New York, NY: HarperCollins.

_____. (2004, June 3). Gender gap: What were the real reasons behind David Reimer's suicide? *Slate Magazine*. Retrieved from http://www.slate.com/articles/health_and_science/medical_examiner/2004/06/gender_gap.html/

Colcombe, S., & Kramer, A. F. (2003). Fitness effects on the cognitive function of older adults: A meta-analytic study. *Psychological Science, 14*(2), 125–130.

Collaborative Institutional Training Initiative. Retrieved from https://www.citiprogram.org/aboutus.asp?language=english/

Collins, L. M., & Graham, J. W. (2002). The effects of the timing and spacing of observations in longitudinal studies of tobacco and other drug use: Temporal design considerations. *Drug and Alcohol Dependence, 68*, S85–S93.

Cooper, C. A., McCord, D. M., & Socha, A. (2011). Evaluating the college sophomore problem: The case of personality and politics. *The Journal of Psychology, 145*, 23–27.

Cooper, H. (2010). *Research synthesis and meta-analysis—A step-by-step approach* (4th ed.). Thousand Oaks, CA: Sage.

Corkin, S. (1984). Lasting consequences of bilateral medial temporal lobectomy: Clinical course and experimental findings in H. M. *Seminars in Neurology, 4*, 249–259.

_____. (2002). What's new with the amnesic patient H. M.? *Nature Reviews: Neuroscience, 3*, 153–160.

Crawford, M., & Unger, R. (2000). *Women and gender: A feminist psychology* (3rd ed.). Boston, MA: McGraw–Hill.

Cronbach, L. J. (1951). Coefficient alpha and the internal structure of tests. *Psychometrika, 16*, 297–334.

Cumming, G. (2012). *Understanding the new statistics: Effect sizes, confidence intervals, and meta-analysis*. New York, NY: Routledge.

Cundiff, J. M., Smith, T. W., Uchino, B. N., & Berg, C. A. (2013). Subjective social status: Construct validity and associations with psychosocial vulnerability and self-rated health. *International Journal of Behavioral Medicine, 20*, 148–158.

Dallery, J., Cassidy, R. N., & Raiff, B. R. (2013). Single-case experimental designs to evaluate novel technology-based health interventions. *Journal of Medical Internet Research, 15*(2), e22. doi:10.2196/jmir.2227

Dallery, J., Glenn, I. M., & Raiff, B. R. (2007). An internet-based abstinence reinforcement treatment for cigarette smoking. *Drug and Alcohol Dependence, 86*, 230–238. doi:10.1016/j.drugalcdep.2006.06.013

Damasio, H., Grabowski, T., Frank, R., Galaburda, A. M., & Damasio, A. R. (1994). The return of Phineas Gage: Clues about the brain from the skull of a famous patient. *Science, 264*, 1102–1105.

Danziger, S., Levav, J., & Avnaim-Pesso, L. (2011). Extraneous factors in judicial decisions. *Proceedings of the National Academy of Sciences of the USA, 108*, 6889–6892. doi:10.1073/pnas.1018033108

Davis, C. M., & Carlson, J. A. (1970). A cross-cultural study of the strength of the Müller–Lyer illusion. *Journal of Personality and Social Psychology, 16*, 403–410.

De Bruin, A., Treccani, B., & Della Sala, S. (2015). Cognitive advantage in bilingualism: An example of publication bias? *Psychological Science, 26*, 99–107.

Dearborn, W. F., Rothney, J. W., & Shuttleworth, F. K. (1938). Data on the growth of public school children (from the materials of the Harvard Growth Study). *Monographs of the Society for Research in Child Development, 3*(Serial No. 14), 1–139.

Deer, B. (2011, January 6). How the case against the MMR vaccine was fixed. *British Medical Journal, 342*, 77–84. doi:10.1136/bmj.c5347

Dehue, T. (2001). Establishing the experimenting society: The historical origin of social experimentation according to the randomized controlled design. *American Journal of Psychology, 114*, 283–302.

DeLoache, J. S., Chiong, C., Sherman, K., Islam, N., Vanderborght, M., Troseth, G. L., . . . O'Doherty, K. (2010). Do babies learn from baby media? *Psychological Science, 21*, 1570–1574.

DeLoache, J. S., Pierroutsakos, S. L., Uttal, D. H., Rosengren, K. S., & Gottlieb, A. (1998). Grasping the nature of pictures. *Psychological Science, 9*, 205–210.

DeLoache, J. S., Uttal, D. H., & Rosengren, K. S. (2004). Scale errors offer evidence for a perception-action dissociation early in life. *Science, 304*, 1027–1029.

Dennis, W. (1940). The effect of cradling practices upon the onset of walking in Hopi children. *Journal of Genetic Psychology, 56*, 77–86.

Denzin, N. K., & Lincoln, Y. S. (1998a). *Strategies of qualitative inquiry*. Thousand Oaks, CA: Sage.

————. (1998b). *Collecting and interpreting qualitative materials*. Thousand Oaks, CA: Sage.

————. (2005). *The Sage handbook of qualitative research* (3rd ed.). Thousand Oaks, CA: Sage.

Diamond, M., and Sigmundson, H. K. (1997). Sex reassignment at birth: Long-term review and clinical implications. *Archives of Pediatric and Adolescent Medicine, 151*(3), 298–304.

Down, J. L. H. (1866). Observations on an ethnic classification of idiots. *Clinical Lecture Reports, London Hospital, 3*, 259–262. Reprinted in *Mental Retardation*, 1995, 33, 54–56.

Downey, G. (2010, July 10). We agree it's WEIRD, but is it WEIRD enough? Neuroanthropology.net. Retrieved from http://neuroanthropology.net/2010/07/10/we-agree-its-weird-but-is-it-weird-enough/

Drake, J. E., & Winner, E. (2011). Superior visual analysis and imagery in an autistic child with drawing talent. *Imagination, Cognition, and Personality, 31*, 9–29.

Drew, A. (2013). APS replication initiative underway. *APS Observer, 26*(9). Retrieved from http://www.psychologicalscience.org/index.php/publications/observer/2013/november-13/aps-replication-initiative-underway.html/

Drisko, J. W. (1997). Strengthening qualitative studies and reports: Standards to promote academic integrity. *Journal of Social Work Education, 33*, 185–197.

Duarte, J. L., Crawford, J. T., Stern, C., Haidt, J., Jussim, L., & Tetlock, P. E. (2015). Political diversity will improve social psychological science. *Behavioral and Brain Sciences, 38*, 1–58.

Dweck, C. S. (1999). *Self-theories: Their role in motivation, personality and development*. Philadelphia, PA: Psychology Press.

————. (2002a). Beliefs that make smart people dumb. In R. J. Sternberg (Ed.), *Why smart people can be so stupid* (pp. 24–41). New Haven, CT: Yale University Press.

————. (2002b). Messages that motivate: How praise molds students' beliefs, motivation, and performance (in surprising ways). In J. Aronson (Ed.), *Improving academic achievement: Impact of psychological factors on education* (pp. 37–60). New York, NY: Academic Press.

Dweck, C. S., & Reppucci, N. D. (1973). Learned helplessness and reinforcement responsibility in children. *Journal of Personality and Social Psychology, 25*, 109–116.

Eibl-Eibesfeldt, I. (1967). Concepts of ethology and their significance in the study of human behavior. In H. Stevenson, E. H. Hess, & H. Rheingold (Eds.), *Early behavior: Comparative and developmental approaches* (pp. 127–146). New York, NY: Wiley.

Eisenberger, N. I., Lieberman, M. D., & Williams, K. D. (2003). Does rejection hurt? An fMRI study of social exclusion. *Science, 302*, 290–292.

Enders, C. K. (2010). *Applied missing data analysis*. New York, NY: Guilford Press.

Erceg-Hurn, D. M., & Mirosevich, V. M. (2008). Modern robust statistical methods: An easy way to maximize the accuracy and power of your research. *American Psychologist, 63*(7), 591–601.

Erceg-Hurn, D. M., Wilcox, R. R., & Keselman, H. J. (2013). Robust statistical estimation. In T. Little (Ed.), *The Oxford handbook of quantitative methods* (Vol. 1). New York, NY: Oxford University Press.

Erdreich, B. L., Slavet, B. S., & Amador, A. C. (1994). *Sexual harassment in the federal workplace: Trends, progress and continuing challenges.* Washington, DC: U.S. Merit Systems Protection Board.

Faden, R., & Kass, N. (1998). HIV research, ethics, and the developing world. *American Journal of Public Health, 88,* 548–550.

Farar, M. (2002). Emerging ethical issues in neuroscience. *Nature Neuroscience, 5,* 1123–1129.

Festinger, L. (1957). *A theory of cognitive dissonance.* Palo Alto, CA: Stanford University Press.

Festinger, L., & Carlsmith, J. M. (1959). Cognitive consequences of forced compliance. *Journal of Abnormal and Social Psychology, 58,* 203–210.

Few, S. (2006). *Information dashboard design: The effective visual communication of data.* Sebastopol, CA: O'Reilly.

Figlio, D., Schapiro, M., & Soter, K. (2013). Are tenure track professors better teachers? NBER working paper no. 19406. Retrieved from http://www.ipr.northwestern.edu/publications/papers/2013/ipr-wp-13-18.html/

Finkel, M. (2011, March). The blind man who taught himself to see. *Men's Journal.* Retrieved from http://www.mensjournal.com/magazine/the-blind-man-who-taught-himself-to-see-20120504/

Fischer, C. T. (2006). *Qualitative research methods for psychologists: Introduction through empirical studies.* Amsterdam, The Netherlands: Elsevier/Academic Press.

Fisher, C. B., & Vacanti-Shova, K. (2012). The responsible conduct of psychological research: An overview of ethical principles, APA Ethics Code standards, and federal regulations. In M. Gottlieb, M. Handelsman, L. VandeCreek, & S. Knapp (Eds.), *Handbook of ethics in psychology* (pp. 335–370). Washington, DC: APA.

Fiske, S. T., & Taylor, S. E. (2013). *Social cognition: From brains to culture* (2nd ed.). Thousand Oaks, CA: Sage.

Fleischman, J. (2004). *Phineas Gage: A gruesome but true story about brain science.* New York, NY: Houghton Mifflin Harcourt.

Floyd, F. J., & Widaman, K. F. (1995). Factor analysis in the development and refinement of clinical assessment instruments. *Psychological Assessment, 7,* 286–299.

Flyvbjerg, B. (2006). Five misunderstandings about case-study research. *Qualitative Inquiry, 12,* 219–245.

Folkins, J. (1992). *Resource on person-first language.* American Speech–Language-Hearing Association.

Folstein, M. F., Folstein, S. E., & McHugh, P. R. (1975). Mini-mental state: A practical method for grading the cognitive state of patients for the clinician. *Journal of Psychiatric Research, 12,* 189–198.

Forgas, J. P., & Bower G. H. (1987). Mood effects on person–perception judgments. *Journal of Personality and Social Psychology, 53,* 53–60.

Forrester, M. A. (Ed.). (2010). *Doing qualitative research in psychology. A practical guide.* London, UK: Sage.

Fortner-Wood, C., & Henderson, B. B. (1997). Individual differences in two-year-olds' curiosity in the assessment setting and in the grocery store. *The Journal of Genetic Psychology, 158,* 495–497.

Fowler, F. J. (2002). *Survey research methods.* New York, NY: Sage.

Fraley, R. C., & Vazire, S. (2014). The N-pact factor: Evaluating the quality of empirical journals with respect to sample size and statistical power. *PLoS ONE, 9*(10), e109019. doi:10.1371/journal.pone.01909019

Frazier, P. A., Tix, A. P., & Barron, K. E. (2004). Testing moderator and mediator effects in counseling psychology research. *Journal of Counseling Psychology, 51,* 115–134.

Gage, S. (2013, May 15). Sifting the evidence. *The Guardian.* Retrieved from http://www.theguardian.com/science/sifting-the-evidence/2013/may/15psychology-registered-replication-reports-reliability/

Galanes, P. (2013, June 14). The mother of all housewives. *The New York Times.*

Gapp, K., Jawaid, A., Sarkies, P., Bohacek, J., Pelczar, P., Prados, J., . . . Mansuy, I. M. (2014). Implication of sperm RNAs in transgenerational inheritance of the effects of early trauma in mice. *Nature Neuroscience, 17,* 667–669.

Gardner, D. G., Cummings, L. L., Dunham, R. B., & Pierce, J. L. (1998). Single-item versus multiple-item measurement scales: An empirical comparison. *Educational and Psychological Measurement, 58,* 898–915.

Gardner, H. (1983). *Frames of mind. The theory of multiple intelligences.* New York, NY: Basic Books.

Gaviria, M., Wright, D., Lyman, W., PBS Home Video, Rain Media, WGBH (Television station), Boston, M., & WGBH Educational Foundation. (2008). *The medicated child.* [United States]: Distributed by PBS Home Video.

Gelman, A., Carlin, J. B., Stern, H. S., Dunson, D. B., Vehtari, A., & Rubin, D. B. (2013). Bayesian data analysis (3rd ed.). Boca Raton, FL: Chapman & Hall/CRC.

Gentner, D., & Namy, L. (1999). Comparison in the development of categories. *Cognitive Development, 14,* 487–513.

Ghasemi, A., & Zahediasl, S. (2012). Normality tests for statistical analysis: A guide for non-statisticians. *International Journal of Endocrinology Metabolism, 10,* 486–489.

Giedd, J., Raznahan, A., Alexander-Bloch, A., Schmitt, E., Gogtay, N., and Rapoport, J. L. (2015). Child psychiatry branch of the national institute of mental health longitudinal structural magnetic resonance imaging study of human brain development. *Neuropsychopharmacology, 40*, 43–49.

Gigerenzer, G. (2004). Mindless statistics. *The Journal of Socio-Economics, 33*, 587–606.

Gillie, B. (2012, October 12). New survey exposes most absurd reasons for skipping work. Examiner.com. Retrieved from http://www.examiner.com/article/new-survey-exposes-most-absurd-reasons-for-missing-work/

Gilovich, T., Griffin, D., & Kahneman, D. (2002). *Heuristics and biases: The psychology of intuitive judgment.* Cambridge, UK: Cambridge University Press.

Giridharadas, A. (2010, August 25). A weird way of thinking has prevailed worldwide. *New York Times.* Retrieved from http://www.nytimes.com/2010/08/26/world/americas/26iht-currents.html? pagewanted=all/

Gladstone, B. (2013, July 5). Retraction watch revisited. *On the Media.* Retrieved from http://www.onthemedia.org/story/304647-retraction-watch-revisited/

Glaser, B. G., & Strauss, A. L. (1967). *The discovery of grounded theory: Strategies for qualitative research.* Chicago, IL: Aldine.

Global Down Syndrome Foundation. (2011). Words can hurt. Retrieved from http://www.globaldownsyndrome.org/about-down-syndrome/words-can-hurt/

Goodman, E. (1999). The role of socioeconomic status gradients in explaining differences in US adolescents' health. *American Journal of Public Health, 89*, 1522–1528.

Goodman, E., Adler, N. E., Kawachi, I., Frazier, A. L., Huang, B., & Colditz, G. A. (2001). Adolescents' perceptions of social status: Development and evaluation of a new indicator. *Pediatrics, 108*(2), E31.

Goodman, S. (2008). A dirty dozen: Twelve *p*-value misconceptions. *Seminars in Hematology, 45*, 135–140.

Gorvine, B. J. (2002). *Fathers and father figures of Head Start children: A study of the effects of involvement on children's socioemotional development.* Ann Arbor, MI: University of Michigan.

Gould, M. S., Marrocco, F. A., Kleinman, M., Thomas, J. G., Mostkoff, K., Cote, J., & Davies, M. (2005). Examining iatrogenic risk of youth suicide programs: A randomized controlled trial. *Journal of the American Medical Association, 293*, 1635–1643.

Grady, C. (2005). Payment of clinical research subjects. *The Journal of Clinical Investigation, 115*, 1681–1687.

Graf, C., Wager, E., Bowman, A., Fiack, S., Scott-Lichter, D., & Robinson, A. (2007). Best practice guidelines on publication ethics: A publisher's perspective. Retrieved from http://www.apastyle.org/manual/related/best-practice-guidelines.pdf/

Granott, N., & Parziale, J. (2002). *Microdevelopment: Transition processes in development and learning.* Cambridge, UK: Cambridge University Press.

Gray, K., & Wegner, D. M. (2013). Six guidelines for interesting research. *Perspectives on Psychological Science, 8*, 549–553.

Greenwald, A. G., McGhee, D. E., & Schwartz, J. K. L. (1998). Measuring individual differences in implicit cognition: The Implicit Association Test. *Journal of Personality and Social Psychology, 74*, 1464–1480.

Gross, L. (2009, May 26). A broken trust: Lessons from the vaccine-autism wars. *PLoS Biology.* Retrieved from http://journals.plos.org/plosbiology/article? id=10.1371/journal.pbio.1000114/

———. (2015, January 20). Parents who shun vaccines tend to cluster, boosting children's risk. *National Public Radio.* Retrieved from http://www.npr.org/blogs/health/2015/01/20/378630798/parents-who-shun-vaccines-tend-to-cluster-boosting-childrens-risk/

Gross, P. R., & Levitt, N. (1994). *Higher superstition: The academic left and its quarrels with science.* Baltimore, MD: Johns Hopkins University Press.

Gunsalus, C. K., Bruner, E. M., Burbules, N. C., Dash, L., Finkin, M., Goldberg, J. P., . . . Pratt, M. G. (2006). Mission creep in the IRB world. *Science, 312*, 1441.

Hagen, R. L. (1997). In praise of the null hypothesis statistical test. *American Psychologist, 52*, 15–24.

Haggerty, K. D. (2004). Ethics creep: Governing social science research in the name of ethics. *Qualitative Sociology, 27*, 391–414.

Haney, C., Banks, C., & Zimbardo, P. (1973a). A study of prisoners and guards in a simulated prison. *Naval Research Reviews, 26*(9), 1–17.

———. (1973b). Interpersonal dynamics in a simulated prison. *International Journal of Criminology and Penology, 1*, 69–97.

Hannaford, A. (2013, April 6). Andrew Wakefield: Autism Inc. *The Guardian.* Retrieved from http://www.theguardian.com/society/2013/apr/06/what-happened-man-mmr-panic/

Harlow, J. M. (1848). Passage of an iron rod through the head. *Boston Medical and Surgical Journal, 39*, 389–393.

Harmon, A. (2010, April 21). Indian tribe wins fight to limit research on its DNA. *New York Times.* Retrieved from http://www.nytimes.com/2010/04/22/us/22dna.html?pagewanted=all&_r=0/

———. (2010, September 19). New drugs stir debate on rules of clinical trials. *The New York Times.* Retrieved from http://www.nytimes.com/

Harris, R. J. (1997). Significance tests have their place. *Psychological Science, 8*, 8–11.

———. (1999). *Information graphics: A comprehensive illustrated reference.* New York, NY: Oxford University Press.

Haslam, S. A., & Reicher, S. (2007). Beyond the banality of evil: Three dynamics of an interactionist social psychology of tyranny. *Personality and Social Psychology Bulletin, 33*, 615–622.

————. (2012). When prisoners take over the prison: A social psychology of resistance. *Personality and Social Psychology Review, 16,* 154–179.

Heath, H., & Cowley, S. (2004). Developing a grounded theory approach: A comparison of Glaser and Strauss. *International Journal of Nursing Studies, 41,* 141–150.

Heffernan, V. (2011, April 17). Too much relationship vérité. *The New York Times.*

Hellerman, C. (2013, December 26). You may not be better off after knee surgery. *CNN.com.* Retrieved from http://www.cnn.com/2013/12/26/health/knee-surgery-study/

Henley, D. (1989). Nadia revisited: A study into the nature of regression in the autistic savant syndrome. *Art Therapy: Journal of the American Art Therapy Association, 6,* 43–56. Illinois Criminal Code. (2012). Article 26,

Henrich, J., Heine, S. J., & Norenzayan, A. (2010). The weirdest people in the world? *Behavioral and Brain Sciences, 33*(2/3), 1–75.

Herbert, W. (2014, January 21). Know thy avatar: Good and evil in the gaming world. *Huffington Post.* Retrieved from http://www.huffingtonpost.com/wray-herbert/know-thy-avatar-good-and_b_4644183.html/

Hess, R., Kashigawa, K., Price, G. G., & Dickinson, W. P. (1980). Maternal expectations for mastery of developmental tasks in Japan and the United States. *International Journal of Psychology, 15,* 259–271.

Hesse-Biber, S. N., & Leavy, P. (2006). *The practice of qualitative research.* Thousand Oaks, CA: Sage.

Higgins, E. T. (2000). Making a good decision: Value from fit. *American Psychologist, 55,* 1217–1230.

Hillman, C. H., Buck, S. M., Themanson, J. R., Pontifex, M. B., & Castelli, D. M. (2009). Aerobic fitness and cognitive development: Event-related brain potential and task performance indices of executive control in preadolescent children. *Developmental Psychology, 45,* 114–129.

Hiltzik, M. (2014a, January 20). The toll of the anti-vaccination movement, in one devastating graphic. *Los Angeles Times.* Retrieved from http://www.latimes.com/business/hiltzik/la-fi-mh-antivaccination-movement-20140120-story.html/

————. (2014b, January 22). More on the unsavory history of the vaccine–autism "link." *Los Angeles Times.* Retrieved from http://www.latimes.com/business/hiltzik/la-fi-mh-vaccineautism-link-20140122-story.html/

Hoaglin, D. C., Mosteller, F., & Tukey, J. W. (Eds.). (2000). *Understanding robust and exploratory data analysis.* New York, NY: Wiley.

Hodge, V. J., & Austin, J. (2004). A survey of outlier detection methodologies. *Artificial Intelligence Review, 22,* 85–126.

Hoekstra, R., Kiers, H. A. L., & Johnson, A. (2012). Are assumptions of well-known statistical techniques checked, and why (not)? *Frontiers in Psychology, 3,* 137. doi:10.3389/fpsyg.2012.00137

Hoff, E. (2003). The specificity of environmental influence: Socioeconomic status affects early vocabulary development via maternal speech. *Child Development, 74*(5), 1368–1378.

Hoffman, J. (2013, June 5). Watchdog halts action on researchers. *New York Times.* Retrieved from http://www.nytimes.com/2013/06/06/health/watchdog-halts-action-on-researchers.html/

Holliday, A. (2001). *Doing and writing qualitative research.* London, UK: Sage.

Holton, G. (1973). *Thematic origins of scientific thought: Kepler to Einstein.* Cambridge, MA: Harvard University Press.

Hoover, K. D., & Perez, S. J. (1999). Data mining reconsidered: Encompassing and the general-to-specific approach to specification search. *Econometrics Journal, 2,* 167–191.

Horn, J. L., & Cattell, R. B. (1967). Age differences in fluid and crystallized intelligence. *Acta Psychologica, 26,* 107–129.

Hubbard, R., & Lindsay, R. (2008). Why *P* values are not a useful measure of evidence in statistical significance testing. *Theory & Psychology, 18,* 69–88.

Iacono, W. G., & McGue, M. (2002). Minnesota Twin Family Study. *Twin Research, 5,* 482–487.

Illes, J. (2006). "Pandora's box" of incidental findings in brain imaging research. *Nature Clinical Practice Neurology, 2*(2), 60–61.

Illes, J., Tairyan, K., Federico, C. A., Tabet, A., & Glover, G. H. (2010). Reducing barriers to ethics in neuroscience. *Frontiers in Human Neuroscience, 4,* 1–5. Retrieved from http://dx.doi.org/10.3389/fnhum.2010.00167/

Illinosi Criminal Code. (2012). Article 26, Illinois Compiled Statutes, Illinois General Assembly. Retrieved from http://www.ilga.gov/legislation/ilcs/ilcs4.asp?DocName=072000050HArt.+26&ActID=1876&ChapterID=53&SeqStart=73400000&SeqEnd=74325000/

Inflation remains in check—Except for the tooth fairy. (2013, August 31). *The Chicago Tribune.* Retrieved from http://articles.chicagotribune.com/2013-08-31/business/chi-tooth-fairy-amount-08302013_1_jason-alderman-single-tooth-young-parents/

Ingraham, C. (2015, January 22). The devastating impact of vaccine deniers, in one measles chart. *The Washington Post,* Wonkblog. Retrieved from http://www.washingtonpost.com/blogs/wonkblog/wp/2015/01/22/the-devastating-impact-of-vaccine-deniers-in-one-measles-chart/

Ioannidis, J. P. A. (2005). Why most published research findings are false. *PLoS Medicine, 2*(8), e124.

Jackman, S. (2009). *Bayesian analysis for the social sciences.* New York, NY: Wiley.

Jacob, T., Tennenbaum, D., Seilhamer, R. A., Bargiel, K., & Sharon, T. (1994). Reactivity effects during naturalistic observation of distressed and nondistressed families. *Journal of Family Psychology, 8,* 354–363.

Jacoby, W. G. (1997). *Statistical graphics for univariate and bivariate data*. Thousand Oaks, CA: Sage.

———. (1998). *Statistical graphics for visualizing multivariate data*. Thousand Oaks, CA: Sage.

Jamieson, S. (2004). Likert scales: How to (ab)use them. *Medical Education*, 38: 1217–1218. doi:10.1111/j.1365-2929.2004.02012.x

Jaschik, S. (2013, September 9). The adjunct advantage. *Inside Higher Ed*. Retrieved from http://www.insidehighered.com/news/2013/09/09/study-finds-students-learn-more-non-tenure-track-instructors/

Jaslow, R. (2013, December 26). Common arthroscopic knee surgery no better than "sham" version, researchers say. *CBS News*. Retrieved from http://www.cbsnews.com/news/common-arthroscopic-knee-surgery-not-effective-no-better-than-sham-researchers-say/

Jerman, P., & Constantine, N. A. (2010). Demographic and psychological predictors of parent–adolescent communication about sex: A representative statewide analysis. *Journal of Youth and Adolescence, 39*, 1164–1174.

Jeynes, W. H. (2002). The challenge of controlling for SES in social science and educational research. *Educational Psychology Review, 14*, 205–221.

Joffe, V., & Varlokosta, S. (2007). Patterns of syntactic development in children with Williams syndrome and Down's syndrome: Evidence from passives and wh-questions. *Clinical Linguistics & Phonetics, 21*, 705–727.

Johnson, S. M., & Bolstad, O. D. (1975). Reactivity to home observation: A comparison of audio recorded behavior with observers present or absent. *Journal of Applied Behavior Analysis, 8*, 181–185.

Jones, J. (1981). *Bad blood: The Tuskegee Syphilis Experiment*. New York, NY: Free Press.

Kaczynski, A. T., Potwarka, L. R., & Saelens, B. E. (2008). Association of park size, distance, and features with physical activity in neighborhood parks. *American Journal of Public Health, 98*, 1451–1456.

Kahneman, D. (2011). *Thinking, fast and slow*. New York, NY: Farrar, Straus and Giroux.

Kahneman, D., & Tversky, A. (1979). Prospect theory: An analysis of decision under risk. *Econometrica, 47*, 263–291.

Kahneman, D., Fredrickson, B. L., Schreiber, C. A., & Redelmeier, D. A. (1993). When more pain is preferred to less: Adding a better end. *Psychological Science, 4*, 401–405. doi:10.1111/j.1467-9280.1993.tb00589.x

Kahneman, D., Slovic, P., & Tversky, A. (1982). *Judgment under uncertainty: Heuristics and biases*. Cambridge, UK: Cambridge University Press.

Kamenica, E. (2012). Behavioral economics and psychology of incentives. *Annual Review of Economics, 4*, 427–452.

Karasik, L. B., Tamis-LeMonda, C. S., & Adolph, K. E. (2011). Transition from crawling to walking and infants' actions with objects and people. *Child Development, 82*, 1199–1209.

Katz, J. (1972). *Experimentation with human beings*. New York, NY: Russell Sage Foundation.

Kazarian, E. (2013, September 23). What the study didn't show. *Inside Higher Ed*. Retrieved from http://www.insidehighered.com/views/2013/09/23/essay-report-comparing-student-learning-instructors-and-tenure-track/

Keane, E., Layte, R., Harrington, J., Kearny, P. M., & Perry, I. J. (2012). Measured parental weight status and familial socio-economic status correlates with childhood overweight and obesity at age 9. *PloS One, 7*(8), e43503. doi:10.1371/journal.pone.0043503

Keppel, G., & Wickens, T. D. (2004). *Design and analysis: A researcher's handbook*. Upper Saddle River, NJ: Pearson.

Kid Nation. (n.d.). In *Wikipedia*. Retrieved from http://en.wikipedia.org/wiki/Kid_Nation/

Kidder, L. H., & Fine, M. (1997). Qualitative enquiry in psychology: A radical tradition. In D. Fox & I. Prillentensky (Eds.), *Critical psychology: an introduction*. London, UK: Sage.

Kim, H., & Markus, H. (1999). Deviance or uniqueness, harmony or conformity? A cultural analysis. *Journal of Personality and Social Psychology, 77*(4), 785–800.

Kirkman, J. (1992). *Good style: writing for science and technology*. London, UK: E & FN Spon.

Kirsch, I. S., Jungeblut, A., Jenkins, L., & Kolstad, A. (1993). *Adult literacy in America*. National Center for Education Statistics. U.S. Department of Education.

Kirsch, I., & Sapirstein, G. (1998). Listening to Prozac but hearing placebo: A meta-analysis of anti-depressant medication. *Prevention and Treatment, 1*, Article 2a.

Kolata, G. (2013, April 7). Scientific articles accepted (personal checks, too). *New York Times*. Retrieved from http://www.nytimes.com/2013/04/08/health/for-scientists-an-exploding-world-of-pseudo-academia.html?pagewanted=all&_r=0/

Krueger, J. (2001). Null hypothesis significance testing: On the survival of a flawed method. *American Psychologist, 56*(1), 16–26.

Krugman, P. (2013, April 18). Excel depression. *New York Times*. Retrieved from http://nytimes.com/2013/04/19/opinion/krugman-the-excel-depression.html?_r=0/

Kruschke, J. (2014). *Doing Bayesian data analysis* (2nd ed.). San Diego, CA: Academic Press.

Kruschke, J. K. (2013). Bayesian estimation supersedes the *t* test. *Journal of Experimental Psychology: General, 142*, 573–603.

Kuhn, T. S. (1962). *The structure of scientific revolutions*. Chicago, IL: University of Chicago Press.

Kulkarni, H. (2009). MRI: What, why, and when? *Health & Medicine, Technology*, http://www.slideshare.net/keshrad/basics-of-mri

Kwak, J. (2013, February 9). The importance of Excel. *The Baseline Scenario*. Retrieved from https://baselinescenario.com/2013/02/

Landsberger, H. A. (1958). *Hawthorne revisited: Management and the worker*. Ithaca, NY: Cornell University Press.

Leslie, M. (2000, July/August). The vexing legacy of Lewis Terman. *Stanford Magazine*. Retrieved from https://alumni.stanford.edu/get/page/magazine/article/?article_id=40678/

Leslie, S-J., Cimpian, A., Meyer, M., & Freeland, E. (2015). Expectations of brilliance underlie gender distributions across academic disciplines. *Science, 347*, 262–265.

Leung, S. (2011). A comparison of psychometric properties and normality in 4-, 5-, 6-, and 11-point Likert scales. *Journal of Social Service Research, 37*, 412–421.

Lewin, T. (2003, October 29). A growing number of video viewers watch from crib. *New York Times*.

Lewis, H. S. (1925). *Arrowsmith*. New York, NY: Harcourt, Brace.

Li, F., Harmer, P., McAuley, E., Fisher, K. J., Duncan, T. E., & Duncan, S. C. (2001). Tai chi, self-efficacy, and physical function in the elderly. *Prevention Science, 2*, 229–239.

Likert, R. (1932). A technique for the measurement of attitudes. *Archives of Psychology, 140* (1), 44–53.

Likert, R., & Hayes, S. P. (1957). *Some applications of behavioural research*. Paris, France: UNESCO.

Lin, T. (2012, June 4). Hitting the court, with an ear on the ball. *The New York Times*. Retrieved from http://www.nytimes.com/2012/06/05/science/a-game-of-tennis-tests-notions-of-blindness.html/

Lit, L., Schweitzer, J. B., & Oberbauer, A. M. (2011). Handler beliefs affect scent detection dog outcomes. *Animal Cognition, 14*, 387–394.

Lloyd, R. (1999, September 30). Metric mishap caused loss of NASA orbiter. *CNN.com*. Retrieved from http://www.cnn.com/TECH/space/9909/30/mars.metric.02/

Lloyd-Fox, S., Blasi, A., & Elwell, C. E. (2010). Illuminating the development brain: The past, present and future of functional near infrared spectroscopy. *Neuroscience and Biobehavioral Reviews, 34*, 269–284.

Lo, B., & Barnes, M. (2011). Protecting research participants while reducing regulatory burdens. *Journal of the American Medical Association, 306*, 2260–2261.

Locke, L. F., Silverman, S. J., & Spiruduso, W. W. (2010). *Reading and understanding research* (3rd ed.). Los Angeles. CA: Sage.

Loftus, G. R. (1996). Psychology will be a much better science when we change the way we analyze data. *Current Directions in Psychological Science, 5*(6), 161–171.

Lowry, R. (2014, March 18). Jenny McCarthy's dangerous anti-vaccine crusade. *New York Post*. Retrieved from http://nypost.com/2014/03/18/anti-vaccine-activist-jenny-mccarthy-mother-of-plagues/

Lynch, S. M. (2007). *Introduction to applied Bayesian statistics and estimation for social scientists*. New York, NY: Springer.

MacKay, D. G., James, L. E., Taylor, J. K., & Marian, D. E. (2007). Amnesic H.M. exhibits parallel deficits and sparing in language and memory: Systems versus binding theory accounts. *Language and Cognitive Processes, 22*, 377–452.

Macmillan, M. (2000). *An odd kind of fame: Stories of Phineas Gage*. Cambridge, MA: MIT Press.

MacWhinney, B. (1987). *Mechanisms of language acquisition*. Hillsdale, NJ: Erlbaum.

Maerz, M. (2011, April 21). You haven't heard the last of the Louds. *Los Angeles Times*.

Maguire, E. A., Woollett, K., & Spiers, H. J. (2006). London taxi drivers and bus drivers: A structural MRI and neuropsychological analysis. *Hippocampus, 16*, 1091–1101.

Mai, X., Xu, L., Li, M., Shao, J., Zhao, Z., Lamm, C., Fox, N. A., . . . Lazoff, B. (2014). Sounds elicit relative left frontal alpha activity in 2-month-old infants. *International Journal of Psychophysiology, 94*, 287–291.

Manuck, S. B., & McCaffery, J. M. (2014). Gene–environment interaction. *Annual Review of Psychology, 65*, 41–70.

Martin, J. (2011, June 30). UW battle over *Baby Einstein* settled, maybe. *The Seattle Times*.

Martin, R. C., & Allen, C. (2012). Case studies in neuropsychology. In H. Cooper (Editor-in-Chief). *APA Handbook of Research Methods in Psychology: Vol. 2. Research Designs* (pp. 633–646). Washington, DC: American Psychological Association.

Mast, F. W., Ganis, G., Christie, S., & Kosslyn, S. M. (2003). Four types of mental imagery processing in upright and tilted observers. *Cognitive Brain Research, 17*, 209–213.

Master, S. L., Eisenberger, N. I., Taylor, S. E., Naliboff, B. D., Shirinyan, D., & Lieberman, M. D. (2009). A picture's worth: Partner photographs reduce experimentally induced pain. *Psychological Science, 20*, 1316–1318.

Masuda, T., & Nisbett, R. E. (2001). Attending holistically versus analytically: Comparing the context sensitivity of Japanese and Americans. *Journal of Personality and Social Psychology, 81*, 922–934.

Mathis-Lilley, B. (2015, May 1). Emails reveal American Psychological Association's role in CIA torture. *Slate Magazine*. Retrieved from http://www.slate.com/blogs/the_slatest/2015/05/01/american_psychological_association_cia_torture_collaboration_documented.html/

Maxwell, S. E. (2004). The persistence of underpowered studies in psychological research: Causes, consequences, and remedies. *Psychological Methods, 9*, 147–163.

Mayer, J. (2005, July 11). The experiment. *The New Yorker*. Retrieved from http://www.newyorker.com/magazine/2005/07/11/the-experiment-3/

McAdams, D. P. (2011). *George W. Bush and the redemptive dream: A psychological portrait*. New York, NY: Oxford University Press.

————. (2013). *The redemptive self: Stories Americans live by*. New York, NY: Oxford University Press.

McAuliffe, W. E., Geller, S., LaBrie, R., Paletz, S., & Fournier, E. (1998). Are telephone surveys suitable for studying substance abuse? Cost, administration, coverage and response rate issues. *Journal of Drug Issues, 28*, 455–481.

Meehl, P. E. (1990). Why summaries of research on psychological theories are often uninterpretable. *Psychological Reports, 66*, 195–244.

Messer, S. C., & Gross, A. M. (1995). Childhood depression and family interaction: A naturalistic observation study. *Journal of Clinical Child Psychology, 24*, 77–88.

Mewhort, D. J. K., Kelly, M., & Johns, B. J. (2009). Randomization tests and the unequal-N/unequal-variance problem. *Behavior Research Methods, 41*(3), 664–667.

Meyer, M. N., & Chabris, C. (2014, July 31). Why psychologists' food fight matters. *Slate*. Retrieved from http://www.slate.com/articles/health_and_science/science/2014/07/replication_controversy_in_psychology_bullying_file_drawer_effect_blog_posts.html/

Micceri, T. (1989). The Unicorn, the normal curve, and other improbable creatures. *Psychological Bulletin, 105*, 156–166.

Milgram, S. (1963). Behavioral study of obedience. *Journal of Abnormal and Social Psychology, 67*, 371–378.

Miller, L., & Spiegel, A. (2015, January 22). Batman Pt. 1. *National Public Radio, Invisibilia*. Retrieved from http://www.npr.org/2015/01/23/379134306/batman-pt-1/

Moberg, P. E. (1982). Biases in unlisted phone numbers. *Journal of Advertising Research, 22*(4), 51–55.

Moens, E., Braet, C., & Soetens, B. (2007). Observation of family functioning at mealtime: A comparison of families of children with and without overweight. *Journal of Pediatric Psychology, 32*, 52–63.

Mone, M. A., Mueller, G. C., & Mauland, W. (1996). The perceptions and usage of statistical power in applied psychology and management research. *Personnel Psychology, 49*, 103–120.

Money, J., & Ehrhardt, A. (1972). *Man & woman, boy & girl: Gender identity from conception to maturity*. Northvale, NJ: Aronson.

Morris, E. (2008, April 10). Play it again, Sam (re-enactments, part two). *New York Times*. Retrieved from http://opinionator.blogs.nytimes.com/2008/04/10/play-it-again-sam-reenactments-part-two/

Mottron, L., Limoges, E., & Jelenic, P. (2003). Can a cognitive deficit elicit an exceptional ability? A case of savant syndrome in drawing abilities: Nadia. In C. Code, C. Wallesch, Y. Joanette, & A. R. Lecours (Eds.), *Classic Cases in Neuropsychology* (Vol. II, pp. 323–340). East Sussex, UK: Psychology Press.

Mueller, C. M., & Dweck, C. S. (1998). Praise for intelligence can undermine children's motivation and performance. *Journal of Personality and Social Psychology, 75*, 33–52.

Must, A., Jacques, P. F., Dallal, G. E., Bajema, C. J., & Dietz, W. H. M. D. (1992). Long term morbidity and mortality of adolescent obesity: A follow-up of third Harvard Growth Study participants of 1922 to 1935. *The New England Journal of Medicine, 327*, 1350–1355.

Naik, G. (2011, August 10). Mistakes in scientific studies surge. *Wall Street Journal*. Retrieved from http://online.wsj.com/news/articles/SB10001424052702303627104576411850666582080/

National Center for Education Statistics. (2006). National Assessment of Adult Literacy (NAAL): A first look at the literacy of America's Adults in the 21st Century. Retrieved from http://nces.ed.gov/pubsearch/pubsinfo.asp?pubid=2006470/

————. (2011). Enrollment rates of 18. Retrieved from http://nces.ed.gov/programs/digest/d11/tables/dt11_213.asp/

National Institutes of Health. (2014). High impact journals. National Institute of Environmental Health Sciences. Retrieved from http://tools.niehs.nih.gov/srp/publications/highimpactjournals.cfm/

Neale, M. C., & Cardon, L. R. (1992). *Methodology for genetic studies of twins and families*. Dordrecht, The Netherlands: Kluwer Academic Press.

Neider, M. B., Gaspar, J. G., McCarley, J. S., Crowell, J. A., Kaczmarski, H., & Kramer, A. F. (2011). Walking and talking: Dual-task effects on street crossing behavior in older adults. *Psychology and Aging, 26*, 260–268.

Newport, F. (2013, June 3). Wives are cheating 40% more than they used to, but still 70% as much as men. *Gallup.com*. Retrieved from http://www.gallup.com/poll/147887/americans-continue-believe-god.aspx/

Nguyen, H. D., & Ryan, A. M. (2008). Does stereotype threat affect test performance of minorities and women? *Journal of Applied Psychology, 96*, 1314–1334.

NICHD Early Child Care Research Network. (1996). Characteristics of infant child-care: Factors contributing to positive caregiving. *Early Childhood Research Quarterly, 11*, 269–306.

————. (2003). Does quality of child care affect child outcomes at age 4½? *Developmental Psychology, 39*, 451–469.

Norman, G. (2010). Likert scales, levels of measurement and the "laws" of statistics. *Advances in Health Sciences Education, 15*, 625–632.

Northcraft, G. B., & Neale, M. A. (1987). Experts, amateurs, and real estate: An anchoring-and-adjustment perspective on property pricing decisions. *Organizational Behavior and Human Decision Processes, 39*, 84–97.

Northwestern University Institutional Review Board. (2012). Form for determining whether a project involves human subjects research. Retrieved from http://irb.northwestern.edu/sites/default/files/templates/human-subjects-determination-form-1336675694.doc/

Nosek, B. A., Greenwald, A. G., & Banaji, M. R. (2007). The Implicit Association Test at age 7: A methodological and conceptual review. *Automatic Processes in Social Thinking and Behavior,* 265–292.

Nowakowski, M. E., Rogojanski, J., & Antony, M. M. (2014). Specific phobia. In S. G. Hofmann, D. J. Dozois, W. Rief, & J. A. Smith (Eds.), *The Wiley handbook of cognitive behavioral therapy* (pp. 979–999). Boston, MA: Wiley–Blackwell.

Nyhan, B. (2014, September 18). To get more out of science, show the rejected research. *New York Times.* Retrieved from http://www.nytimes.com/2014/09/19/upshot/to-get-more-out-of-science-show-the-rejected-research.html?hpw&rref=science&action=click&pgtype=Homepage&version=HpHedThumbWell&module=well-region&region=bottom-well&WT.nav=bottom-well&_r=0&abt=0002&abg=1/

O'Dougherty, M., Story, M., & Stang, J. (2006). Observations of parent–child co-shoppers in supermarkets: Children's involvement in food selections, parental yielding, and refusal strategies. *Journal of Nutrition Education and Behavior, 38,* 183–188.

Oakes, J. M., & Rossi, P. H. (2003). The measurement of SES in health research: Current practice and steps toward a new approach. *Social Science & Medicine, 56,* 769–784.

Obenshain, M. K. (2004). Application of data mining techniques to healthcare data. *Statistics for Hospital Epidemiology, 25,* 690–695.

Oden, S., & Asher, S. R. (1977). Coaching children in social skills for friendship making. *Child Development, 48,* 495–506.

Office for Human Research Protections. (2013, August 28). Matters related to protection of human subjects and research considering standard of care interventions. Retrieved from http://www.hhs.gov/ohrp/newsroom/rfc/Public%20Meeting%20August%2028,%202013/supportmeeting-transcriptfinal.pdf/

Ogden, J. A., & Corkin, S. (1991). Memories of H. M. In W. C. Abraham, M. Corballis, & K. G. White (Eds.), *Memory mechanisms: A tribute to G. V. Goddard* (pp. 195–215). Hillsdale, NJ: Erlbaum.

Oishi, S., Kesebir, S., & Diener, E. (2011). Income inequality and happiness. *Psychological Science, 22,* 1095–1100.

Oransky, I. (2013, December 24). Doing the right thing: Yale psychology lab retracts monkey papers for inaccurate coding. *Retraction Watch.* Retrieved from http://retractionwatch.com/2013/12/24/doing-the-right-thing-yale-psychology-lab-retracts-monkey-papers-for-inaccurate-coding/

Orne, M. T. (1962). On the social psychology of the psychological experiment: With particular reference to demand characteristics and their implications. *American Psychologist, 17,* 776–783.

Pankratz, H. (2007, August 8). *"Baby Einstein"* may be harmful, study says. *The Denver Post.* Retrieved from http://www.denverpost.com/2007/08/07/baby-einstein-may-be-harmful-study-says/

Pariser, D., & Zimmerman, E. (2004). Learning in the visual arts: Characteristics of gifted and talented individuals. In E. W. Eisner & M. D. Day (Eds.), *Research and policy in art education* (pp. 379–408). Mahwah, NJ: Erlbaum.

Parker-Pope, T. (2009, October 22). What clown on a unicycle? Studying cellphone distraction. *New York Times.* Retrieved from http://well.blogs.nytimes.com/2009/10/22/what-clown-on-a-unicycle-studying-cell-phone-distraction/

Parra, M., Hoff, E., & Core, C. (2011). Relations among language exposure, phonological memory, and language development in Spanish–English bilingually developing two year olds. *Journal of Experimental Child Psychology, 108,* 113–125. doi:10.1016/j.jecp.2010.07.011

Parsian, N., & Dunning, T. (2009). Developing and validating a questionnaire to measure spirituality: A psychometric process. *Global Journal of Health Science, 1,* 1–11.

Parsons, K. (2003). *The science wars: Debating scientific knowledge and technology.* Amherst, NY: Prometheus Books.

PBS Video. (2013, September 26). An American family: Revisit the Loud family [Video file]. Retrieved from http://video.pbs.org/video/2045835722/

Pearl, J. (2009). *Causality: Models, reasoning, and inference* (2nd ed.). New York, NY: Cambridge University Press.

Pettit, N. C., Sivanathan, N., Gladstone, E., & Marr, J. C. (2013). Rising stars and sinking ships: Consequences of status momentum. *Psychological Science, 24,* 1579–1584.

Pew Research Center. (n.d.). Question wording. Retrieved from http://www.people-press.org/methodology/questionnaire-design/question-wording/

Pfungst, O. (1911). *Clever Hans (The horse of Mr. von Osten): A contribution to experimental animal and human psychology* (Trans. C. L. Rahn). New York, NY: Holt.

Piaget, J. (1926). *The language and thought of the child.* New York, NY: Harcourt, Brace, & World.

———. (1952). *The origins of intelligence in children.* New York, NY: International University Press.

———. (1964/1997). Development and learning. In R. E. Ripple & V. N. Rosckcastle (Eds.), *Piaget rediscovered* (pp. 7–20). Reprinted in M. Gauvain & M. Cole (Eds.), *Readings on the development of children* (2nd ed.). New York, NY: Freeman.

Pisani, J. (2013, August 30). Tooth fairy inflation: Price of a tooth nears $4. *ABC News.* Retrieved from http://abcnews.go.com/Business/wireStory/tooth-fairy-inflation-price-tooth-nears-20114599? singlePage=true/

Polling Center. (2012). Politico. Retrieved from http://www.politico.com/2012-election/presidential-polls/

Pont, J. (2008). Ethics in research involving prisoners. *International Journal of Prisoner Health, 4*, 184–197.

Pope, K. S. (2011). Are the American Psychological Association's detainee interrogation policies ethical and effective? Key claims, documents, and results. *Zeitschrift für Psychologie, 219*, 150–158.

Power Balance band is placebo, say experts. (2010, November 22). *BBC News*. Retrieved from http://www.bbc.co.uk/news/uk-wales-11805616/

Power Band bracelets "a scam" professor says. (2011, January 5). *CBCNews/Health*. Retrieved from http://www.cbc.ca/news/health/story/2011/01/05/con-balance-bracelet.html/

Price, D. D., Finniss, D. G., & Benedetti, F. (2008). A comprehensive review of the placebo effect: Recent advances and current thought. *Annual Review of Psychology, 59*, 565–590.

Protzko, J., Aronson, J., & Blair, C. (2013). How to make a young child smarter: Evidence from the database of raising intelligence. *Perspectives on Psychological Science, 8*, 25–40.

Public Health Service. (2002). Retrieved from http://grants.nih.gov/grants/olaw/references/phspol.htm#PublicHealthServicePolicyonHumaneCareandUseofLaboratory/

Raiff, B. R., & Dallery, J. (2010). Internet-based contingency management to improve adherence with blood glucose testing recommendations for teens with type 1 diabetes. *Journal of Applied Behavioral Analysis, 43* (3), 487–491. doi:10.1901/jaba.2010.43-487

Ramachandran, V. S. (2002). *The artful brain*. London, UK: Fourth Estate.

Rapport, M. D., Orban, S. A., Kofler, M. J., & Friedman, L. M. (2013). Do programs designed to train working memory, other executive functions, and attention benefit children with ADHD? A meta-analytic review of cognitive, academic, and behavioral outcomes. *Clinical Psychology Review, 33*, 1237–1252.

Ratiu, P., Talos, I. F., Haker, S., Lieberman, D., & Everett, P. (2004). The tale of Phineas Gage, digitally remastered. *Journal of Neurotrauma, 21*, 637–643.

Raven, K. (2014, February 19). Can avatars bring out the good in gamers? *Reuters Health*. Retrieved from http://www.reuters.com/article/2014/02/19/us-can-avatars-gamers-idUSBREA1I21L 20140219/

Razali, N. M., & Wah, Y. B. (2011). Power comparisons of Shapiro–Wilk, Kolmogorov–Smirnov, Lilliefors and Anderson–Darling tests. *Journal of Statistical Modeling and Analytics, 2*, 21–33.

Reicher, S., & Haslam, S. A. (2006). Rethinking the psychology of tyranny: The BBC prison study. *British Journal of Social Psychology, 45*, 1–40.

Reid, O. (2010, December 30). Stanford doctors face down ghost-writing, money scandals. *The College Fix*. Retrieved from http://www.thecollegefix.com/post/5490/

Retraction Watch. (2013, January 15). Retraction record broken, again; University report should up Fujii total to 183. Retrieved from http://retractionwatch.com/2013/01/15/retraction-record-broken-again-university-report-should-up-fujii-total-to-183/

Revelle, W., Humphreys, M. S., Simon, L., & Gilliland, K. (1980). The interactive effect of personality, time of day, and caffeine: A test of the arousal model. *Journal of Experimental Psychology: General, 109*, 1–31.

Rice, M. J. (2011). The institutional review board is an impediment to human research: The result is more animal-based research. *Philosophy, Ethics, and Humanities in Medicine, 6*(12). doi:10.1186/1747-5341-6-12

Richeson, J., Baird, A. A., Gordon, H. L., Heatherton, T. F., Wyland, C. L., Trawalter, S., & Shelton, N. (2003). An fMRI investigation of the impact of interracial contact on executive function. *Nature Neuroscience, 6*(12), 1323–1328.

Righetti, F., Finenaur, C., & Finkel, E. J. (2013). Low self-control promotes the willingness to sacrifice in close relationships. *Psychological Science, 24*, 1533–1540.

Risen, J. (2015, April 30). American Psychological Association bolstered C.I.A. torture program, report says. *New York Times*. Retrieved from http://www.nytimes.com/2015/05/01/us/report-says-american-psychological-association-collaborated-on-torture-justification.html?_r=0/

Rizvi, S. L., & Nock, M. K. (2008). Single-case experimental designs for the evaluation of treatments for self injurious and suicidal behaviors. *Suicide and Life-Threatening Behavior, 38*(5), 498–510.

Roberts, B. W., & DelVecchio, W. F. (2000). The rank-order consistency of personality from childhood to old age: A quantitative review of longitudinal studies. *Psychological Bulletin, 126*, 3–25.

Roberts, B. W., Robins, R. W., Caspi, A., & Trzesniewski, K. (2003). Personality trait development in adulthood. In J. Mortimer & M. Shanahan (Eds.), *Handbook of the life course* (pp. 579–598). New York, NY: Kluwer Academic/Plenum Press.

Roberts, B. W., Walton, K., & Viechtbauer, W. (2006). Patterns of mean-level change in personality traits across the life course: A meta-analysis of longitudinal studies. *Psychological Bulletin, 132*, 1–25.

Robinson, D. H., & Wainer, H. (2001). On the past and future of null hypothesis significance testing. Research Report published by the Educational Testing Service. Princeton, NJ.

Robson, C. (2002). *Real world research* (2nd ed.). Oxford, UK: Blackwell.

Rosengren, K. S. (2002). Thinking of variability during infancy and beyond. *Infant Behavior and Development, 25*, 337–339.

Rosengren, K. S., & French, J. A. (2013). Magical thinking. In M. Taylor (Ed.), *The Oxford handbook of the development of imagination* (pp. 42–60). New York, NY: Oxford University Press.

Rosengren, K. S., Brem, S. K., Evans, E. M., & Sinatra, G. M. (2012). *Evolution challenges: Integrating research and practice in teaching and learning about evolution.* Oxford, UK: Oxford University Press.

Rosengren, K. S., Carmichael, C., Schein, S. S., & Anderson, K. (2009). A method for eliciting scale errors in preschool classrooms. *Infant Behavior & Development, 32,* 286–290.

Rosengren, K. S., Guitiérrez, I. T., Anderson, K. N., & Schein, S. S. (2009). Parental reports of children's scale errors in everyday life. *Child Development, 80,* 1586–1591.

Rosengren, K. S., Schein, S. S., & Guitiérrez, I. T. (2010). Individual differences in children's production of scale errors. *Infant Behavior and Development, 33,* 309–313.

Rosin, H. (2013, August 12). "This app will not harm your baby." *My San Antonio.* Retrieved from http://www.mysanantonio.com/lifestyle/article/This-app-will-not-harm-your-baby-4726676.php/

Roslow, S., & Roslow, L. (1972). Unlisted phone subscribers are different. *Journal of Advertising Research, 12*(August), 35–38.

Rossi, J. S. (1990). Statistical power of psychological research: What have we gained in 20 years? *Journal of Consulting and Clinical Psychology, 58,* 646–656.

Rothman, D. J. (1991). *Strangers at the bedside: A history of how law and bioethics transformed medical decision making.* New York, NY: Perseus.

Rovee-Collier, C. (1999). The development of infant memory. *Current Directions in Psychological Science, 8,* 80–85.

Rozeboom, W. W. (1960). The fallacy of the null-hypothesis significance test. *Psychological Bulletin, 57,* 416–428.

Sample, I. (2011, September 22). Faster than light particles found, claim scientists. *The Guardian.* Retrieved from http://www.guardian.co.uk/science/2011/sep/22/faster-than-light-particles-neutrinos/

Sarsour, K., Sheridan, M., Jutte, D., Nuru-Jeter, A., Hinshaw, S., & Boyce, W. T. (2011). Family socioeconomic status and child executive functions: The roles of language, home environment, and single parenthood. *Journal of the International Neuropsychological Society, 17,* 120–132.

Savory, P. (2008). How do you interpret a confidence interval? Industrial and Management Systems Engineering, Instructional Materials.

Schaefer, P. W., Grant, P. E., & Gonzalez, R. G. (2000). Diffusion-weighted MR imaging of the brain. *Radiology, 217*(2), 331–345.

Scherpenzeel, A. C., & Bethlehem, J. G. (2011). How representative are online panels? Problems of coverage and selection and possible solutions. In M. Das, P. Ester, & L. Kaczmirek (Eds.), *Social and behavioral research and the Internet* (pp. 105–132). New York, NY: European Association of Methodology.

Scheve, T., & Venzon, C. (2015). 10 stereotypes about aging (that just aren't true). HowStuffWorks: *Health.* Retrieved from http://health.howstuffworks.com/wellness/aging/aging-process/5-stereotypes-about-aging.htm#page=0/

Schmidt, F. L., & Hunter, J. E. (1997). Eight common but false objections to the discontinuation of significance testing in the analysis of research data. In L. A. Harlow, S. A. Mulaik, & J. H. Steiger (Eds.), *What if there were no significance tests?* (pp. 37–64). Mahwah, NJ: Erlbaum.

Schmiedek, F., Lövdén, M., & Lindenberger, U. (2013). Keeping it steady: Older adults perform more consistently on cognitive tasks than younger adults. *Psychological Science, 24*(9), 1747–1754.

Schonfeld, Z. (2013, July 2). Wives are cheating 40% more than they used to, but 70% as much as men. *The Wire.* Retrieved from http://www.theatlanticwire.com/national/2013/07/wives-cheating-vs-men/66800/

Schucany, W. R., & Ng, H. K. T. (2006). Preliminary goodness-of-fit tests for normality do not validate the one-sample Student *t. Communications in Statistics Theory Methods, 35,* 2275–2286.

Science Watch. http://archive.sciencewatch.com/dr/sci/09/aug2-09_2/

Scott, E. C., & Bajema, C. J. (1982). Height, weight and fertility among the participants in the Third Harvard Growth Study. *Human Biology, 54,* 501–516.

Scoville, W. B., & Milner, B. (1957). Loss of recent memory after bilateral hippocampal lesions. *Journal of Neurology, Neurosurgery and Psychiatry, 20,* 11–21.

Sedlmeier, P., & Gigerenzer, G. (1989). Do studies of statistical power have an effect on the power of studies? *Psychological Bulletin, 105,* 309–316.

Segall, M. H., Campbell, D. T., & Herskovits, M. J. (1966). *The influence of culture on visual perception.* Indianapolis, IN: Bobbs–Merrill.

Selfe, L. (1977). *Nadia. A case of extraordinary drawing ability in an autistic child.* New York, NY: Academic Press.

————. (2011). *Nadia revisited: A longitudinal study of an autistic savant.* New York, NY: Psychology Press.

Seligman, M. E. P., & Csikszentmihalyi, M. (2000). Positive psychology: An introduction. *American Psychologist, 55,* 5–14.

Sherif, M., Harvey, O. J., White, B. J., Hood, W. R., & Sherif, C. W. (1961). *Intergroup conflict and cooperation: The Robbers Cave experiment.* Norman, OK: University Book Exchange.

Shermer, M. (1997). *Why people believe in weird things: Pseudoscience, superstition, and other confusions of our times.* New York, NY: Freeman.

Shields, D. L., Bredemeier, B. L., LaVoi, N. M., & Power, F. C. (2005). The sport behavior of youth, parents, and coaches: The good, the bad, and the ugly. *Journal of Research in Character Education, 3,* 43–59.

Shores, K. A., & West, S. T. (2010). Rural and urban park visits and park-based physical activity. *Preventative Medicine, 50*, S13–S17.

Siegler, R. S. (2006). Microgenetic analyses of learning. In D. Kuhn & R. S. Siegler (Eds.), *Handbook of child psychology: Vol. 2. Cognition, perception, and language* (6th ed., pp. 464–510). New York, NY: Wiley.

————. (2007). Cognitive variability. *Developmental Science, 10*, 104–109.

Siegler, R. S., & Crowley, K. (1991). The microgenetic method: A direct means for studying cognitive development. *American Psychologist, 46*, 606–620.

Siegler, R. S., & Jenkins, E. (1989). *How children discover new strategies.* Hillsdale, NJ: Erlbaum.

Sihvonen, R., Paavola, M., Malmivaara, A., Itälä, A., Joukainen, A., Nurmi, H., Kalske, J., & Järvinen, T. L. N. (2013). Arthroscopic partial meniscectomy versus sham surgery for a degenerative meniscal tear. *New England Journal of Medicine, 369*, 2515–2524.

Silberman, G., & Kahn, K. L. (2011). Burdens on research imposed by institutional review boards: The state of the evidence and its implications for regulatory reform. *The Milbank Quarterly, 89*, 599–627.

Silver, N. (2012). *The signal and the noise: Why so many predictions fail—But some don't.* New York, NY: Penguin.

Silverman, K., Wong, C. J., Higgins, S. T., Brooner, R. K., Montoya, I. D., Contoreggi, C., . . . Preston, K. L. (1996). Increasing opiate abstinence through voucher-based reinforcement therapy. *Drug and Alcohol Dependence, 41*, 157–165.

Simmons, J. P., Nelson, L. D., & Simonsohn, U. (2011). False positive psychology: Undisclosed flexibility in data collection and analysis allows presenting anything as significant. *Psychological Science, 22*, 1359–1366.

Simons, D. J., & Chabris, C. F. (1999). Gorillas in our midst: Sustained inattentional blindness for dynamic events. *Perception, 28*, 1059–1074.

Sirin, S. R. (2005). Socioeconomic status and academic achievement: A meta-analytic review of research. *Review of Educational Research, 75*, 417–453.

Sleek, S. (2013, August 28). Science reveals the benefits of an aging workforce. *Psychological Science.* Retrieved from http://www.psychologicalscience.org/index.php/news/minds-business/science-reveals-the-benefits-of-an-aging-workforce.html/

Smith, R. (2013, July 11). Digital dogma, deconstructed. *New York Times.* Retrieved from http://www.nytimes.com/2013/07/12/arts/design/simon-dennys-all-you-need-is-data-at-the-petzel-gallery.html/

Sokal, A. D. (1996). Transgressing the boundaries: Towards a transformative hermeneutics of quantum gravity. *Social Text, 46/47*, 217–252.

Soldz, S., Raymond, N., and Reisner, S. (2015, April 30). All the president's psychologists: The American Psychological Association's secret complicity with the White House and US intelligence community in support of the CIA's "enhanced" interrogation program (Full Text Reports). Retrieved from http://fulltextreports.com/2015/04/30/all-the-presidents-psychologists/

Spearman, C. (1904). "General intelligence," objectively determined and measured. *The American Journal of Psychology, 15*, 201–292.

Speckhard, A. (2015, August 16). Why ethical psychologists play an important role in interrogations. *The Washington Post.* Retrieved from https://www.washingtonpost.com/opinions/why-ethical-psychologists-play-an-important-role-in-interrogations/2015/08/16/b8b2df1e-4047-11e5-9561-4b3dc93e3b9a_story.html/

Spelke, E. S. (1985). Preferential-looking methods as tools for the study of cognition in infancy. In G. Gottlieb & N. Krasnegor (Eds.), *Measurement of audition and vision in the first year of postnatal life: A methodological overview* (pp. 323–363). Norwood, NJ: Ablex.

Sroufe, L. A. (1990). Considering normal and abnormal together: The essence of developmental psychopathology. *Development and Psychopathology, 2*, 335–347.

Stanovich, K. E. (2012). *How to think straight about psychology* (10th ed.). Boston, MA: Allyn & Bacon.

————. (2013). *How to think straight about psychology* (11th ed.). New York, NY: Pearson.

Stark, L. (2012). *Behind closed doors: IRBs and the making of ethical research.* Chicago, IL: University of Chicago Press.

Steele, C. M., & Aronson, J. (1995). Stereotype threat and the intellectual test performance of African Americans. *Journal of Personality and Social Psychology, 69*, 797–811.

Stenovec, T. (2013, March 14). Google Glass ban underscores privacy concerns months before futuristic specs are even released. *The Huffington Post.* Retrieved from http://www.huffingtonpost.com/2013/03/14/google-glass-ban-privacy-concerns_n_2856385.html/

Sterling, R. L. (2011). Genetic research among the Havasupai: A cautionary tale. *American Medical Association Journal of Ethics, 13*, 113–117.

Sternberg, R. J. (1992, September). How to win acceptances by psychology journals: 21 tips for better writing. *APS Observer*, 12–13, 18.

Straus, M. A. (1979). Measuring intrafamily conflict and violence: The Conflict Tactics (CT) Scales. *Journal of Marriage and the Family, 41*, 75–88.

Straus, M. A., Hamby, S. L., Boney-McCoy, S., & Sugarman, D. B. (1996). The revised Conflict Tactics Scales (CTS2): Development and preliminary psychometric data. *Journal of Family Issues, 17*, 283–316.

Strong, W. (1991). Writing incisively: Do-it-yourself prose surgery. New York, NY: McGraw–Hill.

Stroop, J. R. (1935). Studies of interference in serial verbal reactions. *Journal of Experimental Psychology, 18*, 643–662.

Sullivan, G. (2014). Cornell ethics board did not pre-approve Facebook mood manipulation study. *Washington Post.* Retrieved from http://www.washingtonpost.com/news/morning-mix/wp/2014/07/01/facebooks-emotional-manipulation-study-was-even-worse-than-you-thought/

Tarkan, L. (2012, June 7). Is ageism widespread in the workplace? *FoxNews.com.* Retrieved from http://www.foxnews.com/health/2012/06/07/is-ageism-widespread-in-workplace/

Tate, D., & Gibson, G. (1980). Socioeconomic status and black and white intelligence revisited. *Social Behavior and Personality, 8*, 233–237.

Taubes, G. (1993). *Bad science: The short life and weird times of cold fusion.* New York, NY: Random House.

Tavernise, S. (2013, April 10). Study of babies did not disclose risks, U.S. finds. *New York Times.* Retrieved from http://www.nytimes.com/2013/04/11/health/parents-of-preemies-werent-told-of-risks-in-study.html?pagewanted=all/

Taylor, A., & Kim-Cohen, J. (2007). Meta-analysis of gene–environment interactions in developmental psychopathology. *Development & Psychopathology, 19*, 1029–1037.

Taylor, S. (2003). Telephone surveying for household social surveys: The good, the bad and the ugly. *Social Survey Methodology Bulletin, 52*, 10–21.

Terman, L. M. (1925). *Mental and physical traits of a thousand gifted children (I).* Stanford, CA: Stanford University Press.

————. (1930). *The promise of youth, follow-up studies of a thousand gifted children: Genetic studies of genius, III.* Stanford, CA: Stanford University Press.

————. (1947). *The gifted child grows up, twenty-five years follow up of a superior group: Genetic studies of genius, IV.* Stanford, CA: Stanford University Press.

Thagard, P. (2012). Coherence: The price is right. *The Southern Journal of Philosophy, 50*, 42–49.

————. (2012). *The cognitive science of science: Explanation, discovery, and conceptual change.* Cambridge, MA: MIT Press.

Thaler, L., Arnott, S., & Goodale, M. (2011). Neural correlates of natural human echolocation in early and late blind echolocation experts. *PLoS ONE.* Retrieved from http://journals.plos.org/plosone/article?id=10.1371/journal.pone.0020162/

The aftermath of measles vaccine scare in Britain. (2013, May 22). *New York Times* [editorial board]. Retrieved from http://www.nytimes.com/ 2013/05/23/opinion/the-aftermath-of-measles-vaccine-scare-in-britain.html/

Thomas, A., & Chess, S. (1977). *Temperament and development.* New York, NY: Brunner/Mazel.

Thomas, A., Chess, S., Birch, H. G., Hertzig, M., & Korn, S. (1963). *Behavioral individuality in early childhood.* New York, NY: New York University Press.

Tinbergen, N. (1951). *The study of instinct.* Oxford, UK: Clarendon Press.

Top 20 party schools for 2015. (2015, May 20). CollegeAtlas.org. Retrieved from http://www.collegeatlas.org/top-party-schools.html/

Tufte, E. R. (1983). *The visual display of quantitative information.* Cheshire, CT: Graphics Press.

Tugend, A. (2013, July 26). Unemployed and older, and facing a jobless future. *New York Times.* Retrieved from http://www.nytimes.com/2013/07/27/your-money/unemployed-and-older-and-facing-a-jobless-future.html?pagewanted=all&_r=0/

Tukey, J. W. (1977). *Exploratory data analysis.* Reading, MA: Addison–Wesley.

Tversky, A., & Kahneman, D. (1974). Judgment under uncertainty: Heuristics and biases. *Science, 185*, 1124–1131.

Underwood, E. (2014, November 11). How blind people use bat-like sonar. *Science magazine.* Retrieved from http://www.sciencemag.org/news/2014/11/how-blind-people-use-batlike-sonar

U.S. Department of Health and Human Services. (2009). Basic HHS Policy for Protection of Human Research Subjects. Retrieved from http://www.hhs.gov/

————. (2009). Institutional Review Board Guidebook, Chapter VI: Special classes of subjects. Retrieved from http://archive.hhs.gov/ohrp/irb/irb_chapter6.htm

Valentine, J. C. (2012). Meta-analysis. In H. Cooper (Editor in Chief), *APA handbook of research methods in psychology: Vol. 3. Data analysis and research publication* (pp. 485–499). Washington, DC: American Psychological Association.

van de Schoot, R., Kaplan, D., Denissen, J., Asendorpf, J. B., Neyer, F. J., & van Aken, M. A. G. (2014). A gentle introduction to Bayesian analysis: Applications to developmental research. *Child Development, 85*, 842–860.

Van Horn, J. D., Irimia, A., Torgerson, C. M., Chambers, M. C., Kikinis, R., & Toga, A. W. (2012). Mapping connectivity damage in the cage of Phineas Gage. *PLoS ONE, 7*(5), e37454. doi:10.1371/journal.pone.0037454

Vincent, J. (2014, February 11). Do you play as Voldemort or Superman? Study shows virtual roleplay affects behaviour. *The Independent.* Retrieved from http://www.independent.co.uk/news/science/do-you-play-as-voldemort-or-superman-study-shows-virtual-roleplay-affects-behaviour-9121831.html/

Viruet, P. (2014, August 29). *Kid Nation*: Looking back on TV's most disturbing reality show. Retrieved from http://flavorwire.com/474701/kid-nation-looking-back-on-tvs-most-disturbing-reality-show/

Visa, Practical Money Skills. (2000–2013). *Financial literacy for everyone*. Retrieved from http://www.practicalmoneyskills.com/resources/polls/

Von Hofsten, C. (1993). Studying the development of goal-directed behavior. In A. F. Kalverboer, B. Hopkins, & R. Geuze (Eds.), *Motor development in early and later childhood: Longitudinal approaches* (pp. 109–124). Cambridge, UK: Cambridge University Press.

Vygotsky, L. S. (1978). Chapter 6: Interaction between learning and development. In M. Cole, V. John-Steiner, S. Scribner, & E. Souberman (Eds.), *Mind in society: The development of higher psychological processes* (pp. 79–91). Cambridge, MA: Harvard University Press.

Wainer, H. (1999). One cheer for null hypothesis significance testing. *Psychological Methods, 6*, 212–213.

Wakefield, A. J. (2010). *Callous disregard: Autism and vaccines—The truth behind a tragedy*. New York, NY: Skyhorse.

Walker, J. (2004, May 24). The death of David Reimer: A tale of sex, science, and abuse. *Reason.com*. Retrieved from https://reason.com/archives/2004/05/24/the-death-of-david-reimer/

Walkington, E. (2010, June 28). Louis Armstrong birthday broadcast, July 3rd, 6:00 p.m., to July 5th, 9:30 a.m. WKCR 89.9FM NY. Retrieved from http://www.studentaffairs.columbia.edu/wkcr/story/louis-armstrong-birthday-broadcast-july-3rd-600-pm-july-5th-930-am/

Walsh, A. (2013, December). Harkonen's Supreme Court petition denied. FDA Law Blog, Hyman, Phelps & McNamara, P.C. Retrieved from http://www.fdalawblog.net/fda_law_blog_hyman_phelps/2013/12/harkonens-supreme-court-petition-denied.html/

Walton, G. M., & Cohen, G. L. (2003). Stereotype lift. *Journal of Experimental Social Psychology, 39*, 456–467.

Ward, M. K. (2015). Careless responding on internet-based surveys: Humanizing the process may improve data quality. *APS Observer, 28*(2), 37–39.

Watson, J. B. (1913). Psychology as the behaviorist views it. *Psychological Review, 20*, 158–177.

Watters, E. (2013, February 25). We aren't the world. *Pacific Standard*. Retrieved from https://psmag.com/we-aren-t-the-world-535ec03f2d45

Weight Loss Pills Network. (2016). Dr. Oz green coffee bean extract: What does he recommend? Retrieved from http://www.weightlosspillswork.com/dr-oz-green-coffee-bean-extract/

Weisberg, D. S., Keil, F. C., Goodstein, J., Rawson, E., & Gray, J. R. (2008). The seductive allure of neuroscience explanations. *Journal of Cognitive Neuroscience, 20*, 470–477.

Weissman, J. (2013a, September 9). Tenured professors make worse teachers. *The Atlantic*. Retrieved from http://www.theatlantic.com/business/archive/2013/09/study-tenured-professors-make-worse-teachers/279480/

———. (2013b, September 25). Are tenured professors really worse teachers? A lit review. *The Atlantic*. Retrieved from http://www.theatlantic.com/business/archive/2013/09/are-tenured-professors-really-worse-teachers-a-lit-review/279940/

Wellman, H. M., & Gelman, S. A. (1992). Cognitive development: Foundational theories of core domains. *Annual Review of Psychology, 43*, 337–375.

Wells, M. (2002, January 24). BBC halts prison experiment. *The Guardian*. Retrieved from http://www.theguardian.com/uk/2002/jan/24/bbc.socialsciences/

Wells, W., Cavanaugh, M. R., Bouffard, J. A., & Nobles, M. R. (2012). Non-response bias with a web-based survey of college students: Differences from a classroom survey about carrying concealed handguns. *Journal of Quantitative Criminology, 28*, 455–476.

WHO Multicenter Growth Reference Study Group. (2006). WHO Motor Development Study: Windows of achievement for six gross motor development milestones. *Acta Paediatrica, Suppl. 450*, 86–95.

Wilcox, R. R. (1998). How many discoveries have been lost by ignoring modern statistical methods? *American Psychologist, 53*, 300–314.

———. (2012). *Introduction to robust estimation and hypothesis testing* (3rd ed.). Waltham, MA: Academic Press.

Wilcox, R. R., & Keselman, H. J. (2003). Modern robust data analysis methods: Measures of central tendency. *Psychological Methods, 8*, 254–274.

Wilkinson, L., & the Task Force on Statistical Inference, APA Board of Scientific Affairs. (1999). Statistical methods in psychology journals: Guidelines and explanations. *American Psychologist, 54*, 594–604.

Willems, R. M., Van der Haergen, L., Fisher, S. E., & Francks, C. (2014). On the other hand: Including left-handers in cognitive neuroscience and neurogenetics. *Nature Reviews Neuroscience, 15*, 193–201.

Willig, C. (2008). *Introducing qualitative research in psychology* (2nd ed.). Buckingham, UK: Open University Press.

———. (2012). Perspectives on the epistemological bases for qualitative research. In H. Cooper (Editor in Chief), *APA Handbook of Research Methods in Psychology, Vol. 1. Foundations, planning, measures, and psychometrics* (pp. 5–21). Washington, DC: American Psychological Association.

Winer, L. (2011, April 25). Reality replay. *The New Yorker*.

Winerip, M. (2013, January 13). Documenting a generation's fall. *New York Times*. Retrieved from http://www.nytimes.com/2013/01/14/booming/set-for-life-documents-crisis-among-baby-boomers.html/

Wolff, L. S., Acevedo-Garcia, D., Subramanian, S. V., Weber, D., & Kawachi, I. (2010). Subjective social status, a new measure in health disparities research: Do race/ethnicity and choice of referent group matter? *Journal of Health Psychology, 15,* 560–574.

Wynn, K. (1992). Addition and subtraction by human infants. *Nature, 358,* 749–750.

Yang, Y., DeCelle, S., Reed, M., Rosengren, K. S., Schlagel, R., & Greene, J. (2011). Subjective experiences in older adults practicing taiji and qigong. *Journal of Aging Research, 2011,* Article ID 650210. doi:10.4061/2011/650210

Yates, D., Moore, D., & McCabe, G. (1999). *The Practice of Statistics.* New York, NY: Freeman.

Yong, E. (2012, October 3). Nobel laureate challenges psychologists to clean up their act. *Nature.* Retrieved from http://www.nature.com/news/nobel-laureate-challenges-psychologists-to-clean-up-their-act-1.11535/

Yoon, G., & Vargas, P. (2014). Know thy avatar: The unintended effect of virtual-self representation on behavior. *Psychological Science, 25*(4), 1043–1045.

Zannad, F., Stough, W. G., McMurray, J. J. V., Remme, W. J., Pitt, B., Borer, J. S., Geller, N. L., & Pocock, S. J. (2012). When to stop a clinical trial early for benefit: Lessons learned and future approaches. *Circulation: Heart Failure, 5,* 294–302.

Zelazo, P. D., & Bauer, P. J. (2013). National Institutes of Health Toolbox Cognition Battery (NIH Toolbox CB): Validation for children between 3 and 15 years. *Monographs of the Society for Research in Child Development,* Serial No. 309, 78, 1–149.

Zimbardo, P. G. (1999). Stanford Prison Experiment. Retrieved from http://www.prisonexp.org/

————. (2006). On rethinking the psychology of tyranny: The BBC prison study. *British Journal of Social Psychology, 45,* 47–53.

Zimmerman, F. J., Christakis, D. A., & Meltzoff, A. N. (2007). Associations between media viewing and language development in children under age 2 years. *Journal of Pediatrics, 151,* 364–368.

Credits

Chapter 1
Inside Research Photo 1: Colby College
Figure 1.1: From *The New York Times*, June 25, 2012 © 2012 *The New York Times*. All rights reserved. Used by permission and protected by the copyright laws of the United States. The printing, copying, redistribution, or retransmission of this content without express written permission is prohibited.
Figure 1.3: Photo by Bill Graham/Barcroft USA/Getty Images

Chapter 2
Inside Research Photo 2: Duke University
Figure 2.1: Agentur Voller Ernst/picture-alliance/dpa/AP Images
Figure 2.2: OJO Images Ltd/Alamy Stock Photo

Chapter 3
Inside Research Photo 3: Courtesy of Kathleen Murphy

Chapter 4
Inside Research Photo 4: Courtesy of Daniel Simons
Figure 4.2: Tim O'Brien/Cartoonstock
Figure 4.3: John Klossner/The New Yorker Collection/The Cartoon Bank

Chapter 5
Inside Research Photo 5: Bryce Richter/University of Wisconsin–Madison
Media Matters 5: Vitalinka/Shutterstock
Figure 5.1: Martyn Shuttleworth

Chapter 6
Inside Research Photo 6: Courtesy of Amy Bohnert

Chapter 7
Inside Research Photo 7: University of Michigan
Figure 7.2: PEARLS BEFORE SWINE © 2015 Stephan Pastis. Reprinted by permission of UNIVERSAL UCLICK. All rights reserved.
Figure 7.4: PEARLS BEFORE SWINE © 2015 Stephan Pastis. Reprinted by permission of UNIVERSAL UCLICK. All rights reserved.

Chapter 8
Inside Research Photo 8: Courtesy of Travis Seymour
Figure 8.1: Created by Amy Milner-Gorvine
Figure 8.2: Created by Amy Milner-Gorvine
Figure 8.3: Created by Amy Milner-Gorvine

Chapter 9
Inside Research Photo 9: Courtesy of Steven Asher
Figure 9.6: Courtesy of Karl Rosengren

Chapter 10
Inside Research Photo 10: Northwestern University
Media Matters 10: Photo by John Dominis/The LIFE Images Collection/Getty Images
Figure 10.2: Shutterstock/Peppinuzzo
Figure 10.3: Copyright © 1989 Routledge

Chapter 11
Inside Research Photo 11: Courtesy of Marie Banich
Figure 11.3: Katherine C. Cohen/Boston Children's Hospital
Figure 11.4: Reprinted from *International Journal of Psychophysiology*, Vol. 94/Issue 3, Xiaoqin Mai, Lin Xu, Mingyan Li, Jie Shao, Zhengyan Zhao, Connie Lamm, Nathan A. Fox, Charles A. Nelson, Betsy Lozoff, "Sounds elicit relative left frontal alpha activity in 2-month-old infants," Pages 287–291, Copyright (2015), with permission from Elsevier.
Figure 11.5: http://www.mind-braintraining.com
Figure 11.6: Reprinted from *Developmental Psychology*, 45, Hillman, C. H., Buck, S. M., Themanson, J. R., Pontifex, M. B., & Castelli, D. M. "Aerobic fitness and cognitive development: Event-related brain potential and task performance indices of executive control in preadolescent children," Pages 114–129, Copyright (2009), with permissions from the American Psychological Association.
Figure 11.7a: Shutterstock/nimon
Figure 11.7b: Cultura Creative (RF)/Alamy Stock Photo
Figure 11.8: Reprinted by permission from Macmillan Publishers Ltd: Nature Publishing Group (doi: 10.1038/npp.2014.236), copyright (2015).
Figure 11.9: Van Horn JD1, Irimia A, Torgerson CM, Chambers MC, Kikinis R, Toga AW. PLoS One.
Figure 11.10: From *Science*, 302, Naomi I. Eisenberger, Matthew D. Lieberman, Kipling D. Williams. "Does Rejection Hurt? An fMRI Study of Social Exclusion," Copyright (2004). Reprinted with permission from AAAS.
Figure 11.11: Reprinted from *Vision Research*, 114, Brian Allen, Daniel P. Spiegel, Benjamin Thompson, Franco Pestilli, Bas Rokers. "Altered white matter in early visual pathways of humans with amblyopia," 48–55, Copyright (2016), with permission from Elsevier.

Figure 11.12: Reprinted from *Vision Research*, 114, Brian Allen, Daniel P. Spiegel, Benjamin Thompson, Franco Pestilli, Bas Rokers. "Altered white matter in early visual pathways of humans with amblyopia," 48–55, Copyright (2016), with permission from Elsevier.
Figure 11.13: Reprinted from *Neuroscience & Biobehavioral Reviews*, 34/Issue 3, S. Lloyd-Fox, A. Blasi, C.E. Elwell. "Illuminating the developing brain: The past, present and future of functional near-infrared spectroscopy," Pages 269–284, Copyright (2011), with permission from Elsevier.
Figure 11.14: Copyright © 2009 by Tobias Gilk. Republished from MRImetalDetector.com

Chapter 12

Inside Research Photo 12: Florida Atlantic University
Figure 12.1: Shutterstock/GagliardiImages and Shutterstock/Tyler Olson
Figure 12.2: Courtesy of the authors.

Chapter 13

Inside Research Photo 13: Campus Faculty Association, UIUC

Chapter 14

Inside Research Photo 14: Photo by Matt Cashore/University of Notre Dame

Chapter 15

Inside Research Photo 15: Courtesy of Stella Christie
Figure 15.1: Copyright 2010, "Where Hypotheses Come From: Learning New Relations by Structural Alignment," *Journal of Cognition and Development*, 11 (3): 356–373. Reproduced by permission of Taylor & Francis LLC, http://www.tandfonline.com.
Figure 15.2: Copyright 2010, "Where Hypotheses Come From: Learning New Relations by Structural Alignment," *Journal of Cognition and Development*, 11 (3): 356–373. Reproduced by permission of Taylor & Francis LLC, http://www.tandfonline.com.
Figure 15.3: Copyright 2010, "Where Hypotheses Come From: Learning New Relations by Structural Alignment," *Journal*

of *Cognition and Development*, 11 (3): 356–373. Reproduced by permission of Taylor & Francis LLC, http://www.tandfonline.com.
Figure 15.4: Copyright 2010, "Where Hypotheses Come From: Learning New Relations by Structural Alignment," *Journal of Cognition and Development*, 11 (3): 356–373. Reproduced by permission of Taylor & Francis LLC, http://www.tandfonline.com.
Figure 15.5: Copyright 2010, "Where Hypotheses Come From: Learning New Relations by Structural Alignment," *Journal of Cognition and Development*, 11 (3): 356–373. Reproduced by permission of Taylor & Francis LLC, http://www.tandfonline.com.
Figure 15.6: Copyright 2010, "Where Hypotheses Come From: Learning New Relations by Structural Alignment," *Journal of Cognition and Development*, 11 (3): 356–373. Reproduced by permission of Taylor & Francis LLC, http://www.tandfonline.com.
Figure 15.7: Copyright 2010, "Where Hypotheses Come From: Learning New Relations by Structural Alignment," *Journal of Cognition and Development*, 11 (3): 356–373. Reproduced by permission of Taylor & Francis LLC, http://www.tandfonline.com.
Figure 15.8: Copyright 2010, "Where Hypotheses Come From: Learning New Relations by Structural Alignment," *Journal of Cognition and Development*, 11 (3): 356–373. Reproduced by permission of Taylor & Francis LLC, http://www.tandfonline.com.
Figure 15.9: Copyright 2010, "Where Hypotheses Come From: Learning New Relations by Structural Alignment," *Journal of Cognition and Development*, 11 (3): 356–373. Reproduced by permission of Taylor & Francis LLC, http://www.tandfonline.com.
Figure 15.10: Copyright 2010, "Where Hypotheses Come From: Learning New Relations by Structural Alignment," *Journal of Cognition and Development*, 11 (3): 356–373. Reproduced by permission of Taylor & Francis LLC, http://www.tandfonline.com.
Figure 15.11: Copyright 2010, "Where Hypotheses Come From: Learning New Relations by Structural Alignment," *Journal of Cognition and Development*, 11 (3): 356–373. Reproduced by permission of Taylor & Francis LLC, http://www.tandfonline.com.

Chapter 16

Inside Research Photo 16: Linda A. Cicero/Stanford News Service
Figure 16.1: Image courtesy of the authors
Media Matters 16: GL Portrait/Alamy Stock Photo

Author Index

Subject Index

Page references referring to figures and tables are suffixed with an *f* and *t* respectively.